HUMAN PALEOPSYCHOLOGY

APPLICATIONS TO AGGRESSION
AND PATHOLOGICAL PROCESSES

HUMAN PALEOPSYCHOLOGY

APPLICATIONS TO AGGRESSION AND PATHOLOGICAL PROCESSES

Kent G. Bailey
Virginia Commonwealth University

LEA LAWRENCE ERLBAUM ASSOCIATES, PUBLISHERS
1987 Hillsdale, NJ   London

Lawrence Erlbaum Associates, Inc., Publishers
365 Broadway
Hillsdale, New Jersey 07642

Library of Congress Cataloging-in-Publication Data

Bailey, Kent.
Human paleopsychology.

Bibliography: p.
Includes indexes.
1. Genetic psychology. 2. Man—Animal nature.
I. Title. [DNLM: 1. Behavior. 2. Human Development.
3. Phylogeny. 4. Psychology. 5. Regression (Psychology).
WM 193.5.R2 B154h]
BF701.B27   1986   155.7   86-19823
ISBN 0-89859-810-9

Printed in the United States of America
10 9 8 7 6 5 4 3 2 1

To Paul D. MacLean, whose theory of the triune brain
forms the core of the New Social Science

Contents

Preface

Neither the motives nor the goals for writing this book may be simply described. At the most fundamental level, the innumerable hours of library research and reading, the years of personal discussions and debates with anyone and everyone from next-door neighbors to well-known experts in the biological and social sciences, and the actual commitment of the ideas of others and my own to writing, have represented a powerful intellectual growth experience. In one respect, then, this book serves as a medium for sharing that growth experience in searching for some small grip on what we call human nature. The book is premised on the overarching assumption that both the hard scientific and softer practical aspects of social science function best when founded upon a credible rationale (Bergmann, 1950) on human nature. Moreover, I believe that any credible view must grapple not only with human distinctiveness (e.g., learning capacity, language, rationality, and culture), but the dark sides of senseless violence and social disorder as well. Any such grappling with the dark side must necessarily confront our animal natures as well as our distinctly human natures.

A comprehensive discussion of the animal aspects of human nature would necessarily address the following questions:

1. Why is so much of human violence gratuitous, that is, far more destructive than is required to achieve instrumental goals?
2. Why does gratuitous violence often seem to have a hedonic component, that is, appears to be enjoyable?

3. Why is gratuitous violence concentrated almost solely in the male sex? And conversely, why is the female of the species far less prone to kill or destroy on a large scale?

4. What are the implications of the predator-prey complex in human affairs, if we are granted the following:

   a. The predator-prey complex (stalk-kill-eat patterns of the predator as they interact with avoidance and escape patterns of prey) is, by a monumentally large margin, the phylogenetically oldest integrated motivational-behavioral system in the animal world.

   b. Predation is the only form of animal aggression characteristically involving the annihilation and destruction of the object of aggression.

   c. Predation is the only form of aggression characteristically involving a hedonic component.

   d. Approximately 99% of human evolution from the earliest hominid types to modern *Homo sapiens* occurred in the hunting-and-gathering phase of development (Chapter 4).

   e. Human beings share approximately 99% of their genetic material with their closest relative in phylogeny, the chimpanzee (Chapter 6), who is a hunter and predator (Chapter 11).

Clearly, a comprehensive analysis of the dark side of human nature is a major goal of the book. Yet, there are several subgoals embedded within the larger one. First, the theory of phylogenetic regression (Bailey, 1978) and progression (Chapters 3, 4, Appendix I) has been refined and elaborated in the present work. Additionally, regression-progression theory has been extended beyond dark side phenomena into the broader realms of personality and psychopathology. Secondly, I have focused, in large measure, on what is perhaps the greatest conundrum in human psychology—sudden changes in behavior where the person temporarily regresses from social propriety into irrational, personally atypical, and often socially reprehensible behavior. Such changes often seem as mysterious and inexplicable to the person exhibiting them as to the social scientists studying them. Thirdly, I have attempted to develop a human paleopsychology to enrich the neopsychology (Chapter 9) of modern social science. Human paleopsychology characteristically focuses on the animal aspects (especially, phylogenetic carry-overs from mammalian and primate phylogeny) of human behavior, while neopsychology typically looks for explanations in the neocortex, rationality, society, and culture. Fourthly, regression-progression theory has attempted to elaborate the dynamics of Paul MacLean's Triune Brain (Chapter 2), by detailing some of the processes of progressing up and regressing down the triune structures. Fifthly, the book implicitly addresses one of the sorest questions in the various bioevolutionary approaches to human behavior—that is, if there are important phylogenetic substructures in human behavior, as human ethologists, human sociobiologists, biocultural anthropologists, ethopsychiatrists, etc. (Chapter 2) suggest, then what are they and how do we *gain access* to them? Generally, the approach has been an either-or one where the biologically-oriented writer states or implies that humans are basically animals, to which the sociocultural determinist counters that we are not really animals in any meaningful psychological sense. The present volume emphasizes *both* the animal and distinctly human aspects of human nature, and attempts a rudimentary analysis of their modes of interaction. Lastly, the book was broadly referenced and fairly content-inclusive, so that those knowledgeable in bioevolutionary issues in human psychology might find a few things of interest for incorporation into their personal paradigms, and neophytes might find enough to stimulate formulation of a paradigm which creatively blends the paleo- and neopsychological levels of analysis.

The above goals are ambitious and each, at best, was only partially realized in the present book. Indeed, time will no doubt show that few and perhaps none of the goals extended beyond a framing of questions that need to be answered. I can only hope that experts in the various disciplines transgressed will have sympathy for a clinical psychologist whose primary qualifications for writing this book were a deep concern about the seemingly accelerating regressive behavior of humankind and a personal struggle with the question of human nature in the light of modern biology.

Kent G. Bailey

Acknowledgments

Many persons contributed to this volume by way of personal support, constructive criticism, and provision of articles, chapters, and other scholarly materials. Several colleagues at Virginia Commonwealth University read specific chapters and gave encouragement along the way. Among these were Stephen Auerbach, Marilyn Erickson, Don Kiesler, John Mahoney, James P. McCullough, and Stanley Strong. I am also deeply indebted to my graduate students Susan Arrington, Linda Bazan, and Steve Burns, who worked closely with me and contributed greatly to my thinking during the writing of this book. Also, undergraduates Dianna Gibbs and Jennifer Wampler provided an important critical dimension. Several colleagues at other universities offered thoughtful criticisms and suggestions, including Jason Brown at the New York University Medical Center, Gerard G. Neuman at the Institute for the Psychodynamics of Mind in La Jolla, California, Robert Hogan at the University of Tulsa, Fred Kozub at the University of Richmond, K. Warner Schaie at the

Pennsylvania State University, Glenn Shean at William and Mary College, David Smille at the New College of the University of South Florida, and Marvin Zuckerman at the University of Delaware.

One of the first persons to comment extensively on the phylogenetic regression-progression model was Michael T. McGuire, Director of the Human Ethology Laboratory at UCLA. His detailed and thoughtful commentary in the early phases of my thinking was crucial, as was his timely personal encouragement. He was one of my best critics in terms of outlining the many problems and complexities inherent in the concept of phylogenetic regression. Professor McGuire also was most generous and cooperative in providing numerous preprints and reprints of his and his colleagues work.

I am also deeply indebted to Paul D. MacLean, to whom this volume is dedicated. His comments on core Chapters 3 and 4 were thoughtful and stimulating, and encouraging at a time when encouragement was needed. He kindly forwarded numerous reprints, preprints, and other materials as needed, and helped rewrite several passages on the triune brain in Chapter 2. Moreover, I had the pleasure to discuss matters of mutual interest with him at a conference in his honor in 1983. Clearly, Professor MacLean's personal support and writings on the triune brain are at the heart of the present work.

One of my closest compatriots during the writing of this volume was Luigi Valzelli, Director of the Mario Negri Institute for Research in Psychopharmacology in Milan, Italy. We have corresponded on a regular basis for the past few years, and his suggestions, criticisms, books, and articles have made a deep imprint on my version of human paleopsychology. Certainly, the formative influence of his excellent book, *The psychobiology of aggression and violence* (1981), may be clearly seen in the pages to follow. Also, I deeply appreciate the speedy manner in which he forwarded photographs of his beautiful drawings of the reptilian and paleomammalian brains (see Figures 2.2 and 2.3 in Chapter 2 of this volume).

My deepest debt of gratitude is to Professor Brendan A. Maher of Harvard who recommended the book to Lawrence Erlbaum Associates in the first place, and who also served as my working editor during the manuscript's evolution from a few rough chapters to the present volume. I am also pleased and honored that he agreed to write the book's foreword. Professor Maher read every word from the preface to the final reference, and provided more thoughtful, incisive, and thorough critical commentary than an author ought to expect. Although not always in personal agreement with my arguments or interpretations, he never wavered from the overriding goal of extracting the best work from me. Despite his efforts, however, many errors of omission and commission remain for which I must assume sole responsibility.

I am also indebted to my editor at Erlbaum, Jack Burton, who was cordial and helpful in every way during the book's writing. He provided interesting and relevant articles and references, made numerous suggestions regarding both style and substance, and he was most generous in giving me enough time to complete the manuscript. Some of the book's contents may prove controversial, and I deeply appreciated the atmosphere of intellectual freedom and support provided by Jack and Lawrence Erlbaum Associates.

The various accommodations made by my department and the College of Humanities and Sciences in support of the present project are gratefully acknowledged. Most noteworthy was the "Scholarly Semester" awarded to me by Dean Elske V. P. Smith in the spring of 1983, which allowed the completion of several important chapters.

Lastly, I deeply appreciated the patience and support of my wife Patricia, who composed the author index, and my daughter Kendra during the years that work on the book cut into family togetherness and recreation time. Moreover, I am more indebted to them than anyone else for showing me, in real life, the true nature of human nature.

Foreword

This is likely to be an important book; it is certain to be a controversial one. *Human Paleopsychology* deals with the possibility that much complex human behavior comes from archaic biological roots. Hence, for most readers it will be seen as falling squarely within the domain of human sociobiology; their assessment of it will be substantially determined by their view of that domain.

I have had the opportunity to review Professor Bailey's manuscript as it evolved, and to correspond with him on our many points of agreement, as well as disagreement. He has invited me to write this foreword, and I am pleased to do so; for it permits me some anticipatory comment about the axes along which the controversy is located.

Bailey states at the outset that his purpose is to "prod the reader to apply his or her wits to the questions of why we love, hate, reason, and reach for the stars with such passion." But his purpose is, of course, not quite as didactically neutral as that statement suggests. He presents a theory upon which he has been working for many years, and in which he believes. His prodding is directed, at those who are unfamiliar with sociobiology or those who criticize it. It is safe to assume that there will be vigorous responses to Bailey's theory. Perhaps we can anticipate some of the discussion here. Two kinds of issue are certain to be the central focus of dispute; one relates to the social/ethical and political consequences of biologizing about behavior, while the other concerns the character of the evidence that would be necessary to establish the sociobiological thesis. We may touch on them here rather briefly.

Sociobiology has been under sharp criticism for its implicit message that there is a biological core of unchangeable human nature. This core, sociobiology seems to imply, is likely to be with us permanently, and the hope that human beings might be perfectible is therefore illusory. Society as it is, and as it has (allegedly) always been, reveals the broad outlines of this core. Crime, warfare, and so forth will always be with us because of human nature. Plans for the fundamental improvement of society are, according to this theory, always doomed to failure. Time is wasted, false hopes aroused, and more harm than good done, by optimistic schemes of reform. Biological constraints are such that little can be done and little more than band-aid remedies are worth undertaking.

Messages of this kind may serve to squelch enthusiasm for social improvement, and can readily be used to justify the maintenance of the *status quo*. Most people seem to agree that crime, poverty, ignorance, and the like are social evils that we would be glad to eliminate; hence writings that discourage the attempt to eliminate them cast doubt upon the extent of awareness of social responsibility on the part of those whose words produce the discouragement. Do they really want us to stop trying to solve social problems and settle for *laissez-faire*?

What about the social responsibility of scientists? Do scientists have a duty to withhold their findings or views from the public if there is some real prospect that these might be used to achieve unethical social purposes? Or can everyone who bears the label "scientist" claim, in the words of Tom Lehrer's song, "I just send them up, I don't care where they come down; that's not my department, says Werner von Braun".

Several stances are possible on this matter. There is a common view, promoted by some scientists, that ethical arguments are irrelevant to science and should not be allowed in the debate. From this point of view, the "truth" is an ultimate good, requiring no further justification for its promulgation. Indeed, this argument sometimes goes further to assert that not only should the truth always be published, but that we collectively have a positive moral obligation to support those who are seeking it, even if we don't like what we get when we get it. Any suppression of the truth by others, or self-suppression by the discoverer of the truth is, according to this, a blatant form of censorship, and an affront to long-cherished values of free speech.

There is an alternative formulation of this argument: This is not a simple matter of science "versus" ethics, it is a matter of two conflicting ethical values. From this standpoint the argument discussed immediately above is really a disguised assertion that the publication of the "truth" has a higher ethical priority than any other ethical principle. This is sometimes based on an article of faith that in the long run the truth can never really be bad for people, no matter how it may seem to be so in the short run. By the same token, withholding the truth is tantamount to lying, and lying is always bad for everybody in both the short and the long run.

The counter view is that the overriding ethical principle is human welfare (defined in terms of individual security), justice, a fair share of the world's goods, and a decent respect for and from others. Scientific truths are valuable to the extent that they provide a means to an end, that is, human welfare, and not because they provide some vision of a metaphysical abstraction called "Truth". If the scientist's reports are used in ways that undercut human welfare, however innocent the intentions, then the lesser ethical value has really prevailed over the greater.

Here we have a situation in which we see opposed views as to which of two conflicting ethical principles is superior to the other. Both principles have strong appeal; much of the time they point towards the same decision in actual cases. Whether or not one is intrinsically superior to the other is a matter for personal, individual reflection. License is not automatically granted to the scientist to win this argument *a priori;* each citizen must decide where he or she thinks that the priorities lie.

There is, I think, a rational basis for opinion on this matter. Anybody familiar with the methods and findings of the behavioral sciences (whether in their biological forms or their psychological forms) knows that the literature reports very few empirically-based findings robust enough to survive serious attempts at falsification. Our observations have substantial margins of error attached to them, and are often confined in their application to the specific circumstances under which they were obtained. Whatever the ethical justification for announcing reliable if unpalatable findings may be, there is much more room for concern about the announcement of findings that are neither palatable nor reliable. Hence, the duty of the scientist lies not so much in the requirement for some kind of self-censorship, but in the clear ethical obligation to be very sure indeed before reporting findings that might be abused for socially malevolent purposes. The more socially disastrous the uses of a finding might be, the more reliable it must be, and the greater the burden upon the reporter to make the limits of reliability clear. Bailey has avoided the risk of oversell. He is well aware of the limitations of the data in his chosen field, and tries hard to make the reader aware of it also. But there is no harm here in adding an additional reminder to the reader on this point.

I do disagree with Professor Bailey, with regard to his assessment of the way in which those opposed to sociobiology have allegedly used *ad hominem* arguments against the sociobiologists. The *ad hominem* fallacy asks us to accept or reject empirical evidence solely on the basis of the alleged characteristics of the person who is reporting it. Critics of sociobiology, such as Richard Lewontin, Stephen Jay Gould, Leon

Kamin, Marvin Harris, and others have not, in my reading of them, argued that good sociobiological evidence should be thrown out because of the personal motives of the sociobiologists. They have pointed out instead that the evidence for sociobiology is very unconvincing on scientific grounds, and should be thrown out on that basis. When we find very intelligent people enthusiastically offering poor evidence in support of their theoretical position, it is important to figure out why they do this. We have little reason to query the cognitive processes that lead somebody to conclude that 2 and 2 make 4, but we have good reason to inquire into the cognitions of somebody who announces that 2 and 2 make 5! Why people rush into print with sweeping generalizations based on marginal evidence is as legitimate a scientific question (particularly for psychologists) as why some people carry a rabbit's foot to protect them from harm.

On the other side of the coin, Bailey is on very solid ground in pointing out that the anti-sociobiologists cannot win the nature-nurture argument by default. Positive convincing evidence for the effects of specific measured environmental factors in producing social ills is as hard to find as is evidence for the sociobiological alternatives. Each side of the issue carries a burden of positive proof; sooner or later the sociobiologist must show us the biological genetic evidence. Reference to the alleged universality of a behavior across cultures is insufficient, for it is congruent with many theoretical models, both social and biological. Analogies in animal behavior are interesting, but can scarcely clinch the matter when we turn to humans with language and other cultural acquisitions. Mathematical models of the way in which assumed genetic units might account for obtained empirical observations are interesting also—but as the modeler is rarely constrained in advance in his choice of assumptions the effect is more provocative than probative.

For those of us, including myself, who are impressed by socio-environmental explanations of most behavior, Bailey's examples of behavior such as gratuitous cruelty and violence present difficulties. Although it is true that retrospectively tracing the long complex of the environmental antecedents of an event is immensely difficult, the fact of the difficulty does not excuse us from the obligation to do so. Nor does the fact that we can demonstrate the power of the environment to induce a very wide range of behaviors permit us to reason backwards from effects to causes in all other cases.

Obviously, we cannot hope to understand human behavior by pitting nature-explanations against nurture-explanations in some winner-take-all contest. It is inevitable that the most useful answers will depend on models that identify the relative contributions of both and will identify them in ways that permit us to use the knowledge to solve social problems rather than submit to them. Lawful forces in nature can be overcome, and indeed must be overcome, if man is to survive. The flight of the airplane is testimony to the truth that we do not have to bow to the force of gravity but can counter it with the intelligent use of aerodynamic forces. Penicillin tells us that we can use the natural properties of some phenomena to counter the undesirable properties of other phenomena. Man has shown that he is not a helpless victim of the limitations of his own biology when face to face with nature; he has shown himself capable of active intervention to transcend them.

So it is with human nature. If, indeed, there are primitive biological propensities in man that are destructive of human life and happiness, then our task is to channel, control, and counter them as effectively as possible. We cannot do this by refusing to recognize their existence. There is no doubt in my mind that the major and lasting contribution of Professor Bailey's book will be in his insistence that we look the data in the eye.

Brendan Maher

HUMAN PALEOPSYCHOLOGY

APPLICATIONS TO AGGRESSION
AND PATHOLOGICAL PROCESSES

1
Introduction

Human nature interests me because it is my nature. My interest in the rest of nature is always tinged with this personal reference, whether I recognize it or not, for we can see the surrounding world only through human eyes, and our apparatus of perception is at best an imperfect instrument. We look at human nature, too, as spectators, but we also have the unique ability to look at it from inside the works. The extraspective and introspective methods of observation have equal scientific validity, and both methods are subject to . . . erroneous interpretation. To understand human nature and so learn to control behavior for our own good, each of these components of experience—the objective and subjective—must be examined separately and in their reciprocal relationships.

—Herrick, 1956, p.1

WHAT IS MAN?

From time immemorial, we humans have wondered "What are we and whence did we come," or as Robert Burns mischievously framed it:

Good Lord, what is man! for as simple he looks,
Do but try to develop his hooks and his crooks,
With his depths and his shallows, his good and his evil,
All in all, he's a problem must puzzle the devil.

Indeed, are we created in the image of God, kin of beasts in body and God in spirit as Francis Bacon mused, or are we, more pessimistically, "in error throughout our strife" and "Nature's sole mistake," as Goethe and W. S. Gilbert respectively concluded? Such questions plague the great thinkers of today as those of yore, and it seems that the answers are as elusive as ever. However, the recent era has seen a remarkable shift in the way such questions are fashioned and their answers sought: Theologians, philosophers and metaphysicians, historians, physicians, and naturalists have been joined by, and perhaps superceded by, social scientists in the endless quest for the essence of humanity. With the advent of highly trained specialists in human behavior, the laity and scientists themselves looked forward to a time of peace and happiness for all, as answers to age-old questions flowed in a steady stream from the social scientists' laboratories.

Certainly, the social and behavioral sciences have produced a multitude of interesting findings, many of which have contributed to the betterment of the species. Through the efforts of anthropologists, sociologists, psychologists, and related disciplines, we have learned much about cultural differences around the world, how groups interact, how social influences condition behavior, how the intellects and personalities of children develop, how the mind works, and so on. But despite greatly expanded knowledge about the specifics of behavior, the perennial problems of crime, warfare, terrorism, divorce, loneliness and alientation, drug and alcohol addiction, and mental illness march on seemingly unchecked. We social scientists seem to have fared well in the laboratory dealing with abstract and often discipline-confined issues, but failure has met us repeatedly in attempting to eradicate the metastisizing evils of society. Within this setting, new models and theories need to be developed and old ones dusted off and re-evaluated. This volume represents an attempt to formulate a biologically based conceptual model incorporating features from several current disciplines, along with ideas from earlier writers and researchers. Any such broad and inclusive approach will lack depth in certain areas, both factually and in terms of theoretical and cross-disciplinary linkages. This work is no exception, but, hopefully, the pages to follow prod the reader to apply his or her wits to the questions of why we love, hate, reason, and reach for the stars with such great passion.

ANIMAL NATURE AND HUMAN NATURE

Because our true nature remains undefined, and we must settle for approximations in the form of theories, assumptions, models. Given the tautology that human study must necessarily be performed by humans, some degree of bias and compromised objectivity will always discolor the loftiest of our formulations (Bailey, 1986a). The object, then, is not to once and for all distinguish the true essence of humanity from competing false essences, but to generate progressively better statements about human nature. Ideas evolve just as do organic and behavioral systems, with most destined to fall by the wayside. Yet, for a time, a precious few will survive the selective forces of empirical research, conceptual criticism, contemporary fads and fashions, and the ravages of obsolescence. Thus, within certain political, social, and historical settings, certain ideas and theories will be granted immediate acceptance, others will be accepted only after acrimonious debate or years of controversy, and still other equally meritorious ones will be doomed to extinction.

Were all ideas about human nature equally true, acceptance or rejection would be based entirely on the vicissitudes of the Zeitgeist. However, just as some organisms are more durable over evolutionary time than others by virtue of superior design, the more accurate formulations about human nature may be expected to emerge and re-emerge again and again throughout history, often in defiance of current ideology. One formulation that has been attacked repeatedly but refuses to die is that of the "animal" nature of man. For many in current American society, the animal part of human nature is repressed or denied, and the causes of human behavior and misbehavior attributed to socialization practices and cultural influences (see chapter 9). In the modern era of rationalism and humanism, the inherent perfectability of humankind is presumed and emphasis is placed on removing environmental obstacles to positive growth and development. From a practical standpoint, the notions of human perfectability and transcendence over our base animal nature have much to commend them. Compassion toward the weak, poor, the mentally ill, social deviants, criminals, and persons of other cultures and ethnicities is facilitated by focusing on their "humanness" and not their "animalness." Prejudice, hatred, and warfare often are premised on real or imputed differences between groups of people (see chapter 7), and what greater difference could there be than for one group to be more "animalistic" than another? Yet, aside from practical considerations, we must ask whether an accurate and comprehensive view of human nature is possible without a thoroughgoing consideration of the animal roots of our humanness.

The notions of human perfectability and transcendence have emerged with far less frequency throughout the course of history than has the antipodal notion of a base animal nature from which humanness develops with the aid of moral instruction and cultural shaping. It is significant that so many of the world's great thinkers over the ages have subscribed to some variation of the man-as-beast assumption, and we must consider the possibility that their assumption was an essentially correct one. Nevertheless, there is no dearth of modern writers who recoil from the implication that our humanness is erected upon a baser nature. J. R. Durant (1981), a critic of the beast-within perspective, documented how writers from Plato, through Darwin, Spencer, Galton, Freud, and more recently Ardrey, Lorenz, and Wilson have perpetuated the "myth" of a basically evil human nature, inherited from the evolutionary past, which is held under tenuous control by the more civilized, rational forces of the mind. Similarly, the philosopher Mary Midgley (1980) says that "in the world there is no such Beast" (p. 37), and she sees the beast concept as a worn and negative abstraction with little basis in reality.

In his scholarly and entertaining book *The Mismeasure of Man,* Stephen J. Gould (1981) strives mightily to discredit the beast-within idea, even to the extent of employing some rather harsh *ad hominem* attacks on the likes of Louis Agassiz, Samuel Morton, Cesare Lombroso, and Paul Broca. Gould reserved some of his harshest criticism for the recapitulationists and Lombroso who were forever finding evidence of phylogenetically primitive and atavistic physical characters, especially among the lower classes, among criminals, and among "inferior" racial groups. Gould is, of course, to be applauded for exposing the invidious elitist and racialist applications of these views, but this is not the same as forever laying to rest the man-as-beast concept. The way to permanently consign the idea to the infernal depths is to develop a superior and at least equally parsimonious formulation. Unfortunately, Gould disappoints us at this juncture by shifting from brilliant and incisive criticism to rather worn and loose sociological speculation about the "true" causes of human evil (e.g., oppression, unemployment, and blaming the victim). Such imputed causes are certainly of no higher scientific or philosophic order than the notion that human beings are motivated, in varying degrees, by tendencies, predispositions, species-typical drives, and so forth, derived from our millions of years of phylogenetic shaping through natural selection.

We find ourselves here on the horns of a dilemma: Shall we accept the beast-within idea on the basis of its acceptance by many of the world's great thinkers since the dawn of history, or by its common-sense appeal, or by its implicit validation each day on the front page of every newspaper; or, should we stand with many modern intellectuals and social scientists who reject the idea as socially dangerous, scientifically unfounded, or a useless abstraction? In my opinion, the man-as-beast concept cannot be rejected because of its scientific invalidity or its lack of empirical referents in human behavior; indeed, we are forced to conclude that the concept has never been scientifically disproven, but merely disapproved of for personal, professional, and moral reasons. Nonetheless, the modernist is correct in asserting the social dangers of presuming and publicizing the carnal nature of man. History has shown that once human beings are reduced to "beasts" through scientific or military propaganda, imperialism, exploitation, tyranny, and genocide are not long to follow. One wonders if the mighty intellectual protests against the Beast do not perhaps belie a deep inner belief that it really does exist; indeed, the reasons often given for suppressing the view revolve around the preconscious cognition "We must not expose laypersons to the idea that they have a beastly nature, for if we do, the floodgates of beastly behavior will be opened and all is lost." This fear is a real one, but, again, it is not, *ipso facto,* a scientific justification for dismissing man's animal nature.

It is unquestionably incorrect to assume that man is a beast, for it is not an either–or question. As is evident in the chapters to follow, human beings appear to possess both phylogenetically old or animal characteristics, and distinctively human ones as well. The challenge of this book is to analyze how these older and newer characteristics blend and interact in supernumerous ways, whereas at the same time encouraging the reader to think more deeply and compassionately about what a human being really is. To find a beast within is not to condemn the human race, but instead represents an appropriate acknowledgment of our essential nature, and our place in Nature.

The Mythical Beast

Ancient mythology bristled with stories of part human and part animal creatures, some of which were transcendent gods and others demons of the deep. As projections of real inner fears and concerns, these nonexistent beings leapt from the unconscious of men not yet capable of distinguishing between the real world and the world of imagination. The renowned classicist, Edith Hamiliton (1942), tells us that prehistoric peoples and precivilized tribes of today incorporate few romantic visions in their myths, but, instead, tend to focus on horrors lurking in the forest that only can be appeased through magical rituals and human sacrifice. Perhaps because of his closeness to Tennyson's jungle, red in tooth and claw, primitive man easily envisioned horrible possibilities in the form of attacks by night, children stolen by hungry animals, and adversity visited upon the village by angry gods.

Gradually, the myths of early civilized societies took on a romantic tone, and many of the gods became heroic superhumans rather than anthropomorphized animals whose blood lust required the ultimate sacrifice. With what Hamilton (1942) called the "Greek miracle," "Old things passed away; behold all things are become new" (p. 14). The Greeks had their roots in primitive savagery as did other peoples, but somehow they developed a civilized and beautiful mythology that brought the first true literature into being. In Homer's *Iliad,* for example, the gods for the first time are created in the image of man rather than in the image of inanimate objects or animals. Certainly, these new Greek gods were often petty, selfish, unpredictable, and less civilized than their human counterparts, but they nevertheless transcended the animal world. Yet, despite these grand steps toward rationality and humanism, the early Greeks could not totally divorce themselves entirely from fantasies of man's animalistic nature. Their stories still included beast gods—satyrs, centaurs, minotaurs, chimeras, gorgons, and hydras—but these lower gods were mere foils for the hero to defeat in battle.

References to the man-beast or beast-within are evident throughout the history of literature, from Homer to the present time. Some of the more dramatic examples include Nathaniel Hawthorne's retelling of the minotaur legend in his *Tanglewood Tales,* Robert Louis Stevenson's *Dr. Jekyll and Mr. Hyde,* Mary Shelley's *Frankenstein,* Bram Stoker's *Dracula,* H. G. Wells' *The Island of Dr. Moreau,* and John Gardner's highly acclaimed *Grendel,* a retelling of the Beowolf legend from the monster's point of view. To these we might add the reptilian, humanoid creatures from outer space so frequently seen in modern science fiction novels and movies, the murderous and predatory demons and monsters of the horror genre of films, and the monsters of our nightmares, which Carl Sagan (1977) suggests may arise from primordial memories of times when we humans were preyed upon by large predators. A recent popular film, *Altered States,* addressed the beast-within idea in a novel way, much to the delight of the ticket-buying public. The hero, by a process of "genetic regression," gradually lost all vestiges of humanness as he reverted to a Neanderthal-like creature, and then, stage by stage, down to a complete merging with the cosmos.

Apart from the literary or artistic merit of the mythical man-beasts that have pervaded human consciousness from earliest times, we must ask why the Beast holds such fascination for us. Is it because we tend to project our own passions onto innocent animals as some argue? Is it because we possess memory traces deep in our brains of times when large animals stalked us as prey? Is it because an animal nature continues to reside within us, living in "schizophysiological" disharmony with our higher nature, as Paul MacLean (1954a) and Arthur Koestler (1967) suggest? For whatever reasons, the mythical beast continues to emerge in our dreams and in the entertainment media, and continues to fascinate modern man as it did his primeval ancestors. Let us now shift from fantasy and imagination to rational analysis and see how philosophers and scientists have dealt with the Beast throughout the ages.

Plato and Aristotle

Charles Duff (1930) argues that Greek civilization, at its zenith during the Golden Age of Pericles, came the closest to the ideal of human perfection. During this brief episode in history, science, philosophy, and the arts flourished, and lofty concepts of freedom, justice, and democracy were implemented as never before or after. Duff credited the Golden Age Greeks with liberating the mind from the shackles of political tyranny and biological destiny; for the first time, the spiritual nature of man rode supreme over his animal nature. Plato was born during this era, and eventually became the brightest pupil of the master teacher Socrates. During Plato's lifetime, perhaps due to his frustrated political fortunes and first-hand observation of the Greek people's inability to maintain their earlier Golden Age spirituality, he developed a rather puritanical and aristocratic political theory that emphasized self-control and social order. In the *Republic,* Plato defined the Ideal State as one composed of a ruling class at the highest level, guardians who keep order and defend society at the middle level, and ordinary citizens (craftsmen, merchants, laborers) at the lowest level. Only members of the ruling class were to be educated, the most brilliant of which became philosopher kings, *le permier rang* of the Ideal State. Plato's view of the soul directly paralleled the constitution of the Ideal State, with the highest level, reason, ruling over the will at the middle level, and the impulses and passions occupied the lowest level. Thought or reason was seen as locked in eternal battle with animal passion, and only through willpower and self-denial could the passions be contained. Even under the best of circumstances, however, eruptions of evil and unpleasant animal desires occur, as seen in this quote from Book 9 of the *Republic:*

[These] bestir themselves in dreams, when the gentler part of the soul slumbers, and the control of Reason is withdrawn. Then the Wild Beast in us, full-fed with meat and drink, becomes rampant and shakes off sleep to go in quest of what will gratify his own instincts. As you know, it will cast off all shame and prudence at such moments and stick at nothing. In phantasy it will not shrink from intercourse with a mother or anyone else, or from forbidden food or any deed of blood. It will go to any lengths of shamelessness and folly. (Cited in Midgley, 1978, p. 37)

Aristotle was 37 years old when Plato died in 347 B.C. Like Plato and the other thinkers of his time, Aristotle assumed the basic animal nature of man, but ranked man above all other animals due to possession of a soul or rational intellect. In his *Nicomachean Ethics* (Commins & Linscott, 1947) Aristotle makes frequent reference to man's progress or lack of progress above the animals in the areas of self-control and moral sensibility. Aristotle liked to think in terms of levels and hierarchies, and in Book I of *Ethics* he postulated three levels of life—a hedonic life governed by vulgar pleasures, a political life devoted to honor, and a contemplative life devoted to wisdom and truth. He expressed contempt for the vulgar masses of mankind who tended to be slavish in their pursuit of pleasure, "preferring a life suitable to beasts" (Commins & Linscott, 1947, p. 7). In Book II, the questions of morality and virtue are duscussed from the perspective of the soul and its component structures—the passions shared with the beasts and generally accompanied by feelings of pleasure or pain, the natural faculties of structure whereby the passions are experienced, and states of character by which a person may be morally judged vis-à-vis the animal passions. Of these three, only states of character are distinctly human, for the former two are "natural" and do not involve rational choice. Thus, we cannot be judged good or bad regarding our natural passions and the mechanisms for experiencing them, but we are morally culpable regarding our states of character where freedom of choice and will come into play. For Aristotle, temperance in expressing the animal passions was one of the great virtues, and in Book III he says, "self-indulgence would seem to be justly a matter of reproach, because it attaches to us not as men but as animals" (Commins & Linscott, 1947, p. 620).

In Aristotle's *Historia Animalium,* we see his penchant for hierarchy most clearly etched. He suggested that all animals, from the lowliest creature up to man at the topmost extreme, could be ranked on a single graded scale *(scala naturae).* Using various criteria, such as possession of blood, number of legs, and breeding habits, Aristotle deduced 11 grades ranging from the zoophytes to man (Yarczower & Hazlett, 1977). Just as creatures in the external world are hierarchicalized, the workings of the soul are graded in similar fashion. In his treatise, *On the Soul* (Kerferd, 1967), Aristotle defined the soul and treated its functions one by one. The primary functions of the soul are the nutritive, the perceptive, the power of initiating movement, and the intelligence *(Nous)*. As Kerferd tells us, the functions form a hierarchy, with the lower animals possessing few functions, the higher animals possessing most of them, and man possessing all of them. Most importantly, man is the sole possesser of the highest function of the soul, intelligence. Aristotle's writings on the soul are complex and subject to differing interpretations, and some writers see active reason, the most refined aspect of the Nous, as a transcendent entity that places man closest to God and farthest from the animals (Kerferd, 1967).

Descartes and 17th-Century Philosophy

One of the most novel and controversial theories of man's animal nature is that of René Descartes. He postulated that animals act as pure machines and are subject to the universal laws of physics. Lacking a mind or soul, the animal operates in terms of reflexes unaffected by reason or will. Man, likewise, has an animal nature analogous to a biological machine, but he alone, as a creature made in the image of God, possesses a soul or rational mind. Although Descartes believed that most human actions do not involve mind (e.g., physiological functions, reflexive actions, and feelings or passions), man nevertheless had the capability, in better moments, to speak and think on profound matters, and to rise above creatureliness. Descartes' mind–body dualism was especially attractive to theologicans, for now the God-implanted soul could be a pure thing totally separate from the sinful and worldly body. Young (1967) tells us that Descartes' attractive yet awkward dualism probably arose in the first place as a means of solving scientific problems while remaining firmly within a Christian point of view.

Descartes attempted to maintain a rigid dualism, but even he occasionally lapsed into ascribing mental functions to animals—sensation, memory, passions, imagination (Young, 1967). Some of his critics and contemporaries went much further and based their arguments on some form of animal–human continuity. Descartes most formidable opponents in the 17th century were the Peripatetics, who, drawing upon Aristotle, explained animal behavior as something intermediate between matter and mind. Animals were said to possess a rudimentary soul endowed with all mental attributes except reason and will. Later in the century, Leibniz (Young, 1967) elaborated a philosophy based on the principle of continuity wherein animals possessed various levels of mentality but were denied the defining attributes of the souls of men: self-consciousness and the power to recognize eternal truths. Slowly developing was the idea that many attributes of humans and animals were continuous, and that man differed from the animals only in degree. The debate carried over into the 18th century, and a heightened interest in apes and savage tribes was evident. Many of the great philosophers of that era—Locke, Condillac, Hartley, and La Mettrie—addressed Cartesian dualism either to defend, refute, or modify it in accordance with current thought. It was not until the 19th century, however, with the advent of evolutionary theory, that the question of man's animal nature came fully to the forefront of human consciousness.

Evolution and its Proponents

Charles Darwin

Young (1967) tells us that the formulation and general acceptance of the theory of evolution has been the most important single factor in the debate on the mind since Descartes. In the theory's wake, the principle of continuity became more than a way of viewing the scale of beings; it became a necessary consequence of the fundamental law of life. Now whatever was said of men could only differ in degree from what was said of animals, and the mind became less a transcendent instrument of knowing and progressively more an adaptive function of the organism. Mind and intelligence were, thus, no longer seen as supernatural implants, but biological functions to be studied scientifically like other functions of the body. Debates on the animal soul became irrelevant as biological materialism and the scientific method came to supplant speculative philosophy and metaphysics.

Just as Freud did not discover the unconscious mind but recovered it from oblivion with his genius, Darwin took the age-old idea of biological evolution and gave it new life and respectability. The early Greek thinkers had held the view that life had gradually developed out of a primeval slime, and Diderot, Buffon, and Maupertuis in the 18th century thought in evolutionary terms as well (Burrow, 1968). Darwin's own grandfather, Erasmus Darwin, also held evolutionary views, as expressed in the following verse:

> First, forms minute, unseen by spheric glass
> Move on the mud, or pierce the watery mass
> These, as successive generations bloom
> New powers acquire and larger limbs assume.

(Cited in Burrow, 1968, p. 27)

Evolution was discussed in the early 19th century, but was not an accepted concept in the biological sciences. Jaynes (1969) provides an interesting analysis of the historical origins of ethology and comparative psychology, tracing them back to the debates between Baron Cuvier, the leading biologist of his day and champion of the immutability of species, and Etienne Geoffry-Saint-Hilaire, a brilliant young evolutionist. The debates reached their peak at the Academie des Sciences in 1830, and the Baron's reputation and his mountains of facts proved too much for the creative but unprepared upstart evolutionist. As Jaynes (1969) summarized, Geoffry-Saint-Hilaire was right in principle and wrong in facts, whereas Baron Cuvier was right in facts but wrong in principle. It was only a year after the debates that Charles Darwin, at age 23, departed on his famous voyage on the Beagle. While on the voyage, he began to question the immutability of species, and after returning made this famous entry in his journal:

> In July [1837] opened first notebook on the Transmutation of Species. Had been greatly struck from the previous March on character of South American fossils and species on Galapagos Archipelago. These facts (especially latter) origin of all my views. (Cited in Burrow, 1968, p. 26)

The stage was now set for the drama to unfold, but it would be many years before the play would open. Darwin had returned to England from the voyage of the Beagle in October 1836. By 1837, he had become an evolutionist and had firmly accepted evolution by common descent (Mayr, 1977). From that time, he never questioned the fact of evolution, but spent the rest of his life collecting supporting evidence and defending his position. Mayr (1977) refers to Darwin's initial conversion to evolutionary theory as the *"first Darwinian revolution,"* and the *"second Darwinian revolution"* corresponded to the formulation of the theory of natural selection. Natural selection provided a means of explaining the method by which evolution generates new species and dooms others to extinction, and represented "an entirely new way of explaining the world" (Mayr, 1977, p. 321). In his autobiography, Darwin (Barlow, 1958) describes how he developed and rejected one formulation after another until, finally, on September 28, 1838, the decisive insight occurred after reading Thomas Malthus's *Essay on Population:*

> Fifteen months after I had begun my systematic inquiry, I happened to read for amusement Malthus on Population, and being well prepared to appreciate the struggle for existence which everywhere goes on, from long-continued observation of the habits of animals and plants, it at once struck me that under these circumstances favorable variations would tend to be preserved, and unfavorable ones to be destroyed. The result of this would be the formation of new species. Here, then, I had at last got a theory by which to work. (p. 120)

As Mayr (1977) says, the theory of natural selection was a daring innovation because it proposed to explain, through natural causes, how species come into being, how they are maintained, and how those of lesser adaptive capacity waver or die out. In Darwin's time, both natural theologians and scientists were aware that animals struggle to exist in the wild, but it was seen as a benign struggle designed to maintain the proper balance of nature. Darwin's formulation was devoid of such teleological implications and the struggle anything but benign. In Darwin's eyes, nature was extravagant in the production of offspring but frugal in allowing survival up to or beyond reproductive age, thus setting the stage for fierce competition in the struggle for life. The goal of this struggle was to maximize the survival probabilities of single individuals, not to maintain the balance of nature or the viability of species. By virtue of individual differences or interindividual variability within populations, the mechanism of natural selection would determine which of the supernumerous offspring would be winners or losers in the game of life. Those species' members equipped with structural and behavioral characteristics more suited to prevailing environmental constraints and demands would have the advantage in the struggle, whereas less adapted ones would, on a probabilistic basis, tend to fall by the wayside. As Mayr (1977) summarizes, "Here we have the fortuitous coming together of two important concepts—excessive fertility and individuality—which jointly provide the basis for an entirely new conceptualization" (p. 325).

About 20 years following the formulation of the theory of natural selection, and after much urging from his friends to publish before priority was accorded to A. R. Wallace for his parallel version of the theory, Darwin finally published his masterwork, the *Origin of the Species,* in 1859. A year earlier, Darwin and Wallace had co-presented the theory of evolution by natural selection in an invited series of papers before the Linnean Society. In these papers, the basic principles of the *Origin of the Species* were eloquently stated by both Darwin and Wallace, but to an unenthusiastic and unreceptive audience. As Burrow tells us, much hind-sighted amusement arose from an unfortunate comment by Thomas Bell in his presidential address to the Society toward the end of the year in 1858: "[this year] has not, indeed, been marked by any of those striking discoveries which at once revolutionize, so to speak, the department of science in which they occur" (cited in Burrow, 1968, p. 15). As the reader is no doubt aware, no such ennui and nonchalance greeted the publication and initial reception of the *Origin*.

The ideas contained in the *Origin* were viewed as socially and morally dangerous not so much because of the scientific principles embodied in them, but because of the threat they represented to established ideologies. Mayr (1972) lists six cherished ideas of Darwin's time that were placed in mortal jeopardy by literal acceptance of the theory of evolution: (a) the idea that the earth was created no more than 6,000 years ago; (b) catastrophism and the notion of a harmonious, steady-state world; (c) the concept of automatic upward evolution; (d) the Genesis account of creation; (e) essentialism, nominalism, and typological thinking; and (f) anthropocentrism, the idea of man's uniqueness in nature. Mayr suggests that the replacement of typological thinking ("essentialism") by population thinking was possibly the most revolutionary change of all, for the doctrine that the changeable world of appearances was based on fundamental immutable essences (with each particular class of objects or living creatures emanating from its own particular essence) was well entrenched in continental Europe in the early part of the 19th century. Although essentialists would concede that animals vary within species at the level of observation, at the level of ultimate reality all members share equally in the essence from which they are derived. It is easy to see why Darwin's emphases on "real" variability in populations, on the individual instead of the type, and on a changeable universe governing by materialistic probabilities produced such panic in philosophical and scientific circles.

Many writers consider the *Origin* to be not only Darwin's greatest work, but, perhaps, the most important book of the last century. Not only did it explicate the theory of natural selection with convincing clarity and provide such extensive scientific documentation that many earlier critics and detractors were swayed, it rescued the concept of instinct from the metaphysicians and teleologists (Burrow, 1968; Ghiselin, 1973) and helped provide the foundation for, along with certain of Darwin's other works (Darwin 1865, 1875), the phylogenetics and genetics of behavior (Ghiselin, 1973). The book was not without its weaknesses, however, among which three are particularly noteworthy: (a) Darwin was woefully ignorant of the mechanisms of heredity. At one place in the *Origin* he lamented, "The laws governing inheritance are quite unknown" (1859/ 1968, p. 76), and later commented, "Our ignorance of the laws of variation is profound" (p. 202); (b) lacking knowledge of the laws of heredity, Darwin had no reason to reject the then popular Lamarckian theory of inheritance of acquired characters. Consequently, the *Origin* and Darwin's other writings are flawed with frequent references to inherited habits, and he included Lamarckian inheritance—along with natural selection and sexual selection—among the three main causes of variation within species; and (c) Darwin avoided the controversial issue of human evolution in the *Origin,* although he faced the question squarely in later psychological works, *The Descent of Man* (1871/1981) and *The Expression of the Emotions in Man and Animals* (1872/1896). Darwin was, as Burrow (1968) says, the least combative of men, and he seemed to dread the controversy and uproar that was sure to follow publication of the *Origin.* It would be more than a decade before he fully confronted the animal nature of human nature in *The Descent*.

Darwin and Evolutionary Psychology

Rather than reviewing Darwin's psychological works separately and in detail, we, instead, focus on certain themes of particular relevance to the thrust of the present book. As Ghiselin (1973) points out, Darwin's psychology was not confined to any one of his works, but was interspersed throughout the 10,000 or so pages of the entire Darwinian corpus. Darwin's most straightforward psychological writings, however, are found in the *Descent* and *The Expression of Emotions,* and these serve as our primary reference sources here. In outlining Darwin's human psychology and his views on human nature, we focus on the questions of animal–human continuity, human instincts, emotional expression and nonverbal behavior, intellect and morality, and phylogenetic reversion.

Animal–Human Continuity.   From the standpoint of the 19th-century Victorian traditionalists, the idea that animals and humans were related in any way was an anathema. Darwin's theory was superbly threatening to the status quo because of the clear implication that humans and lower species, such as apes and monkeys, shared a common heritage and were thus related. Darwin did not address this issue directly in the *Origin,* but the implication was clear. In the *Descent* (1871/1981), however, Darwin minced no words: "man must be included with the other organic beings in any general conclusion respecting his manner of appearance on this earth" (p. 1), and, later, "It is notorious that man is constructed on the same general type or model with other mammals" (p. 10). Humans not only shared their genesis and their physical morphology with the animals, however, but their behavioral (instinctive) and mental characteristics as well:

> It has, I think, now been shewn that man and the higher animals, especially the Primates, have some few instincts in common. All have the same senses, intuitions and sensations—similar passions, affections, and emotions, even the more complex ones; they feel wonder and curiosity; they possess the same faculties of imitation, attention, memory, imagination and reason, though in different degrees. (pp. 48–49)

A careful reading of Darwin's psychological writing reveals a recurrent theme of phylogenetic continuity between animals and humans, with no clear line of demarcation between the highest ape and the lowest human. Man was not so much special as different, and then different only in degree: "In a series of forms graduating insensibly from some ape-like creature to man as he now exists, it would be impossible to fix on any definite point where the term 'man' ought to be used" (*Descent,* p. 235). Likewise, the difference between the lowest savage and the highest man was again a matter of degree: "Differences [in intellect and moral disposition] between the highest men of the highest races and the lowest savages, are connected by the finest gradations" (*Descent,* p. 34). Organisms, as they become increasingly better adapted by natural selection, will tend to become more differentiated and complex, but they will not lose their rootedness in earlier phases of phylogeny; whether it be progress from ape to man or from savage to savant, the process is one of elaboration of old characters and slow accretion of new ones, with little loss of the original stuff.

Human Instincts.   Darwin's contemporaries used the term *instinct,* but in a way consistent with the essentialism and theological mandates of the times. Instincts were appropriately seen as complex, unlearned behavior patterns, but due to their apparent rational and species-appropriate nature they could only be the result of God's miraculous powers (Ghiselin, 1973). In the *Origin,* Darwin shied away from defining instinct, but he noted the ways in which they resemble habits, vary only slightly in wild species but considerably moreso in domesticated ones, are constant throughout life, involve an orderly sequence of actions, and involve "mistakes" and never progress to the point of perfection. Moreover, instincts may benefit a particular species indirectly, but the direct effects are on the particular individual performing the instinctive action. Likewise, no instinct was ever produced for the good of other animals, although it is common for animals to parasitize each other and to take advantage of each other's instincts. The most important point in the *Origin* was that instincts are produced by the slow, accumulative effects of natural selection operating, under conditions of changing circumstances of life, to shape innate behavior patterns in a useful direction: "I can see no difficulty in natural selection preserving and continually accumulating variations of instinct to any extent that it may be profitable. It is, thus, as I believe, that all the most complex and wonderful instincts have originated" (*Origin*, p. 236). Although Darwin speculated on Lamarckian habit and reversion (see following) as determinants of instinct, natural selection was correctly seen as the primary cause.

As discussed previously, in the *Descent* Darwin postulated phylogenetic continuity between animal and man in instincts and many other areas. Crucial to our argument (chapter 4) was the fact that he also postulated a psychological continuum proceeding from simple instincts at the primitive pole, on through mixtures of instinct, reason, and voluntary action in the middle range, and then on to reason and intellect minimally mixed with instinct at the upper pole. This continuum is seen not only in humans but in the more advanced primates also: "The anthropomorphous apes, guided probably by instinct, build for themselves temporary platforms; but as many instincts are largely controlled by reason, the simpler ones, such as this of building a platform, might readily pass into a voluntary and conscious act" (*Descent*, p. 53). Man never totally transcends instinct, for some degree of instinct–intellect mixture is always present in the form of instinctive elaborations (such as human language building upon innate imitative processes, animal cries and gestures, etc.), the occasional reappearance of ancestral patterns (reversion) that mix in with ongoing processes, or the blending in of emotional feeling with higher cognitive processes. Within these assumptions of instinct continuity, instinct elaboration, instinct–intellect blending, and reversion to instinctive patterns lie many foundation principles for a rich and powerful human paleopsychology.

Emotions and Expressions.   Darwin's primary goal was to show that anatomical structures such as fins, wings, hands, and eyes represented successful adaptations of different species to different types of environments, but he also was interested in the evolution of "mind" and expressive behavior as well. He assumed that the mental processes of intelligence, reasoning ability, memory, and emotions all evolved through the process of natural selection, and that all could be identified at different phylogenetic levels (Plutchik, 1980). The emotions and their expressions were especially intriguing because of the dramatic way they reveal man's kinship with the animals:

> With mankind some expressions, such as the bristling of the hair under the influence of extreme terror, or the uncovering of the teeth under that of furious rage, can hardly be understood, except on the belief that man once existed in a much lower and animal-like condition. The community of certain expressions distinct through allied species, as in the movements of the same facila muscles during laughter by man and by various monkeys, is rendered somewhat more intelligible, if we believe in their descent from a common progenitor. (*The Expression of Emotion*, 1872/1896, p. 12)

All of the emotions are more phylogenetically primitive than reason, intellect, or memory, but some emotional expressions are more primitive than others. In the final chapter of *The Expression of Emotion*, Darwin speculated on the relative primitiveness of differing human emotions, as defined by degree of similarity with lower animals, and concluded that expressions associated with rage, fear, and laughter are quite phylogenetically old, whereas signs of grief and weeping, frowning, furrowing the brow while in deep thought, and blushing are more recent acquisitions. Darwin found blushing to be "the most peculiar and most human of all expressions" (p. 310), and he noted that women blush more than men, blushing runs in families, a certain "mental confusion" accompanies the reaction, and the reaction is probably common to all races of man. Darwin believed blushing reflected a self-conscious concern about appearance and social evaluation, a concern that seems totally absent in the rest of the animal world.

Darwin believed that most of the expressions and gestures involuntarily used by man and the lower animals occur under the influence of "emotions" and "sensations." In speculating on the relationship between emotion and behavior, Darwin was heavily influenced by Herbert Spencer's "general law" that "feeling passing a certain pitch, habitually vents itself in bodily action;" and that "an overflow of nerve-force undirected by any motive, will manifestly take first the more habitual routes; and if these do not suffice, will next overflow into the less habitual ones" (cited in *The Expression of Emotion*, p. 9). Thus, the emotions and sensations (feelings), when experienced in sufficient intensity, will typically spill over into habitual patterns of action (we might say species-typical patterns) and much of the energy is dissipated by virtue of performance of the actions themselves, or the need-reducing consequences of the behavior. When such normal, habitual outlets are blocked, it would seem that expressive behavior is displaced from usual channels to unusual and perhaps abnormal ones. Spencer asserted that liberated nerve-force produces strong feeling that *must* expend itself in some direction, whether it be in specific goal-directed action or "intense sensations, active thought, violent movements, or increased activity of the glands" (cited in *The Expression of Emotion*, p. 71). Darwin basically agreed with the proposition that strong feeling generally leads to behavior, but he was aware that, in humans, emotional expression can be blocked or modulated by will and intellect. As evident in succeeding chapters, the superior human capacity to bind, sublimate, block or otherwise interrupt emotion→expression or drive→behavior linkages is one of the major characteristics distinguishing animals and mankind.

It is clear that Darwin considered most emotions and their linked expressions to be innate or unlearned, and he also thought that the ability to recognize certain expressions in others might be innate as well. This is a crucial point, for it bears upon the relationship between emotional expression and the processes of communication. Interestingly, Darwin viewed the communicative aspect of emotional expression as an epiphenomenon of the emotional states themselves; for example, the morphological and physiological structures subserving rage were originally designed to facilitate attack behavior, and only later, in secondary fashion, did the violent movements, bared teeth, accelerated breathing, savage sounds, erection of dermal appendages, and so on, achieve communicatory status. We may presume that once animals within a given population began to perceive "meaning" in certain expressive behaviors, e.g., aggressive "intentions" in the animal experiencing rage, those most capable of sensing the probability of attack would enjoy an adaptive advantage. In this way, natural selection would favor those animals most capable of recognizing emotional expressions in other members of their species, and, eventually, such capacity for recognition would become a general characteristic of the species.

Phylogenetic Reversion.   In speculating on the genesis of morphological structures and behavioral phenomena, Darwin generally relied on four modes of explanation: Lamarck's theory of acquired habits, natural selection, sexual selection, and reversion. The first three modes were favored by Darwin, but the reversion argument was invoked with some frequency in his psychological works. When faced with explaining a troublesome phenomenon, such as the near-complete but not totally complete domestication of dogs, Darwin often was forced, with some reluctance, to cite reversion as a probable cause. In *The Origin,* for example, Darwin asserts that "Natural instincts are lost under domestication" (p. 240), but then qualifies the statement by admitting that domesticated dogs do occasionally revert to wildness and attack poultry, sheep, and pigs. Because such reversions undoubtedly occur, and probably with greater frequency than Darwin assumed, we may ask why he was less than comfortable with the topic: First, the principle of reversion to ancestral states was popular in Darwin's day, but it was not his concept; second, he no doubt preferred the even more popular theory of acquired hereditary characters and his own concepts of natural and sexual selection to that of reversion; third, most proponents of the principle of reversion believed in the fixity of species and the idea that the animal or person reverts to a single, prototype ancestor; and fourth, Darwin seemed more concerned with how things come into being in the first place than with the re-emergence of pre-existing traits or characters.

Darwin's ambivalence about the principle of reversion to ancestral characters was reflected in the numerous and varied ways he used the term. It would be instructive to briefly review some of his major usages:

1. Although Darwin used the term *reversion* throughout the text of the *Origin,* he rather mysteriously omitted the term from the glossary at the end, and substituted the term *retrogression.* As defined in the glossary, retrogression was more akin to ontogenetic regression (*qua* Freud) than ancestral reversion.

2. Darwin more often invoked the principle of reversion when discussing the genesis of morphological traits than of behavioral traits. In *The Descent,* for example, Darwin defined reversion thusly: "Whenever a structure is arrested in its development, but still continues growing until it closely resembles a corresponding structure in some lower and adult member of the same group, we may in one sense consider it as a case of reversion" (p. 122). Here the character is arrested in development rather than recovered through reversion, and Darwin cited the microcephalous idiot as an example such reversion at the human level. This was an instance of phylogenetic reversion only in the oblique sense that the brain of the retarded person was assumed (inappropriately so) to be homologous with that of his ape progenitor.

In the *Origin,* Darwin used the principle of reversion rather literally in explaining why the distinctive coloring patterns of the wild rock-pigeon often are acquired suddenly in domestic varieties—even in instances where two different breeds are crossed, neither of which, themselves, possess the specified markings. Darwin concluded—assuming that the domestic varieties did, in fact, descend from the rock pigeon—that these phenomena could be best explained by "reversion to ancestral characters."

In discussing morphological structures, Darwin often blended the concepts of rudimentary organs, reversion, and recapitulationism in a confusing manner. In the first chapter of *Descent,* Darwin discussed the matter of rudimentary organs in considerable detail. Rudimentary organs are those that were once functional at some point in phylogeny, but are retained in current species as useless or near-useless vestiges. Such rudiments in humans include the wisdom teeth, certain muscles for moving or twitching the skin, and the veriform appendix. Being "useless," rudiments are extremely variable and tend to be suppressed by the processes of natural selection. Nevertheless, once suppressed, rudimentary organs may occasionally reappear through the process of reversion (see chapter 1 *Descent*). In a later chapter, Darwin states that it is very difficult to distinguish between genuine rudimentary organs and those that arise through reversion. The true rudimentary organ in man often represents the same organ in its normal state in lower species (recapitulation) and may be present in all members of the species, e.g., the os coccyx in both sexes and the mamme in the male sex. By contrast, vestigial organs that reappear on an unpredictable, sporadic basis are best explained as products of reversion. Although Darwin was somewhat indecisive about the differences between rudimentary conditions and those caused by reversion, he minced no words on the relevance of these concepts to the animal nature of man: "These several reversionary, as well as strictly rudimentary, structures, reveal the descent of man from some lower form in an unmistakeable manner" (*Descent,* p. 130).

3. Darwin was, perhaps, more variable in his applications of the principle of reversion to behavioral phenomena than in any other area. In the *Origin,* he spoke of how the child often reverts in certain characters to its grandparents or more remote ancestors, providing us with yet another type of reversion. Here a normal, but infrequently expressed genetic (as opposed to phylogenetic) trait is assumed to sporadically arise within families. Such within-family reversions also may be responsible for the reappearance of pathological traits that have lain dormant for generations: "with mankind some of the worst dispositions, which occasionally without any assignable cause make their appearance in families, may perhaps be reversions to a savage state, from which we are not removed by very many generations" (*Descent,* p. 173).

Darwin also spoke freely of phylogenetic kinds of behavioral reversions, such as teeth-baring and the snarl that represent carry-overs from our animal progenitors (see both *Descent* and *The Expression of Emotion*). This kind of reversion includes both morphological and behavioral characters, and is premised on the idea of phylogenetic continuity—if we are phylogenetically continuous with the animals and thus share certain structure-function relationships with them, then remnants of these relations will be evident in some of our more primitive kinds of behavior. Although we humans no longer use our teeth as weapons, when provoked we still "expose them ready for action, like a dog prepared to fight" (*Descent,* p. 127). Darwin believed that the "playful sneer or ferocious snarl, is one of the most curious [expressions] which occurs in man" (*The Expression,* p. 253), one that clearly reveals animal descent. As subsequent chapters show, this type of "phylogenetic regression" is one of the major forms emphasized in the present book.

The occasional reversion to wildness in domesticated animals discussed earlier is another type of phylogenetic regression. Here, the natural wildness of the animal is overlain with new habits and arbitrary constraints which, with varying degrees of success, serve to suppress natural tendencies. The suppression is not complete, however, and reversions to natural behavioral tendencies sometimes occur. In a recent review of feralization in the laboratory rat, Boice (1981) marvelled at the readiness with which the effects of prolonged captivity, often going across many generations, could be reversed by simple priming procedures like allowing rats to raise litters in sizes similar to those in nature, or allowing litters to be raised in burrows instead of cages. Boice commented that a couple of uncomplicated techniques of feralization were enough to undo a significant degree of the tameness and curiosity that make captive rats ideal research subjects. It is unfortunate, as Boice points out, that the research literature on feralization is virtually nonexistent, but if the findings on captive rats generalizes to other populations, and possibly even to humans, the implications for behavioral science are enormous.

Darwin believed that such regressive behavior was particularly evident in the insane, and in *The Expression* he quoted a Dr. Maudsley at some length on the topic. Dr. Maudsley asserted that the "animal-like traits in idiots" were due to the "reappearance of primitive instincts," and he questioned, "Why should a human being, deprived of his reason, ever become so brutal in character, as some do, unless he has the brute nature within him?" (*The Expression,* p. 246). This is a question we address ourselves in subsequent chapters. However, instead of proceeding from the basically recapitulationist perspective of Darwin and Maudsley (e.g., with emphasis on phylogenetically arrested development), we employ the phylogenetic regression–progression model as outlined in this volume.

A final type of behavioral reversion is that of group or social regression. Like most 19th-century writers, Darwin saw the human being as a brutal and savage animal redeemed and transformed by civilization. Through the inculcation of moral values and the development of mind and intellect, man was able to place a thin veneer over his basic animal condition and become truly human. Through the rigorous processes of civilization, man was domesticated and his wildness tamed. Yet, like the domesticated dog that slips and kills a chicken or two, reversions to the savage state occur in man as well. In some respects, such reversions are more severe in man, for entire populations may revert or retrogress from a high level of civilization and domestication to barbarism, savagery, or even primitive animality. Despite the ever-present possibility of turning the evolutionary clock backward, Darwin held a sanguinary view of the possibilities for human progress: "progress has been much more general than retrogression; that man has risen, though by slow and interrupted steps, from a lowly condition to the highest standard as yet attained by him in knowledge, morals, and religion (*Descent*, p. 184).

The Darwinians: Huxley, Spencer, Romanes, Haeckel, and Lombroso

Thomas H. Huxley has been described as "the most versatile man of science of nineteenth-century England" (Goudge, 1967). As a young man he held antievolutionary views, but after reading the *Origin of the Species* he became an ardent supporter of Darwin's theory. Unlike the anxious and self-effacing Darwin, Huxley reveled in the controversy surrounding the new theory of evolution, and his public lectures and writings on the topic were unrivaled. He believed the "most ingenious hypothesis" of natural selection provided a credible scientific explanation for the transmutation of species, and he once reflected, "How exceedingly stupid not to have thought of that." Huxley championed the idea of phylogenetic continuity in the organic world and was intrigued with the similarities between humans and the higher apes:

> In view of the intimate relations between Man and the rest of the living world, and between the forces exerted by the latter and all other forces, I can see no excuse for doubting that all are co-ordinated terms of Nature's great progression, from the formless to the formed—from the inorganic to the organic—from blind force to conscious intellect and will. (Huxley, 1896, p. 151)

> So far as cerebral structure goes, therefore, it is clear that Man differs less from the Chimpanzee or the Orang, than these do from the Monkeys, and that the difference between the brains of the Chimpanzee and Man is almost insignificant, when compared with that between the Chimpanzee brain and that of a Lemur. (Huxley, 1896, p. 140)

Like many of his contemporaries, Huxley believed that man was a base creature by nature, and only through the redeeming and transforming powers of intellect, will, and culture could any semblance of humanness be achieved. Man is born to the "ape and tiger" struggle for existence, within which he must exert "coercive self-assertion" in order to survive; yet, "the ape and tiger methods of the struggle . . . are not reconcilable with sound ethical principles" (Huxley, 1896, p. 52). In order to progress from his original Hobbesian condition, man must "escape" from his place in the animal kingdom and establish a kingdom of man governed upon the principle of moral evolution rather than biological evolution (Huxley, 1896). Yet, the victory of ethical man over natural man is not a bloodless coup; as Huxley says, intellectual progress brings its own set of miseries whereby the simple, the sure, and the familiar are transmuted into the complex, the unpredictable, the unknowable. Moreover, social progress requires that man deny his animal desires, and if the goal is moral perfection, the self-denial must be total: "having reached the point of absolute self-negation, and having nothing but moral perfection to strive after, peace will truly reign, not merely among nations, but among men, and the struggle for existence will be at an end" (Huxley, 1896, p. 209).

Huxley questioned whether humankind will ever reach this stage of moral perfection, for it is clear that the stage has heretofore not been reached "by a very long way." Not only has man never reached the stage of moral perfection, he often retrogresses from modest gains already attained. As Huxley poetically states it, man would gladly kick down the evolutionary ladder by which he has climbed, and would gladly see "the ape and tiger die." But the ape and tiger refuse to die, and often represent "unwelcome intrusions" into our everyday lives. Escape from our animal nature has never been total, and there is always some threat or provocation to reset the struggle for existence back into motion once it has been temporarily suspended. When the masses of mankind are cast into misery, as in the French Revolution, "society becomes as unstable as a package of dynamite, and a very small matter will produce the explosion which sends it back to the chaos of savagery" (Huxley, 1896, p. 214). In this regard, Huxley believed that evolution could be retrogressive as well as progressive, and he once commented that "the return of a species to one or other of its earlier forms, is a possibility to be reckoned with" (1896, p. 88). For the most part, however, Huxley was a champion of evolutionary progress, progress predicated on the refinement of intellect, on the one hand, and renunciation of animal desire on the other.

Herbert Spencer was an English philosopher and intimate friend of Huxley who applied evolutionary theory to all branches of knowledge. In 1850 Spencer published his first book, *Social Statics,* which advocated a theory of evolution similar to that of Darwin, but with an even greater emphasis on Lamarckian principles. Four years later, he published *Principles of Psychology,* but it was not until reading Darwin's *Origin of the Species* that his evolutionary zeal really caught fire. He was so enamored with Darwin's theory that he resolved to develop a synthetic philosophy that would bring all the sciences under the superordinate principle of evolution. He decided to write a series of volumes on the topic that would incorporate methods and data from metaphysics, biology, psychology, sociology, and ethics, and devoted himself to the project from 1860 to 1893. The recurrent theme running through these diverse essays was that every state of being—both physical and mental—reflects the organism's constantly evolving attempts to adjust to the environment: "Life is 'the definite combination of heterogeneous changes, both simultaneous and successive, in correspondence with external co-existences and sequences;' and . . . Life is 'the continuous adjustment of internal relations to external relations' " (Spencer, 1879, p. 20).

Evolution is a progressive process whereby organisms, in the process of adjusting inner demands to outer realities, proceed from primitive and elementary functions to those more complex and differentiated. As the organism progresses, both physical and mental functions, and their combinations, become not only more complex and differentiated, but more coherent, definite, and integrated as well. From primitive simplicity involving few component structures and few intercoordinations among them, there evolves, in the higher organisms, "coherent combinations" of physical, biological, and psychological functions that allow both flexible and efficient ways of effecting adaptive means-ends contingencies. Although Spencer disavowed teleological implications in his approach, at times he seemed to imply that evolutionary progress was toward the goal of a balance or equilibrium where the internal structures integrate themselves optimally for reliably effective adjustment. This equilibrium was not the dissolution of structures as occurs in death, but a "moving equilibrium" maintaining a balanced combination of actions in the face of an environment tending to overthrow it (Spencer, 1879).

For Spencer, the "ideally moral man," or most phylogenetically advanced human, "is one in whom the moving equilibrium is perfect, or approaches nearest to perfection . . . one in whom the functions of all kinds are fulfilled" (1879, p. 85). The ideally moral man, through his complexity and integration of structure and the application of superior intelligence, is able to properly satisfy needs in three basic areas: (a) needs pertaining to self; (b) the needs of offspring; and (c) the needs of other members of society. The ideally moral man is, therefore, more than a wonderfully complex and efficient machine designed for maximizing self-preservation, he also is a moral and reflective creature concerned with the "good" of relatives and society as well. The moral man restrains immediate impulse, reflects on the consequences of his acts, imagines future contingencies, emphasizes indirect as well as direct effects, and thinks in general rather than specific terms. In effect, man achieves unprecedented flexibility in adaptation through the use of intelligence, which, for Spencer, was the *sine qua non* of human adaptive capacity. With human intelligence, adjustments to the environment are both more "involved" and "appropriate," conscious co-ordinations are more deliberate and analytical, and actions may be emancipated from the coercive effects of immediate stimulation.

George John Romanes was a British biologist and comparative psychologist who became best known for his writings on the evolution of mind. Romanes was a close friend of Charles Darwin, who encouraged him to apply the logic of natural selection to mental processes of man and animals. Three major works were subsequently completed on the topic: *Animal Intelligence* (1882), *The Mental Evolution in Animals* (1883), and *Mental Evolution in Man* (1888). The leitmotif in these works was one that also frequently revealed itself in Darwin's psychological writings: Phylogenetic continuity exists between the animal and human mind, and differences are a matter of degree not kind. In chapter 1 of *Mental Evolution in Man,* entitled "Man and Brute," the argument for continuity is defended with considerable vigor and counterarguments subjected to detailed disvaluation. Romanes believed that the *prima facie* evidence for the general principle of evolution, and for its corollary assumption of animal–human continuity, was so overwhelming that only "very convincing evidence" could put it into question.

Some of the points adduced by Romanes (1888) in support of the continuity concept included: (a) the close morphological similarity between the higher apes and man; (b) instinct is well-marked in both man and animals, and is "identical" in basic function. However, instincts play a larger part in animals, children, and primitive humanity than in civilized human adults; (c) the emotions of man and brute are virtually identical and provide striking evidence for evolutionary descent; (d) the will or volitional capacity of man is similar in kind to that of animals, but the former surpasses the latter at the point where "complexity, refinement, and foresight" come into play; (e) intelligence is fundamentally the same in man and animal up to a point, but from there on certain "superadded" powers give man a distinct advantage. Nevertheless, the superadded powers arise through evolution just as did the more primitive ones; and (f) all psychological functions come into being ontogenetically through a slow process of graduated, incremental development, and it is therefore eminently reasonable to assume that the phylogenesis of traits followed an analogous pattern of development. Explicit in Romanes's line of argument is that all human psychological traits, with the exception of those pertaining to "religion and the perception of the sublime," arise through the process of evolution whereby fundamental animal characters are elaborated and refined into their human counterparts. Why the "religious instincts" were excepted from naturalistic explanation is not totally clear; however, as he got older, there was a tendency for Romanes's "youthful rationalism" to give over to a "hesitant espousal of theism" (Goudge, 1967).

Ernst Heinrich Haeckel was a German zoologist, philosopher, and zealous Darwinian who is best known for his theory of recapitulation. Recapitulation, which Haeckel called the "fundamental biogenetic law," is stated thusly: *"Ontogenesis is a brief and rapid recapitulation of phylogenesis,* determined by the physiological functions of heredity (generation) and adaptation (maintenance)" (Haeckel, 1900, p. 81). Haeckel believed that ontogeny, the history of the embryo, and phylogeny, the history of the stock, stand in intimate relation to one another, and one cannot be understood apart from the other. The relation between the two is not merely apparent or superficial, but of an intrinsic, causal nature. Haeckel summarized the theory in his *Anthropogenie* (1874), a work on the development and evolution of man:

> The series of forms through which an individual passes during its development from the egg-cell to its adult state is a short, compacted repetition of the long series of forms that the animal progenitors of the same organism (or the ancestral forms of its species) have passed through from the earliest times of so-called organic creation up to the present day. (Cited in Baker, 1974, p. 132)

Recapitulation was an intriguing idea that quickly gained many converts, and became one of the most influential ideas of late 19th-century science (Gould, 1981). According to Baker (1974), Darwin accepted the idea but was rather lukewarm to it, whereas others, such as Huxley, who translated many of Haeckel's writings, received it as a major evolutionary principle. The concept, or "dogma" as Oppenheimer (1973) calls it, still has its supporters in the present age, despite the wealth of technical criticisms that have accrued over the years (Baker, 1974; Gould, 1981; Handy, 1967; Oppenheimer, 1973). The concept is so attractive because it provides a conceptual means of deducing the characteristics of long-lost ancestors through analysis of the developmental characteristics of living organisms. If the theory were correct in general principle and in specific facts, one could, for example, deduce the probable adult characteristics of extinct progenitive species from the embryological or infantile characteristics of contemporary forms. Moreover, given the corollary assumption that recapitulation is based on an orderly succession or hierarchy of characteristics from earliest phylogeny up to latest ontogeny, the temptation to rank groups as higher or lower is a natural consequence. For example, the theory predicts that adults of inferior groups should be like the children of superior groups, for the child represents a primitive adult ancestor. Gould (1981) provides an excellent critical summary of the excesses and abuses of 19th-century recapitulationists who habitually compared "inferior" groups—blacks, women, lower socioeconomic classes, "savage" tribes, and so on—to the children of "superior" white males.

Recapitulation was an apparent truism that never lived up to its promise. By the early 20th century, embryologists had begun to concentrate more on experimental research and less on evolutionary explanations, and, more directly, the basic assumptions of recapitulationism were being challenged by accumulating experimental evidence. Exceptions to the biogenetic law were found at every turn; for example, in some groups of insects, species unlike in adult form have similar larvae (de Beer, 1958), and in one order of molluscs, the cephalopods, development is unique and noncomparable to closely related species (Oppenheimer, 1973). We must agree with Baker (1974) that there is no general biogenetic "law" in effect in nature, but this is not to say that Haeckel's theory is wrong in all respects. If recapitulation theory has any explanatory power at all, it is likely to be in the realm of mind and not morphology; whereas Haeckel's zoology was fraught with complications and exceptions, his psychology may rest on firmer conceptual ground. Certainly, his ideas on continuity and gradualism are congruent with the thrust of the present book:

> The psychic life of man obeys completely the same laws as the psychic life of other animals. . . . Like all complicated phenomena in higher organisms, so the mind, as the most complicated and highest function of all . . . can be understood only by comparing it with simpler and less complete phenomena of the same sort in lower animals and by following its gradual development step by step. We must return here not only to the biontic but also to phyletic development. (Haeckel, 1866; cited in Oppenheimer, 1973, p. 58-59)

Cesare Lombroso was a noted Italian physician and psychopathologist who is credited with establishing the field of criminal anthropology. His approach was based on a somewhat loose mixture of evolutionary principles that revolved around the then popular concept of *atavism,* or the sudden reappearance, in offspring, of mental or physical traits seen in earlier generations. Such atavisms, or *reversions* to use Darwin's term, may emanate from earlier human ancestors or from subhuman ancestors in phylogeny. Whereas Darwin, Spencer, Romanes, and Haeckel were primarily concerned with progressive evolution (although Darwin dealt with reversion in special instances), Lombroso founded his criminology, and broader psychopathology, on the phylogenetically regressive nature of human behavior. Proceeding from the typical Eurocentric perspective of his time, Lombroso found virtually everyone but the white male as throwbacks, of one sort or another, to our apish ancestors. He found the criminal particularly intriguing, for such asociality and barbarity in an age of civilization could only arise through a return to the natural inclinations of savages and lower animals. Criminals are born and not made, and they are characterized by:

> an absence of moral sensibility, in general instability of character, in excessive vanity, excessive irritability, a love of revenge, and, as far as habits are concerned, a descent of pleasures and customs akin in their nature to the orgies of uncivilized tribes. In short, the habitual criminal is a product, according to Dr. Lombroso, of pathological and atavistic anomalies; he stands midway between the lunatic and the savage; and he represents a special type of human race. (W. D. Morrison, in Introduction of Lombroso's *The Female Offender,* 1897, p. xvi)

Up to this point, Lombroso appears little different from other 19th-century evolutionists, save for his focus on criminality and regressive rather than progressive evolution. However, Lombroso took evolutionary reasoning one large and dangerous step further than his contemporaries: He asserted that the phylogenetic primitiveness or advancedness of individuals could be inferred from deviant physical characteristics or *stigmata*—the peculiar shape and structure of the brain, skull, face, and so forth. As Morrison stated in the Introduction just cited, "Dr. Lombroso's distinctive merit consists in the fact that he has devoted a laborious life to the examination . . . of anthropological anomalies" (Lombroso, 1897, p. xv). Lombroso thus assumed, logically but incorrectly, that a meaningful correlation exists between physical functions and psychological ones, and, further, that primitive physical characters were indicative of equally primitive mental functioning. Among the apish stigmata were greater skull thickness, simplicity of cranial sutures, large jaws, large face relative to cranium, long arms, low forehead, large ears, absence of baldness, darker skin, diminished sensitivity to pain, and absence of blushing (from *The Criminal Man,* 1887; cited in Gould, 1981, p. 129).

Obviously, Lombroso's theory of the stigmata held great potential for abuse, and Gould (1981) does an admirable job of documenting the social mischief that occurred during the heyday of criminal anthropology. Moreover, Gould does an equally adept job of subjecting Lombroso's theoretical model and research methods to devastating technical criticism. However, Gould fails badly in the central thrust of his mission; that is, to demonstrate, through withering criticism of 19th-century evolutionists and anthropometrists, that the beastly element of human nature is nonexistent. As long as beastly behavior exists, theories will be developed to address the problem.

The Legacy of the Early Evolutionists

Perhaps the chief legacy of the early evolutionists was their intensive focus on the animal nature of man. They aspired to develop a comprehensive philosophy of mind, one that took due account of both the lower animal traits and the higher human faculties. For the 19th-century thinker, arriving at the "truth" was the overriding issue, and how one got there a lesser consequence. Consequently, common sense reasoning, rational introspection and intuition, arguments from authority, and bits and pieces of empirical data were blended in often ingenious ways to derive far-reaching generalizations of man's true nature. Although we may question the sometimes personalistic and anecdotal methods of a Darwin, Spencer, or Lombroso, we are left with the larger question of how essentially right or wrong, in principle, they were. Methodological issues aside, how much of human nature is, in fact, due to physical and mental carry-overs from the animal world, and how much due to transcendent processes of social learning and enculturalization? Moreover, assuming the existence of significant evolutionary carry-overs, how do they blend in with and otherwise interact with more-or-less distinctive human characters?

These are difficult questions; ones that cannot, it seems, be totally answered with mountains of the purest empirical data. Thus, we must resort to theory and a degree of speculation in order to construct a workable and comprehensive model of human nature. The goal of this volume is to construct such a model of human nature, one that incorporates both the speculative wisdom of the 19th-century writers and the theories and empirical findings of 20th-century behavioral scientists. To aid the reader, some of the major 19th-century conceptual building blocks for the phylogenetic regression-progression model are listed in Table 1.1.

TABLE 1.1
Nineteenth-century Ideas on the Animal Nature of Man

Animal–human continuity exists in physical morphology and mental functioning.

To achieve full humanity, man's animal nature must be tamed through exercise of intellect and enculturalization.

Humans possess instincts as do other animals, but perhaps a fewer number.

Animal instinct in humans is opposed by and modulated by exercise of mind and intellect.

Rational intellect is distinctively human, while the emotions are more clearly shared with the animals.

Human language is more phylogenetically advanced than are emotional expressions and nonverbal communication.

Man's animal nature is not lost in ontogeny, but is elaborated, modified, controlled, and differentiated during psychological development.

Physiological and psychological functions blend and intermix during ontogeny, both within and between hierarchic levels of functioning.

Evolution is generally progressive, but reversions, atavisms, and phylogenetic regressions also occur.

Humans are characterized by a thin veneer of culture and humanity, which can easily rupture and allow the primitive "beast" underneath to escape.

THE PHYLOGENETIC
REGRESSION–PROGRESSION MODEL

In line with the 19th-century writers, this book is based on the idea that *Homo sapiens* is really two beings rather than one: The first, the animal being, is comprised of our phylogenetically old characteristics, both structural and behavioral, whereas the second, the human being, encompasses the first but adds measures of self-consciousness and intelligence unknown anywhere else in nature. In this view, the animal nature is normally subdued through learning and enculturalization, and blends in with our distinctively human characteristics (see chapter 4) to produce a "normal" human being. Yet, the powerful animal nature is never totally and permanently tamed, and under sufficient stress or provocation, phylogenetic regression may occur where the old motives and emotions re-assert themselves, sometimes with fury. By contrast, we phylogenetically progress when the higher functions of reflective thought, self-control, and refined moral sensitivity take over and the animal nature is, at least temporarily, left behind. As we shall see, it is much easier to phylogenetically regress than progress, for the animal nature is much older, more well-established in the genotype, and more well-established in the brain, than are the fragile and very recent acquisitions that define our distinctive humanness.

We are thus, from many important perspectives, more animal than human, and it is an open question as to which of our inner beings is master over the other. In recent times, it has become fashionable to revel in our distinctive human qualities, and to ignore, deny, and even suppress the obvious fact of our omnipresent animal heritage. In an era of vicious and cold-blooded rapes and murders, burgeoning crime rates in other areas, increasing social disruption and malaise, explosive international conflict in the forms of terrorism, warfare, and the threat of global nuclear destruction, it is interesting to note that the experts in such matters, the social scientists, have had fairly little to say. The social sciences continue to generate important empirical findings on these problems, but the question of what defects in human nature cause these sad events to occur in the first place is seldom addressed.

The phylogenetic regression–progression model was specially designed to address the causes of violence, psychopathology, and the more general problem of human evil, but it is not restricted to those issues. The model applies with equal vigor to the parameters of human goodness—love, altruism, kinship, parenting, cooperation, play, and so on—at the regressive level (see chapter 5), and intelligence, creativity, self-reflection and self-consciousness, cultural advancement, and spiritual fulfillment at the progressive level (see chapter 9). Because most contemporary behavioral scientists favor progressive over regressive explanations, it was decided to focus on the latter in the present work. Even the 19th-century writers emphasized evolutionary progress over regress, and it seems the human mind is more inclined toward looking to its rosy future than its sanguinary past. Yet, according to the phylogenetic regression–progression model, the greater part of our human nature is erected upon this long-forgotten and generally ignored animal past.

SUMMARY

Human nature is yet to be defined, and the question of man's kinship with the animals continues to be controversial. For many in contemporary American culture, the animal part of human nature is repressed or denied, and the causes of behavior attributed to environmental influences. Modern writers tend to denigrate the man-as-beast philosophy, but the idea refuses to die. In fact, most of the great thinkers throughout recorded history, including the likes of Aristotle, Plato, Darwin, Freud, Lorenz, and Wilson, have subscribed to some variation of the man-as-beast theme. The antipodal notions of human transcendence and perfectability are relative newcomers on the scene, and have enjoyed precedence only in the modern era. Indeed, we are forced to conclude that the man-as-beast concept has never been disproven scientifically, but has been merely disproved of at different points in history for nonscientific reasons.

Ancient mythology was replete with part human–part animal creatures that, among other things, represented projections of real concerns about large and dangerous predators. With the early Greeks, mythological creatures became more human in form, but various beast gods—centaurs, chimeras, gorgons, etc.—still roamed the countryside. The Greeks tamed the mythological beast, but did not destroy it. References to the beast-within continue to be found in modern literature, plays, and movies. The question naturally arises, why are people to fascinated with the mythological beast-within? Are these just fantasies, or do they tell us something about the deep recesses of human nature?

Plato believed that human thought and reason were locked in an eternal battle with the beast-within. Even under the best of circumstances, however, the animal nature breaks through, as in dreams where shame and prudence are cast off and the "Wild Beast" in us emerges to gratify its forbidden desires.

Aristotle also assumed the basic animal nature of man, but he ranked humans at the topmost rung of nature's ladder due to possession of the soul or rational intellect. We share our passions with the animal world, but we become virtuous human beings through temperance, moderation, and exercise of intellect. Aristotle suggested that all animals could be ranked on a single graded scale from the lowliest creature to the most advanced, depending on relative intellect (the soul or *Nous*) and self-control.

Descartes dealt with the beast-within by positing a dualistic nature in man. Man has an animal nature analogous to a biological machine, but he alone, as a creature fashioned in the image of God, possesses a soul or rational mind. This dualistic approach was awkward and problematic, but it did accomplish the seemingly impossible feat of recognizing man's animal nature while still preserving human distinctiveness and Godliness. Cartesian dualism was hotly criticized from its genesis in the 17th century, and the debate continued into the 18th century. Dualism eventually slipped well into the background in the 19th century with the advent of evolutionary theory, which revolved around the theme of animal–human continuity.

With the publication of *The Origin of the Species* in 1859, the issue of man's animal nature was placed, once and for all, at the forefront of human consciousness. Once Darwin finally decided on natural selection as the *modus operandi* of the evolutionary process, he had a means of explaining, through natural causes, how species come into being, how they are maintained, and how those of lesser capacity, in the struggle for existence, waver or die out.

Darwin's theory not only explained life, death, and survival in the animal world, it also served as a firm foundation for an innovative human psychology. In the *Descent of Man* in 1871 and the *Expression of Emotion in Man and Animals* in 1872, Darwin addressed the issues of animal–human continuity, human instincts, emotional expression and nonverbal behavior, intellect and morality, and phylogenetic reversion. Darwin used the term *reversion* in several different ways—reappearance of characteristics not seen in the family for one or more generations, reappearance of characteristics from earlier stages of phylogeny, descent from the domesticated to feral state, and group regressions. Reversions occur with either morphological or mental traits, although Darwin usually spoke of the former.

Darwin's theory attracted some of the great minds of the nineteenth century. Among some of his avid supporters were Huxley, Spencer, Romanes, and Haeckel. The Italian physician, Lombroso, also could be considered a Darwinian. All of these writers were evolutionists who were very much concerned with the animal nature of man. Huxley was an articulate exponent of the principle of animal–human continuity, and Spencer attempted to build a grand synthetic philosophy around evolutionary theory. Romanes applied Darwin's principles to the evolution of mind, and published three books on the topic. Haeckel, of course, is known for his famous "fundamental biogenetic law," more commonly known as recapitulation. According to Haeckel's theory, "ontogenesis is a brief and rapid recapitulation of phylogenesis"; viz., the history of the embryo is equivalent to the history of the species. Whereas most of the early writers focused on progressive evolution, Lombroso erected his theory, instead, on backward evolution or atavism. He believed that criminals, for example, were evolutionary throwbacks to early human savagery and some throwbacks even to subhuman ancestors. Even more controversial was Lombroso's assumption that the presence of primitive physical characters or "stigmata" was predictive of primitive or atavistic behavioral traits.

Despite the excesses and abuses of the 19th-century evolutionists, they provided us with many rich insights about human nature. Table 1.1 summarizes some of the 19th-century ideas which are of particular relevance to the phylogenetic regression–progression model.

The phylogenetic regression–progression model assumes that *Homo sapiens* is really two beings instead of one. First, there is the animal being comprised of our phylogenetically old characteristics, and second, the human being that includes the animal nature plus intelligence, self-consciousness, and culture. In our everyday behavior, we humans normally act like human beings, but under sufficient stress or provocation we can "phylogenetically regress" in a fraction of a second. Such regressions may be benign or beneficial, or they may be malignant or pathological. The phylogenetic regression–progression model deals with both types, but is especially sensitive to irrational and inhuman kinds of behavior. The model hopefully represents one means of integrating the Beast and man, the phylogenetically old and the phylogenetically new, in a comprehensive approach to the human condition.

2

The New Biology

Developments in the knowledge of the brain promise to have a profound influence on epistomology. In scientific and philosophic writings, it has been customary to regard the human brain as a global organ dominated by the cerebral cortex which serves as a tabula rasa *for an everchanging translation of sensory and perceptive experience into symbolic language, and which has special capacities for learning, memory, problem solving, and transmission of culture from one generation to another. Such a view is blind to the consideration that in its evolution the human brain has expanded along lines of three basic patterns which may be characterized as reptilian, paleomammalian, and neomammalian. Radically different in structure and chemistry and in an evolutionary sense countless generations apart, the three formations constitute, so-to-speak, three brains in one, a* triune *brain.*

—P. D. MacLean, 1977b, p. 308

THE NEW DARWINIAN REVOLUTIONS

The First Revolution

In the prior chapter, we discussed Mayr's (1977) first and second Darwinian revolutions. The first revolution represented Darwin's conversion to evolutionary theory, and the second corresponded to his formulation of the theory of natural selection. In this chapter, we focus on the broad implications of the two most recent Darwinian revolutions: First, the incorporation of evolutionary theory into the mainstream of biological science, and second, the incorporation of evolutionary theory into the mainstream of modern social science. With these two new revolutions, evolutionary theory has slowly, and often imperceptibly, become the foundation stone of the biological and social sciences. As Dobzhansky (1973) tersely summarized, "Nothing in biology makes sense except in the light of evolution" (p. 125). To this we might add that little in the social sciences—anthropology, psychology, sociology—makes sense as well without due consideration of the evolution of the brain, of behavior, of mind and consciousness (Crook, 1980).

According to Stebbins (1982), Dobzhansky introduced the first model for a successful synthesis of the diverse strands of evolutionary theory in his *Genetics and the Origin of Species* (1937; revised in 1941, 1951, 1971). In developing what is now called the *modern synthetic theory of evolution,* Dobzhansky brought genetics, selection theory, quantitative population biology, and field research on natural populations into a comprehensive evolutionary framework. Now geneticists, biochemists, paleontologists, biogeographers, cellular biologists, population biologists, and other specialists shared a common conceptual base and common language. With Dobzhansky's modern synthesis, the first recent Darwinian revolution was inaugurated, but it did not reach its apogee until the publication of E. O. Wilson's *Sociobiology: The New Synthesis* in 1975. The introduction of the sociobiological model not only capped off the first revolution, but also brought evolutionary theory squarely into the realm of the social sciences. Thus, from a historical perspective, the field of sociobiology bridges both of the recent Darwinian revolutions.

The Second Revolution

If there is any validity in the study of human nature, it is most likely in the dialectic of nature and nurture, or more specifically, in the synthesis of the two (Vale, 1980). According to the historian Hamilton Cravens (1978), a true nature–nurture synthesis will require a new model of evolutionary science that emphasizes the mutual interdependence of both biological and cultural evolution. To simply mouth interactionism or dismiss the issue by sloganizing that "behavior is a function of heredity and environment," or "genes provide the limits and learning provides the outcomes," is patently unproductive. What happens too often is that the nature-oriented biologist will talk of interaction yet act as if all behavior is the outward manifestation of genetic effects, whereas the nurture-oriented social scientist will similarly affirm interactionism and then proceed as if a person were nothing more than a clump of matter molded by circumstances. A true synthesis must go further, and necessarily incorporate and systematically integrate the following three levels of information:

The Phylogenetic Level.   Each species has its own particular evolved morphological characteristics and behavioral dispositions that determine its essential nature. This is true of all living species, including species *Homo sapiens*. These fundamental morphological and behavioral characteristics are *conditioned* by evolution—to use Dobzhansky's term—and are under the control of genes carried in the particular species' gene pool. Phylogenetic development of a species implies a progressive attunement of organism-niche interrelationships over evolutionary time, whereby surviving species adapt to environmental demands and unsuccessful ones do not. Generally, the behavioral characteristics and the organism-niche interplay are more genetically fixed and limited in primitive, less evolved species, whereas more evolved species exhibit more behavioral eccentricity and adaptational flexibility. Of course, the human species is the most flexible and least gene-controlled of all species, but its freedom is only relative (see chapter 9 and Rensch, 1971). Despite our braininess and relative freedom from the harsh imperatives of instincts and rigid fixed-action patterns, we are a species nonetheless, and much of what we are emanates from that fact.

The Neurophysiological Level.   Most living beings possess some form of nervous system to mediate between the urgencies of the organism and the demands of the environment. Some heavy-handed biologists write as if an organism may be understood in terms of a simplistic genes → behavior model, which is analogous to the equally simplistic stimulus → response model of the early learning theorists. The sociobiologists, for example, have been criticized (Washburn, 1978a) for minimizing the role of the nervous system in behavior, a mistake that naturally leads to an erroneous overemphasis on direct gene control of responses. Genes do indeed influence human behavior, but they must always act through the neural, hormonal, and muscular systems of the body, all of which leave their imprint on final behavioral output. Of these mediating systems, the nervous system is by far the most important in humans, and it is fair to say that the whole of psychology may, in the last analysis, be reduced to the vicissitudes of brain functioning. Given its role as the connecting link between the genes and the outside world, the brain must be duly considered in any approach to personality or psychopathology.

The Cultural Level.   The environment, society, culture, and civilization all refer to aspects of that part physical and part social outside world that exerts an enormous shaping and directing effect on human behavior.

More correctly, man shapes the world and the world shapes man in a dynamic, ongoing feedback relationship, and it is impossible to determine which exercises the more influence on the other. For purposes of convenience, however, many scientists think in terms of external stimuli "causing" behavior in a linear, unidirectional fashion, but this is overly simplistic for several reasons. First, stimuli, just as genes, do not act on muscles and glands directly, but rather act through the nervous system prior to eventuating in behavior. This complex central mediation and information-processing prevents us from thinking in rigid cause-effect terms, and thus serves as a major obstruction to a lawful science of behavior. Secondly, stimuli only affect organisms whose innate physical and perceptual equipment have the capacity to respond; that is, stimuli can only act within the sensory, central, and motor limits of the animal. And thirdly, an organism is extremely selective in what it will respond to, even when its response range is very great, as with the human species. Despite these qualifications, there is little question that the environment affects behavior, albeit in complex and indirect ways.

For humans, one of the greatest environmental influences is culture. Culture is not a thing, but rather a system of symbolically organized patterns based largely on the distinctive human capacity for language (Parsons, 1966). No individual can create a cultural system, for cultural systems develop over many generations and are shared by relatively large groups. At the individual level, culture must be learned, although each individual makes a lesser or greater contribution to subsequent cultural change. Parsons says that cultures evolve just as do species of organisms, with relatively stable, general cultural patterns acting much like genetic materials do in determining species type. He further suggests that the cultural system serves as an "environment" to society by providing ideological legitimization of the society's normative order.

From tools to technology, from kinship to society, and from ritualization to institutions, we see the growth of culture as the medium for virtually all of the collective forms of achievement and progress. The physical anthropologist A. J. Kelso (1970) states the case very well:

> Culture is the basic unifying concept of anthropology. To study man without a consideration of culture is analogous to studying fishes without an understanding of the properties of water. Culture is the medium in which man resides. It presents simultaneously its own adaptive challenges and also the primary means by which the human species meets these challenges. . . . (p. 1)

To understand culture is to understand much of what man is all about, but not all. The secrets of nature are to be found, rather, in the interplay of phylogenetic, neurological and cultural influences as they combine to produce the wonders of human behavior. An understanding of this dynamic interplay between our species heritage, brain functioning, and learned culture is imperative if we are to understand human social behavior, personality, psychopathology, and human nature in general. Given that our species heritage and neurohumoral functioning are difficult, if not impossible, to understand apart from evolutionary theory, it is evident that the second new Darwinian revolution must reach fruition prior to a full maturing of the social sciences.

THE NEW BIOLOGY AND NEW SOCIAL SCIENCE

The recent renaissance of Darwinism in the biological sciences has affected virtually all areas of Western thought, and the social sciences are just beginning to accommodate to the movement's impact. One indicant that resistance is crumbling is dramatically illustrated by the recent controversy between the eminent learning theorist, B. F. Skinner, and his erstwhile prize student and fellow environmentalist, Richard Herrnstein. Herrnstein (1977a, 1977b) argued that Skinner's theory is obsolete due to its failure to assimilate the phylogenetic, or species–specific component of behavior. Herrnstein further called for the merger of behavioristic and ethological theories, thus producing "a more complete science of behavior than either one alone has been" (1977a, p. 593). He upbraids Skinner for being an "environmentalist" who ignores the "innate motivational dynamics" in behavior while proceeding on the false assumption that all significant behavior is learned according to the general principles of operant conditioning. Herrnstein pictures "Skinnerianism" as "a movement dedicated to the study of behavior as behavior, to environmentalism as opposed to naturism, and to the primacy of the law of effect in guiding the behavior of higher organisms, especially human beings" (1977a, p. 593). Skinner (1977) rejoins that he is as good an ethologist as anyone, and points to several articles he has written on "nativist" topics, i.e., on the innate susceptibilities to reinforcement (Skinner, 1966a), on the relation between phylogeny and ontogeny of behavior (1966b), and on the shaping of phylogenic behavior (1975). As to this later paper, Skinner asserts that it represents "a much stronger statement on the inheritance of behavior than is commonly made by many ethologists" (Skinner, 1977, p. 1008). When the Godfather of the environmentalists endorses the ultra-Darwinian discipline of ethology with such conviction, we are perhaps correct in predicting that a new era of social science is at hand. Let us now look at some emergent trends in this New Social Science.

The Emergence of Human Ethology

Many social scientists were introduced to human ethology by the popular writings of Konrad Lorenz (1952, 1964, 1967), Desmond Morris (1967, 1969, 1971), Anthony Storr (1968), and Robert Ardrey (1961, 1966, 1970, 1977). Much of popular ethology has concerned itself with various aspects of "innate" aggression in the form of predatory carry-overs, territoriality, and dominance-consciousness, but attachment, affiliation, and bonding also have been included in the phylogenetic wellsprings of behavior. The popular approaches have been controversial and hotly criticized (Berkowitz, 1969; Leaky & Lewin, 1977; Lewis & Towers, 1972; Montagu, 1968) for their dogmatic tone and impetuous extrapolations from phylogenetically distant animals to the human level. Behind the hyperbole, however, the popular writings provide us with hints, suggestions, and speculations that often are heuristically intriguing and consistent with common sense. This is particularly true of the originator of the ethological movement, Lorenz.

Robert Lockard (1971) traces the history of ethology from Darwin through the intermediary contributions of Wallace Whitman, Oscar Heinroth, and Wallace Craig, on to the christening of the true movement with the early publications of Lorenz (1931, 1935) and Niko Tinbergen (1936a, 1936b). Additional historical material may be found in excellent articles by Jaynes (1969) and Beer (1963, 1964). In the early stages of development, the word "ethology" connoted a European movement within zoology concerned with the evolution of behavior, detailed and objective observational methodology, and the study of instinctive behavior in relation to habitat. In recent years, ethology has broadly expanded its purview, and is today linked with numerous biological disciplines including genetics, ecology, developmental biology, physiology, and sociobiology. As Lockard (1971) points out, ethology is in danger of losing its name—it is often called the *biology of behavior*—by virtue of being as broad as biology itself.

How might this burgeoning biology of behavior apply to the human species? First, let us examine the ethological theory of instinct, and see whether it applies at the human level. From its early history, ethology has focused on the concept of instinct, and Lorenz is credited with reviving the term following its "demise" due to withering criticism in the 1920s and 1930s (Bernard, 1924; Dunlap, 1919; Kuo, 1921). Prior to Lorenz, the term *instinct* had been used in contradictory, inconsistent and "experimentally useless" ways (Eggan, 1926), and had fallen into total disrepute. Approaching the problem from the field rather than the laboratory, Lorenz found convincing evidence for instincts throughout the animal world. In contrast to earlier usages, Lorenz, and later Tinbergen (1951), molded the term *instinct* into a rich and empirically rooted theoretical concept that went to the core of animal behavior in the wild. For Lorenz, an instinct is an inherited, species–specific, stereotyped pattern of behavior that is adaptive and contributes to the survival of the organism. The instinct itself is relatively fixed and generally refers to the terminal or consumatory phase of a motivational act, whereas the "instinctive behavior" that precedes and leads to this terminal phase is more broad and variable. When an animal is motivated to perform a specific instinct, its pre-consumatory instinctive behavior brings about "by *variable* movements, an *invariable* end or goal . . ." (Lorenz, 1950, p. 248) in ways characteristic of its species. Lorenz (1973) postulates that the specific instinct has its own "reaction specific energy" that accumulates in the animal's nervous system leading to an "appetite" (appetitive behaviors) for instinctive action, and finally the goal-oriented "searching" behaviors eventuate in the instinctive "fixed-action pattern" under appropriate stimulus conditions. This final discharge of the instinct occurs when an environmental "releaser" acts on the internal IRM (innate releasing mechanism) which in turn unleashes the fixed action pattern.

Although elegant and provocative, the classic ethological conception of instinct is fraught with problems (Cofer & Appley, 1964) even when applied to relatively primitive, stereotyped animal behavior. The conceptual problems multiply greatly, of course, when we talk of human instincts or species–specific patterns of behavior. We defer detailed analysis of human instincts and innate behaviors until later, but suffice it to say— problems notwithstanding—that something like instinct may be seen at the human level. For example, Lorenz speaks at length of the aggressive instinct and the aggression-inhibiting instinct (1967), the parental instinct that responds to stimuli emanating from the human baby (1943), and the bonding instinct which goes "hand in hand with the emotions of love and friendship in their purest and noblest form" (1967, p. 211). One might say that instincts such as these exist only in the eyes of the beholder, but Lorenz garners a wealth of observation and anecdotal data to support his views, and his sweeping generalizations, if not totally convincing, are certainly food for thought.

The Dutchman, Niko Tinbergen, is second only to Lorenz in the history of ethology, and he, Lorenz, and Karl von Frisch received the 1973 Nobel Prize for their respective contributions to the study of animal behavior. Tinbergen's master work, *The Study of Instinct,* (1951), helped establish ethology as a major new discipline in natural science, as did his *Social Behavior in Animals* (1953a) and *The Herring Gull's World* (1953b). In recent years, he has focused on human behavior, and has formulated one of the competing theories of childhood autism (Tinbergen & Tinbergen, 1972), written one of the most discriminating essays extant on aggression and war (1968), and provided the final commentary chapter in the anthology, *Growing Points in Ethology* (Bateson & Hinde, 1976). In this commentary, Tinbergen (1976) takes a large step away from classical ethology, and urges that ethology be applied to the diagnosis and remediation of human social problems. The application of ethological principles to a "sick, greatly impoverished and damaged society" (p. 524) is a far cry from the microbehavioral analysis of courtship patterns in the male stickleback or speculations on the umwelt of the wood tick! He reflects upon the damage that overpopulation, psychological stressors, and pollution have exacted upon modern society, but he is most concerned about "Man's Agonism to Man," that "supermotivation," or admixture of intraspecific and inter-specific aggressive tendencies that has plagued our species from its beginning, and now threatens to annihilate the race. We only can be saved when we understand our "true nature" in relation to a changing and progressively demanding environment. Tinbergen believes that ethology, and its twin sister ecology, can contribute much to this understanding.

The work of Irenäus Eibl-Eibesfeldt represents another serious attempt to develop a human ethology. In his well-known text, *Ethology: The Biology of Behavior,* (Eibl-Eibesfeldt, 1975) a chapter on the "ethology of man" was included, which dealt with fixed-action patterns in infants, species–specific behaviors of children born blind, instinctive releasing mechanisms in man, and so forth. In the preface to an earlier edition of the book (1970), Eibl-Eibesfeldt defines the thrust of human ethology: "The realization that phylogenetic adaptations determine the behavior of animals in a definable manner has increasingly led even those sciences which deal exclusively with man to search for the biological bases of human behavior" (p. vii). In his highly acclaimed (Kalat, 1975) introduction to human ethology, *Love and Hate,* Eibl-Eibesfeldt (1972) outlined his argument regarding the preprogrammed, phylogenetically determined elements of behavior, and then proceeded to incorporate a remarkable array of human social behaviors into his two-factor model based on the interaction of innate altruistic (love) and aggressive (hate) tendencies. Further, Eibl-Eibesfeldt's anthropological studies with Hans Hass (1970) rank among the most innovative cross-cultural analyses done to date, and their covert photographic technique (where their subjects were presumably unaware of being photographed) provided convincing evidence for the existence of universal, presumably innate patterns of behavior and social-signaling. More recently, Eibl-Eibesfeldt (1979) has discussed peace and war from the human ethological standpoint. Again, he emphasized the phylogenetic underpinnings of both our warlike and peaceful, cooperative tendencies, but also was careful to acknowledge the contributions of culture in constraining violence and aggression.

The study of child development represents one of the most fruitful offshoots of human ethology, and has helped establish beachheads in child psychology and pediatric psychiatry. W. C. McGrew's (1972) *An Ethological Study of Children's Behavior* showed that ethological theory could be tested in the free play situation, and interesting data were generated on dominance hierarchies, introduction of strangers into established groups, and effects of group density on behavior. Another important source in this area is Blurton-Jones' (1972) anthology entitled, *Ethological Studies of Child Behavior,* which covers such topics as nonverbal behavior, reactions to strangers, mother–infant interaction, attachment behavior out of doors, and the social behavior of normal and problem children. The main purpose of the Blurton-Jones volume was to apply the ethological–observational methods in the classroom and on the playground. In another offshoot, the various works on child development by John Bowlby (1952, 1958, 1969, 1973), Eckhard Hess (1959, 1970, 1973), and Daniel Freedman (1961, 1964, 1965, 1971, 1974), are heavily indebted to ethology, with their emphases on attachment behavior, human "imprinting," and critical periods of development. To a somewhat lesser degree, a substantial number of other developmentalists have incorporated ethology into their theories and perspectives (Ainsworth, 1969; Ambrose, 1963, 1969; Gray, 1958; Rheingold, 1967).

Human Sociobiology

The field of sociobiology saw a meteoric rise to popularity in the last decade, earning itself a featured article and accompanying photograph in *Time* magazine ("Why You Do," 1977). As *Time* says "few academic theories have spread so fast . . . with so little hard proof" (p. 63). The movement's originator, E. O. Wilson (1975), in his famous treatise *Sociobiology: The New Synthesis,* raised hackles by asserting that sociobiology will "cannibalize" the social sciences as it proceeds to discover the neurobiological bases of social behavior. In the more radical forms of sociobiology, the gene rules all (see Dawkins, 1976a) and the phenotypic organism is little more than a robot-like gene carrier obsessed with genetic immortality. Proceeding from a hardcore evolutionary perspective, the sociobiologist weaves fascinating theories regarding human sex differences, dominance, territoriality, warfare, maternal and parental care, attraction and altruism, and the model extends even into the domains of ethics and religion (Trivers, 1971, 1972, 1974; Wilson, 1975, 1978).

Barash (1977) emphasizes the multidisciplinary, integrative nature of sociobiology, and he sees ethology and population biology as especially formative influences in this new field. From ethology, sociobiology has inherited emphasis on natural, species–specific behavioral structures, and from population biology emanates general principles of social behavior, and, at the highest level of abstraction, analysis of the structure of whole societies. Actually, all biologically related sciences may be viewed as falling on a continuum going from cellular biology at the reductionistic end to population biology at the molar extreme, and neurophysiology and sociobiology, now at respective ends of this continuum, are quietly waiting to subsume all intermediary fields like ethology, and physiological and comparative psychology (Wilson, 1975). At the most fundamental paradigmatic level, however, sociobiology involves the "application of evolutionary biology to the social behavior of animals, including *Homo sapiens* (Barash, 1977, p. 2), and that would seem quite sufficient challenge for the moment.

Conceding the speculative nature of his argument, Barash (1977) applied the Central Theorem of Sociobiology (social behavior has evolved to assure personal survival and perpetuation of one's genes) to humans, and subsequently concluded that many universal species–specific behavioral tendencies exist, including such things as altruistic self-sacrifice, gender differences, mate selection, parent–child conflict, incest aversion, hostility toward outsiders, and even obsessive aversion to cuckholdry! The clear implication is that many phenomena previously thought to be learned, actually radiate from a phylogenetic base, a preparedness (Seligman & Hager, 1972) to respond in species-characteristic ways. In other words, there may exist genetic predispositions to play certain broad roles (Wilson, 1975) in terms of dominance, leadership, helping others, and possibly intelligence and mental ability. These assertions may seem rash to some, but Wilson, undaunted by controversy and blistering attacks from all sides (see Caplan, 1978), went considerably farther in his more recent popular work, *On Human Nature* (1978). Emboldened by the apparent defeat and humiliation of his critics (Wallace, 1979), Wilson spared neither humanist, nor theologian, nor philosopher as he placed thought, love, charity, and religion as sacrifices at the altar of Darwinian selection. If his new naturalism is true, then "no species, ours included, possesses a purpose beyond the imperatives created by its genetic history" (Wilson, 1978, p. 2), and the human mind is nothing more than "a device for survival and reproduction, and reason is just one of its various techniques" (p. 2). Wilson makes clear that all higher activities may be reduced to their genetic base: "innate censors and motivators exist in the brain that deeply and unconsciously affect our ethical premises; from these roots, morality evolved as an instinct . . . science may soon be in a position to investigate the very origin and meaning of human values, from which all ethical pronouncements and much of political practice flow" (1978, p. 5). In these statements we see the biological ethic in its most extreme, depicting man as a creature of instinct, a pawn of heredity, or, as Dawkins (1976a) concretely put it, a virtual gene machine.

In recent years, Wilson has softened his biological determinism somewhat, and he now focuses on cultural as well as genetic influences on behavior. In *Genes, Mind, and Culture* (Lumsden & Wilson, 1981), Wilson and Lumsden integrated material from several disciplines—neurobiology, population genetics, cognitive psychology, and cultural anthropology—in their attempt to bring sociobiology into the mainstream of modern social science. In so doing, the authors developed a comprehensive theory of gene-culture coevolution in which individuals assimilate the basic units of inheritance, termed *culturgens,* in accordance with epigenetic rules based on cognitive processing. Culture itself is defined as "the sum total of mental constructs and behaviors, including the construction and employment of artifacts, transmitted from one generation to the next by social learning" (p. 3). The social patterns which comprise culture are formed by gene-culture translation, a process whereby choices of individual members (via the epigenetic rules) are related to the distribution of culturgens in society as a whole. Culturgen choice, as influenced by the process of gene-culture translation, is essentially reducible to "the effect of genetically determined epigenetic rules of individual cognitive and behavioral development on social patterns" (p. 100). Thus, genes do not specify social behavior directly, but act through the intermediary epigenetic rules laid down in the innate organic processes of the body. How we are built and function physiologically, neurophyschologically, and cognitively affects what and how we learn and what choices we make. It is evident that the Lumsden and Wilson model is, at basc, a genetic one, but the determinism is more muted and the multidisciplinary integration richer than in Wilson's earlier writings.

Biosocial Anthropology

It is difficult to characterize anthropology under a single heading because the discipline ranges so widely into primatology, human evolution, archaeology, and other related areas. Robin Fox (1975) greatly simplified matters by coining the term, "biosocial anthropology," which encompasses a number of biologically oriented disciplines including comparative sociology, comparative zoology, physical anthropology, and primate biology. For Fox, this, "Biosocial analysis . . . is an analysis of the interplay between biological 'givens'—whatever their nature—and cultural responses" (1975, p. 3). This new field focuses on the full panorama of human experience, but converges on three major concerns: (a) development and the life cycle, with emphasis on the unfolding of innate programs, ease of learning, and critical period phenomena; (b) pathologies where there is a breakdown of normal life-cycle contingencies; and (c) biogrammatical universals, either institutions or processes, which go across cultures and societies. Fox (1971) feels that a new thrust is necessary because anthropology has, in the past, been obsessed with cultural differences that are used to explain every aspect of human behavior, including other cultural differences, *ad infinitum*. Anthropology traditionally has embraced cultural determinism while eschewing other, possibly more refined, explanations based on racial variation, history, ecological pressures, or biological universals. As Fox (1971) asserts, however, "Once one gets behind the surface manifestations, the uniformity of human behavior and of human social arrangement is remarkable" (p. 281).

Ethology represented a fertile source of theory for the anthropologist interested in behavioral or species–specific universals, and the anthropologist Fox and the sociologist Lionel Tiger were among the first to introduce this perspective in anthropology with their joint publications (Tiger & Fox, 1966, 1971) and separate endeavors (Fox, 1971, 1972, 1975, 1980; Tiger, 1969, 1970a, 1970b, 1975, 1979; Tiger & Shepher, 1975). Their best-known joint work is the *Imperial Animal* (Tiger & Fox, 1971), in which they defined and developed the concept of biogrammar, and then applied it to the problem of human bonding and sociality. Building on the notion that most of the bewildering complexity of culture can be reduced to relatively few biogrammatical or "wired-in" behavioral universals, they interpreted group behavior and politics in terms of primate sexual competition, and the mother–infant bond was traced to its powerful mammalian roots. Indeed, primate mother–infant, male–female, and male–male bonds serve as the foundations of marriage, family, and kinship systems, with male togetherness being the most important cohesive element in social cooperation, group defense, war, and many other vital community activities. This notion of the "male mystique" had been exploited earlier in Tiger's (1969) controversial monograph *Men in Groups,* much to the consternation of feminists and cultural determinists.

Fox (1975, 1979) is particularly concerned with kinship systems, and he assumes that kinship is a universal classification like human language capacity. He argues that our primate cousins have kinship systems fundamentally like our own, but no other primate combines elements in the ways we do. Essentially, our human systems contain little that is new structurally; we all have kin, recognize kin, and behave differentially to different kin and nonkin, as occurs throughout nature. However, humans differ from animals in several important ways: (a) humans are unique in that naming, prescribed rules, and classification schemes play major roles in kinship relations; (b) humans are uniquely exogamous, a factor of immense significance in homind evolution and social organization; and (c) humans have used their large neo-cortices to constrain sexual and aggressive drives so that simple breeding systems could evolve into complex, stylized kinship systems (Fox, 1972). Thus, culture is largely based on these highly corticalized inhibitions, customs, mores, and so forth, which oppose our natural sexual and aggressive proclivities, and allow for orderly, nonincestuous relations among immediate kin, and exogamic extension of kinship relations into larger and larger social units. In the early phases of cultural development, extension of kinship to larger units was accomplished by exchange (marriage) of females between groups, which resulted in cooperative alliances and consanguineous relations otherwise impossible. The natural inclination of unfamiliar males is hostility or xenophobia (Holloway, 1974), and exchange of females provided the basis for economic reciprocity and the politics of restraint. In essence, kinship has helped to form individuals into "one happy family" within a given classification, which is itself, a part genetic and part psychological entity.

Sociobiologists (Alexander, 1975; Dawkins, 1976a; Wilson, 1975) view kinship in fundamentally genetic terms, following W. D. Hamilton's (1964) theory of kin selection. Kinship selection means that behavior by an organism that may reduce its own Darwinian fitness can be favored by natural selection if the resulting effect increases the fitness (survival) of close relatives; in other words, our self-sacrificing altruism to close kin serves to perpetuate our genes in them through succeeding generations. The object, then, is for genes themselves to survive, whereas the fate of individual phenotypes is of lesser consequence. Success is measured in terms of inclusive fitness, an individual organism's genetic representation in descending generations as a result of its own reproduction and that of genetically related individuals (Hamilton, 1964). Kinship selection theory assumes that all behavior is genetically selfish, working with varying degrees of subtlety toward two all-encompassing goals: (a) inclusive fitness, and (b) reciprocal altruism (Trivers, 1971), or reciprocity (Alexander, 1974), where a given beneficial act is performed on the presumption that the recipient will return the favor in kind. Many sociobiologists believe that these principles characterize human kinship systems just as they do for animals, and are, in fact, the roots from which the vagaries of social behavior—sexual and reproductive processes, parenting, dominance, intergroup relations—grow.

The combination of Hamilton's (1964) kinship selection theory and Triver's (1971) reciprocal altruism concept represents a new way for anthropologists to answer the question of why kinship is important in every human society, but we must remember that not every single human act is altruism-related, and, further, that recognition of relatives often must be learned (Alexander, 1977). For example, parents must learn who their offspring are, and all individuals must learn who their relatives are by virtue of the type, frequency, and timing of social interactions with them (Irons, 1979). What seems to be innate or biogrammatical is the pervasive readiness to effect kinship ties, whereas the definition, recognition, and classification of kin is more intertwined with learning, experience, and culture. Nevertheless, it is probable that kinship ties are more easily effected when true genetic affiliation exists, as between parents and offspring, siblings, and other family members and close relatives. The single fact, however, that an adopted child can be truly loved reminds us that kinship selection theory cannot be applied to humans in a simple, cause–effect fashion.

Kinship selection theory and the broader sociobiological model were addressed in Chagnon and Iron's (1979) excellent edited text, *Evolutionary Biology and Human Social Behavior: An Anthropological Perspective*. Chagnon and Iron's text was an outgrowth of a symposium entitled "Sociobiology and Human Social Organization" held at the 1976 meeting of the American Anthropological Association. The papers were of high technical quality, and the sociobiological argument was exploited to the fullest, both theoretically and empirically. Most of the authors proceeded from a single, overriding thesis: Animal and human social behaviors are means toward the end of reproduction and genic survival, and sexual selection, kin selection, nepotism, parenting strategies, and even culture, in disguised forms, are all part and parcel of this quintessential process. As Dickemann (1979) summarizes, "Behind the surface complexity of human cultural forms, a general mammalian model, maximizing reproductive success through male competition and the manipulation of sex ratios, is clearly visible" (p. 367).

Reproductive success, then, is the fundamental criterion whereby the adaptive value of morphological traits or social strategies may be determined. Application of this logic to the questions of population regulation (Bates & Lees, 1979), sex-ratio variation in primitive societies (Chagnon, Flinn, & Melancon, 1979), female infanticide (Dickemann, 1979), reproductive variation in egalitarian societies (Chagnon, 1979), sexual dimorphism (Alexander, Hoogland, Howard, Noonan, & Sherman, 1979), concealment of ovulation in the human female (Alexander & Noonan, 1979), human ornamentation (Low, 1979), and parental investment in the offspring, led to many ingenious insights and explanations. These works are among the first real technical applications of biosocial anthropology, and the provocative theories and data generated presage the birth of a new field and a powerful mode of anthropological study.

Space limitations preclude detailed discussion of the various directions taken in the Chagnon and Irons (1979) text, but we may permit ourselves a closer look at one particularly intriguing topic, analyzed in depth by

Dickemann (1979), female infanticide. The current orthodoxy in anthropology (Divale, Harris, & Williams, 1978; Harris, 1977) assumes that female infanticide is a method contributing to population regulation, whereby numbers may be adjusted to local resources and population equilibrium maintained. Harris (1977), for example, sees warfare and male "supremacy" as excuses for female infanticide, which, in turn, reduces population to desirable levels: "War and female infanticide are part of the price our stone age ancestors had to pay for regulating their populations in order to prevent a lowering of living standards to the bare subsistence level. I feel confident that the causal arrow points from reproductive pressure to warfare and to female infanticide rather than the other way around" (p. 43). Bates and Lees (1979) consider these Malthusian, materialistic assumptions to be without empirical support, and they refer to them collectively as "The Myth of Population Regulation." Bates and Lees prefer the alternative sociobiological argument articulated by Alexander (1974), who sees female infanticide, the male status hierarchy, sexual dimorphism, and other "family-related" phenomena in terms of parental investment strategies. It is rather success in reproducing ones genes—and not prevention of reproduction—that motivates parents in one situation to murder their daughters, in another to murder their sons, and in still another, to shower both sons and daughters with exquisite forms of love and affection. The reproductive demands differ from situation to situation, giving rise to a myriad of parental strategies for achieving a single purpose—inclusive fitness. Female infanticide, for example, is only one of many techniques for assuring inclusive fitness in societies where males must compete for mates; other correlative traits include celibacy, polygamous breeding, hypergyny, status-correlated wealth exchange, matrilateral cross-cousin marriage, and seclusion of women (Dickemann, 1979).

At this point, it may appear that biosocial anthropology glorifies biological determinism and ignores the cultural roots of behavior. Actually, the biosocial anthropologist is more likely to assume that both natural selection and cultural selection work together to best enhance the inclusive fitness of individuals (Durham, 1979). Cultural selection refers to a process of selective retention of those cultural variants whose net effect is reproductively adaptive for the individuals involved. Campbell (1975), for example, refers to the process of "sociocultural evolution" whereby "a *selective* cumulation of skills, technologies, recipes, beliefs, customs, organizational structures, and the like, (are) retained through purely social modes of transmission, rather than in the genes" (p. 1104). Further, this "cultural inheritance can, on evolutionaly grounds, be regarded as adaptive, and treated with respect" (Campbell, 1975, p. 1105). Human phenotypes thus evolve subject to both biological and cultural conflu-

ences, and, given the combined effect of these two processes, we should
be thinking in terms of a "coevolutionary" theory of human behavior
(Durham, 1979).

Biosocial anthropology addresses itself to the fundamental question of
how biology and culture interact protagonistically, antagonistically, and
synergistically to produce observed consistency and variation among the
over 3,000 cultures of the world. As with most human questions, the
complexities are enormous: First, it is difficult to distinguish between
cultural traits that are targeted toward inclusive fitness (genetically adaptive) and those that are purely arbitrary and based on momentary reward
or symbolic belief (Durham, 1979); second, separating biological from
cultural causality is severely complicated by the fact the former is more
linked to ultimate (long-term) causes, and the latter to proximate (short-
term) causes (Wilson, 1975); third, culture may represent an important
selection pressure that has "produced an animal wired for the processing
of various cultural programs" (Fox, 1971, p. 292); fourth, culture may be
viewed as a mechanism for extending, modifying, and modulating herita-
ble characteristics (Mead, 1971); fifth, biology and culture normally are
adaptively coupled in order to effect reproductive maximization, but
uncoupling often occurs, especially in modern urban society (Alexander,
1979); and sixth, culture affects the genotype more or less directly
through its control of reproductive practices, viz., courtship and mating,
parenting, and degree and type of exogamic, intergroup relations. Alexander (1979) believes that the most important cultural attribute affecting
differential reproduction in early man was intergroup competition, and he
asserts that "eventually culture became the chief vehicle of competition"
(p. 440).

Ethopsychoanalysis and Ethopsychiatry

Darwinian theory has had significant influence in the field of psychoanalysis. As a young man, Freud (1935/1952) was "strongly attracted" to
Darwin's theories, which seemed to hold out "hopes of an extraordinary
advance in our understanding of the world" (p. 14). Freud (1935/1952)
acknowledges that his reflections on the meaning of the totem feast (1913/
1938) were based on Darwin's speculations on the primal horde (see Fox,
1980), and smatterings of Darwin are seen in many of his other works.
However, like Darwin, Freud knew little of the mechanisms of genetic
transmission, and he seemed to be basically a Lamarckian at heart. For
example, Freud (1920/1969) considered both ego and libido to be "at
bottom inheritances" (p. 309), but he was apparently thinking here in
Larmarckian rather than Darwinian terms. Whereas the strict evolutionary links between Darwin and Freud were tenuous, both men shared a

penchant for biological materialism and reductionism. In his Project in 1895, Freud (1957) clearly implied that all psychic activity ultimately could be reduced to neuronal processes, and biological determinism is a central theme throughout his writings.

As did Darwin, Freud looked to the past to explain the present, and naturally he turned to paleontology and evolutionary theory for the dark secrets of man's origins. Thus, it was not surprising that Darwin's idea of a primal horde, where the oldest and strongest male prevented sexual promiscuity among his inferiors, was so fascinating to Freud. Proceeding from the primal horde metaphor, Freud (1913/1938) went on to reconstruct the genesis of Oedipus and less directly weave an anthropological argument for man's inherent aggressiveness:

> One day the brothers formed forces, slew and ate the father, and put an end to the father horde. Together they dared and accomplished together what would have remained impossible for them singly . . . The totem feast, which is perhaps mankind's first celebration, would be the repetition and commemoration of this memorable, criminal act with which so many things began, social organization, moral restrictions, and religion (pp. 915-916)

Freud's pessimistic beliefs about human nature would put Ardrey or Dart to shame, as exemplified in his essay *Reflections on War and Death* (1915/1963a): "The very emphasis of the commandment *Thou shalt not kill* makes it certain that we spring from an endless ancestry of murderers, with whom the lust for killing was in the blood, as possibly it is to this day in ourselves" (p. 124). Later, in his famous letter to Albert Einstein entitled "Why War," Freud (1932/1963b) reiterated the same depressing, fatalistic theme: "the attempt to replace actual force by the force of ideas seems at present to be doomed to failure . . . law was originally brute violence" (pp. 140-141). Though repulsive to many, these ideas have been given new credence by virtue of recent findings on primate violence (Fossey, 1984; Goodall, 1979; Hausfater & Hrdy, 1984), violence in early man (Roper, 1969), and cannibalistic rituals and ceremonies in Neanderthal man (Constable, 1973). These matters are discussed in greater detail in later sections, but, for now, we may conclude that many of Freud's ideas on aggression and human nature are in sympathy with some of the more pessimistic theories and findings of the New Biology (see chapters 10 and 11).

Fundamental similarities between the New Biology and psychoanalysis are not limited to the areas of aggression and violence. In 1959, a group of psychoanalysts met to discuss the implications of ethology for psychoanalysis at the 21st Congress of the International Psycho-Analytical Association in Copenhagen (Bowlby, 1960; Kaufman, 1960; Tidd, 1960). It was concluded that ethology and psychoanalysis share many fundamental similarities including a fondness for careful description and classification, emphasis on direct observation of subjects, focus on developmental processes and early attachment, and a theoretical proclivity for thinking in terms of relations, sequences, and connections. In another context, Hinde (1959) lists the three basic orienting attitudes of ethology: "What causes it to be here?", How does it work and what is its function?", and "What is its evolutionary origin and history?" In answering these questions, one uses causal, functional, and historical explanations, modes of reasoning ever familiar to the psychoanalyst.

Basic similarities between ethology and psychoanalysis exist at the "metapsychological level" also. Rapaport and Gill (1959) formulated five metapsychological assumptions that encompass the various aspects of psychoanalytic theory: They conclude that psychoanalysis is dynamic, economic, structural, genetic (developmental), and adaptive. One might argue that each of these apply equally well to ethology, at least to the classical, hydraulic version as postulated by Lorenz, with its action-specific energy, innate-releasing mechanism, and heavy emphasis on developmental and adaptive processes. Also, several psychoanalysts have drawn parallels between certain ethological concepts and the Freudian mental structures, but there is inconsistency as to what specific behaviors fall under "ego" and "superego." For example, Menaker (1956) and Weigert (1956) included inhibitory, submissive, and other aggression-reducing survival behaviors under the heading of ego, whereas Schur (1960) suggests that instinctive inhibitory mechanisms in animals might be forerunners of the superego. Schur (1953, 1955, 1960) also has employed evolutionary theory and ethology in a sophisticated discussion of instincts, anxiety, the repetition compulsion, and the problem of affect and structure formation in general. Similarly, Meerlo (1962) and Bailey (1978) have drawn heavily from psychoanalysis and evolutionary theory in their theoretical papers on the topic of phylogenetic regression.

A number of etho-analytically oriented books have emerged in the last two decades. Peterfreund's (1971) amalgamation of information, systems, and evolutionary theories is a prime example, and represents the most serious attempt to synthesize psychoanalysis with modern biology. He sees the human organism as a complex, hierarchical arrangement of control systems capable of processing phylogenetic, ontogenetic, current, and self-monitoring kinds of information. The phylogenetic subprograms or subroutines that underlie behavior are central in the theory, and these include not only autonomic, reflexive processes but psychological ones as well, including sexuality:

In an information-systems frame of reference, sexuality can easily be conceptualized in terms of a genetically-ordained, extremely complex group of structures or subroutines which form a system that unfolds according to a motivational blueprint, and which is based on information inputs and selections through eons of evolutionary time. The phenomena referred to as orality, anality, and genitality can be viewed as phenomena which correspond to the hierarchial levels of the over-all maturing control-system program . . . it is quite well established that sexual control centers do exist in the phylogenetically older parts of the brain such as the hypothalmus (Peterfreund, p. 152).

Rado's (1964) theory of adaptational psychodynamics also emphasizes the phylogenetic foundations of personality (see chapter 3). He assumes that the human psychodynamic cerebral system involves several hierarchically arranged levels of integration roughly corresponding to the phylogeny of the human species. Going from the most phylogenetically primitive to the most refined, distinctively human levels, we find: (a) the hedonic, pleasure-seeking level that is common to all animals; (b) the brute-emotional level of social emotions such as fear, rage, love, and grief; (c) the emotional-thought level where primitive tendencies are brought under cognitive control and behavior reflects mixtures of "older" emotions and "newer" thought patterns; and (d) the unemotional-thought level that appears to be distinctively human, and represents the capability to use insight, reflection, and to solve problems by intellectual means alone. With both Peterfreund and Rado, we see highly integrative theories which aspire to a comprehensive understanding of the human organism as an evolved mammal and primate on the one hand, and as a reflective, linguistic human being on the other.

In 1974, the psychoanalyst Louis Breger published an integrative textbook entitled, *From Instinct to Identity: The Development of Personality*. As with Peterfreund and Rado, human behavior and motives are seen as erected upon phylogenetic foundations, with the fundamentals of social behavior (sexuality, love, play, aggression and its control, curiosity, fantasy, rebellion, and even conscience) representing elaborated derivatives of our primate heritage. Breger focuses on developmental processes, and his integrative model synthesizes basic concepts from evolutionary theory, psychoanalysis, and Piagetian psychology.

There are several edited texts of interest devoted to bringing evolutionary theory into the mainstream of psychiatry. In 1974, White published an anthology entitled *Ethology and Psychiatry,* and many discriminating papers by eminent ethologists and primatologists were included that addressed development, social behavior, and evolutionary processes. Although the readings were interesting and many had been previously published elsewhere, few suggestions were given as to how ethological and primatological concepts could be applied to understanding personality or psychopathology. Hutt and Hutt's (1970) *Behaviour Studies in*

Psychiatry dealt more with applied issues, but childhood autism was the only clinical syndrome discussed in detail. Although Hutt and Hutt's book offered little by way of application, the theoretical synthesis was convincing, and the first chapter by S. J. Hutt, "The Role of Behaviour Studies in Psychiatry: An Ethological Viewpoint," was a conceptual gem. Hutt says that the ethologically oriented psychiatrist deals with natural units of behavior, i.e., endogenous, patterned, and stereotyped "action chains" that arise from fundamental, and often innate, motivational systems. In understanding these motivational systems, the psychiatrist can learn much from "phylogenetic comparisons" of physiological states underlying abnormal behaviors in human beings, and from animal–human differences and similarities at the morphological and action levels as well.

Ethological psychiatry has begun to fulfill its promise through the efforts of Michael McGuire and his associates at the Human Ethology Laboratory at the University of California. In an edited text (McGuire & Fairbanks, 1977) entitled *Ethological Psychiatry: Psychopathology in the Context of Evolutionary Biology,* the foundation for a new field was laid, and the reader is left taken with the exciting possibilities at hand. It is clear that ethology more readily complements psychiatry than either experimental or clinical psychology, in its emphasis on internal causes, multiple determination, and the biological-rootedness of behavior. McGuire and Fairbanks (1977) summarize their central theme: "We believe it is in recognizing species-typed tendencies, exploring their ontogeny, their tenacity, and their modifiability as well as observing the consequences of thwarting them that ethology gains interpretive leverage over current theories of normal and abnormal behavior" (p. 15).

Since the 1977 book, McGuire and his colleagues have generated a great quantity of publications in evolutionary psychopathology, and their theoretical emphasis has broadened to include sociobiology as well as ethology (McGuire, 1979; Essock-Vitale & Fairbanks, 1979; Essock-Vitale & McGuire, 1979; Essock-Vitale & McGuire, 1980). Their focus on research methodology and empirical data, as well as theory, sets a new standard in evolutionary psychopathology, and has helped give birth to a new subdiscipline within psychiatry. Whether one calls this new subdiscipline ethopsychiatry, sociobiological psychiatry, or simply biological psychiatry, McGuire and colleagues have built a convincing case for its legitimacy. In a triad of seminal papers on psychiatric disorders in the context of evolutionary biology (McGuire & Essock-Vitale, 1981, 1982; McGuire, Essock-Vitale, & Polsky, 1981), psychiatric disorders were redefined in terms of reduced ability to achieve biologically-relevant goals (suboptimization), and a new functional classification of behavior was developed. Examples of adaptive goals (McGuire & Essock-Vitale, 1981) include those important to sexually reproducing species (live in optimally dense environment, have optimal number of offspring, establish and maintain pair bonds, have adequate defenses, and so on), those important to social species (communicate fluently and develop and maintain social support networks), and those especially relevant to higher primates, including humans (behavioral and learning flexibility and optimization of investment in offspring and other kin). The hypothesis that reduced likelihood of achieving such goals is a major correlate of psychiatric illness (McGuire & Essock-Vitale, 1981) has strong intuitive appeal, and has received initial empirical support (Essock-Vitale & Fairbanks, 1979; McGuire & Essock-Vitale, 1982). From these and other findings, it is clear that McGuire and colleagues have opened up a vast new area of inquiry.

THE EVOLVED NERVOUS SYSTEM

Gross Brain Size

If one were to pick a single place where the differing strands of the New Biology converge, it would be the nervous system. The nervous system sits at the center of all activity, and once the interrelationships between brain and behavior are understood, human nature will be essentially understood as well. We are far from that goal, but intensive study of the brain is required for making sense of the complexities of thought, consciousness, motivation, intelligence, language, and, indeed, the totality of human experience and behavior. The relation between gross brain size and behavior is a good place to begin our study. The relative size of the brain in hooved and carnivorous mammals has increased and become diversified as these animals evolved over the past 50 million years (Jerison, 1976), and the hominid brain has approximately tripled in the past 1.5 to 4.5 million years (Jerison, 1977; Tobias, 1971). Although absolute size is a poor measure of functional capacity (Gould, 1981; Tobias, 1971), no doubt the observed increases—especially the dramatic increases in man—are correlated with greater information-processing capacity and more refined integration of perceptual–motor–cognitive systems.

According to Jerison (1973, 1977), mind or intelligence arises from natural selection for encephalization, whereby greater brain enlargement results than would be expected from corresponding increases in body size. This "extra" brain tissue, above that needed to mediate body functions, serves as the basis for the evolution of higher cognitive functions (Jerison, 1976). Only about 20% of the variance in mammalian brain size is attributable to encephalization, while the remainder is tied to the body size factor (Jerison, 1977). Yet, it is this critical 20% that accounts for much of the mental superiority higher primates exert over other mammals, and also for the fact that the human species has a brain about six times the size of the average living mammal. Little or no such extra brain tissue is seen in the lower vertebrates (e.g., fish, amphibians, and reptiles) whose brains remained small relative to higher vertebrates and of lesser relative importance for adaptation to environmental niches (Jerison, 1977). We return to this issue in chapter 3 in distinguishing between biological and abstract forms of intelligence.

Generally, those species possessing larger brains also appear to have more complex brains as well. Differences in gross brain size are highly correlated with numerous microscopic characteristics of the brain as a whole, including total number of cells in the cerebral cortex, concentration of acetycholine, total amount of cortex, the ratio of neurons to glial cells, and the size of the various subcortical structures of the brain (Jerison, 1977). If one knows the size of the brain, then, it is possible to estimate other features of the brain with reasonable accuracy. Laughlin and d'Aquili (1974) caution, however, that the correlation of brain size to complexity is a variable one—that is, increased brain size may be positively related to progressive neural reorganization, progressive neural reorganization may occur with no increase in brain size, and brains may get larger with no resultant increase in neural complexity. Nevertheless, they say that significantly increased brain size indicates a high probability of an overall increase in neural complexity or "intelligence."

Laughlin and d'Aquili (1974) speculate that neural reorganization, and not simply larger brains, was the crucial factor in the evolution of higher mental functions in humans. Moreover, their argument is premised on a rather startling assumption: The neural reorganization underlying human abstractive, problem-solving, and possibly even language abilities was developed at the prehominid level, not during the hominid phase of marked increase in brain size in the Pleistocene! For Laughlin and d'Aquili, the organization of the brain, and not size per se determines human intelligence, and the rudiments of our brain organization were established in the prehuman, "animal" phase of evolutionary development. Later and dramatic increments in brain size "resulted only as a progressive elaboration of the systems laid down at the prehominid level" (Laughlin & d'Aquili, 1974, p. 20). The notion of elaboration of pre-existing, prehuman structures is a major feature of the phylogenetic regression model, as is evident in chapter 8.

Our discussion thus far has focused on between rather than within species factors in the evolution of brain size and complexity. There is a negligible relationship between brain size and intelligence in living humans (Tobias, 1971), and this fact has led some writers to question whether between and within-species variations in the brain result from similar mechanisms. Jerison (1977) suggests that within-species variation in brain size is probably of a nonadditive type not affected by natural selection, and following this logic, one would expect the IQ test to measure something quite different from the "intelligence" evolving when the hominid brain was increasing at so great a rate from *Australopithecus* to Neanderthal. Indeed, the IQ test requires far more than increased information-processing and integration of neuropsychological systems, which presumably characterized the intelligent adaptive strategies of early man. One might say that modern man uses his brain for reflection, abstract thought, intellectual competition, and other forms of mental work for its own sake, while early man used his to successfully adapt—mentally and physically—to a demanding environment.

Hemisphericity

The corpus callosum, the cerebral commissure connecting the right and left hemispheres, was an enigma to neurologists up through the 1940s and 1950s (Gazzaniga, 1977). In the early 1950s, however, this cloud of ignorance began to lift with the inauguration of the famous split-brain studies on cats performed by Ronald Meyer and Roger Sperry at the University of Chicago. It was not long thereafter before split-brain surgery was performed on human subjects, producing some of the most dramatic findings in modern brain research (Gazzaniga, Bogen, & Sperry, 1962, 1963, 1965; Gazzaniga & Sperry, 1967). The most important initial finding was that information exchange between the two hemispheres was totally disrupted following commissurotomy. For example, information presented to the left hemisphere could be described verbally with ease, whereas information presented to the right hemisphere went undescribed. Using a complex array of psychological tests designed by Michael Gazzaniga, these researchers found that the heretofore neglected right hemisphere possesses some language capacity, can initiate its own response, and can carry out many of the normal processes of life—without the left hemisphere knowing anything about it. Further, these researchers validated a long-standing clinical tradition that the left hemisphere is primarily attuned to processing verbal information, whereas the right hemisphere specializes in visual–spatial activities such as drawing cubes and arranging blocks to make a design. These findings on the "two brains," and subsequent research in the area, have generated tremendous excitement, and revolutionized thinking in neurology and neuropathology.

The left hemisphere is "dominant" over the right hemisphere by virtue of its mediation of handedness and the "higher functions" of language and speech, linear cause–effect thinking, temporality, and propositional-analytic reasoning. By contrast, the right hemisphere is predominantly nonverbal, synthetic, imagistic, and mediates appositional, relational, experiential, and intuitive forms of thought. The psychologist Neisser (1966) summarizes views on the dichotomous nature of mental functioning, many of which were formulated before the neurological substrates were recognized:

> Historically, psychology has recognized the existence of two different forms of mental organization. The distinction has been given many names: "rational" vs. "intuitive", "constrained" vs. "creative", "logical" vs. "prelogical", "realistic" vs. "autistic", "secondary process" vs. "primary process". To list them together might be misleading . . . nevertheless, a common thread runs through all the dichotomies. (p. 297)

Bogen (1977) provides an excellent summary of the supernumerous left vs. right dichotomies which exist in the literature (see Table 4.3 in chapter 4), and it seems clear that the rational, abstract, controlled functions of the left brain are more highly valued in our technological culture than are the more "primitive" experiential functions of the right brain. Indeed, we revere and shower rewards upon the physical scientist, mathemetician, or space technologist, whereas the artist, the person who "understands" others, the emotionally expressive individual, or the creative but not intellectually brilliant person are seemingly of lesser value. The apparent differential valuing of the two cognitive styles has led several writers to claim widespread discrimination against the nondominant right hemisphere in society, science, and education (Bogen, 1977; Fincher, 1976; Gazzaniga, 1977; Ornstein, 1977), and several of them call for major educational reform (see especially Gardner, 1983).

Value considerations aside, it appears true that left hemisphere functioning is more phylogenetically advanced than that of the right hemisphere.

First, we must consider the fact that a high degree of lateralization or specialization of the hemispheres is basically a human characteristic, especially where specialization involves centers for speech. For example, monkeys show little evidence of lateralization for cognitive functions, and only the apes show similar (though smaller) left–right asymmetries of the brain in the peri-Sylvian regions where speech is mediated in humans (see discussion in Bradshaw & Nettleton, 1983). This absence of clear-cut phylogenetic continuity of brain lateralization for the higher cortical functions emphasizes the distinctiveness of human speech and the neuroanatomical specializations which go with it.[1]

---

[1]Bradshaw and Nettleton's (1983) conservative approach to animal-human phylogenetic continuity in cerebral lateralization is shared by many neuroscientists. However, several recent writers (Geschwind & Galaburda, 1984; Glick, 1985) have argued strongly for animal-human homolgies in cerebral asymmetry. Both of these publications were greatly influenced by the master neuropsychological theorist, Norman Geschwind, who considered a neurobiology of brain lateralization across species an emergent probability.

Second, given the distinctive nature of human speech, one would presume that evolved neuroanatomical structures governing speech and related functions, e.g., Broca's and Wernicke's areas, would be "phylogenetically advanced" by definition (see chapter 3). Indeed, the left hemisphere appears to have specialized in mediating the "highest" human functions of speech and reason, those characteristics that most distinguish us from the animals. In other words, the human–animal differential is probably greater for the hyperspecialized areas of the left brain governing speech and rational thought than for any other areas of the brain.

Third, given the second point, the right hemisphere is presumed to be more phylogenetically continuous with lower species than the left, and, thus, more involved in lower survival functions than with abstract issues. According to what Laughlin and d'Aquili (1974) call the *specialization hypothesis,* a number of writers have reasoned that hemispheric asymmetry was coterminous with the development of speech and existed far back in the hominid record, perhaps as far back as *Australopithecus.* This view further holds that the prehominid brain was essentially bilaterally symmetrical and was, as a whole, predominantly devoted to survival functions. With language specialization, the right lobe remained basically the same, while the left lobe lost many of its prior functions, replacing them with higher ones. Consistent with this idea is the right brain's involvement in the "lower" functions of emotional reactivity (Ley & Bryden, 1981), nonverbal ideation and simple language comprehension (Berent, 1981), facial identification (Milner, 1967), awareness and orientation (Springer & Deutsch, 1981), vigilance and sustained attention (Dimond, 1979), sensitivity to novel or degraded stimuli (Bradshaw & Nettleton, 1983), and perceptuo–spatial as opposed to verbal–symbolic forms of thinking (McGee, 1979). All of these are real world functions necessary for survival, to be contrasted with inner world of verbally mediated thoughts and reasoning processes associated with the left brain.

Laughlin and d'Aquili (1974) also summarize the *preadaptation hypothesis,* which states that cerebral asymmetry existed in prehominids as a general system of alternating survival functions; that is, the two hemispheres had specialized prior to the onset of language, but underwent additional specialization in accommodating it. This view would deny the uniqueness of cerebral asymmetry in humans, and would otherwise assert that asymmetry of function is a fundamental characteristic of the vertebrate nervous system. Its fullest expression, however, is in the primate nervous system, most notably man's.

Although the preadaptation hypothesis sounds plausible, the supporting evidence is weak. Crucial is the fact that little hard data exist for consistent lateral asymmetries at the population level in nonhuman species (Laughlin & d'Aquili, 1974), although, as previously noted, chimpanzees exhibit a small degree of laterality possibly analogous to that in humans (Bradshaw & Nettleton, 1983). Until the facts prove otherwise, it seems prudent to assume that extreme hemispheric specialization is a unique adaptation of the human species.

Various theorists and researchers have approached the problem ontogenetically as well as phylogenetically. According to *progressive lateralization theory* (Lenneberg, 1967; Orton, 1928), the higher mental functions in human infants initially are controlled by both sides of the immature brain. Gradually, with maturation and learning, the ultimately dominant hemisphere assumes a superordinate share of control of the higher functions. This view implies that failure to achieve lateralization, or incomplete lateralization, results in less-than-optimum cognitive functioning and possibly pathological processes. Until recently, most theorists have favored the progressive lateralization idea, in conjunction with the idea that sublateralization or some other kind of deviant lateralization is pathological (Kinsbourne, 1981).

Kinsbourne (1981) proposes an alternative called *invariant lateralization theory*. This theory holds that the developmental sequences that characterize acquisition of each higher function originate and terminate on the same side of the brain, right or left. Thus, the formative structures are there originally in the proper hemisphere in inchoate form, and there is no need for a shift to another hemisphere in ontogeny. Thus, for Kinsbourne, cognitive pathology is not the result of incomplete lateralization, but, rather, due to "a lower plateau of ultimate capability," slower acquisition of information, or, in the extreme case, delayed onset of the appropriate developmental sequence. From this perspective, the role of insufficient or deviant lateralization is obviously minimized.

For our purposes, it is not necessary to choose between Lenneberg's or Kinsbourne's formulations. Whether or not lateral asymmetry is absent at birth and must be developed, or whether it is initially present in rudimentary form, is less important than the fact that lateral asymmetry is more highly developed in man than other animals, and is correlated with numerous normal and abnormal behaviors (Bradshaw & Nettleton, 1983; Springer & Deutsch, 1981). Furthermore, the evidence strongly supports the notion that the highest and most phylogenetically distinctive mental traits in man are housed in the left hemisphere, whereas the right hemisphere occupies a slightly lower position in the hierarchicalized brain. Still, the right hemisphere occupies a relatively advanced position, compared to the limbic and reptilian structures, in the phylogenetically tiered human brain.

The Hierarchical Brain

Although the horizontal differences between the right and left lobes are important, they pale in comparison to the violent interplay of vertical forces in the hierarchically arranged, dynamic cerebral system. It is largely this vertical interchange between the old and the new, the animal and the human, which serves as the conceptual basis for the ideas developed in this book.

When addressing the hierarchical brain, one is naturally led to the decades of research and writing by the eminent chief of the Laboratory of Brain Evolution and Behavior at the National Institute of Mental Health, Professor Paul MacLean. According to MacLean, the brain is something like an archaeological site, with the outer layer composed of the most recent brain structure, the cerebral cortex, while the deeper layers contain structures inherited from our evolutionary forbears, the mammals and the reptiles. Thus, we humans have not one brain, but three—the "triune brain" (MacLean, 1970, 1973a, 1978b, 1982b), as is shown schematically in Fig. 2.1

As Valzelli (1981) aptly summarizes, thinkers from antiquity have tended to classify human characters in threes: the concept of the trinity in religion; the triad of physical, psychological, and spiritual components

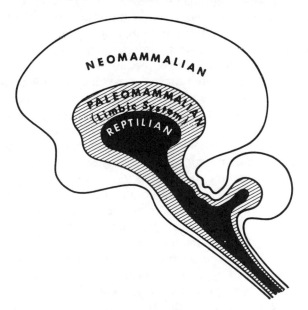

FIG. 2.1. The triune brain (from MacLean, 1967).

outlined by Hermes Trismegistus some 15 centuries ago; the vegetative, motive, and intellectual souls of Aristotle; the Freudian tripartite of id, ego, and superego; and more recently, in Yakovlev's (1970) postulated systems of the body—organs, the brain, and behavioral structures. Of the many tripartite systems, MacLean's stands foremost as a comprehensive, integrated, and evolution-based theory of human nature and behavior. Indeed, the theory of the triune brain has implications for human study that transcend disciplinary boundaries and provide rich insights in many areas including personality (MacLean, 1976, 1977b), psychopathology (MacLean, 1977b), the self-concept (MacLean, 1970), aggression and power (MacLean, 1978b, 1982a), empathy (MacLean, 1976), epistomology (MacLean, 1977b) and even the evolution of law (MacLean, 1982a).

In the process of human brain evolution, new tissue and connections were added in two ways: (a) brain size increased as body size increased, and (b) "extra" brain matter was added through the process of encephalization, allowing for the emergence of higher cognitive functions. As discussed previously, a far greater proportion of hominid brain increase was associated with body size increase than with encephalization. This implies that most of the larger evolved brain was designed to mediate modal or "lower" survival activities (viz., biological intelligence—see chapter 3), whereas a quite small proportion of the increase was allocated to the "higher" functions. Thus, despite its overall size, the human brain is far more old in its morphology and function than it is new; as primates, we continue to be phylogenetically programmed mainly for adaptation to the environment. As MacLean has repeatedly noted (1976, 1977b), our brains are much more devoted to "paleopsychic processes" and "prosematics" (nonverbal behavior) than to neopsychic, verbal processes.

Rather than simply old and new, our three brains could best be classified as oldest, old, and new, corresponding to the reptilian, paleomammalian, and the neomammalian segments. Each of the three cerebrotypes has its own kind of intelligence, its own specialized memory, its own sense of time and space, its own motor skills and special functions, and its own neural architecture and biochemical setting (Valzelli, 1981). Within each of us, then, are three distinct "minds," one inherited from our reptilian ancestors, one from our mammalian ancestors, and one from our primate and hominid ancestors. And just as three phylogenetically distant species might experience conflict in a zoo cage, our three brains coexist in an atmosphere of uneasy harmony. Typically, the three brains operate protagonistically and complement one another, but it nevertheless requires considerable socialization and cultural shaping to avoid bothersome and sometimes pathological regressions and dissociations. We see that the triune brain represents a dynamic, ongoing process of interrelationships between the hierarchicalized component brains, and out of these interrelaionships emerge the driving forces of behavior.

The Reptilian Brain

Anatomically, the human counterpart of the protoreptilian brain is composed of a complex of structures including the olfactostriatum, corpus striatum (caudate nucleus and putamen), the globus pallidus, and satellite collections of gray matter (MacLean, 1982b, 1986). Since there is no term that applies to all these structures, MacLean has referred to all of these collectively as the *striatal complex,* or in a comparative context, as the R-complex (see Fig. 2.2). In neurological texts, some of these structures are included among the so-called basal ganglia that are variously defined by different authors (P. D. MacLean, personal communication, April 29, 1986). The functions of these structures are poorly understood. Having little hard data available, early researchers assumed the striatal structures were merely part of the motor system dominated by the motor

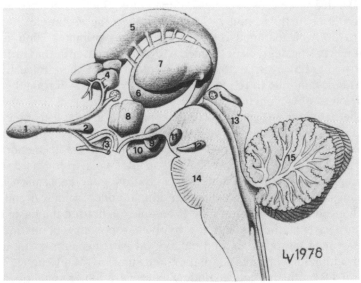

1) Olfactory bulb	9) Mammilary body
2) Olfactory tubercule	10) Amygdala
3) Optic chiasma	11) Interpeduncular nucleus
4) Septal nuclei	12) Substantia nigra
5) Caudate	13) Quadrigeminal bodies
6) Putamen + globus pallidus	(Tectum mesencephali)
7) Talamus	14) Pons
8) Hypothalamus	15) Cerebellum

FIG. 2.2   The reptilian brain (from Valzelli, 1981).

areas of the neocortex. However, large destructions of the mammalian R-complex often result in no obvious impairment of movement (MacLean, 1976), and, similarly, electrical stimulation of extensive portions of the R-complex fail to elicit movement (MacLean, 1982b). Rather than subserving movement, the R-complex appears to play a central role in primitive forms of motivation in both animals and humans.

Recent developments in biochemistry have helped in identifying corresponding parts of the brain in reptiles, birds, and mammals. Staining procedures for cholinesterase bring out the ganglionic structures of the striatal complex in sharp detail, and application of a special histoflorescence method reveals the same neural structures in bright green due to the presence of dopamine (MacLean, 1982b). These same regions also are rich in other neurochemicals including serotonin (Paasonen, MacLean, & Giarman, 1957) and the opiate receptors and endorphins (Pert & Snyder, 1973). Clearly, the R-complex has its own distinctive neurochemistry, allowing researchers to map the anatomical loci of the striatal structures and make definitive cross-species comparisons. Such comparisons reveal the lizard's or turtle's brain as little more than the R-complex, whereas the birds, lower mammals, higher mammals, primates, and humans exhibit increasing degrees of "added" forebrain matter in that order. The crucial point, however, is that even humans, with their hypertrophied neocortices, continue to retain the basic neural chassis in roughly similar proportion to phylogenetically lower species.

At the behavioral level, the reptilian brain is a "slave to precedent" (MacLean, 1970), calling, as it does, upon rigid, stereotyped, and preprogrammed responses steeped in ancestral learning and memory. The sea turtle returns to the same place year after year to lay its eggs, and birds migrate incredible distances, generation after generation, to the same geographic location, even when climatic and ecological conditions have changed radically. Within the R-complex is housed the basic behavioral hardware of the animal, the evolved repository of instincts and species-typical motivational and behavioral patterns subserving individual and, ultimately, species adaptation and survival. MacLean (1976) lists a pentad of reptilian traits including perseveration, re-enactment, tropisms (both positive and negative), deception, and isopraxic behavior. Thus, reptiles, and humans when they "regress" to reptilian levels of behavior, exhibit repetitive obeisance to daily routines and subroutines, ceremonial re-enactments and compulsive ritualism, mechanical reactions to minimal stimuli and partial representations (tropisms), nonconscious misrepresentation of motivation or intention (deception), and slavish conformance to species standards of behavior. The last fundamental parameter, isopraxis, is particularly interesting, for it is through imitation and mimicry of species-appropriate behavior that species members act in accordance with species standards and achieve a sense of "identity" of sorts. As MacLean (1978b) says: "It cannot be overemphasized that isopraxis is basic for maintaining the identity of a species or social group" (p. 320).

MacLean (1982b), lists 25 special forms of behavior mediated by the reptilian brain, and these are discussed in more detail in chapter 4 (see Table 4.4). For the present, however, note that reptilian behavior falls into a number of general categories including imitation and species conformity, establishment and defense of territorial areas, home-site selection, foraging and feeding, courtship, mating and reproductive behavior, ritualistic display, group formation, and competition, dominance, and aggression (MacLean, 1962, 1964, 1972a, 1982b). In considering this formidable list, we must acknowledge that our species possesses the neural hardware and many of the motivational–emotional "proclivities" (MacLean, 1978b) of our reptilian ancestors, and, thus, our drives, inner subjective feelings, fantasies, and thoughts are thoroughly conditioned by emanations from the R-complex. The reptilian carry-overs provide the automatic, compulsive urgency to much of human behavior, where free will steps aside and persons act as they have to act, often despising themselves in the process for their hatreds, prejudices, compulsions, conformity, deceptiveness, and guile.

The Paleomammalian Brain (Limbic System)

From the cold-blooded repulsive world of the reptile, we move a step up to that mammalian hotbed of emotion, the paleomammalian brain. The evolution of the paleomammalian brain was nature's way of providing a "thinking cap" (MacLean, 1968a, 1968b) for the reptilian brain system, thereby freeing animals from a sorely limited repertoire of more-or-less automatic responses and behavioral patterns. As the suprareptilian brain structures of birds and mammals increased in size and complexity over evolutionary time, the older structures remained essentially intact, repositories of millions of years of hard-won wisdom. It is important to note here that the mammalian mesocortex grew upon and not beyond the reptilian system, producing two distinct yet interdependent levels of mental functioning. This new two-component brain system allowed for greater flexibility in adapting to the environment, but it also suffered from a serious side effect called *schizophysiology* (MacLean, 1954b).

Schizophysiology refers to dis-integrations and antagonisms between phylogenetically disparate brain levels, producing, among other things, "conflicts between 'what we feel' and 'what we know' " (MacLean, 1977b, p. 319). Here MacLean is apparently referring to conflicts between the lower centers (reptilian and limbic) and the higher neocortical centers. Similar conflicts can occur, however, between the lowest (reptilian) and the next highest (mammalian) levels without significant involvement of the neocortical level. In humans, for example, psychic conflict could occur between the different consciousnesses of the two lower systems, e.g., between rigid stereotypy, on the one hand, and impetuous emotionality on the other. Reptilian mental content also may interact with the limbic emergency system in fearful nightmares in children; the R-complex provides the monsters and dragons (Sagan, 1977), and the limbic system the overpowering fear and anxiety.

MacLean (1977b) sees schizophysiology behind many forms of human psychopathology, including certain aspects of psychosis—depersonalization, distortions of perception, paranoid delusions, and hallucinations. He says that the psychotherapeutic drugs primarily owe their salutary effects to a selective action on the limbic system and the R-complex. Although the three cerebrotypes always act in concert, each one's dominance or subservience varies from behavior to behavior, with the two lower systems being more dominant when primitive, nonintellectual and irrational responses prevail. Bailey (1978, 1985) refers to this type of schizophysiology as phylogenetic regression, where the lower systems become dominant and the inhibiting and modulating forces of the neocortex are temporarily diminished or suspended. Such regressions may involve any of the numerous permutations of three variables, but most of them seem to represent conflicts between the emotional, pleasure-seeking limbic system and the rather cold, moral, and intellectual computer called the *neocortex*. Thus, throughout this volume we generally focus on neocortical-to-limbic regressions, while keeping in mind that the deepest regressions, especially the pathological ones, must include a significant reptilian component.

Reptiles possess very little cortex, but considerable cortical material was added with the mammals, producing the "great limbic lobe" described by Broca (1878). In 1952, MacLean defined this area as the "limbic system," a complex anatomical web including the hypothalamus, amygdala, septal nuclei, septum, hippocampus, hippocampal gyrus, and certain cerebellar structures (see Valzelli, 1980, 1981). The various components of the limbic system are shown in Fig. 2.3.

The limbic system is considered the seat of emotional life in both animal and man, and is a center for the integration of visceral inputs, sensations, perceptions, and affects. Valzelli (1981) provides an excellent summary of the integrative functions of the limbic system, and the central role played by the hippocampus:

In 1949 MacLean elaborated Papez's theory of emotion (1937) and suggested that impulses from intero- and exteroceptive systems reach the hippocampus through the hippocampal gyrus; the hippocampal structure was viewed as

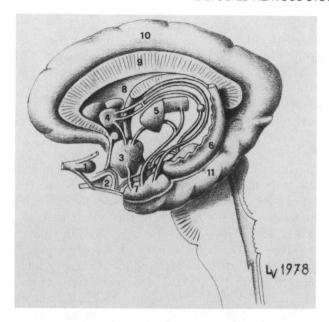

1) Olfactory tubercule
2) Optic chiasma
3) Hypothalamus
4) Septal nuclei
5) Thalamic nuclei
6) Hippocampus

7) Amygdala
8) Septum
9) Corpus callosum
10) Cingulate gyrus
11) Hippocampal gyrus
(Temporal lobe)

FIG. 2.3.   The paleomammalian brain (from Valzelli, 1981).

capable of combining internal and external information into affective feelings. The latter was further elaborated and expressed through connections
with amygdala, septal area, basal ganglia, and hypothalamus; they then
reentered the limbic lobe and completed the 'Papez circuit'. Thus the
hippocampus can be considered the key structure of the entire system, and
the amygdala-hippocampal complex the functional key unit responsible for
normal or abnormal feelings and behavior . . . (p. 36)

MacLean (1977b) outlines three subdivisions of the limbic system, two
of which, the amygdaloid (1) and septal (2), are phylogenetically oldest
and related to the olfactory apparatus. MacLean's experimental work
indicates that these two subdivisions are involved in oral and genital
functions. Subdivision 1 (amygdaloid) appears primarily concerned with
self-preservation, namely, searching, feeding, fighting, fear, and self-
protection (MacLean, 1952). Monkeys that have had portions of the

amygdala system surgically removed become docile, pick up and eat objects indiscriminantly, and are unable to defend themselves (Dicks, Myers, & Kling, 1969; Klüver & Bucy, 1937). As contrasted with subdivision 1, subdivision 2 (septal) seems to be more involved with species rather than self-preservation (Fishbein, 1976), and primarily mediates primal sexual and sociosexual expression (MacLean, 1973a, 1982a). Although the amygdaloid and septal subdivisions have fairly distinct functions, MacLean (1977b) emphasizes the interplay and mixing of "orosexual manifestations" in feeding, mating, and aggression.

The third, or anterior thalamic subdivision, has no counterpart in the reptiles, and is a far more recent phylogenetic acquisition than were the first two subdivisions. This subdivision bypasses the olfactory apparatus and has connections, via the nucleus of the thalamus, with the frontal neocortical areas. Electrical stimulation of parts of the thalamocingulate division in monkeys produces a variety of sexual responses including genital tumescence. Stimulation of related intralaminar nuclei may result in genital scratching and seminal discharge. Interestingly, MacLean (1978b) also reports that in hamsters the neocortex may be eliminated at the time of birth without interfering with any basic hamster-typical behavior. If, however, the cingulate cortex is also destroyed, playful behavior fails to develop, and adult females show marked deficits in maternal behavior (P. D. MacLean, personal communication, April 29, 1986). The absence of the quintessential mammalian traits of maternal and play behavior led MacLean (1978b) to comment, "It was as if these [lesioned] animals had *regressed* towards a reptilian condition" (p. 377; italics added).

By virtue of bypassing the older olfactory system and emphasizing vision over smell (MacLean, 1977b), the third district advanced phylogenetically beyond the two more primitive districts. Moreover, it became more phylogenetically advanced in the sense of mediating heretofore negligible concern for offspring and a primitive kind of love. As Sagan (1977) says, "love is the invention of mammals," and the rudiments of love and responsibility toward other members of the same species owes much to the third subdivision of the limbic system (MacLean, 1982a). It also is possible that the third subdivision, in conjunction with the prefrontal cortex of the neomammalian brain, serves as a neural substrate for the evolution of human empathy (MacLean, 1977b). Given the importance of empathy and positive feelings toward others in the dynamics of human social behavior, this limbic-neocortical interplay becomes a huge piece of the human puzzle. No doubt, the evolution of a primitive concern for others was a major step in transcending our animality and becoming human in the first place.

MacLean (1978b) points to three key behavioral changes in the transition from reptiles to mammals: nursing, parental care, and play. These residues of limbic evolution are the primal parameters of the concept of family, and MacLean (1982a) tells us that the evolution of mammals can be viewed as the history of the evolution of the family. Of all the mammalian traits, parenting is perhaps the most significant, for "parental care of the young eventually generalizes to other members of the species, a psychological development that amounts to an evolution of a sense of responsibility and what we call conscience" (MacLean, 1978b, p. 325). When we speak of parenting at the mammalian level, we refer basically to the mother–infant attachment–separation complex, from which radiates all aspects of love, togetherness, and kinship in mammals, nonhuman primates, and human beings (Mellen, 1981). In discussing the joys of attachment and the agony of separation, MacLean (1978b) says, "We can divine in this situation the evolutionary roots of unity of the family, unity of the clan, unity of larger societies, as well as the emotional intensity of feelings attending separation, isolation, and the threat of annihilation" (p. 325).

By virtue of its fundamental roles in mediating motivation and emotion in general, and, more specifically, pleasure and aversion, attachment and love, sexuality, aggression and fear, and play, the limbic system should stand at the center of any comprehensive theory of animal and human behavior. Certainly, it occupies center stage in the phylogenetic regression model, for most regressions in humans are limbic-emotional ones, although reptilian ones occur as well. In fact, as outlined in chapter 3, most phylogenetic regressions occur in the emotional–subjective realm of mental functioning, and far fewer behavioral regressions are seen where persons actually act upon their fears, desires, and hatreds. Although beneath our conscious awareness, "the limbic cortex is constantly bombarded by impulses from the internal environment" (MacLean, 1970, p. 345), meaning that our inner subjective worlds, our selfhood, our sense of reality, are being constantly conditioned by ancient mammalian imperatives. A major role of the neocortex is to interpret, modulate, elaborate, or repress or deny these limbic urgings and feelings. Thus, in many respects, the neocortex is passive and reactive, a pawn of the millions of years of reptilian and limbic evolution that preceded it. Except for the highly educated and enculturated, the neocortex basically is an organ of survival phylogenetically, and an organ of satisfaction ontogenetically. There are those moments of "progression," however, where the neocortex prevails over its scaly and furry forbears, and rises above instinct for dispassionate thought and intellectual work. It is to such rare moments, when a few great minds in human history (Cattell, 1971) produced their "progressive" and creative insights, that modern culture and technology are so deeply indebted.

The Neomammalian Cortex

The neomammalian cortex is the most phylogenetically recent of the three brain systems, and it reaches its quintessence in man. As C. Judson Herrick once commented (1933; cited in MacLean, 1977b, p. 320–321), "Its explosive growth late in phylogeny is one of the most dramatic cases of evolutionary transformation known to comparative anatomy." Despite its vastly increased size and complexity, the modern human neocortex has not transcended nor achieved independence from the two lower brain systems; all incoming information must be processed through the two lower systems with the result that response output always has an emotional coloring (Valzelli, 1981). Nevertheless, the human neocortex is a magnificent thinking machine possessing capability for language and speech, greatly increased sensory capacity, greatly refined motor skills, spatial and perceptual–motor ability, and more advanced attention and memory. In a general sense, the greatly enlarged neocortex allowed for more improved processing of survival-relevant information (Jerison, 1973), or "biological intelligence" (see chapter 3). Certainly with more complex and variable physical and social environments, the oversized neocortex conferred considerable adaptive advantage: "In general, the greater the knowledge that members of a species have about the environment in which they will develop the more effective will be their chances of surviving and reproducing, i.e., the higher will be their Darwinian fitness" (Fishbein, 1976, p. 88).

MacLean (1958b) sees the neocortex as a kind of television set that provides the organism with a clear view of the outside world to which it must adapt. Thoroughly connected with the highly refined human sensory apparatus, the neocortex specializes in processing information from the outside world, and is apparently less internally oriented than are the two lower paleopsychic systems (MacLean, 1977b). Focused on the outside world and "servant" (Plutchik, 1977) to the limbic and reptilian systems, the neocortex is somewhat like a coldly reasoning, giant computer (MacLean, 1982a) that has the capacity to be infinitely destructive, or loving and kind, depending on motives emanating from the lower systems.

Anatomically, the neocortex is an impressive structure consisting of cell bodies, 50 to 100 deep, organized into six levels or strata of gray matter (Boddy, 1978). All animals with cortex exhibit a similar grouping into six layers (Gardner, 1963), suggesting a homologous formation. The human neocortex is unique, however, in terms of its weight, surface area relative to weight, the ratio of neocortex to subcortical matter, complexity of organization, and far-reaching functional capability. By virtue of its richly convoluted surface, the human neocortex can accommodate approximately 10 billion neurones, three-quarters of the total number of the entire human brain and four times the number found in the brain of our closest nonhuman relative, the chimpanzee (Boddy, 1978). Using an index of cephalization, Stephan and Andy (1970) found that relative to basal insectivores, the prosimian neocortex increased on the average by a multiple of 15, the simian neocortex (including the apes but omitting humans) by a factor of about 40, and man's neocortex increased by a whopping multiple of approximately 156. Although it is not entirely clear to what extent subneocortical structures have increased or decreased in primate phylogeny (Andy & Stephan, 1974), the vast enlargement of the human neocortex is unambiguous.

Given that the human neocortex increased greatly in phylogeny, and that it differentiated into several lobes or subdivisions, we may ask if certain parts increased more than others. Blinkov and Glezer (1958) did a comparative study of the brain in a series of primates from macaques to man, and concluded that the relative size of the frontal, temporal, and inferior parietal (the language area) divisions increased in phylogeny, whereas the relative size of the occipital division decreased. They also found that the relative size of the primary motor area of the brain remains fairly constant in phylogeny, although as Fishbein (1976) points out, following Woolsey (1958), the motor regions subserving the production of speech and those of the fingers and hands are much larger in man than in other primates. These conclusions are not incontrovertible, and following his study of fossil endocasts and other data, Holloway (1968a) concluded that relative increases occurred in the temporal and inferior parietal areas, but not in the frontal lobes.

Holloway's conclusions are particularly significant because many writers traditionally have considered the frontal lobes to be the most phylogenetically advanced areas of the brain, presumably mediating the highest human intellectual capacities. Kolb and Whisaw (1980) agree that the human frontal lobes changed little functionally in phylogeny, and further say that they are not really special organs at all when compared to other animals. Apparently, all mammals have a frontal lobe composed of regions receiving projections from the thalamus (Rose & Woolsey, 1948), although the sheer mass of frontal tissue reaches its acme in humans. Although the similarities between animal and human frontal lobes may outweigh the differences, humans appear unique in that lesions in the frontal area produce significant behavioral effects (Kolb & Whisaw, 1980), as the spate of psychosurgery in the 1950s and modern neuropsychology have shown. In fact, damage to the frontal lobes in humans is often associated with pathological changes in personality functioning and specific deficits in intelligence test performance (McFie, 1975).

Perhaps the mystery of the frontal lobes is mitigated somewhat if we distinguish between the frontal and prefrontal areas (Fuster, 1980). Mac-Lean (1982b), for one, believes that the prefrontal cortex serves as a communicative link with the internal world (mainly the limbic system), allowing one to interpret "inner feelings," look ahead to the future, and to empathically "experience" the feeling of others. He says that the prefrontal cortex is intimately geared in with the third great subdivision of the limbic system (anterior thalamic division) that has been found to be implicated in parental behavior, play, and social affiliation. Thus, as the presumed seat of personality, empathy, and foresight, the prefrontal area might be the phylogenetically latest and most advanced of the various neocortical areas. This must remain tentative and speculative, however, due to the overall lack of phylogenetic specialness of the prefrontal area, and worst still, the possibility that the ventrally situated temporal lobes may be a more recent phylogenetic acquisition (Jerison, 1973). Certainly, the temporal lobes deserve high phylogenetic status by virtue of their proximity to and involvement with the language and speech area, which Geschwind (1965) sees as probably the only unique feature of the human brain.

Human speech was indeed something new; it was controlled primarily by specialized structures in the neocortex, including those sensitive to complex auditory stimuli and those capable of appropriate processing of such auditory information. Whereas the primarily visual, gestural social signaling of many animals remained tied to the lower brain centers, human speech became more neocorticalized, on the one hand, and more sound- rather than sight-focused on the other. Even for those animals capable of complex vocal communication, such as monkeys and apes, the controlling centers remain basically tied to the motivational-emotional areas in the limbic system (Washburn & Moore, 1980). Whereas the limbically controlled facial expressions and vocalizations of nonhuman primates are tied to immediate eliciting stimuli and act solely in the service of "lower" drives such as hunger, sex, fear, and aggression, the human being, possessing highly specialized neocortical speech centers in addition to the lower ones, was alone able to develop spoken language. Exactly how humans developed this unique capacity is somewhat a mystery, but many theorists assume that the human neocortex became highly specialized first for exquisite motor skill and hand-eye coordination, as were required for tool-making and successful hunting, and only later did the giant leap occur from grunts and gestures to true language (see Kimura, 1979; Springer & Deutsch, 1981). Hewes (1977) reviewed the various language origin theories and concluded in favor of the language-from-gesture model, citing two reasonable supporting assumptions: (a) as primitive man became more facile with tools, gesticulation as the sole means of communication became increasingly awkward, and (b) as communication became increasingly more complicated, even refined manual and facial gestures were insufficient to the task, and words were required.

Laughlin and d'Aquili (1974) emphasize the phylogenetic continuity of communication systems, and they question the popular assumption that language capacity, in the general sense, is unique to humans. They cite Hockett (1960), who pointed out that of the 13 "distinctive" features of human speech, 12 are shared with other species. Hockett concluded that only "duality of patterning," the capacity to link meaningless sounds into meaningful utterances, was truly unique to human speech. Yet, even the uniqueness of duality of patterning has been challenged (Altmann, 1967), and something akin to this feature may exist in the complex patterning of songs in certain song birds (Smith, 1969a, 1969b). Laughlin and d'Aquili (1974) discuss the similarities of animal and human communication at some length, and they accuse behavioral scientists of a systematic bias in favor of finding or stipulating language design features that set humans apart from the rest of the animal kingdom. There appears to be more than a grain of truth to their assertions, and it is likely that greater rather than lesser phylogenetic continuity of language will emerge as we learn more about the phylogenesis of language capacity.

The Dynamic Cerebral System

In MacLean's system, brain structures increase in complexity of function according to an upward growth of more advanced and highly evolved neural components. However, these new functions are not merely transferred from below to above or added on like boxes stacked on a shelf; instead, we should think of progressively greater cortical involvement in the overall cerebral system as new structures come to "share" in the responsibility of helping the organism adapt to the environment (Brown, 1977). Newer levels of functioning are thus derived from preceding ones, and the old and new work together in expanding the repertoire of adaptive responses. Yet, the new never completely transcends the old in the nervous system, for to do so would involve a grievous wastage and net loss in terms of overall adaptive capacity. So, rather than being a fully autonomous organ of thought divorced from the instinctive apparatus, the neocortex mediates *"complex processes of sensory input, evaluation, symbolization, comparison with memory stores and the like—those processes we call cognitive—(which act) in the service of emotions and biological needs"* (Plutchnik, 1977, p. 203).

The neocortex not only serves the lower needs, however, but also acts to inhibit instinctive responses through cultural programming of prescribed beliefs, norms, and values, on the one hand, and the intellectual control of asocial and antisocial impulses on the other. Stenhouse (1973) argues that the power to delay or withhold instinctive responses is a necessary precondition for the emergence of instinctive variability, and ultimately, the evolution of human intelligence. This postponement, or "P-factor," allows for release from the automaticity of the R-complex, and the binding of limbic emotionality, so that intelligence could proceed up the scale to learned habits and finally human thought. It should be noted, however, that Stenhouse assumes that human behavior always involves a mixture of instinct and intelligence, and neither one nor the other is ever exhibited in pure form.

To recapitulate, the hierarchical-interactive components of the dynamic cerebral system basically run from the most ancient reptilian on through the intermediary and compelling limbic structures, and up, finally, to the neomammalian cortex. Going one step beyond MacLean's triune brain concept, we might add a fourth level, the "asymmetric symbolic" which takes hemisphericity and lateralization into account. Following Brown (1977), the four levels of structural organization and cognitive functioning are outlined below:

Species Level	Functional Level	Genetic Level
human	symbolic (asymmetric, neocortical)	onto- & phylogenetic
neomammalian	representational (cortical)	phylogenetic
paleomammalian	presentational (limbic)	phylogenetic
reptilian	sensori-motor (subcortical)	phylogenetic

In MacLean's conceptual system, and in Brown's elaboration of it, we have a simple yet elegant model for understanding the vicissitudes of human behavior. In using the model, we must realize that a vast universe of psychoneural complexity theoretically has been compressed into a few finite categories for the sake of convenience. MacLean's enticing hierarchy of the mind is a convenient abstraction, a general metatheory that arches across specific theories of behavior, points of view, and even disciplinary boundaries. Its potential as a grand theory of theories is obvious, radiating as it does out into all aspects of the New Biology. All behavior in the last analysis reduces to neuroelectric and neurochemical processes occurring in the brain, and any ultimate "truth" about the human condition must be sought within our own crania, and not in economics, society, culture, or even the genes per se. How the brain processes input, from both internal and external sources, appears more important than the input itself.

SUMMARY

In the 19th century, two Darwinian revolutions occurred: First, Darwin's conversion to evolutionary theory, and second, his discovery of the principle of natural selection. In this century, two additional Darwinian revolutions are in progress, constituting a New Biology: First, the incorporation of evolutionary theory into the mainstream of biological science, and second, a similar incorporation into the social sciences. E. O. Wilson's (1975) *Sociobiology: The New Synthesis* stands astride the culmination of the recent revolution in biology and the true beginning of the revolution in social science.

In attempting to understand human nature, the New Biology must incorporate and systematically integrate three levels of information: the phylogenetic level, the neurophysiological level, and the cultural level. All three levels are required if we aspire to a truly integrative and synthetic approach to human behavior.

Out of the New Biology is developing a New Social Science thoroughly wedded to what Cravens (1978) calls the *new evolutionary science*. This New Social Science is proceeding up many avenues including human ethology, human sociobiology, biosocial anthropology, ethopsychoanalysis, and evolutionary psychiatry. Each of these new trends is discussed in some detail in this chapter.

More than anywhere else, the diverse strands of the New Biology and New Social Science converge at the nervous system. The present writer contends that once the interrelationships between brain and behavior are understood, human nature will be essentially understood as well.

The human brain has approximately tripled in size in the past 1.5 to 4.5 million years, and the increase in neocortical matter has been especially astounding. Although individual differences in size do not correlate highly with functional measures such as IQ or academic achievement, there is no question that the information-processing capacity of the human brain has increased in phylogeny since the Pleistocene. These increases in "intelligence" were apparently due to natural selection of "extra" brain tissue for mental and cognitive activities.

The split-brain research of Roger Sperry and his colleagues in the 1950s revolutionized neuropsychology. This and subsequent research on brain hemisphericity revealed that the neocortex is really two brains rather than one. The left brain specializes in language, speech, and linear-rational functions, whereas the right brain is more imagistic, holistic, intuitive, and spatially oriented. It is not clear as to why or how the human brain became lateralized, but several contending theories were discussed.

The interplay between brain structures is not only basically horizontal, as with left–right brain interaction, but vertical as well. Paul MacLean views the human brain as like an archeological site composed of the recently evolved neocortex, the mammalian brain, and the reptilian brain. Our brain is thus really a "triune brain" composed of a phylogenetically primitive reptilian structures, upon which are situated the paleomammalian structures, and, finally, sitting at the top of the hierarchy is the phylogenetically advanced neocortex. Although distinct neurochemically and behaviorally, the three brains interact functionally and dynamically, both protagonistically and antagonistically. It is important to note that we humans share much of the reptilian and mammalian brain matter with lower animals, and only at the neocortical level is the animal–human differential great.

Perhaps more than anything else, human speech enabled man to phylogenetically progress beyond the animals. Human speech was something new in the evolutionary process; communication was now a basically neocortical phenomenon involving transfer of auditory symbols rather than transfer of gestural information in the visual modality. It was now possible to communicate something other than emotional states or rudimentary intentions mediated by the limbic system; it became possible to separate thought and symbol from needs and emotions, and thereby to communicate in distinctive human fashion. Still, as Laughlin and d'Aquili (1974) point out, human language is based on animal forms of communication and is only distinctive to a degree.

The phylogenetic regression–progression model is heavily indebted to MacLean's hierarchical brain concept. Following MacLean, we may think of the brain as a dynamic cerebral system involving reptilian components, mammalian components, and right and left neocortical components, all intertwined in a mutually interactive symphony of excitation and inhibition as behavior occurs. Moreover, when the neocortex predominates we may say that phylogenetic progression occurs, whereas phylogenetic regression occurs when the lower centers take the upper hand.

3

Ape and Angel Revisited:
A Theoretical Perspective

*Can you imagine language, once clear-cut and exact, soft-
ening and guttering, losing shape and import, becoming
mere lumps of sound again? And they walked erect with
increasing difficulty. Though they evidently felt ashamed of
themselves, every now and then I would come upon one or
other running on toes and fingertips, and quite unable to
recover the vertical attitude. They held things more clum-
sily; drinking by suction, feeding by gnawing, grew com-
moner every day. I realised more keenly than ever what
Moreau had told me about the "stubborn beast flesh". They
were reverting and reverting rapidly.*

—H. G. Wells, *The Island of Dr. Moreau*

PHYLOGENETIC REGRESSION AND PROGRESSION

Overview

The basic theme running through the diverse topics in chapters 1 and 2 is
that man is, first and foremost, an evolved, biological organism whose
mammalian and primate heritage comprise the inner core of being from
which the vagaries of humanness radiate. Each person is the beneficiary
of eons of natural selection where the style and character of the human
race slowly evolved in progressive attunement to the demands of the

environment. The human structural organism, with its many interrelated functions, is a highly tuned instrument of adaptation, and coping with environmental stresses, threats to survival, and ecological imbalances is just as important now as in the evolutionary past. Thus, we may view the physical organism, intelligence, language, learning capacity, and culture as integral components of a biobehavioral matrix of factors working together to assure adaptation in the form of a successful person-niche fit. So rather than viewing various somatic and psychological functions as independent and unrelated (e.g., as "innate" vs. "acquired") we are led instead to analyze how they combine forces for the ultimate good of the individual and the species. This approach forces us to think in terms of populations as well as individuals, of "ultimate" as well as "proximate" causes of behavior (Wilson, 1975), and of complex person-niche relationships rather than simple cause–effect relationships.

A person may be organized to behave in adaptive ways in the evolutionary sense, but this does not mean that actual emitted behavior is always adaptive in the modern social context. Indeed, the socially maladaptive behavior of modern man is strikingly reflected in marital turmoil and divorce, family breakdown, rising crime rates, war and threats of war, and rising rates of stress-related diseases and disorders (Engel, 1977). Human beings have the capacity to rise to great heights of technological progress and cultural achievement, but the tendency to regress to earlier, more primitive, and often more pathological modes of functioning is ever with us. If we are to properly characterize the human condition, tendencies to regress as well as progress must be duly considered; in so doing, we must confront the Beast in each of us in order to understand the Man. As the 19th-century writers correctly argued—and news events of the day continue to confirm their argument with dreary regularity—the human psyche is composed of a thin veneer of cultural control and moral proscription, under which lies a smouldering cauldron of phylogenetically primitive drives and emotions ready to erupt into behavior at the slightest pretense. Even the most vigorously held and thoroughly ingrained moral and ethical values may be temporarily by-passed in emergency conditions, as the ancient survival imperatives "learned" in phylogeny push the arbitrary acquisitions of culture aside.

The phylogenetic regression–progression model attempts to resolve the Man–Beast paradox by postulating a conceptual continuum going from primitive, regressive, basically unlearned responses at one pole, on to those refined, socialized, enculturated, and distinctly human characteristics at the upper pole (Bailey, 1978, 1985; also see Appendix I). It is assumed that most, if not all, human behaviors, traits, and attributes fall along this phylogenetically primitive-advanced continuum, and further that "progression" up and "regression" down the continuum occurs on a momentary basis. Thus, like mercury in a thermometer reacting to fluctuations in temperature, human behavior is constantly moving up and down the continuum in response to inner urges and outer stresses. What we humans are, in large measure, is a function of the type and quantity of our dynamic and ongoing phylogenetic regressions and progressions.

Psychoanalysis and Regression

A paper by Bailey (1978) drew heavily on Arlow and Brenner's (1964) excellent historical overview of how Freud's ideas grew out of his two earliest and deepest interests, biology and neurology. Freud was greatly influenced by the concepts of biological atavism and retrogression of morphological structures current in the late 19th century, and it is not surprising that the neurological–evolutionary theories of Hughlings Jackson held a special attraction for him. Jackson (Taylor, 1931) applied the doctrine of evolutionary levels to different pathological forms such as illusions, hallucinations, and delusions, and theorized that these phenomena were occasioned by a process of dissolution of the higher nerve centers and reactivation of more phylogenetically primitive levels of functioning. Freud (1891/1953a) borrowed Jackson's concept of functional retrogression and performed a brilliant analysis of speech problems in his *On Aphasia*. However, Freud was not to use the term *phylogenetic regression* until the publication of the late 1918 edition of the *Interpretation of Dreams,* wherein he used the concept to analyze racial memories in dream formation (cited in Arlow & Brenner, 1964). Later, in a *General Introduction to Psychoanalysis* (1920/1969), Freud stated:

> Both of them (ego and libido) are at bottom inheritances, abbreviated repetitions of the evolution undergone by the whole human race . . . In the development of the libido, this phylogenetic origin is readily apparent, I suppose . . . One sees in animals all the various perversions, ingrained, so to speak, in the form taken by their sexual organizations. (pp. 309–310)

Despite Freud's occasional reference to the phylogenetic origins of certain mental structures and instinctual motivations, it is surprising that such considerations virtually have been ignored in the development of psychoanalytic theory. For example, Arlow and Brenner (1964) distinguish between five different types of regression—genetic, systemic, instinctual, phylogenetic, and biogenetic—and then go on to say that the latter two have little relevance to psychoanalysts. Both phylogenetic (the archaic racial heritage of man) and biogenetic (evolutionary carry-overs from subhuman forms of life) kinds of regression are seen by Arlow and Brenner as little more than "suggestive analogies" that "are of limited use scientifically, and have no proper place in our current framework" (pp.

70–71). Much has happened in evolutionary theory, field biology, and neurobiology since Arlow and Brenner penned these lines 2 decades ago, and perhaps today they might take a more sanguinary view toward the significance of phylogenetic regression as it is defined in the present work.

Phylogenetic Regression

For the concept of phylogenetic regression to be meaningful, we must look beyond Freudian theory and build upon the firm ground of the new biology, the findings of social science, and our own observations of the world around us. A first step in developing such a multidisciplinary, integrative formulation would be to view regression as a general process of primitivization, dissolution, hierarchical disintegration, and so on, which involves both phylogenetic and ontogenetic components. Theorists typically have viewed these two components as separate, nonoverlapping phenomena, although some writers have emphasized their mutuality and complementarity. Meerlo (1962), for example, differentiated between phylogenetic and ontogenetic regression, the former reflecting archaic biological patterns of functioning, and the latter resulting from infantile fixations and early experience. For Meerlo, the phylogenetic and ontogenetic components are conceptually distinguishable, but they are still part and parcel of a general process of regression. He sees regression as a process where "both the phylogenetic and ontogenetic clocks are turned back" (p. 79) in response to danger, stress, and fear. Such regression can occur individually or collectively as in group panic or riots, and may be classified into three categories: physical regression, in which entropy and inertia increase and minimal energy expenditure takes place; biological regression, in which loss of biological differentiation takes place; and psychological regression, in which learned habits and behaviors deteriorate. Meerlo further asserts that regression occurs more easily than does progression, and goes on to say that "regressive behavior is so much more seductive and contaminating than civilized, restrained behavior" (p. 78). Although the negative aspects of regression are obvious, Meerlo says that both the phylogenetic and ontogenetic forms may be either adaptive or counteradaptive, and both are involved in psychopathology, particularly in the psychosomatic disorders. Meerlo states that phylogenetic regression is often at the root of many stress-related disorders involving hyperstimulation of the autonomic fight-or-flight defense system where the person resorts to older, basically unlearned, physiological methods of dealing with threat.

Meerlo's distinction between phylogenetic and ontogenetic regression is similar to Lewin's (1951) two-fold classification of *regression,* meaning primitivization, especially in the perceptual sphere, and *retrogression,* which refers to the resumption of infantile modes of speech, dress, gesticulation, and the like. For Lewin, both forms presumably arise ontogenetically, but it is implied that regression is a far more subtle, somatic, and universal process than is retrogression that involves more in the way of learning and enculturalization. It is unlikely, however, that the various forms of regression operate independently from each other, and it is reasonable to assume that a phylogenetic component is always involved in the regressive process, interacting in complex ways with a myriad of ontogenetic variables. The development of sexuality, for example, illustrates this complex, interactive process: "we may view the manifestations of sexuality in terms of ontogenetic development of inborn sensorimotor patterns, achieving a maturational, hierarchical, unitary structure by progressive synthesis of components through a series of transactional experiences" (Kaufman, 1960, p. 324).

A guiding assumption, then, is that regression may be viewed simultaneously as both a phylogenetic and an ontogenetic phenomenon, and the proportionate loading of each serves to determine the distinctive character of the physiological and behavioral results. When one reverts from conscious, rule and role-governed self-control to uncontrolled rage, hysterical crying, paralyzed fear, or even anger, peevishness, or anxiety on a milder scale, the result is a new balance of phylogenetic and ontogenetic relationships. Regression, thus conceived, becomes more phylogenetic and less ontogenetic as greater levels of primitiveness are reached, as learned habits collapse, and as the neocortex yields to lower brain centers. Metaphorically, we might say that atavistic "animal" urges and tendencies rise to the surface as more distinctly "human" features are lost in the regressive process. It is important to note, however, that regression never reaches such depths where all human vestiges are lost and the pure animal takes over; human thought, feeling, and language are never totally suspended, but are intermixed with lower elements, even in the deepest and most pathological forms of regression.

Illustrative Example—Oral Regression

Regression to orality is discussed widely in the psychoanalytic literature, generally in exclusively ontogenetic-developmental terms. The phylogenetic regression–progression model takes a slightly different view. Regression from adulthood to primitive orality does appear to involve a retreat to ontogenetically pre-existing infanthood, but upon reaching the deep oral level, one has, *ipso facto,* also fallen farther back into the instinctive core common to all humanity. The oral phase itself is built upon phylogenetically primitive substructures shared with the animal world, and includes a host of "partial instincts" such as crying, clinging, and following that can be explained in ethological–evolutionary terms

(Schur, 1960). Moreover, an infant of several months is a behaving organism with a fairly large, wired-in response repertoire including sucking, mouthing, crying, biting, chewing, and so forth (Bowlby, 1969). None of these behaviors is purely learned, and none, for that matter, is distinctly human. Indeed, such behaviors are observed in a variety of mammalian species, and certain of these, especially biting and chewing, descend far down the phylogenetic scale to organisms only faintly related to species *Homo sapiens* (Hiiemae, 1978; Hiiemae & Kay, 1973). If these behaviors are basically unlearned, universal in human and many subhuman species, and are phylogenetically continuous across species, then they are, to a significant degree, innate in their structure and instinctual in their function.

We might speculate a bit further here on the matter of orality, to emphasize the broad implications of the concept of phylogenetic regression. Let us look at two correlates of orality, fear of being eaten and destructiveness. These two phenomena traditionally are seen (Fenichel, 1945) as reflecting the vicissitudes of oral eroticism, but there are other explanatory possibilities. Fear of being eaten, for example, is the overriding daily concern for most animals of the earth, and is probably one of man's deepest subconscious fears. Sagan (1977), for example, asks the question, "Could the pervasive dreams and common fears of 'monsters', which children develop shortly after they are able to talk, be evolutionary vestiges of quite adaptive—baboonlike—responses to dragons and owls?" (p. 151). If Sagan is even partially right, the horror-filled dreams of the child, the more subtle fear of mutilation and death in the normal adult, and the raw oral imagery of the psychotic are partial reversions back to a time when life was, as Hobbes stated, nasty, brutish, and short, and man was preyed upon by fearsome creatures of the jungle.

But man was also a predator as well as preyed upon, and it is here that "oral destructiveness" may be taken somewhat literally. Rather than being simply a function of early frustration or redirected libido, oral destructiveness, whether in fantasies, dreams, or actual behavior, may reflect, in part, the phylogenesis of the human race as well. Fenichel (1945) tells us that analysis "of sexual perverts often reveals that at the bottom of their symptoms there is a fixation on the oral sexual aim of biting" (pp. 64–65). Further, serious forms of aggressive biting may be seen in both normal and disturbed children, in regressed mental patients, and even in the "peaceful" African Bushmen (Eibl-Eibesfeldt, 1972, 1979). At a deep psychological level we may be touching on something fundamental to the human character; for much of our existence as a species we were predatory, omnivorous hunters (Freeman, 1964; Washburn & Hamburg, 1972), even to the point of being cannibalistic many times along the way (Hogg, 1958). Although it is true that biting and mouthing have virtually disappeared in human play behavior, and the teeth and mouth are only rarely used as instruments of aggression, the age old predatory motivation system still seems to exist, and may lie at the base of certain "cold-blooded" forms of sadism involving torture, killing, and body mutilation (Bailey, in press 1985; also see chapters 9, 10, and 11). In these instances, is it not reasonable to assume that a mostly motivational but partly behavioral regression to the predatory system has occurred where killing becomes pleasurable and destruction the inexorable result? Phylogenetic regression need not be total across the various systems of motivation, perception, and behavior to be theoretically significant; how the regressive recovery of species patterns interacts with the total human being is the issue.

Emotion, Behavior, and Regression

Generally, phylogenetic regression is more tied to motivational and emotional systems than to overt behavioral systems. When overt muscle responses are the focus of attention, it is natural that situational causes be sought, but gut-level emotionality calls for subtler analysis. Simply stated, overt behavior often is capricious and the pawn of circumstances, whereas emotion is phylogenetically archaic, closer to the core of the personality, and thus more "regressed." Outward manifestations, then, are more likely to be learned, consciously controlled, and culture-specific, whereas inner automatic responsivity, feeling, and emotionality reflect nature more than nurture (see Breger, 1974). Wilson (1978) summarizes the situation very well: "The less rational but more important the decision-making process, the more emotion should be expended in conducting it. . . . Because the brain can be guided by rational calculation only to a limited degree, it must fall back on the nuances of pleasure and pain mediated by the limbic system and other lower centers of the brain" (p. 68).

Imagine, for example, a situation where a stranger verbally or physically abuses each of a variety of persons from very disparate cultural and experiential backgrounds. Whether these hypothetical individuals react outwardly with counter-attack, appeasement and submission, or helpless resignation will be determined largely by their individual learning experiences and cultural value systems. It is likely, however, that each individual will feel anger and rage and will wish to retaliate against the aggressor, regardless of what his overt responses might be. Furthermore, these feelings and wishes represent, to a significant degree, phylogenetically conditioned, adaptive, and survival-related motivational–emotional responses to threat and danger that are more or less universal in the species. Fear of the stranger (xenophobia) is considered to be universal in the species (Holloway, 1974), and it is likely that antipathy to strangers, especially where threat is involved, is equally universal.

Many phylogenetic carryovers in man are, thus, more likely to manifest themselves emotionally than behaviorally. Therefore, as William McDougall (1926) observed, if we analyze what a person feels or desires, we are more likely to discover archaic patterns of "instincts" than if we merely observe what a person does:

> Hence in man, whose intelligence and adaptability are so great, the afferent and efferent parts of each instinctive disposition are liable to many modifications, while the central part alone remains unmodified: that is to say, the cognitive processes through which any instinctive process may be initiated exhibit a great complication and variety; and the actual bodily movements by which the instinctive process achieves its end may be complicated to an indefinitely great extent; while the emotional excitement, with the accompanying nervous activities of the central part of the disposition, is the only part of the total instinctive process that retains its specific character and remains common to all individuals and all situations in which the instinct is excited. (p. 35)

Similarly, Nash (1970) says that, "the emotional component is an essential part of an instinct, and this aspect . . . is increasingly more important as one moves up the phylogenetic scale. Instincts in man are largely feeling" (p. 59). Emotion, broadly defined, is not only essential, but probably the most fundamental component of an instinct. Schur (1960) infers that the ethological and psychoanalytic instinct theories are different in many ways, but they are largely in agreement on the fundamental significance of internal drive states (affects, emotions, urges, desires, etc.) In his classic essay on affects in psychoanalytic theory, Rapaport (1953) postulated "inborn-affect-discharge channels" that lie at the core of the instinctual apparatus. These inborn channels act as safety valves at the rudimentary level, but progressive "training" by the ego ultimately transforms them into neutralized cathexes or controlled "affect signals." Actually, as Rapaport tells us, affects exist on a continuum that ranges from massive affect attacks and abreactions up to mere signals or meta-signals at the highest level.

Emotions obviously are very important and are rooted deeply in the survival mechanisms of mammalian and primate species. In *The Expression of the Emotions in Man and Animals,* Darwin (1872/1896) provided many examples of continuity of emotional expressions from lower animals to human beings. As we recall from chapter 1, Darwin correlated the human sneer with the baring of fangs in wolves and dogs, and he discussed how many animals, including humans, try to look terrible and fierce in agonistic encounters. Many animals appear more ferocious by virtue of apparent increases in size accomplished through piloerection, expansion of air pouches, facial swelling, or postural exaggeration. Darwin felt that the energizing and nonvocal signaling aspects of emotions and expressions are adaptive in emergency situations, and serve to increase the organism's chances of survival. Carroll Izard (1977) and various other writers (Plutchik, 1979; Tomkins, 1963) maintain that not only are the emotions adaptive in the evolutionary sense, they constitute the primary motivation system of human beings. So viewed, the emotions play an important role in organizing, motivating, and sustaining behavior, and the evidence is strong that basic emotional expressions and their experiential qualities are virtually the same in every part of the world, even across widely differing cultures. These clear cross-cultural similarities in emotional expression led Izard to conclude that the fundamental emotions are built upon "innate neural programs." The innate programs are modifiable by experience, however; "Almost anyone can learn to inhibit or modify the innate emotional expressions" (Izard, 1977, p. 6). For the most part, the emotions may be seen as neuropsychological constants that are inhibited, modified, elaborated upon, and/or triggered by social and environmental stimuli.

There are many comprehensive theories of emotion, but the broad, integrative, "psychevolutionary" scheme of Plutchik (1980) is particularly interesting. Plutchik assumes that emotions are the by-products of biological evolution, and he identifies eight primary emotions and traces them back to their original survival functions. His theory defines an emotion as a complex sequence of events involving elements of cognitive appraisal, subjective feeling, impulses to action, and overt behavior. An emotion is thus a coordinated sequence that is set off or triggered by environmental stimuli such as threat, sexual stimulation, absence of the love object, and numerous other forms of arousal and emergency. It is noteworthy that cognitive factors play a large role in the emotional sequence, particularly by way of enabling the organism to appraise the environment and then predict the future contingencies (e.g., whether there is food, a mate, or an enemy in its environment). Further, Plutchik says that cognition and "intelligence" in the form of complex processes of sensory input, evaluation, symbolization, and comparison of new information with stored memory, normally act in service to the emotions and biological needs of the organism. From this standpoint, the hypertrophied human neocortex may be viewed in less-than-transcendental terms; its primary function is to serve the deeper, older, and survival-related motivational systems of the person, rather than serving merely as an autonomous organ of cognition and reflection. This point is a crucial one as we elaborate the phylogenetic regression concept in subsequent sections.

As Spinoza, Darwin, James, and others have done in the past, Plutchik sees emotions as comparable to colors, which may be of primary types, secondary types, or mixtures of types. Like colors, emotions vary in intensity, in degree of similarity to one another, and they exhibit polarities. Intensity is reflected in the distinctions we make, for example, between fear and panic, irritation and rage, or pensiveness and grief. In terms of similarity, we instantly recognize that emotions like disgust, loathing, and anger are closely related, whereas anger and adoration or disappointment and joy are not. Polarities are readily evident as well, as seen in the polar opposites of love–hate, joy–sadness, or optimism–disappointment. Plutchik's model for depicting relative intensities and similarities of the primary emotions is shown in Figure 3.1. In their most extreme forms, the eight primaries are grief, amazement, terror, adoration, ecstasy, vigilance, rage, and loathing. Each primary may be expressed in relatively pure form (e.g., grief or terror) or in milder versions of a pure primary such as boredom, annoyance, or apprehension. Each primary describes a hierarchy of intensity going from the most extreme expression on up through various milder levels. For most of Plutchik's eight primaries, there appears to be increased neocortical involvement and decreased raw emotionality proceeding up from the most extreme to the mildest expressions. This implies that the pure, extreme emotions are

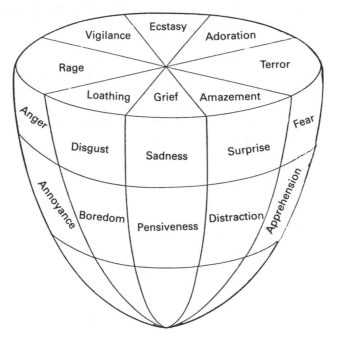

FIG. 3.1   Plutchik's multidimensional model of the emotions (from Plutchik, 1980).

more phylogenetically loaded than are the milder ones; further, we might presume that in the heat of an argument, for example, a person might regress from mere annoyance to lethal violence under sufficient provocation.

In human beings, emotions are rarely expressed in pure, extreme form, and we more often see various mixtures of components: "corticalized" emotions with a heavy controlling, inhibiting cognitive element, combinations of pure primaries, or more complex mixtures of primary and secondary, extreme and mild elements (Plutchik, 1980). The notion of "mixture" is important theoretically (see McDougall, 1926; chapter 8), for as Izard (1977) says: "It is possible that the whole brain participates in the emotion process, with some mechanisms contributing more than others and playing different roles in different emotions" (p. 16). Again, we see the importance of the proportional loading of phylogenetically older versus newer neuropsychological, emotion–cognition-behavior coordinations. Depending on the relative loading of reptilian, limbic, and neocortical components in a given action sequence, for example, the emotion–cognition-behavior blends operating may be relatively regressive or progressive, relatively "animal" or "human."

In lower animals, adaptive emotion–motivation-behavior patterns (instincts) are wired into the nervous system and operate in a generally, smooth, coordinated fashion with little blending of components of separate instinctive systems. Tinbergen (1976), for example, says that aggression acts in the service of a number of different functional and motivational systems, but in animals the systems tend to exclude each other and act independently. Man, however, has the capacity to fuse and mix systems, *ad infinitum,* into what Tinbergen calls *supermotivations*; he believes that these grand motivational systems subserve the phylogenetically distinctive, bittersweet "accomplishments" of the human race— technological warfare and mass killing, art, religion, and science. Thus, in humans, we rarely see a pure instinctive pattern analogous to nest-building in birds or territorial defense in the hedgehog, but old stereotyped patterns still intermix with the most lofty human endeavors. Under circumstances of extreme stress and provocation, however, our phylogenetically advanced supermotivations tend to defuse into approximations of their original instinctive components, as when the acquisitions of culture melt in the heat of the copulatory response or anger overwhelms the rational senses.

Definitional Issues

So far we have characterized phylogenetic regression as a general primitivization and emotionalization of the phylogenetic–ontogenetic interplay, but it is possible to be a bit more specific. Let us now look briefly at several subdefinitions, most of which are at least roughly congruent with the general definition.

The Metaphorical Definition

The metaphorical definition is the weakest and most informal of the various definitions and is, for the most part, based on intuitive and loosely analogical comparisons between human beings and the "lower animals" (see chapter 1). Here we see the man-as-beast idea expressed in often superficial and politically dangerous terms, where the criminal, the social malcontent, those of lower social standing, or opponents in war are seen as "acting like animals," "brutes," "savages," and the like. Gould (1981) correctly implies that Cesare Lombroso made his original "discovery" of the relationship between atavism and criminality at the metaphorical level before proceeding to develop a rather specific theory based on anthropometric data. Upon examining the skull of a famous criminal, the following insight came in a flash of inspiration to Lombroso: "At the sight of that skull, I seemed to see all of a sudden, lighted up as a vast plain under a flaming sky, the problem of the nature of the criminal—an atavistic being who reproduces in his person the ferocious instincts of primitive humanity and the inferior animals" (in Taylor, Walton, & Young, 1973, p. 41).

From Plato to the 19th-century evolutionists and recapitulationists, and to ourselves in the present age, there is a strong temptation to employ the metaphorical definition in attempting to explain the more egregious forms of human misbehavior. This tendency was evident in the journalistic hyperbole that followed the infamous power outage in New York in the summer of 1977 (*Night of Terror,* 1977). As we recall, roving bands of men, women and children reportedly looted at will and engaged in what was described as wanton destructiveness. One witness said they acted as if a "fever struck them," and a policeman referred to the carnage as "the night of the animals." Even the educator Kenneth Clark was quoted as saying, "We have reduced the people of the ghetto to the point where they function on the level of predatory animals." These examples show rather clearly how intuitive and impressionistic the metaphorical definition is, and, further, how it is so often misapplied.

The Anthropometric Definition

Once Lombroso actually began to collect anthropometric data, "regression" became almost totally associated with physical signs, or *stigmata* as he called them. As Gould (1981) so aptly points out, the notion of physical atavisms and their putative connection with behavioral dispositions was largely discredited in Lombroso's time, and no reputable scientist would subscribe to such views today. The situation is not so clear, however, where behavior, motivation, emotion, and mentation are concerned. The phylogenetic regression–progression model assumes that part-atavisms, mixed in with higher neocortical functions, can and probably do occur in some and possibly all of these response systems. This does not at all imply that the model subscribes in the slightest to the anthropometric definition; the regression–progression approach is thoroughly psychodynamic, intrapsychic, and a theory of mind and not physique.

Regression as Hierarchic Disintegration

Razran (1971) provides a brilliant evolutionary analysis of higher and lower learning processes, and he postulates 11 different hierarchically arranged levels proceeding from rudimentary habituation and sensitization, on through various types of associative and perceptual learning, and finally on up to the most phylogenetically advanced forms of cognitive learning. In the human being, all of these forms of learning are present, functional, and systematically interrelated. Razran assumes that during the process of evolution higher levels arose from lower ones, lower levels continue as subsystems within higher levels, higher levels are more functionally efficient but lower levels are more universal and less disrupted by environmental stimuli, higher systems typically but do not invariably control lower systems, and higher and lower systems interact both antagonistically and synergistically. Although this complex, interactive model was designed to explain learning processes, it applies to many other functional systems as well. It is likely that most psychological and neurological systems are hierarchically arranged and functionally interrelated as outlined in Razran's model. If so, then "regressing down the hierarchy" would involve a progressive loss of higher functions and proportionate recovery of lower ones, and differentiation would yield to more universal processes.

As all theories of development state or imply, developmental progress involves moving from lesser to greater complexity, from concrete to more abstract modes of thinking, from emotional to intellectual predominance, from lesser neocortical to greater neocortical control and inhibition, from asocial to cultural behavior patterns, from the "grammar" of behavior to the "literature" of behavior (Tiger & Fox, 1971), from narcissistic self-centeredness to object cathexis and some on to higher levels of altruistic other-centeredness, from the unlearned, rigid and stereotyped to the more learned and flexible modalities, from short latencies to longer ones, and, in general, from lesser self-control to greater response inhibition. When regression occurs, then, the genetic process is reversed and the individual returns to earlier, more primitive stages of the developmental sequence. Along with such genetic reversal, some degree of hierarchic disintegration is involved in the regressive process. The systems theorist,

Ludwig von Bertalanffy (1968) sees regression as a "loosening of the hierarchical mental organization," a disintegration of the personality wherein primitive states reappear (dedifferentiation) and "functional dysencephalization" (decentralization) occurs. Many writers (Breger, 1968; Peterfreund, 1971; Powers, 1973; Werner, 1948) view the human being as a tiered system of hierarchically arranged subsystems, and personologists and developmentalists often speak of ordered stages and sequences in physical and psychological growth. Generally, the more advanced human behaviors are those associated with "higher" subsystems, or later and more complex stages of development, as is especially clear in the hierarchic nature of the nervous system (see chapter 2). However, evolved "autonomic information-processing control systems" operating at the lower levels of functioning are of fundamental importance, as Peterfreund (1971) points out:

> These control systems can be viewed as genetically ordained, 'wired-in' subroutines . . . they are each subroutines or hierarchical levels of an over-all organismic progression . . . these control systems . . . represent the programming that has evolved through phylogenetic time, instructions from which are transmitted to successive generations through the genetic code. They have emerged as a result of mutations and natural selection, and they serve the goals of survival and adaptation. (p. 151)

Peterfreund goes on to say that sexuality, for example, is a complex amalgamation of genetically ordained subroutines, and phenomena such as orality, anality, and genitality correspond, in large measure, to differing hierarchical levels of the overall control-system program (see chapter 2). He also speaks of "regression" in the overall system, which is a benign process of "disordering" and "randomization" whereby a wide variety of information-processing levels are activated and new arrangements (learning) effected. Such regression is similar to Ernst Kris' (1952) idea of regression in the service of the ego, although Peterfreund emphasizes learning more than creativity.

Proceeding on the assumption that personality is arranged hierarchically, with lower levels being more phylogenetically loaded than higher ones, several relevant theories will now be analyzed from the perspective of the phylogenetic regression–progression model. Of course the structural trichotomy of id, ego, and superego represents an ordered, hierarchical system, and descent through the structures implies greater access to the evolved instinctive apparatus, and, consequently, greater involvement of the lower phylogenetic programs. There are other theories, however, that provide much clearer examples of the process of phylogenetic regression. Sandor Rado's (1969) theory of adaptational psychodynamics is a perfect case in point. As we recall from chapter 2, he postulates a "psychodynamic cerebral system" that is dominated by the action of pleasure, pain, emotion, and reason, and is hierarchically arranged into four levels of functioning: hedonic, brute emotional, emotional thought, and unemotional thought. All of these levels work simultaneously and in combination (are mixed, "interlocked," and interact in various proportions, ratios, etc.), and phylogenetic influence is diminished as higher levels gain precedence. As Rado (1969) states, "These four superimposed levels correspond roughly to the phylogeny of the human species" (p. 32), with the lower levels being guided by primitive, subcortical emotional centers and higher levels by the rational intellect of the neocortex. Although in perfect concert with the present writer on many essential points, Rado fails to carry his argument to its logical conclusion: if one can progress up the hierarchy to lesser emotionality and greater intellectual control, then one can also regress down the scale to greater emotionality and lesser intellectual control! The word "regression" is mentioned only once in Rado's book, and even there it is unclear as to whether the process is basically ontogenetic, phylogenetic, or a combination of the two. Although he failed to exploit an idea for which such excellent groundwork was laid, the following quote shows he was on the right track: "This regressive tendency is characteristic of life. The most general mechanism that brings about regression is the failure of higher patterns. When more recent, higher organization fails, the organism reverts to more elementary patterns" (p. 56).

The reasoning developed thus far leads us to a principle of remarkable simplicity: Not only does one regress to lower phylogenetic levels as well as progress to higher ones, but descent, disintegration, dedifferentiation, decentralization, and so forth, are often more pleasureable and invariably more quickly and easily accomplished than is ascent to higher levels which require oft-resisted excesses in terms of enculturalization, education, and cortical programming. Abraham Maslow's (1943, 1954) famous need-hierarchy theory popularized the notion that greater pleasure is to be found in the higher as opposed to the lower needs, but common sense and the statistical rarity of the "self-actualized" personality suggests the contrary. The work of Buchenholtz (1956, 1958; Buchenholtz & Naumberg, 1957) provides ample empirical evidence that lower instinctual pleasures, especially sex, are far more significant than are higher pleasures for most subjects, and the work of Bailey and associates (Bailey, Burns, & Bazan, 1982; Bazan, 1980; Burns, 1979) with college students revealed that activities presumably mediated by lower brain centers (viz., sex, eating, swimming, sleeping, being massaged, etc.) were highly pleasurable, whereas higher activities such as work, intellectual study, organizing time, attending the ballet, composing a computer program, etc., were typically rated as aversive. It is noteworthy that studying for classes was consistently rated as very subjectively aversive across several different subject samples.

The phylogenetic regression–progression model applies almost as well to Maslow's theory as to Rado's hierarchical model. From his initial grounding in primatological research under the tutelage of Harry Harlow (Lowry, 1973), Maslow went on to study dominance patterns in human females (Maslow, 1942), and ultimately achieved fame upon publication of the need-hierarchy theory (Maslow, 1943). Maslow's background made him aware of the fundamental similarities between subhuman primates and humans, and he spoke of "behavioral universals" (Maslow, 1937) in expressing dominance and subordination, and he noted similarities in certain aspects of homosexual and copulatory behavior across primate species. Also, in his 1942 paper on self-esteem and sexuality in women, he concluded: "In general, it is fair to say that human sexuality is almost exactly like primate sexuality with exception that cultural pressures added to the picture, drive a good deal of sexual behavior underground into fantasies, dreams, and unexpressed wishes" (Maslow, 1942; cited in Lowry, 1973, p. 134). It was from these core ideas that the need-hierarchy theory developed.

Six general need systems comprise the Maslovian hierarchy: physiological needs, safety needs, love needs, self-esteem needs, self-actualization needs, and aesthetic needs. Common sense assures us that this hierarchy is properly ordered and that the levels are meaningful and valid ones, but we must take this on faith. Given his hierarchical assumptions, it is herewith proposed that Maslow's higher needs are more phylogenetically advanced, cortically dominated, more rational, conscious, abstract, and distinctly human than the lower needs, and, once we are as low as the love needs we are approaching the mammalian base of behavior, and once we get to the safety and physiological needs the animal–human differential becomes negligible. To an extent, self-esteem with its implication of conscious self-evaluation vis-à-vis culturally determined criteria for goodness and superiority tends toward the distinctly human end of the continuum, and certainly self-actualization and aesthetic appreciation have no parallels in the animal world. It seems then that the subneocortical–neocortical ratio increasingly favors the neocortical as one moves up Maslow's hierarchy, and, consequently, there should be decreasing proportions of archaic emotionality in the expression of the higher needs (see E. O. Wilson's 1975 chapter, "Man: From Sociobiology to Sociology," for a similar analysis of Maslow's theory). Like Rado, Maslow spoke often of movement up the scale to higher units of growth and actualization, but he mysteriously neglected the equally obvious matter of regression or moving down the scale. The phylogenetic regression–progression model would appear to be one way of enrichening Maslow's theory by providing a schema for analyzing bidirectional movement in the need-hierarchy.

In summary, there are many forms of hierarchical regression including genetic reversal of stages, hierarchic dissolution, dedifferentiation, decentralization, and so forth. All of these share a common characteristic, however: All involve a temporary loss or diminution of cortical control which consequently leaves the more primeval urges less constrained. The phylogenetic regression hypothesis carries this reasoning a step further and postulates that what is released in the regressive process is of major theoretical significance. Regression may bring out bits and pieces of previously acquired habits, thoughts, and feelings, but mixed in with them are likely to be elements of vestigial, survival-related patterns of response that are released when the cortex steps aside. A newer rationality thus gives way to an older one, as the individual falls back on pre-established and pre-cultural strategies not random irrationality.

Regression as Diminished Cortical Control

The concept of phylogenetic regression implies a restructuring of brain relationships whereby the individual moves from higher, rational, predominantly neocortical involvement, to lower levels of cortical or even subcortical mediation. If we assume that the brain's structures work in concert and all levels are functionally involved in any and all forms of response output, it is more correct to say that the ratio of phylogenetically "older" to "newer" forms of mediation varies with the amount and degree of regression operating. As regression deepens, then, neocortical control is progressively diminished relative to the more primitive and archaic brain structures such as those of the limbic-hypothalamic complex or the even more primitive reptilian system.

There are numerous writers who allude to regression down the hierarchically arranged brain, although few actually use the term *regression*. Several illustrative quotes may be listed here.

Arthur Koestler (1967), in his *Ghost in the Machine,* drew heavily upon Paul MacLean's theory of the triune brain, and used it to reformulate the psychoanalytic notion of "regression in the service of the ego." "Poetry could thus be said to achieve a synthesis between the sophisticated reasoning of the neocortex and the more primitive emotional ways of the old brain. . . . This . . . process, which seems to underlie all creative achievement, may reflect a temporary regression from overconcrete, neocortical thinking to more fluid and 'instinctive' modes of limbic thinking" (p. 288). Such regressions are not always beneficial; they may be pathological as well. In fact, following MacLean (see chapter 2), Koestler argues that a fundamental antagonism exists between the old and new brains—the limbic system and the neocortex—which has produced a blight on the human species, a condition which MacLean calls *schizophysiology*. This fundamental split between the old and new brain structures is responsible, Koestler thinks, for a wide range of pathological symptoms in modern man including delusional thinking, irrational fears and phobias, and the "paranoid streak running through human history" (p. 296).

Konrad Lorenz (1972) addressed the regressive aspect of the neocortical-limbic system interplay in his well-known essay on the *Enmity Between Generations:*

> Anyone familiar with the ethological facts need only observe the hate-distorted faces of the more primitive type of rebel students in order to realize that they are not only unwilling, but quite unable to come to an understanding with their antagonists. In people wearing that kind of facial expression the hypothalamus is at the helm and the cortex completely inhibited. . . . (p. 102)

More recently, Holloway (1974) argued that human beings are little different from animals in many respects, and he took the universal phenomenon of xenophobia as a point of departure. He believes that xenophobia is built upon a firm phylogenetic foundation, and he comments on the perceptual readiness with which all human groups recognize themselves as different from other groups:

> Surely the roots for this basic, perceptual style are very deep in our evolutionary history, and not easily overcome. We can only assume some eufunctional basis for these kinds of perceptual stances, which are hardly human specific, but shared throughout most of the animal kingdom. We overcome this to some extent through cultural learning, and a pride in and positive value on tolerance and goodwill. *But put stress on the system, and the age-old dispositions are dominant.* (p. 8; italics added)

Phylogenetic regression in the form of downward displacement in the hierarchical brain has particular relevance in the area of episodic and uncontrolled rage and violence. Following an extensive review of primate neuroanatomy, Andy and Stephan (1974) concluded that:

> These combined anatomic and physiologic observations imply that the complex physiologic and behavioral changes which together make up aggression were predominantly integrated through rudimentary brainstem and diencephalic structures which revealed very little change in phylogenetic development from lower to higher primates, including man. The progressively increased control of the aggressive state, as the primate evolved, was predominantly due to increased neocorticalization in phylogeny. (However), a developmental abnormality or lesion implicating those rudimentary structures may activate physiologic mechanisms, resulting in aggressive states

which cannot be controlled by inhibitory mechanisms of neocortical origin. (pp. 326–327)

The Andy and Stephan review reveals several important considerations: (a) aggression in primates is primarily mediated through brainstem and limbic-hypothalamic structures; (b) aggression is held in check largely by inhibiting mechanisms in the neocortex; and (c) uncontrolled or dyscontrolled aggression may result when brain damage occurs or the neocortex malfunctions. Research models based on principles similar to these have been used in the study of violent behavior in mental patients and criminal populations. Mark and Ervin (1970) believe that a number of disease states—both inherited and acquired—can disturb limbic brain function and predispose the afflicted individual toward violent behavior, giving rise to what they call the "dyscontrol syndrome" (see chapter 10). Similarly, Monroe (1978) refers to an "epileptic mechanism" that generated episodic dyscontrol reactions in the violent criminals studied. This mechanism is thought to be associated with excessive neuronal discharges in sub-neocortical structures, especially in the limbic system. In between their epileptoid seizures, Monroe's prisoners were generally well-behaved, but in a brief moment they would "regress" to dangerous, lethal forms of violence.

The Polish psychologist Kosewski (1979) also emphasized phylogenetic regression in prison violence, although his approach focused more on animal-human behavioral analogies than neuropsychological factors:

> The differentiation of group roles and of status in the group on the basis of physical domination and fighting competence is a typical feature of highly organized animal communities. We might therefore say that human groups that are organized on this pattern have suffered a primitivization of social organization: they have *regressed* to a more primitive developmental stage, one marked by physical coercion as the differentiating factor in group role and status. (p. 208; italics added)

> These similarities in the social functioning of highly organized animal groups and violence-prone human groups entitle us to speak of the primitivization of human social behavior and its regression to an evolutionarily earlier stage. (p. 209)

A favorite quote in the area of aggression comes from the book, *Psychobiology of Aggression and Violence* (1981), by the noted Italian neuropharmacologist, Luigi Valzelli, who clearly draws his impetus from Professor MacLean's theory of the triune brain:

> In man, the neocortical mantle is thought to be the seat of logical and mathematical reasoning, knowledge and understanding, analytical and synthetic processes, invention and fantasy, philosophy and religion, meditation

and intuition. However, in man, too, some behaviors and aspects of mental disease suggest a *regression* of brain functioning to a predominantly paleomammalian (limbic) or reptilian level. In this last instance, as has been observed in animal experiments, the breakdown of social, familial, parental behavior, and personal care is often accompanied by the emergence of asocial, hostile, and aggressive behaviors, and "reptilian" man emerges. (p. 38; italics added)

The most definitive and sweeping statements on the issue were made by Sagan (1977), in his Pulitzer prize-winning *Dragons of Eden,* and by Bailey in the 1978 essay on phylogenetic regression. Interestingly, Sagan's comment was made in discussing epileptic behavior:

Indeed, *grand mal* epilepsy can, I think, be described as a disease in which the cognitive drivers are all turned off because of a kind of electrical storm in the brain, and the victim is left momentarily with nothing operative but his neural chassis. This is a profound impairment, *temporarily regressing the victim back several hundreds of millions of years.* (pp. 57–58; italics added)

Although Bailey's (1978) essay contained some remarkably similar quotes, it was written without knowledge of Sagan's book. Following is a sample quote:

The main point emphasized here is that in a matter of seconds, a culturally refined, cortically controlled individual can regress to the emotionality characteristic of his evolutionary forebears, and at that moment he is little different from them. We are normally far different from *Homo erectus* or *Australopithecus,* or a baboon or chimpanzee for that matter, but under severe stress, threat, provocation, or loss of "control" through alcohol ingestion, drugs, and so forth, we temporarily lose our humanity, our culture, and rationality. (p. 22)

The previous citations lead to several conclusions about phylogenetic regression as it is defined from the perspective of diminished cortical control: (a) there is a continuing interplay between neocortical brain structures and phylogenetically older structures; (b) this interplay may be antagonistic or protagonistic, beneficial or pathological; (c) regressions from the new to the older structures sometimes occurs; (d) the regressions may occur very quickly and appear to underly certain types of episodic violence; and (e) both internal conditions (brain dysfunction, developmental abnormalities, drug and alcohol intake, etc.) and external conditions (stress, threat, etc.) may act as elicitors or facilitators of regression. These conclusions apply most clearly to sudden, epileptoid kinds of dyscontrolled violence, but the phylogenetic regression model, when defined according to the notion of diminished cortical control, is, as subsequent chapters show, applicable to a much wider range of both aggressive and non-aggressive behaviors.

As we end this section on diminished cortical control and regression, it is tempting to conclude that, "As the cortex goes, so goes human behavior." At the subcortical level, individual differences are minimal, and as a species we are little different from our close phylogenetic relatives in limbic functioning. In discussing the transition from ape to human, Washburn and Moore (1980) remind us that, "the control of emotions is one of the ways in which humans differ from their nearest relatives. We are so used to living in a world in which people's emotions are under control that we think of uncontrolled behavior as criminal. But the sexual or aggressive acts we think of as unacceptable are common in societies of monkeys and apes" (p. 150). They further point out that the cortex succeeds in binding such unacceptable behavior both through direct neural control and through culturally programmed customs, mores, and prohibitions. Certainly, the *uncommited cortex,* to use Arieti's (1976) term, provides us with limitless opportunities to creatively rise above our phylogenetic origins. Yet, once its vigilance is relaxed to the slightest degree, the threat of regression arises, and, not infrequently, the imprisoned beast breaks forth in dyscontrolled and uncivilized forms of behavior.

Phylogenetic Progression[1]

So far, emphasis has been on the human being's capacity to phylogenetically regress under threat, particularly threat to survival, but there is another side to the coin, that of phylogenetic progression. Thus, not only

[1]*Phylogenetic progression,* as defined here, is basically an active process of transcending our basic animality through neocortical inhibition of our generally amoral and acultural natural tendencies on the one hand, and cultural reshaping on the other. Without such active inhibition and reshaping, individual human beings are likely to remain "fixated" at pre-cultural and certainly pre-technological levels of functioning; that is, phylogenetic inertia exerts a stronger pull backward than any "natural," noncultural pull forward. Nevertheless, as suggested by an anonymous reviewer of this book, phylogenetic progression is "passive" in many respects; e.g., it can be viewed as the passive, natural, and spontaneous outcome of rearing and socialization experiences, subconscious identification with significant others, situational pressures, punishment for "primitive behavior," moral and religious exhortation, and so on. To a degree, this follows from PRP theory, but only for phylogenetic progress up to the midpoint of the PRP continuum (see chapter 4; Appendix I) or slightly beyond, e.g., at or around the level of culture (see chapter 9). Thus, phylogenetic progression may be partly passive up through the lower levels of cultural conformity, but becomes distinctly active on through the higher sublevels of cultural innovation and technocultural advancement, and more active still on through the last two levels of philosophical and spiritual expression (see chapter 9). We see, therefore, that while passive and spontaneous phylogenetic progression is crucial to achieving humanhood, it is the active form that subserves our highest human endeavors and distanciates us most from our basic animality.

may a person regress to the archaic emotionality and primitive drives of the limbic and reptilian systems under stress or threat, it is possible to phylogenetically progress from lower levels of functioning to cortically dominated, conscious, rational, abstract, and distinctly human levels of functioning as well. In fact, most theories of development in psychology are of the progressive sort, where the individual gradually moves from lower to higher units of development by virtue of the combined effects of maturation and learning. Freud's theory of psychosexual development, Erickson's eight stages of psychosocial development, Jane Loevinger's various stages of ego development, Kohlberg's stages of moral development, and so forth, all assume a gradual rising above the simple, primitive, and selfish demands of the infant organism. One should not get the impression, however, that regression and progression are identical processes, one merely moving down the scale and the other up.

As outlined in Appendix I and also in chapter 4, the dynamic processes of regression and progression are quite different. We may briefly summarize some of these differences here:

1. It is far easier to regress than to progress. In essence, just acting naturally and gaining access to one's animal nature is to phylogenetically regress according to our definition. To regress is to return to pre-established patterns of response that were established in phylogeny and that are typically self-reinforcing and pleasurable to perform (see chapter 8). By contrast, to phylogenetically progress, one must often oppose natural, pleasurable tendencies for the sake of social conformity and obeisance to arbitrary cultural imperatives. Phylogenetic progression requires massive amounts of intellectual control and neocortical inhibition, neither of which are as natural nor as pleasurable as yielding to regressive processes. Moreover, intellectual work and neocortical inhibition not only lack natural, self-reinforcing properties, but are actually perceived as aversive by many people (Bailey, Burns, & Bazan, 1982; Bazan, 1980; Burns, 1979, 1984).

2. In phylogenetic regression, much of the content of the response or response pattern is innate, encoded in the nervous system, and universal in the species. In humans, examples include the sucking and rooting reflex, sexual foreplay and the copulatory response, and certain aspects of fighting behavior (see chapter 5). By contrast, most of the content of phylogenetic progression is supplied by the customs, mores, and fads and fashions current in a particular social group or culture at a particular time. Such socially inculcated mandates often are arbitrary, changeable, and not necessarily adaptive in the ultimate sense. We find, therefore, that the basic content of regression is fairly predictable and uniform across cultural groups (e.g., all individuals who perform sexual intercourse perform in fundamentally similar fashion and derive similar pleasure from

it), whereas at the progressive cultural level of deciding when, where, and who shall enjoy sexual intercourse we see great cultural variability. In regression, we conform to inner and generally universal mandates, whereas in progression we conform, in varying degrees across individuals within a given social classification, to outer pressures and demands that often go against our wishes and natural proclivities.

3. All human beings possess similar biological needs and desires, and, therefore, in phylogenetic regression, individual differences are reduced in the regressive process (see chapter 5). We humans all start at basically the same place, and when we regress we regress to basically the same place. By contrast, to reach even a moderately high level of progression in modern technological society numerous requirements must be met: The individual must be reasonably "intelligent" compared to peers, the lower needs in Maslow's sense must be minimally satisfied, opportunity for formal and informal education must be present, the individual must exhibit sufficient motivation and cultural compliance to benefit from educational opportunities, the individual must live in a society that provides sufficient political freedom to grow and develop, progression is a financially expensive process and, thus, the individual must be financially secure, and so on. Clearly, there are many more parameters for variation at the progressive, as contrasted to the regressive, level of functioning.

4. Phylogenetic regression and progression differ on the time dimension. Generally, momentary regressions are far more common than momentary progressions. For example, after having slowly brought oneself to a lofty stage of philosophic reflection, a young man might immediately lose his hard-won progress with the mere sight of an attractive woman. Once the sight of the woman elicits regressive sexual fantasies, the young man might not be able to psychologically progress again until some sexual relief is achieved. On the other hand, how many young men are likely to be distracted from a scantily clad young woman by the intrusion of a creative thought? In this example, we see how the more intrinsically powerful and momentarily urgent lower motives must be repressed and constrained so that the higher, progressive processes may enjoy a brief period of dominance. Such constraining processes take time and effort, and aside from the sudden, creative "Aha" experiences discussed by the Gestaltists, we typically see little in the way of momentary progressions.

The Regression–Progression Continuum

The regression–progression model assumes that all behavior exists on a conceptual continuum going from phylogenetically old, primitive, regressive, unlearned responses at one pole, up to refined neocortically mediated, socialized, and distinctly human responses at the other pole (see Appendix I). Theoretically, each response a person makes can be placed at a point on the regression–progression continuum (actually, one can only speak of a response in the abstract, for even the smallest unit of "behavior" is, in reality, a combination of motivational, emotional, cognitive, and motorial subunits). At the highest levels, we might find activities such as philosophical contemplation, mathematical reasoning, or writing a complex computer program. Here, neocortical activity would be maximal and involvement of lower systems would be minimal; correspondingly, intellectual output would be maximal and emotional output minimal. By contrast, at the lower "paloepsychic" (MacLean, 1976) levels we might find things such as violent homicides, tantrum and rage reactions, the heights of sexual passion, panic reactions, active defense of self or kin, symbiotic reactions, and so on. Here, rational mediation of behavior is minimal, and the individual is compelled by powerful motives that are difficult or impossible to control once they are set into motion. At the middle or "mixed" level, we find such things as courtship and marriage patterns, patterns of hunting behavior, aggressive sports activities, kinship togetherness, group cooperation, "love," and a multitude of everyday activities that are motivated neither by primitive drives nor emotionless thought alone. It is from this middle band of mixed activities that we typically regress to lower emotion-bound compulsions or progress up to reflection and thought involving minimal emotion.

A brief example relevant to the topic of aggression would be appropriate at this point. Proceeding from the assumption that behaviors within a particular class (e.g., "acting against others") can be hierarchicalized according to the logic of the regression–progression continuum (see chapter 9 on hierarchical analysis), we might construct the following theoretical hierarchy for aggressive responses: predatory aggression—dominance aggression—assertiveness—intellectual aggression. It is noted that these four types are ranked in terms of phylogenetic remoteness and recentness, and level of neocortical involvement as well. Further, note that the two lower levels (predatory and dominance aggression) are shared between man and the lower animals, whereas the upper two levels (assertiveness and intellectual aggression) are predominantly human as far as we know. It follows from this reasoning that "predatory" aggression, for example, and "assertiveness" are fundamentally different, in that the former resonates more to the heritage of the species, whereas the latter resonates more to the individual's cultural heritage. We are faced here with the possibility that two different psychologies may be required to accommodate these considerations; a *paleopsychology* for the primitive, phylogenetically regressive aspects of behavior, and a *neopsychology* for advanced forms of aggression.

Active and Passive Regression

Human intellect provides the capability for phylogenetic progression, but it does not guarantee it. Intellectual functioning is typically associated with higher, progressive processes, but only when it serves an inhibitory role and acts in opposition to the lower systems. However, intellect sometimes sides with and facilitates the lower limbic and reptilian systems, producing what might be called *active phylogenetic regression.* *Passive phylogenetic regression,* by contrast, refers to an uncontrolled or dyscontrolled loss of neocortical ability to inhibit archaic compulsions and imperatives. Here one effortlessly slips back, often unconsciously, into species and subspecies patterns of behavior. Being provoked into male-to-male combat, more or less against one's will, would exemplify the passive form, whereas the use of Nazi propaganda to incite violence and persecution against the Jews would illustrate the active form. The human capacity for such active regression makes our species, at one and the same time, the most resourceful and destructive on earth, for our great intelligence allows us to manufacture lofty rationalizations and justifications for every sort of inhumanity imaginable (MacLean, 1982a). Without such rationalizations—of aggression actually motivated by the primitive lower centers—one wonders whether organized warfare, religious persecution, or racial antipathy would be the scourges they are today. The world is not threatened by passive regressions in the form of tantrums, fighting, or even violent criminality; the greater threat comes from the use of human intellect to fan the flames of our phylogenetically old tendencies and dispositions. We discuss the issues of passive and active regression further in the following section on intelligence.

INTELLIGENCE AND THE REGRESSION–PROGRESSION CONTINUUM

Intelligence is possibly our most valued, misunderstood, and controversial behavioral trait. Although everyone seems to intuitively know what it is and each wants a goodly share of it, intelligence is difficult to define and the term has only been in general use since the turn of the century (Matarazzo, 1972). Through the ages, though, people have ranked and rated themselves in terms of wisdom, genius, accomplishment or whatever, but only with the development of the Binet–Simon scale and subsequent IQ tests was a numerical measure available. Despite the growth of elaborate psychometric technology, there is still widespread disagreement about what the "it" is being measured. Fortunately, our concern here is not with psychometric or sociopolitical issues, but rather with the assumed role that intellectual functioning plays in the phylogenetic regression–progression system. Accordingly, there are six basic assumptions of interest here (see also Appendix I).

Intelligence as an Evolved Character. Human intelligence is an evolved, biologically based adaptive characteristic (process) that is phylogenetically continuous with lower species and is (has been) crucial to species survival.

Consistent with other 19th-century writers, Darwin (1871/1981) devoted considerable attention to the similarities in "mental powers" between animals and humans. His intention was to demonstrate that mental powers of animals and humans exist on a phylogenetic continuum with differences between the highest man and lowest savage, and between the lowest savage and the highest animal, being "connected by the finest gradations" (p. 35; see also chapter 1, this volume). Indeed, he strove to show that there is "no fundamental difference between man and the higher mammals in their mental faculties" (p. 35). Darwin, thus, disagreed with Cuvier that instincts and intelligence necessarily stand in inverse relation to one another (viz., that the more elaborate an animal's instincts the less elaborate its mental powers). Darwin argued to the contrary, for example, that insects with wonderfully complex instincts are more intelligent than those with more primitive instinctive patterns. Still, complex instincts and intelligence are not the same thing, for they originate from different sources: Instinct from "natural selection of variations of simpler instinctive actions" (1871/1981, p. 38) and intelligence from "the most intricate patterns of intercommunication" (p. 38) between various parts of the brain. By virtue of these intricate patterns of brain activity, man is able to rise, to a degree, above his instincts and enjoy a modicum of cognitive freedom not available to other animals.

In chapter 1, we found that Darwin believed instinct and intelligence interact in humans in various ways including intellectual elaboration of instinctive patterns, mixing and blending of instinct and intelligence, and occasional opposition of the two. Moreover, we might add that Darwin was remarkably prescient in his belief that intelligence is, ultimately, based on the brain's capacity to elaborate upon and extend the inherent adaptive capacities of the individual.

Many writers credit Herbert Spencer (1985) with introducing the term *intelligence* in his *Principles of Psychology* (Guilford, 1967). He defined life as the "continuous adjustment of internal relations to external relations," and this adjustment is achieved by intelligence in humans and instinct in animals (see chapter 1, this volume). This intelligence was basically "the power of combining separate impressions," or in modern terms, the capacity for processing large quantities and qualities of information. The acquisition of intelligence was clearly tied to the process of evolution, and some feel that Spencer's ideas on the topic gave impetus to the Social Darwinist movement. Spencer did help popularize the idea of the survival of the fittest, which translates ever so easily to "survival of the smartest" at the human level.

Various writers over the years have viewed intelligence as a biologically adaptive trait in humans (Count, 1973; Halstead, 1951; Piaget, 1964; Stenhouse, 1973) and virtually all behavioral scientists agree that more rather than less intelligence is generally adaptive and desirable. As a basically biological characteristic of limited within-person environmental variation except under the most extreme circumstances, intelligence would be expected to have a significant genetic component, and a wealth of evidence indicates that IQ scores, for example, are strongly influenced by heredity (see Osborne, Noble, & Weyl, 1978, for a review of the area). Estimates of the genetic contribution to measured IQ usually range between a minimum of 45% on up to 80% (Jensen, 1972), and even 90% for Cattell's (1971) neurologically based "fluid ability."

Along with this apparent high degree of within-species genetic variability, human intelligence, broadly defined, appears to be phylogenetically continuous with earlier hominid species and closely related subhuman primate species (Jolly, 1972), and certain rudimentary functions descend far down the evolutionary scale (Razran, 1971). That intelligence has an evolutionary history is incontrovertible, as many lines of evidence attest. Jerison (1973), for example, has built a powerful case for the progressive evolution of brain size, and with more neural matter and interconnections available higher animals are able to integrate larger amounts of adaptation-relevant information and, thus, behave more intelligently. Köhler (1925), Warden (1951), Rensch (1957), Bitterman (1965), Warren (1977) and others have studied living species, including reptiles, mammals, and primates, and it is clear that intelligence is highly correlated with the evolutionary scale (viz., lower animals are less intelligent and higher ones more intelligent). Using various neuroanatomical criteria, such as the ratio of brain weight to body weight, or the ratio of brain weight to spinal cord weight, produces a rough phylogenetic hierarchy with primates and humans toward the top, but analomies are encountered, e.g., the superior ranking of the squirrel monkey relative to humans (Passingham, 1982), and an analogous brain "superiority" of dolphins over humans on several criteria (Fichtelius & Sjölander, 1972).

Before proceeding further, we should distinguish between *biological intelligence* and human *abstract intelligence* as measured by the IQ test. Biological intelligence refers to the evolved, neurologically based, primarily innate information-processing equipment that a given species employs in adapting to its own unique environmental demands. This biological intelligence has been defined in many ways: "animal" as opposed to human intelligence (Romanes, 1882, 1883, 1888), the "ability to adapt" (Barnett, 1967), "purposive adaptation" as contrasted with "purposive intelligence" (Cattell, 1971), practical intelligence versus rational intelligence (Viaud, 1960), behavioral adaption versus cognitive adaption (Laughlin & D'Aquili, 1974), ethologically adaptive behavior versus rational intelligence (Barkow, 1983), and so on. Biological intelligence, as defined here, refers to the breadth of capability a given animal has to effectively adapt to modal environments for its particular species. It refers to what Charlesworth (1979) calls the "other half of intelligence"— the capacity to overcome environmental problems that thwart optimal adaptation and survival.

At lower phyletic levels, biological intelligence is correspondingly low, e.g., simple animals are capable only of adapting to simple, stable environmental demands. Intelligent reactions may be limited to rigid fixed-action patterns or instincts, where little central mediation is required. As we move up the scale, however, the ratio of cortex to total brain mass increases, and at the human level, neocortical development has progressed to where a new kind of self-conscious, verbal, and symbolic intelligence is possible. This new human intelligence not only allows for seemingly limitless adaption to both present and unforeseen problems, more importantly, it enables man to step from the world of reality to one of imagination, from immediate fact to anticipation of future contingencies. Modern technological man went one step further, however, and created a new and oftimes oppressive demand on the brain to do intellectual work for its own sake, and it is the capacity to do this work that the IQ test measures. With this new human intelligence man could no longer be content to survive, reproduce, or merely be happy; he must achieve, "keep his nose to the grindstone," and not let his "mind go to waste." Consequently, the new human intelligence required, in short spurts at least, that the brain be used to maximal capacity to generate ever-increasing quantities of abstract intelligence. Neither the natural intellectual functions nor the motivational–emotional functions of the human brain were phylogenetically prepared for this eventuality; thus, in modern intellectual meritocracies such as the United States and Japan, we find great masses that must struggle to keep up with the pace set by the "deviant," brilliant few. Through eons of evolution nature had no need for mathematicians, philosophers, or computer programmers, and it should come as no surprise that abstract intelligence is a recent, rare, fragile, and unnatural capacity that few possess in abundance and even fewer enjoy putting to use (Bailey, Burns, & Bazan, 1982). To achieve it, however, is to rise from biological adaptation to transcendent thought, and to "phylogenetically progress" in the intellectual sphere.

Intelligence and the Nervous System.   Species intelligence is closely tied to the functioning of the nervous system, and, in humans, the cerebral cortex plays the central role in intelligent behavior.

Throughout history intelligence has been associated with the brain, but there is no one-to-one relationship between neural structures and specific forms of intelligent behavior (Bindra, 1976; Gibson, 1977). Nevertheless, as we recall from chapter 2, it is assumed that sheer evolved brain size is roughly correlated with species intelligence (Jerison, 1969, 1973), and the relative size of the neocortex to lower brain structures also is an important consideration (Stephan & Andy, 1969). As Stephan and Andy tell us, the proportion of neocortex to total brain size is estimated at 50% in prosimians, 67% in monkeys, 75% in apes, and 80% in humans, but just as important as neocortical mass is the relative size of the different functional areas of the neocortex. For example, humans have extremely overdeveloped motor areas for controlling hand movements, and that part of the cortex mediating thumb use is far larger than corresponding areas in other primates (Washburn & Moore, 1980). Washburn and Moore say that such ample cortical representation "makes hand skills possible and pleasurable to learn" (p. 167). Even more impressive than man's manual dexterity, however, are the massive association areas spread throughout the neocortex that mediate functions other than simple sensory input and motor output. These brain areas have expanded greatly in mammalian brain evolution, and are responsible for the "complex cognitive functions" associated with human intelligence (Kolb & Whisaw, 1980). By contrast, nonhuman species are limited in associational cortex, and once we descend the phylogenetic scale to rats and opossums, for example, most of the neocortex is involved in fundamental sensory and motor functions (Diamond & Hall, 1969).

Given that the prefrontal neocortex in humans is one of the last areas to develop phylogenetically and ontogenetically (Fuster, 1980), we are not surprised that it is an important seat of intellect and also important in distinguishing advanced primates from lower species. Gibson (1977) describes the major functions of the frontal areas:

> The frontal association area, more than any other area of the cortex, mediates the active aspects of intelligence: flexibility of relationship between sensation and response, internalization, anticipation of perceptions, and the comparison of expected perceptions to actual perceptions. The ability to inhibit responses and sensations is . . . a prerequisite to flexible perceptual/ response relationships. The frontal lobes clearly have inhibitory functions, as patients with frontal lesions suffer from behavioral pathologies based on the inability to inhibit actions and/or perceptions, including the return of

infantile reflexes (i.e., grasp, visual following, and urination reflexes). (p. 125)

Flexibility, anticipation, the ability to internalize stimuli rather than merely respond to them, and the ability to inhibit inappropriate thoughts or behaviors are basic parameters of intelligence, and it appears these functions are mediated in large degree by frontal areas, especially the prefrontal cortex (Fuster, 1980). Significantly, response inhibition is a major function of the prefrontal area, and we recall that Stenhouse (1973) lists the "P" or postponement factor among the basic components of intelligence. According to Stenhouse, the P-factor enables the organism to rise above instinct and releaser-bound reflexivity, and even purportedly serves to foster "creative motivation" and creative reflection. Stenhouse says the P-factor was one of the last major intelligence factors to evolve, and as such may be considered one of the higher types of intellectual functioning. If his reasoning is correct, then loss of inhibition normally exerted by the prefrontal lobes should lead to phylogenetically regressive forms of intellectual functioning and behavior. However, lesions in the frontal lobes, unless extremely large, are associated with minimal intellectual deterioration as measured by IQ tests, but major changes in personality are frequent (McFie, 1975). Thus, rather than being an area devoted strictly to intellectual activity *per se,* the prefrontal cortex may primarily serve to modulate other intellectual and motivational structures of the brain. Certainly the widespread connections of the prefrontal cortex with other parts of the brain (viz., the diencephalon, mesencephalon, and limbic region) are consistent with a role of synthesizing "cognitive and motor acts into purposive sequences" (Fuster, 1980).

The Hierarchical Nature of Intelligence.   As is true of other neuropsychological systems, the intellectual system is hierarchically arranged both structurally and functionally.

Because it is impossible to locate general intelligence in the brain, or to pinpoint its component neuroanatomical substructures with any degree of accuracy, it is difficult to demonstrate the hierarchical nature of intelligence anatomically. Yet, there is still a rough correlation between putatively more evolved brain structures and the higher intellectual functions. First of all, we may safely presume that the neocortex as a whole is the primary mediator of cognitive and intellectual functions in humans, and is, thus, the closest thing to a "seat" of intelligence. Nevertheless, within the neocortex itself, there is little clear evidence that "higher" structures are always found progressively toward the more anterior regions culminating in the theoretically most advanced prefrontal lobes. Although the prefrontal cortex is viewed as phylogenetically advanced by many writers, many other areas mediating advanced motor, verbal, or associational functions are scattered about the cortex. For example, the capacity for speech and language often is cited as the most definitive and distinctive characteristic of the human species, but structures mediating speech functions are situated more posteriorly and ventrally than might be expected according to the principle of encephalization (see Passingham, 1982; chapter 2, this volume). Actually, language, in its many vocal and written forms, is not a single entity capable of a single location in the `brain; rather, language is an extremely complex phylogenetic, ontogenetic, motivational, sensory-motor, and cognitive system involving a host of higher and lower components. For example, there are fairly specific cortical areas for dealing with seen words, heard words, the speaking of words, and the writing of words (Brown, 1977; McFie, 1975), which are found in disparate cortical regions including Broca's and Wernicke's areas and surrounding tissues, and parts of the occipital lobes. Certainly, as Bindra (1976) correctly states, the language system, and other systems of the brain, are not organized into simple, unidirectional hierarchies, but, instead, into complex, integrated, and flexible "hierarchical arrangements."

Even though specific cortical structures do not arrange themselves into simple, clear-cut hierarchies, the gross neuroanatomy and neurofunction of the entire brain conforms to what Paul MacLean calls the "triune brain," a hierarchical arrangement composed of the phylogenetically ancient reptilian brain, the phylogenetically newer mammalian brain, and the phylogenetically newest human neocortex. As discussed in chapter 2, each of MacLean's hierarchical levels has its own peculiar neurochemistry, its own consciousness, and its own "intelligence." We further recall that Brown (1977) extended MacLean's cerebral hierarchy by dividing the neocortex into the left and right lateralized portions, producing the following advanced-to-primitive phylogenetic hierarchy: left neocortex, right neocortex, paleomammalian cortex, and reptilian brain system. According to MacLean (1977b), the hierarchical brain systems are characterized by three forms of mentation: protomentation, emotomentation, and ratiomentation. Protomentation is seen primarily at the reptilian level of functioning, and includes basic, stereotyped behavioral patterns, propensities, drives, compulsions, and obsessions. Emotomentation (emotional mentation) is mediated primarily by the paleomammalian cortex and refers to the experience of emotion and feeling. Ratiomentation, of course, refers to the rational, self-conscious activity of the human neocortex. Note that virtually all of the brain matter in the MacLean–Brown cerebral hierarchy is implicitly devoted to what we call *biological intelligence*—the use of brain to effect the best fit of organism to environment. For most people most of the time, even the advanced neocortex is used for mundane adaptive purposes, but in rare instances of creative reflection or intellectual work it rises above its natural purpose to a higher calling.

Human intelligence clearly appears to have higher and lower functional components even if the anatomical loci are not obvious. McFie (1975) distinguishes between lower perceptual-motor functions, middle levels of integrated skills and memory processes, and higher level intellectual abilities including verbal fluency, verbal reasoning, numerical ability, spatial ability, and "g," or general intelligence. Generally speaking, perception, motor skill, and memory are integrated by complex subcortical and cortical interconnections in the brain, and, as McFie tells us, general intelligence is a result of the activity of the entire cerebrum. By contrast, the higher intellectual functions are more often highly specialized, are located in specific areas of the neocortex, and are lateralized to a great degree. It would seem, then, that higher intellectual functions reflect the increasing specialization and differentiation of the neocortex, and one suspects that they are rather recent acquisitions from the evolutionary standpoint. Roughly speaking, we may say that phylogenetically and anatomically older sensory-motor and perceptual processes underly and subserve the newer conceptual, rational, and abstract aspects of intelligence.

The underlying hierarchical nature of intelligence is reflected in most of the existing theories of intelligence. In most theories a continuum is implied going from concrete, sensory-motor, attentional, and simple retentive processes at the lower end, on up to various forms of abstract intelligence at the upper end. A sampling of these stated or implied continua is provided in Table 3.1, and one can easily discern higher from lower functions in most instances. It also is abundantly obvious that the higher functions are more highly valued than lower ones in our modern technological society; indeed, excellence in rote memory, skill in carpentry, or athletic prowess are intuitively perceived as signifying low intelligence in the minds of many people, while the accomplishments of an Einstein, von Braun, or Newton are listed among the great achievements of the human race. Money, fame, and honor are readily accorded those heavily endowed with refined, abstract cognitive skills, and as Jensen (1973) and as Herrnstein (1973) have pointed out, social class standing is often predicated upon one's IQ score. Abstract intelligence is the ultimate triumph over our animal nature, and its possessors are rewarded accordingly.

Intelligence in Regression and Progression.   Human intelligence is the trait most implicated in the phylogenetic regression process; when its trait expression is low, regression is more probable, and, conversely, progression is more probable when its expression is high.

TABLE 3.1
Representative Hierarchies of Intelligence

Aristotle	*Descartes*	*E.L. Thorndike*	*Freeman (1962)*	*Piaget*
Multiple Souls	*Mind-Body Dualism*	*Three Types of Intelligence*	*Descriptions of Intelligence*	*Developmental Stages*
1. Soul or "nous"	1. Mind (God-given; free will)	1. Abstract	1. Ability for abstract thinking	1. Formal operations
2. Motive soul	2. Body (animal; reflexive machine)	2. Social	2. Capacity for learning	2. Concrete operations
3. Vegetative soul		3. Practical	3. Adaptation to environment	3. Preoperational thinking
				4. Sensorimotor functioning

A.R. Jenson	*D. Wechsler (and others)*	*R.B. Cattell*	*C. Burt*	*P. Vernon*
Two Types of Intelligence	*Verbal vs. Performance Function*	*Two-Factory Theory*	*Hierarchy of Abilities*	*Hierarchy of Abilities*
1. Cognitive ability (conceptual reasoning)	1. Verbal intelligence (abstract, conceptual, left-brained)	1. Crystallized intelligence (culturally-loaded, complex skills)	1. General factor—"g" (present in all abilities)	1. General factor—"g"
2. Associational ability (rote memory)	2. Performance intelligence (concrete, perceptual, right-brained)	2. Fluid intelligence (speed of response; largely genetic and physiologically-based)	2. Group factors (present in some tests)	2. Verbal-educational group factor
			3. Specific factors present in specific tests	3. Spatial-mechanical group factor
			4. Error factor (test error)	4. Minor group factors
				5. Specific factors

Human intelligence is the trait that most clearly separates man from beast, and the intellectual achievements of a handful of super-endowed geniuses along the way have created a world unlike that of any other living creature. We may have even become too intelligent for our own good, as Koestler (1967) argues, for man's conquest of nature has brought with it the ecological catastrophies of technological warfare, urban blight, and every sort of physical and psychological pollution imaginable. Intelligence is, no doubt, a two-edged sword, but through its inhibiting properties and emphasis on the mental as opposed to the physical, our species possesses the potential, at least, to enjoy peace and prosperity in a technological age. But, unfortunately, man's potential for creative imagination and refined intelligence is rarely used; man more often relies on the easier and lower level trial-and-error, rote memorial, and imitative processes (Humphrey, 1976).

When we speak of human abstract intelligence, "potential" and "probability" are the key words, for there is no one-to-one relationship between intellectual ability and phylogenetic regression or progression. Each normally endowed person has the potential to use his or her neocortex and its associated intellectual powers for good or ill, for lofty purposes or mundane ones. Similarly, each normal person has the capacity to use his or her intelligence to merely adapt and maximize pleasure in the old sense, or strive for new vistas of enlightenment in the progressive sense. Having a normal or above-normal intellectual endowment allows a great range of response, but the actual emission of intelligent behavior is generally more a function of motivation than sheer mental ability (Hayes, 1962). Intellectual functioning is dependent on the lower emotional and motivational centers for activation and direction, and, given normal ability and an intact nervous system, conative factors are likely to be more potent causes of behavior than are cognitive ones. Indeed, just as the cortex is servant to the lower brain structures (Plutchik, 1977), we may assume that intelligence is normally servant to body needs and demands. Despite the fundamental dependence of cognition on motivation, intelligence makes higher, progressive responses possible, and the higher the intellectual capacity, the more probable phylogenetic progression becomes. Obversely, the lower the endowment (whether this endowment is primarily genetic or environmental is not especially important here), the less likely cognitively advanced responses are to appear, although some progression may be realized through cultural enrichment and intensive training and educational programs.

At the lowest end of the human intelligence scale lies the profoundly retarded individual. Although these persons are seldom dangerous or a threat to others, they are, theoretically phylogenetically regressed (or fixated) to the utmost degree. They suffer from a severely impaired capacity for enculturalization (MacAndrew & Edgerton, 1964), have a greater reliance on subcortical mechanisms such as territoriality and dominance ranking (Hereford, Cleland, & Fellner, 1973; Paluck & Esser, 1971), and appear to be especially sensitive to phylogenetically conditioned releasing stimuli such as the threatening stare (Bailey, Tipton, & Taylor, 1977). In the absence of learned strategies and coping skills, the profoundly retarded person seems to fall back on ontogenetically older and phylogenetically older patterns of response, but they are not true replicas of either subhuman primates or early hominids. By virtue of brain damage or poor heredity, they are abnormal types and only similar to lower species by virtue of the absence of normal neocorticalization, not the presence of true vestigial characteristics. Nevertheless, they are an instructive population from the standpoint of regressive and proto-adaptive behaviors.

Whereas the retarded individual may lack sufficient intelligence for social mischief, the male of low-to-moderate intelligence appears to be at high risk for regressive acting-out in the form of juvenile delinquency (Gordon, 1980; Moffitt, Gabrielli, Mednick, & Schulsinger, 1981), and physical violence and murder (Heilbrun, 1982; Holcomb & Adams, 1982; Holland, Beckett, & Levi, 1981; Simonds & Kashani, 1979). The phylogenetic regression–progression model interprets these findings as reflecting two mutually interacting processes. First, below average intelligence handicaps the person in our competitive society, producing frustration, helplessness, and rage. Second, below average intelligence handicaps the person in inhibiting his own limbic and reptilian compulsions, thereby increasing the probability of reverting to phylogenetically old strategies (acquisitive, defensive, or offensive aggression) under provocative circumstances. In similar vein, Heilbrun (1982), in his study on the relationship between low IQ and violence, described the highest risk factor as a combination of low IQ and proneness to psychopathy, producing a person of low empathy, low impulse control, and low inhibition over physical aggression.

In the intellectually normal or superior person, intelligence sits at the very center of the personality (Matarazzo, 1972; Wechsler, 1958), and it enables the person to mediate between different internal and external demands in the adaptive sense. For a select few, it enables the mind to phylogenetically progress into a world of supraorganic reflection and imagination, and it provides the opportunity for the merely normal mortal to rise above his species for short periods of time. Phylogenetic progression is a tenuous thing, however, and regressive processes take over ever so quickly. Once again, purely and simply, it is very difficult to move up the scale, and remarkably easy to regress into older, species or prespecies forms of behavior.

Intelligence in Active and Passive Regression. Intelligence provides the capability for phylogenetic progression, but does not guarantee it. Greater trait expression of intelligence is typically associated with higher, progressive processes, but higher mental functions sometimes serve to facilitate rather than inhibit lower systems. Intelligence can, thus, set itself in opposition to lower systems (progression), or it can ally itself with them (regression). Such alliances with the lower systems makes the human species, at one and the same time, the most resourceful and dangerous creatures on the face of the earth.

It is tempting to categorize the higher systems as basically inhibitory and the lower ones as excitatory, but the actual state of affairs in nature is far more complex and unpredictable. In subhuman organisms, particularly those far down the phylogenetic scale, the total brain is used with near complete efficiency, for there is little or no "extra" neural tissue beyond that needed for day-to-day survival (see chapter 2). The human species, by contrast, possesses more extra brain than any other animal, and the "why" from the evolutionary standpoint remains one of the great mysteries of modern anthropology. As Restak (1979) asks us, can natural selection alone account for the sudden acceleration of brain growth during the last few million years, or can it explain our present oversized brain with its extra tissue? Somewhere along the way, whether through the development of tools, language, culture, or all three, the brain had new, unnatural, and arbitrary pressures placed upon it, and these led to a rate of growth unprecedented in nature (Restak, 1980). In a general sense, then, "unnatural" cultural pressures came to exert a more significant selective effect on brain development than did the demands of mere survival. A. R. Wallace seemed to hint at this possibility many years ago in his famous quote: "Natural selection could only have endowed the savage with a brain a little superior to that of the ape, whereas he possesses one very little inferior to that of an average member of our learned society" (cited in Restak, 1980, p. 76).

In the area of intelligence more than any other man has freed himself from the hegemony of natural selection, but this freedom is a mixed blessing that allows the individual to inhibit or excite his lower animal nature almost at will. This fact forces us to make a distinction between passive and active forms of phylogenetic regression (see earlier section). In the passive form, the individual is faced with sudden stress or threat to survival, and spontaneous and sudden regression occurs where the lower, survival levels of the brain more or less come automatically into play. Such regression in the area of violence, for example, may produce a temporarily dangerous person who acts out limbic agonistic patterns until "he is himself again." Although such violence may be involved in hot-blooded homicides, domestic fighting, child-battering, spontaneous rioting, and so forth, the danger to society is minimal in the broad sense. Active phylogenetic regression, however, is possibly the greatest threat of all to species survival, for it allows man the capability to plan and implement mayhem on a grand scale through organized warfare and other forms of collective violence. Rather than pitting man against man in mortal combat, modern warfare pits the great military minds and techno-logical geniuses of one nation against those of another, and the modern soldier serves more as technologist than fighter. Still, war is not merely an intellectual abstraction; it must draw upon ancient reserves of xenopho-bia, male togetherness, and territoriality to provide the motivational basis for its implementation.

Active phylogenetic regression, then, refers to instances where the individual uses his cortical powers to augment or exacerbate primitive survival systems, and, in extreme forms, this may lead to exploitation and cruelty of the worst sort. Not all forms are harmful or dangerous, however, as we see in attempts to increase sexual arousal through fantasy or mental imagery, or in forcing oneself to get in a "killing" frame of mind for a tough tennis match. Of the many cortical stimulators of regression, values and belief systems, especially those held by particular in-group collectives, are among the most potent, and without them there would have been no Skull Cults among the Neanderthal, no Nazi holocaust, and no decimation of the peaceful Cambodian people in recent times. The neocortex can be treacherous in providing the lower centers with conven-ient excuses and rationalizations for the most gratuitous forms of "totali-tarian egotism" (Greenwald, 1980), greed, and inhumane treatment of others.

At times, the rational intellect may totally capitulate to ancient impera-tives, but human intelligence is resourceful enough, through the process of rationalization and self-deception, to transform the worst vice into a sacred virtue. The historian Henry Thomas (1937) illustrates this process very graphically in his classic chronicle of man's inhumanity to man throughout the ages. He shows, time and again, how the "lofty values" of the likes of Alexander, Hannibal, Charlemagne, Chief Inquisitor Torque-mada, and a host of other "heroes" of the past have perpetuated blood-shed beyond comprehension. Even Martin Luther, who championed reason and justice so fiercely during the "protestant" phase of his career, actively regressed once in power himself. Outraged by peasant rebellion against the king, Luther once urged the princes to "stab, smite, and throttle" the miscreants into submission, and he likewise broke venom-ously with the Jews who refused to forsake their faith and accept his brand of Christianity. He exhorted the true believers to "Burn their synagogues and schools. . . . Take away their prayer books and Talmuds. . . . Forbid their Rabbi to teach, on pain of life and limb . . . and if they persist, tear out their tongues'' (cited in Thomas, 1937, p. 326). Here we see belief system against belief system, neocortex against neocortex, and in Luther's case ideology and instinct mixed in deadly combination.

Intelligence and "Cortical Supplementation." Natural neocortical inhibition must be supplemented in at least two ways if the modern individual is to grow into a civilized human being: (a) the individual must be thoroughly socialized, enculturated, and infused with customs, values, and moral prohibitions, and (b) added to this cultural programming must be constant social and cultural pressure to behave in prescribed ways. To be civilized is to be unnaturally constrained and self-denying, and cortical supplementation of various sorts is required to keep lower more spontaneous and pleasurable centers in check.

In most societies, there are socially proscribed actions that, if only emitted once in an individual's lifetime, would result in banishment, imprisonment, or even death. One needs only to commit treason, heresy, or murder once to find one's head on the chopping block, but severe social sanctions are not limited to grievous offenses against other persons or the state; rather, every civilized person in every civilized society lives under countless rules, regulations, and prohibitions, which underly social order and give particular cultures their distinctiveness. Consequently, cultural man must, of necessity, be sufficiently intelligent to learn rules, understand them, and inhibit actions contrary to those rules (Humphrey, 1976). Further, this must be an extremely reliable, fail-safe process, for the slightest error may prove fatal. Achieving such error-free status is not an individual matter, however; all of the correcting processes of culture—parents, extended kin, the community, social institutions, the legal structure, policing agencies, and so forth—stand constant guard and are ready with immediate punishment for the smallest infraction. The goal of culture, it appears, is to condition the most reliable conformity in its members, and to discourage forms of individuality and self-expression which represent threats to group stability. The civilized person is, thus, "free" in only the most abstract sense, for none of us satisfy our needs at will and precious little latitude is given to be different from the norm even in the most democratic societies.

Despite culture's concerted effort to extract conformity from its members, it never totally succeeds, and history provides us with ample testimony to the ongoing dialectic between cultural inertia, on the one hand, and individual genius and radical innovation on the other. For modern civilized man, however, life is not so complicated and he is content to survive, adapt, and enjoy a little pleasure and happiness. Modal man is more than ready to merge his individuality into the group belief system, and to actively *escape from freedom,* to use Eric Fromm's

(1941) term. Indeed, modal man has precious little neocortex truly his own; because of the multifarious communal pressures already discussed, and the aggressive advertising, propaganda, and creation of heroes and antiheroes in the modern media, the brain of modern man suffers from stifling oversupplementation. Whereas person-to-person cortical supplementation in the form of parental discipline, or friendly advice from your minister, therapist, or stockbroker may be beneficial, supplementation at the level of the larger group often is both oppressive and regressive (see Meerlo, 1967).

The humanistic view of rational man going back to Locke, Comte, and Rousseau, proceeds on the fundamental premise that reason and intellect have the inherent power to control destiny, and, further, that man is only superficially wicked and there resides in each of us a core of goodness waiting to be released. Modern biology and the phylogenetic regression–progression model suggest a different picture of the state of mankind; we are, by nature, rather selfish, xenophobic, regressive, and pleasure loving creatures who possess the potential for the most wicked and vile acts, and the most lofty and inspiring ones. Rather than being slightly lower than the angels, or, conversely, only slightly above the animals, we are both ape and angel, and this fact explains the extreme range and unpredictability of human behavior. And to channel and mold this unpredictability into full personhood is a task too great for any single individual—it requires cortical supplementation from many sources, and even then, as history shows, phylogenetic regressions are all too frequent.

SUMMARY

The human organism is a highly tuned instrument of adaptation, and threats to survival and ecological imbalances are just as important now as in the evolutionary past. At one level, man is a product of a vast phylogenetic heritage, and at another level a creature of reason and culture. Consequently, human behavior may be viewed on a conceptual continuum going from primitive, regressive responses at one end up to distinctly human ones at the upper pole. Where a particular action falls on this continuum determines its phylogenetic "regressive" or "progressive" nature.

Psychoanalysis uses the term *regression* in several ways: genetic (developmental), systemic, instinctual, phylogenetic, and biogenetic (Arlow & Brenner, 1964). Phylogenetic and biogenetic regression generally have been ignored by psychoanalysts, with some exceptions (Meerlo, 1962). The present writer argues, however, that all forms of regression incorporate a phylogenetic component in some degree. "Regression to orality" was discussed in terms of its interacting ontogenetic and phylogenetic components.

Phylogenetic carry-overs in man are more likely to be emotional than overtly behavioral, and consequently phylogenetic regression represents, to a great degree, a recovery of older, emotion-laden patterns of response. More specifically, regressive patterns set in when emotionality gains control over rational processes, and our animal nature is free to assert itself in a context of diminished cortico-cultural control. Still, emotions are rarely expressed in pure form in human beings; we more often see mixtures of thought and feeling (Plutchik, 1980).

The concept of phylogenetic regression implies a restructuring of brain relationships whereby the person moves from predominantly neocortical involvement down to lower cortical or even subcortical levels of functioning. Actually, because the brain works as an integrated unit, it is more correct to say that the ratio of phylogenetically "older" and "newer" forms of mediation varies with the degree of regression operating. This principle is seen in the writings of diverse authors, including Koestler (1967), Lorenz (1972), Sagan (1977), and the various works of MacLean on the triune brain. Such neurological regressions are most clearly seen in sudden, episodic forms of violence (see Monroe, 1978), but are evident in many other contexts as well.

It is presumed that all neurological and psychological processes are hierarchically arranged, and "regression down the hierarchy" becomes a significant consideration. Ludwig von Bertalanffy (1968), for example, sees regression as a "loosening of the hierarchic mental organization" where primitive states reappear and "functional dysencephalization" occurs. Likewise, Peterfreund (1971) sees the human organism as a complex information-processing control system with higher cognitive systems holding sway over lower, phylogenetically programmed subroutines such as sexuality, aggression, and self-protection. Many theories of development and personality revolve around the idea of higher and lower processes and a phylogenetically ordered hierarchy of responsivity, but the theories of Sandor Rado (1969) and Abraham Maslow are noteworthy in this regard. As we recall, Rado postulates four psychological levels of integration that "correspond roughly to the phylogeny of the human species"; these levels, in order, are the hedonic, brute-emotional, emotional thought, and unemotional thought. A phylogenetic hierarchy also is clearly seen in Maslow's motivational theory that postulates six ordered need systems: physiological needs, safety needs, love needs, self-esteem needs, self-actualization needs, and aesthetic needs. The physiological needs, for example, would be at the phylogenetically regressive end of the continuum, whereas the self-actualization and aesthetic needs would be at the advanced end.

Intelligence sits at the core of the personality, and is the most important psychological variable mediating the phylogenetic regression–progression process. There are two fundamental types of intelligence, biological intelligence and abstract intelligence. The former type is present, in some degree, in most animals, and is tied to the innate, neurologically based information-processing equipment a given species employs in adapting to the environment; the latter type, by contrast, is seen primarily in humans, and represents a rather arbitrary demand by culture for its members to do intellectual work. Abstract intelligence is, thus, a fragile and unnatural capacity that may contribute to, or detract from, an individual's ability to adapt to the environment. Abstract intelligence requires great amounts of training and education for its full actualization and, even then, only a few develop it in significant measure, as the IQ test has shown.

Species intelligence is closely tied to the nervous system, and the cerebral cortex plays the major role in human beings. In humans, the exaggerated neocortex provides the wherewithal for advanced cognitive functions not seen in most other animals. These include a refined self-consciousness, well-developed memory functions, language, anticipation, response flexibility, response inhibition, and, in the general sense, a capacity for culture. Also, intelligence appears to be hierarchically arranged—as is true of most other neuropsychological functions—although the higher and lower elements are more obvious functionally than anatomically. Several hierarchical theories of intelligence were mentioned including those of Aristotle, Descartes, Thorndike, Piaget, Jensen, and Vernon.

Intelligence provides the individual the potential to rise above his or her species heritage, but the higher mental functions can excite the lower systems (regression) as well as inhibit them (progression). This fact makes the human being, at one and the same time, the most resourceful and dangerous creature on earth. Not only do we passively regress under stress or provocation, we also may actively regress by allying the cortex with the lower, more primitive systems. The most extreme forms of phylogenetic regression are likely to occur when the neocortex actively releases its hold on the lower centers, and simultaneously uses ideology and rationalization to aggravate the beast within. Only through extreme and sustained cortical supplementation via cultural and religious programming, the learning and obeying of rules, social pressure, and the temporary use of other's cortices, as when a mother's firm, calm voice halts her infant's outburst in mid-tantrum, may we be fully human and civilized in any stable sense.

4
Regression-Progression and Human Evolution

Finally, it will be noted that the genetic approach is of essential importance even in the study of the mental life of the adult normal man, *for the following reason. Even if such states of consciousness as the dream are disregarded, the normal man does not always function on the same level of mental activity. The same normal individual, depending on inner and outer circumstance, may be characterized by entirely different levels of development. His mentality, genetically considered, is not the same when he is utterly distracted as when he is in a state of perfectly organized concentration. It varies as he moves from sober scientific or practical work to an emotional surrender to people or things. It may be said that mental life has different strata. At one time man behaves "primitively" and at another he becomes relatively "cultured" or "civilized"....*

—Heinz Werner (1948, p. 4).

THE CONTINUUM

The Behavioral Scale

As postulated in the last chapter, human experience and behavior may be seen as existing on a conceptual continuum going from primitive, phylogenetically old characteristics at the low end on up to refined, phylogenetically newer, more distinctly human ones at the upper end (see Appendix

I). This presumption, of course, represents an extremely oversimplified view of what actually occurs in the complex human animal, but much of what we do can be meaningfully analyzed in terms of the older and newer components operating at a given time. More specifically, a given unit of behavior is presumed, at a given moment in time, to fall on a point somewhere between the purely "animal" and purely "human" poles on our hypothetical scale. Furthermore, this unit of behavior, or more accurately unit of total experience, is viewed as the momentary end result of the multitude of internal and external "causes" (see chapter 9) operating at that instant. The true nature of this momentary experience, however, is far beyond our comprehension, encompassing, as it does, the supernumerous dynamic and hierarchical systems and subsystems (hormonal, neuropsychological, neuromuscular, situational, etc.) that interact among themselves in incredibly complex ways. It is therefore necessary for us to impose some order on this dynamic flux, and it is here that theory offers consolation while we wait for the empirical facts to accumulate. We may never completely comprehend the totality of a single instant of human experience, but we may reasonably assume that response output during that instant is attributable to all of the internal and external contemporaneous influences acting on the individual.

It is assumed that response output is the net product of the many excitatory, inhibitory, and mutually interacting influences in effect at a given instant; in other words, a given thought, feeling, or action arises by a subtractive process in which the essential causes are those that survive numerous inhibitory obstacles along the way toward experience. Experience is, thus, not an effect attributable to a single cause, but is, rather, the end product of many interacting forces operating both prior to and during the response output in question. Human experience is dynamic and ongoing, however, and we may speak of a "given response" only in the abstract. Therefore, rather than occupying a single given point on the regression-progression continuum, or even fluctuating closely about a given point, human behavior constantly moves up and down the scale depending on the state of the organism and prevailing circumstances. The major purpose of this chapter is to ennumerate and describe some of the evolutionary substrates involved in this movement.

Assuming a physically intact individual under basically normal circumstances, movement up and down the scale would reflect flexible, adaptive response variability in meeting environmental demands. So conceived, the regression-progression continuum is similar, in certain respects, to the behavioral scale described by Wilson (1975). In illustrating this notion, Wilson recalled that the vervet monkey, for example, has been described by some researchers as highly territorial and prone to rigid dominance hierarchies, whereas other observers failed to see these characteristics. Some of these differences might be due to geographic variation of a genetic nature, but "a substantial percentage of cases do not represent permanent differences in populations at all: the societies are just temporarily at different points on the same *behavioral scale*" (Wilson, 1975, p. 20). Behavioral scaling refers to variation in the magnitude or in the qualitative state of a behavior as it resonates in sympathy with influences such as stages of the life cycle, population density, or environmental demands. A species or individual animal is thus characterized by a range of responses from which it selectively draws to adapt to prevailing ecological conditions. In more advanced vertebrates, it is the entire scale—and not isolated points on it—that is the genetically based trait shaped by natural selection (Wilson, 1971). Wilson (1975) uses the hypothetical example of an animal genetically pre-programmed to cope with varying degrees of population density and crowding: at low densities all aggressive behavior may be suspended, at moderate densities mild forms of territorial defense may appear, and at high densities territorial defense is sharp and rigid dominance hierarchies appear. Environmental stress may go beyond the scale, however, to a point where the animal is phylogenetically unprepared to cope with the situation. As Calhoun (1962) demonstrated with his "behavioral sink" studies with rats, severe social pathology may emerge at abnormally high population densities where adaptive aggression degenerates into random violence, homosexuality, and cannibalism.

It is probable that human beings possess behavioral scales as do other animals. Social scientists generally agree that man is the most flexible, variable, and intelligent of all animals, and the human being has no peer in terms of breadth and depth of responsivity. Yet, human behavior is neither infinitely variable nor random, and many of our behavioral systems (sex, bonding, status-consciousness, parenting, etc.) appear to be genetically scaled so that we are prepared to meet a great number of contingencies as they arise. In the area of sexuality, for example, we are scaled such that incest, group sex, and homosexuality are generally avoided, whereas exogamy, heterosexuality, and assortative mating are positively valenced. Pleasure versus pain, health versus unhealth, and social organization versus disorganization are, to a great degree, contingent upon whether we stay within scaled limits or not, for adaptation and ecological fit are fundamentally matters of congruence between scaled tendencies and fluctuating environmental conditions. More simply, we will be happier, healthier, and more socially adaptable when we operate within our natural, scaled limits.[1]

---

[1]In nonhuman animals, behavioral output is confined within the genetic scales or limits of a given species. Humans appear unique in their ability to move outside of or decouple from natural imperatives and genetically-defined limits. For example, humans are capable of a wide range of sexual responses within natural scaled limits, limits that evolved in circum-

Although similar, the phylogenetic regression-progression continuum differs in several important ways from Wilson's concept of behavioral scale. First, Wilson is concerned with behavioral scaling in populations of animals, whereas our concern is with the range of responsivity or genetic limits within a single individual. Second, behavioral scaling typically deals with a single motivational-response system (e.g., aggression), whereas the present view emphasizes the net result, or response product, of all systems operating at a given time. So construed, response output is multiply determined, extremely complex, and a kind of "behavioral figure" embedded in the phenomenal field. Third, the behavioral scaling notion implies a genetically fixed trait with limited variability beyond that more or less built into the organism. By contrast, central mediation, learning, and enculturalization play major roles in movement up or down the regression-progression continuum, and intelligence becomes the trait that defines the limits of movement, especially at the upper, advanced pole. Fourth, behavioral scaling implies that behavior is stable if the governing parameters of the environment are likewise stable; for example, at low population density aggression will be diminished proportionately, and so on. The present view, however, emphasizes the momentary nature of behavior, and the suddenness of regressive and progressive movement depending on the balance of internal and external forces operating at a given time.

An Operational Measure

Although definitions may differ from writer to writer, the notion of scaling is indispensable to the study and analysis of human behavior. Numerous writers state or imply that various aspects of human behavior exist on continua, but at some point units of measurement must be derived for scientific research and analysis. At the conceptual level, continua and hierarchies may be postulated *ad infinitum,* and the phylogenetic regression-progression model encourages the student of behavior to postulate meaningful and heuristically rich hierarchies as a first step in conceptual analysis. In empirical research and formal analysis, however, the process requires quantitative units of measurement. Thus, if the phylogenetic

---

stances of few sexual partners, little knowledge of sexual anatomy or physiological processes, and little in the way of aids (pornography, mechanical aids, sex therapy, and so forth) to facilitate copulatory performance or pleasure enhancement. By contrast, modern humans not only fully exploit the comparatively broad limits, phylogenetically, of natural, scaled human sexuality, but descend (regress) below them in certain areas of violent and child pornography and ascend (progress) above them in other areas of romantic and Platonic sexual expression. Yet, even though humans possess the capacity to go beyond the limits of natural sexuality, we normally do not because of phylogenetic inertia and the apparently greater satisfaction, ultimately, of being our natural selves sexually.

regression-progression continuum is to be studied empirically, it must be operationalized in tangible terms. Several years ago, the present writer and one of his students (Burns, 1979) addressed the problem, and a rating scale (see Table 4.1) was derived. As shown, the phrase "Gut Level Experiencing" describes the lower, primitive pole, whereas the phrase "Involves Detached Objective Thinking" describes the upper pole. These phrases are not presumed to describe the actual, absolute poles of emotion versus thought, but are, rather, convenient and meaningful phrases on the hypothetical emotion-thought, regression-progression continuum. The previous phrases, although obviously face valid at the outset, were selected following a rather elaborate selection procedure. We began with 30 phrases (15 nominally "primitive" and 15 nominally "advanced" phrases) that were generated using Bailey's (1978) phylogenetic regression hypothesis as a frame of reference. Examples of primitive phrases included "emphasizes high degree of sensuality," "involves great self-indulgence," "features bodily feelings and sensations," "implies satisfaction of low-level survival needs," and "reflects gut-level experiencing." The advanced phrases, by contrast, included "highly abstract conceptually," "suggests a philosophical, reflective attitude," "involves a high degree of analytical awareness," "oriented toward the world of ideas," and "involves detached, objective thinking."

Once generated, the 30 phrases were submitted to 15 clinical psychology graduate students who rated each of them on a 7-point "Primitive" Scale and a similar "Advanced" Scale (see Table 4.2). Each rater was trained in advance as to our definition of *primitive* and *advanced*. Each phrase was, thus, rated twice: once on the Primitive Scale and once on the Advanced Scale. Correlated t tests were then computed to determine whether the phrases differed significantly in their "primitiveness" or "advancedness." It was hoped, of course, that the differences would be significant and large, showing that a given phrase would be either highly primitive or highly advanced. The results were as expected, and all phrases differed at the .005 level or better. The phrase "reflects gut level experiencing" received the highest t value for the primitive items ($t = -10.98$), whereas the phrase "involves detached, objective thinking" received the highest value for the advanced items ($t = 18.33$). Following extensive reliability analyses and actual use of the scales in rating subjects' pleasure and aversive responses on a projective-type test, we finally decided on the single bipolar scale shown in Table 4.1. This scale and elaborations of it (Bailey & Millbrook, 1984; Brockett, 1982) have proved to be very effective in rating the primitiveness and advancedness of self-reported pleasures and aversions, which themselves are correlated with personality (Bailey, Burns, & Bazan, 1982), psychopathology (Burns, 1984), and IQ scores (Bailey & Millbrook, 1984). Although

TABLE 4.1

Scale for Rating "Primitive" and "Advanced" Characteristics

Gut Level Experiencing	1	2	3	4	5	6	7	*Involves Detached Objective Thinking*
				Involves both about equally				
1. Features bodily feeling and sensations 2. Concrete 3. Basically subcortical 4. Nonverbal 5. Involves little or no mental concentration								1. Does not feature bodily feelings and sensations 2. Abstract 3. Basically neocortical 4. High degree of verbal mediation 5. Involves sustained mental concentration

Note: For more detailed information on scale and its application, see Burns (1979, 1984) and Bazan (1980).

TABLE 4.2
"Primitive" and "Advanced" Scales Used in
Rating the Initial Item Pool

Primitive Scale						
1	2	3	4	5	6	7
not primitive; not ruled by emotions and needs						very primitive; ruled by emotions and needs
Advanced Scale						
1	2	3	4	5	6	7
not advanced; lowest degree of neocortical expression; rational thought						very advanced; highest degree of neocortical expression; rational thought

Note: For more detailed information on scales, see Burns (1979).

effective, the primitive-advanced rating scale (Table 4.1) requires considerable training of raters and exceptionally time consuming item-by-item ratings of each subject's projective responses. To ameliorate these problems, Burns (1984) has recently developed an objective Pleasure-Aversion Scale that provides stronger results than the older method, but does not require rating of subject responses.

Our purpose here has been to show that the logic of the phylogenetic regression-progression continuum may be used to generate interesting hypotheses, to develop new research methods, and to produce provocative findings. The pleasure-aversion approach is only one of a multitude of research applications of the phylogenetic regression-progression model, and hopefully the present volume will stimulate additional research and methodological innovation in the area.

The General Theoretical Continuum

Both Wilson's behavioral scale and Bailey's operational rating scale are similar to and consistent with the general theoretical continuum, but are not identical with it. The general primitive-advanced, "animal-human," regression-progression continuum is broad and inclusive, such that it includes and subsumes all lesser continua. Theoretically, what a person is and does is a function of the combined effects of all the hierarchically arranged systematic processes of the body (thought, emotion, motivation, neurohumoral processes, etc.), and, at any given moment, the balance of interacting forces falls somewhere on the regression-progression scale. Ongoing behavior is, of course, comprised of a steady stream of moments, and, thus, reflects a dynamic process of regressions and progressions or movement on the general continuum.

A surprisingly large number of deductions about human behavior may be derived from the simple premise of the regression-progression continuum. To avoid burdening the reader here, these deductions are outlined in proposition form in Appendix I. However, we may pause briefly here to consider the extreme limits or poles of the general continuum. Theoretically, the primitive pole for humans would describe the most "animalistic" behavior possible within the neurohumoral and motoric capabilities of the organism. Rather than attempting to imagine the most animalistic act possible in the abstract, let us look for a concrete example. Because thorough discussion is provided in chapter 9, let us choose here the senseless, "animalistic" actions of the serial killer, Ted Bundy, in his infamous attack in the Chi Omega House on January 14, 1978. In this orgy of rape, murder, and mutilation, the horrible details of the death of Lisa Levy stand out among the most "regressed" and inhuman acts imaginable. Amid the frenzy of his maniacal attack on Lisa, Bundy plumbed the depths of inhumanity as he bit and tore at her buttocks with his teeth (Rule, 1980).

The advanced pole of the regression-progression continuum describes something akin to what Sandor Rado (1969) calls "emotionless" thought. Here the lower reptilian and paleomammalian centers are operating at minimal capacity, leaving the individual free to apply his or her distinctly human abstract intelligence to seeking truth for its own sake, apart from self-advantage, deceit, or guile. Only the human being can operate toward this upper pole on the scale, and the gap between the human being and the highest animal at this juncture is large indeed. Unfortunately, by virtue of ability factors, level of education, level of enculturalization, and so on, only a few humans are capable of operating toward the upper pole, and even then petite regressions easily draw one away from the rarified atmosphere of pure thought. Ideally, the fully advanced person would have no interference from the reptilian or mammalian systems, and the resulting "living brain" of science fiction could work at its fullest apart from petty concerns of survival and adaptation. This, of course, is not possible, but there is a living counterpart to Ted Bundy at the advanced end of the scale who comes close to meeting the emotionless thought criterion. He is the brilliant physicist, Stephen Hawking, who has been described as the nearly perfect "cerebral being" (Boslough, 1984). He is a 42-year-old man suffering from the crippling and deadly disease amyotrophic lateral sclerosis, who is now confined to a wheelchair, suffers almost total paralysis of the body, and must be fed, dressed, and otherwise cared for by others. Yet, his mind is not dimmed in the slightest, and during the course of the disease he has emerged as one of the most creative and brilliant scientists living, and appears to be the heir apparent to Einstein (Boslough, 1984). Prior to the disease, Hawkings was casual about his studies, but since then he has achieved the stature of true genius, and some physicists believe he could pull off one of the greatest coups in scientific history—the creation of a single theory reconciling the twin pillar of modern physics, Einstein's theory of general relativity and the modern quantum-mechanics theory (Boslough, 1984). Although we cannot say for sure that Hawking's genius is attributable to suspension of interference from the lower centers, he certainly makes an interesting exemplary for the upper pole of the regression-progression continuum.

THE CONTENT OF HUMAN EVOLUTION

Higher and Lower Functions[2]

So far we have discussed the process of regression-progression at some length, described an experimental scale for measuring primitive and advanced characteristics, and have described the poles of the phyloge-

---

[2]The question of whether the phylogeny of organisms allows scaling or ranking into categories of primitive-advanced or lower-higher is highly controversial (Demarest, 1983), as is the related question of whether or not evolution is progressive (Dobzhansky, 1970). Despite the numerous technical complications surrounding the notions of directional evolution and phylogenetic continuity (see Demarest, 1983 for a thorough discussion), Stebbins (1982) says that the complete denial of evolutionary progress is to court absurdity. As both Dobzhansky and Stebbins point out, evolution may be either progressive (gain over ancestral species in complexity, breadth of adaptive function, and so forth) or regressive (loss of complexity or breadth of adaptive function present in ancestral species). With some reluctance, Demarest (1983) concedes the possibility of progressive trends in evolution (e. g., he sees some merit in Julian Huxley's criteria of greater integration of biological systems, and increased control over and independence of the environment), but deems unlikely any general principle of evolutionary progress.

In the present volume, the issue of progress or phylogenetic advancedness has been approached in various ways: amount of extra brain tissue in relation to expected brain tissue estimated from body size (encephalization quotient—Jerison, 1973), various ratios of amount of neocortical-to-subneocortical brain matter (Passingham, 1982), complexity of brain organization (Laughlin & d'Aquili, 1974), increased intelligence, left-over-right hemispheric dominance, verbal over nonverbal functions, capacity for more complex forms of learning (Razran, 1971), capacity for refined self-consciousness, foresight and planning ability, capacity for denial of impulse and self-control, capacity to elaborate and extend basic behavioral software programs, capacity to control movement on PRP continuum, capacity for emotionless thought, behavioral flexibility and capacity for alternative solutions, and so on. Some of these criteria extend across organisms, some are limited to

netic regression-progression continuum. However, we have only touched indirectly on the issue of what "primitive" and "advanced" means in terms of content. Following Jerison (1973), we may assume that some rudimentary form of "consciousness" is involved at even the most phylogenetically primitive levels of functioning, and following Brown (1977) we may also assume that "cognitive" elements are present, to some degree, at all levels of neuropsychological functioning. Further, psychological phenomena such as imagery, dreaming, fantasy, perception, thoughts, ideas, reflection and so forth, are not pure, circumscribed events in nature, but are, instead, convenient abstractions that we use to make sense of complex, dynamic mental processes. We shall not, therefore, attempt to force a false precision on these phenomena by relegating events into discrete, well-defined categories. Because all mental phenomena represent mixtures of processes, we content ourselves here with the rough categories of "higher" versus "lower" levels of functioning. What, then, are some of the higher functions that fall toward the upper end of the regression-progression continuum, and some of the lower functions that fall toward the lower end?

Throughout the ages there has been concern with higher and lower processes, although the methods of study and the phenomena focused upon have varied greatly. Table 4.3 includes a sampling of the many bipolar adjectives and conceptual continua that have been set forth in a variety of contexts. Generally, at the higher levels we find refined self-consciousness and self-awareness, verbally mediated rational thought, self-control, a sense of reality, selflessness and altruism, individuality, empathy, and cultural refinement. In addition to the absence of these things, at the lower levels we find a generalized nearness to the biological

---

mammals and primates, some to primates and humans, and some apparently only to humans. More problematic yet is the issue of circularity of definition: viz., is the organism advanced because of possessing these characteristics, or do these characteristics come with being advanced? How may we distinguish causes from effects?

A major first step in addressing these issues is to disgintuish between evolved progressive characters (e. g., enlarged neocortex) and the advanced behaviors emanating from those characters (e. g., flexibility, foresight). Strictly speaking, behavior does not evolve nor do behavioral tendencies; rather, evolutionary change occurs at the level of biochemical genetics which, in turn, produces change at the levels of brain neurostructure and organization. It would appear that structure precedes function in this sequence, for the organism could not perform the first, newly evolved action-pattern without the necessary underlying neurostructures. Thus, it appears that the brain is the best unit for defining phylogenetic progress, since the genome is more-or-less inaccessible and behavior a result rather than cause. In this scenario, extra brain tissue, neocortical hegemony over subneocortical centers, the overall quantity of neocortical matter and the quality of its behavioral programming, and so forth, loom large as criteria of phylogenetic progress. With progress so construed, it seems reasonable, and certainly intuitively appealing, to speak of certain species as being higher or lower than another.

TABLE 4.3
Examples of Primitive and Advanced Functions.

Primitive	Advanced	Author
manas	buddi	Akhilinanda
single-loop learning	double-loop	C. Agyris
cultural decoupling	coupling	R. Alexander
intuition	intellect	Assagioli
divergent	convergent	Austin; Guilford
regression	progression	K. Bailey
instinct	intelligence	S. A. Barnett
analogic	digital	Bateson & Jackson
senuous	intellectual	Blackburn
right brain	left brain	Bogen
Flesh	Spirit	Bible
Satan	God	Bible
evil	good	Bible
imaginative	deductive	Bronowski
metamorphic	rational	Bruner
nonpurposive	purposive	R. B. Cattell
mythopoetic	logic-empirical	Cassirer
power	empathy	K. Clark
relational	analytic	Cohen
horizontal	vertical	DeBono
receptive	active	Deikman
continuous	discrete	Dieudonne
biogrammar	culture	Fox & Tiger
primary process	secondary process	Freud
fused drives	defused drives	Freud
"off" behavior	"on" behavior	I. Goffman
concrete	abstract	Goldstein
infraculture	supraculture	E. T. Hall
impulsive	realistic	Hilgard
free	directed	Hobbes
closed thinking	open thinking	Horton
imaginative	propositional	Humphrey & Zangwill

(Continued)

roots of the organism, neurologically, perceptually, psychologically, and socioculturally. Some sources imply that "evil" exists at the lower levels, while good is on a higher plane. We see later that this is a gross simplification, but one of some essential truth. There is little doubt, however, that to be civilized is to regularly conform to higher mandates, and to maintain reliable control over the lower centers.

Relations Between Process and Content

In a rather literal way, the phylogenetic regression-progression process implies content in the following fashion: As we descend the phylogenetic ladder we lose certain capacities, and when we ascend the ladder there is

TABLE 4.3 *(Continued)*

Primitive	Advanced	Author
postural communication	facial communication	C. Izard
existential	differential	W. James
associative	transformational	A. Jensen
relational	analytic	Kagan & Moss
"wild"	"domesticated"	Levi-Strauss
prelogical	logical	Levy-Bruhl
gestalt	analytic	Levy & Sperry
Bios	Zoe	C. S. Lewis
differentiation	integration	Lomas & Berkowitz
autistic	realistic	McKellar
subcortical	cortical	MacLean
intuitive	rational	Maslow
private	public	Mehrabian
multiple	sequential	Neisser
timeless	historical	Oppenheimer
holistic	analytic	Ornstein
first signaling	second signaling	Pavlov
assimilation	accommodation	Piaget
ampliative	explicative	C. S. Pierce
tacit	explicit	Polanyi
compositionist	reductionist	Price
eidetic	discursive	Reusch
simultaneous	successive	Schenov (Luria)
subjective	objective	Schopenhauer
gross	atomistic	C. S. Smith
heterarchical	hierarchical	Wells
syncretic	differentiated; integrated	Werner
selfishness	reciprocal altruism	E. O. Wilson
irrationality	rationality	B. R. Wilson
selfishness	selflessness	P. Vitz

Note: Adapted and extended from the *Human Brain* by M. C. Wittrock et al. (1977) by Prentice-Hall, Inc. Reprinted by permission of the publisher Prentice-Hall, Inc., Englewood Cliffs, New Jersey.

an analogous gain in higher functions and capacities. The challenge thus becomes one of identifying and defining these losses and gains by comparative analysis across species. Using MacLean's system, for example, we may ask the question, "How much of human neuropsychological functioning is based on reptilian patterns of behavior?"

MacLean (1978b) addressed this issue, and he listed no less than 24 primal patterns of reptilian behavior, including many that are fundamental parameters of human behavior (see Table 4.4). MacLean considers the establishment and defense of territory as possibly the most important reptilian carry-over in humans, and he interprets this conclusion in the light of Nietzsche's concept of will-to-power. So construed, the omnipresent will-to-power, which Nietzsche likened to a veritable life force in

TABLE 4.4
MacLean's Reptilian Behavior Patterns

1. Selection and preparation of homesite
2. Establishment of territory
3. Trail making
4. "Marking" of territory
5. Showing place-preferences
6. Patrolling territory
7. Ritualistic display in defense of territory, commonly involving the use of coloration and adornments
8. Formalized intraspecific fighting in defense of territory
9. Triumphal display in successful defense
10. Assumption of distinctive postures and coloration in signaling surrender
11. Foraging
12. Hunting
13. Homing
14. Hoarding
15. Use of defecation posts
16. Formation of social groups
17. Establishment of social hierarchy by ritualistic display and other means
18. Greeting
19. "Grooming"
20. Courtship, with displays using coloration and adornments
21. Mating
22. Breeding and, in isolated instances, attending offspring
23. Flocking
24. Migration

human beings, would draw its essential motive force from the dim recesses of reptilian phylogeny. MacLean argues that many other human behaviors are reptilian in origin, including certain forms of ritualized behavior, imitation (isopraxis), perseveration, superstitions, and deceptiveness (see chapter 2).

As we move to the mammalian level, an even greater number of human functions and activities are subsumed. Among the distinctive mammalian characteristics are body hair, the diaphragm separating the chest from the abdomen, warmbloodedness, complex teeth, the placenta, and, of course, the mammary glands. The development of the mammary glands is far more momentous than it might first appear. With these glands came the mother-infant nursing interaction, more refined maternal behavior, and, most importantly, parenting, a phenomenon unknown to reptiles. As MacLean (1978b) says, "With the evolution from mammal-like reptiles to mammals, there appears to have come into being a primal commandment stating: 'Thou shalt not eat the flesh of thy young or the flesh of thine own kind' " (p. 325). So, with mammals there came a more advanced sense of kinship and sociality that would later reach full flower in the primate species. This distinctive mammalian sociality expresses itself most fully in that important pastime of warm-blooded animals known as *play*. Indeed, play is one of the most practically important and theoretically significant biogrammatical parameters to arise in the mammals. The play complex goes to the very roots of many forms of normal and pathological behavior in humans.[3]

Mammals also possess a more complex and elaborate cerebral system than their predecessors, and the old mammalian brain, or limbic system, is particularly well developed. Generally, the mammalian limbic system provides us with a capacity for emotion, and its subdivisions are involved in many vital behavioral activities including feeding, fighting, and self-preservation (amygdala), sexual arousal and affection (septum), and parenting, nursing, and maternal behavior (mammillary bodies). It is here that "biological intelligence" is seen in its most urgent forms, as the organism is impelled and compelled by strong emotion to follow pathways of self-preservation.

Obviously, many of the emotional and motivational substrates of human behavior may be accounted for by carry-overs from our mammalian heritage. We now move up to the level of the primates, where many more biogrammatical substrates are found. We must now, however, try to distinguish between substrates that *originate* with the primates and those that are merely carry-overs or elaborations of basic reptilian and mammalian characteristics. This is a difficult conceptual task, but based on the notion of the hierarchically arranged brain, we would expect most primate biogrammar to be erected upon older structures and relatively little would be truly new or distinctive. Anthropologist Count (1973), for example, argues that many human behavioral complexes are erected upon the foundation of a vertebrate-tetrapod-mammalian-primate "biogram" that provides the basic structures to which particularly human embellishments

---

[3]The phenomenon of play is absent in reptiles, but assumes a position of great functional importance in mammals and primates. Among its many functions are performance of survival-relevant behavior, practice of subroutines which will be later combined into species-adaptive behavior patterns (Bruner, Jolly, & Sylva, 1976; Reynolds, 1981), practice in dominance and redirection of aggression (Aldis, 1975; Fishbein, 1984), shaping of sexual and reproductive skills (Breger, 1974), development of intellectual skills and creativity in children (Fishbein, 1984; Piaget, 1962), and development of moral sensibility in children (Piaget, 1932; Huizinga, 1976). Play activities are seen in all human cultures, and dominance forms of play (rough and tumble play and chasing) are noteworthy in their cross-cultural similarities (Schwartzman, 1978). Social play, especially among peers, is necessary for healthy psychological development in primates (Fishbein, 1984), and its absence is associated with pathological responses such as depression, separation anxiety, and many other forms of pathology (Harlow, 1969; Harlow & Mears, 1979). Given the role of play in normal socialization, play deprivation also may be an important correlate of pathological syndromes involving asocial or antisocial behavior—psychosis, sociopathy and criminality, sex perversion, social inadequacy, reclusiveness, and so on.

are added in phylogeny. For example, the lactation complex in primates is an evolved configuration of anatomical, physiological, biochemical, and psychological characteristics that flowered in mammalian phylogeny, but may even have some features traceable to the reptilian level. Count further says that little embellishment of the basic lactation complex occurs from ape to human *physically,* but, nursing in humans is far more rich and complex psychologically. This is a good example of how the basic reptilian and mammalian foundation structures are elaborated psychologically at the primate and human levels. Given this analysis, how would we answer the question, "Is nursing distinctive to the human species?" Clearly, the nursing complex is not distinctive to the human species, but its mode of expression is, indeed, distinctive. That is, the human nursing complex involves performing the same basic actions as other mammals and primates, but due to the mediating and elaborating effects of self-consciousness, cultural learning, abstract intelligence, and so on, the psychobehavioral end product is distinctive in richness, complexity, and meaning. However, when *distinctive* is defined as "absent in any form in animals lower on the phylogenetic scale," we would expect very few human characters to be distinctively human.

Table 4.5 lists some of the important physical characteristics of nonhu-

TABLE 4.5
Basic Physical Characteristics of Nonhuman Primates

Primitive muzzle development lost or reduced

Sense of smell poorly developed

Tactile hairs lost

Reduction in size and loss of mobility of external ears

Canine teeth are well-developed in males

Shoulder joint is mobile, especially in ape species

Limited wrist movement in monkey, but greater movement in apes

Structure of hands and feet more complex than in mammals; allows grasping and climbing; more complex locomotor adaptations
  a. small but usable thumb
  b. instead of claws or hooves, nails on ends of fingers and toes
  c. hands rather than mouth used to pick up and manipulate objects

Hand and foot area are represented about equally in nonhuman primate's brain

Eyes situated in front of face; binocular depth and color vision; fovea active during daytime

Life phases (gestation, infanthood, juvenile era, and adulthood) very different from other mammals
  a. long life span; life span increases positively correlated with phylogenetic scale in primate order
  b. prolonged immaturity and generally slow growth rate

man primates that are more or less phylogenetically distinctive. As shown, nonhuman primates lost several primitive characteristics and gained a number of advanced ones in the process of evolution. Although the "losses" and diminutions were significant, e. g., the primitive muzzle, smell sense, tactile hairs, and size and mobility of the external ears, the "gains" were even more noteworthy. The nonhuman primate could do much more than its predecessors, due to greater flexibility and complexity in musculoskeletal, perceptual-motor, and cerebro-behavioral systems. The shoulder and wrist joints allowed greater movement, and the advanced structure of hands and feet permitted complex locomotor adaptations including grasping and manipulating objects, and climbing. In addition, daylight vision was well developed and allowed for processing of depth and color. Many of those phylogenetic gains are significant ones, but the advances in life phases were even more dramatic. Compared to its mammalian ancestors, the nonhuman primate lived longer, grew at a slower rate, and enjoyed a far longer period of immaturity. These gains allowed the primate to become a creature of learning who used its prolonged immaturity to become more social and intelligent than any other animal.

Some of the more salient behavioral and social characteristics of nonhuman primates are shown in Table 4.6. The range and complexity of nonhuman primate behavior is remarkable, and it is abundantly clear that we humans sprang from the primate family and share much with our cousins the monkeys and apes. Our omnivorous eating habits, freedom from predator pressure, mother-infant and parent-infant behavioral systems, emphasis on social modeling and role behavior, kinship relations, aversion to incest, group loyalties, sex-role differences, status consciousness and aggressiveness, and highly developed systems of nonverbal communication are not unique to ourselves, but deeply rooted in our primate heritage (see Gallup & Suarez, 1983). Even our most revered trait of intelligence is likewise erected upon phylogenetic foundations laid down in the nonhuman primates.

Table 4.7 briefly summarizes the basic mental abilities of monkeys and apes. As Gibson (1977) has noted, the cerebral cortex is particularly well developed in the primate order, and it appears that the basic neuropsychological substrates of human intelligence are present in monkeys and apes. However, despite their considerable potential for intelligent behavior, primates in the wild generally exhibit little more than biological intelligence, viz., organism-niche maximization and maximally effective survival tracking. The relatively large and complex brains of the higher primates nevertheless suggest that potential for "abstract intelligence" is present, only needing appropriate stimulation and enrichment to be expressed (see Passingham, 1982). Specially trained and "humanized" chimpanzees, for example, have demonstrated the capability for fairly

TABLE 4.6
Behavioral and Social Characteristics of Nonhuman Primates

Eating habits are omnivorous—will eat leaves, fruit, insects and even meat on occasion. Only chimpanzees are known to actively hunt for meat

Most nonhuman primates are arboreal; all New World monkeys are tree dwelling, while a few Old World monkeys (primarily the Cercopithecidae, esp. the baboon) and apes (chimpanzees and gorillas) live on the ground

Generally, little interspecific predator pressure exists; some predation may occur within species

Males generally play special role in protecting (esp. the young) against predation and external threat

Seasonal breeding occurs in some species (langurs, macaques, and hamadryan baboons), but not in others (howler monkeys and chimpanzees)

Female primates have a repeating estrus cycle of 20-35 days. Estrus is often accompanied by pronounced genital swelling and coloration

Birth process involves labor and expelling of the placenta. Initial response of mother to offspring is variable; however, virtually all lick infant and eat the placenta

Learning plays an important role in effective mothering; viz., prior experience is needed

Mother-infant bond is very strong and involves great amount of physical contact

Early disruption of mother-infant bond can have long-lasting pathological effects on offspring

Infant responds with extreme upset to mother absence

Infant's stages of attachment resemble imprinting in birds: first reflex clinging, then recognition of mother, followed by unease at strangers, and then increasing independence (Jolly, 1972)

Mother often reacts differently according to sex of infant; e.g., males are treated more aggressively and allowed more independence

Paternity is usually unclear in nonhuman primates; "fathering" is therefore not well-developed. However, adult males protect infants and allow them special liberties

In all social primates, females take interest in other females' infants ("aunt behavior")

Rudimentary kinship relations exist which typically revolve around the mother; relationships with mother often persist into adult life

(Continued)

132

TABLE 4.6 *(Continued)*

Sibling relationships are seen in muted forms, esp. in the chimpanzee

Fairly well-developed incest taboos are seen in most species for mother-son relations, but not for brother-sister or father-daughter pairings

In-group (group loyalty) and out-group (xenophobia) dynamics are clearly seen in most species

Gender differences are pronounced in many species; adults take note of newborn's genitals by peering, touching, sniffing, etc.
   a. males are more aggressive than females; this difference is seen early in the context of rough-and-tumble play
   b. female infants are more frequently involved in associative behaviors, such as grooming, and they stay in closer physical proximity to other animals than do males
   c. females are likely to spend their entire life within the group, but males are likely to leave or be driven off in the process of peripheralization
   d. males tend to play harder, begin play earlier and cease at a later age, and play for longer periods than do females
   e. males are usually larger and physically stronger than females
   f. observation on chimpanzees suggest that young males do more general object manipulation, but females seem to have superior manipulatory skills
   g. females of many species reach socio-sexual maturity earlier than males, thereby quickening the termination of play

Social bonding is continuous and ongoing, and basically unrelated to sexual behavior

Grooming is an important variable in primate social bonding

Social role-taking, social recognition, and imitative behavior are seen in most primates

Aggression plays many adaptive roles in primate societies
   a. in well-developed dominance systems, esp. for males
   b. in promoting proper spacing between individuals, groups, and populations
   c. in protecting young from predators
   d. in allowing "leaders" to maintain social order

Sexual and dominance systems may sometimes intermix (as with dominance mounting, penile display, etc.)

The primate's complex social behavior revolves around well-developed systems of nonverbal communication involving primarily the visual and auditory modalities. The various forms of communication include display and rituals, intention movements, and dominance-submission postures. Primates are characterized by a variety of vocalizations, postural signals, and an extremely wide range of facial signals.

TABLE 4.7
The Mental Abilities of Monkeys and Apes

The primate brain is large in the phylogenetic sense, ranging from approximately 88 grams in monkeys to 350 grams in chimpanzees. Primates also score well in terms of the ratio of brain to body weight:1:12 for the small squirrel monkey, 1:70 for monkeys in general, 1:200 for the gorilla, and 1:45 for humans (Cobb, 1965)

The cerebral cortex is particularly well-developed in the primate order, providing the following basic substrates of mental functioning (Gibson, 1977):

a. fine differentiation of motor acts and perceptual data
b. ability to coordinate motor actions and perceive simultaneous relationships among perceptual data
c. ability to coordinate sequential actions and sequential perceptual relationships
d. ability to develop flexible stimulus-response relationships
e. ability to internalize perceptual and motor data
f. ability to anticipate future contingencies
g. ability to compare expected with actual perceptions

The increased brain capacity and brain organization in primates allows for a broad range of flexible and adaptable behavior in meeting ecological demands in the wild-"biological intelligence"

There is considerable variability in mental ability across the different primate species—generally the less phylogenetically advanced monkeys score lowest on most tasks, while the more advanced apes do best. With rare exception, the chimpanzee appears to be the brightest of the nonhuman primates. See footnote 4.

The chimpanzee is the star tool-user of the monkeys and apes. They use sticks for termite fishing, use sticks for "olfactory aids," use leaves as sponges to sop water from tree holes and to wipe sticky substances off the body, and sticks and stones are sometimes used as weapons (Jolly, 1972)

Köhler's classic experiments with chimpanzees on Teneriffe island suggest:

a. wide variability in mental ability among chimpanzees; one "genius,"Sultan, emerged and consistently outperformed his peers
b. the presence of reasoning, purposive behavior, and problem-solving ability in chimpanzees
c. the capacity for sudden solutions, or "insight" in chimpanzees

Nonhuman primates perform well on man-made animal "IQ" tests, with chimpanzees being generally superior. Sometimes the gorilla does best, however, particularly when a

(Continued)

134

TABLE 4.7 *(Continued)*

calm, deliberate, and persistent approach is required

Chimpanzees in captivity excel in the use of implements and their"tool use" is frequent; however, such behavior is seen less frequently in the wild. This suggests that *learning* and richness of experience are implicated in the superior performance of the captive chimp

Anecdotal accounts of home-raised chimpanzees suggest the presence of imaginary play, "artistic ability" in the form of aesthetically pleasing painted pictures, and an apparent understanding of human misery or illness; this suggests that the higher mental processes of imagination, creativity and sympathy may be present in simple form (Reynolds, 1967)

Chimpanzees can be *taught* a wide variety of behaviors, including such things as complex circus tricks, operating complex laboratory manipulanda, playing tic-tac-toe, and the rudiments of "language"

Whether the chimpanzee possesses true language is a highly controversial question. Efforts at teaching them vocal speech have been unsuccessful, but extensive work with sign language suggests the capacity for symbolic communication. The Gardner's Washoe was able to master 160 word signs, while Penny Patterson's gorilla Kiko extended her vocabulary to 250, signs. Some even suggest that ape communication obeys the basic laws of grammar and syntax. This appears particularly true for the pygmy chimp (Savage-Rumbaugh, 1984)

Nonhuman primates have an exceptionally well-developed capacity for social learning. Hall and Goswell (1964) say, for example, that "The essential learning-how-to-learn socially is a fundamental adaptation of the monkey and ape . . ." (p. 61). This capacity may be involved in primitive forms of culture in certain species. Much of primate behavior is transmitted by learning from generation to generation (Jolly, 1972)

Although intelligent, the chimpanzee seems to lack the capacity for cooperative teamwork that characterizes the human species. However, some research (Savage-Rumbaugh, Rumbaugh, & Boysen, 1978) indicates cooperative symbolic communication between chimps, and cooperative forms of hunting have been observed in the field (Teleki, 1973)

The higher apes, esp. the chimpanzee, possess the rudiments of *abstract intelligence*— consciousness, self-awareness, reasoning ability, symbolic communication, and foresight. Through extensive communication training, social and environmental stimulation, and attempts at humanization of chimpanzees, etc., it is suggested that apes can rise above purely species—specific adaptation processes (biological intelligence) and be intelligent in the human, abstract sense high-level problem-solving, purposive behavior, and even "insight." Further, a variety of primate species have performed fairly well on arbitrary laboratory tasks and animal "IQ" tests (Reynolds, 1967), and, thus, may be said to possess "abstract intelligence" as it is defined by the present writer. Even language is no longer the hallowed domain of the human species, for both the gorilla and chimpanzee appear to possess the capacity for symbolic, albeit nonvocal communication (Desmond, 1979; Passingham, 1982; Rumbaugh, 1970, 1977)[4].

Given the many fundamental behavioral and mental similarities between nonhuman primates and humans at the deep, paleopsychological levels of functioning, we are faced with the question of what—if anything—is exclusively human and totally transcendent over our animal nature? The facts reveal a very blurred line between animal and human at many important junctures—morphology and structure, social behavior, mental functioning, and perhaps even language—and it seems that the more we learn about our primate cousins the less unique the human species becomes.

Content Features of Human Evolution

Ramapithecus. Table 4.8 summarizes the basic characteristics of the hominid creatures that stand between the nonhuman primates and modern man. Although the fossil evidence is sketchy, and particularly so for earlier hominids such as *Ramapithecus* and *Australopithecus,* the overall picture of phylogenetic gains and losses over evolutionary time is convincing. Many writers consider *Ramapithecus* the first hominid, whereas others deny it the status of human ancestor. The few dental fragments available do not allow factually based reconstructions of the creature's physical, social, and mental characteristics, and we are not even sure that it walked upright, used tools, or possessed the barest rudiments of symbolic communication. Following Leaky and Lewin's (1977) reasoned argument, however, we may presume that the creature's greatly reduced

---

[4]Recent evidence suggests that the pygmy chimpanzee, *Pan paniscus,* may be the brightest and most phylogenetically advanced of the nonhuman primates. Preliminary research on the pygmy chimp (Savage-Rumbaugh, 1984) indicates a clear conceptual/ communicative superiority over the common chimpanzee, *Pan troglodytes.* Some of the more dramatic findings were summarized in a two-part series in the *New York Times,* June 24 and 25. Particular noteworthy pygmy-common chimp differences are: A smaller, more humanlike face, a greater frequency of upright gait, female receptivity throughout the menstrual cycle, occasional face-to-face copulation, and an unprecedented capacity for learning and using human language. At age 2½, the pygmy chimp Kanzi began to "spontaneously" use geometric word symbols that were being taught to his mother. Now at age 4 Kanzi has far surpassed the linguistic accomplishments of any other nonhuman primate. Although results are preliminary, Kanzi appears to understand complex sentences in

canine incisors and fairly broad geographic range imply several advanced characteristics. Reduction of the canines, for example, implies a vegetarian diet, and Clifford Jolly (1970) pictures *Ramapithecus* as a seed-eater who developed a precision grip for picking up tiny morsels of food. The small canines also imply that protection against predators and interspecific dominance conflicts were handled in other ways than brandishing buccal weaponry. Leaky and Lewin (1977) speculate that *Ramapithecus* may have stood up to throw objects at adversaries as modern chimpanzees do, and the upright posture may have developed in the process. Whether or not these speculations are valid, we may be fairly certain that *Ramapithecus* favored forested areas traversed by rivers, and no doubt ventured on occasion out into the open woodlands bordering the savannas in search for food.

Most early writers on *Ramapithecus* presumed it had descended from the ape-like creature *Dryopithecus* somewhere between 10 and 15 million years ago (Simons, 1977). This left a tremendous temporal gap between the genesis of the hominid line, qua *Ramapithecus,* and the next apparent stage of hominid progression, *Australopithecus afarensis,* around 3.5 million years ago. Sherwood Washburn (1978b) summarized the consensus of opinion in the late 1970s, which held that our human ancestors diverged from the African line of apes much less than 10 million years ago. Calculating immunological distances from the immunological reactions of the blood proteins of humans and other primates suggests an even more recent date of divergence. Sarich and his colleagues (Sarich, 1968; Sarich & Cronin, 1976; Sarich & Wilson, 1967), using the immunological methdology, estimated that chimpanzees and humans shared a common ancestry as recently as 4 million years ago. Although the immunological approach is subject to methodological criticisms, and it seems improbable that the entire record of human evolution could be compressed into a mere 4 million years (Passingham, 1982), a short time scale rather than a long one appears most likely.

The issue of the short or long time scale bears indirectly on the

English such as "Will you go get a diaper for your sister Mulika?" or "Do you want to get out the hose and play in your swimming pool?" (*New York Times,* June 24, 1985). What all this means for human evolution is unclear. Savage-Rumbaugh (1984) finds the pygmy chimp-human similarities remarkable, but difficult to explain phylogenetically. She asks, "Why would evolution operate this way, giving an animal an ability to understand human speech when it would never use that in its own world?" (Eckholm, 1985, p. B1). Also, Vincent Sarich (1984) points out that the pygmy chimp separated from the common chimp far too late (about 1.5 MYA) for there to be any special evolutionary relation to humans, and others (Johnson, 1981; Latimer et al., 1981) argue strongly against the pygmy as kind of missing link. Until the data say otherwise, it seems most prudent to view *paniscus* as a subspecies of chimpanzee that, because of convergent evolution, developed a form of biological intelligence from which abstract intelligence is more easily derived than from any other ape.

TABLE 4.8
Basic Characteristics of Intermediary Hominid Ancestors

Ramapithecus

Known only from a few dental fragments that date from 9 to 14 million years ago

Fragments reveal a reduction in snout and anterior teeth (incisors and canines), and U-shaped dental arch rather than the V-shaped arch seen in apes

Some writers believe that the reduced canines are correlated with primitive tool use and bipedalism, but this is highly speculative

It is not known whether *Ramapithecus* walked upright or what it looked like. Its status as a true hominid is subject to considerable controversy

The faunal context of *Ramapithecus* implies a riverine forest and possibly a move to more open woodland bordering the savanna. All of this suggests that a great amount of time was spent foraging for food on the ground

---

Australopithecus

The link between *Ramapithecus* and later hominids was apparently *Australopithecus afarensis*. This hominid lived 3 to 4 million years ago, walked upright in human fashion, but was rather ape-like in facial appearance (Pfeiffer, 1980). The body was small (approximately 4 feet tall and 50-70 pounds in weight), as was the brain (300-500 cc). Despite the small brain, *afarensis* was more socially intelligent than the apes, and is credited with many phylogenetic advances in *male-female relationships* and *parenting* (Johanson & White, 1979)

Following *afarensis,* there were two subsequent forms, *Australopithecus robustus* and the smaller *africanus*. *Africanus* is the likely ancestor to man, and it existed in southern Africa over 3 million years ago. Body size (height 3 to 4 feet; weight 49-80 pounds), and brain size (400-500 cc) were both small. Leg bones of *africanus* indicate upright gait and the capacity to both walk and run

Australopithecine brain *organization* was more human-like (large temporal and parietal lobes, but relatively small occipital lobes) than ape-like (the opposite pattern). Leakey and Lewin (1977) believe that the human-like brain *predated* tool-making and serious hunting; the human brain evolved, instead, in response to selective pressures of a *social* type. Barkow (1980) says that hominids adapted to a *cultural* environment from *Australopithecus* on to the present

Crude stone tools (choppers) go back at least 2.6 million years to the Lake Turkana australopithecines. More complex tools have been associated with later finds; Swindler (1980) reasons that the advanced tool and social culture of *Australopithecus* implies a rudimentary *language* capacity

The hunting-gathering adaptation became well-developed during the australopithecine stage, and with it came emphasis on meat-eating, food-sharing, cooperative group behavior, and a reinforcement of the sexual division of labor

---

Homo habilis

This was a contemporary of the australopithecine, discovered by the Leakeys and christened *Homo habilis,* the "handy man." They argued that *habilis* was the first true man,

(Continued)

138

TABLE 4.8 *(Continued)*

while others saw him merely as an advanced form of *africanus.* He lived between 2 and 1.5 million years ago.

The teeth of *habilis* were more human-like than those of *Australopithecus,* and the brain was considerably larger (650-700 cc)

The cultural achievements of *habilis* appear to far transcend his relatively small brain. Finds by Mary Leakey at Olduvai Gorge reveal *habilis* as an advanced tool maker and user. Implements in his "tool kit" include choppers, picks, cleavers, awls, anvils, and spheroids. Evidence of primitive forms of shelter were seen also

It is presumed that the elaborate tool culture of *habilis* was accompanied by a similarly elaborate social culture. The hunting and gathering adaptation was central as with *Australopithecus*

Homo erectus

Homo was only slightly larger than *Australopithecus,* but his brain was much larger. The range of brain size is from 750 to 1400 cc, overlapping with modern man at the upper level. It is likely that greatly advanced brain organization accompanied the increase in brain size

A curved spine, short pelvis and head more nearly centered allowed erect balance for efficient walking. *Erectus* was five feet tall or more, and sturdily built. Skeletal frame is similar to modern man except for smaller head and shorter legs

Face and teeth were reduced, though not to the extent of modern humans. Smaller teeth probably reflects eating of tender cooked food once fire was discovered. The vocal apparatus was primitive by modern standards, but would have allowed slow, clumsy forms of speech (Leakey & Lewin, 1977)

Homo is credited with the discovery of fire 500,000 to 750,000 years ago. Fire was a major cultural advancement in many ways:

a. food could be cooked
b. tools and weapons could be tempered
c. survival could be achieved in colder geographic regions
d. family relationships, group social behavior, domesticity, and a sense of home were encouraged by fire and more stable campsites
e. it is probable that language was facilitated also by extended interaction around the campfire
f. fire may have played a role in the earliest rituals, e.g., the "cannibalistic feast of Choukoutien" (White & Brown, 1973)

Tool use and hunting became greatly advanced, and *erectus* was able to bring down the largest game animals through refined hunting methods, group cooperation, and tactical skill. Using his greater memory, attentional skills, and reasoning ability, *erectus* was able to outwit prey

A crude forerunner of family was evident with the australopithecines, but it became a social reality with *erectus.* The division of labor and the hunting-gathering adaptation remained in force, but male-female and parent-infant interrelationships became more subtle and refined. Sexual habits, mate selection, and child-rearing were becoming increasingly more human. More elaborate kinship ties developed, intergroup relationships became more complex, and exogamy was generally practiced phylogenetic regression-progression model. Although the model does not stand or fall on the recentness-remoteness issue, the short scale, by implication, strengthens the regression argument. The reasoning goes thusly: If we diverged from the apes only recently, then we have had little time to phylogenetically "progress" beyond our essential apeness or to develop a large number of distinctively advanced characteristics. If the short scale is the true one, then humans are not "as different from other animals as one might like to suppose. The beast might still exist in us as part of our essential nature—and being civilized would demand considerably more than doing what comes naturally" (Pfeiffer, 1980, p. 91).

Australopithecus. Whereas controversy surrounds the question of whether *Ramapithecus* is ancestral to man, there is fair agreement that *Australopithecus* (or variations thereof) is a true human ancestor. The earliest variation appears to be *Australopithecus afarensis,* a small, ape-like creature discovered by Donald Johanson and his colleagues in the Afar region of Ethiopia in November 1974. The creature discovered was the famous "Lucy" (Johanson & Edey, 1981) whose skull fragments, mandible, arm bones, several ribs, partial pelvis, and fragments of leg bones represented the most complete australopithecine skeleton ever found. Lucy was thought to have been about 40 years old when she died, and she stood little more than a meter high. The remarkable Lucy and other findings by the Johanson team help to paint an exciting picture of the morphology and probable behavioral patterns of *afarensis.* As Table 4.8 shows, *afarensis* lived 3 to 4 million years ago and apparently walked upright. The first two *afarensis* bones found by Johanson indicated an erect posture, and subsequent findings have supported this conclusion (Pfeiffer, 1980). Although basically human in character, *afarensis* was primitive in most of its features. The face resembled that of a chimpanzee and its very small brain fell well within the chimpanzee range as well. The body was quite small, with males apparently being 50-100% larger than females (Pilbeam, 1984), implying significant sex differences in adaptive patterns and social behavior.

Despite its small brain, *afarensis* was well on the way to humanhood in several respects. Pfeiffer (1980) says that infant survival was a crucial issue for *afarensis* as it was for other slow breeding and slow growing primates, and, consequently, the male-female bond and male participation in parenting became important new adaptive strategies. It seems, then, that *afarensis* can be credited with important phylogenetic gains in male-female relationships and social organization. They were apparently able to rise above, so to speak, the rigid sex roles of earlier primates and to introduce a more flexible arrangement maximizing attachment and minimizing aggression, especially in the males. Their male-female bond may have been even stronger than that of modern humans: "Monogamy and everything that went with it seem to have been established by *afarensis* times. In fact, if the strength of the male-female bond is any index . . . modern humans could be said to represent a devolution rather than evolution in this respect" (Pfeiffer, 1980, p. 96).

It is reasonable to assume that *Ramapithecus* was the ancestor of *Australopithecus,* and, for convenience, the line between them may be drawn at about 6 million years ago (Campbell, 1979). Between 6 and 4 million years ago, *Ramapithecus* slowly merged into the primitive australopithecine forms, which later divided into at least three types, *afarensis,* the gracile *africanus,* and the larger *robustus. Australopithecus afarensis* was apparently the first to evolve, with the more advanced gracile and robust forms coming later. According to Campbell (1979), the gracile *africanus* gradually evolved into *Homo* during the 4 to 2 million-year period, while *robustus* and his similarly large cousin *Australopithecus boisei* were on the pathway to extinction. By the 2 million-year point, the robust forms had disappeared, and *africanus* had evolved into the "handy man" *Homo habilis.*

Assuming that the gracile *africanus* was ancestor to man, with what phylogenetic advances may it be credited? As shown in Table 4.8, *africanus* was more advanced than *afarensis* in several respects: a slightly larger brain capacity and probably more complex brain organization, crude tool use, and probably more refined social behavior (hunting, sexual division of labor, larger and more complex social structures in general). Campbell (1979) suggests that *africanus* was a keen-sighted, agile, and alert creature who moved in compact bands and possibly carried sticks, bone clubs, and crudely chipped rocks. There was a strong sense of group defense that enabled the group to search for insects, berries, and roots without the constant fear of being eaten by a large predator. Campbell further suggests that the gracile ape-man, although not capable of spoken language, was no doubt capable of a number of expressive nonverbal sounds and a rich repertoire of gestures, body movements, and facial expressions. *Australopithecus africanus* was clearly on the road to humanity, but was not quite there—that distinction awaited its more brainy and competent successor, *Homo habilis.*

Homo Habilis.   The rudimentary tool use of the australopithecines was greatly extended by the handy man, *Homo habilis.* His achievements went far beyond his small brain (see Table 4.8), e. g., the development of the first "tool kit," a modest collection of primitive stone implements unearthed by Mary Leaky in Bed I at the Olduvai Gorge in Tanzania. The tools were mainly what Leaky called choppers—small, primitive, but distinctly human implements made by using a small round or oval stone to knock large chips off a larger rock. Among the resulting chips were sharp and jagged ones capable of cutting meat, scraping hides, or sharpening the point of a stick. Smaller chips knocked off in the process of making choppers, called flakes, were sharper and probably used for slicing and cutting. These and several other primitive tools (see Table 4.8) comprised the ancient tool kit of *Homo habilis*. Perhaps more important than the tools themselves was the more complex and elaborate culture that came with them. With a larger brain and emergent tool technology, *habilis* was able to take all that he had inherited, both phylogenetically and culturally, from *africanus* and cross the gap between ape and human. With the contributions of *habilis*, human evolution began in earnest and at a phenomenally fast pace (see Lumsden & Wilson, 1983).

Homo Erectus.   As Table 4.8 shows, the brain of *Homo erectus* was much larger than that of *habilis*, and it was put to good use in inventing new phases of human development and elaborating upon and expanding old ones (e. g., fire was discovered, food cooked for the first time, tool invention and use became more extensive and sophisticated, new geographic areas were explored, and social organization and culture vastly increased in complexity). The numerous and varied accomplishments of *erectus* reveal a high level of biological intelligence that allowed for greater tactical skill in hunting, greater subtlety and refinement in social organization, and an increasing mastery over nature. A true human culture was in the making, with the rudiments of group identity, social cooperation, ritual, and perhaps even religion now a part of the human experience. Moreover, it is likely that *erectus* was able to sufficiently rise above the natural selfishness and xenophobia of his predecessors and develop cooperative and reciprocal arrangements, both within primary kinship group and intergroup relations. We see here that phylogenetic gains involve not only inventions and elaborations of old tendencies, but inhibition and modulation of old tendencies as well.

Homo Sapiens Neanderthalensis and Cro-Magnon.   *Homo erectus* was succeeded by the Neanderthals, whose body size, general physiognomy, and brain capacity were in the modern range (see Table 4.9). This increased brain size and more complex neural organization (Laughlin & d'Aquili, 1974) allowed for many advances over *erectus,* including more refined tool technology, increased sensitivity in interpersonal relations, and religio-philosophical concerns about life and death. Perhaps Neanderthal was the first true philosopher, who devoted brain and intelligence to higher concerns than day-to-day survival and ecological adaptation. Still, perhaps because of relatively small frontal lobes, something was lacking that his successor, Cro-Magnon, possessed in great abundance—initiative.

Despite the possibility that gross brain size favored Neanderthal, those newcomers, the Cro-Magnons, with their small faces, vertical foreheads and well-developed frontal lobes, were the ones to take the last giant step to full humanhood starting about 50,000 years ago. Their hypertrophied frontal lobes aided them greatly in the process, providing the much needed initiative on the one hand, and greater cognitive control over the primitive lower centers on the other. Modern man now had the motivation for intellectual work and abstraction, and just as importantly, he had the capacity to more effectively control and inhibit interference from the lower limbic and reptilian neuropsychological systems. Intellect and emotion were now fully set into a sometimes antagonistic, sometimes protagonistic, and always complementary interrelationship that provided the wherewithal for advances heretofore unknown in nature. Increasing refinement of the emotion-intellect, lower center-higher center complementarity, is possibly the most important correlate of hominidization. Earlier hominids had already stood upright, developed tools and culture, and developed the rudiments of language, but Cro-magnon added that "something extra" for full human status. The final section of Table 4.9 shows just how far the astounding advances of modern humans progressed beyond our not fully human predecessors.

But by no means did Cro-Magnon, nor we humans of today, totally transcend the Beast, the limbic and reptilian whispers of the phylogenetic past. Certainly Cro-Magnon was progressive in many ways, and his advances shook the world to its very foundations. Yet, he could be phylogenetically regressive at times, and passively lapse into violence, obsessions with reproduction and fertility, and, no doubt, overvaluation of kin and devaluation of nonkin. Certainly he also actively regressed as well by allying, for example, belief systems and mythology with the lower centers to whip up enthusiasm for warfare or to provide religious rationales for sexual obsessions. To become fully human was not to foresake the limbic and reptilian wisdom of the past, but to build upon it and at the same time keep it under control. Only in the technological-intellectual sphere do we, on rare occasion, temporarily transcend our animal nature, while in the social sphere we often do little better than the apes. As Pfeiffer (1980) puts it. "Technologically, and in many other ways, *Homo sapiens* ranks supreme. Socially, the species may leave some room for debate" (p. 182).

Brief Overview

From the foregoing considerations, we may deduce that evolution and phylogenetic progress, from ape to protohominid and from protohominid to modern man has involved, among other things, the following interacting processes: (a) increased brain capacity; (b) accelerated neocortical growth; (c) increased complexity of brain organization; (d) increased

TABLE 4.9
Basic Characteristics of Modern Hominids

Homo sapiens neanderthalensis

The Neanderthals emerged as a new hominid species around 100,000 years ago and then disappeared 35,000-40,000 years ago. His geographic range was much larger than that of *erectus*, with key sites in Europe, the Near East and Far East, and in southeast Africa. The Neanderthal period coincided largely with the Riss glacial period; this frigid, forbidding environment represented a supreme test for hominid endurance and ingenuity

Neanderthal's brain size was as large (and perhaps larger-up to 1450 cc) as that of moderns, and body size and shape were similar. He was slightly shorter than *Homo sapiens*, however, and was thicker-boned and more massively built. Although structurally similar, he *looked* very different due to huge eyebrow ridges, a sloping forehead, receding chin, and relatively long skull in proportion to breadth. Frontal lobes were small relative to overall large brain size (Baker, 1974)

Considerable controversy surrounds the question of Neanderthal's species status. Brace (1967) sees him as an intermediary link between the Pithecanthropines and moderns, Coon (1939) suspects considerable hybridization between Neanderthal and *sapiens*, and Leakey and Lewin (1977) consign him to extinction. Swindler (1980) distinguishes between an earlier "progressive" Neanderthal which merged into *sapiens* and a later primitive form which became extinct. Final extinction may have come due to overspecialization during the ice age or due to failure in competition with *sapiens*

Special accomplishments of Neanderthal:

a. Neanderthal used the previously invented Acheulean and Levallois methods of toolmaking, and also developed new techniques such as the diskcore method (Constable, 1973). He became an expert stonecrafter, and many new special purpose tools were designed for increasingly elaborate and varied tool kits

b. Neanderthal hunted less haphazardly than *erectus*, and apparently knew a great deal about animal behavior. Cooperative hunting became more advanced, and a great variety of large, dangerous animals were hunted

c. Neanderthal made efficient use of animal products. All of the red meat and internal organs were probably eaten, and skins no doubt were used for clothing and advanced forms of tent-like shelters (Constable, 1973). It is also probable that certain animals—such as the dog and reindeer—were domesticated by Neanderthal (Campbell, 1972)

d. Neanderthal was a creature of *symbols* who understood the meaning of life and death. The dead were often buried with considerable ritual and fanfare, and Neanderthal may have practiced a primitive form of *religion*. Cults of various types were formed including an "ibex cult," "bear cult," and "skull cult" (Constable, 1973; Pfeiffer, 1969). Body decoration was also prevalent and Neanderthal may be the first hominid to use jewelry. Clearly, he was able to see beyond himself into the world of *abstract thought*

e. Perhaps more importantly, Neanderthal seemed to be a sensitive, caring creature who mourned loved ones, cared for the sick and the elderly, and experienced empathy in rudimentary form (Constable, 1973)

Although Neanderthal was caring, he could also be extremely *violent* as were his predecessors. Ample evidence of killing, body mutilation, and cannabalism exist at many Neanderthal sites. Much of this violence was probably associated with ceremonies, rituals, and religious practices

Despite many achievements, Neanderthal was denied full humanhood in the area of *speech*. Although clearly right-handed and presumably lateralized, he lacked a modern pharynx and was, consequently, limited in vocal range (Constable, 1973). His speech was quite impoverished by modern standards

The last link in the hominid chain appeared 30,000 to 35,000 years ago during the Würm glaciations. The Combe-Capelle and Cro-Magnon fossil finds ushered in the era of Cro-Magnon man, and all

(Continued)

TABLE 4.9 *(Continued)*

Homo sapiens sapiens

present humans are descendants of this branch of the hominid tree. Early versions of Cro-Magnon and transitional types overlapped with Neanderthal for at least 20,000 years

Compared to Neanderthal, Cro-Magnon had small teeth, lighter bones, a smaller face with higher, more vertical forehead, and brow ridges all but disappeared. The cranial capacity was equal to or slightly smaller than Neanderthal's, but the skull was more advanced in several respects (Baker, 1974). Most notably, the frontal lobes were extremely well-developed, but the occipital lobes reduced compared to Neanderthal

Cro-Magnon dispersed into all habitable regions of the globe, and was the first to move into the arctic regions, North and South America, and Australia. He had the capacity to adapt to all terrestrial environments. As Cro-Magnon spread geographically, great population increases were realized, and varying adaptations led to racial variation and other trait variation across populations. Although remaining one species, *Homo sapiens sapiens* became the most diverse and complex hominid of all

The Cro-Magnon period was the "supreme age of hunters and gatherers," and can be seen as the last stand of "natural man" (Solecki, 1973). His great brain power and capacity for *true speech,* however, enabled man to make the ultimate transition from primitive but natural hunting and gathering to advanced but unnatural agricultural and technological modes of adaptation. *Cultural evolution* came to supplement physical evolution as the primary agent of change

Cultural achievements of Cro-Magnon:
   a. Tool use and manufacture were extremely advanced, and one invention led to another. Among his inventions were coal burning kilns for making pottery, woven baskets, the needle, and increasingly elaborate forms of housing. Advanced weaponry was also invented, including the spear-thrower and the bow and arrow. Tools were made from a variety of materials including bone, antler, ivory, wood, and, of course, stone. Cro-Magnon was the master stonecrafter, and the invention of the blade technique (Prideaux, 1973) led to more refined tools and tools to make tools. Over 100 tools might be found in his tool kits, whereas the best Neanderthal kit contained less than 70
   b. Of great importance was the transition from tool technology to *art.* Art is the great cultural contribution of Cro-Magnon, for it represents going beyond the functional and utilitarian into a world of abstraction. According to many experts, the subtlety of line, form, and color in his cave paintings, statuettes, and decorated artifacts ranks with the best of modern art (Prideaux, 1973). Much of Cro-Magnon's art was apparently associated with magic, religious practices, and ritual. Content tended to center on hunting themes and sexual symbolism
   c. Concern for life after death far transcended that of Neanderthal. Unearthed burial grounds in Russia revealed unprecedented funerary luxury and symbolic ritual. These findings suggest persons of love and sensitivity who understood life and death in the most abstract sense
   d. Religion based on nature worship was developed which included fertility rites and a host of fertility goddesses. It is probable that Cro-Magnon believed in beneficent and malevolent spirits, and his elaborate symbolic rituals often represented appeals to supernatural powers
   e. As was true of earlier hominids, Cro-Magnon engaged in fighting and killing, but of a more refined sort. Several scenes in Spanish Levantine art (Prideaux, 1973) show bands of archers attacking each other in disciplined combat. This early warfare involved simple forms of military ranking, military dress, and honor codes. Cro-Magnon's proficiency in organized warfare may be implicated in the sudden disappearance of Neanderthal 30-35,000 years ago
   f. Despite a firm division of labor associated with the hunting-gathering economy, women played important roles in Cro-Magnon society. Families were presumably small and close-knit (Prideaux, 1973), and women were revered because of their "magical" reproductive powers. Women exerted great social influence in their domestic and parental roles, and they also took part in feasts and religious ceremonies. With Cro-Magnon, phylogenetically prepared sex-role distinctions broke down to some degree

specialization of cortical structures; (e) more well-defined hemisphericity; (f) more refined control over the lower centers; (g) more intensive cultural programming of the neocortex (cortical supplementation); and (h) progressively better integration of all these interlocking variables. Human distinctiveness, it seems, rests less on absolute brain size or cultural invention than on the complex interaction of the phylogenetically old, the phylogenetically new, and the cultural. Of all the variables in this complex matrix, the present writer has chosen to focus on the antagonistic-protagonistic interaction between the so-called lower and higher centers, but many insights are to be found in other combinations of variables. Most would agree, though, that an analysis of the animal-human, lower-higher function interplay is a good starting point, given the remarkable range of human responsivity from the most regressive to progressive levels. Indeed, the breadth of the regression-progression continuum (see Appendix I), and the ability to move up and down that continuum, are among our most distinctive attributes.

The Hunting-Gathering Modality and Human Nature

During most of human evolution, natural selection operated within an ecological medium dominated by the hunting and gathering modality. The hunting and gathering modality was both a means of adapting to broad environmental demands and itself an environment within which man was constantly evolving. For at least 1 million years, and perhaps for 2 to 3 million years (Campbell, 1979), our ancestors were hunter-gatherers, and many of our physical traits, emotional predispositions, and mental characters were formed or elaborated during this period. Of the 3 to 4 million years of human evolution, approximately 99% were in the hunting and gathering mode (Campbell, 1979), meaning that around 90% of all the people who have ever lived were hunter-gatherers (Lee & DeVore, 1968). Further, even a scant 10,000 years ago 100% of the world's population were hunter-gatherers, while at present a mere .003% fall into this category (Coon, 1971). It is generally agreed that little or no biological evolution has occurred in humans since the demise of Neanderthal 35,000 years ago (Coon, 1971), and we can be reasonably confident that natural selection operated feebly if at all during the rise of agriculture, civilization, and, finally, modern technological culture in the past 15,000 years. Thus, we must agree with Lee and DeVore (1968) that the origin of all common characteristics in humans must be sought in preagricultural times. Indeed, as (Coon, 1971) says, "We and our [hunting and gathering] ancestors are the same people" (p. xvii).

If we were to choose a single phrase to characterize the human species, "man the hunter" would be most apt. Laughlin (1968) summarizes the situation quite well:

> Hunting is the master pattern of the human species. It is the organizing activity which integrated the morphological, physiological, genetic, and intellectual aspects of the individual human organisms and of the population who compose our single species. Hunting is a way of life, not simply a 'subsistence technique', which importantly involves commitments, correlates, and consequences spanning the entire biobehavioral continuum of the individual and of the entire species of which he is a member. (p. 304)

From *Australopithecus, Homo habilis, Homo erectus,* and on up to Neanderthal and Cro-Magnon, the hunting and gathering way increasingly dominated all phases of human life—diet, mating, reproductive behavior and parenting, social behavior and kinship ties, perceptual and mental functioning, social and political organization, in-group and out-group relations, and so on. Table 4.10 summarizes some of the many biobehavioral correlates of the hunting and gathering modality. As Table 4.10 shows, the rudiments of virtually every human behavioral complex can be traced to the hunting and gathering phase, and it follows, then, that human nature is, to a great extent, defined by that phase.

That we moderns are hunter-gatherers at heart has direct implications for the phylogenetic regression-progression model. The reasoning goes thusly: If virtually all of human evolution occurred in the hunting and gathering modality, and if evolution defines the essential nature of the human species, then two conclusions follow: (a) the biological nature of man was designed for hunting and gathering (and not for modern civilized life), and (b) post-agricultural cultural evolution, involving an extremely short time period within which the neuropsychological systems of the body remained essentially unchanged, has contributed little to the fundamental nature of man, and represents "a thin veneer" over the quintessential hunter-gatherer lying underneath. It furthermore follows that when we phylogenetically regress—under stress, provocation or threat (see chapters 6 & 7)—we are most likely to regress to some aspect of our essential hunting and gathering nature. In such regression, we shed the superficial cloak of culture, with its infinitude of often arbitrary rules and presses, and return to wired-in and reliable modes of adaptation that have served our species for millions of years. When our lives or the lives of our offspring are at stake, the cultural mode is short-circuited and we nonconsciously and reflexively call upon the ancient wisdom of our essential human nature to see us through the crisis. Once the smoke of the crisis clears, however, we return to "normal," never once reflecting upon our short brush with our deeper nature.

Table 4.10 summarizes some of the phylogenetic content that is likely to

TABLE 4.10
Behavioral Correlates of the Hunting-Gathering Modality

Increased intelligence
  1. increased cranial capacity from *Australopithecus* to Cro-Magnon
  2. increased complexity of cerebral organization
  3. progression from biological intelligence (adaptation) to abstract intelligence (mastery)
  4. progressive development from primitive tool use to complex tool technologies, from "unspecialized hunting-gathering" to "highly specialized hunting-gathering" (Wymer, 1982)
  5. progressive insight into behavior of animals and primitive conservation strategies (Campbell, 1979)
  6. both hunting and gathering required progressive development of memory skills and knowledge of animals and the environment (Laughlin,1968: Washburn & Lancaster, 1968)
  7. domestication of animals, especially the dog (Coon, 1971)
  8. development of progressively more complex planning strategies; consideration of future contingencies
  9. many adversities were faced requiring intelligent solutions (clothing, shelter, food storage, possible weapons competition between neighboring groups, etc.)
  10. parents progressively refined methods for training offspring in hunting and gathering strategies
  11. primitive gesticulation and vocalization gradually developed into spoken language
  12. hunting and gathering technologies transmitted to succeeding generations by oral tradition?

Evolution of family
  1. a clear division of labor by gender possibly from *Australopithecus* and certainly by *Homo erectus*—men did virtually all of the hunting and women virtually all of the gathering
  2. parenting became increasingly more complex with progressively more father involvement and involvement of siblings, aunts, uncles, etc. (Campbell, 1979; White & Brown, 1973)
  3. incest was discouraged and exogamy probably practiced by time of *erectus* (Campbell, 1979)
  4. strict monogamy was probably not practiced but males and females were "partnered" (Campbell, 1979)
  5. extended and extensive kinship ties developed
  6. the "family" became less nomadic and more associated with a home base (Wymer, 1982)
  7. increased social interdependence—babies on mothers and vice-versa, mothers and fathers on each other, youngsters on adults, etc.(Campbell, 1979)
  8. increased control of aggression among family members

Other major achievements of hunting and gathering stage
  1. more refined sense of sharing and cooperation
  2. refinement of empathy and psychological mindedness
  3. more refined group organization—emergence of strong leaders (Wymer, 1982)
  4. emergence of "humanitarian tendencies"—concern for old, weak, crippled (Wymer, 1982)
  5. more elaborate clothing and adornment—clothing and adornment come to define social status and position
  6. increasing concern with death, burial, religion
  7. the emergence of artistic sensibility

be recovered in the regressive process. Particularly noteworthy in Table 4.10 is the dual nature of the human species—on the one hand, the primeval hunter-gatherer is a cooperative, sharing, and loving creature, whereas on the other he is a creature who makes a living through killing. This is the paradox of the carnivore—the largest and most powerful killers of prey are often the most gentle and group-centered of creatures in the areas of parenting and intraspecies social intercourse (Lorenz, 1967). Given that human nature is primarily defined by evolutionary innovations and elaborations during the hunting-gathering phase, we see that human nature is clearly dualistic, embracing cooperation and competition, in-group affections and out-group antipathies, and pacifism and contention at the same time. Should we be surprised, then, that a Mother Teresa and a Ted Bundy are both of the human race, or that a single individual can change from a peaceable, law-abiding citizen to a dangerous instrument of violence in a mere fraction of a second? We should not be surprised, for our very nature commands that we be that way.

In our deepest and most pathological regressions, the Platonian beast emerges again, but, fortunately, this rarely occurs. More often, we are likely to regress nonpathologically and often salubriously to our real hunter-gatherer selves in our dietetic preferences, our camping and fishing trips, our competitive athletic rituals, our elaborate courtship and mating rituals, our so-called "traditional" gender-based division of labor, our powerful attachments to kin and attraction to in-group collectives, our ways of training and socializing the young, our reliance on increasingly complex "tool technologies," and perhaps even our proclivity for religion. All of this means that the hunting and gathering phase produced a great amount of phylogenetic inertia whereby it is difficult, if not impossible, to totally escape or transcend the wired-in tendencies and predispositions of that period. Moreover, the greater the phylogenetic inertia in a given area, the greater the likelihood that phylogenetic regressions will gravitate to that area. Thus, we see that our hunting and gathering nature is extremely difficult to transcend to begin with, but once transcended the powers of regression are waiting in the wings. Indeed, much of the paleopsychology of human behavior is predicated upon progressions from and regressions to the hunting and gathering way of life.

Phylogenetic Regression
and Sex-Role Divergence

Human sex roles illustrate the theme of this chapter very well. Human phylogeny, as summarized in the foregoing tables, reveals that male and female roles have been highly and consistently divergent throughout most of human evolution. Therefore, we would expect modern trends toward androgyny, which represent advanced, learned deviations from the phylogenetic norm, to be fragile and transient acquisitions. "Traditional," or more phylogenetically based sex-role differences, would be expected to re-emerge frequently, particularly when survival threats (poverty, warfare, social disorganization, etc.) are involved. By virtue of phylogenetic inertia and phylogenetic regression, evolved sex roles are extremely difficult, if not impossible, to totally transcend, at least in any permanent sense.

As we recall from earlier discussions, phylogenetic regression is a general process that mainly reflects the MacLeanian psychoneural dynamics operating at a given moment, but it also involves elements of ontogenetic regression, hierarchic disintegration, primitivization of perception, emotion-controlled thinking, and so forth. Thus, when such regression brings older sex role differences to fore, it is in a dynamic, nonmechanical, and nonspecific way. One does not, for example, regress back to specific Neanderthal forms of maleness and femaleness, regress a little more to *erectus* forms, and so on; rather, as regression deepens, progressive losses at the neocortical and cultural levels occur, and proportionate gains are realized at the lower phylogenetic levels. The object is not to determine exactly where a person has regressed, but, rather, to estimate how much a person has regressed. This inferred quantity of regression embodies reduced cortical, self-conscious, and willed control on the one hand, and increased reliance on older, lesser learned, adaptive strategies on the other. In the regressive process, we behave more like our primate and hominid ancestors, but not exactly like any of them. Phylogenetic regression is predicated on approximation and not isomorphy.

What does all this mean for human sex roles? Perhaps the issue can be clarified if we compare and contrast regressive and progressive sex roles in contemporary humans. Our foregoing analysis of human evolution revealed widespread sexual asymmetry in prehuman primates and our hominid ancestors, and the parameters underlying this divergence have remained fairly stable throughout primate phylogeny: greater size and aggression in the male, greater sociality and reproductive-centeredness in the female, prominent differences in reproductive physiology, and so on. By virtue of culturally imposed sex-role customs and ideologies—most of which extend rather than transcend phylogeny—it sometimes appears that the older divergences have been lost. However, they have not disappeared, but merely lie dormant waiting to re-emerge at the first threat to survival. It follows, then, that men will tend to recover aggressiveness in the regressive process whereas women will tend to recover more in the way of affiliativeness or sociality. Of course, the situation is far more complex than this, and Table 4.11 outlines some of the intricate

TABLE 4.11
"Regressive" and "Progressive" Sex Role Characteristics in Contemporary Humans

Behavior		Regressive		Progressive
		Passive	Active	
Concern with	Females	High	Higher	Probably high; Possibly low
producing offspring	Males	High	Higher	Probably high; Possibly low
Concern with	Females	High	Higher	Probably high; Possibly low
rearing offspring	Males	Low	Lower	High for male mammal; Possibly low
Interest in	Females	High	Higher	High; Unlikely to be low
own baby	Males	Moderately low	?	High; Possibly low
Interest in	Females	High	Higher	High or low
other babies	Males	Low	Low	Possibly high; Generally low
Concern with	Females	High	Higher	Generally high; Possibly low
mate selection	Males	Moderately low	?	Generally high; Possibly low
Pursued as	Females	High	Higher	Generally high; Possibly low
sex object	Males	Low	Lower?	Possible high; Generally low
Tolerance of	Females	Moderately high	?	Moderately high; Possibly low
infidelity	Males	Low	Lower	Unlikely to be high
Multiple sex	Females	Moderately high	Higher	Low; Possibly high
partners	Males	Moderately high	Higher	Moderately high; Possibly low
Affiliativeness	Females	High	Higher?	High; Possibly low
and sociality	Males	Low	Lower	Low or moderately high
Domestic	Females	High	Higher?	Usually high; Possibly low
activities	Males	Moderately low	Low	Probably low; Possibly high
General agg.,	Females	Low	Lower	Low; Possibly moderately high
competitiveness	Males	High	Higher	High or moderately high
Dominance	Females	Low	Lower	Possibly high; Low
agg., power	Males	High	Higher	High; Rarely low
Predatory	Females	Low	Lower	Low; Rarely high
agg., "hunting"	Males	High	Higher	Generally high; Possibly low
Defense of	Females	Low	?	Low; Possibly high
group	Males	High	Higher	High; Rarely low
Alpha leader	Females	Low	Lower	Low; Higher in recent years
role	Males	High	Higher	High or low
Yield dominance	Females	High	Higher	Generally high; Low
to opp. sex	Males	Low	Lower	Low; Rarely high
General activity	Female	Low	Lower	Low or high
level	Males	High	?	Generally high; Low
Exploratory	Females	Low	Lower	Low; Possibly high
behavior	Males	High	?	High or moderately high
Geographic	Females	High	Higher	High or low
restrictedness	Males	Low	Lower	Low or high

Note: This table is theoretically-based but is subject to empirical verification. This issue is addressed in detail in a later chapter.

Passive regression = loss of neocortical inhibition leading to reversion to "natural" sex roles

Active regression = neocortical augmentation of reversion to "natural" sex roles.

High = *relatively* frequent in expression for sex in question

Low = *relatively* infrequent in expression for sex in question relationships between the old and new for males and females from the standpoint of the phylogenetic regression-progression model.

To clarify Table 4.11, the reader is reminded that passive regression refers to more or less automatic, natural recovery of phylogenetically older predispositions and patterns under stress or other elicitors, that the active form refers to neocortical facilitation and augmentation of the regressive process (e. g., reinforcement of natural sex roles with cultural stereotyping, "traditional" role modeling, etc.), and that progression refers to the achievement of relative independence from the lower centers through the exercise of intellect and imagination. Theoretically, it follows that active regression would usually yield the greatest recovery of older patterns, because the neocortex willingly abdicates its normal control functions and actively allies itself with the animal emotions and drives. Accordingly, the largest sex-role differences are found in the Active Regression column in Table 4.11. By contrast, virtually all of the cross-sex similarities and behavioral convergences are under the Progressive column, which underlines our theoretical premise that primitiveness is associated with sex-role divergence, whereas advancedness can go in either direction depending on socialization practices and cultural programming.

Of the various behaviors listed in Table 4.11, dominance stands out as an excellent choice to illustrate regression-progression issues in sex-role divergence. As shown, females are rated low in dominance in both the passive and active regression categories, but it can go either way at the higher progressive levels depending on what is reinforced and deemed desirable in a particular culture. Even in egalitarian societies, however, phylogenetic inertia restricts large gains in dominance for females, as Tiger and Shepher (1975) revealed in their sociological study of women in the kibbutz. The kibbutz movement showed a great upsurge in the 1940s and 1950s and its leaders pursued a policy of complete sexual equality and freedom from sex-role restrictions. The first generation of women quickly moved into the heretofore male bastions of politics, management, and labor, but as Wilson (1978) observed "they and their daughters have *regressed* somewhat toward traditional roles, despite being trained from birth in the new culture" (p. 134; italics added). This reversion seemed to be based more on a desire to return to phylogenetically conditioned maternal, nurturant roles than it was an avoidance of dominance conflict or lack of ability to compete with men. Pure and simply, it was more pleasurable (see chapters 5 & 8) for many of the women to emphasize parenting and domestic involvement than to participate in the power structure or to pursue dominance as an end in itself.

Males, by contrast, seem compelled to pursue dominance and power irrespective of cultural conditioning, even when survival and economic stresses are minimal. Under circumstances of wealth and abundance, men do not happily retreat from dominance conflict, but instead construct for themselves "artificial status races" to structure their extra leisure time (Maclay & Knipe, 1972). It seems that dominance seeking is a cardinal pleasure and pastime and indeed a veritable obsession for the male of the species, whereas power for power's sake is more likely viewed with nonchalance, disdain, and puzzlement by the human female. Given the evolutionary argument for the phylogenetic-rootedness of this major sex difference (Freedman, 1979; Savin-Williams & Freedman, 1977; van den Berghe, 1979; Wilson, 1978), we see that passive phylogenetic regression would tend the man toward greater and the woman toward lesser expressions of dominance behavior. At the ideological-progressive level of functioning, men and women may believe in dominance equality, and actually may achieve it in a tenuous way, but tension, pressure, or provocation make it ever so easy to slip back into older gender-divergent strategies.

When male dominance and female nurturance are not merely passively accepted but actively supported and reinforced by cultural pressure, then we have active phylogenetic regression. It is this kind of extreme and often stifling sex-role divergence that has been the target of feminists and other civil rights groups in recent years. Although mistaken in their view that sex roles are nothing more than the product of arbitrary socialization practices, feminists are correct in their assertion that rigid and exaggerated sex-role stereotyping is undesirable and unhealthy from the standpoints of personal growth and self-expression. However, such unhealthy extremes cannot be attributed totally to domineering men who force compulsive masculinity on themselves and submissive femininity on women; much more important is the readiness in both sexes to regress deeper into the pleasure and security of biological gender when culture allows it, or moreover, encourages it.

Social sicentists often belittle or ignore the biology of sex differences (Durden-Smith & deSimone, 1983), but politicians, propagandists, and advertisers are quick to exploit the inherent differences between male and female. Such exploitation represents one of the myriad of ways that most cultures—including our own—conspire with phylogeny to keep the sexes well within their phylogenetically conditioned and adaptive role limits. This reasoning helps explain, for example, the paradox that "millions of American women spend billions of dollars in response to TV and magazine ads that make them feel stupid and worthless" (Callen, 1980, p. 5). On June 25th, 1980, Dr. Muriel Cantor, a sociologist at American University and a noted scholar of the media and television, held a seminar in Washington, DC, entitled, "The Portrayal of Women in the Media" (Callen, 1980). She pointed out that advertising is a $40 billion a year industry that directs much of its efforts toward women. According to Cantor, many of the ads suggest that women should strive toward two ideals: one, the eternally young sex object (see Symonds, 1979) with no wrinkles, skin pores, or facial expression, and, second, the "moronic housewife who is obsessed with cleanliness." Clearly, advertisers know what appeals to the lower levels of consciousness (Key, 1974, 1981), and even for relatively liberated American women, the older modalities of sexual attraction and domestic success remain powerful sources of motivation as they were for our ancestors in the hunting and gathering period. We see here, as with the kibbutzim experiments, that the forces of culture are extremely effective when they support or augment pre-existing sex-role characteristics, but it is quite another matter when culture attempts to alter or eradicate characteristics that are correlated with reproductive success and heavily rooted in phylogeny.

The previous argument does not assume that traditional sex roles must forever remain the same nor that men and women will necessarily passively or actively regress when their newfound liberation is tested by threats to survival. What the argument does imply, however, is that rising above the older roles will be difficult, and a great amount of phylogenetic inertia must be overcome in the process. An additional complication is that female dominance itself constitutes a threat to men, and once this threat reaches sufficient intensity, men characteristically revert to physical violence to re-establish dominance. As Wilson (1978) states, "The physical and temperamental differences between men and women have been amplified by culture into universal male dominance. History records not a single society in which women have controlled the political and economic lives of men. Even when queens and empresses ruled, their intermediaries remained primarily male" (p. 128). Yet a page later Wilson says that societies could probably cancel the modest genetic differences between the sexes through careful planning, but we do not know at present how to go about it. Whatever we do, our strategy will have to take into account the natural divergence of the sexes and the ready willingness of men to employ physical violence to maintain male dominance. To do so will require a fuller understanding of the phylogenetically regressive processes operating, often in complementary fashion, in both sexes.

The Question of Human Distinctiveness

The question of human distinctiveness is addressed at numerous junctures in the chapters to follow, but a brief word on the subject is an appropriate way to end this chapter. As we have seen, the human species differs in many ways from nonhuman primates and from the early ape-men and man-apes, but not because we are phylogenetically distinctive to any great degree. As biochemical genetics has shown (see chapter 6, and Passingham, 1982), the human species is very similar to the chimpanzee and gorilla in DNA and blood proteins, but it is obvious that we look differently, act differently, and possess cognitive capacities far beyond those of our primate cousins. But exactly what is unique about the human species? We certainly have large, complexly organized brains, and highly specialized neocortices that mediate language, abstract thought, and refined self-consiousness, but that is not the whole story. Modern humans developed culture to its highest form, and through recorded knowledge and powerful techniques of socialization, each person is controlled from within (natural, basically unlearned cortical controls), and from without (pressure to conform to group, obey rules, etc.). We humans are, thus, both cortical and cortically supplemented beings. But there is even more to the human animal: Below our over-developed neocortices lies the limbic and reptilian systems that provide much of the motive force of behavior. Where amid the complex interlocking systems is our distinctiveness to be found?

Experts have labored long on the question of human distinctiveness, and one of the better efforts is a paper by Richard Alexander and Katherine Noonan (1979). They list and discuss a number of putative distinctive human attributes shown in Table 4.12. The first five attributes listed are those seen by many writers as unique to the human species, but Alexander and Noonan point out that all occur in other primates, and chimpanzees alone may possess all five, although not in the form nor to the degree that they are expressed in humans. There do appear to be a number of distinctive human traits, or traits distinctively expressed in humans as compared to other primates, and these may be either *cultural* or *noncultural* or *universal* or *nonuniversal* (see Table 4.12).

Several important conclusions follow from Alexander and Noonan's list of 30 attributes. First, most of the distinctive attributes are sexually asymmetrical or involve special interactions between the sexes: "They [attributes] suggest that the human male is not particularly unusual among the primate males, except that he is generally more parental than the males of other group living species. On the other hand, the human female is distinctive in several regards, most dramatically in undergoing menopause and concealment of ovulation" (Alexander & Noonan, 1979, p. 436). Second, the authors say that these and several other distinctive attributes for both sexes (e. g., length of juvenile life and helplessness of the young) indicate that increasing emphasis on parental care was one of the major accomplishments of human evolution. Third, it seems that few attributes are both distinctive (d) and noncultural (nc), meaning that few of the traits are predominantly phylogenetically determined ones. Aside from attributes 5 (longer juvenile life) and 13 through 16 (distinctive

TABLE 4.12
Alexander and Noonan's List of "Distinctively Human Attributes"

1. Consciousness (self-awareness)
2. Foresight (deliberate planning, hope, purpose, death-awareness)
3. Facility in the development and use of tools (implying consciousness and foresight)
4. Facility in the use of language and symbols in communication (implying consciousness and foresight)
5. Culture (a cumulative body of traditionally transmitted learning—including language and tools, and involving the use of consciousness and foresight)
6. Upright locomotion usual (de, nc, u, s)
7. Frontal copulation usual (de, c & nc, u, as)
8. Relative hairlessness (de, nc, u, as)
9. Longer juvenile life (d, nc, u, as)
10. Greater infantile helplessness (de, nc, u, as)
11. Parental care frequently extending into and even across the offspring's adult life (d, c, u?, as)
12. Unusually extensive parental care for a group-living primate (de, c?, nu?, as)
13. Concealed ovulation in females (sometimes described as continuous sexual receptivity, continuous estrus, "sham" estrus, or lack of estrus (d, nc, u, as)
14. Greater prominence of female orgasm (d, nc?, u, as)
15. Unusually copious menstrual discharge (d, nc, u, as)
16. Menopause (d, nc, u, as)
17. Close association of close kin of both sexes, sometimes throughout adulthood (de, c, u?, as)
18. Extensive extrafamilial nepotism (de, c, u?, as)
19. Extensive extrafamilial mating restrictions (de, c, u?, as)
20. Socially imposed monogamy (d, c, nu, as)
21. Extreme flexibility in rates of forming and dissolving coalitions (d, c, u, as)
22. Systems of laws imposed by the many (or powerful) against the few (or weak) (d, c, nu, as)
23. Extensive, organized, intergroup aggression; war (d, c, u?, as)
24. Group-against-group competition in play (d, c, u?, as)
25. Ancestor worship (d, c, nu, as)
26. Political and other kinds of appointed, elected, or hereditarily succeeding leaders (d, c, nu, as)
27. The concepts of gods and life-after-death (d, c, nu, as)
28. Organized religion (d, c, nu, as)
29. Nationalism; patriotism (d, c, nu, as)
30. Polities of thousands or millions of nuclear families (d, c, nu,s)

Note: Attributes 1-5 are those considered distinctively human by most writers; however, Alexander and Noonan (1979) say that none of these five are exclusively human characteristics. They code attributes 6-30 the following way:

(d) = distinctive to humans
(de) = distinctively expressed
(u) = universal among humans
(nu) = nonuniversal among humans
(c) = basically cultural in origin
(nc) = noncultural in origin
(s) = attribute is sexually symmetrical
(as) = attribute is sexually asymmetrical

This table is a modified version of material in Alexander and Noonan (1979). Reprinted by permission.

reproductive attributes of females), most are culturally loaded in one way or another. It seems, then, that we transcended the animals by virtue of culture, and not so much by biological evolution. In other words, our basic natures differ little from other nonhuman primates, and we must therefore look to culture for our uniqueness. Or, more accurately, we should look to how culture has elaborated and extended the basic structures, tendencies, and dispositions that we share so fully with lower species (see chapters 8 and 9).

SUMMARY

The regression-progression continuum is similar to the concept of behavioral scale described by Wilson (1975). The behavioral scale is a species-specific, genetically based range of responsivity from which a given animal draws to adapt to a changing environment. Humans no doubt possess phylogenetically conditioned scales as do other animals, and happiness and health may be contingent upon staying within these naturally scaled limits. Although similar in many ways, the phylogenetic regression-progression continuum differs from behavioral scaling in several respects: (a) it deals with individuals rather than populations; (b) it emphasizes the immediate, total functioning of the organism rather than single response systems such as territorial defense or parenting behavior; and (c) its limits (especially upper limits) are defined, to a great extent, by the individual's intelligence.

An empirically derived scale was described that was designed to operationalize the phylogenetic regression-progression continuum in psychometric terms. Following an elaborate selection procedure, a 7-point scale was chosen with the phrase "Gut Level Experiencing" describing the primitive pole, and "Involves Detached Objective Thinking" describing the advanced pole. This scale has proved to be reliable and effective in assessing the "primitiveness" and "advancedness" of pleasures and aversions in college students (Bailey, Burns, & Bazan, 1982; Bailey & Millbrook, 1984; Bazan, 1980; Burns, 1979, 1984), and appears to have considerable research potential in many other areas as well. According to phylogenetic regression-progression theory, virtually any behavior can be viewed in terms of its primitiveness or advancedness, and the present scale represents one way to address the problem.

Movement up and down the regression-progression continuum implies that the content of behavior varies with the process. That is, phylogenetically lower kinds of behavior are emitted when we regress, and higher forms emerge when we progress up the scale. The issue becomes, then, one of defining what lower and higher mean. One approach is to perform a rough losses and gains analysis on the primate phylogenetic ladder. Based on what we know about primate phylogeny, we may ask for example, "Exactly what physical and mental characteristics were lost in the transition from *Homo erectus* to Neanderthal, and what characteristics were gained?" With each new gain the continuum is extended at the upper pole and new behavioral content is added to the species repertoire. We must remember, however, that human evolution is characterized by few true "losses" or "gains." More often, new structures or processes are built upon old ones, and the gain is really an amalgram of the old and the new.

To facilitate comparative content analysis, a series of summary tables is provided going all the way from reptilian species up to modern hominids. Although sketchy, these summaries helped dramatize some of the specific losses and gains that have characterized the ascent of man. Perusal of the summaries shows that the slow, treacherous march toward humanhood was the consequence of many factors, but advances in brain size and organization were particularly crucial. As we proceed from *Australopithecus* to *habilis* or *erectus,* and then on to the modern hominids Neanderthal and Cro-Magnon, we see remarkable advances in numerous areas: reproductive, male-female, and parenting behavior; social organization and self-control; tool-making and technology; art, aesthetic sensitivity, and a fuller appreciation of the world; concern with the afterlife and religion; and, of course, language and symbolic thought. These great achievements were due primarily to progressive evolutionary changes in the brain that occurred in the process of hominidization. Among these changes were: (a) increased overall brain growth; (b) accelerated neocortical growth; (c) increased neocortical control over the lower centers; (d) more intensive cultural programming of the neocortex; and (e) better integration of all these variables.

The greatest advances in human evolution occurred during the 1 to 3 million-year hunting and gathering phase. The hunting and gathering modality represented the primary eco-behavioral medium within which natural selection exerted its shaping effects on our ancestors. Beginning perhaps as far back as *afarensis* and reaching its acme with *erectus,* the hunting and gathering way served as the evolutionary bridge from animal to human, and represents the single most important defining element of human nature. Approximately 99% of human evolution occurred during the hunting and gathering phase, and to this phase we owe much of our intelligence and cognitive skills, technological mentality, refined capacity for family and kinship, sex-role characteristics, capacity for complex and coordinated social and political arrangements, and our psychological-mindedness and ability to empathize with others. The hunting and gathering phase endowed us with many important tendencies and predispositions, producing a great amount of phylogenetic inertia. Given this inertia, it has been extremely difficult for we humans to phylogenetically progress beyond our hunting and gathering characters, and it is to these characters that we most frequently regress under stress or provocation.

Sex-role divergence was one of the primary precipitates of the hunting and gathering phase. Consequently, this variable was chosen for detailed analysis from the standpoint of the phylogenetic regression-progression model. This analysis was premised on the assumption that movement down the continuum leads to natural divergence of sex roles, whereas progress up the scale allows for greater diversity of roles. Actually, the picture is more complicated than this, especially because people can actively as well as passively regress. In the former type, the neocortex actively supports the regression, and in the latter type it merely steps aside and allows older motives to return. It logically follows, then, that active phylogenetic regression leads to unnaturally divergent roles where sex-role stereotyping and cultural pressure accentuate pre-existing, phylogenetically conditioned tendencies. It also follows that sex-diversity and cross-sex similarities are most probable under progressive circumstances where the neocortex is relatively free from subcortical interference. The various theoretical possibilities involving active and passive regression and progression are detailed in Table 4.11.

The tabular summaries also show that modern humans are not phylogenetically distinctive to any large degree, aside from superior brain power. As Alexander and Noonan (1979) have argued, even language, foresight, tool use and culture are shared with the chimpanzee. They do point out, however, that many human characteristics are distinctively expressed; in other words, we humans often do the same things our primate cousins do (reproduce, protect our young, develop dominance hierarchies, fear strangers, etc.), but we do them in more elaborate and complex ways. Only longer juvenile life and certain reproductive attributes in women (concealed ovulation, orgasmic capacity, copious menstrual discharge, and menopause) appear truly new phylogenetic advances. Interestingly, this implies that women have progressed farther from the apes than men—at least in terms of reproductive physiology. However, far more important than these few "distinctive" characteristics are the seemingly limitless ways we distinctively express and culturally extend our primate heritage.

5

Fundamental Paleopsychology:
Correlates and Consequences
of Phylogenetic Regression

*I have endeavoured to show that no absolute structural line
of demarcation, wider than that between the animals which
immediately succeed us in the scale, can be drawn between
the animal world and ourselves; and I may add the expression of my belief that the attempt to draw a psychical
distinction is equally futile, and that even the highest faculties of feeling and intellect begin to germinate in lower
forms of life.*

—Huxley (1896, p. 152)

CORRELATES

Overview

In preceding chapters, we reviewed 19th century theories of atavism and
reversion, discussed recent trends in the New Biology, defined the
phylogenetic regression-progression model and compared it to similar
concepts, described and analyzed the regression-progression continuum
in reference to the progressive stages of human evolution, and applied our
newfound insights to the questions of human distinctiveness and sex-role
divergence. We saw that simple bioevolutionary, genetic, behavioral,
situational, learning, or cultural explanations, when taken singly, are
incapable of grasping the most rudimentary realities of immediate experi-

ence. Not only does reality embrace all these variables simultaneously in response output, it is accomplished smoothly, continuously, and dynamically. This is not to say, however, that the human being is a chaotic collection of cells or that behavior is inherently unpredictable or unlawful. Order can indeed be found in human behavior, but it is a relativistic, probabilistic order; we cannot predict exactly what a person will do at a given moment although we may surmise what is likely with some degree of accuracy.

· Possibly the most important element in predicting behavioral likelihoods is having a thorough knowledge of an organism's essential characteristics—its morphology, neurobiochemical makeup, phylogenetic behavioral programming, current biological state, ecological pressures, learning history, and so forth. Failure to take all of the organism's essential characters into account in explanation or prediction will necessarily lead to incomplete knowledge and incomplete understanding. By this criterion behavioral scientists have failed rather badly in studying the human animal, especially where phylogenetic programming and ecological considerations are concerned. Consequently, we have failed to confront the primitive, irrational, sometimes "animalistic" side of human nature by viewing ourselves as fully and sublimely "human" in all respects—creatures of will and intellect capable of mastering our passions and rendering the phylogenetic past irrelevant and obsolete. Phylogenetic regression-progression theory makes no such presumptions and asks, rather, "in what ways have eons of natural selection acting upon structure and function, morphology and behavior, come to exert influence upon modern man?" Moreover, "How is the essential nature of modern man influenced by paleopsychological carry-overs from the dim phylogenetic past," and, "What are some of the things that happen when a person phylogenetically regresses"? We turn now to the correlates and consequences of phylogenetic regression.

Primitivization of Consciousness

Primitivization of consciousness is one of the main correlates of phylogenetic regression. As with the concept of intelligence (see chapter 3), however, the problem of definition is a serious one. In *An Essay Concerning Human Understanding,* John Locke (1690/1952) defined *consciousness* basically as the perception of what goes on in one's own mind. For Locke, consciousness was essentially introspection, or reflection upon the internal processes and operations of the mind. By such means a person acquires the "ideas" of perceiving, thinking, doubting, reasoning, knowing, and willing, and by which the self and world are known and understood. Locke was little interested in the physical structure of the mind, or the essence of consciousness; rather, he concentrated on the process whereby ideas are generated and associated with each other in the mind. Simply speaking, the mind is initially furnished with ideas through sensations or sensory perceptions of objects in the external environment. Once the mind is sufficiently furnished, new ideas occur internally through reflection on pre-existing simple ideas and the combining of simple ideas into complex ones.

Locke's view of mind and consciousness was and continues to be exceptionally influential in the predominantly empiricist, associationist, English-speaking world. With its singular emphasis on function to the exclusion of structure, Locke's formulation represented a repudiation of Descartes' earlier doctrine of innate ideas and also succeeded in avoiding the mind-body dilemma. Prior to Locke, Descartes had dominated the philosophy of mind with his view that animals were automata and man alone possessed a true conscious soul: "The greatest of all prejudices we have retained from our infancy is that of believing that beasts think" (quoted in Wells, Huxley, & Wells, 1934, p. 1273). In Descartes' philosophy, human mind and consciousness were not only fully separated from the animal world, they were generally separate and distinct from the working of the body itself. The mind is a pure and God-given substance that interacts with, or forms a "substantial union" with the body in various poorly understood ways. Even though some interplay between the mundane body and transcendent soul was conceded, the latter was the truly human character.

Although Locke and Descartes disagreed on most matters pertaining to human consciousness, they fully agreed on one issue—the fundamental significance of thinking in defining the essence of humanness. Whether it be called *thinking* or *reflection*,—or to use de Chardin's (1959) favorite metaphor, "The power acquired by a consciousness to turn in upon itself" (p. 165)—most writers agree that advanced forms of cognition clearly separate man from animal. As Jaynes (1976) avers, higher consciousness is primarily verbally mediated and metaphorical in humans, but we may speak of lower levels operating within the process of sensation, perception, and the immediate sense of awareness or being (Crook, 1980). To merely perceive and experience the world about us, and to even enjoy a rudimentary self-awareness, is not to rise a great degree from the higher animals; indeed, some see animals as having extremely rich perceptual worlds, or unwelts (von Uexküll, 1909). However, to logically analyze, reflect upon, and philosophize about the world is to use our brains and consciousness to the fullest for the most human endeavor, the performance of intellectual work. Thus, intelligence and consciousness, as defined in the present book, are not separate and distinct, but are the intermixed, quintessential defining elements of our species.

Despite definitional problems and the perennial mind-body dilemma, we may safely presume that richness of consciousness increases as we ascend the phylogenetic scale (Boddy, 1978; de Chardin, 1959), that consciousness is correlated with brain size and function (Jerison, 1973), and that mental experience and awareness in humans are phylogenetically continuous with analogous precesses in lower animals (Crook, 1980; Darwin, 1871/1981; Hobhouse, 1901; Razran, 1971; Romanes, 1888). Contrary to the age-old solipsistic prejudices of humankind, consciousness, in some form and degree, exists in other animals and is not the sole possession of our species. It follows, then, that if richness of consciousness correlates with the phylogenetic scale, and if mental experience and awareness are continuous between man and animal, then we have yet another hierarchical scale to progress up and regress down. Human consciousness may thus be viewed as primitive or advanced, regressive or progressive, depending on its manifestation at a given time.

The concepts of consciousness and hierarchy seem to enjoy a natural affinity, as we see in Razran's (1971) hierarchy of awareness, affects, images, and meanings, or in Griffin's (1976) hierarchically arranged components of mental experience. Griffin places consciousness at the acme of his hierarchy, as shown in Table 5.1. It is noteworthy that Griffin lists consciousness as the ultimate taboo in humans—that putatively exclusive characteristic that we most resist sharing with animals. From the standpoint of human intuition, it is perfectly permissible to share lower functions like pattern recognition, affect, expectancy, or even feeling with animals, but mind, will, and consciousness are ours alone. Unfortunately, such presumed discontinuities at higher levels are neither logically nor empirically defensible. Rather than asserting that humans have certain mental capacities that are entirely absent in lower species, it seems more reasonable and heuristically expedient to assume phylogenetic continuity for even our most cherished higher faculties of self-awareness, consciousness, and thought. Indeed, the richness of human experience and thought is probably due to the fact that cognition and consciousness embody the phylogenetically old and new in infinite variation, not in spite of it.

The relationship between phylogenetic regression and consciousness may be illustrated with the postulated aggression hierarchy discussed at various points in this volume and elsewhere (e.g., chapters 2 & 10; Bailey, 1985). Proceeding from the logic of the phylogenetic regression-progression continuum, the aggression hierarchy might go like this: undifferentiated rage→predatory aggression→dominance aggression→assertiveness→intellectual aggression→mastery. At the lower pole of undifferentiated rage, the neurological centers controlling behavior would be phylogenetically older ones, and cortical inhibition, self-awareness, and consciousness would be at a minimum. A person experiencing over-powering

TABLE 5.1
Griffin's Hierarchy of Mental Experience

Advanced Mental Characters: Taboo to Share with Animals

consciousness
free will
choice
thought
mind (mental)
mental experience
awareness
feeling
intention
understanding
concept
internal image
covert verbal behavior
expectancy
spontaneity
affect
search image
sollwert
neural template
pattern recognition

Primitive Mental Characters: Acceptable to Share with Animals

Note: Adapted from *The question of animal awareness: Evolutionary continuity of mental experience,* 1976, by copyright permission of The Rockefeller University Press.

rage would, of course, not literally metamorphose into a hairy animal or Mr. Hyde, but the older, more primitive systems would virtually dominate the newer, cortical ones, and consciousness of oneself and the immediate surroundings would be severely diminished.

As we proceed up the scale to predatory and dominance aggression, factors like learning, awareness, and self-control enter in, but a heavy instinctual component remains. The "predatory" criminal who "hunts," lies in wait for his victim, and then attacks, is, of course, conscious of his actions to a degree, but the powerful irrational urges operating overshadow the cognitive component. In other words, the regressive elements are the determining ones in such behavior. At the next stage, we see that dominance aggression takes many forms—winning a contest, getting promoted, having a larger car than the Jones' and so forth—but underlying each is an instinctive motive component rooted in phylogeny. It is well-known that the dominance, status, and ranking motif is seen throughout the animal kingdom and reaches full flower in the primates (see chapter 11).

Phylogenetic regression theory assumes that this upward thrust provides much of the motive force for even refined dominance behaviors like winning a debate or getting your work published before another. In the midst of a challenging exchange of ideas, the ideas often become lost in the challenge; a specific idea that may be subjected to exquisite conscious reflection in a relaxed context, loses its coherence and reality when emotion (e.g., the need to win, prevail) takes over. Likewise, the heights of refined consciousness reached in writing one's masterwork fade into the background at the victorious moment when prizes, recognition, promotion, or winning over detractors or competitors enters the picture. Rather than consciousness turning in on itself for reflection, it is more often buffeted to and fro by the hedonic and self-aggrandizing motive forces of the subneocortical centers.

Moving up to the next level, assertiveness, we see a substantial increase in the cortical component and a diminution in the limbic-affective dominance component. Still, even in assertiveness, with its self-conscious strictures about fairplay and propriety, a certain motive force remains. Assertiveness presumably builds upon and emanates from the older dominance complex, but the heavy cognitive and ideological element masks this regressive aspect except for the keen observer. Assertive persons generally pride themselves in being "nonaggressive," "respecting the rights of others," "being able to say 'no,' " and so forth, and they view the assertive encounter in highly intellectualized terms. They seem to be conscious of all ramifications and implications of the encounter, except why it is so important to them that they be assertive! The extreme need to be assertive requires explanation, and that is where the older, regressive component comes in.

At the level of intellectual aggression, the infusion of lower motives is even more difficult to detect in oneself and others. Professors and intellectuals, for example, often convince themselves that vigorous attacks on the theories or research findings of others are solely based on the most honorable motives, and they are seldom conscious of the roles that competing for priority, professional envy, and one-upmanship may play in the process. Not infrequently, anonymous journal reviewers will indulge in pomposity and bullying tactics, and editors sometimes seem to enjoy a little too much the mighty powers accorded to them—rationalizations of hard-mindedness or quality control often seem insufficient to explain the motive force behind such forms of intellectual aggression. Similarly, we have all witnessed situations where guest speakers or lecturers have been gleefully "torn to shreds" and humiliated by audiences whose motives seemed to involve more than a dispassionate search for truth. Indeed, young applicants for assistant professorships often are required to go through a stress test sanguinely referred to as the "required research colloquim," a process not unlike the feared doctoral oral examination. In moments of deep reflection, senior faculty members may be mildly conscious of the fact that they enjoy the role of inquisitor and having the career of another in their hands, but the insight passes quickly.

Finally, at the level of mastery we see primate dominance at minimum and cultural man in full dress uniform marching to the drums of achievement and progress. To the cultured, educated person of the 20th century, the pursuit of change and progress are self-evident goals requiring little justification; we are, indeed, duty-bound to combat the evils and adversities that surround us—hunger, poverty, ignorance, disease, warfare, waste, pollution, and so on, *ad infinitum*. Yet, even at this high level of abstraction and ideology, a smidgeon of the primate dominance complex remains. This phylogenetic residue is heavily masked by a multitude of complex cognitions, but underneath it all is the older, omnipresent need to win, to prevail, to bring Mother Nature to her knees. Not surprisingly, this obsessive need to prevail over nature seems to be considerably more well-developed in men than in women (de Riencourt, 1974). Paradoxically, as our consciousnesses have been raised and decoupled (Alexander, 1979) from our phylogenetic roots, the problems seem to have gotten worse rather than better. Human consciousness and intelligence, when separated from the phylogenetic wisdom of the past, often become unwitting enemies of the natural order of things. By definition, the higher our consciousnesses are raised, the more alienated we become from our animal heritage, our phylogenetic past. We see here what is, perhaps, the fundamental dilemma of our technological age.

Before leaving the topic of consciousness, a word should be said about unconscious motivation, thoughts, images, and perceptions. Given that we are primarily creatures of reptilian automaticity and limbic emotionality, and further that our day-to-day adaptive behavior seems to emanate more from our primate heritage and millions of years in the hunting and gathering modality than our conscious will, it follows that exquisite consciousness is a rare thing in humans. How often do we really understand or perceive why we love, hate, act irrationally, or choose a red dress over a white one? Human consciousness is analogous to the captain of a 100-ton vessel who can do little directly to guide the ship to its proper destination; instead, the captain, as an absurdly small energy source, must rely on more powerful energy sources (e.g., the crew and the dynamic design characteristics of the vessel) over which he has few direct perceptual or behavioral links. We humans, first of all, have little access to the inner mechanics of the motives, feelings, and thoughts that guide us to our destinations, but, more importantly, we seldom ponder those things that are accessible to us. It seems that we exist in relative degrees of unconsciousness rather than consciousness, but with considerable effort and education we are capable of occasionally turning our minds back on ourselves for objective self-observation.

In summary, phylogenetic regression and consciousness are related in a fundamental, theoretically important way: Movement toward the advanced pole brings with it a flexible, refined, and sensitive awareness of oneself in the world, both in the concrete and abstract senses; by contrast, regression produces a diminished sense of the social self and the cultural environment, but a heightened awareness of bodily needs, urges, and imperatives. Once again, we see the fundamental antithesis of thought and feeling, intellect and emotion, in slightly different terms.

Reduced Inhibition

Reduced inhibition is another correlate of the regressive process. By virtue of learned social and moral proscriptions, rules of etiquette, and obeisance to the abstractions of law, justice, rightousness, and the like, modern humans lead a generally constrained and ordered existence. Were it not for these reliably imposed inhibitions, society would quickly degenerate into chaos and disarray. Even with order imposed upon us at every turn by parents, peers, teachers, institutions, government, policing agents, and such, slippage and breakdowns occur with regularity. Due to the population and information explosions, crowding, dwindling resources, environmental degradation, and many other ecological stresses and imbalances, breakdown of internal and/or external inhibitions has become a greater problem now than in any time in human history.

As Midgley (1980) tells us, primitive man possessed natural inhibitions against things like cold-blooded homocide, severe neglect of infants or rebellion against authority, but these controls were weak and unreliable. Our weak paleopsychological inhibitions must thus be cortically supplemented by powerful cultural programming and external controlling agents if modern society is to exist. The phylogenetically advanced person is, therefore, one who exerts mental control over his own impulses and is able to successfully traverse a variety of socially defined situations; the regressed person, by contrast, has less control over behaviors emitted or roles played, and must rely, instead, on genetically conditioned tendencies and dispositions. Take, for example, the gastronomic habits of the advanced and regressed person. Our hypothetical, well-fed, portly, and probably priviledged "advanced" person typically makes a major production of food consumption—just the right entree and courses must be chosen, the guests must be properly matched, the wine served at just the right temperature, and all amenities observed throughout. The whole production may take from 1 to 3 hours, while actual food consumption is limited to minutes. The regressed person—who needs food for survival of self and kin—pursues nutrition with consistency and desperation. With survival at stake, there is no time for frills and frivolity—his quest is direct and unerring, a virtual compulsion over which he has little or no control. We recall the tragic effect on the social behavior of the Ik, an African pygmy tribe numbering 2,500 or so, when bare subsistence gave way to starvation: social structures collapsed, brother was set against brother, and affectional relations all but disappeared (Turnbull, 1972). Rasmussen (1931) describes how hunting was a never-ending pursuit for the subsistence-level Netsilik Eskimos: "The man that is wise never lolls about idle when the weather is good; he can never know when bad days may eat of his meat caches, and drive him and his family into starvation" (p. 134). The point here is that the fundamental causes of behavior—the interacting motivational and inhibitory systems involved in a behavioral act—are both qualitatively and quantitatively different in regressive and progressive states. Most notably absent in severely regressed actions are the learned values and inhibitions that normally keep tight rein on the lower instincts. Meerlo (1967) says it very well: "The tolerance for frustration and inhibition in man is of the highest importance. It is the only way to learn to control the animal reactions and to develop a moral society. Moral examples teach us to sublimate our animal past" (p. 11).

Along with diminished inhibition in regressed states, there appear to be reduced latencies in response to phylogenetically conditioned stimuli or *releasers,* to use the ethological term. For example, Ellsworth, Carlsmith, and Henson (1972), demonstrated reduced latencies for flight behavior in response to a stranger's stare, and Bailey, Tipton, and Taylor (1977) showed that a threatening stare involving postural, facial, and eye-contact components produced immediate escape behavior in profoundly retarded adult patients. Van Hooff (1967) and many primatologists agree that the threatening stare is a releaser in most if not all primates, including the human being, and this makes the aforementioned findings especially provocative. It seems reasonable to assume that other equally strong releasing stimuli in sexual and aggressive areas would produce a similar speed of response effect in human beings (see chapter 6).

Along with reduced inhibition and immediacy of response, we may expect our primitive animal side to produce more extreme, all-or-none (Werner, 1948) forms of responding in terms of physiological arousal, motoric output, and motivational level. Extremity of response is most clearly observed when the person's survival is threatened by physical danger. It is here that fight or flight supercedes all other considerations, and as Schur (1958, 1960) and Wickler (1972) point out, danger is a major stimulus for the more extreme forms of regression in both humans and animals. When faced with extreme and lethal danger, the person responds in a holistic fashion, bringing into play an integrated system of attack, defense, and flight responses. In the fight or flight situation we see phylogenetic regression most clearly, with its diminished inhibitions, reduced response latencies, minimal cognitive mediation of behavior, extreme all-or-none responding, and high energy mobilization. All of this is to be expected, of course, if increasing proportions of emotionality are elicited in phylogenetic regression, as was argued in chapter 3.

Evolved Behavior Patterns

Segments and part-segments of evolved behavioral patterns are elicited in phylogenetic regression that intermix with the highly energized motivational and affective components called into play (see chapter 8). These so-called *fixed-action patterns* are, thus, not elicited in pure form, but are rather part of the motivational-emotional-behavioral primitivization that occurs in phylogenetic regression. There are a number of evolved behavioral patterns to draw from, in addition to the elaborate and highly coordinated patterns of nonverbal communication discussed in the next section. For example, the sucking and rooting reflex has an innate basis (Eibl-Eibesfeldt, 1970) as apparently does the smile (Gray, 1958; Hass, 1970). To these we might add the vicissitudes of sexual foreplay and the copulatory response (Morris, 1967; Schur, 1960) as well as the distinctive grimaces, postures, and offensive and defensive maneuvers that accompany both play fights (Aldis, 1975) and actual hand-to-hand combat.

Behavior is seldom studied with sufficient precision to analyze the micro-components of a complex sequence of responses. We have only a rudimentary understanding of the sequential and interactional components in a barroom seduction, the playful banter of mother and child, or even the simplest action; we cannot, therefore, prove or disprove whether evolved patterns are interwoven in certain of our regressive activities. Nevertheless, several studies involving detailed analysis of filmed interactions have built a strong case for evolved behavior patterns in humans. Eibl-Eibesfeldt and Hass (Eibl-Eibesfeldt, 1970; Hass, 1970) used a special camera with a right-angle prism to film people without their awareness as they went about their normal activities. According to Eibl-Eibesfeldt, the lawfulness of complex behavioral sequences became evident when they were subjected to "true transformations" (i.e., time acceleration or slow motion). These procedures revealed a variety of behaviors thought to be phylogenetically inherited in man—protecting oneself from behind, intermittent scanning of the environment while eating, the flirting pattern in females, the universal raised eyebrow greeting, the "arrogance and disdain" pattern, exhibiting the tongue to show disdain and rejection, offering food to appease another, dominance and submission displays, and so on.

In the course of his study, Aldis (1975) filmed and analyzed over 700 hours of animal play and 1,500 hours of human play. Slow motion analysis revealed the complex interactional and sequential aspects of such "simple" actions as wrestling, swimming, pool play, peek-a-boo, chasing, and acrobatics. Comparisons between animals and humans suggested, moreover, that certain components of play like laughter, chasing, wrestling, and competition for objects may have a phylogenetic basis.

Along with the positive atavisms seen in play behavior, there are negative kinds of phylogenetically conditioned behavior patterns seen in the area of human psychopathology. For example, Gallup and Maser (1977) employed the "animal" concept of tonic immobility in discussing the evolutionary underpinnings of human catalepsy and catatonia. Sometimes viewed as a type of animal hypnosis, tonic immobility is a well-documented but not particularly well-understood phenomenon. In experimental situations, the animal is placed under manual restraint and, after struggling for about 15 seconds, it assumes a relatively motionless, immobilized posture. In addition to paralysis, other symptoms often are involved including suppression of vocal behavior, changes in heart and respiration rate, altered electroencephalographic patterns, muscle tremors in the legs, and diminished responsivity to external stimuli. Some evidence suggests that animals farther down the phylogenetic scale may be more susceptible to the tonic immobility syndrome than those high on the scale; chickens, for example, average around 500-600 seconds in the state (Gallup & Maser, 1977), whereas in lizards the response may last 8 hours or more (Prestrude, 1975). Further, tonic immobility is a robust, naturally occuring response found in a wide variety of animals, including insects, crustaceans, and primates. The syndrome has been attributed to death feigning, fear, cortical inhibition, sleep, spatial disorientation, and hypnosis (Gallup, 1974; Gallup & Maser, 1977; Ratner, 1967).

Gallup and Maser say that the tonic immobility syndrome is similar to the constellation of symptoms often ascribed to catatonic schizophrenia, catalepsy, and cataplexy. They further suggest that the syndrome is an adaptive, evolved response system in both animals and humans. The reasoning goes like this: When a weaker animal is in the clutches of a powerful predator—and there is no possibility for fight or flight—chances for survival are increased when the prey remains immobilized and "frozen with fear." Such behavior is adaptive because it serves to diminish or turn off the predators kill responses, and thereby avert the imminent coup de grace. Because hominids were not immune to the effects of predation during their evolution, it is reasonable to assume that tonic immobility is an evolved, built-in response system in humans as well as lower animals.

However, the modern human is largely emancipated from predator pressure, and the tonic immobility syndrome has, in all probability, become a maladaptive anachronism. Yet, under extreme stress, the catatonic schizophrenic, and perhaps even normal persons may phylogenetically regress to the syndrome in whole or in part. Gallup and Maser (1977) state the case thusly:

> Maybe there are elements contained in catatonia that represent fragments of primitive defenses against predators that now misfire under conditions of exaggerated stress. Today man is not prey but predator and the veneer of civilization may obscure many of his natural defenses. It is only under conditions of unusual stress, combined with a particular constitutional makeup that tonic immobility may be triggered in man. Possibly such situations prevail on the field of battle, in situations in which the person is "frozen with fear", and in some unfortunate person's overall aversive life conditions—where withdawal from social intercourse takes the form of depressed motoric involvement as a predominant defense against an experience containing elements of predation. (p. 357).

The example of tonic immobility shows how once normal and adaptive behavior patterns may be regressively recovered under extremely evocative conditions, and, further, how these patterns may be pathological in the modern context. Indeed, all atavisms were "normal" or species-typical in their original contexts, but things are not so simple for modern, phylogenetically advanced human beings. Our task is to control, modulate, sublimate, or otherwise mold our vast array of primal patterns into socially acceptable forms of behavior; certainly, in most cultures, the re-emergence of unmodulated or minimally modulated atavisms generally is seen as pathological or deviant.

Increased Nonverbal Communication

A proportionate increase of nonverbal forms of communication is expected when people slip from culture-typical to paleopsychological forms of behavior. The human being is commonly seen as a uniquely verbal creature, and one frequently hears the refrain that only man is capable of speech, or that speech is our one, true species-specific characteristic. However, in recent years language-training experiments with chimpanzees and monkeys (see Desmond, 1979; Passingham, 1982) suggest a rudimentary language facility in the higher apes, and it seems reasonable to assume that such findings reflect a degree of phylogenetic continuity. Yet, although language may not be completely unique to humans, its complexity of function is, and it is clear that words and symbols virtually define our humanity. Therefore, when the mediating and controlling powers of human language are lost or diminished, the door is left open for phylogenetic regression. Indeed, when involved in restrained scholarly debate or discussion of lofty abstract issues, we are at the acme of our humanness, whereas at other times, like our infrahuman ancestors, we may emit groans of pleasure during the sexual act, screams of fright when endangered, or savage growls when angered or attacked. At certain times, then, our external speech or internal verbal statements may occur with little or no involvement of the lower centers, whereas at other times our communications may reflect mixtures of primitive and advanced elements, or in rare instances, the rational-linguistic element may be lost for all practical purposes.

Meerlo (1967) refers to "concealed" or archaic communication in humans that "intrudes into our clear semantic and rational thinking and troubles the higher abstractions" (p. 2). Archaic communication is essentially innate, nonverbal, emotional language that not only interferes with objectivity but also serves as the basis for regressive crowd phenomena such as mental contagion, mass hysteria, susceptibility to propaganda and many other forms of group pathology. Further, "the more an emotional expression reflects regression to the archaic biological sign code, the more contagious the expression will be" (Meerlo, 1967, p. 9). It will be recalled from chapter 3 that Meerlo (1962) developed a form of phylogenetic regression theory, and that theory is evident in his notion of archaic communication:

> The behavioral intercourse established by innate bodily signal codes held in common by man and beast forms part and parcel of archaic communication. Everyone understands and reacts to distress calls of animals. Certain emotional expressions are immediately understood. Crying, laughing, rhythmic tapping, fright reactions, shouting, fainting, itching, dancing movements, sneezing, convulsions, erotic gestures—they all evoke immediate understanding and response. (Meerlo, 1967, p. 8)

As might be expected given its long phylogenetic history, nonverbal communication is far more prevalent in human behavior than is verbal communication. Even with the most talkative individual, information transmitted through supernumerous nonverbal channels vastly outweighs the output of speech signals. Voice inflections, postural movements, facial cues, gestures, and the like, not only account for a greater quantity of communication, they often serve to betray and subvert our conscious speech as well. Freud (1901/1960), in his *Psychopathology of Everyday Life,* provided a psychodynamic explanation for many forms of communication leakage, and Ekman and Friesen (1975) and many other modern psychologists have described the complexity and subtlety of nonverbal leakage. The idea is that what is leaked is more basic, deeper, and more primitive than consciously willed communication. It seems, then, that nonverbal (and generally nonconscious) communication is not only more prevalent than strictly verbal forms, it also more deeply mirrors the inner person.

Given that virtually all nonhuman and most human communication is nonverbal, we would do well to highlight some of the pertinent literature here. Our approach is a comparative one, and draws heavily from Roger Peters' (1980) book, *Mammalian Communication: A Behavioral Analysis of Meaning*. The book is organized by phylogeny rather than message content *per se,* and it analyzes communication processes from tree shrews to human beings. Peters' phylogenetic analysis of communication builds upon W.N. Tavolga's (1970) six hierarchic levels of animal interaction:

1. Vegetative interaction—These are physical interactions that are understood in terms of physical constructs such as force and mass. One animal accidently bumping into another would illustrate the vegetative mode of interaction. Obviously little in the way of communication is involved at this level.

2. Tonic interaction—This level includes situations where the continuous metabolic process in one organism influences the behavior of another. An example might be where the body heat of one animal induces another to dive into the pond to cool off. Again, as in level one, this level falls short of true communication. Tavolga reserves the term *communication* for the next four higher levels of interaction.

3. Phasic interaction—These occur when discontinuous, more or less regular stages or events in the development of one animal influences the behavior of another. For example, if one animal is an adult male, his reaction toward a second male will be influenced by the other's age, size, demeanor, odor, and so on. Clearly, a considerable amount of complex information is processed in such interactions. Further, what cues and constellations of cues that a particular animal responds to will be largely a function of the species to which it belongs.

4. Signal interaction—Communication by signals involves specialized morphological structures and highly specialized forms of behavioral output. The classic ethological notion of releasing stimuli falls into this category, with the male stickleback's highly stylized and specific response to his male conspecific's red abdomen serving as a prime example. The important point here is that certain animals have evolved some very specific responses to specific stimuli, and especially noteworthy is the fact that the releasing stimuli are extremely effective even when embedded within a complex array of stimuli. Human beings communicate at this sign level as do other animals, but generally with less rigidity and

specificity. Examples of possibly innate sign-stimuli in humans include a baby's smile (Gray, 1958), infant crying and screaming (Wolff, 1969), the primate stare (Bailey, Tipton, & Taylor, 1977), various sexual cues (Morris, 1967), physical size and intimidation value (Bailey, Hartnett, & Gibson, 1972), and perhaps even a man's beard! (Freedman, 1979).

5. Symbolic interaction—This refers to abstract communication that is largely freed from morphology or instinct, and that employs conventional rather than universal signs (Peters, 1980). For example, when a chimp learns to "point" to direct attention, this is symbolic communication, whereas its species-typical means of directing attention (vocalizing, touching object, etc.) would not be. As Jolly (1972) tells us, signs are concretely tied to the situation and to things whereas symbols operate at a distance from the objects they represent. There is little argument that such representational communication is highly phylogenetically advanced and limited, for the most part, to primate species. However, signs and symbols are not always mutually exclusive, but rather they exist on a continuum as do most events in nature: "There is a gradation from the uninhibited yell through the whimper, through a culturally conditioned stiff upper lip, through saying 'Ouch' in various tones of voice to the symbolic report 'I banged my finger' [with a hammer]" (Jolly, 1972, p. 327).

6. Language interactions—This, of course, is the most phylogenetically advanced form of communication and is limited to humans and some specially trained chimpanzees and gorillas. Yet, as distinct as human language is, it is erected upon phylogenetically older systems of nonverbal communication:

> Our ability to use language ·did not replace older systems but incorporated them. These older systms provided the context within which language evolved and they may provide some insights as to how this process took place. Moreover, we still share with other mammals most or all of the types of communication." (Peters, 1980, pp. 7-8)

According to Branigan and Humphries (1972), human nonvocal signals, including facial expressions, postures, gestures, and physical contacts, number about 136. Peters (1980) says that when various nonverbal sounds such as grunts, moans, gasps, whistles, shrieks, and several kinds of cries are added, the number of nonverbal signals is 150 or more. When the multiplicity of human signals is categorized by meaning, however, most fit into the 30 message types seen in infrahuman human species. In fact, Peters believes that some human signals transmit basically the same information as the messages of our mammalian cousins. Peters (1980) concludes his review of human nonverbal communication with the comment that, "especially in our neonatal, integrative, agonistic, and sexual behavior, we are still mammals" (p. 273). Certainly, mother–infant, infant–mother, play, contact, agonistic, male and female sexual advertisement, courtship and many other interpersonal interactions are guided by and modulated by the ongoing, dynamic interchange of nonverbal information.

Phylogenetic regression theory assumes that the omnipresent nonverbal element in live interactions is phylogenetically older, more fundamental, and more revealing of human motivations and character than is the verbal element, and is, along with limbic emotions, one of the royal roads to the core of the personality. Only through noninteractive use of language and verbal-representational thinking, as in higher forms of scientific or philosophical writing or solitary thinking, may the nonverbal modes be temporarily suspended. And such rare occurrences are arbitrary and unnatural from the evolutionary standpoint. As with abstract intelligence, structures did not evolve to perform these higher functions; instead, structures originally developed to perform other functions are opportunistically exploited for cultural reasons. In other words, the language capacity that evolved up through *Australopithecus, Homo erectus,* Neanderthal, and Cro-Magnon was a literal, functional, and interpersonal form of communication, and not a means of generating and pondering abstract concepts for their own sake. All of this suggests that refined, advanced forms of speech or writing are recent and tenuously held acquisitions, as are the higher forms of abstract thought or intelligence. Consequently, regressions from these tenuously held higher levels to the more pervasive, intermediate levels of concrete interpersonal language, and on down to the primitive, nonverbal levels of communication, should be both easy and frequent. Indeed, how much easier it is to grimace with pain, or to posture and make threatening faces at a misbehaving child, than it is to compose a lasting poem or derive a new mathematical theorem.

Perhaps we can best illustrate the ideas just discussed with a specific example. Facial expression is probably the most phylogenetically advanced and psychologically significant of the various forms of human nonverbal communication. Ekman and Friesen (1975) tell us that human emotions are shown in the face not the body, and, further, there are specific facial patterns for each emotion but not specific body movement patterns. Izard (1977) points out that facial activity, as compared to postural activity in emotion and emotion differentiation, becomes more important with advances in both phylogenetic and ontogenetic development. Facial communication is thus more advanced than postural communication, and, not surprisingly, human beings have the richest repertoire of facial expressions in nature. Yet, despite their relative advancedness, complexity, and diversity (see Vine, 1970 for an extensive review), many human facial expressions are phylogenetically continuous with the display behaviors of lower organisms (Izard, 1977), and many are apparently universal in the species as well (Darwin, 1872/1896; Ekman & Friesen, 1975; Izard, 1971). Although certain facial expressions may be innate and universal, the stimuli that elicit them and the circumstances under which their expression is permissible differs from culture to culture (Ekman & Friesen, 1975). Thus, culture serves to control and modulate the action of universal facial patterns, but it does not have the capacity to produce them nor erase them.

Let us now place these relatively advanced yet fundamentally innate and universal facial expressions into our theoretical perspective:

1. First, let us construct a theoretical hierarchy going from emotionless abstract thought down to the most natural and primitive nonverbal behavior-emotion linkages. The hierarchy might look like this: an abstract thought about snakes with no observable emotion or facial expression; the same thought with a suppressed facial expression; the same thought with perhaps a fearful facial expression; a clear mental image of a snake (as in deep fantasy or a dream) accompanied by exaggerated facial expression and body movement; and, finally, the actual presence of a snake accompanied by exaggerated facial expression and actual escape or attack behavior. In moving down the scale, one phylogenetically regresses by forsaking arbitrary abstract thought for lesser learned and universal communicational-emotional-behavioral systems of response.

2. If the previous reasoning is valid, certain assumptions and researchable hypotheses may be derived. First, consonant with earlier sections of this chapter, we may assume that consciousness becomes less acute as the hierarchy is descended, and the presentation of the snake moves one rather quickly from the intrapsychic to the behavioral realm. Second, inhibitions are reduced with descent, with response to the real snake being immediate and automatic. Third, evolved defense or attack behavior are elicited at the lower levels that are absent from higher ones. Fourth, the pain–pleasure, approach–avoidance system becomes increasingly obvious with descent down the hierarchy. And last, we may draw an example from the previous chapter for purposes of illustration: Gender differences appear to be accentuated with descent from the abstraction of snake to the real thing. There are many other assumptions that could be derived here, but suffice it to say that facial communication in humans is the most advanced and important of the nonverbal modes, and, as such, it stands between distinctive human speech and thought on the one hand, and phylogenetically primitive postural forms of communication on the other.

Increased Pleasure-Seeking and Pain Avoidance

Hedonism, or pleasure-seeking, and pain avoidance or withdrawal are major correlates of phylogenetic regression. Some writers believe that pleasure and pain avoidance are the two most fundamental parameters of an organism's functioning, and Schneirla (1959) argues that approach and withdrawal tendencies are present in all organisms down to the unicellular level. In Rado's (1969) hierarchic psychodynamic cerebral system, we recall that the hedonic (pleasure vs. pain) level is the most primitive phylogenetically, and lies at the foundation of the organism's response to the environment. Delay of impulse gratification, on the other hand, is antithetical to the nature of the organism and, in the human being, requires massive enculturalization and generous amounts of parental admonition. Impulse modulation and control are thus progressive whereas immediate gratification is likely to be regressive and more analogous to non-human modes of response.

According to the sociobiologist Dawkins (1976a), not only is man pleasure seeking and inherently selfish, he is little more than a gene-carrying robot programmed with powerful survival needs. Dawkins' thesis of the "selfish gene" is probably correct, but only at regressed levels of functioning; human beings can and often do rise above the inherent selfishness programmed in the genotype (Singer, 1982). Perhaps our rampant tendencies toward narcissism and egocentrism do emanate from this inner core of sociobiological selfishness, and perhaps we should recognize this flaw in human nature. Nevertheless, selfishness and hedonism are generally kept within manageable bounds by a variety of internal (inhibition, sublimation, repression, altruistic values, and so forth) and external (socialization practices, customs, rules or order, and so forth) controls. Further, it is theoretically possible to progress to sufficiently advanced levels of moral or ego development where selfishness, in its rawer forms, is replaced by refined sorts of individualism (Graves, 1966; Kohlberg, 1964; Loevinger, 1976). Still, even at the highest levels of moral individualism, vestiges of primal selfishness remain to provide the motive force to seeking and avoidant behaviors of various kinds. We see, then, that it is not merely a matter of whether Dawkins or Kohlberg is right—indeed they both are when the regressive or advanced level of functioning is taken into account.

The aforementioned issues suggest that a significant relationship exists between pain, pleasure, and motivation. Certainly the relationship between pleasure, pain, and motivation has intrigued many great writers of the past—Aristippus, Epicurus, Hobbes, Hume, Locke, J.S. Mill, Darwin, Spencer, and many others. Jeremy Bentham summarizes thusly: "A motive is substantially nothing more than pain or pleasure operating in a certain manner" (cited in Young, 1973, p. 317). Similarly, McDougall (1926) concludes, "Further, we seem justified in believing that the continued obstruction of instinctive striving is always accompanied by painful feeling, its successful progress toward its end by pleasurable feeling, and the achievement of its end by a pleasurable sense of satisfaction" (p. 29). More recently, biologists and evolutionists have emphasized the innate, species-specific aspects of motivation, and several writers see pleasures and aversions as nature's way of assuring the performance of adaptive forms of behavior (Fishbein, 1976; Herrnstein, 1977a, 1977b; Washburn & Hamburg, 1972). Herrnstein (1977a, 1977b) provides the most persuasive argument that organisms find especially pleasurable those phylogenetically prepared behaviors that are important for survival. The sociobiologist Barash (1977) states a similar case for humans:

> What behaviors do we find satisfying and why? Sex, good food, rest, the respect of others, physical comfort, personal power and autonomy, coordinated and successful movements (athletics, dancing), and accomplishments of ourselves and offspring, all these pleasures contribute eventually to our own fitness, and, therefore, we have been selected to engage in them. We find them sweet. (p. 289)

It seems that pleasure-seeking has deep phylogenetic roots, but withdrawal activities in the form of avoidance and escape behavior may lie deeper still. Indeed, withdrawal appears to be more primal than pleasure from the evolutionary standpoint; that is to say, avoidance or escape on a day-by-day, encounter-by-encounter basis is more likely to assure survival for most animals in the wild than is approach. Hediger (1964) summarizes the situation:

> By far the chief pre-occupation of wild animals at liberty is finding safety, i.e., perpetual safety from enemies, and avoiding enemies. The be-all and end-all of its existence is flight. Hunger and love occupy only a secondary place, since the satisfaction of both physical and sexual wants can be postponed while flight from the approach of a dangerous enemy cannot. In freedom, an animal subordinates everything to flight; that is the prime duty of an individual, for its own preservation, and for that of the race. (p. 20)

In a world governed by predator–prey dynamics and fight-or-flight contingencies, certainly flight is the more common strategy. The concept of flight is no simple matter, however; it involves a rich array of species–specific behavioral systems with high survival value. Under the heading of *antipredator behavior,* for example, Alcock (1975) includes such complex behaviors as death feigning, evasive behavior, hiding, misdirecting attack, startle displays, and vigilance. Eibl-Eibesfeldt (1970) assumes that complex flight systems such as these are basically phylogenetically conditioned adaptations, and, further, that the direction and goal of flight are innate as well. For example, a squirrel flees to the top of trees, a mouse into its hole, a fish to deeper water, a pheasant flies up, and so forth. Again, let us look to Hediger (1964) to put the matter in perspective:

> in the presence of an enemy, an animal or bird doesn't simply run or fly away; the escape reaction is subject to definite laws, quantitatively and qualitatively. These facts . . . may be summed up like this: on suddenly encountering an enemy, an animal shows a characteristic escape reaction, specific for sex, age, enemy, and surroundings, as soon as the enemy approaches within a definite distance (the flight distance). (p. 19)

Our purpose here is not to analyze predator-prey dynamics in detail, but, rather, to underline the fundamental significance of aversive-withdrawal tendencies in the motivational-behavioral systems of animals, including humans. A further purpose is to emphasize the richness, complexity, and diversity of what Schneirla (1959) broadly includes under the heading of withdrawal processes—that is, any motivated behavior that involves moving away from rather than toward a stimulus source. Of course, such withdrawal processes involve a seemingly limitless number of "moving away from" behavioral complexes that are described by many diverse, yet related terms—*aversion, avoidance, escape, flight, fear,* and so forth. Amid this diversity lies a central truth of utmost significance for the phylogenetic regression–progression model: "moving away from" noxious, excessive, or threatening circumstances is the most fundamental and powerful form of motivation in living organisms. So viewed, many aspects of aversive or withdrawal behavior—both human and animal, normal and abnormal—fall somewhere on our postulated primitive-advanced continuum, and more often than not they fall toward the primitive end of the scale. Whether one speaks of protecting one's genes at all costs (Dawkins, 1976a), fleeing from danger (Schur, 1960), avoiding noxious foods or excessive stimulation (Cofer & Appley, 1964), avoiding punishment (Razran, 1971), defending one's geographic territory (Carpenter, 1958) or body territory (Lyman & Scott, 1967), experiencing incest avoidance (Fox, 1967) or fear of the stranger (Holloway, 1974), the primitive withdrawal theme comes through loud and clear. Given the hegemony of withdrawal throughout the animal kingdom, we are compelled to ask, "How much of human behavior can be accounted for by phylogenetically primitive withdrawal tendencies in the form of aversions, fear, defenses, and patterns of flight?"

Diminished Control Over Aggression

At regressed levels of functioning, the potential for loss of control over aggressive and violent impulses increases with the depth of regression (see chapters 10 & 11). Aggression may be viewed as an adaptive (Lorenz, 1967) form of approach behavior as is pleasure-seeking, but its neural (Holloway, 1974), hormonal (Moyer, 1976; Valzelli, 1981), and species–specific (Eibl-Eibesfeldt, 1975) modes of expression are quite different. In the animal world, aggression takes many forms, yet all share the common purpose of increasing the chances of survival for the individual or the individual's kin through acting against real or imagined enemies—predators, territorial interlopers, competitors for nutritional or sexual resources, and so forth. Aggression, indeed, plays a major role in the grand scheme of things, and an animal or person lacking in this characteristic operates at a severe adaptive disadvantage. Given that man shares some of the predatory heritage (Ardrey, 1961, 1966; Dart, 1953; Freeman, 1964; Washburn & Hamburg, 1972), territoriality (Ardrey, 1966; Esser, 1971), and rank-consciousness (Ardrey, 1970; Wilson, 1975, 1978) of lower animals, it is not surprising that aggression is so readily elicited nor that it escalates with such ease. The motivational and behavioral substructures of aggression are phylogenetically wired-in for most animals, including humans, and are in that sense natural; thus, following Herrnstein's (1977a, 1977b) argument that behaving naturally is pleasurable, we must conclude that expressing aggression is often pleasurable. This is a fundamental conclusion that, as we shall see in later chapters, goes to the very heart of the human condition. We cannot ignore Washburn and Hamburg's (1972) admonition that "man has been a predator for a long time and his nature is such that he easily learns to enjoy killing other animals . . . (and) . . . man easily learns to enjoy torturing and killing other human beings" (p. 294).

An important point about the fusion or mixing of behavioral elements should be made here. We have emphasized throughout how primitive emotions and advanced cognitions intermix along the regression-progression continuum, but there are mixtures of other sorts. As Plutchik (1980) theorizes, the primitive emotions themselves often blend and intermix in an additive fashion, and Tinbergen (1976) uses the term *supermotivation* to refer to potent blends of several emotional–motivational subsystems in humans. Nowhere is the fusing of basic urges more evident than in the phenomenon of *agonistic behavior*. This concept refers to a complex, interrelated, and adaptive set of responses involving several patterns of behavior: fighting, escape, defensive posturing, and passivity (Scott, 1981). From this viewpoint, aggression is not always a pure and independent pattern, but typically is part of a larger and highly adaptive system of fight and flight responses. We must, therefore, be cautious in speaking of "phylogenetically regressing to primitive aggressive responses," and so forth. As pointed out in chapter 3, phylogenetic regression is a general process of primitivization where older emotional and motive systems not only increasingly emerge but increasingly fuse with depth of regression. Such fusions are not random, however, but generally involve adaptive and evolved response systems for dealing with ecological stresses and other threats to survival. The agonistic response system is a major case in point: It apparently evolved to help animals cope with conflict, both within and between species.

It is evident that aggression can rarely be separated from its evolutionary *frere d'arme,* fear. Actually, fear often serves to inhibit gratuitious expressions of aggression, and the aggression (attack) ↔ fear (inhibition) balance is the prime consideration in both understanding and controlling human forms of violence (Valzelli, 1981). That the agonistic response system is innate in man as in other animals is made clear by Tinbergen (1976):

> Our present agonistic behavior is in my opinion unlikely to be a purely cultural phenomenon; its roots must be sought in our animal ancestry, for it is obviously highly environment resistant. I am convinced that it will soon be more generally recognized that primitive man had already long ago evolved the machinery for various forms of agonistic interaction. (p. 516)

Phylogenetic regression theory assumes that an evolved agonistic response system does exist in humans, but we must regress to it for it to be evident. At advanced levels of functioning (such as a recondite debate on whether anything in human behavior is innate) aggressive and fear systems are de-emotionalized and discoordinated, but at primitive levels of functioning (such as being attacked by a mugger or hearing an intruder downstairs) both subsystems' strength and intercoordination are recovered in the regressive process. Thus, when fairly deep regression occurs, we are more likely to revert to a highly coordinated system of agonistic responses than we are to aggression or fear taken alone. When faced with a physical threat to survival in the form of intraspecific dominance aggression or, moreover, interspecific predatory aggression, powerful, phylogenetically tuned flight and fight responses are set into motion. Generally, flight responses will dominate, but eventual escape from harm will usually involve an oscillating series of flight (fear) and fight (aggression) responses.

It is important to recognize that whereas aggressive behavior alone may be pleasurable, the agonistic experience may be perceived as basically unpleasurable depending on the amount of fear operating. Although there are no doubt exceptions to this rule, fear is generally antagonistic to gratuitous, excessive, enjoyable forms of aggression and violence. It is when the attacked is too weak or powerless to respond that gratuitious aggression is likely to occur. It is in attacks on the weak, the vulnerable, and the defenseless that we see the most pernicious forms of pleasurable, predatory aggression; by contrast, the worthy opponent often sets fear and flight patterns into effect that culminate in withdrawal or inhibited and ritualized forms of attack.

Sex and Regression

One of Freud's greatest contributions was his realization that sex plays a focal role in human social life. For him, sexual energy, or libido, was a basic life force uniquely capable of undergoing transformations denied the other instincts: If frustrated in achieving gratification in its original form, it could alter its objects and aim (Fenichel, 1945); it could migrate from its original energy source (id) and redistribute itself in other mental structures (ego and superego); once transformed in the higher mental structures the original excitatory potential (cathexis) was then capable of being transformed into inhibitory potential (countercathexis); and, once primal energy became checked by this transformed, countercathectic energy (e.g., repression), it continued to seek expression through indirect means (dreams, symptomotology, "slips" and "accidents," rationalized, displaced, or sublimated activities, etc.), or through more direct, abreactive expressions (dyscontrolled behavior, acting out, etc.). For Freud, the development of personality was largely a matter of distribution and transformation of libidinal energy, and psychological health and maturity depended on how effectively one mastered the psychosexual crises of life and found socially appropriate outlets for excess libido.

Freud did not assume that the sexual instinct was the only instinct, but it was clearly first and foremost in psychoanalytic theory (Freud, 1969). He carefully distinguished between the self-preservative or ego instincts and the sexual instinct, and argued that neurosis resulted from the war between these two instinctive systems. Nevertheless, the sexual instinct was more general, powerful, and less modifiable than the ego instincts, and more inextricably tied into psychic functioning (Freud, 1969). Moreover, the ego instincts more readily come under the control of the Reality Principle and are less subject to the Pleasure Principle and regressive processes than is the sex instinct. During development, portions of the libido tend to remain fixated at primitive stages of "polymorphous perverse sexuality" and primary narcissism, whereas other portions fixate at progressively higher levels (orality, anality, oedipality, adolescent genitality) along the way. When the individual faces frustration of libidinal satisfaction at a given stage of development, there is a tendency to regress to earlier levels where constellations of libidinal energy were previously fixated.

Holzman (1970) comments on the similarity between Freud's fixation-regression theory and the Jackson (Taylor, 1931) model that emphasized dissolution, the yielding of higher to lower psychoneural systems, or reverse evolution in Spencer's sense, when higher systems suffer injury (see chapter 3). For both Freud and Jackson, regression meant a return to older, simpler, more automatic, and more neuropsychologically primitive modes of response under physical or psychological stress. Although the theories of Freud and Jackson were similar in defining the process of regression, their approaches were quite divergent in terms of content, or what was recovered when regression occurred. Although Freud often hinted at the phylogenetic bases of the sexual instinct in his writings, his emphasis was clearly on the ontogenetic aspects of development and the regressive recovery of infantile sexual patterns. By contrast, Jackson emphasized the loss of higher intellectual and mental functions and the partial return of phylogenetically older patterns in epilepsy, dementia, aphasia, and insanity in general.

The Sexiest Ape. The phylogenetic regression-progression model finds Freud's focus on the centrality of sex well-placed, but Jackson's reverse evolution scheme seems to represent a better bridge into the paleopsychology of human sexuality. This suggests that contemporary human sexuality may be productively viewed in terms of the phylogenetic gains and losses analysis outlined in chapter 4 (e. g., our sexual natures are defined by structures, tendencies, and predispositions carried over, with little modification or elaboration from prehuman and premodern hominids, by carryovers more extensively modified and elaborated, by the addition of novel characters, and from the loss of certain characters along the way). Our phylogenetically advanced sexual natures are not static, however, but are subject to fluctuating regressions and progressions as outlined in chapter 3 and Appendix I. To fully comprehend our sexual natures, then, it is necessary to consider the phylogenetically old and normally latent tendencies as well as the overt, culturally typical behavior which may appear caused by purely environmental factors.

We are inherently sexy apes because sex plays such a central role in the reproductive process, and as we know, differential reproduction is the prime *modus operandus* of evolution. Ghiselin (1974) quotes Erasmus Darwin to the effect that, "Sexual reproduction . . . is the master-piece of nature" (p. 49). Similarly, Wilson (1978) comments that, "Sex is central to human biology and a protean phenomenon that permeates every aspect of our existence and takes new forms through each step in the life cycle" (p. 121). Sex is an inherently "risky, gratuitously consuming" (Wilson, 1978) and "wasteful" activity (Ghiselin, 1974), but one that is worth the trouble in terms of mobilizing genetic variability and diversity that allows greater adaptability in a world governed by natural selection. In a world of sexual creatures, our species is thoroughly devoted to sex (Fisher, 1982) and, with our hypertrophied secondary characters and capability for constant arousal, we are the sexiest of the apes (Morris, 1967). We have lost little in the way of sexuality in phylogenetic development and have realized several gains, most of which have contributed to greater rather than lesser expression (e.g., the capacity for constant arousability, greater capacity for female orgasm, thought and word-induced arousability, etc.).

Reverting to Natural Sexual Patterns.   Like most of our other human characters, sexuality reflects our evolutionary heritage, especially that during the hunting and gathering phase (see chapter 4). One way that we gain access to these natural patterns is through the process of phylogenetic regression (see chapter 3). In chapter 4 we discussed active and passive forms of phylogenetic regression in the sexual area, and in chapter 6 the relation between stress and regression is discussed. Simply stated, we tend to phylogenetically regress to older survival patterns when faced with threat to survival, and it follows, then, that archtypal "maleness" and "femaleness" are likely to emerge under stress. For example, Bokun (1977) comments that, "The behavior of human beings today in certain revolutions and catastrophes is comparable to the behavior of our human ancestors in the savannah. A rejected or displaced person is closer to our human ancestors than a human fossil or aborigine could be ever be" (p. 28). There is some evidence that men and women do revert to basic gender patterns in catastrophes, with men striving "to tough it out" and play the protector role, and women exhibiting "selfless concern for others," helplessness, and despair (McLeod, 1984); moreover, wives accused husbands of being insensitive and foolhardy, and husbands complained that their wives were hysterical and overemotional.

From another perspective, it is well-known that traditional, stereotypical gender roles are associated with the lower social classes, poverty, lack of education, and social underdevelopment in general. This is graphically illustrated by the present oppression of women in certain famine-ravaged areas of Africa:

> The status of women is a matter of great concern in Africa. Perhaps the rural African woman is the most underpriviledged of all human beings. Various social roles, cultural practices, and the biological tasks imposed by fertility have combined to keep the average rural African woman close to a beast of burden. (Sai, 1984, p. 804)

Assuming the process of reversion to natural sexual patterns, we have the question of "What constitutes the natural patterns?" To answer this question would require a book in itself, but some of the basic patterns are summarized in Table 5.2. Clearly, males and females differ genetically, neurohormonally, neurologically, behaviorially, and cognitively, with men generally being more active, aggressive, "passionate," variable, and prone to disease and psychopathology, and women being more gentle, less aggressive, more inclined toward attachment, bonding, and social relationships, and lesser degrees of deviance and psychopathology. In the area of sex, the male is the pursuer and the female the pursued, a fact that underlies much of the sexual behavior of mature humans. In general, there seems to be a compulsive urgency to male behavior that makes the male of the species a feared and dangerous creature, especially when he is in a regressed state. Thus, in phylogenetic regression, the male often becomes more dangerous and threatening—as primitive aggression and sexuality rise to the surface—whereas this need not be true for the female who may become more dependent and passive in the regressed state.

Social Approach Behavior

Social approach and prosocial behavior are related to the regressive process, but in complex and sometimes unexpected ways. As a rough generalization, we may say that regressions from emotionless abstraction at the progressive end-point of our theoretical scale, down to the "warm-blooded," mammalian levels, allows access to love and human concern (at least toward own kin) on the positive side of the coin, as well as temper, aggression, fear, and anxiety on the negative side. Indeed, the cold, distant, detached, rigid intellectualist who has lost contact with the emotions is one of the most despised of persons, whereas the flighty hysteric, the compulsive playboy, or even the street fighter or war hero are objects of sympathy or even admiration. Recall Guasconti's comment in Nathaniel Hawthorne's (1981) *Rappaccini's Daughter:* " 'Methinks he is an awful man indeed', remarked Guasconti, mentally recalling the cold and purely intellectual aspect of Rappaccini'' (p. 40). Everyone really does seem to love a lover, and we make gallant efforts to at least understand the child molester, the murderer who "lost control," or the alcoholic who cannot control his passion for drink. As long as primitive emotion or feeling accompanies an act, it is accepted or reluctantly tolerated; it is for the cold, aloof pedant at the super-advanced end of the continuum that we reserve our distaste, while for the sublimbic, reptilian forms of detachment we feel deep revulsion and hatred. We see, then, that it is possible to both regress and progress beyond optimal motivational and emotional functioning.

The phylogenetic regression model further tells us that regression works differently in "positive" versus "negative" areas of behavior. With

TABLE 5.2
Basic Features of Human Sexuality

General Features

Human sexuality is a complex, intercoordinated system composed of evolved, wired-in
structure-function relationships that is extended, modulated, and/or inhibited by learning,
experience, and social pressure
Human sexuality plays the central role in the mating and reproductive strategies essential to
survival of the species
Human sexuality is adaptively integrated with and intercoordinated with other limbic-
survival, motivation-emotion systems: fear, aggression, affection and kinship, etc.
Although interacting components of the limbic matrix, human sexuality and kinship are
distinctly different systems with distinctively different ultimate causes (Symonds, 1979)

Basic Sex Differences

Male and female human embryos develop identically during the first phase of gestation. No
gonadal hormones are required for female development in embryogenesis, but testosterone is required for male phenotype development (Wilson, George, & Griffin, 1981)
Testosterone is not only a major factor in differential development of the reproductive
system, it is also a major determinant of extragenital dimorphism as well—e. g., size,
strength and muscular development, secondary sexual characters, and gonadotropin
regulation (Bardin & Catterall, 1981; Naftolin, 1981)
In higher vertebrates, including humans, hormonally-induced changes early in development
lead to essentially irreversible differences in central nervous system function (MacLusky
& Naftolin, 1981)
Human males and females differ in brain structure and function, and in terms of a wide range
of neuropsychological variables (Durden-Smith & deSimone, 1983); however, only a few
of these differences may be conclusively attributed to prenatal hormonal influence
(Ehrhardt & Meyer-Bahlburg, 1981)
Some of the postulated male-female differences in brain function include:
1. Male-female differences in sexual behavior in subhuman mammals are largely mediated subcortically. Given the anatomical and histological similarities between the subcortical sexual centers in subhuman mammals and analogous centers in humans, it is likely
that roughly similar regulation occurs in humans as well (Erhardt & Meyer-Bahlburg,
1981)
2. Male and female brains are similar in gross anatomy, although the male brain is slightly
heavier due to larger body size, and the female cerebral cortex may be slightly less
convoluted (Durden-Smith & deSimone, 1983)
3. The male brain appears to be more clearly laterally asymmetrical in terms of function,
while the female is characterized by greater bilateral symmetry (Springer & Deutsch,
1981). Recent findings indicate that females have a larger corpus callosum, presumably to
allow for greater transmission of information between the hemispheres (de'Lacoste-
Utamsing & Holloway, 1982). Generally, males process verbal information predominantly

(Continued)

186

TABLE 5.2 *(Continued)*

in the left hemisphere and spatial information predominantly in the right hemisphere, while females are less lateralized for these processing skills

4. Generally, males appear to be slightly superior in spatio-mathematical skills, while females are slightly superior in the verbal area. Levy (Durden-Smith & deSimone, 1983) speculates that this gender difference evolved in the hunting and gathering phase, where male visuo-spatial skills were at a premium in the hunt, and the female communicational skills were highly adaptive in child rearing and in maintaining order at the home base

5. Males and females appear to differ in the relationship between stress, the brain, the immune system, and behavior. Generally, it appears that testosterone tends to reduce immunological efficiency, while estrogen seems to promote it. Thus, males are more vulnerable to a wide assortment of diseases, while females are more likely to suffer the auto-immune syndrome which is caused by over-efficiency of the immune system (Durden-Smith & deSimone, 1983)

There are a number of psychological and behavioral differences between the sexes:

1. Males appear to have "gone beyond" the basic mammalian model more than females in some respects; e. g., the more neotonous female is analogous to the young male (Darwin, 1871/1981) and additional hormonal intervention is required for maleness but not femaleness. However, females appear to have advanced beyond the primate model more than males in certain areas of reproductive physiology—e. g., menopause, concealment of ovulation (see chapter 4, Table 4.12)

2. Males appear to be more active and energetic at many levels of functioning. This difference is even evident at the level of the gamete (sperm vs. egg)

3. Male characters are generally more extreme and variable than those of females. Darwin (1871/1981) commented on the "greater passions" of males. Almost all sexual perversions or paraphilias occur in males—bestiality, exhibitionism, fetishism, voyeurism, child molestation, etc.

4. Males are generally more aggressive, power-oriented, and dominance-oriented than are females (Symonds, 1979; Wilson, 1978). Testosterone is associated with higher levels of aggressiveness, whether in male or female phenotypes (Rubin, Reinisch, & Haskett, 1981)

5. Males are generally more vulnerable to psychopathology and social pathology than are females—mental retardation, childhood autism, schizophrenia, alcoholism, suicide, crime, delinquency, etc. (Mitchell, 1981). However, females may be more prone to depression (Mitchell, 1981)

6. Males are generally more promiscuous than females (Symonds, 1979) and more interested in sex (Durden-Smith & deSimone, 1983). Males tend to "pursue" and females tend to "escape" (Darwin, 1871/1981). Aggression in the service of sexual access (e. g., rape, forced copulation) is frequently seen in males, but rarely in females (Zillmann, 1984)

7. The male orgasm is universal and virtually 100% efficient in terms of orgasm per copulation, while the female orgasm is neither universal nor efficient (Symonds, 1979)

8. Attachment, parenting, and sociality appear to be more well-developed in the female than the male (Symonds, 1979; Wilson, 1978)

9. The two main factors in sexual selection are male competitiveness and female choice (Darwin, 1871/1981). However, sexual selection appears to have acted more on the male than the female in producing evolutionary change (Symonds, 1979)

aggression, for example, one may regress in more or less linear fashion all the way from a bloodless thought of aggression, down through various feelings of hostility, and further on down to the almost automatic, emotionless ripping and tearing of a scaly predator at the reptilian level. By contrast, it is difficult to conceive of altruism (in the nonsociobiological sense), love, or kinship existing at all at sublimbic levels, and we are thereby forced to make some qualifications in the area of positive regression:

1. In regressing from advanced cognition to limbic emotionality, an increase in prosocial motivation may or may not occur. It will not occur, of course, when the regressive process leads to a greater proportion of negative relative to positive response tendencies, as when the love-hate ambivalence or balance shifts decidedly toward the hate side. Moreover, given that primal hate tendencies (e.g., predatory aggression) have been with us since the dawn of life (Valzelli, 1981) and mammalian love tendencies only for a few million years, we may speak of the *primacy of the negative*. In accordance with this primacy principle, it follows that regression is generally more likely to produce "negative" than "positive" effects. We must turn to custom, morality, and rule of law to help shift the inherently negative balance in favor of positive outcomes.

2. In regressing from limbic levels to reptilian levels, negative motivation is likely to increase, but positive motivation will not increase, for there is no reptilian prosocial content to recover! Withdrawal, fear, escape, defense, predatory attack, and so on, predate even avian attachment (imprinting) by a large margin, mammalian attachment by even a greater margin, and human love is a very recent phenomenon indeed. So we see that what humans generally value as good forms of behavior are quite recent derivatives of the evolutionary process, and, as such, are less ingrained in the human psyche than are the bad forms. As we all intuitively know, it takes more effort and cultural pressure to produce a noble spitit than an evil one. Evil seems to generate itself with help from no one.

Another reason for the prosocial paradox is that what is good and desirable is culturally defined in great measure, and thus is at least moderately advanced by definition. Adherence to customs, mores, and morals is a crucial element in prosocial behavior, and one cannot regress too far and still be a part of the cultural main. However, we recall from chapter 3 that concepts and ideas can be used to rationalize primitive behavior (active regression), but that is quite another matter theoretically. Our concern here is with the theoretical continua themselves, and it is evident that the continuum for attachmental or positive motives and behaviors is truncated at the lower levels compared to aggression and withdrawal.

That aggression and withdrawal are older, deeper, and more pervasive than positive approach tendencies may explain why *regression* is such a pejorative term. Meerlo (1967) says that the word "regression," as used in areas like pathology, psychiatry, and psychology, almost always has negative connotations, but he concludes, "Many times people must regress to progress" (p. 20). Many years ago the psychoanalyst Kris (1952) spoke of "regression in the service of the ego" where creative energies are released from the bondage of repression and inhibition. Similarly, Meerlo and the present writer argue that certain forms of regression are not only beneficial but necessary for the full realization of human potential. So, despite the primacy of the negative, moderate and controlled regression can be healthy, invigorating, and desirable in its effects.

The same pessimism and despair that surrounds the concept of regression surrounds biologically based theories as well. There is widespread apprehension among both scientists and laypersons regarding ideas like innate aggression, human instincts, human imprinting, and so on, which seem to reduce human beings to little more than animals. From this perspective, the phylogenetic regression-progression model is particularly guilty because it involves the twin bedfellows of regression and biological determinism. Yet, as we have argued, to regress is not always dehumanizing, even when that regression calls up the primeval wisdom of our phylogenetic forbears. What is called up is the issue, not merely whether our motives and behavior are colored by or determined by preprogrammed tendencies from the past. Tiger's (1979) book, *Optimism: The Biology of Hope,* has helped put biological theorizing on a higher plane, and he is convinced that even a sanguinary term like *optimism* is rooted in our animal nature:

> I've already begun to claim that optimistic practices may be easy for people to learn, pleasurable to engage in, and indeed may often be necessary for the conduct of long-term social relationships. Thinking rosy futures is as biological as sexual fantasy. Optimistically calculating the odds is as basic a human action as seeking food when hungry or craving fresh air in a dump. (p. 35)

Proceeding on the assumption that neither regression—at least suprareptilian regression—nor nature is *ipso facto* negative or pathological, let us look at some of our natural, positive correlates of regression: imprinting, attachment, love, kinship and family relations, play, cooperation, and submission to authority.

Imprinting and Attachment.   Imprinting is perhaps the most primitive building block for attachment in higher animals, and it may have implications for human attachment as well. Since the publication of Lorenz's (1935) famous *Der Kumpan* paper, the concept of imprinting has generated considerable research and controversy. Lorenz originally used the term to refer to the early, sudden, almost automatic, and apparently irreversible process of establishing species identity in precocial birds, and he considered the process to be distinctly different from all known forms of learning (Evans, 1975; Lorenz, 1982). Subsequent research has supported the uniqueness of imprinting, but it is now widely accepted that the process is not irreversible (Cairns, 1979; Hess, 1973). Imprinting differs from traditional learning in the following ways (Hess, 1959): (a) it occurs most efficiently during a critical or sensitive period, often in the first day of life of the animal; (b) it obeys the law of primacy rather than recency (the first-learned object is learned most completely); (c) massed practice produces stronger learning than distributed practice; (d) imprinting is reduced to zero with tranquilizing drugs whereas traditional learning is unaffected; (e) and most dramatically, imprinting is facilitated rather than inhibited by punishment and aversive stimuli. Hess (1970) concludes that imprinting is a special, adaptive, and phylogenetically ancient form of learning that promotes species survival by raising the probability that certain fundamental preferences will be acquired early in life. Hess (1973) says that such preferences include members of one's own species, the mothering one, certain food objects, certain olfactory stimuli, certain auditory stimuli, and environmental or locality imprinting (Thorpe, 1945). Such primal preferences are not just limited to infant animals, however: maternal forms of imprinting exist in herd animals such as sheep and goats (Collias, 1956; Smith, 1965), and may exist in other species as well. Obviously the range of imprinting objects is extensive, and it is equally obvious that a properly imprinted animal will enjoy an adaptive advantage over the animal that mal-imprints (Morris, 1969) or fails to imprint at all.

The question of human imprinting is a controversial one, and after a review of the literature, Taketomo (1968) concluded that the question remains unanswered. Hess (1973) similarly concluded that neither imprinting nor critical periods, when strictly defined, are clearly evident at the human level, but he conceded that there is a strong resemblance between the primary socialization of human infants and the analogous process in precocial birds. Hess says that if we speak of sensitive and susceptible periods in humans, rather than of critical periods in the avian sense, then we are on firmer ground conceptually. A sensitive period in humans might be of 2 or 3 months duration, and would lack the primacy and suddeness of the avian critical period that often occurs minutes or hours after birth. The susceptible period would be even longer as in, for example, the period (0-2 1/2 years) for primary socialization in humans as set forth by Money, Hampson, and Hampson (1957). All this suggests some degree of phylogenetic continuity in imprintability between lower species and humans, but in the latter case less rigid genetic programming, greater cerebral mediation, and considerable experiential learning characterize the phenomenon.

Phylogenetic regression theory assumes weak vestiges of imprinting do exist in human beings that play important roles in the developmental process, and that serve as the foundation for various forms of attachmental behavior. Gray (1958) was probably the first to seriously address the issue of human imprinting. He reviewed studies on the smiling response, early deprivation, and institutionalization, and suggested that imprinting could likely be at the foundation of personality. He proposed that the period between the age of 6 weeks and 6 months was the period for primary socialization, and, further, that the smiling response was homologous to the following response in young precocial birds. Although credible, these were radical suggestions, and Ambrose (1963) was quick to provide criticisms of the specifics of Gray's thesis. Despite having reservations, Ambrose agreed that the analogy between the human smiling response and the avian following response is a reasonable one, and he went on to refine Gray's hypothesis and correct some of its weaknesses.

Our purpose here is not to defend the notion of human imprinting, but to point out that human beings have many primal preferences of presumed high survival value that are learned quickly and strongly during early sensitive phases of development. In all probability, many of our likes and dislikes, attractions and repulsions to both inanimate objects and persons, are conditioned early, rather automatically, and with minimal cognitive mediation. Some of these are possibly variations of human imprinting, broadly conceived, whereas others are merely reminiscent of the phenomenon. Such preferences would appear to encompass far more than those reflected in the crying and smiling responses discussed by Gray and Ambrose, and would seem to go right to the heart of the bonding process. The work of Bowlby, Harlow, Schaffer, Spitz, Rheingold, Wolff, and many others come to mind here, for they have dramatically shown how crucial the healthy infant–mother bond is and how devastating and pathological its absence can be. It is clear that failures in the bonding area are at the root of much human misery (Bolton, 1983; Fairbanks, 1977).

Morris (1969, 1971) has speculated at length on human imprinting and mal-imprinting, and even suggests that the fetus may imprint to the symphony of stimuli in the womb: "The very first impressions we receive as living beings must be sensations of intimate body contact, as we float snugly inside the protective wall of the uterus" (1971, p. 14). He goes on to say that prolonged fetal exposure to these rich sensations leaves a "lasting impression on our brains" that spells security, comfort, and passivity. Once experienced, this intrauterine bliss is never forgotten, and is, for all practical purposes, imprinted on the human psyche. The fetus–womb interrelationship thus appears to serve as a prototype for all later relationships; it, along with primary socialization that occurs during the first 2 years or so *ex utero,* represent the core components of human social behavior. It is to these core components that we regress when faced with survival stresses in later life. For example, Morris (1969) suggests that "falling in love" in the adolescent has "all the properties of an imprinting process" (p. 165). He says that falling in love generally occurs during a sensitive period early in adult life; it is a relatively rapid process; its effects often are long-lasting; and it may persist even in the conspicuous absence of rewards. We assume here that the newer developing sexual–reproductive social system had reverted back to the core infant–mother system to draw from its vast reserves of tenderness, compassion, and primal love. Perhaps this positive regression to primal love is required to make courtship and the sex act something more than a strict reproductive encounter.

Before ending this section, some mention should be made about mal-imprinting, or pathological types of attachment. It is well-known that many species, especially avian species, will imprint on a variety of animate and inanimate objects that bear little resemblance to the natural imprinting objects (e.g., the parent organism). Such accidents usually are maladaptive, and as Morris (1969) said, "The world of the mal-imprinted animal is a strange and frightening place" (p. 163), a world of piteable and frustrating contradiction. One is reminded here of the sad case of the quail that suffered grievous punishment in order to approach its mal-imprinted chicken hawk "mother" (Melvin, Cloar, & Massingill, 1967). And, there are, of course, numerous examples of animals sexually imprinting on their human keepers and other inappropriate objects, toward whom they direct their amorous desires (Meyer-Holzapfel, 1968; Sluckin, 1965). In mal-imprinting, the animal performs normal species patterns of behavior, but directs them toward inappropriate objects. Morris (1969) suggests that certain sexual fetishes in humans may arise through mal-imprinting, and he provides several interesting examples to bolster his case. He argues that salient objects present or involved in the first sexual experience may become fetishes, and the sex drive then becomes directed toward them rather than copulation with a human partner (see chapter 12). He includes some types of homosexuality in this category, where the first sexual experience occurred with a member of the same sex. Folklore tells us that the first love, or more specifically, the first true sexual encounter— whether it be heterosexual or homosexual—holds a specialness for those involved, and may set the stage for subsequent relationships.

Primate and Human Love.   The primate capacity for love not only builds upon the imprinting–attachmental complex of lower species, it draws heavily from the emotions and behaviors developed during the age of mammals as well. This period lasted from 200 million years or so ago to about 65 million years ago when the prosimians entered the scene and the age of primates began. In *The Evolution of Love,* Mellen (1981) outlines the paleopsychological origins of human love from the mammals on up through monkeys, apes, protohominids, *Homo erectus,* Neanderthal, and modern *Homo sapiens.* At the mammalian level, quality of offspring became more important than quantity, and with this new emphasis came the basic rudiments of mother love—feeding through the mother's body, close physical intimacy, and a relatively long infancy with extreme dependency on the mother. From what we know, it was during this period that touch, closeness, and intimacy became extremely powerful and pleasurable mediators of behavior. As Mellen (1981) tersely states, "These ancient mammalian traits lie at the root of the profound and special emotional intimacy between the average mother and her baby today" (p. 4). At the mammalian level, parents began to invest in their young, and their first real concern with "other" served as the stepping stone for more advanced love and kinship relationships to follow.

With the dawn of the primates, the mammalian foundation structures were greatly elaborated upon, and a variety of essentially new morphological and behavioral components were added as well (see chapter 4). Of all these progressive changes, the elaboration of the mammalian mother–infant bonding system was possibly the most important, providing the lietmotif for evolutionary processes leading to human love. Mellen (1981) says that these powerful young-protecting tendencies were necessary and adaptive due to the prolonged infanthoods and extreme dependency of monkey and ape offspring. Monkey and ape mothers normally spend large amounts of time licking, nursing, grooming, manipulating, and playing with their infants, whereas the infants respond with strong clinging, grasping, and nuzzling reflexes that are probably the result of "rigid genetic programming" (Mellen, 1981). Harlow (1971) concluded that maternal love is the most fundamental affectional system in primates, including humans, but it is followed closely by the infant affectional system that emerges with the infant's ability to recognize and respond to the mother. These two interlocking and mutually enhancing affectional systems serve as the building blocks for the peer and heterosexual systems that come along later in development.

Family and Kinship Relations.   We now move from the topics of species identification, infant–mother attachment, and primate love to the variegated tapestry of human family and kinship relations. As early hominids and finally modern humans emerged from the din of the evolutionary process, love became a more complex biocultural phenomenon. Still, the basic rudiments remained and kept their fundamental integrity despite the bending, molding, and elaborating effects of culture. With our large brains to augment their effects, the joy of love and the agony of its absence became more acute in humans than any other creature. It was within this context that human family and kinship relations developed.

Family relations begin with the mother–infant relationship and most primate offspring maintain special ties with their mother, even into adult life (Jolly, 1972). Radiating from this primal mother–infant bond are primitive interrelationships involving brothers, sisters, fathers, aunts, uncles, peers, and others within a given troop. Incest taboos, rank and status, age, sex, and individual personality traits mediate these simple social networks, but underlying them all is a special feeling of attraction, a "love" of sorts. From these humble beginnings a deep sense of family gradually emerged that has reached its fullest expression in the human animal. Despite arguments by some anthropologists and sociologists that the human family is a mere cultural symbol (Schneider, 1968), or that its origins are overwhelmingly cultural (Goode, 1963; Lévi-Strauss, 1968; Parsons & Bales, 1954), we have seen that its roots are deeply embedded in mammalian and primate evolution. Pierre van Berghe (1980) makes three important points in this regard: (a) the human family is a biologically evolved form that, although unique in many ways, is analogous to family groups in other species; (b) the human family, while showing considerable diversity across cultures, exhibits certain underlying universal characteristics; and (c) so-called cultural universals often are biologically based ecological adaptations. We see then, that our concept of family is deeply rooted in our phylogenetic heritage, and no doubt our ancient capacity for love lies behind the remarkable success of family as an adaptive strategy.

Although the family is the most fundamental social unit beyond the mother–infant relationship, the range of human social interactions extends far beyond these necessary but limited strategies. Mellen (1980) provides eloquent commentary on this issue:

> In the evolution of genus *Homo* as one of the most social primates, emotional tendencies to form . . . attachments have been developed . . . notably enduring affection among members of extended families, fellowship among male companions, and solidarity among members of larger social groups, from tribes to nations. Most of us today seem to have a latent emotional affinity with members of our groups, in some cases very large groups, our own kind collectively; *such feelings show up in times of crisis or in evocative situations.* (pp. 272-273; italics added)

This capacity to progress beyond and rise above our primal familial and kinship networks and engage in complex social activities with acquaintances and even strangers is a distinctive characteristic of our species (Alexander & Noonan, 1979). Yet, as Mellen implies in the aforementioned quote, we tend to regress into the primeval security of our own kind when faced with threatening circumstances (Bailey, 1986b). It appears that the regression–progression continuum outlined in chapter 4 has ready applicability to the many lingering questions that surround the viscissitudes of human kinship relations and social behavior.

Before addressing theory, however, we need to flesh out the presumed continuum more fully. Moving from primitive to advanced, we start with the primal mother–infant relationship and move on to the levels of the family, extended family, kinship relations, and supra-kinship relations with acquaintances and strangers. We have discussed the first two levels, so let us look briefly at the next level, that of the extended family. Presumably, in early man the extended family was a natural consequence of genetic relatedness and family consanguinity, and thus conformed pretty much to the sociobiological notions of kinship selection and inclusive fitness; that is, family extended little farther than the strict sharing of genes and relationships with nonkin were extremely limited. With "love" limited to close family members, social relations and cultural progress were likewise limited. However, as primitive man advanced both intellectually and culturally, the notion of family came to mean more than immediate kin; indeed, at some point in development, the concept of family merged into the concept of kinship in the abstract sense. In modern parlance we speak of the "family of man" or "we are all God's children," both of which suggest a common kinship tie in all humanity. This progression from sociobiological kinship to oneness with humanity represents one of the great leaps in human evolution, and today it serves as the foundation assumption of many moral and religious beliefs.

All this suggests that kinship may be viewed in the concrete sense as genetic relatedness or within-family togetherness, or in the abstract or metaphorical sense as proposed by Wittgenstein (1963) and Wilson (1980). In the latter sense, kinship is what Wittgenstein (cited in Needham, 1971) calls an odd-job word; that is, a word possessing a variety of functional uses, but one that defies definition itself. As we have seen in various other contexts, things get far more complicated and differentiated at advanced as compared to primitive levels of functioning, and this is particularly true of the notion of kinship. For example, Wilson (1980) states that, "The natural, determinate female/offspring tie among all mammals remains a universal model" (p. 167) for the metaphor of kinship, but he believes that the primary metaphor of fatherhood must be added to explain human kinship at the cultural level. For him, the female/offspring bond is primal, biologically determined, and thus more or less invariable in all mammals, whereas the father relation is distinctly human, culture-bound, and in our terms, more phylogenetically advanced. In contrast to Wilson's position, phylogenetic regression theory implies that a bifurcation of animal and human kinship is not required; rather, even the most advanced forms of human kinship are seen as elaborations and refinements of older systems. Thus, the father system would not replace the infant/mother system, but would build upon it, enrichen it, and give it greater variety.

As seen here and in chapter 2, kinship relations appear universal in the human species, and they serve many adaptive functions. Kinship helps us distinguish between loved ones, mere acquaintances, strangers, and enemies, and it helps produce order and stability amid the intricate, complex interactions that underly society and culture. As we recall from chapter 2, kinship is largely predicated upon cortical inhibitions overtly expressed in customs, mores, taboos, and so forth, which oppose our natural tendencies to be selfish and indulge our own preferences at the expense of the larger group (Fox, 1972). As such, human kinship relations are considerably more advanced and cortical than the love and quasi-familial relationships of nonhuman primates, and far more advanced still than the highly specialized and often automatic imprinting responses of avian species. Nevertheless, our ancient need for love, closeness, and kinship remains with us more or less intact at deeper levels of functioning. To be "a part of" is a fundamental prerequisite of every human being, but, for some, the love imperative remains unsatisfied with often grievously pathological consequences. Loneliness, alienation, and depression are the whelming burdens of our age, and all of us long for those adaptive regressions to the furry, warm, secure world of the infant–mother bond and familial togetherness. Yet, as modernization and forever burgeoning technology envelop us further, these longings are doomed to even greater degrees of frustration. The extended family has already been replaced by the nuclear family in many countries (Dumond, 1975), producing numerous pathological consequences (Uzoka, 1979). The traditional roles of parents, other caretakers, and children have been drastically altered, and age segregation has severely reduced opportunities for the young and elderly to fully involve themselves in the family (Robinson, Woods, & Williams, 1979). Increasingly, the roles of the extended family and kinship community, so vital in the process of hominization, have been eroded as institutional child care and educational programs have proliferated (Aries, 1962). We can only speculate on the long-term effects of these unnatural conditions of child rearing. It is clear, however, that we humans can phylogenetically progress to the point of alienation from our deepest needs and wishes.

Cooperation, Competition, and Play.   The hominid proclivities for love and kinship left many new and largely prosocial behavior patterns in their wake. Probably the most important of these was the capacity to cooperate to meet common goals within family and kinship groups. This was no easy accomplishment, given the limited precedent for cooperation in lower primates, the limited brain power of early hominids, and the stultifying effects of genetic self-interest. Yet, in order to enjoy reasonable success in the quest for larger and larger game animals, early man had to put self-interest and intra-family exclusivity aside, and join in with friends and even barely familiar male acquaintances on the hunt. Thus, the genesis of human cooperation owes much to the social and economic imperatives of the hunting strategy (Bigelow, 1972; Crook, 1971; Lee & Devore, 1968); but, as Fisher (1982) so aptly points out, cooperation between early men and women probably predated the male-to-male bonding system (Fox & Tiger, 1971; Tiger, 1969) involved in hunting. Fisher suggests that the "sexual contract" probably goes back at least 4 million years to the time of *Australopithecus afarensis,* and it, rather than the male bond, led to the advanced forms of cooperation. Regardless of where one stands on the sexual contract versus male bond issue, it is clear that human beings have evolved as deeply cooperative animals, and cooperation, is thus, a significant component of human nature.

Like so many other human traits, however, cooperation seldom acts as a pure character. There is considerable evidence that love and hate (Eibl-Eibesfeldt, 1972), and cooperation and competition (Bigelow, 1972; Crook, 1971) work in concert and have the capacity to fuse and defuse, and to intermix in a fashion analogous to the Life and Death instincts (Freud, 1924/1948, 1937/1964). Assuming that such fusion and defusion occurs, many elements of early hominid and modern human behavior could be conceptualized in terms of the relative weighting of cooperation versus its counterpart, competition. Perhaps the controversy surrounding who contributed most to the evolution of cooperation—men or women—could be re-evaluated from the perspective of the cooperation–competition interplay rather than one or the other taken alone. First, let us assume that women are inherently more love-centered and cooperation-oriented and men are inherently more aggressive and competitive, an assumption for which there is considerable supporting opinion. If this assumption is basically true, then it resolves the question of who started the ball rolling toward more advanced forms—women primarily begat the rudiments of cooperation through the love complex and men the rudiments of competition through the aggression complex. This, of course, does not mean that women are totally cooperative nor that men are totally competitive, but, rather, that their proportions of both traits differ in predictable ways. Therefore, it becomes a question of how these traits are blended in a given individual, rather than who generated them in the first place.

The loveless psychopath, the doting mother, the dutiful soldier, the playful child, and the canonized saint all combine the positive (love, cooperation, attachment, etc.) and negative (hate, aggression, dominance, power, etc.) in varying proportions, and Crook (1971) argues that "competition-contingent cooperation" lies at the foundation of in-group membership, self-esteem, compassionate empathy and many other social phenomena. From the standpoint of phylogenetic regression theory, love and hate and cooperation and competition may defuse or decouple in the advanced modern human, but in the normal life of primitive man (and in regressed states today) these traits combined and complemented each other in a generally adaptive fashion.

Play is another example of a healthy fusion of cooperation and competition (Bruner, Jolly & Sylva, 1976), which occurs within a context of make-believe interactions (see footnote 3 in chapter 4). Play is a natural, spontaneous and highly social instrument of learning whereby the juvenile acquires skill in the arenas of sex and dominance, and the adult may regressively recover a few moments of lost youth. Because play is an evolved, adaptive system of responses in virtually all warm-blooded animals, and, further is especially well-developed in all primate species, we may conclude that regression-into-play in humans moves us closer to our phylogenetic roots, and often serves to make us more interesting and creative people as well. We might also surmise that the abstractions of justice, fairness, and respect for others arise, in significant measure, from the give-and-take of play: "Civilization will, in a sense, always be played according to certain rules, and true civilizations will always demand fair play. Fair play is nothing more than good faith expressed in play terms" (Huizinga, 1976, p. 687).

It is largely through play that the young are socialized and prepared for their adult roles in a make-believe context less fearful and threatening than the real ones they will encounter later. The play context allows for experimentation with new motor skills, new forms of communication, and new combinations of activities (Bruner, 1972), and, as such, it is the Great Educator of the young. Play requires no incentive other than itself, and it conforms beautifully to the notion that spontaneous pleasure associated with a given act reflects the phylogenetic rootedness of that act. Children love to play and as they indulge this ancient pleasure they are primates to the fullest—cooperative, competitive, and noticably distinctive in their maleness and femaleness. In play, both children and adults are truly themselves perhaps more than at any other time; whether it be on the playground, in the bedroom, or in corporate gamesmanship, primate play remains a central feature in human behavior.

Conformity and Submission.   Conformity and submission to authority are two rather bittersweet precipitates of the evolutionary process.

Roughly speaking, the more one moves down the phylogenetic scale within the primates, the more rigid and invariable social structures become. With the more primitive primates mother–infant bonding, dominance interactions, territorial defense, and mating patterns are relatively simple and fixed, often operating under the control of neurophysiological conditions within the animal and specific releasing stimuli in the environment. Conformity was, in those terms, an instinctive response to internal and external stimuli. In prosimians and monkeys, for example, behavorial repertoires are limited and the combinatorial richness of behavior is not great (Bruner, 1972); consequently, social structures are tightly bound. Structures are only loosened through the avenues of play (Bruner, 1972), but even play is irreversibly gone by adulthood. By contrast, the more advanced great apes are allowed far more freedom of action in general, greater amounts of play in both juveniles and adults, and greater independence from strict, instinctual kinds of conformity. Still, this freedom is relative and each ape knows its place in matters of dominance, sexual and food priorities, group structure, and so forth.

Schaller (1963) describes how the silver-backed male mountain gorilla maintains strict discipline and order in his group by stylistic posturing, facial threat, and limited vocalizing. The primate leader in most species is usually the alpha male who typically governs his followers by threat signals rather than violent confrontation (Dolinow, 1972). As leader he is accorded rapt attention (Chance, 1967), is followed without question, and exerts great authority over much of the group's daily routine. Given the form and structured character of nonhuman primate leader–follower relationships, several writers have speculated that submission to authority may have an innate basis in humans (Erickson, 1950; Waddington, 1967), and others discuss the central role of the leader in mob violence (Kolb, 1971), the "war game" (Toch, 1969), and so on. The psychology of leadership also was a central theme in Freud's writings, from his reconstruction of the death and cannibalization of the primal father (1913/1938), to his pronouncement that religion was nothing more than the "figure of an enormously exalted father" (1930/1961, p. 74). Alexander (1960) stated that: "Freud was thoroughly impressed by the indestructability of the profound emotional need of humanity for strong leadership, which is the cornerstone of all his sociological speculations" (p. ix).

Given this background, it seems reasonable to speak of an innate need to submit to authority, or to likewise speak of phylogenetically regressing to this need for protective leadership when under threat. Perhaps more problematic is the question of whether things like the need for leadership, the need to submit, and the need to conform are prosocial or pathological forms of behavior. For nonhuman primates, there is no question that these needs were effective adaptive strategies in the dim phylogenetic past, but the liberated human primate of today—especially in Western culture—tends to denigrate following, conformity, sacrifice of self for the group, and submission of any sort. Yet, with such independence comes solitude, loneliness, and alienation from the warm, secure comforts of primate togetherness. Perhaps we have moved too far from our primate roots in this regard, and for many persons regression to submission and conformity, within accepted cultural bounds, would be welcome relief from the wearing demands of independence.

SUMMARY AND COMMENT

We have seen that phylogenetic regression has a multitude of correlates and consequences, among which are primitivization of consciousness, reduced inhibition and self-control, the elicitation of segments and part-segments of atavistic behavior patterns, increases in nonverbal and proportionate decreases in verbal–linguistic modes of communication, increased reliance on pleasure and pain to guide behavior, increased reliance on aggression and violence to mediate social conflict, increased emphasis on culturally disinhibited sexuality and "traditional" male and female sex role functioning, and a host of prosocial, social-approach forms of behavior.

Phylogenetic regression theory assumes that modern humans demonstrate these behavioral primitivizations only at times, most often when under stress or highly evocative circumstances. Under normal circumstances, our older predispositions and tendencies remain latent or are expressed in sublimated or oblique forms that escape notice; yet each of these carryovers was once a part of the adaptive response repertoire of species ancestral to *Homo sapiens*. It is, of course, probably impossible and certainly beyond the scope of the present work to ascertain exactly what species originally developed what trait, and then trace the trait, step-by-step, up to the human level. Granting that our case is circumstantial and that many steps are left out between the birth of a response pattern or motive tendency and its eventual expression in human behavior, there is still good reason to believe that the correlates listed above really do play a role in human personality and social functioning.

Again, we must remind the reader that none of the correlates is likely to emerge in anything resembling pure form except under the most extreme evocative circumstances. The problem is that actual behavior is always infinitely more complex than behavior theoretically construed or studied in the laboratory, and the true essence of the fathomless within- and between-system interactions characterizing the simplest human act continue to elude us. Thus, it is not surprising that considerable within- and between-system interaction characterizes even simple instances of phylogenetic regression; that is, the correlates themselves interact with each other in the process of regression, as well as interacting, lower system versus higher system, with advanced, cognitive elements of the personality (see chapters 7 and 8).

The various themes of chapter 5 may be illustrated with a specific example. Imagine a situation where a mother has just returned from visiting a neighbor across the street, only to see her 8-year-old child being dragged away, screaming and struggling, by three strange men. Imagine ·further what raging emotions the mother must experience and the thoughts that course through her mind as she helplessly watches the car speed away with her beloved child. We would certainly not expect only one correlate—let's say increased aggression—to completely characterize the pitiful scene; much to the contrary, it is obvious that many, if not most, of the correlates discussed in this chapter would play some part in the mother's highly agitated state. Certainly primitivization of consciousness would be involved, replete, no doubt with fleeting images of death, rape, mutilation, and the like. For the first few moments, this human mother is again the loving, doting primate mother whose feelings, thoughts, and very existence are devoted to the safety and survival of her offspring. Before long, however, she would likely regain her bearing and put her social and cultural learning to work in summoning help and alerting proper authorities. Even then the deep anguish of the primate mother would remain until the child was safely returned.

Along with primitivization of consciousness, other of the correlates would rise to the surface in the mother's regressed state. She would, of course, be disinhibited and in poor control of herself; she would likely clench her fists, flail at the air, run about and loudly vocalize; she would call (or signal) for help, perhaps hoping that a protective male was nearby; she would emit an assortment of "helpless" or "need help" nonverbal postural and facial communications; her behavior would be strongly guided by the extreme emotional pain of the immediate situation and the prospective ectasy attendant to the child's safe return; she would feel hatred and revulsion toward the abductors, and would entertain violent fantasies centering on rescue and revenge; and all of this would fall under the superordinate motive—or better still, obsession—to re-establish the rudely broken primate bond between mother and child. We see from this illustration that phylogenetic regression typically calls up admixtures of primitive elements or correlates, to meet the demands of a threatening situation, rather than single elements in a one-to-one fashion. Remember also that primitive elements, singly or in combination, never totally divorce themselves from the advanced, cortical, human level of functioning. At no time did the mother in the illustration become an ape mother; she did, however, temporarily call upon the vast reserves of phylogenetic wisdom that resides today in all of us.

6

The Primers and Elicitors
of Phylogenetic Regression

We note an orderly sequence of actions in the movement of animals, even in cases where every observer admits that the coordination is merely reflex. We see one act succeed another without confusion. Yet, tracing this sequence to its external causes, we recognize that the usual thing in nature is not for one exciting stimulus to begin immediately after another ceases, but for an array of environmental agents acting concurrently on the animal at any moment to exhibit correlative change in regard to it, so that one or the other group of them becomes—generally by increase in intensity— temporarily prepotent. Thus here dominates now this group, now that group in turn. It may happen that one stimulus overlaps another in regard to time. Thus each reflex breaks in upon a condition of relative equilibrium, which latter is itself reflex. In the simultaneous correlation of reflexes some combine harmoniously, being reactions that mutually reinforce.

—Sherrington (1947, p. 120)

Throughout the history of philosophy the question of free will has burdened and challenged the greatest minds of the human race. Are we humans the masters of our own destinies and fully responsible for our actions, or are we buffeted helplessly about by releasers, stimuli, the environment, primitive internal drives, or other forces beyond our control? In essence, we are asking, "What are the true causes of human behavior, and are those true causes under the conscious, willful control of the individual emitting the behavior, or are they determined by forces external to human will and volition?" (see chapter 9, this volume; Mark & Ervin, 1970; Rensch, 1971, for further discussion of this issue).

The phylogenetic regression–progression (PRP) model has clear implications for the freedom issue, especially from the Platonic perspective that postulates man is free when the rational part of his soul governs the animal feelings and passions. Plato believed that when man is enslaved by his inner passions and compulsions, he is no longer free and exists in a state of unnatural disharmony (Berofsky, 1973). In earlier chapters, we discussed the many genetic, biochemical, anatomical, neurological, and behavioral characteristics that we humans share with nonhuman species, and these similarities define the animal nature Plato alluded to 2,400 years ago. Further, the dynamics of regressing down to or progressing up from this animal nature was analyzed from a number of perspectives, including the triune brain concept and the notion of diminished cortical control. Also, some of the more important correlates of phylogenetic regression were described, including both adaptive and maladaptive correlates and consequences. In this chapter, we proceed a step further, and look at the primers and elicitors of regression and progression, those events or circumstances that make movement down or up the regression–progression continuum more probable.

Freedom, determinism, choice, and *causes* become rather relative terms in the context of the phylogenetic regression model, but this does not imply that all is disorder; in fact, order and predictability are presumed to fluctuate hierarchically as does most of nature, and further, they are presumed to resonate with the regression-progression continuum in predictable ways. This leads to a major assumption derived from the PRP model: Human action is more free, conscious, and variable toward the progressive end of the scale, and, following Razran's (1971) complex hierarchical model, behavior becomes more universal, less disrupted by environmental stimuli, and more functionally efficient at lower levels of functioning. This implies that elicitative causes operating at higher levels of human functioning are highly unpredictable and variable due to: (a) greater cognitive mediation between eliciting circumstances and resulting responses; (b) a greater number of systems involved in output (viz., both lower and higher systems, and their interactions); and (c) the vastly greater number of response alternatives possible in the higher systems. By virtue of our complex nervous systems and extensive central mediating capacities, we humans generally behave relatively "far from" our genes (Symonds, 1979), and clear-cut genetic causes of specific behavior patterns are difficult to isolate. As Scheller and Axel (1984) tell us, "The central nervous system integrates and filters the dictates of genes in ways that for the most part are inaccessible to experiment. The more complex the nervous system, the more elusive the relation between a set of genes . . . and observable traits" (p. 54).

By contrast, distance-from-the-genes is reduced when lower systems are predominant, and highly efficient, relatively simple, and thoroughly wired-in structures behave more or less independently of the higher, more variable systems. At the moment of orgasm, for example, neocortically mediated variability is drastically reduced, and the individual is little more than a Cartesian creature of instinct for a few blessed moments. If strict cause–effect relationships exist for human beings, they are discernible only for these simpler, primitive response systems (e. g., orgasm, the pupillary response, the startle response, simple reflexes, simple associative learning, and so on). At higher levels of social behavior, personality, and psychopathology, strict linear models fail us and we are forced to speculate about multiplicative and interacting causes.

Thus, circumstances that elicit regressive responses, or maintain primitive responses after regression has occurred, are more easily discerned than are the advanced causes that lead us to vote for Democrats rather than Republicans, to favor Nukes over no Nukes, to favor free will over determinism, or to abhor the very notion of the death penalty. Ease of identifying the elicitors of regressive behavior is only relative, however, and even here the partitioning of true causes is difficult. Discerning the true causes of isolated behavioral events, or worse still of movement on the regression–progression continuum, is especially difficult for the following reasons: (a) a multiplicity of interacting causes is involved in even the simplest adaptive behavior patterns; (b) the causes themselves may emanate primarily from within the behaving organism or, conversely, from the external environment; (c) causes may be relatively complete or incomplete in their effects; and (d) causes may have immediate or delayed effects. The phylogenetic regression–progression model postulates that primitive behavior patterns generally involve a relatively small array of primarily internal causes that are relatively complete and immediate in their effects; causes of advanced behavior patterns, in contrast, are seen as proportionately more external, delayed, and piecemeal in their effects. For example, the sight of a male robin's red breast is likely to have immediate and relatively complete control over the fighting and territorial display of a male conspecific, whereas the complex stimulus array of a verbal insult may produce no immediate effect in a human being, and the ill feeling engendered might never reach the behavioral system. Although the verbal insult was insufficient to promptly *elicit* an overt behavioral response, it no doubt *primed* the person for aggression or retaliation.

We see that the causes of behavior may originate primarily within the organism or primarily within the environment, and, further, that causes may be relatively incomplete and delayed (primers) or relatively complete and immediate (elicitors). *Primers*, or priming conditions, are stimuli that contribute to states of readiness to respond, but are, themselves, insufficient to elicit a response. *Elicitors* are stimuli that are (more or less) sufficient to set off or release a response or response pattern; often, they serve to release previously primed readiness or tendencies of the organism. A given class of stimuli (i. e., sexual urges, verbal insults, or alcohol intake) may act as either primers or elicitors, depending on the immediacy and completeness of their effects. A primer or elicitor is distinguished entirely by its consequences; a primer contributes to readinesses short of overt response whereas the elicitor releases readiness into behavior. Generally, primers originate internally and elicitors externally, but this distinction is not a hard and fast one. In fact, our distinction between primers and elicitors is basically a conceptual convenience that only roughly approximates the true causes operating.

INTERNAL PRIMERS

Often, it is difficult to clearly distinguish between internal and external primers or elicitors because, for example, a threatening external circumstance first acts upon the sensory apparatus and then quickly sets many internal processes into motion that serve as elicitors for further reactions in the sequence. For present purposes, the internal primer or elicitor is defined as one that arises primarily from inside the person and one that requires little or no external stimulation to produce significant behavioral consequences. For example, the individual's genetic material, which may produce major behavioral consequences irrespective of environmental circumstances, as with Huntington's chorea or familial mental retardation, would qualify as an internal primer, whereas drugs or alcohol would not. Alcohol or other drugs certainly exert major effects on the internal environment, but they initially act from the outside and are not generated by the internal structures of the body as is the genetic material or the hormonal secretions. So defined, there are relatively few internal primers, but they nevertheless exert powerful control over behavior, and are major mediators of phylogenetic regression.

For the most part, the internal priming conditions do not produce phylogenetic regression directly, but, instead, act to facilitate regression through strengthening response readinesses, as with the testosterone-aggression relationship, or through dys-releasing effects where brain damage or dysfunction allows chaotic sexual or aggressive behavior to emerge in unmodulated form. We see that internal primers or elicitors may operate within the context of normal or abnormal body structures and functions in facilitating the regressive process. We recall from earlier chapters that regression can be either adaptive or maladaptive, and certainly the internal primers and elicitors often serve to facilitate adaptive regressions of various sorts. For example, when one experiences extreme sexual tension after a long period of sexual abstinence, a benign and possibly adaptive phylogenetic regression results that owes much of its motive force to the biochemistry of the body. Note that the now sexually aroused individual has relinquished considerable freedom regarding feelings and emotions, and may be compelled to masturbate (perhaps against his will) to relieve tension, or to search for a sexual partner even though this may produce high levels of anxiety and guilt. The individual, no doubt, accepts all of this with aplomb, and never stops to ponder the "why" of the ancient imperatives operating. Indeed, we do not experience sexual lust by virtue of having simply learned to do so; rather, the sexual urge is defined more by its evolved neurological and hormonal substrates and the internal primers and elicitors that go with them, than by the external stimuli that release or set them off.

Genotypic Primers

Proceeding from the logic of the phylogenetic regression–progression argument, we may deduce that our genes influence us in two major ways:

1. First, the great mass of our genes make up the *phylogenotype,* those genes that we share with our ancestors in phylogeny. These genes define our animal nature, and provide us with the basic physical body and its supernumerous structural components. Those of nativist persuasion believe that much of our behavioral, emotional, and motivational equipment is also innate, and shared with lower animals. The phylogenotype generally has been ignored by social scientists because their concern is more with individual differences than similarities, and they prefer conceptual models that emphasize human distinctiveness rather than similarities between us and phylogenetically related species. Yet, if we are to truly understand the human species, we cannot ignore the great genetic overlap between humans and mammalian, and even reptilian species, and we absolutely cannot ignore the almost complete overlap between us and the great apes, most notably the chimpanzee (King & Wilson, 1975; Yunis & Prakash, 1982).

2. Secondly, only a small proportion of our overall genotype (1% or so—Washburn & Moore, 1980) is concerned with differences between us and our closest primate relative, the chimpanzee, and the resemblance between the DNA of man and chimpanzee is greater than that between the DNA of mouse and rat! (Kohne, 1975). Further, when the sequence of

blood proteins or immunological methods are used, man again is closer to the chimp and gorilla than they are to the other apes, the orangutang and the gibbon (Goodman, 1975). This small difference in genetic relationship between us and the higher nonhuman primates might be called the *transgenotype,* because by it we have transcended the great apes.

Several writers (Gould, 1977; Passingham, 1982) have noted that humans and chimpanzees differ anatomically far more than genetic (transgenotypic) differences would predict. For example, the body shape of humans and chimps is vastly more different than their respective differences in structural genes (Cherry, Case, & Wilson, 1978), and the same apparently holds true for brain size (Passingham, 1982). The DNA-trait relationship is complicated by the fact that not all genes are structural ones; the genotype also includes control genes that regulate growth and development by turning processes on and off (Kohne, 1975). Small changes in the regulating effects of such genes can effect dramatic alterations in anatomical structures (Gould, 1977), and perhaps in behavioral structures as well. Obviously, the transgenotype cannot account for all of the anatomical and behavioral differences between man and ape. Nevertheless, any comprehensive theory of human behavior must confront the small ape-human difference, and further confront the question of "How much do we need to know about our close genetic relative, the chimpanzee, in order to truly understand the human organism?".

In all sexually reproducing organisms, including humans, genetic material is transmitted from the parental organisms to offspring. Through the process of reductive gametogenesis in each parent organism, and eventual genetic recombination at fertilization, the offspring receives its appropriate complement of genetic material. The offspring genome may be described by the simple formula:

$$P + T = G$$

Where: P = phylogenotype
        T = transgenotype
        G = total genotype

Thus, the total genotype, G, of the human offspring is comprised of the phylogenetic factor, P, which is equal to the total genotype of the offspring's nearest living relative down the phylogenetic scale (e.g., the chimpanzee for human offspring), and, T, those inherited characters unique to the species. Taking into account that each parent's genetic contribution may be divided into P and T components, our basic formula may be expanded to read:

$$\text{Parent}_1 \ 1/2(P + T) + \ \text{Parent}_2 \ 1/2(P + T) = \text{offspring} \ (P + T) = G$$

This formula implies that individuals (e. g., the parent organisms just cited) within species vary on the P:T ratio, where one might be a smidgen closer to the nearest ancestral species, on the average, than the other. Actually, it is likely that characters within individuals also vary in their P:T ratios, as when, for example, a given human male is more chimpanzee-like in aggressiveness (higher P: lower T) than a given human female (lower P: higher T). Assuming P:T variation between traits within individuals, we may define the total P:T ratio for a given individual as the arithmetic mean of all the separate P:T ratios for innate characters. Thus, a given P or T, is, in actuality, an average of all the various phylogenetically nondistinctive or phylogenetically distinctive characters of the person.

From earlier discussion, we know that total P is very large for humans and total T very small, whether one speaks of individuals or populations. To the extent that T is large relative to P for an individual or group, we may say that P has been "transcended" to that degree. Given an estimated average P:T ratio of about 98:2 in human populations, we might assume, for example, that individuals vary, say, roughly within a range of P:T values from 97:3 to 99:1 for innate characters. Thus, the lower value would reflect less than average phylogenetic distinctiveness, whereas the higher value would reflect greater than average distinctiveness. Once biochemical and behavioral geneticists develop precise and valid measures of P and T for individuals—which seems likely in the future— then individual P:T ratios may be regressed against a boundless number of criterion measures in the areas of social behavior, personality, and psychopathology.

Table 6.1 contains theoretically derived P:T ratios for a number of phylogenetically conditioned characters. It is evident that many of our innate characters are shared with our closest living nonhuman relative, the chimpanzee, and only a few are species–specific for humans. Thus, the "chimpanzeeness" or P factor appears to be very large in humans for most innate characters, suggesting that the animal component of human nature is very large compared to the human part of human nature. This large P factor defines the phylogenetic inertia that makes progressing above our animal natures extremely difficult, and regressing to it extremely easy and frequent. And it is the phylogenotype that serves as the internal milieu, the internal set of priming and eliciting conditions that, below our conscious awareness, make many of our overt behaviors more or less probable.

Hormonal Priming Conditions

As Konner (1982) avers, the "humour" metaphor of the Elizabethans is intrinsically closer to the truth than was the "drive" metaphor of the early 20th century. Contrary to drive theory, the nervous system is not a

TABLE 6.1
Hypothetical P:T Ratios for Certain "Innate" Human Characters

Human Character	High P:T	Low P:T
Type of DNA strands	*	
Type of blood proteins	*	
Basic body structure	*	
Absolute brain size		*
Brain organization and specialization		*
Neocortex to total brain volume		*
Size of hindbrain and midbrain	*	
Size of diencephalon and striatum	*	
Within-species variation in brain size	*	
Amount of brain growth following birth	*	
Neocortical specializations for speech		*
Long life span	*	
Prolonged immaturity; slow growth rate	*	
Pronounced gender differences	*	
Omnivorous eating habits	*	
Meat-eating propensities	*	
Upright walking, bipedality		*
Reduced sense of smell	*	
Well developed sight and hearing	*	
Refined manual dexterity		*
Biological intelligence (Chapter 3)	*	
Abstract intelligence (chapter 3)		*
Well-developed nonverbal communication	*	
The primate "grin"→ human smile	*?	
Rudimentary affection and kinship	*	
Mothering behavior	*	
Fathering behavior		*
Separation anxiety	*	
Predatory aggression	*	
Hunting behavior	*	
Dominance aggression	*	
Territorial aggression	*	
Xenophobia	*	
Cooperative social behavior		*
Rudimentary tool use	*	
Rudimentary "cultural transmission"	*	

Note: P = phylogenetically conditioned characters in chimpanzees; T = phylogenetically conditioned characters unique to humans. "High" vs. "Low" ratios are relative: actually, all P:T ratios are "High", regardless of the size of T, given the magnitude of P (e. g., probably between 97% and 99% for innate characters).

The High P:T and Low P:T classifications in Table 6.1 were derived theoretically, based on the author's extrapolations from existing literature.

Passingham (1982) was a major source for much of Table 6.1, as were Tables 4.6 and 4.7 of the present book. However, the present author must take full responsibility for the P:T classifications.

High P:T ratios for human characters imply homologous trait formation. The author is aware of the highly inferential nature of this conceptual approach (see von Cranach, 1976).

hydraulic system where energy periodically builds up that requires reduction through prescribed actions. Of course, no fluid corresponding to the Elizabethan humour exists either, but the secretions of the endocrine system and the neurotransmitters represent rough analogies to the humours.

Behavioral scientists are turning more and more to concepts like "state," "arousal," and "excitation," that refer to general activation tendencies and specific ones as well, such as activation of the sexual, anger, or fear systems. Konner anticipates that the hope of the Elizabethans may be realized some day as we are able to effectively characterize both the stable aspects of temperament and short-lived changes in terms of the action of a few dozen hormones and neurotransmitters. Even the mysteries of long-term "personal growth" may eventually be unraveled through detailed analysis of what Konner calls the "subtle mixing" of these body and mind controlling substances. Such mixes appear to play prominent priming and elicitative roles in the complex matrix of causes controlling the dynamic stream of human behavior.

In chapter 5, we saw that gonadal hormones exert powerful effects on prenatal gender development in humans; specifically, the absence of testosterone in embryogenesis is associated with female development and its presence with male development. Also, we recall that testosterone not only effects differential gender development prenatally, but many other functions as well following birth—size, strength, secondary sexual characters, and gonadotropin regulation. Testosterone, however, is only one of many hormonal secretions, as is evident in Table 6.2.

In Table 6.2 we see that the major hormones may be classified into three major types, the amines, polypeptides, and steroids. The amines and peptides usually bind to specific receptors on the surface of target cell membranes, whereas the steroid hormones pass through the membrane and bind to specific receptor proteins in the cytoplasm. Then the steroid–protein complex enters the cell nucleus and interacts with the genetic

TABLE 6.2
Major Hormones Classified by Type of Chemical Compound

Amines	Polypeptides	Steroids
Epinephrine	Adrenocorticotropic hormone (ACTH)	Estrogen
Norepinephrine	Follicle-stimulating hormone (FSH)	Progesterone
Thyroxine	Luteinizing hormone (LH)	Testosterone
	Thyroid-stimulating hormone (TSH)	Glucocorticoids
	Insulin	
	Glucagon	
	Oxytocin	
	Antidiuretic hormone (vasopressin)	

Note: Table is exerpted from Rosenzweig and Leiman, 1982.

material, leading to the production of specific proteins (Rosenzweig & Leiman, 1982). Through these two primary modes of action, the hormonal system, in conjunction with the central nervous system, maintains control over a bewildering array of complex body functions, including sexual-reproductive processes, body growth, metabolic processes, glycogen formation and storage, secretion of gastric juices, immunological functions, emotional responses, and fight-or-flight reactions. All of these functions involve the subtle interaction of the endocrine communication system and the brain communication system working together to maintain physiological and psychological homeostasis. The pituitary gland, hypothalamus, limbic system, and the endocrine glands situated in various parts of the body, all comprise a superordinate negative-feedback control system designed to promote balance and order in a growing, changing, and often stressed human organism (Rosenzweig & Leiman, 1982).

Although the hormonal status of the body seldom acts as a direct elicitor of specific behavior patterns, it often serves as a priming or potentiating condition for phylogenetically regressive behavior. In contrast to the neural communication system that acts quickly and directly via a fixed network of channels, the hormonal system is slower and spreads messages broadly throughout the body that may be picked up by any cells possessing receptors for them (Rosenzweig & Leiman, 1982). The endocrine–aggression relationship illustrates the regressive hormonal priming effect very well. Despite protestations that the evidence is largely circumstantial and primarily based on research with nonhuman subjects (Quadagno, Briscoe, & Quadagno, 1977), it appears that androgenic hormones may prime humans for higher energy expenditure (Quadagno et al., 1977), aggressiveness (Zillmann, 1984), and dominance behavior (Mazur, 1983). Most researchers in the area (Hines, 1982; Mazur, 1983) agree that the hormone–aggression relationship in humans has not been decisively proven at present, for the following reasons: (a) weak and inconsistent findings; (b) weak experimental designs or anecdotal data (c) the hormone–aggression relationship may be indirect (e. g., via masculine body build); and (d) ethical constraints on research with human subjects. Nevertheless, one suspects that more refined future research will produce greater rather than lesser support for the hormonal mediation of aggression in humans. Until then, it seems best to view androgenic hormones as real, but weak primers for regressive aggressive behavior.

Neurotransmitters as Primers

Various biochemical neurotransmitters contribute to behavioral output by facilitating neural transmission at the synapse. Neural transmission may be quick and efficient at a particular synaptic junction, or it may be blocked depending on the neurochemical environment at the presynaptic terminals (Rosenzweig & Leiman, 1982). Because all behavior is ultimately mediated neurologically, we see how crucial synaptic transmitters are in the complex infrastructure of internal causes governing subjective experience and overt action. Along with genetic mechanisms and their effects on metabolism and protein synthesis, hormonal effects, and numerous other internal causal agents, the neurotransmitters make their own special contribution to output probabilities. No one knows exactly how many neurotransmitters exist, but a few substances have been definitely identified as synaptic transmitters (Rosenzwieg & Leiman, 1982) such as acetycholine, norepinephrine, epinephrine, and gamma aminobutyric acid (GABA). Table 6.3 summarizes the main transmitters and transmitter candidates and their associated behavioral functions. Obviously, the neurotransmitters are implicated in a wide variety of normal and pathological effects, ranging from simple neuromuscular innervation to pathological aggression and psychosis.

Some synaptic transmitters are widely distributed throughout the mammalian nervous system whereas others are not (Rosenzweig & Leiman, 1982); for example, the two major inhibitory transmitters, GABA, and glycine, account for about half of all synapses in the brain. The well-known excitatory transmitters (acetycholine, norepinephrine, serotonin, and dopamine) account for only a small proportion of the excitatory synapses, but it is thought that certain major excitatory transmitters await discovery—likely candidates are the amino acids glutamate and aspartate (Snyder & Bennett, 1976). The phylogenetic regression–progression model places great emphasis on inhibitory processes in the brain that serve to constrain and modulate motivation-emotion-behavior linkages mediated by the primitive reptilian and limbic systems (see chapter 8). Clearly, the brain's inhibitory and excitatory neurotransmitters play important roles in the more general processes of response inhibition and excitation in the central nervous system. Of course, the special enzyme acetycholinesterase also plays an important role in response inhibition by inactivating the neurotransmitter acetycholine at the synapse.

Biorhythmic and Biometereological Primers

The 24-hour fluctuations observable in the activity and metabolic processes of plants and animals are referred to as *circadian cycles,* from the Latin words meaning "about a day." Circadian rhythms are valuable because they synchronize bodily states and behavior to changes in the environment, such as the day–night sequence, oceanic tides, and other changes associated with the revolving earth. These biorhythms subserve certain species-typical action programs of living creatures, including rest and activity cycles, sleep cycles, primary diurnality or nocturnality, biochemical fluctuations, hunger–thirst patterns, and timing of vital metabolic processes. These orderly and stable fluctuations help keep the animal within its prescribed species-typical range of response, and within its appropriate adaptive limits. One measure of the adaptive success of a given creature is its ability to integrate the multitudinous circadian production lines, or internal timekeepers, which are involved in ongoing basic life processes—enzymatic and hormonal activity, production of blood cells, body temperature, fluid intake and excretion, and so on. Luce (1971) summarizes how we humans are governed by these internal timekeepers in our daily life as are other animals:

> Man, no exception to this daily ebb and flow, may be unaware that his body temperature, blood pressure, and pulse, respiration, blood sugar, hemoglobin levels, and amino acid levels are changing in a circadian rhythm. So too, do the levels of the adrenal hormones in his blood and concentrations of essential biochemicals throughout his nervous system. Urine also shows the influence of the circadian cycle. We excrete rhythmically, not merely according to time of liquid intake . . . there is a rhythmic fluctuation in the contents of the urine, along with almost every physiological function, from the deposition of fat or sugar in the liver to the rate at which cells are dividing. (p. 1)

Normal functioning for human beings is largely premised on these biological clocks, and disruptions of the individual's normal cycle may cause malfunctions of various sorts, including somatic and psychosomatic complaints (Coleman, Butcher, & Carson, 1980). A report prepared for the National Institute of Mental Health by Weitzman and Luce (1970) noted the adverse effects of rapid technological change on "the invisible circadian cycle that may govern our susceptibility to disease or shock, our emotions, our performance, our alertness or stupefaction" (p. 279). Studies by Stroebel (1967, 1969) further suggest that disturbances in periodic processes may contribute to human psychopathology even though such asynchronies may not be available to clinical observation. Stroebel hypothesizes that disturbances in the rest–activity cycle may be the temporal common denominator in human neuroses and possibly other pathological reactions. Stroebel (1967) also suggests that neocortical cognitive responses may be minimally responsive to circadian variations, whereas emotions appear to be strongly affected. In regression–progression terminology, the phylogenetically advanced cognitive sphere may have transcended primitive temporal regulation to a degree, whereas the more primitive limbic-emotional system continues to be temporally regulated.

In circadian synchronicity we see an internal response system that affects the overall condition of the body, the level of activation, and the

TABLE 6.3
The Primary Neurotransmitters and Their Functions

Neuromuscular Transmitter

Acetycholine (ACh)

The neurotransmitter at nerve–muscle connections for all voluntary muscles of the body as well as at many of the involuntary (autonomic) synapses. Also located in CNS, but role is unclear

Acts as an excitatory transmitter at synapses between motor nerves and skeletal muscles

Acts as an inhibitory transmitter between vagus nerve and heart muscle

Catecholamine Transmitters

Norepinephrine

Is produced mainly in neurons whose bodies lie in brainstem nuclei; however, the axons of these nuclei project widely in the brain

One of the two catecholamine neurotransmitters; serves both excitatory and inhibitory functions

Neurotransmitter of the sympathetic nerves of the ANS which mediate emergency responses—e.g., acceleration of heart, dilatation of bronchi, and elevation of blood pressure

Involved in arousal and wakefulness, control of eating, intracranial self-stimulation, learning, and memory

Norepinephrine is a hormone as well as a neurotransmitter; elevated levels may be correlated with intensity of emotional encounters (Elmadjian, Hope, & Lamson, 1957)

Norepinephrine may produce a metabolic byproduct called adrenochrome. Adrenochrome has hallucinatory properties, suggesting a possible link between norepinephrine and schizophrenia

Dopamine

Dopamine is produced mainly by neurons whose bodies lie in the basal forebrain and brainstem; the axons project to the basal ganglia, the olfactory system, and limited parts of the cerebral cortex. Highest concentration of dopamine is in hypothalamus

A major transmitter in the corpus striatum, a part of the brain which regulates motor behavior. Destruction of the dopamine neurons in the corpus striatum is apparently responsible for the symptoms of Parkinson's disease, such as rigidity and tremor

In circuits involved in the control of voluntary movement, emotional arousal, learning, and memory

Many clinical and research findings strongly suggest that abnormal levels of dopamine are associated with schizophrenia. The dopamine hypothesis is among the leading theories on the causes of schizophrenia

The Serotonergic Transmitter

Serotonin

Serotonin is produced in the CNS, mainly by cells in the midline of the brainstem. The neurons that produce serotonin form the *raphe nuclei*. These neurons send long axons to structures throughout the cerebral hemispheres

Serves both excitatory and inhibitory functions. Involved in circuits mediating sleep and emotional arousal

Changes in the activity of serotonin neurons are related to the actions of psychedelic drugs

Serotonin inhibits aggressive behavior in rats; thus, decreased serotonin is associated with

(Continued)

TABLE 6.3 *(Continued)*

increased aggression (Mandel, Kempf, Mack, Haug, & Puglisi-Allegra, 1981). Reduced brain serotonergic control also correlates with aggression in humans (Valzelli & Morgese, 1981) and also possibly with the intense self-mutilative behavior seen in the Lesch-Nyhan Syndrome (Mizuno & Yugari, 1975)

Amino Acids

Gamma-aminobutyric acid (GABA)

This is one of the amino acid transmitters in the brain. It has no known function other than serving as a neurotransmitter and is found almost exclusively in the brain

GABA is the main inhibitory transmitter in the brain. It acts to reduce the firing of neurons and is found at 25 to 40% of all synapses in the brain

Glycine

Serves as a conventional amino acid in protein synthesis and general metabolism, but also serves as an inhibitory neurotransmitter in small neurons in the spinal cord and brainstem. In these locations it is the transmitter for 25 to 40% of the synapses and predominates over GABA that is more prominent in the higher centers

Glutamic acid

Is one of the major amino acids in general metabolism and protein synthesis, but is also a major neurotransmitter. It appears to be the neurotransmitter of the major neuronal pathway that connects the cerebral cortex and corpus striatum. It is also the neurotransmitter of the granule cells, which are the most numerous neurons in the cerebellum

It stimulates the neurons to fire and is probably the principal excitatory neurotransmitter in the brain. It may also be the primary neurotransmitter of the visual pathway

Neuropeptides

The Endorphins

The term *endorphin* is a contraction of "endogenous morphine." Have been called the "body's own narcotics"

The endorphins act on narcotic receptors located in specific areas of the brain. These include the pain-processing regions in the medial thalamus, the periaqueductal gray of the brainstem, and specific layers of the spinal cord

The endorphins also act on the narcotic receptors abundant in the amygdaloid nuclei. Stimulation of this area may be related to the euphoria that narcotics produce

The endorpins influence a variety of behavioral and physiological processes in addition to pain: temperature regulation, respiration, cardiovascular response, and possibly certain epileptic seizures

The endorphins have also been implicated in reinforcement or reward, memory consolidation, attention, and male copulatory response (Bolles & Faneslow, 1982)

The Enkephalins

The enkephalins are endorphins composed of two peptides, each containing five amino acids. Enkephalin neurons are localized to areas of the brain that regulate functions that are influenced by opiate drugs

The enkephalins are mostly inhibitory, especially in circuits involving pain. They can mimic the effects of opiates (e.g., can relieve pain, addiction in animals)

Note: The contents of Table 6.3 are based on material from Rosenzweig and Leiman (1982) and Snyder (1980) unless otherwise noted.

ability to cope with stress. Consequently, the biological clock may be viewed as a subtle and invisible mediator or primer of phylogenetic regression by augmenting the adverse effects of threatening and stressful external stimuli. The hormones, neurotransmitters, and the biorhythms all act similarly in these respects: They all may heighten activity and tension levels; they all may be implicated in pathological reactions; and they all may prime the individual for regressive behavior. Note here that internal and external primers (or eliciting conditions) interact with one another, and seldom, if ever, act independently. Even if an individual is highly internally primed for a certain behavioral reaction, an external elicitor is usually required to set it off.

Biorhythms are not limited to circadian regulation, but may occur monthly, seasonally, annually, and in many other sequences. Thus, the rhythmic temporal regulation of body processes and behavior runs both wide and deep. Those many instances where biorhythms and external environmental conditions interact represent good examples of how internal, primed readinesses are released into behavior by special external elicitors. The effects of biometeorological variables on behavior (Campbell & Beets, 1978) represents a good case in point. Research in the area has suggested numerous interesting relationships such as variation in suicide rates with season of year (Cerbus, 1970) and degree of weather turbulence (Tromp & Bouma, 1973), variation in psychiatric hospital admission rates with season of year (James & Griffin, 1968) and geomagnetic disturbances (Friedman, Becker, & Bachman, 1963), and variation in cosmic ray activity with ratings of psychiatric patient behavior (Friedman, Becker, & Bachman, 1965). Briere, Downes, and Spensley (1983) examined 4,025 visits to a psychiatric emergency room in relation to meterological variables for the summer months across 2 consecutive years. Weather involving low barometric pressure and high cloud cover was related to emergency room visits for depression, and air pollution was correlated with schizophrenia and total visits. Briere et al.'s correlations are interesting and provocative, but we are left in the dark regarding the causal variables (if any) operating.

Other behavioral variables correlated with meterological conditions include automobile accidents (Moos, 1964), reaction time (Wilson, 1974), brightness discrimination (Beal, 1974), mental test scores, (Cerbus & Travis, 1973), and criminal behavior (Sells & Wills, 1971). Moreover, the phases of the moon reputedly affect a wide range of human pathologies—homocide, suicide, alcoholism, pyromania, somnamulism, lycanthropy, and so on, but the empirical support for "moon madness" or "lunacy" is very slim (Campbell & Beets, 1978; Rotton & Kelly, 1985).

Overall, it is clear that external biometeorological variables and internal biorhymic variables interact in significant ways, but determination of the specific causal mechanisms operating must await much further re-search. Nevertheless, it is reasonable to place circadian rhythms and the biometerological-biorhythm interaction into the category of primers of regressive and sometimes abnormal behavior.

Brain Damage as Priming Condition

Although psychiatrically normal people may regress to primitive levels of functioning under threat or provocation, the brain-damaged person is particularly primed for phyloregressive behavior. This regression-prone-ness may emanate from diminished capacity of the neocortex to inhibit the lower centers, or the lower centers themselves may be damaged producing pathological disinhibitions and excitations. For example, certain types of brain damage may produce sexual hyperexcitation where the individual may masturbate almost constantly and other response systems, particularly the higher ones, fade completely into the background. Mark and Ervin (1970) describe the sexual aspects of the temporo-limbic dyscontrol syndrome, epitomized by the patient, Theresa L. At the time she was seen in the psychiatric ward of the Boston City Hospital, she was masturbating 18 to 20 times a day, and was being assaultive and abusive with patients and attendants as well. She had a history of chaotic and compulsive homosexual and heterosexual sexual relations, and was de-scribed as willing to use anything and anybody for sexual gratification. Mark and Ervin commented that her behavior was reminiscent of the hypersexual behavior of monkeys subjected to bilateral temporal lobecto-mies (Klüver & Bucy, 1937). Thus, it was not surprising when brain wave examination revealed that Theresa suffered from generalized brain abnor-malities with a focus of abnormal waves in the right frontal temporal region.

Theresa's case does not clarify for us whether the hypersexuality was due to loss of cortico–temporal inhibitory capability, or whether direct damage to the limbic system was at fault. Although the symptoms of temporal lobe lesions in animals often qualitatively resemble those in humans (Kolb & Whisaw, 1980), temporal lobectomies in humans do not always produce uniform outcomes. For instance, Kolb and Whisaw say that unilateral temporal lobectomies in humans do not produce the hypersexuality seen in bilateral lobectomies with animals, and, further, that bilateral lobectomies in humans are so rare that generalizations are not possible. To complicate things further, Blumer and Walker (1975) found that 70% of their temporal lobe epileptics did exhibit sexual abnormalities, most commonly a *decrease* in sexual interest! Several writers (Kolb & Whisaw, 1980; Mark & Ervin, 1970), suggest that destruction of the amygdala may be the most important factor in the

Klüver–Bucy syndrome of excessive tameness, hypersexuality, and hyperphragia, for the amydala and several other limbic structures are removed in the bilateral temporal lobectomy. If so, the problem is more due to hyperexcitation and/or disinhibition within the amygdaloid nuclei, rather than diminished temporal lobe control of the lower centers.

The example of dyscontrolled sexuality reveals the complexity of the brain mechanisms involved. Yet, despite the forbidding complexity, it is clear that brain damage, whether to lower or higher centers, can prime a person for primitive outbursts or regressions that circumvent rational control on the part of the afflicted individual. We return to this point in later chapters, especially chapters 10 and 11.

Cognitive Primers and Elicitors

This category is uniquely human as far as we know. Here thoughts, images, ideas, concepts, values, and a host of other mental stimuli may act from within the individual to retard or facilitate phylogenetic regression. Although regressive phenomena are emphasized in this chapter, it should be noted that mental stimuli play crucial roles in phylogenetic progression as well: In fact, neocortically mediated cognitive "elicitors" of phylogenetic progression (i. e., rational thoughts that beget other rational thoughts in meaningful and complex sequences) are the main factors that distinguish humans from lesser intelligent species. The hegemony of cognitive–linguistic processes in species *Homo sapiens* generally is recognized by layman and expert alike, so let us concentrate more acutely on the dynamics of regression.

As usual, let us first construct a reasonable hypothetical hierarchy to accomodate the various forms of mentation. A possible hierarchy might be: dreams→images→fantasies→emotional thoughts→emotionless thoughts. Freud (1900/1953) viewed the dream as a primitive, primary process kind of thinking motivated by energy generated by the id. Such thinking occurs in the sleeping state, is saturated wtih primitive drives like sex and aggression, and, while occuring, is subject to little or no critical modification by the rational ego (neocortex). Imagistic thinking is only a bit more progressive than the dream because it occurs in the waking state and is subject to some conscious awareness within the fleeting and temporary nature of the images themselves. Fantasies often have a dream-like quality and incorporate a multiplicity of images, but they are subject to considerable conscious control and often are tied to real objects in the world. Further, fantasies may involve either regressive or progressive content (Bailey, Burns, & Bazan, 1982), and, all in all, seem to fall toward the middle of the proposed hierarchy. Emotional thoughts involving a modicum of rationality are a step further up the scale, and sometimes may be quite advanced as occurs, for example, when scholars debate the relative virtues of their own disciplines, political views, and so on. The most reserved professors will occasionally "lose their cool" over issues like the innateness of intelligence, how to solve economic crises, and almost any other conceivable difference of opinion. The main point is that—immediately prior to the emotional thought entering consciousness—the reserved professor was placidly puffing on his pipe pondering the mysteries of the universe, but once stimulated by the provocative thought he regresses to limbic feelings of ego-threat, anger, or retribution. Of course, the unemotional thought, following Rado (1969), defines the upper pole of the cognitive hierarchy. This level of functioning approaches the philosopher's notion of pure thought, a condition rarely experienced by the human species with its ever-present passions and animosities.

Our main point here is that mentation below the level of unemotional, rational thought is likely to induce regressive processes, and the more primtive the mentation operating, the more regression should occur. Regression feeds on itself and one primitive cognitive indulgence is likely to lead to another.

EXTERNAL ELICITORS

Whereas most primers are internal, most elicitors are external in that they literally derive their energy from outside the body. However, external elicitors vary greatly in terms of phylogenetic primitiveness, in terms of strength of the elicitor-behavior pattern relationship, in terms of the sensory–motor systems they primarily affect, and so forth. Receiving a painful burn to the hand or having the words "I love you" whispered in your ear both represent stimulus conditions that may elicit phylogenetically regressive responses, but there the similarities end. The painful burn obviously operates at a more primitive level of the nervous system than does the verbal endearment, as could be easily tested by applying a painful stimulus to a wild wolf's paw and noting the animal–human response differential, and then whispering "I love you" in its ear and computing a similar differential! This absurd example reveals how external elicitors differ dramatically along a primitive-advanced continuum, proceeding from evolved elicitor-reflex and elicitor-fixed action pattern responses at the primitive pole up to verbal or imagistic stimuli that provoke regressive fantasies and thoughts at the mental level.

Pain, Injury, and Fear

Approach and avoidance are the most fundamental parameters of all behavior, and writers from antiquity to the present have tried to characterize human motivation bifactorially, usually concentrating on some

variation of the pleasure–pain theme. In the previous chapter, we discussed the pleasure–pain dialectic and concluded that pain-avoidance was
more phylogenetically primitive and more important in the day-to-day life
of animals than is pleasure-seeking. In that discussion, increased pleasure-seeking and/or pain-avoidance were analyzed as correlates or consequences of phylogenetic regression, but let us now look at them as
elicitors of regression. Although pleasurable circumstances often serve as
elicitors of regression, it is likely that pain-avoidance is the more significant elicitor across situations. Purely and simply, to avoid threat to
survival is probably the most powerful motivational imperative known to
man or animal, and we therefore find that the experience of pain, and to a
lesser extent, the threat of pain can quickly elicit regressive behavior.

Numerous studies have assessed the effects of painful electrical shocks
on the aggressive behavior of experimental animals. The most common
paradigm involves placing two rats in a box with an electrical grid floor
and then applying shock to their feet at periodic intervals. Upon being
shocked, the rats typically face one another, rear up on their hind legs,
and assume what is called the *boxing posture*. Some writers (Ulrich &
Azrin, 1962) have referred to this post-shock posturing as stereotyped or
reflexive fighting, but the response pattern observed is more likely
defensive than aggressive (Johnson, 1972; Moyer, 1976). To complicate
matters further, the boxing posture is moderated by a number of variables
including the intensity of shock, the size of the experimental chamber, the
length of the testing session, age of the animal, and strain of the subject
population (Ulrich, 1966). Despite these complications, it is clear that a
significant elicitor-response pattern relationship exists between painful
shock and defensive aggression in rats, and many other species as well
(Moyer, 1976). That the elicited behavior in the boxer rat research is not
pure aggression nor completely reflexive does not nullify the relationship;
qualifications notwithstanding, the animal manifestly regresses to more or
less species–specific and adaptive methods for protecting itself when
faced with an alien and painful stimulus.

It is important to distinguish here between the experience of pain when
the source is evident versus when it is not evident. Compare, for example,
an animal being shocked by a strange and nonidentifiable stimulus, as
with the boxer rat research, versus a prey animal being attacked by its
normal predator in the wild. In the former case, the animal may emit a
very generalized defensive response pattern upon receiving a strange
shock from a strange source, while in the latter case the pain of being
wounded by the predator feeds into the phylogenetically conditioned
flight-or-fight software of the animal. The wounded animal would thus
exhibit a more clearly distinguishable relationship between the painful
elicitor and the action patterns of its species than would the albino rat
responding to painful shock under rather artificial laboratory conditions.

Although the laboratory studies on foot shock in rats leave many questions unanswered, there is little doubt that under certain circumstances pain can lead to intense attack (Moyer, 1976). It has been observed that a wounded animal is much more irritable than a healthy one (Scott, 1958), and is more likely to react aggressively to a wide range of nonspecific stimuli that are typically ineffective in arousing aggression in normal animals (Valzelli, 1981). Also, pain-elicited aggression has been demonstrated in a variety of species including the monkey (Plotnik, Mir, & Delgado, 1971), the cat (Ulrich, Wolff, & Azrin, 1964), the wild rat (Karli, 1956), and the gerbil (Dunstone, Cannon, Chickson, & Burns, 1972). Little laboratory research on pain-elicited aggression has been done with humans, but our own introspections and every day observations suggest that the pain-aggression response pattern holds for us as well. Yet, as always, the picture is vastly more complex for us than for the albino rat or even the monkey. Certainly the "ouch dammit!" response is frequently seen, but what about the pain-elicited attack of one human being to another? For humans, learning, context, the affiliative and power relations between the two individuals, and a host of other factors would mediate and obscure any pain-attack tendencies that might exist. Yet, in highly regressive encounters, such as a fist fight, for example, the underlying pain-aggression relation is likely to assert itself.

From the phylogenetic standpoint, the subjective, emotional counterpart of pain and wounding is fear. Literally speaking, pain is a noxious perception actually experienced by the animal or person, whereas fear is a noxious emotion often based on the anticipation of pain or injury. As such, pain only can be perceived when an actual noxious stimulus is present, but the emotion of fear, at least in the higher animals, can be stimulated by the mere anticipation of danger. Indeed, most animals flee from danger due to fear and not pain: If a given species was phylogenetically prepared to flee only upon the perception of pain, it would be at a great selective disadvantage. In fact, in moving up the phylogenetic scale from one-celled creatures to human beings, it is clear that fear becomes more important and sheer pain less important as reliable motivators of attack or escape behavior. At the human level, we see the fear system developed to such an exquisite degree that it can be activated not only by real threats to life and limb but by vague anticipations and even thoughts as well.

Chemical and Drug Effects

There are numerous chemical substances that affect the functioning of the nervous system and many of them can prime or elicit regressive behavior. Unfortunately, progressive behavior is more difficult to elicit chemically because the action of psychoactive drugs on the cerebral cortex is at present so poorly understood (Julien, 1981). Certain chemical substances may inhibit neocortical functioning, but, except for the mild energizing effects of caffeine, nicotine, and amphetamine, it is unclear as to which substances serve to facilitate higher mental functions such as intelligence, logical thinking, or creativity. Throughout the ages, however, people have sought higher truths and spiritual fulfillment through the use of chemical agents that affect the lower rather than the higher centers.

In contrast to the neocortex, both the inhibitory and facilitory effects of a large variety of drugs on brain stem and limbic functions are well known (Julien 1981). Tranquilizers, hallucinogenic drugs, antipsychotic drugs, hypnotics, depressants, and stimulants all primarily affect the lower emotional and motivational systems, and are therefore often implicated in regression as we have defined it. Such drugs may influence regression in at least four ways: (a) reptilian and limbic regressions may be inhibited or even reversed by antianxiety or antihallucinogenic substances; (b) regressions may be retarded by the paradoxical effects of certain neural excitants (e. g., the effects of amphetamines in controlling some types of hyperactivity in children); (c) certain substances may facilitate regressive behavior through their direct excitatory effects (e. g., as with the confused and disorganized behavior, irritability, fear and suspicion, etc., in the amphetamine psychosis); and (d) the inhibitory and constraining effects of the neocortex may be diminished so that lower drives and emotions are released into behavior. As we see, drug-related regressive behavior is complex and may be produced in a number of ways, although diminution of neocortical control over the lower centers often is an important part of the picture.

According to Julien (1981), there are five major classes of psychoactive drugs that may be classified according to their behavioral effects (see Table 6.4). These include the sedative-hypnotic compounds, behavioral stimulants, the opiates, the antipsychotic agents, and the psychedelics and hallucinogens. Julien makes several important points regarding the above classification: (a) the action of psychoactive drugs is seldom restricted to any one functional or anatomical subdivision of the brain; (b) the action of any given psychoactive drug is explained by alterations in the synthesis, release, action, and metabolism of a specific neurotransmitter chemical—in other words, the drug acts upon the neurotransmtiter and then the transmitter chemical acts upon the brain which, in turn, produces behavior change; (c) it is important to understand that psychoactive drugs do not produce new physiological or behavioral responses—they simply modify ongoing processes. Most experts agree that the behavioral effects of psychoactive drugs is secondary to their blocking or modification of synaptic transmission in the brain; (d) the classification of psychoactive drugs given in Table 6.4 is not a rigid one because different drugs may sometimes exert similar effects, and the same drug may produce different effects depending on dosage level; and (e) the use of centrally acting drugs often creates pleasurable states of consciousness and pleasurable mood changes that are capable of inducing psychological dependence hazardous to the well-being of the individual. Such dependencies may become powerful compulsions in some persons; so powerful, in fact, that the need for the drug and its "high" may come to dominate the very existence of the person to the extent that all other motives, both higher and lower, are overridden.

Julien's (1981) discussion of the sedative–hypnotic drugs is especially relevant to phylogenetic regression, for he postulates a continuum of behavioral sedation where progressively primitive systems of the brain come into operation with increased drug intake. The continuum goes as follows, proceeding step-by-step downward from absence of the drug (normality) to lethal dosage (death): normality → relief from anxiety → disinhibition →sedation → hypnosis (sleep) → general anesthesia → coma → death. Of particular relevance to phylogenetic regression is the level of disinhibition that occurs fairly early in the sequence. This means that a relatively small dose of the appropriate central nervous system (CNS) depressant, such as ethyl alcohol, has the potential to relax the restraining power of the neocortex and allow limbic and reptilian material to slip through.

The mild sedatives or tranquilizers such as meprobamate or the benzodiazepines (e. g., Librium and Valium) are also very interesting from the phylogenetic standpoint. These drugs are extremely popular because they produce relief from anxiety, the neurotic scourge of modern society. But what is anxiety? The phylogenetic regression model views anxiety as the hyperfunction of the limbic system that, among other things, is designed to produce the powerful emotion of fear when actual danger or even the threat of danger is present. For animals and for primitive man, danger was external and perceived through the senses, and once the pangs of fear were felt, flight behavior was elicited and fear diminished with escape. What happens, however, when the individual possesses the intellectual capacity to imagine lethal threat when only the ego is threatened, or when internal threats are diffuse, overdetermined, or not even subject to conscious awareness at all? The result of this rather messy, excessive, and distinctly human frailty is the experience of anxiety, a vague, subjectively painful apprehensiveness from which there is no easy escape. So viewed, anxiety is a neocorticalized elaboration of the limbic fear response, and as such is literally a mild form of active phylogenetic regression. However, it is active only in the sense that there is cortical complicity, for the psychological mechanisms underlying the production of anxiety operate unconsciously.

TABLE 6.4
Five Major Classes of Psychoactive Drugs

Sedative-hypnotic Compounds (CNS Depressants)

Barbiturates

Long-acting: phenobarbital (**Luminal**)
Immediate-acting: amobarbital (**Amytal**)
Short-acting: pentobarbital (**Nembutal**), secobarbital (**Seconal**)
Ultrashort-acting: pentothal (**Thiopental**)

Nonbarbiturate hypnotics

Glutethimide (**Doriden**)
Methyprylon (**Noludar**)
Methaqualone **Parest, Quaalude, Somnafac, Sopor**)

Antianxiety agents

Meprobamate (**Miltown, Equanil**)
Chlordiazepoxide (**Librium**)
Diazepam (**Valium**)

Others

Ethyl alcohol, Bromide, Chloral hydrate, Ether, Chloroform

Behavioral Stimulants and Convulsants

Amphetamines

Benzedrine, Dexedrine, Methedrine

Clinical antidepressants

Monoamine oxidase (MAO) inhibitors: **Parnate**
Tricyclic compounds: **Tofranil, Elavil**

Cocaine

Convulsants

strychnine, **Metrazol, Picrotoxin**

(Continued)

TABLE 6.4 *(Continued)*

Caffeine

Nicotine

Narcotic analgesics

Opiates

  Opium, heroin, morphine, codeine, **Demerol**

Antipsychotic agents

Phenothiazines

  chlorpromazine **(Thorazine)**

Reserpine

  (Serpasil)

Butyrophenones

  haloperidol **(Haldol)**, droperidol **(Inapsine)**

Lithium

Psychedelics and Hallucinogens

LSD (lysergic acid diethylamide)

Mescaline

Psilocybin

Cannibis

  marijuana, hashish, tetrahydrocannabinol

From *A primer of drug action* (3rd ed.) by Robert M. Julien, W. H. Freeman and Company. Copyright © 1981.

The compounds usually classified as CNS stimulants are drugs that increase the behavioral activity of the individual. These drugs differ widely in their molecular structure and mechanisms of action, and do not fall on a neat, graded continuum of effects as do the sedative compounds. Nevertheless, the central stimulants may be subdivided into several groups of agents that are similar enough in sites and mechanisms of action to be discussed together (Julien, 1981). These are summarized in Table 6.5. The first two groups of central stimulants—behavioral stimulants and clinical antidepressants—share the ability to augment the action of the neurotransmitter norepinephrine. As we know, norepinephrine and its close relative epinephrine (adrenalin) play well-established roles in the body's response to stress and are important features of the fight/fright/ flight response pattern. Norepinephrine is much more abundant in the brain than is epinephrine, however, and several researchers (Bunney, Pert, Rosenblatt, Pert, & Gallaper, 1979; Schildkraut, 1965) have suggested that a deficiency of norepinephrine is associated with depression whereas an oversupply is associated with mania. Julien (1981) postulates a continuum of norepinephrine effects with depression and mania at the extremes and normality in the middle.

Of the various stimulants, amphetamine is perhaps the most clear-cut example of an elicitor of phylogenetic regression. Structurally, amphetamine closely resembles norepinephrine, and at low doses it evokes an alerting, arousal, or behavior-activating response similar to the normal reaction to an emergency or to stress. This would, by definition, represent a mild regression characterized primarily by an activation of the limbic system and an emotional readiness to fight or flee as the situation

TABLE 6.5
Classification on CNS Stimulants

Class	Mechanism of Action
Behavioral Stimulants	Augmentation of norepinephrine neurotransmitter (e.g., cocaine, amphet.)
Clinical antidepressants	Blockade of norepinephrine uptake (e.g., **Tofranil, Elavil**) Increased norepinephrine secondary to MAO inhibition (e.g., **Parnate**)
Convulsants	Blockade of inhibitory synapses (e.g., **Metrazol**)
General cellular stimulants	Activation of intracellular metabolism (Caffeine) Stimulation of certain acetycholine synapses (Nicotine)

Note: From A primer of drug action (3rd ed.) by Robert M. Julien. W. H. Freeman and Company. Copyright © 1981.

requires. A mild phylogenetic progression also is simultaneously involved by virtue of increased alertness of the neocortex and small but perceptible improvements in mental concentration and intellectual performance may be seen. At high dosage levels, however, a pattern of psychosis is induced that may be indistinguishable from schizophrenia. The affected individual demonstrates confused and disorganized behavior, compulsive repetition of meaningless acts, fear, irritability, suspiciousness, hallucinations and delusions, and also may exhibit extremely aggressive and antisocial behavior. Moreover, a "whole body orgasm" may be induced that produces a subjective experience of sexual ecstasy in the user. All of these pathological or deviant responses are part-segments and mixtures of limbic and reptilian content that have been released through the action of the drug. Thus, the content of the amphetamine psychosis is not manufactured by the drug's effect on the brain, but, rather, the drug, in high enough dosage, serves to release pre-existing emotions and response patterns encoded in the brain in phylogeny. In the amphetamine psychosis we see a caricature of our phylogenetically old tendencies and predispositions in extreme form: fear, sex, aggression, and xenophobia.

The convulsants are interesting in that they appear to act at the most primitive levels of neural functioning, acting primarily on the spinal cord and brain stem and exerting minimal effect on the cortex. These drugs, in effect, operate at the level of physical behavior, and their psychological effects and treatment applications are minimal. Moreover, they do not exert their effects through the norepinephrine synapses as do most of the other psychoactive drugs, and therefore do not activate the limbic emergency syndrome nor do they produce the continuum of behavior states seen in the sedative compounds. Thus, the convulsants produce the greatest amount of phylogenetic regression literally, but the gross spinal and brain stem motor patterns elicited are not very meaningful theoretically nor do they tell us much about human behavior.

Lastly, the general cellular stimulants deserve a word of mention. Caffeine and nicotine fall into this category and are among the most widely used stimulants in the world. The main pharmacological actions of caffeine are exerted on the CNS, the heart, lungs, kidneys, and the arteries supplying the heart and brain. Most of these effects appear to result from the caffeine-induced augmentation of the rates of cellular metabolism. Caffeine acts as a powerful stimulant to nerve tissue, and the cortex, being the most sensitive, is affected first followed by the lower centers. Thus, the earliest effects of caffeine are increases in mental alertness, restlessness, and wakefulness, which are produced without the disruptions of intellectual and motor activity that usually accompany liberal use of amphetamine, cocaine, or the convulsants. Caffeine is not particularly interesting from the phylogenetic standpoint, but it is capable of producing mild regressions and progressions like those seen at low doses of amphetamine. Nicotine also is a potent component that exerts powerful effects on the brain, spinal cord, the peripheral nervous system, and various other body structures. These effects occur indirectly due to the drug's capacity to excite receptors that are involved in the production of acetycholine. This stimulation of acetycholine receptors produces effects similar to those of caffeine, but the release of epinephrine also is facilitated thereby bringing the fight/fright/flight emergency system into play. Thus, heavy smoking and probably excessive coffee drinking (and their combined use) appear to activate or set into readiness the limbic emergency system, and this may explain why excessive use of these drugs is associated with anxiety, nervousness, and tension.

The Special Case of Ethyl Alcohol.   In concluding our discussion of psychopharmacological elicitors of phylogenetic regression (and progression), let us take the drug ethyl alcohol and analyze its behavioral and psychological ramifications. Of all the psychoactive drugs, alcohol constitutes the greatest social problem due to its capacity to disinhibit neocortical functioning and release primitive behavior and emotion from their normal constraints. A vast literature has developed around the relationships between alcohol consumption, release of aggressive behavior, and criminality. Despite the accumulation of a wealth of empirical facts bearing on these relationships, theory is almost totally lacking in the area (Collins, 1981). What is eminently clear, however, is that alcohol is strongly associated with aggression and criminality, either as a direct cause or as a significant moderating variable (Valzelli & Morgese, 1981). Wolfgang's (1958) research on 588 cases of homicide in Philadelphia for the years 1948-1952 is typical. Using police homicide records, Wolfgang found that alcohol was present in either offender, victim, or both in 64% of the cases. Similarly, Voss and Hepburn (1968) found alcohol present in 53% of the 370 cases of homocide studied, and Amir (1967) found alcohol implicated in 34% of the rapes he analyzed from Philadelphia for the years 1958-1960. Johnson, Gibson, and Linden (1978) found that alcohol was involved in 72% of their rape cases, either on the part of the offender, victim or both, and Rada (1975) found that 50% of the convicted rapists studied were drinking at the time of the crime. These studies, and many more that could be cited (see Collins, 1981; Pernanen, 1976), provide ample support for the assumption that alcohol plays a central role in aggression, violence, and antisocial behavior. Moreover, alcohol appears to be implicated in nonviolent crimes as well, including robbery, burglary, larceny, motor vehicle theft, forgery, and arson (Collins, 1981; Roizen & Schneberk, 1978).

Phylogenetic regression theory postulates (see chapters 4 and 5, especially Tables 4.11 and 5.2) that male and female sex roles are purer or more clearly divergent in states of regression, and this seems borne out in the alcohol literature. Macho behavior and hypermasculinity go hand-in-hand with both alcohol abuse and criminality (Zucker, 1968), and in the young, drinking male delinquent we see strutting, cocky, and violent maleness at its most pathological extreme. Such young males are responsible for a large disproportion of serious crime, and they contrast sharply with the female delinquent who is much less violent, less apt to commit serious crimes, and more likely to be a runaway, sexual delinquent, or drug abuser (Gandossy, Williams, Cohen, & Harwood, 1980). Statistics from several federal crime reports for the period from 1981 to 1983 (Cantwell, 1983) revealed that half of all persons arrested for serious crimes were youths under age 20 and 80% (property offenses) to 90% (violent crimes) of these were male. The sex differential is even more pronounced in the following percentages of males arrested for Uniform Crime Reports Index Crimes (Cantwell, 1983): murder 87%, rape 99%, robbery 93%, aggravated assault, burglary 94%, larceny–theft, motor vehicle theft 91%, and arson 89%.

Men tend to drink more than women, have much higher arrest rates for alcohol-related offenses, have higher rates of hospitalization for alcoholism, and, in general, are more prone to act-out when drinking (Wechsler, 1980). Whereas men tend to act-out "sociopathically" when under the influence, women, in contrary, tend more toward "passive" forms of behavior such as depression and suicide (Hill, 1980). Men may drink because of a need for personalized power that expresses itself in violent forms of acting-out (McClelland, Davis, Kalin, & Wanner, 1972), whereas a pattern of personal loss, clinical depression, low self-esteem, and mental illness is seen more often in women (Wolin, 1980). In response to the phylogenetically regressive priming and eliciting effects of alcohol ingestion, we see the classic sexual archetypes of male aggressiveness and intrusiveness in bold contrast to the emotional sensitivity, interpersonal centeredness, and passivity of the female. Alcohol, of course, is not the direct cause of these stereotyped gender differences, but it helps widen the gap by weakening neocortical inhibitory controls and learned social roles, and regressing individuals more deeply into their natural modes of behaving.

Hierarchical Levels of Study.   Collins (1981) suggests that the various disciplines studying the alcohol-crime relationship can be arranged on a conceptual continuum proceeding from the medical–pharmacological level at the lower pole up to the sociodemographic level at the upper pole (see Table 6.6). Although we might argue with certain of Collins' orderings, the continuum is a meaningful one, and it serves to show that the

TABLE 6.6
Collins' (1981) Levels of Analysis in the Alcohol-Crime Relationship

Higher Levels

Sociodemographic
Sociocultural
Social Psychological
Psychological
Psychophysiological
Behavioral-Cognitive
Biochemical
Medical-Pharmacological

Lower Levels

Used with permission of National Institute of Justice.

alcohol-crime relationship, like so many others in nature, conforms to a hierarchical interpretation. The phylogenetic regression approach would go one step further and analyze the intraindividual dynamics of the relationship hierarchically as well. In fact, one suspects that the most significant question of all is, "How does one explain how a normal, law-abiding husband, wife, or adolescent is, within a brief period following the ingestion of large amounts of alcohol, transformed into an angry, hyper-emotional, and perhaps criminal creature?" No theory can lay claim to the alcohol problem until it addresses the question of how and why behavior can devolve so quickly and frightfully under the influence of drink.

Special Releasing Stimuli in Animals and Humans

Each living creature is exposed to innumerable stimuli impinging on its sensory structures at any given moment, but of all the possibilities of response only a miniscule few ever reach the motor system and emerge into behavior. Moreover, the responses that do eventually emerge are hardly random, but are more likely to be adaptive and species-typical modes of coping with internal demands and the demands of the external environment. That is, living organisms do more than just passively respond to stimuli impinging on them; they are phylogenetically prepared to first select certain specific stimuli from the welter of possibilities confronting them and then to respond with an adaptive response pattern typical for its particular species.

The aforementioned certainly holds true for phylogenetically primitive species whose limited response-pattern repertoire is well-attuned to specific eliciting stimuli in their simple environments, but what about more phylogenetically advanced species that enjoy a modicum of freedom and flexibility in both selecting and responding? This question leads us once again to the logic of the primitive–advanced continuum for analysis. The elicitor-response pattern relationships in nature can be placed on a continuum proceeding from the "innate" and highly reliable releaser-fixed action pattern couplings described by the ethologists (Eibl-Eibesfeldt, 1970; Lorenz, 1950; Tinbergen, 1951) at the primitive pole, on through various mixtures of elicited behavior and learning in the middle ranges, up to what appears to be conscious response choice in humans at the advanced pole. The highest selectivity and least freedom of choice occurs with the pheromones, chemical elicitors that exert powerful control over the behavior of certain insects. The male silk moth, for example, detects odors with its antennae that are remarkably sensitive to the chemical bombykol, a sexual attractant secreted by the female silk moth in very minute quantities. Approximately 70% of the adult male's sensory receptors respond to this chemical only, and only one molecule of bombykol is required to generate significant action potential (Alcock, 1975). This exceptional sensitivity and extreme specialization may appear puzzling until we realize that the male silk moth does little more in its brief life span beyond avoiding predators until mating can occur. Thus, for this hyperspecialized and phylogenetically primitive creature, the attunement of elicitor and response pattern is nigh perfect leaving little room for chance or choice. The eliciting stimulus in this case appears to be both necessary and sufficient to produce the species-specific response in proverbial one-to-one fashion.

It is entirely possible that the silk moth could more effectively adapt to the environment, in the ontogenetic sense, if it possessed more behavioral flexibility and were not so unremittingly tied to its chemical elicitors. Indeed, the very inflexibility of the elicitor-response pattern coupling is a major clue to its innateness and phylogenetic primitiveness. Tinbergen (1951) cites the behavior of the carnivorous water beetle, *Dysticus marginalis,* as an example of a creature capable of visual discriminations that could be used to advantage in its hunting and feeding activities; nevertheless the water beetle persists in responding exclusively to chemical and tactile stimuli even when prominent food objects are in clear view. For example, the beetle will ignore a tadpole presented in a glass tube, whereas a meat solution will elicit species-characteristic searching and grasping behaviors (Tinbergen, 1936b). "The occurrences of such 'errors' or 'mistakes'," Tinbergen (1951) observes, "is one of the most conspicuous characteristics of innate behavior" (p. 27).

Releasers in the visual and auditory modalities are more advanced than are the chemical elicitors, but certain of these are quite primitive, inflexible, and wired into the organism. Tinbergen's (1951) classic studies of male stickleback attack responses to experimental models of other male sticklebacks provide good illustrations of this point. In these experiments, dummy fish were presented that retained only one characteristic of the natural stimulus, whereas, the remainder of the characteristics were markedly distorted. Thus, the releasing power of each model characteristic could be established with considerable precision. The results led Tinbergen to conclude that the red belly was the specific stimulus eliciting attack behavior, and this releaser retained its power even on the crudest models which bore little resemblance to a real male stickleback. Tinbergen (1951) presents a wealth of evidence from studies of insects, fish, and birds to support the hypothesis that certain stimulus situations serve as releasers for species-specific patterns of behavior. Examples of such releasers in the visual modality include the stickleback's red belly just cited; the English robin's red breast, which releases defense of territory behavior; sight of a model representing a flying bird of prey, which releases escape behavior in gallinaceous chicks; moving legs in small mammals, which releases predatory responses in the tawny owl; and the red patch on the herring gull's bill, which releases food begging behavior from newly hatched chicks (Tinbergen, 1951).

Auditory stimuli also can serve as releasers, and one of the most powerful is the distress call. Brückner (1933; cited in Tinbergen, 1951) studied the social relationships of domestic fowl and found that a hen's rescue behavior was attuned to her chick's distress call and not its movements. Peters (1980) says that the first signals used by mammalian infants are cries of distress, and most species have more than one cry, each corresponding to a different level of distress. Obviously, the larger repertoire of cries and greater contextual flexibility seen in mammals illustrates the greater complexity but weaker elicitor-response pattern relationship expected with higher organisms.

Alarm calls represent another category of auditory releasers seen in a variety of species. For example, throughout the entire reproductive period, the black-headed gull adults are extremely sensitive to the presence of predators and other intruders and will emit distinctive alarm calls at the slightest disturbance (Alcock, 1975). In fact, most animals capable of vocalization emit distinctive cries when danger is present (e.g., the ultrasonic chirps of the infant albino rat pup, the snorting or coughing of mule deer and whitetail deer at low levels of alarm, the alarm barks of wolves and domestic dogs, the elaborate repertoire of specific alarm calls of the vervet monkey, the bark of the baboon, the single, loud "crack" of the dolphin, and the highly emotionalized words and phrases of human beings; Peters, 1980). In humans, distress calls and alarm signals at low levels of stress involve a heavy cultural component, but at high levels of stress phylogenetic regression theory predicts that older patterns of vocalization are likely to emerge in the form of loud squeals and screams. One merely needs to observe a person in severe crisis, such as in a major accident or natural disaster, to see that such highly vocal but minimally verbal screams are an inherent part of the picture.

This is a good point at which to clarify terms before proceeding further. Lorenz (1982) uses the term *releaser* to refer specifically to anatomical characters or motor patterns, or more often combinations of both, which have evolved in the service of sending a signal or transmitting information. Thus, the physical structures and/or movement patterns of one animal may serve as releasing stimuli for behavioral responses in the protagonist animal. Subsequently, the elicited behavior of the receiver animal may include embedded releasers that serve to augment mutual information exchange and lead into lengthy behavioral interactions. So defined, the term *releaser* is rather general, and, for our purposes, the following subdivision is adopted for added specificity: elicitors that are based on simple structural characters or movements that set off a single, stereotyped response pattern are referred to as *sign stimuli* (see Hinde, 1974), whereas more behaviorally complex elicitative stimuli that set off complex and relatively variable patterns and combinations of patterns are referred to a *social releasers*. Thus, sign stimuli are relatively primitive phylogenetically, and are involved in the more rigid and inflexible elicitor-response pattern relationships. By contrast, social releasers are more advanced phylogenetically by virtue of their greater complexity, variability, and richness of informational content. The general term *elicitor* is used to encompass sign stimuli, social releasers, and any other stimulus conditions that have the capacity to bring out, in whole or in part, phylogenetically loaded responses.

The concept of social releaser usually includes more than just complex elicitors designed by natural selection to induce action in other animals. In fact, in phylogenetically advanced animals, one-to-one sign stimulus-response relations are rare, and, instead, one more often observes animals in conflict where two or more incompatible and competing response systems are simultaneously present. For example, Hinde (1974) describes the conflict between three or more incompatible tendencies involved in the courtship activities of chaffinches. Early in the mating season, the male chaffinch establishes a territory and threatens all intruders, including prospective mates. Slowly, his behavior changes from attack to courtship, and he uses a posture that resembles head-forward threat, but is oriented laterally to the female. This behavior exemplifies a characteristic typical of relatively advanced social releasers—that is, behavior originally designed for one purpose is freed to play new roles in new behavior systems. During this phase of the mating sequence, the female begins to assume dominance over the male and she may drive him away from food sources. Later, the female starts to solicit for copulation, and the male hesitantly approaches in an upright posture with an unusual pattering walk. Many attempts at copulation are unsuccessful because the fearful male flees at the crucial moment. Eventually, copulation occurs, after which the male suddenly flies off and emits a call usually elicited by a flying predator.

Hinde's example shows that the female chaffinch's behavior may elicit attack, flight, sexual activity, or mixtures of the three in the male. Hinde speaks of how the balance of motives fluctuates in fairly predictable ways over the course of the courtship season. He says that analyses of such conflicting tendencies provide some understanding of the nature of much complex display and ritualized behavior. In fact, many animal behaviorists believe that movements such as those seen in chaffinch courtship, which were originally borne of conflict, have themselves, over the course of evolution, come to serve signaling functions as social releasers. Social releasers, so evolved, are thought to be important factors in the elaborate ritualized and display behavior in many animals. Eibl-Eibesfeldt (1970) states that, "Whenever it is of advantage for an animal that some of its incidental behavior be understood by another, selection operates to transform the behavior pattern in question into a conspicious signal. This modification of a behavior pattern to serve communicative function is called *ritualization*" (p. 97).

Eibl-Eibesfeldt (1970) outlines some of the specific modifications that take place during the process of ritualization:

1. The original behavior undergoes a change of function. For example, many avian species exhibit various food-calling and feeding behaviors that play important roles in care of the young. In some species, however, these expressive movements have become ritualized and serve a courtship signaling function. Eibl-Eibesfelt (1970) explains that many adult songbirds feed one another during courtship as if the partner were a young bird. In other species, the original function may be entirely lost, as in the cuckoo, which no longer feeds its own young, but, nevertheless, exhibits mutual feeding between partners during courtship.

2. The ritualized expressive movement may become independent of its original motivation and develop its own motivating mechanisms. Eibl-Eibesfeldt gives the example of the presenting behavior of female baboons, which has become ritualized into a greeting gesture.

3. The ritualized movements are frequently exaggerated with respect to frequency and amplitude, although they may become simplified as well due to the deletion of certain components from the original sequence.

4. The threshold values for releasing stimuli often are altered with the effect that the ritualized pattern is more easily released than the original

behavior. The presence of highly ritualized behavior, then, would imply that strong releasing stimuli are in operation.

5. A behavior pattern that previously varied in terms of intensity of motivation and stimulus, may occur with a constant intensity even if the animal is highly motivated. In this manner behavior becomes stereotyped and unambiguous.

6. In addition to behavioral changes in ritualization, very conspicious morphological changes may occur as well, such as ornamental plumes, enlarged claws for waving, manes, sailfins, and so on.

Eibl-Eibesfeldt's analysis clearly reveals how some of the most conspicious and functionally significant animal behavior represents displacements and elaborations of movements and motive tendencies that were originally designed for other purposes. Again, we see how a relatively small number of original components can serve as the foundations for considerable development and elaboration. The concept of phylogenetic ritualization is indeed a rich one, and when we realize that ritualized behavior also can be modified ontogenetically through learning and experience (Eibl-Eibesfeldt, 1970), the conceptual possibilities become enormous. Eibl-Eibesfeldt (1970, 1972, 1979) has long argued that the cultural ritualizations of man follow the pattern of phylogenetic ritualization, and he garners a wealth of anecdotal examples to support this view. Included in these are teeth baring in humans (and monkeys) as a ritualized threat, flirting behavior that is largely based on ritualized approach and flight movements, the smile that may be an elaboration of the primate fear face, face covering during embarrassment as a "hiding" movement, contests and tournaments based on phylogenetically older aggressive tendencies, ritualized infantilisms in adult courtship behavior, greeting rituals originally based on submissive responses, and so forth. Eibl-Eibesfeldt uses the ritualization model to explain a wide range of human activities, but he is always careful to point out that cultural transmission of ritualized behavior is no doubt more important than is phylogenetic transmission in humans. Nevertheless, he challenges the social scientist to look carefully for those fairly numerous instances when human ritualized behavior does, in fact, emanate from phylogenetically older tendencies.

We have dwelt on the issue of ritualization at some length because as Eibl-Eibesfeldt (1979) says, "the concept of ritualization refers to the improvement of a signal—to the development of releasers" (p. 102). Thus, all innate behavior in animals and humans is not based on simple species-specific, releaser-fixed action patterns that developed in phylogeny for a single adaptive purpose; rather, most innate behavior appears to be of the secondary, ritualized type, where the evolutionary process has selected out certain incidental movements (conflictual and displacement activities), sign-stimuli (stimuli effective on only one response;), intention movements, or autonomic responses (nonmusculoskeletal movements controlled by the ANS—movements of hair or feathers, urination and defecation, changes in skin coloration due to changes in surface blood vesals, etc.), and molded them into often complex ritualized and display behavior. The control of such behavior is due to the effects of social releasers that mediate much of the behavior of both animals and human beings.

Some of the social releasers that have been postulated for humans are shown in Table 6.7. The sample of human social releasers shown reveals the numerous social behaviors which are presumably under the control of, or at least strongly influenced by, special phylogenetically conditioned eliciting stimuli.

What is the importance of all this for the theory of phylogenetic regression? The fact that phylogenetically conditioned eliciting stimuli exist in humans and, further, that there appear to be so many types and forms of them, leads to the following reasoning. An educated, middle-class person may exist in a rarified social atmosphere relatively free of stimulation from primitive releasing stimuli, and would, consequently, behave in a controlled, advanced fashion much of the time. Conversation is polite, the neighborhood is quite and serene, and the thought of threat to life and limb only crosses the mind now and then. Recall, however, the hypothetical example of the child kidnapped from the desperate mother outlined at the end of the prior chapter. The sight and sounds of the screaming child would act as powerful elicitors of more or less innate fear and separation patterns, and the sight of the strange and threatening men would additively augment the fear response, as well as setting rage and aggressive feelings and behaviors into motion. By virtue of the sudden onslaught of these almost overwhelming elicitative stimuli, the erstwhile refined and polite matron now phylogenetically regresses into the mammalian mother who is virtually compelled by her evolutionary heritage to make any desperate effort necessary to defend and protect her offspring. In this illustration, the eliciting stimuli served primarily to set off the initial regression, while internal thoughts and emotions served to maintain the fear, agony of separation, and murderous rage long after the sights and sounds of the actual abduction had abated.

SUMMARY

The phylogenetic regression model has certain implications for the free will-determinism issue. The model postulates that feelings and behavior at the primitive pole of the regression-progression continuum are more

TABLE 6.7
Some Probable Social Releasers in Humans

Releaser	Reference
Infant-mother Relationship	
Characteristics of infants	
Short face relative to large forehead	Lorenz (1943)
Protruding cheeks	Lorenz (1943)
Short, thick extremities	Lorenz (1943)
Maladjusted limb movements	Lorenz (1943)
Soft, elastic body surfaces	Lorenz (1943)
Cries of distress	Wolff (1969)
The infant's smile	Eibl-Eibesfeldt (1970)
Characteristics of mother	
Odor of mother's breast	MacFarlane (1977)
The mother's heartbeat	Morris (1971)
Fear and Appeasement Signals	
Armpit odors	Peters (1980)
Fearful facial expressions	Tomkins (1963)
Crying or weeping	Peters (1980)
High-intensity distress screams	Peters (1980)
Appeasement signals	Eibl-Eibesfeldt (1970)
Physical withdrawal	
Gaze aversion	
Cringing or kneeling	
Head lowering	
Raised eyebrow greeting	
Aggression, Dominance, and Threat Signals	
Deprivations, frustrations	Eibl-Eibesfeldt (1979)
Fist-shaking	Peters (1980)
Fist clenching, foot stamping, frowning	Eibl-Eibesfeldt (1979)
The threatening stare	Van Hooff (1967)
Male genital display	Wickler (1967)
Sight of stranger or outsider	Holloway (1974)
Physical size of male	Bailey, Caffrey, & Hartnett (1976)
Invasion of "body territory"	Bailey et al. (1976)
Personal space encroachment	Bailey, et al (1976)
Extreme or lethal danger	Wickler (1972)
Sexual Signals	
Female vaginal odors	Comfort (1971)
Female breasts and buttocks	Morris (1967)
Female genitals	Symonds (1979)
The male genital "bulge"	Morris (1971)
Healthy-looking skin	Morris (1971)
Vocalization during copulation	Peters (1980)
Sexually revealing clothing	Morris (1971)
Pseudo-sexual signaling with the mouth	Morris (1971)

"determined" and less subject to conscious will than are feelings and behaviors at the advanced pole. This assumption is discussed from the perspective of Razran's (1971) complex hierarchic model.

Behavior at the primitive pole is determined, in large measure, by primitive primers and elicitors that often are part of innate stimulus-response pattern relationships. Behavior at the advanced pole is highly cognitive, variable, and seldom involves strongly coupled elicitor-response pattern relationships. Private and internal thoughts often serve as elicitors at the cognitive level of functioning.

Primers or elicitors may originate either internally or externally. The internal primer or elicitor arises from inside the person and requires little or no external stimulation to produce behavioral effects. Certain aspects of genetic and hormonal functioning fall into this category, along with many other psychophysiological processes. The external primer or elicitor derives its energy from outside the body, and can be any stimulus, stimulus complex, or environmental condition that affects the processes of regression and progression. Pain, chemicals, drugs, social releasers, and a multitude of other variables fall into this category.

There appear to be fewer internal than external primers or elicitors, but their effects are extremely important. Among these are certain genetic processes, the hormones and neurotransmitters, biogeological and biometerological phenomena, CNS damage and dysfunction, and cognitive elicitors in the form of strongly held values, beliefs, and ideologies. The cognitive elicitors are phylogenetically unique as far as we know, for only humans can regress and progress themselves through conscious thought. Following Freud, we presume that unconscious wishes, images, fantasies, and thoughts also serve as elicitors for regression, and perhaps progression also in some cases.

There are a number of external elicitors that are especially relevant to the PR model. Pain, injury, and fear are important components of the withdrawal complex, and they are very powerful elicitors of phylogenetic regression. Regression also can be elicited by a variety of chemical substances, including the sedatives, the hallucinogenic compounds, and the amphetamines. The effects of ethyl alcohol in eliciting regression was discussed in some detail, and literature on the alcohol-criminality relationship was briefly reviewed.

Due to their central theoretical significance, evolved releasing stimuli were discussed in some detail. The most phylogenetically primitive releasers are the pheromones, chemical substances that elicit species-specific response patterns in insects. There are quite primitive visual and auditory releasers as well as chemical ones, including the red spot on the male stickleback's belly, which elicits territorial aggression in other male sticklebacks, and a variety of distress and alarm calls across diverse species. Of particular interest are the social releasers, which are typically found in more advanced species. The social releaser is defined as a complex pattern of stimuli emanating from the sender animal's physical structures and movements that set off complex patterns of behavior in the receiver animal. Social releasers play important roles in the ritualized and display behavior of many animals, and possibly humans as well.

7

Some Special Theory-Derived
Primers and Elicitors

*Not only parts of the body can, under conditions of stress,
assert themselves in harmful ways, but mental structures as
well. The* idée fixe, *the obsession of the crank, are cognitive
holons running riot. There is a whole gamut of mental
disorders in which some subordinate part of the mental
hierarchy exerts its tyrannical rule over the whole; from the
relatively harmless infatuation with some pet theory, to the
insidious domination over the mind of 'repressed' complexes, . . . and so to the clinical psychoses in which large
chunks of the personality seem to have 'split off' and lead a
quasi-independent existence.*
—Koestler (1967, pp. 231-232)

STRESS-RELATED ELICITORS

Phylogenetic regression theory posits that *stress,* broadly defined, is
perhaps the most potent elicitor of regression. The reasoning goes like
this: Stress usually represents a real or imagined threat to survival, and
any threat to survival immediately regresses the individual down to
phylogenetically ancient patterns of adaptive response. Pelletier (1977)
points out how "information perceived through the senses or through the
rational–intellectual cerebro-cortical centers in the brain is transmitted to
lower brain centers concerned with emotional activity, and then to the

hypothalamus, which initiates impulses based on this information to the body's physical stress-response systems" (p. 77). Pelletier further informs us that human stress reactivity is an essential psychophysiological process that is one of the body's most sensitive and vital survival systems.

Physiologically, humans and animals are equipped with essentially the same fight or flight neuropsychological systems for responding to actual external threat, but man is further blessed and burdened with higher centers of awareness that have the capacity to generate threat from within. Whereas the animal may reduce stress by physical flight from the threatening elicitor, we humans must live with great amounts of stress that cannot be dissipated motorically. Such accumulated tension serves as a major internal priming condition of the type described in an earlier section. Persons under constant tension stimulated by conscious and unconscious psychological threat are well primed to over respond to threatening elicitors from the external environment. In view of the brain's capacity to "amplify" small stimulus events (Eccles, 1970; Pelletier, 1977), even the smallest perceived threat may set off an extensive neuropsychological defense response.

Life is full of *stressors,* as Selye (1978) calls them, stimulus conditions that activate the body's defensive apparatus and lead to states of stress and tension. According to Selye, a stressor is "that which produces stress," meaning anything in the environment capable of triggering the body's defense systems. Virtually any stimulus can act as a stressor if it disturbs the body's homeostatic balance, but certain conditions are particularly potent for human beings. Selye (1978) discusses numerous potential stressors for humans, including air and water pollution, social and cultural stressors, diet, physiologic states, vibration, genetics, race, physical and/or cognitive effort, urbanization, travel, catastrophes and disasters, captivity, isolation and loneliness, sensory deprivation and boredom, and meteorologic factors in the form of cosmic rays, solar eruptions, magnetism, and variations in temperature.

The list of potential stressors is endless, but they all share a common characteristic: They all represent deviations from a hypothetical range of stimulus conditions that are readily within the evolved coping capabilities of the individual. Stimuli falling outside this range produce stress and force the individual to adapt in some way. When adaptation is sufficiently successful a return to normal homeostatic balance is achieved and stress is relieved. The natural physiological and psychological make-up of the individual is crucial here, in terms of defining the normal band of stimuli, the limits of adaptation, and the range of coping skills available.

For human beings, there are some obvious categories of stimuli that deviate from the norm and produce stress.

1. First, there are those stressors that are based on changes in the environment. Human beings were designed for a relatively simple life with minimal variation in social and environmental stimulation. The daily life of primitive man was no doubt repetitive, simple, and familiar by modern standards, and in those respects less stressful than the bustling, changing world we live in today. Given the relative stability that characterized hominid evolution, i.e., as in the long hunting and gathering phase, we must conclude that modern man is poorly prepared phylogenetically to cope with a changing environment. Marris (1974) argues that people possess a natural "conservative impulse," a natural tendency to resist change and the stress and sense of loss that comes with it.

2. Second, stress may result from either over- or understimulation. Many of the stressors discussed by Selye (1978) fall into this category, including extremes of temperature, noise, diet, physical activity such as work or exercise, mental effort, and so on. Virtually any stimulus may act as a stressor in its extreme, even ones that are typically pleasant or innocuous in milder form. One can engage in sex to stressful excess or suffer discomfort and frustration in the absence of sexual outlet, one may eat too much or too little, and one may pursue causes to the point of fanaticism or languish in the throes of boredom and nihilism. In each instance, the body and its adaptive processes have been stressed and flight-or-fight mechanisms are set into motion. Once the limbic defense systems are activated, the individual may actively attempt to restore balance, or may merely lapse into passivity and suffer the subjective discomfort of anxiety.

3. Third, and perhaps most important theoretically, any deviation from our phylogenetically prepared modes of experiencing stimuli and responding to them is likely to produce stress and attempts to adapt. By way of exaggeration, imagine the life-threatening stress of landing on the moon, only to discover a malfunction in your life-support system. Your only hope of survival is to repair the mechanical support system immediately, for there is absolutely nothing you can otherwise do to remain alive in this totally alien environment. Nevertheless, you will immediately phylogenetically regress to older patterns of struggling, gasping for breath, and screaming for help, in a futile attempt to adapt. Tragically, the evolved coupling of stressors and adaptive responses to them (e.g., fighting or fleeing) has been irretrievably broken through the unnatural advances of modern space technology. One does not have to fly to the moon, however, to find similar instances of such organism-ecology decoupling; one merely needs to observe children struggling in the classroom to master booklearning (for which there is precious little phylogenetic preparation to build upon), or to take note of the disastrous effects of growing up unloved (which reflects imbalance in an amply phylogeneti-

cally prepared system), or to experience the crowded deprivations and deprecations of prison camp existence. In each of these situations the discrepancy between what is and what existed throughout our evolutionary development is vast, leading to stress and limbic attempts to restore the older balance. Failure to restore a semblance of the prior balance is at the root of many forms of physical and psychological pathology, as we see in chapter 12.

Having briefly discussed the problem of stress, let us now look at a sampling of stressors, or stress-eliciting stimulus conditions, which are of special relevance to the phylogenetic regression–progression model. These stressors are presumed to affect the regressive process in one or the other of the following ways: (a) as direct causes of regression in instances where clear survival threat is involved. For instance, being attacked by a rabid dog would elicit a full-blown regression in all modalities—emotional, cognitive, and behavioral; or (b) as primers that regress the person neurologically, emotionally, and/or cognitively, but do not, at the time, elicit an obvious behavioral response. With sufficient priming, however, the person develops an increasing readiness for motoric response and may exhibit explosive limbic outbursts. Being in a constant state of readiness for flight-or-fight also is responsible for wear and tear on the body and the diseases of adaptation described by Selye (1978). Chronic anxiety, as discussed earlier, is likewise attributable to chronic hyperactivation of the limbic defense system (Malmo, 1975).

Overpopulation and Crowding

Overpopulation and crowding are major elicitors of phylogenetically regressive stress responses in both animals and human beings. The effects of abnormally high levels of population density often are catastrophic, and a formidable list of individual and social pathologies attributable to crowding has accumulated over the years. Extensive research with animals has confirmed the relation between crowding and pathology, but the situation is less clear for humans. Hard data are meager for humans, and there has been a tendency in recent years for both the popular press and scientific journals to catastrophize about the perils of overpopulation. The presumed pathologies for humans include physical and mental disease, crime, riots, war, drug addiction, alcoholism, family disorganization, psychological withdrawal and social alienation, increased aggression, and a decreased quality of life (Freedman, 1973). Freedman doubts that these numerous pathologies are directly caused by density *per se,* and he avers that context is crucial as to whether crowding will produce harmful effects in humans. In *Crowding and Behavior,* Freedman (1976) reviews research indicating that high density may sometimes be perceived positively, and may produce positive behavioral consequences in certain situations. In his zeal to prove that crowding is not always harmful to humans, Freedman devotes an entire chapter to praising city life and the virtues of togetherness.

The regression–progression model assumes that crowding, especially in natural as opposed to laboratory surroundings, has a priming effect on many types of pathology, and may directly elicit pathological responses in certain contexts. Further, although crowding may occasionally elicit phylogenetically advanced responses as Freedman asserts, far more often the effect will be regressive (e.g., increased aggressiveness and social disruption). In natural contexts, particularly where strangers are involved or resources are limited, excessive numbers serve to prime individuals for conflict as well as to provide supernumerous opportunities for covert and overt antagonisms to occur. Among a familiar group of students working on an intellectual task in Freedman's laboratory, the stressful effects of high density may be negligible, but in most day-to-day situations, especially in our large cities, the mere presence of others in close proximity may be stressful. Even in the laboratory, the close approach of another person, as compared to an inanimate object, appears to be stressful (McBride, King, & James, 1965), and there is a tendency to view strangers as "nonpersons" (perhaps as a way of reducing stress) when they invade our personal space (Sommer, 1969). Personal space invasions, territorial encroachments, and even the mere presence of a stranger in close proximity serve, in varying degrees, to stimulate and activate the limbic defense system and to produce a readiness to regress at the slightest pretense. So primed, eliciting stimuli from other sources (e.g., alcohol, body odors, threatening gestures, etc.) are more likely to have significant effects on overt behavior.

There are numerous concepts and theories based on the premise that excessive social contact affects behavior, usually deleteriously. For animals these include Calhoun's (1962) behavioral sink–social refractory hypothesis, Christian's (1950) social stress theory, Wynne-Edwards' (1962, 1965) social convention theory, and Chitty's (1957, 1960) genetic-feedback formulation. However, aside from the popular theorizing of Lorenz, Ardrey, Morris and others, little has been done in the way of systematic theories of human crowding, although Milgrim's (1970) theory of social overload, Freedman's (1976) density–intensity theory, and Verbrugge and Taylor's (1976) interactionist approach are notable exceptions. Milgrim defines *overload* as "a system's inability to process inputs from the environment because there are too many inputs for the system to cope with, or because successive inputs come so fast that input A cannot be processed when input B is presented. When overload is present adaptions occur" (p. 1462). These adaptive responses include giving less time to each input, disregarding unimportant inputs, shifting the burden of social interaction to the other party, blocking inputs before they enter the system, filtering the inputs so that all interactions are weak and superficial, and creating special institutions to handle some of the inputs. These reactions to overload "deprives the individual of a sense of direct contact and spontaneous integration in the life around him. It simultaneously protects and estranges the individual from his social environment (Milgrim, 1970, p. 1462).

Obviously, Milgrim sees high density living as inherently stressful and as a severe obstacle to healthy and spontaneous social behavior. In marked contrast, Freedman (1973, 1976) argues that density *per se* bears little clear relationship to any kind of pathology in humans, but, instead, merely serves to intensify whatever behavioral response the individual emits. Although Freedman's assumption of minimal relationship between density and pathology is overdrawn, he is certainly correct regarding the priming and energizing effects of high densities. The regression–progression model would carry his reasoning one step farther, however, and states that the "intensification" attendant to high densities arises primarily from the emotional and motivation centers of the limbic–hypothalamic complex. So viewed, high densities are more likely to produce regressive than progressive consequences, and more pathological effects than salubrious ones.

The interactionist approach (Verbrugge & Taylor, 1976) fits the facts most adequately, for it neither favors the popular negative stress model of population density nor the positive model of Freedman. Using careful reasoning and sophisticated research methodology, Verbrugge and Taylor found that high population density can have both negative and positive effects depending on the setting and individuals involved. However, their research produced a much stronger pattern of results for the negative as opposed to the positive model. Their study suggests that as conceptual models and research methods improve, additional support for the negative model can be expected.

Deprivation and Frustration

According to Thomas Malthus, and a host of contemporary population doomsdayers, population growth is associated with diminishing resources and eventually a crisis point will be reached where social structures collapse. Thus, along with the personal space provocations and territorial encroachment expected with high social density, the added stress of increased competition for resources must be considered. Failure to provide for the basic survival needs of the body is a powerful elicitor of phylogenetic regression of both the priming and direct response types. Just as pain is the evolved biological signal that informs the organism of immediate physical threat, frustration is an evolved psychological response designed to forcefully inform the organism that basic needs are not being met. Once frustration is keenly felt, the animal or person is motivated to reduce the frustration through goal-seeking behavior. If need satisfaction is achieved, frustration is correspondingly diminished, but if need-satisfaction is blocked, frustration is increased and heightened aggression often results. Kahn and Kirk (1968) tell us that aggressive drive is an inborn, directionally oriented energizer of behavior that is elicited by frustration of other drives and needs necessary for self and species survival. Thus, the subjective experience of frustration and the behavioral system of aggression have been yoked together in phylogeny with the result that frustration elicits aggression when survival needs are unmet. We see here why increased aggression is a major correlate of overpopulation and crowding—with increased population the per capita share of resources is correspondingly diminished, levels of frustration are increased, and aggression becomes a major means of assuring need satisfaction.

Freedman (1976) argues that overpopulation, where humans are concerned, probably always interacts with other factors, such as food or water deprivation, to produce pathological effects. He employs this argument to support his contention that crowding is not, in and of itself, pathological in human beings. In contrast, we have asserted that crowding alone can be stressful and regressive for humans, but certainly its effects can be greatly augmented by the frustrations of needs that often accompany high density living. No doubt, to be both crowded and hungry is going to be more regressive than suffering one or the other alone.

Although crowding fans the flames of frustration and aggression, one can be deprived and frustrated irrespective of amount of space and numbers of people. Regardless of mediating conditions, the deprivation of basic needs (e.g., food, water, sleep, oxygen, elimination, temperature regulation, etc.) can produce frustration and activation of the limbic emergency system, and the person will be primed for regressive behavior. While our stomachs are filled and we enjoy freedom from life-threatening threat, we may operate at a high, phylogenetically advanced level of functioning; but once our lives and the lives of our loved ones are threatened through poverty, oppression, or even through the potential loss of "necessary" benefits, as is occasionally seen in union violence, the mantle of culture and self-control is easily shed.

The most extreme example of phylogenetic regression in the face of subsistence living is described in brutal detail by Colin Turnbull (1972) in his classic work, *The Mountain People*. The mountain people were the Ik, a small-statured, reddish-brown skinned African tribe that Turnbull expected to be enjoying their traditional hunting and gathering existence. Much to his dismay, Turnbull found them cloistered in their mountain villages, desperately but unsuccessfully trying to provide food through farming the arid, rocky soil. With their stomachs empty and their traditional social structures in disarray, the Ik had descended to such depths of degradation and inhumanity that even Turnbull was left stunned and puzzled. He found that:

> they were not hunters, they were farmers, their mountain villages were far from liveable, the food was uneatable because there was not any, and the people were as unfriendly, uncharitable, inhospitable, and generally mean as any people can be. For those positive qualities we value so highly are no longer functional for the Ik; even more than in our own society they spell ruin and disaster. It seems that, far from being basic human qualities, they are superficial luxuries we can afford in times of plenty. . . . Given the situation in which the Ik found themselves . . . man has not time for such luxuries, and a much more basic man appears, using much more basic survival tactics. The much vaunted gap between man and the 'lesser' animals suddenly shrinks to nothingness, except that in this case most 'lesser' animals come off rather well by comparison, displaying many more of those 'human' qualities that the Ik did. (Turnbull, 1972, p. 32)

Further, Turnbull speaks of how quickly the change from kindness and goodness to the animal survival instincts can occur: "The Ik, like the rest of us, are kind and generous and light-hearted and jolly when they can afford to be. I saw the last vestiges of that in the first month or two, and I saw those vestiges replaced almost overnight, it seemed, by the basic survival instincts that lie in all of us" (Turnbull, 1972, p. 33).

What did Turnbull observe in the Ik that would provoke such commentary? For one thing, the Ik appeared to regress far below even the limbic level of functioning we have emphasized in the present book, even down to a totally selfish, survival-obsessed, level devoid of human feeling and emotion. Their behavior perhaps descended further into the MacLean's reptilian system than one could ever expect or want to observe. Relationships were based on self-interest and mutual exploitation, and the most brutal forms of "individualism" reigned. As the Ik sank deeper and deeper into their obsession with sheer survival, virtually all of the characteristics we consider distinctly human were slowly peeled away: love and compassion, family and kinship relations, restraints against cruelty and violence, sex with affection (actually sexual relief often was achieved nonsocially through masturbation), concern for elderly, social rituals and religious beliefs, concern for personal hygiene and sanitation, and so on.

With the Ik, we see deprivation-elicited phylogenetic regression in its most extreme form, but what of the lesser deprivations and frustrations that plague even the most affluent and privileged of our species? From the poverty-stricken ghetto to the high-rise penthouse, frustration, in varying degrees, hovers like an albatross over the affairs of men, sparing none the anguish of unmet needs. Not only is the world replete with real deprivations, our inner world of needs, wishes, fantasies, and aspirations provides infinite resources for unremitting frustration. Except for rare moments, each of us lives in a state of mild frustration, a mild regressive readiness to compete with others for the resources that surround us. However, when resources are scant and people abundant, the mild frustrations of the privileged classes turn into fury, or worse still, the capitulation to animality seen in the Ik.

OTHER THEORY-DERIVED ELICITORS

Most of the elicitors discussed so far are rather obvious ones from the standpoint of regression-progression theory. There are other possibilities, however, which may be derived deductively, or at least commonsensically, from the theory. First, recall that elicitors fall on a continuum going from those that exert virtual one-to-one control over overt behavior at one pole (e.g., the red belly of the male stickleback or certain drugs in humans) to stimulus conditions that do not produce an immediate behavioral response, but rather prime the individual cumulatively for probable future behavior (stress, frustration, threatening circumstances not requiring immediate response, arousing thoughts and fantasies, etc.). Recall also that both elicitors and priming conditions have the potential to produce phylogenetic regression by diminishing neocortical controls, on the one hand, and augmenting function of the lower centers on the other. Phylogenetic regressions may thus be major ones where behavior is under the direct control of the eliciting agent, or mild ones where the regression is experienced subjectively as emotion or motivation, comfort or discomfort, or not consciously experienced at all. When experienced subconsciously, the person is unaware of the elicitor's significance, but, instead, experiences anxiety, dread, and tension of unknown origin, sexual discomfort, repressed hostility, or other "unexplainable" feelings. Here the optional neocortical awareness centers are temporarily suspended, whereas the nonoptional limbic and reptilian centers continue to process information and respond to elicitors as they have throughout phylogeny.

Groups and Crowds

There is something about being in a group that often brings out the worst in people, something that submerges the superego and peels off the proverbial "thin veneer" with astonishing rapidity. Whether it be in riots, terrorist activity, gang warfare in the cities, gang rapes, or the mere misbehavior of children in the classroom, or the sometimes vicious confrontations between factions of opposing political or moral views, the role of the group in the phenomenon is central. Much of the silliness and irrationality of fads, fashions, and manias, the self-delusion seen in mass political and religious movements, and the perniciousness of collective violence owe their existence to the inherent readiness for individual human minds to merge into what McDougall (1920) calls the *group mind*. Seldom does such merger of minds advance the human intellect, but, rather irrationality, unpredictability, impulsiveness, and loss of the higher virtues of self-control, concern for social refinement and amenities, and concern for others are the more likely consequences. Thus, it seems that merger of neocortices for intellectual endeavor is an exception, although a Henry Murray or Gordon Allport in the classroom, or a Carl Sagan or an Alistair Cooke on television may incite some occasional thought about man and the universe. Unfortunately, however, the preponderance of evidence indicates that the lower brain centers are most likely to gain control in groups and crowds, with the higher centers slipping into the background. In other words, using the diminished cortical definition (see chapter 3), it seems that phylogenetic regression is a probable response to the eliciting effects of the group situation. If so, it follows that the lower reptilian and paleomammalian centers are primarily where the merger of minds occurs, not in the more human neocortex.

The aforementioned reasoning leads us to a very important conclusion: Phylogenetic regression is more likely to occur in groups than individuals, and, further, occurs more quickly in the group situation, especially where crowding and large numbers of people are involved (Bailey, 1978). The idea that man's animal nature more readily rises to the surface in crowds is an old one, and only in recent years has scholarly interest in the phenomenon waned (Brown, 1965). In 1895, Gustav Le Bon (1895/1960) published his classic *Psychologie de Foules* (The Psychology of Crowds), and for many years thereafter social scientists debated his thesis that, in crowds, normally peaceful, civilized people are transformed into primitive, brutal beings overcome by primal passions. In the regressed state, as suggested in chapter 5, individual differences are minimized or lost and more universal processes come to fore; Le Bon implies the same thing regarding behavior of crowds: "Whoever be the individuals that compose it, however like or unlike be their mode of life, their occupations, their character, or their intelligence, the fact that they have been transformed into a crowd puts them in possession of a sort of collective mind" (1875/ 1960, p. 27). Not all writers accepted Le Bon's thesis, and numerous alternative concepts have emerged including McDougall's concept of "primitive sympathy" (1920), Freud's (1921/1955) group suggestibility, Allport's (1924) social facilitation, Park and Burgess' (1921) "rapport," and Blumer's (1951) "circular reactions." Nevertheless, as Brown (1965) points out, all of these ideas are essentially the same as Le Bon's "mental contagion."

In a paper by the present writer (Bailey, 1978), several dramatic examples of crowd-elicited regression were cited that Le Bon's conceptualizations explain as well as any:

The primitive, animalistic quality of the more perverse forms of group regression is, unfortunately, becoming more obvious to the expert and layperson alike, due to dramatic news reporting of warfare, terrorism, and mob violence in recent years. One can easily cite supernumerous examples of the most outrageous and uncivilized excesses, but few can rival the mindless destructiveness that followed the power outage in New York this summer. According to a feature article in *Time* (July 21, 1977) magazine, roving bands of men, women, and children wrenched steel shutters from storefronts and scooped up everything they could carry and destroyed what they could not. One witness said the looters acted as if a "fever struck them," and a policeman referred to the carnage as "the night of the animals." Educator Kenneth Clark was quoted as saying, "We have reduced the people of the ghetto to the point where they function on the level of predatory animals," and the psychologist Ernest Dichter similarly commented, "It was just like the *Lord of the Flies*. People resort to savage behavior when the brakes of civilization fail." It is ironical that two weeks before (July 11, 1977) *Time* did a feature article on youth crime, and the picture that emerged was one of devastating proportions involving sadistic homocides, gang rapes, gang attacks on old people, gang warfare, reprisals against witnesses, and other assorted forms of mayhem. If all this fails to convince the reader of the human being's capacity to phylogenetically regress to subhuman modes of behavior, I would like to cite one more example which, I think, provides the strongest evidence for the phylogenetic regression hypothesis. Nine Chicago policemen now stand accused of murdering a 19-year-old youth by dragging him from his car following a dispute, and then beating him to death. According to an eye-witness interviewed on national television, "They began beating him, while he screamed. . . . They pushed and tore at each other to get at the boy. . . . Once they got the taste of blood they were like wild animals tearing apart game. . . . Finally they bashed his head in and killed him." (pp. 28–29)

Wechsler (1971), in his paper on *Collective Intelligence,* refers to Le Bon and likewise concludes that people often behave in archaic, unpredictable, and "stupid" ways in the group. But why is this so? Why is the whole of stupidity in groups far greater than the sum of the individual stupidities? Phylogenetic regression theory assumes that the hierarchically arranged individual personality, with its reptilian, mammalian, and neomammalian components, exists in a state of uneasy balance between the primitive and the advanced, the phylogenetically old and new. Moreover, the older components are far more powerful and pervasive where the emotions and motivation are concerned, and are constantly threatening to break through the defenses and constraints of the higher, culturally bound systems. When the individual is alone, balance and order among the personality's components are relatively easily maintained; one is simply required to control one's own appetites, drives, and emotions. In the group, however, there is a sympathetic intermeshing of reptilian, limbic, and neocortical systems across individuals and a "collective mind" emerges. This emergent collective mind rarely gravitates upward toward higher units of creativity or abstraction, but, rather, slides ever so easily downward into what Rado (1969) calls the hedonic level of functioning where behavior is ruled solely by primitive pleasures and aversions.

The effect of the group on the individual is twofold: (a) the primitive reptilian and limbic excitement of individuals in the group seems to add together or accumulate, and then very quickly, through some sympathetic process, the excitement experienced by each individual comes to approximate that of the group, and (b) the higher controlling centers are disinhibited as individuals observe others perform behaviors normally held in check. Thus, the group experience typically serves to excite primitive centers on the one hand, and disinhibit higher constraining centers on the other. All of this makes perfect sense if we accept a cardinal assumption of the regression–progression model: Human beings possess numerous animal desires and passions that were thoroughly encoded in the brain in phylogeny, and these desires stand ready to be released at any time. Thus, the behavior of groups, mobs, and crowds is not something truly "new," as Le Bon implied, but is instead a release of the "old" in varying mixtures and extremes.

In concluding this section, a word should be said about the leader's role in mob behavior. If people in mobs and crowds are often highly suggestible, irrational, and regressive, then they should be especially susceptible to the whims of their leaders. As individuality and self-control are submerged in the crowd, the neocortex of the leader is in an excellent position to temporarily substitute for the suspended neocortices of those comprising the crowd. As Hitler addressed the frenzied German populace at the height of his influence, many were so taken by the elicitative effects of his words, actions, and deadly charisma that their intelligence and humanity were temporarily forsaken. In the place of an internal self-defined reality, an imposed external reality swept across the mind taking with it all decency, personhood, and personal freedom. This is an example of extreme *cortical supplementation,* to use a term discussed earlier in chaper 3; in effect, as Hitler's words were immediately perceived, or recalled with their accompanying emotions at a later time, the products of his neocortex were the eliciting causes of behavior. We see here how the cortical supplementation of the leader can be regressive or progressive; the leader, with his almost hypnotic control of the collective mind, can, with word or gesture, easily regress followers to limbic emotionality, or with somewhat greater difficulty progress them to higher levels of functioning.

Anonymity and Deindividuation

While fully conscious of oneself and under the immediate scrutiny of other members of a shared normative group, behavior is likely to be well-controlled and consistent with prevailing social norms. Here we see the difference between a normative or reference group, which is defined by shared rules and regulations that serve behavior-controlling functions, and the spontaneous disinhibition and rule dissolution of the mob or crowd. In the crowd, or, with strangers as well, normal constraints may be abandoned as self-consciousness and self-identity are diminished and *deindividualization* occurs (Dipboye, 1977; Zimbardo, 1969). Individuation, conversely, is a desirable condition defined as "the development of the psychological individual as a differentiated being from the general, collective psychology. Individuation, therefore, is a process of differentiation having for its goal the development of the individual personality" (Jung, 1946, p. 561). So defined, *individuation* may be viewed as a phylogenetically advanced state whereby the individual rises above the animal desires of his species and becomes a self-conscious and self-controlled human being. By virtue of this neocortical hegemony in the personality, impulses may be delayed, alternative responses considered, behavior may be properly adjusted to accepted norms, and a certain amount of personal "freedom"experienced. By contrast, deindividuation is seen as a dysfunctional and pathological process by most writers; some of the social symptoms attributed to a deindividuating culture discussed in Dipboye's (1977) review include violence in urban areas, the lack of creativity in large organizations, the conventionalization of consumer tastes, the dehumanization of women, and student alienation.

An even longer list of individual pathologies and antinormative behaviors is associated with deindividuation: unrestrained and uncontrolled behavior (Festinger, Pepitone, & Newcomb, 1952; Zimbardo, 1969), loss of personal identity (Jung, 1946), increased aggression (Dion, 1970; Watson, 1973; Zimbardo, 1969), increased diffusion of responsibility and willingness to take risks (Dipboye, 1977; Pincus, 1969), increased use of sexually explicit language (Singer, Brush, & Lubin, 1965), increased stealing and cheating (Diener, Fraser, Beaman, & Kelem, 1976), and increased touching, hugging, and sexual arousal in a darkened room (Gergen, Gergen, & Barton, 1973). Clearly, the anonymity of the group, and the deindividuation that goes with it, often serves as an eliciting condition for a wide variety of nonnormative and sometimes pathological behaviors.

Social psychological research on deindividuation has been based mainly on the classic theories of crowd behavior postulated by Le Bon (1895/1960), Sighele (1901), and McDougall (1920). These theories were themselves based on the assumption that primitive, atavistic, and animalistic tendencies were released from their normal state of inhibition in the crowd. Of these early writers, only McDougall (1920) recognized that humans may progress in groups as well as regress:

> We seem then to stand before a paradox. Participation in group life degrades the individual, assimilating his mental processes to those of the crowd, whose brutality, inconstancy, and unreasoning impulsiveness have been the theme of many writers; yet only by participation in group life does man become fully man, only so does he rise above the level of the savage. (pp. 27–28)

Thus, to be in a group or crowd does not, *ipso facto,* result in pathological disinhibition, and the group in some instances, as in the classroom or the church sanctuary, may help the individual rise above his instincts; nevertheless, when a given personality is prone to disinhibition to begin with, and other priming elicitors are present, such as drug or alcohol intake, deprivation and frustration, high temperature, inciting leaders, rumors, and so forth, the probability of disrelease becomes very great. Again the complexity of human behavior defies simple explanations and the quest for one-to-one elicitor-response pattern relationships continues to elude us. Still, anonymity and deindividuation appear to be strong and consistent elicitors of phylogenetic regression as we define it.

Differences Between People

Perceived differences between people are among the most potent elicitors of phylogenetic regression. Indeed, one of the prime social correlates of phylogenetic regression is the partitioning of persons into in- and out-groups. The typical state of affairs throughout most of human evolution was for individuals to be part of larger family, kinship, and tribal aggregations where each constituent group member was similar to and familiar with all other group members. Those rare strangers who were encountered elicited fear and hostility, for as Holloway (1974) argues, xenophobia is an innate and universal quality in man. If the basic premises of sociobiology are valid (see chapter 2), the stranger could only represent threat to self or threat of loss of resources in primitive man, for the natural course of things is to be selfish, self-protective, and "altruistic" only to blood kin or those nonkin with whom reciprocal relations are essential. It is therefore adaptive and in the best evolutionary interests of the individual to fear and detest the stranger who, as a competitor for resources, is far more likely to reduce individual fitness than to increase it.

Assuming the aforementioned reasoning, we would expect that, in the course of evolutionary development, hominids would have become extremely sensitive to "differences" that facilitate speedy classification of familiars versus strangers, and in-group members versus out-group members. Moreover, given the central role of pleasurable and aversive feeling in guiding adaptive behavior (see chapter 5), we would expect that encountering and interacting with familiars would be inherently pleasurable whereas the opposite would hold for the stranger, until which time he or she achieves in-group status. Stated another way, there is a great amount of phylogenetic inertia to overcome in relating to strangers, and regressions are all too frequent; indeed, how easy it is to love friends and family, but how difficult it is to overcome our natural antipathy to those different from us. Such inertia is even difficult to overcome in the phylogenetically advanced and sanguinary setting of the counseling relationship, as (Sue, 1981) has so ably documented in his book, *Counseling the Culturally Different.* If our prejudice, raciocentrism, and ethnocentrism continue to pervade even the cross-cultural counseling relationship, imagine how difficult it is for the poor, the uneducated, the consciously prejudiced, or persons under stress to feel truly kindly toward the stranger.

We have already discussed the pervasive stress and tension that characterize our modern, crowded society, where we often are exposed to thousands of strangers in a single day. We maintain our social order and sanity only because of geometrically increasing rules, laws, moral prescriptions, and policing agencies that essentially force us to respect the rights of others and show a modicum of decency to the stranger. In recent years, the social order of our own country has been severely stressed by population, information, and technological explosions, on the one hand, and on the other the proliferation of quasi-tribal "special interest" groups that are often perceived as "strangers" by the majority populace. As our country has ceased to be one, big happy family, as it was when we faced a mortal threat from the outside in World War II, conflict has increased to the point where the republic is threatened by internal warring forces. Much of this conflict is based on the antipathies of "strangers," either real or metaphorical, as in the cases of management versus labor, minorities versus the police, or heterosexuals versus homosexuals. Thus, the differences that elicit a significant portion of these conflicts may be physical characteristics, behavioral characteristics, or mere differences in beliefs. For sure, the elicitative stimuli (the "differences") may be learned in many instances, but the internal, self-protective limbic responses they release are far older than the human race.

What are some of the specific stimuli that are perceived as "differences" by most people? Most of the perceived differences fall into the categories discussed here.

Physical Differences.   Virtually any perceivable anatomical characteristic or set of characteristics can elicit regression by contributing to the placement of an individual into the feared stranger category, or by marking the individual as "sick" or "deviant" in some way. One defining feature of love is that the blemishes and deviancies of the loved one are conveniently overlooked to the point of delusion; with unfamiliars, persons of different races, nationalities, and so forth, the tendency is to do exactly the opposite and look for the slightest excuse for limbic hysteria and sociobiological selfishness. Given the wide variation in human characters, such excuses are easily found.

Human beings differ greatly in size and weight, the relations between body parts, head size and shape, facial features, eye color, skin pigmentation, texture and amount of body hair, body odors and many other characteristics (Baker, 1974). Such variation occurs within in-group designations such as family, tribe, or nation, but differences are likely to be even more accentuated when persons are compared across racial boundaries. Although anthropologists agree that all extant humans are members of a single species, *Homo sapiens,* subspecies or racial differences have arisen during evolution as geographically separated gene pools attuned themselves to differing environmental demands. At this point in history, however, race is extremely difficult to define due to interbreeding and the rarity of truly isolated populations, and a number of writers have advised that the term be abandoned altogether. Further, there is a tendency for scientists and laypersons alike to employ sociological classifications, e.g. Negroes, as if they constitute biological racial classifications, even when the actual degree of African ancestry is minimal (Mead, 1968). These caveats notwithstanding, a residue of real racial characters remains, and between these and the far greater corpus of imputed and projected characters, people have ample opportunity to engage in antipathy.

Of the real racial characters, skin pigmentation is the most obvious, and it is no accident that American blacks have been exposed to such monumental prejudice and discrimination. For the more rabid racist, the mere sight of black skin is sufficient to elicit a fury of fear and tribal hostility; at the moment elicited, the consuming xenophobic response may be little distinguishable from that of primitive man or even lower primates. Here the black is not hated because of the color of his skin, but because he is different; the black skin serves merely as an elicitor for a deeper and more profound xenophobic response. Such responses are not limited to ignorant racists, but dwell in the hearts of all men, even those we consider paragons of racial equality. Baker (1974) and Gould (1981) have amply documented attempts in 18th and 19th century science to "prove" Negro inferiority, and it is clear that hysteria often reigned, as exemplified in the following quote by no less than Abraham Lincoln:

> There is a physical difference between the white and black races which I believe will forever forbid the two races living together on terms of social and political equality. And inasmuch as they cannot so live, while they do remain together there must be the position of superior and inferior, and I as much as any other man am in favor of having the superior position assigned to the white race. (cited in Gould, 1981, p. 35)

With Lincoln we see a concern for self and kin, a concern for priority of resources, an implied concern for cross-racial mating, a probable concern for Negro aggression, and a more general fear of the unknown. These are the concerns that underlie our so easily elicited xenophobia, the concerns that so easily transform perceived differences into deadly rationalizations for prejudice, racism, and genocide.

Behavioral and Mental Differences.   People vary in their psychological proclivities just as they do in their physical characteristics. As we see in the next chapter, variation in behavior can be a function of genetically mediated tendencies, learned habit patterns, or more likely, a combination of both. Regardless of the genesis of particular behaviors, the result is that people differ in behavior across randomly selected individuals, between family members, between racial groups, societies, cultures, and so on. Not all behavioral differences necessarily act as elicitors of regression, but through the learning of prejudicial stereotypes, even trivial differences may be used to rationalize ostracization and oppression.

For many 17th and 18th century writers, the physical, behavioral, and mental inferiorities of blacks were self-evident and required no scientific justification (Baker, 1974; Gould, 1981). Further, the existence of these alleged differences has led to oppression—itself a variation of sociobiological selfishness—of every type imaginable. Civilized people could apparently accept physical differences between they and blacks more readily than the assumed psychological differences in the moral and intellectual areas. The black was seen as a "savage" closer to the apes than the quintessential European in the Great Chain of Being, and, consequently, he was aggressive, unpredictable, animalistic in his sexual appetites, and totally incapable of reason and imagination. As long as the black held the status of savage, the role of slave was justified, his "threat value" was reduced to near zero, and he consumed precious few white resources. There can be no doubt that such prejudice was adaptive for whites, and served to put them at an overwhelming selective advantage.

Differences in Thinking and Beliefs. Although values, attitudes, and beliefs are woven into the behavior of the individual, they deserve to be discussed in their own right. Nature is borne of conflict, and although civilized man claims to have transcended physical conflict as a prime *modus operandus,* he continues to wage ideological warfare at every level. As long as one thought or one argument merely elicits thoughts and arguments in the beholder, violence, war, racial oppression and the like are avoided; that is, as long as neocortices interact with minimal intrusion from lower centers, phylogenetic regression and its apocalyptic hand-maidens are kept in check. Unfortunately, even relatively slight ideologi-cally elicited regression, either where the evocative cognition releases limbic responses in the speaker or the hearer, can snowball quickly into a full-blown confrontation. How often we read of differences of opinion leading to deadly aggression between friends, marital partners, racial and ethnic groups, political groups and nations. Many persons experience the urge to kill (and some act on it) over abortion, civil rights issues, school integration, political policies, governmental structure, and almost any other notion imaginable. Moreover, once the idea-elicited agonism has run its course, few stop to question the naturalness or appropriateness of the feeling or act; intuitively, all seem to agree that "standing up for one's rights," "fighting oppression," "conquering the world for the Father-land," and so forth, are actions too human to be denied.

Building on the dialectic of Hegelian philosophy, Karl Marx and Friedrich Engels saw conflict as the central theme in human relationships, pervading all areas of functioning—social, economic, political, and ideo-logical. Indeed, save for the haven of "pure communism" (Duke, 1976), life is little more than a perennial struggle between different classes, each with its own ideology, wants, and style of life:

The history of all hitherto existing society is the history of class struggles. Freeman and slave, patrician and plebian, lord and serf, guildmaster and journeyman, in a word, oppressor and oppressed stood in constant opposition to one another, carried on an uninterrupted, now hidden, now open fight, a fight that each time ended, either in a revolutionary reconstitution of society at large, or in the common ruin of the contending classes.

In the earlier epochs of history, we find almost everywhere a complicated arrangement of society into various orders, a manifold gradation of social rank. In ancient Rome we have patricians, knights, plebians, slaves; in the Middle Ages, feudal lords, vassals, guildmasters, journeymen, apprentices, serfs; in almost all of these classes, again, subordinate gradations.

The modern bourgeoise society that has sprouted from the ruins of feudal society has not done away with class antagonisms. It has but established new classes, new conditions for oppression, new forms of struggle in place of the old ones.

Our epoch, the epoch of the bourgeoise, possesses, however, this distinctive feature: It has simplified the class antagonisms. Society as a whole is more and more splitting up into two great hostile camps, into two great classes directly facing one another—bourgeoise and proletariat. (Marx & Engels, 1848/1976, p. 485)

Marx and Engel's quote is a powerful reminder of how ideologically defined "differences" between individuals and groups of people are used to justify inequitable distribution of resources and hierarchical class structures. As long as those in power see the poor and lower classes as different in the sense of being inferior and deserving of their fate, oppression is justified and the rich are absolved of all guilt and responsibility. Whether the ideological justifications employed have any basis in fact is irrelevant to their elicitative capability; the fact that the rich and powerful believe their justifications is sufficient. Wars, class antagonisms, oppression of "inferior groups," and the like, all have their genesis in the human capacity to unlock the door of passion with the keys of ideology. Again, as we saw in chapter 3, the ability of the human species to "actively phylogenetically regress" is the one thing that makes us the most dangerous creatures on earth; we do not have to wait for provocation from the outside or from our own internal physiological processes— we may provoke ourselves to passion at any moment by merely allowing a provocative thought to pass across the mind's eye.

Power, Riches, and Money

In a world of vast differences in access and opportunity, we confront an interesting paradox: the poor often phylogenetically regress because they have to in order to survive, as we saw earlier with the Ik, but the rich and powerful often regress in order to further maximize their material resources or to maximize pleasure through hedonic pursuits. The rich and powerful are apt to rationalize their rapacity and pleasure-seeking with racialist, nationalist, intellectualist, faddist, and other ideas that clothe their behavior with meaning and social rectitude. In present-day South Africa, for example, the policy of apartheid is viewed as an unquestioned truth by most Afrikaners, but underlying this neo-cortically mediated value lies the deeper realities of acquisitiveness, power, territorial control, oppression, and the urge to maximize fitness of one's own genes and those of close kin through maintaining strict "racial purity." Thus, at the neocortical level, the Ik and the Afrikaners appear ever so different, the former behaving in the absence of clearly articulated ideology and the latter basking in it, but at the motivational–emotional levels of the limbic and reptilian systems they differ little at all. We might say that the Ik think and act regressively, whereas the Afrikaner thinks progressively (neocortically) and behaves regressively.

Albert Schweitzer was aware of the regressive aspects of power, as evidenced in his comments upon receiving the Nobel Peace Prize in 1952: "Man has become a superman. . . . But the superman with the superhuman power has not risen to the level of superhuman reason. To the degree to which his power grows he becomes more and more a poor man. . . . It must shake up our conscience that we become all the more inhuman the more we grow into supermen" (cited in Fromm, 1976, p. 3). In this statement, Schweitzer implicitly acknowledged that power is a cardinal precondition for inhumane behavior; that is, the mere opportunity for regression is often sufficient for it to occur, and the possession of power provides opportunity for the most egregious forms of regressive self-interest. How seldom do we hear of individuals fighting to gain power so that it might be used for selfless and altruistic pursuits! The very object of obtaining power is to gain access to resources, to gain priority over others, to "win" in the game of life. Even Christian exhortations to meekness, love of enemies, and selflessness could not stem the tide of imperialism in our own forbears: "European-North American history, in spite of the conversion to the church, is a history of conquest, pride, greed; our highest values are: to be stronger than others, to be victorious, to conquer others and exploit them" (Fromm, 1976, p. 142).

The lust for power is neither distinctly European-American, nor is it distinctly human for that matter. In the introduction to de Waal's (1982) *Chimpanzee Politics,* Desmond Morris says of chimps: "Their social life is full of take-overs, dominance networks, power struggles, alliances, divide-and-rule strategies, coalitions, arbitration, collective leadership, privileges and bargaining. There is hardly anything that occurs in the corridors of power of the human world that cannot be found in embryo in the social life of a chimpanzee colony" (p. 14). This is a crucial point, for if our nearest primate relatives fail to exhibit any evidence of power orientation, then the notion of human phylogenetically "regressing-to-power" would be little more than metaphor.

As with power, material riches may facilitate progression or regression, but the latter is the far more likely possibility. Certainly there are many genuinely philanthropic and charitable individuals and institutions, although even there, mildly regressive trends often are seen in publicity-seeking and ego gratification, misuse of funds (tax loopholes, padded expense accounts, ridiculously high overheads, inflated salaries, etc.), and other forms of selfishness. More often, it seems, we hear of the sexual profligations of the rich, their excesses of material consumption, and their use of riches to gain more riches. Moreover, it is not uncommon for thrill criminals (see chapter 10), vandals, drug abusers, terrorists, and other regressive types to come from the upper social classes. Again, we see that the rich and poor are hardly different at subcortical levels of functioning, save for the fact that the rich have opportunity for a wider range of regressions.

The pursuit of riches is obviously one of the great regressors, but what of the nouveau riche, the beneficiaries of sudden riches? Jane Goodall (1971), in her research on the Gombe Stream, showed that sudden riches, in the form of stalks of bananas, produced hyperaggressiveness and social disorder in a normally peaceful group of chimpanzees. Eventually, the practice of providing bananas for group feeding had to be abandoned due to its disruptive effects. De Waal (1982) similarly found it necessary to separate chimpanzees in the Arnhem Zoo at feeding time in order to defuse tension and avoid violent confrontations. De Waal points out that chimpanzees, in their natural habitat, forage for food on their own or in small groups. The berries and leaves searched for are evenly scattered about the terrain, and competition for food is atypical. But when humans disturb the natural order of things by providing large quantities of highly valued food in a circumscribed geographic area, the peace is quickly disturbed.

At the risk of being anthropomorphic, can we really say that humans react that much differently at the disposition of a large will or when money is thrown in a large crowd? Certainly Mackay's (1841/1980) dramatic examples of "money mania" and rampant greed make the chimps look rather tame by comparison. Extrapolations between humans and chimpanzees may be controversial regarding greed and money madness, but one thing is for certain—humans were adapted for adversity not affluence throughout their evolutionary history, and when sudden riches present themselves one may generally expect the worst to follow. Indeed, it takes a person of great character to receive a great financial windfall, and then use his or her good fortune to rise to higher planes of humanity.

So far we have spoken of power and riches as general elicitors, or more accurately, general preconditions for phylogenetic regression, but actual money may serve as an immediate stimulus for subneocortical excitation. As the saying goes "money is the root of all evil," and many a crime of passion has been precipitated by the thirst for money. This fact was recognized by the Roman philosopher and statesman Seneca some 2,000 years ago:

> He that duly considers the subject Matter of all our Controversies and Quarrles, will find them Low, and Mean, not worth the Thought of a Generous Mind; but the greatest Noise of all is about Money. This is it, that sets Fathers and Children together by the ears; Husbands and Wives. (cited in Toch, 1983, p. 1022)

Of course, money has no direct reward or need-reducing capabilities in and of itself, but it sufficiently represents power and access to goods to serve as one of the most powerful motivators and regressors of behavior. In sufficient quantities, money allows for the perennial satiation of primitive needs that were rarely satiated in either lower animals or primitive man. In the monied human, pleasures that were designed to assure elicitation of species–specific adaptive behavior, and that were satisfied incompletely and intermittently in the natural state, can be indulged to the point of pathology and unpleasure (see Solomon, 1980). Yet, money not only causes people to kill, steal, and sacrifice themselves on the altar of hedonism, it can also regress us away from higher morals and values. As Dawes (1980) tells us: "most people in the world will compromise his or her altruistic or ethical values for money or survival" (p. 191). A research study by Damon (1977) revealed just how tenuous human sharing and altruism really are. Damon found that children may, in a hypothetical situation, recommend equal division of candy with peers, but when actual candy is present selfish behavior emerges. In our terms, the actual candy served as an elicitor for regression, where professed higher motives gave way to lower ones at the moment of truth.

The social implications of economically induced regressions is grave indeed. Even in America, unquestionably the most charitable and liberal-minded nation ever known, we often see well-meaning programs of social action rent apart internally by greed and financial malfeasance; we see popular religious figures initially solicit funds for the highest motives, only to have them slowly transmuted into means for personal aggrandizement; we see parents lavish money on wayward adolescents, only to have them worsen in proportion; and we see every phase of our democracy reel and rock in resonance with an ever changing economy. No aspect of our individual or collective lives seems immune from the regressive effects of monetary concerns. Senator Nancy Kassebaum recently commented on economics and the feminist movement: "If the economy doesn't turn around nobody is going to care about feminist issues. The economy far overrides any questions of gender" *(Los Angeles Times,* January 2, 1981). The phylogenetic regression–progression model would phrase it somewhat differently—economic stress tends to regress people back to "traditional," hunting-and-gathering modes of stereotypical maleness and femaleness (see Sai, 1984). Added to this reversion from learned androgynous roles also would be a retreat from ideological commitment in general, when that commitment is "expensive" in hard times. In economic stress, we see a tendency to regress down the Maslovian hierarchy from the lofty and the conceptual to the adaptive and the mundane. Indeed, thinking, philosophizing, and self-actualizing are reserved for a precious few people on this earth who have the time and money to engage in such nonsurvival pursuits.

In closing this section we quote from McDougall (1926), who realized that although acquisitiveness is an unquenchable instinct, its unbridled expression was necessary for the development of civilization:

> Although in highly civilized societies the motives that lead to the accumulation of capital become very complex, yet acquisitiveness, the desire for mere possession of goods, remains probably the most fundamental of them, blending and co-operating with all other motives; this impulse, more than all others, is capable of obtaining continuous or continually renewed gratifications; for while, in the course of satisfaction of most other desires, the point of satiety is soon reached, the demands of this one grow greater without limit, so that it knows no satiety. How few men are content with the possession of what they need for the satisfaction of all other desires than this desire for possession for its own sake! It is this excess of activity beyond that required for the satisfaction of all other material needs, that results in the accumulation of the capital which is a necessary condition for the development of civilisation. (p. 330)

SUMMARY

Phylogenetic regression theory posits that stress, broadly defined, is a potent elicitor of regression. Stress usually represents real or implied threat to survival, and this threat serves to activate the emergency centers of the limbic-hypothalamic complex, thereby "regressing" the person. Life is full of stressors, as Selye (1978) says, although the most potent ones are those that represent threat to survival, sudden change, under- or overstimulation, or deviations from species-typical modes of coping. Overpopulation and crowding, and deprivation and frustration are especially strong stressors, and their effects were analyzed in some detail.

Along with stress, there are many other elicitors derivable from theory, and a sampling was chosen for analysis. The regressive effect of groups and crowds on individual behavior was discussed, drawing heavily from the classic writings of Le Bon and McDougall, and a number of modern writers. In similar vein, anonymity and deindividuation were cited as facilitators of regression in both crowds and individual contexts. When anonymous or deindividualized, the person can open the door on primitive behaviors which would be held in tight control normally. Indeed, numerous research studies have implicated deindividualization in a broad range of pathologies of the impulsive, dyscontrolled type.

Perceived "differences" between people also were cited as powerful elicitors of phylogenetic regression. The issue of group differences was discussed in terms of relations with "strangers," in-group versus out-group relations, racial conflict, and the dynamics of power and oppression. The theme of power and oppression was carried through in analyzing the roles of power, riches, and money as elicitors of regression. It was speculated that the poor exhibit regressive behavior in order to survive, whereas the rich often regress in order to become richer or to indulge themselves in animal pleasures. Further, the rich and powerful often rationalize their exploitation of the poor with racialist, nationalist, intellectualist, and other "active" forms of regression.

Actual money in hand or sight also is a powerful elicitor that people kill for, abuse their bodies for, forsake their morals and ideals for, and forsake their humanity for. Yet, as McDougall (1926) rightly said, money is the root of both man's worst and greatest accomplishments; the same species that degrades itself for money and the access to resources that it represents, has used it to transcend the animals and build a world unlike any other in creation.

8

The Paleopsychology
of Motivation and Learning

*The key factors in the programming of mammal behaviors
go under names like motivation, reward and learning. Subjects* learn *to do things, if they are rewarded for doing them;
and if they are motivated to do them. There is, of course, a
continuum from higher to lower motives. The lower end of
the continuum is the one we have most in common with the
laboratory rat. At this end there are four key factors. First,
there are drives, that is, special states created by alarming
or dangerous deficits. Second are the incentive mechanisms,
that is, reactions to promising stimuli which guide behavior
even though deficits are not alarming. Third there are rewards, that is, targets that become objects of pursuit under
either of the two kinds of motivating conditions, and which
modify behavior repertoires a little or a lot when they are
achieved (or when they are brought to bear as stimuli).
Fourth, and finally, there are the learning mechanisms, that
is, the set of built-in rules for modifying the repertoire with
or without rewards.*

—Olds (1976, pp. 1–2)

MOTIVATION AND BEHAVIOR

The foundation of the phylogenetic regression–progression (PRP) model
has now been laid, and hopefully it will be sturdy enough to support the
discussion of motivation and learning to follow. Our approach has been

analytic and explicative, with the goal of developing an integrative model of present explanatory–heuristic value and future predictive–empirical value. Emphasis has been on exploiting interesting animal–human analogies, cross-disciplinary linkages, and brain-behavior relationships. In developing the logic of the PRP model, evolutionary biology has stood forth as the massive planetary body about which the gravity-drawn lesser satellites of ethology, sociobiology, biocultural anthropology, behavioral psychology, neuroscience, and sociology revolve. Although attempts to integrate diverse strands along the way were not always successful, one inescapable fact remains: We humans are more defined by our animal nature than anything else, and any comprehensive theory or model of human behavior must, at some point, come face-to-face with the Beast. As we shall see, phylogenetic carryovers, pre-programmed tendencies, and so forth, bear heavily upon the psychological constructs of motivation and learning as they do in other areas of functioning. The present chapter attempts to characterize and, in some instances, reformulate these constructs within the regression–progression model.

The Centrality of Motivation

The principles of motivation must, of necessity, lie at the core of any theory of the causes of behavior.[1] It is tautological that adaptive behavior must be motivated to occur, and in the evolved motivational structures of

---

[1]Two issues are raised here, motivation and causality. As Brodbeck (1963) tells us, to understand a human action is to know its motive. Nevertheless, she avers that motive explanations are not equivalent to causal explanations, for understanding the meaningfulness and purposefulness of action and identifying specific causes are not the same thing. Although not equivalent, motivation and causality often overlap and are mutually compatible, and motives are generally embedded within the causal matrix "determining" complex, adaptive human behavior. Brodbeck (1963) discusses the causes involved in buying a house: For example, the motive to gain privacy might be one of many interlocking causes operating, whereas going-to-the-bank-for-money, as a required rule-governed action, might involve little motivation. The distinction here between "doing something" (motivated behavior) and "having something happen to you" (little or no motivation) is important.

Clearly, human action is caused by more than motives, but a psychological understanding of the meaning of human action requires motivational explanations (Weber, 1947). Whereas motivational constructs might not be needed in reference to normatively compelled (aside from the motive to conform) or reflexive action, they are required for explaining spontaneous forms of human social behavior, e.g., playfulness, sexuality, aggressiveness, affiliation. A motive is "spontaneous" when it is premised on specific, evolved neurohumoral structures designed to guarantee behavioral outputs necessary for survival; conversely, their absence would imply inability, or severely diminished ability, to successfully adapt. These spontaneous motivational causes are often nonconscious, affectively toned, and irrational (see Weber, 1947), and only partially influenced by conscious will. The phylogenetic regression model emphasizes such phylogenetically old, spontaneous motivational processes, and accords them a central place in analyzing the causes of human action. Without recourse to them, "meaningful" causal explanations of human social behavior do not seem possible.

both animals and human beings we see the defining characteristics of living creatures most clearly etched. Each organism capable of survival is, by virtue of its evolved structural components and behavioral equipment, programmed to respond adaptively to environmental demands in ways generally characteristic of its species. Thus, each species, and each species member varying around the species norm, act in predictable and characteristic ways as they attempt to meet threats and challenges from the environment.

Some organisms are provided with extremely simple structural components and motivational systems for adaptation. Von Uexküll's (1957) eloquent description of the brief life cycle of the wood tick is an excellent case in point. From the egg the small creature emerges lacking legs and sexual organs. After shedding its skin several times, it acquires the missing organs, mates, and begins the hunt for warm-blooded animals. After mating, the female climbs to the tip of a bush or twig, and lies in wait for her prey passing underneath. Lacking hearing or sight, she hurls herself downward on her quarry once the smell of butyric acid, which emanates from the skin glands of all animals, reaches sufficient intensity. Now there is nothing left for her to do but to enjoy a feast of warm blood, deposit her eggs, and die. By contrast, more advanced organisms, such as the mammals and primates, are characterized by extreme complexity, especially where social behavior is concerned. Still, even with the most complex and advanced social creatures, including humans, behavior continues to be quite predictable in the population sense and is, ultimately, predominantly adaptive (survival-targeted) as it is with other animals. Even human behavioral capacity is far from infinitely flexible, and numerous writers have referred to species-typical, innate, phylogenetically prepared, and so on, motivational and behavioral patterns in humans.

Motivation and the Regression–Progression Continuum

As is true of all behavioral systems, motivation can be characterized in terms of the regression–progression continuum. Thus, it follows that there are primitive motivational structures, advanced ones, and mixed ones between the two poles. At the most primitive pole, we find rigid instincts composed of innate, species–specific releaser-action pattern linkages, such as those seen in the wood tick or the male silk moth whose sexual action potential is elicited with as little as one molecule of the chemical bombykol (see chapter 6). In these primitive linkages we see cause–effect in stark terms, where the mere presentation of the releasing stimulus will reliably elicit a specific response pattern across individual species members across differing conditions. At the advanced pole, as with human sexual motivation, for example, behavior may appear infinitely variable, culture-bound, and cognitively controlled, and innate motivational structures and releaser-action linkages nowhere to be seen. A person may choose to be celibate, for example, leading the naive observer to conclude that the individual has completely "transcended" the lower sexual motives or somehow rendered the evolved "wiring" nonfunctional. Such transcendence may only be metaphorical, however, for the wired-in sexual and reproductive programs are not eliminated, only suppressed. Along with the rich sublimative behavior expected from a Freudian perspective, we often find the celibate fighting a mighty inner moral battle against his or her still-present alien sexual drives, and how this battle is fought describes the unique character of the person in great degree. Indeed, the person living in a state of perennial sexual frustration may become more obsessed with sexuality than the profligate! So, rather than sexuality having been transcended, it has been merely suppressed, modified, and cognitively redefined, but its essential character remains as a constant burden for the celibate to bear. Moreover, the threat of regression always lurks in the background, urging the person to forsake arbitrary moral proscriptions and to yield to phylogenetically older natural mandates. So it seems to be with much if not all of human behavior— our overt actions, even the highly advanced ones, emanate from and are derivative of a relatively small number of phylogenetically programmed motive systems. It is from these few motive systems that we phylogenetically progress, and to them that we phylogenetically regress.

The Basic Motive Systems

In previous chapters, the fundamental significance of approach–withdrawal, pleasure–pain, and reward–punishment polarities were emphasized. Thus, in postulating the basic motive sources in humans, we follow Schneirla's two-factor classification of behavior, approach and withdrawal (Schneirla, 1959). Table 8.1 summarizes the fundamental motive systems that appear to underlie most of the behavior in higher animals and humans.

There are two noteworthy factors to consider regarding the postulated motive systems in Table 8.1. First, approach systems appear more numerous and variegated than do withdrawal systems. Despite the exceptions of playing possum and tonic immobility, the general goal of withdrawal or escape is to merely render the painful or aversive stimulus null and void by removing the phenotype from the stimulus field (see Hinde, 1970, pp. 349–350, for discussion of distinctions between withdrawal, immobility, and fear). Once sufficient distance (perceptual or physical) is put between the animal and the aversive or threatening stimulus object, the behavioral

TABLE 8.1
The Basic Motive Systems

I. Approach types
  A.   Procurement of nutrition
      1. Predation
        a. seeking (hunting)
        b. killing
        c. eating
      2. Other food-seeking
        a. seeking and eating small animals and insects not requiring hunting
        b. seeking, gathering, and eating various forms of plant life—leafy plants, fruit, nuts, berries, etc.
  B.   Aggression—subserves all other motive systems (see chapter 9)
      1. Predatory aggression (interspecic)
      2. Dominance aggression (intraspecific)
      3. Protective aggression (territorial, spatial, fighting for food, protection of young, etc.)
  C.   Reproductive and sexual
      1. Mate seeking and bonding (as opposed to social attachment)
      2. Ritualized courtship behavior
      3. Copulation
      4. Primitive parenting (nest building, sitting on eggs, protective behavior, etc.)
  D.   Social-affiliative (limbic affectional)
      1. Advanced parenting
        a. Maternal care and attachment
        b. Infant attachment
        c. Peer attachment
        d. Paternal care and attachment (not present in most animals)
      2. Friendships, alliances, and kinship relations in higher mammals and primates
      3. Play behavior
  E.   Curiosity and exploration
II. Withdrawal types
  A.   Pain avoidance (proximal stimuli)
  B.   Threat avoidance (distal stimuli)
  C.   Fear

Notes:

Table 8.1 represents a summary of the typically cited motives in the biopsychological literature.

The motives listed seldom act independently; interaction of motives is the rule (e.g., although predominantly social-affiliative, play draws from many systems—predation, dominance, sexual-reproductive, threat avoidance, fear, etc.)

See Table 9.1 regarding "advanced" elaboration of the basic motives in Table 8.1.

interaction is for all practical purposes terminated. With approach behavior by contrast, only the first phase of interaction between the animal and the positively valenced stimulus object is completed with entrance to the perceptual field. The animal may see, hear, or smell the stimulus object at a distance, and then emit a wide variety of approach and consumatory responses before leaving the field. Thus, the consumatory response for withdrawal is to escape or avoid the stimulus object, whereas the approach consumatory response(s) entails doing something to (kill prey, eat prey, etc.) or with (mother the offspring, play with peers, fight with peers, etc.) the object. Secondly, one is struck by the relatively small number of basic motive systems postulated in the biopsychological literature defining the wellsprings of animal and human behavior. Ethologists, sociobiologists, and other biologically oriented writers are fairly consistent and economical in framing their motive constructs, perhaps because of within- and between-species regularities of animals in the wild. Because human ethologists, human sociobiologists, and other human biopsychologists often tend to focus on phylogenetic continuities in analyzing human behavior, their postulated motive systems are both few in number and derivative of animal motive systems.

By virtue of often working on arbitrary conceptual problems in arbitrary laboratory settings, emphasizing advanced cognitive and cultural determinants, and emphasizing individual differences, social scientists tend to see far more motive forces at work than do the biopsychologists. Who, then, is correct, the biopsychologist with few motives or the social scientist with many? Actually, the PRP model would say that both are right; the biopsychologist generally concentrates on the primitive pole of functioning, where the basic, physiologically rooted motivational mechanisms are few, whereas the social scientist favors the advanced pole where learned habits, preferences, attitudes and values, and so on do influence behavior. Nonetheless, it is unlikely that advanced "motives" or "drives" ever totally transcend their primitive energy sources. It appears more fruitful to view the numerous and varied advanced motives as *derivatives* and *elaborations* of primitive neurophysiological motive sources (Reynolds, 1981) that are, ultimately, the driving forces in behavior. Indeed, we may ask just how much human uniqueness, how much transcendent motivation, would remain once the ancient imperatives of food procurement, sex and mating, dominance and protective aggression, danger avoidance, exploration and curiosity, and mammalian parenting and affiliation were to be totally subtracted from the system? Certainly, the basic motives listed in Table 8.1 are not the whole of human motivation, but the basic motives and their numerous derivatives and elaborations would seem to encompass much of what we call human nature.

The Elaboration of Basic Motive Systems

If there are so few basic motive systems in animals and humans, how can we explain the complexity of behavior, especially in upper level primates and *Homo sapiens?* This is where the previously mentioned notions of inhibition-release and elaboration come in.

First of all, it is presumed that most meaningful behavior of animals and humans in natural situations is nonarbitrary and adaptive, and is, thus, motivated primarily by drives and dispositions emanating from neurophysiological structures "built in" to the organism in the course of evolution. Such readinesses and predispositions remain inactive most of the time even in the most primitive creatures, and only emerge into behavior when they are released for some good reason (e.g., presentation of adequate stimulus appropriate to the organism in question). The mating response of most animals, for example, is in a state of inhibition most of the time, and only comes into effect when seasonal factors, situational conditions, internal chemistry, and social releasers are conducive to response output. Species-appropriate mating behavior is therefore released from inhibition by the cumulative effects of response priming (see chapter 6) and releasing stimuli. The male rat's sexual behavior, for example, involves reflexive responses such as penile erection and thrusting movements of the pelvic musculature, which probably depend on neural circuits in the medulla and spinal cord (Hinde, 1970). However, as Hinde points out, the organization of the diverse reflexes involved in functionally effective behavioral patterns in male rats depends on more anterior parts of the brain, most likely areas of the hypothalamus. These brain centers are inhibitory in great degree (Beach, 1967; Hart, 1967), and apparently are sensitive to the disinhibiting effects of androgens circulating in the bloodstream. At higher levels of cortical functioning, experience and learning may exert a modifying effect on the entire process, resulting in fluctuations of sexual responsivity not apparently directly attributable to hormonal level or the primitive sexual centers of the brain. In the foregoing example, we see that primitive sexual behavior in the male rat is actually quite complex and multiply determined, involving intricate interactions among inhibiting and releasing forces at several different levels of functioning.

It is evident that the male rat's sexual response system is, among other things, comprised of reflexive behavior mediated by lower brain structures, hormonal input, and central mediating inputs. We are faced with the question now of whether human sexual behavior is similarly organized, or whether it is a qualitatively different phenomenon entirely. Most laypersons and many social scientists seem to assume human uniqueness a given in this matter, but the law of parsimony exhorts us to accept the simplest and most obvious explanations when possible. One way to accomplish this is to carefully ascertain which animal models of behavior apply to human functioning (Davey, 1983; Harlow & Mears, 1979; von Cranach, 1976), and then to erect explanations upon them. That is the approach taken in the present book: Phylogenetic continuity of structure-function relationships from nonhuman organisms to humans is presumed for many aspects of behavior, with the basic parameters of motivation (see Table 1.1) leading the list. Proceeding from these presumptions, the complexity of human motivation becomes a matter of how the phylogenetically old aspects of motivation are retained in the brain, how these old motive systems inhibit and/or facilitate each other, under what circumstances and to what degree are they released into behavior, and how they are elaborated upon and modified by experience. So construed, the complexity of motive system organization and the multiplicity of motives ascribed to humans primarily arise from elaborations and modifications of old systems rather than the evolution or development of new and unique characters.

The approach just described is clearly premised on what Rose (1983) calls "monist selection hypotheses," which assume that human social behavior is built upon a foundation of primate behavior that is never completely superceded. The "bifurcationist" hypotheses, by contrast, conjecture that human social behavior has evolved away from the animal pattern and man essentially belongs to a kingdom of one species. Rose seems to favor the bifurcationist model himself, but admits that science cannot presently prove one better than the other. When such conceptual standoffs occur, Ockham's razor becomes the criterion for choosing the proper alternative, and the monist selection position has the edge because it implies the fewest assumptions and abstractions regarding animal–human differences and human uniqueness. In deference to William of Ockham, it would seem prudent to view genus *Homo* as a super-primate up to the point where new models and theories are required to make sense of the more phylogenetically advanced behavioral phenomena. Unfortunately, many scientists, especially social scientists, begin with elaborate higher order constructs and then use them to deny or explain away unpleasantries in human behavior (see chapter 10).

The simplest approach to human motivation is first to assume phylogenetic continuities in the basic motive systems, and then to analyze increasing complexity in terms of elaborations and modifications of these systems as long as the facts will allow (Reynolds, 1981). Once the point of diminishing returns is reached, then the scientist should prudently add new concepts and models as they are needed. Unfortunately, the idea of primitive system elaboration has never been sufficiently exploited so that the limits of its applicability could be determined. A major goal of this volume is to conceptualize as much human behavior as possible in terms of offshoots of vestiges, tendencies, readinesses, and dispositions inherited from our phylogenetic forebears. Complementarily, the fewest possible higher order constructs are employed in dealing with the complexities of human behavior.

The Interaction of Motives

Motives and motive systems seldom act independently of one another, except in the most rudimentary releaser-behavior patterns in primitive organisms. More typical is a complex, adaptive, dynamic flow of inter-mixed releaser-action patterns in response to ongoing, momentary changes in a demanding environment. Even rigid instinctive responses involving distinct fixed action patterns, such as egg-rolling movements in the greylag goose (Lorenz & Tinbergen, 1957) or the soliciting posture of the female chaffinch (Hinde, 1970), occur within the flow of fairly rich organism-environment interaction and interblending of motives. In more advanced organisms, such as upper level primates and humans, the release (or more likely part-release) of segments of primitive motive systems may be difficult to discern within the flow of extremely rich behavioral content and the complex intermixing of primitive–primitive, advanced–advanced, and primitive–advanced motivational components. Nevertheless, the PRP model assumes that primitive motive systems are always there in some form, however, quietly providing the whys of behavior—no matter how well disguised they may be.

The notion of mixed emotions and motivations was discussed in earlier chapters, but there are several other points to be made. Much of the following discussion was inspired by the comments of Konrad Lorenz on mixture of motives (Lorenz, 1982; Lorenz & Leyhausen, 1973), but other sources are cited as appropriate.

Unmixed Motivation.   First, it is important to note that unmixed motivation is quite rare. Lorenz (1982) says that behavior activated by a single motivation is just as rare as hybrids differing in only one gene, and, in higher animals especially, final behavioral output "is almost always a compromise made among several necessities" (p. 242).

Coordination of Behavior.   Behavior is highly coordinated and inte-grated, even in organisms possessing clear-cut genetically coordinated movements or fixed action patterns. As Lorenz (1982) tells us, these innate movement patterns often, but not always, form a functional unit together with their appropriate releasing mechanisms that, without prior experience, respond selectively to stimulus situations in adaptive ways. Such functional units are themselves integrations that mix with other integrations in the ongoing flow of behavior. Further, the strict fixed motor patterns and releasing mechanisms, although not functional units in and of themselves, "can be incorporated into complex behavior systems independently of each other and in varying combinations" (Lorenz, 1982, p. 149; see also Reynolds, 1981). The innate motor patterns, moreover, do not follow an all-or-nothing law, but "appear in forms of all the possible transitions from a very slight indication, called an 'intention movement,' to the full telenomic performance that occurs at the high intensity of specific excitation" (Lorenz, 1982, p. 149).

Motivation and Conflict.   By virtue of motive forces that are capable of addition, subtraction, mutual inhibition or facilitation, and many other forms of integration, the organism may behave in a smooth and coordinated manner, or it may oscillate in a state of conflict. In fact much, if not most, animal and human behavior involves some degree of conflict, in the sense that final behavioral output often reflects a compromise solution among opposing forces. Also, given the omnipresence of inherently conflictual inhibition-release mechanisms in the nervous system, we might say that behavior is almost always borne of conflict. Certainly, understanding the essential nature of a given behavioral phenomenon typically involves an analysis of dynamic opposing forces.

Strictly speaking, conflict is defined as a condition where two incompatible drives are simultaneously present, but this simple formula covers a wide range of behavioral phenomena falling under various combinations of approach and/or avoidance (Hinde, 1970):

1. States of neural inhibition where forces of expression are opposed by forces of suppression.

2. The complex dynamisms seen in agonistic and ritualized behavior.

3. Responses where behavioral inhibition is not complete, such as intention movements.

4. Alternation behaviors, such as the zigzag courtship dance of the three-spined stickleback.

5. Ambivalent behavior, where intention movements appropriate to two different tendencies are combined into a single pattern (e.g., pecking and swallowing movements in a frightened moorhen as it edges away from the food source).

6. Autonomically mediated conflict behavior, where, for example, a fearful animal defecates or urinates under stress.

7. Displacement or "substitute" (Kirkman, 1937) behavior, where the highly conflicted animal emits "irrelevant" or inappropriate responses (e.g., in many sexual or aggressive situations passerine birds may wipe their beaks, preen their feathers, emit feeding or drinking behavior, or otherwise engage in activity unrelated to context). Hydraulic model theorists like Tinbergen and Lorenz initially explained displacement in terms of "sparking over" effects, where thwarted motivational energy served to activate different, but closely related motivational systems. This conceptualization is quite similar to the Freudian notion of displace-

ment. Hinde (1970) considers this form of explanation passé, and concentrates instead on several variations of the "disinhibition hypothesis"; in simplest form, this hypothesis assumes that certain strong drives normally inhibit weaker ones, but when the stronger drives are in "balanced conflict" the weaker ones may slip out of inhibition and into behavior.

8. Redirection activities, where the motor patterns appropriate to one of the conflicting tendencies is shown, but are directed toward an "inappropriate object." This concept is directly analogous to psychoanalytic displacement; substitution of the object of the motivated behavior is the crucial issue here.

9. Certain kinds of sexual inversion in animals may occur in conflict situations. Under high sexual arousal, male birds may adopt the female copulatory posture when courtship gestures are frustrated, and assumption of the female presenting posture as an appeasement gesture in male primates is well-documented. The prevalence of homosexual behavior in animals under highly crowded conditions is also relevant here.

10. Regressive behavior, where adult animals revert to juvenile patterns, is also quite common in high conflict situations (Wickler, 1972).

11. Tonic immobility, a condition where the animal deals with conflict or threat by ceasing all overt behavioral activity (see chapter 5 for discussion of this phenomenon).

Motivation and Hierarchy. As we have seen, there are weak and strong motives that interact in various ways in a constant state of dynamic conflict. Such interactions are not random nor anarchical, however, but are typically hierarchical in form. As has been argued throughout, the concept of hierarchical organization is central to the phylogenetic regression–progression argument, and is, indeed, central to the whole of biology (Koestler & Smythies, 1969; Thorpe, 1974; Weiss, 1969). Moreover, it is a likely candidate principle for unifying the broad field of ethology (Dawkins, 1976b). The concept is most often employed by researchers dealing with complex interactions of neurohormonal motivational systems and subsystems; Satinoff's (1982) analysis of the motivational underpinnings of the extremely complex process of thermoregulation is a good case in point. She proceeded from a Jacksonian framework of levels of integration with each level adjusting and regulating the activities of lower levels. In the Jackson–Satinoff approach, the hypothalamus is "near" but not "at" the top of the hierarchy, directing the activities of thermoregulatory systems lower down.

In terms of the postulated primitive–advanced hierarchy, there are rigid fixed action patterns subserved by rigidly linked survival-targeted motivational systems operative at the lower pole, whereas supernumerous emotion-drive-behavior possibilities exist at the advanced upper pole.

Given this conceptual hierarchy, certain hypotheses about motivation may be derived. For convenience, our hypothetical hierarchy is sectioned into three molar levels of functioning roughly corresponding to Mac-Lean's model of the triune brain.

At MacLean's level of the reptilian brain, species–specific fixed action patterns are yoked to equally fixed and specific motive sources, and mixing or intercoordination amongst these innately coupled motivation-behavior systems is minimal. Reptiles, as we know, possess very limited behavioral repertoires compared to mammals and primates due to few and highly specialized innate programs to begin with, and severe limitations in the capability to elaborate upon these pre-existing systems. Thus, the reptile has preciously few behavioral components to elaborate upon, and even less in the way of cortical material to mediate such elaborations. In other words, a reptile can do what it was designed to do through natural selection, but can do little else.

By contrast, the mammal, possessing not only the reptilian neural chassis but the limbic thinking cap as well, is now capable of vastly greater mixing and intercoordination of motivation-behavior pattern relationships. Moreover, mammalian response potential not only overshadows reptilian response potential quantitatively, but qualitatively as well: The mammal not only behaves adaptively in response to environmental challenges, but its actions are influenced by feelings and emotions too. Furnished with the reptilian brain, and new tissue providing additional innate species-typical coordinations, capability to elaborate both old and new motivation-response systems in myriad ways, and the capacity for felt emotion, the range of mammalian response became overwhelming.

With animals possessing large amounts of neocortical tissue, in addition to the reptilian and mammalian structures, the potential for response elaboration was magnified even further, and in the human being we see seemingly infinite response potential. The neocortex served to free or decouple rigid stimulus-response linkages, and opened the way for more flexible and cognitive approaches to adaptation. Such de-bonding or decoupling of phylogenetically integrated sequences and motivation-response mixtures has contributed to human as well as animal evolutionary development: "Our [human] ability to adjust to new environmental challenges is often hampered by powerful bonds of reaction. Nevertheless, during the approximately 100,000 years that *Homo sapiens* has existed, small groups of humans have repeatedly broken these bonds and pioneered new ways of life" (Stebbins, 1982, p. 321).

With development of the neocortex, the rigid bonding of motivation and behavior was broken. Whereas specific motivation inevitably produces specific motivated behavior in the reptile, the mammals and primates have the capacity to exert some modificatory and regulatory control over motivation-behavior linkages. Of course, the super-sized human neocortex expanded this cognitive control even further; in humans, motivation may be repressed, suppressed, denied and otherwise transformed and dissipated through sheer conscious and/or unconscious mental activity. Certainly, the neocortically mediated ability to inhibit and transform motivational energy into behaviorally passive mental activity, as in dreams, daydreams, fantasies, and so on, is a quintessential human characteristic, one that perhaps separates us from the animals as much as any other.

Hormonal and Neural Interaction.   There is strong evidence that neural and hormonal systems interact in the production of complex adaptive behavior. However, the behavioral scientist seldom sees or measures true integration of behavior because of its inherent complexity and inaccessibility to observation. *In vivo* behavior involves many hierarchically organized components and subcomponents, all of which are elicited with proper timing and magniture, whereas inappropriate ones are simultaneously suppressed (Satinoff, 1982). These principles are aptly illustrated in Fahrbach and Pfaff's (1982) detailed analysis of the hormonal and neural mechanisms underlying maternal behavior in the rat. Behavioral changes associated with pregnancy, parturition, and lactation in the rat are legion, and are accompanied by numerous physiological changes. A summary of the more significant changes is provided in Table 8.2. It is evident from Table 8.2 that the highly coordinated behavioral and biochemical changes in rat maternality defy simple explanation in linear cause-effect terms.

Although highly complex, rat maternal behavior does not consist of novel responses, but is instead comprised of components already in the animal's repertoire—carrying objects, nest-building, and licking (Fahrbach & Pfaff, 1982). Here basic behavioral elements are coordinated into meaningful sequences with the result that pups are appropriately nurtured and given their species' insurance for survival. How is all this accomplished biochemically and neurologically? What are the underlying causes providing the motive thrust behind these species-typical patterns?

These are imposing questions, but the accumulated body of research on rat maternal behavior provides some answers. First, as Fahrbach and Pfaff (1982) convincingly argue, rat maternal behavior is motivated behavior. They garner a number of facts to support this assertion: (a) the goal object (rat pup) elicits strong approach responses with short latencies; (b) the rat mother remains alert to cues from the young; (c) she actively searches when cues are distal; (d) maternal behavior is easily elicited by suboptimal cues; (e) maternal drive is highest when the litter is young, and diminishes as the litter gets older; (f) maternal behavior can serve as a

TABLE 8.2
Physiological-Behavioral Changes in Female Rat During Pregnancy,
Parturition, and Lactation

Lower threshold for performance of thermoregulatory behavior during pregnancy
Inhibition of sexual activity during pregnancy
Onset of lactation
Rise in core body temperature during lactation
Suppression of pituitary-adrenal response to stress during lactation
Emission of a fecal maternal pheromone
Specific object-directed behavior
   Nest building
   Tail carrying
   Choice of safe nest location
   Consumption of fetal membranes and placenta
Self-directed behavior
   Self-licking, especially of nipples
   Ingestion of pup urine
   Alterations of food intake
   Decline in gross motor activity during pregnancy
Pup-directed behavior
   Freeing from fetal membranes
   Licking, especially of the ano-genital region
   Retrieval (carrying)
   Crouching over (nursing)
   Attraction to pup-related stimuli
   Eventual rejection of young
Behavior toward adult conspecifics
   Postpartum aggression
   Successful coordination of mating with maternal behavior during postpartum estrus

---

Note: This table is a condensation of Tables 9.2 and 9.3 in Fahrbach and Pfaff, 1982. Used
with permission.

"reward" in learning instrumental responses; (g) maternal drive does not
satiate like most other drives; and (h) maternal drive is extremely strong
compared to other drives like hunger and thirst. Rat maternal behavior is
clearly a strongly motivated response system, and, at its peak expression
following parturition, may override other competing response systems.

Massive endocrine changes occur at the end of pregnancy in the rat
(Morshige, Pepe, & Rothchild, 1973), and the onset of maternal behavior
is associated with the birth of the pups (Fahrbach & Pfaff, 1982; Kristal,
1980). The final days of gestation are marked by a decline in elevated
progesterone levels characteristic of pregnancy, with an accompanying
increase in the level of circulating estrogens. Increases in estrogen level
are evident around day 15 of pregnancy (the rat gestation period is
approximately 22 days), and a sharp increase in circulating prolactin
begins around day 21. These major hormonal changes help prepare the
mother for her first exposure to the pups, which might otherwise be

rejected or cannibalized without these endocrinological supports. These changes at the physiological level guarantee a heightened responsiveness to the newborn pups that is generally absent in females not recently pregnant. Apparently, this heightened responsiveness, or "maternal readiness," does not even require parturitional stimuli in the form of birthing or pup exposure to be evidenced (Fahrbach & Pfaff, 1982). Thus, the data indicate that the maternal action system in the rat is based on a hormonally induced readiness to perform a variety of component maternal behaviors under appropriate eliciting conditions. At this hormonal level of functioning, we see rather primitive, physiological causes acting to prime and otherwise mediate complex organism–environment relationships.

At a slightly more advanced level of internal causality, we find an intricate network of neural substrates supporting the rat's maternality. These neural substrates are, through phylogenetic shaping, blended in with and coordinated with hormonal substrates such that mother rats can be expected, with great likelihood, to behave appropriately toward their young. It is through the neural substrates that the strict behavioral components of maternality are encoded, and additional motive supports as well. In fact, hormones are not even necessary for maternal behavior; they appear to serve primarily a facilitory function, and maternality can be seen in the relative absence of hormonal influence (Fahrbach & Pfaff, 1982).

Lesions in many brain areas have been shown to impair the performance of maternal behavior in the rat (Slotnick, 1975). Although the neocortex, dorsal hippocampus, and septum are involved, recent research has focused on the medial preoptic area of the rostral hypothalamus. Fahrbach and Pfaff (1982) say that a strong case can be made that an intact medial preoptic area is essential to the performance of the commonly studied components of rat maternal behavior, and they cite numerous supporting studies. We may assume, then, that the medial preoptic area is a "center" of sorts for rat maternality. Lesions in this area made 5 days postpartum severely disrupt maternal behavior in rats (Numan, 1974). Once normal nest building, retrieval, and nursing behaviors are disrupted, the lesioned mothers cannot be induced to mother even with prolonged exposure to pups. Hormone implants in the medial preoptic area represent another line of evidence for a hypothalamic maternal center. For example, short latencies for sensitization were found in ovariectomized and hysterectomized pregnant rats receiving an estrogenic solution directly to the medial preoptic area, whereas longer latencies were associated with implants in other areas of the brain (Numan, Rosenblatt, & Komisaruk, 1977). Fahrbach and Pfaff (1982) conclude that research findings support the notion that the medial preoptic area is "a major site in the estrogen facilitation of maternal behavior" (p. 276). Here we see an excellent example of how hormonal and neural structures complement one another in the development of adaptive motivational and behavioral systems.

Although the medial preoptic area mediates rather specific maternal behaviors in the female rat, it also exerts control over other important activities including timing of ovulation and thermoregulation. The specific neuroanatomical loci involved in the control of these activities lie in close physical proximity, and, not surprisingly, there are times when functional overlap occurs. Fahrbach and Pfaff (1982) state that the potential for overlap of neural control mechanisms is particularly striking in the cases of maternal behavior and thermoregulation. For example, it appears that maternal temperature determines length of nursing bouts in the rat (Leon, Croskerry, & Smith, 1978), and nest building is a thermoregulatory response to lowered ambient temperature (Kinder, 1927). All rats build nests in the cold, but rats in the physiological states of pregnancy and lactation go one step further—they build maternal nests. This is a miracle of response system coordination from the neurophysiological standpoint, and Fahrbach and Pfaff (1982) say that the mechanics of this selective switching on and off remains a mystery. It is clear, however, that functional overlap of neurophysiologically proximate control centers in the diencephalon of the rat subserves a great amount of complex adaptive behavior.

In the maternality syndrome in the rat we see how endocrinological and neurophysiological substrates mix and interact to produce complex sequences of adaptive behavior. Moreover, we saw that functional overlap occurs among motivational–behavioral systems lying in close physical proximity in the rat's brain. This latter point is crucial to the phylogenetic regression–progression argument, for as we see later in the chapter, overlap, "sparking over," short-circuiting, and so forth, are presumed to occur among anatomically proximate centers of the brain, especially in the limbic system.

Motivation and Emotion

As Pfaff (1982) tells us, comparing the roles of motivational and emotional processes makes sense from both the neuroanatomical and evolutionary viewpoints. For one thing, there is great neurohumoral and neuroanatomical overlap between the motivational and emotional systems, and it often is difficult to distinguish one from the other. Response systems we call *motivational* and those we call *emotional* generally are mediated by lower brain centers in the hypothalamic-limbic axis, and may be viewed as part and parcel of essentially the same end result—the arousal, activation, and energizing of species adaptive behavior. Hypothalamic neurons control behavioral, endocrine, and autonomic states and are basic to the motivational hardware of the animal. As we saw in the section on maternality in the rat, the hypothalamus is a major neurological center for motivation, and it is similarly so for the human being. Further, limbic–emotional structures project heavily to the medial hypothalamic groups, and the hypothalamic cell groups likewise project back to the limbic system (Pfaff, 1982). Stellar (1954, 1982) provides an excellent discussion of the interrelatedness of hypothalamic and limbic functions, and reminds us that the hypothalamus is just a "part of a larger limbic system operating in motivated behavior" (Stellar, 1982, p. 378).

In nonhuman animals capable of emotional response, motivation and emotion generally remain thoroughly intertwined in adaptive behavioral output, but in humans disjunctions between the two systems is commonplace. For example, an animal has little choice regarding its actions (Rensch, 1971), its feelings, or the interaction of the two in the midst of a violent agonistic encounter, whereas humans in an analogous encounter may "feel" like hitting someone else but nevertheless suppress the behavior. This ability to separate motives and feelings, and to deny one or both access to overt behavior, appears to be a unique human characteristic. Thus, the animal behaves in a symmetrical, integrated way where drives and feelings join forces to assure adaptive behavioral output, whereas humans may behave cold-bloodedly without strong feeling, may experience strong feelings but not act on them, or may actively suppress both motivation and feeling. As was pointed out earlier (chapter 2), human beings have the ability to decouple themselves from natural imperatives in a fashion impossible in any other animal; unfortunately, this distinctive human quality is a two-edged sword, as is evident when we discuss psychopathological processes in chapter 12.

Pleasure, Aversion, and Motivation

For all but the most primitive of creatures, the basic approach–avoidance tendencies are accompanied by the experiences of pleasure and aversion. Although all motivation cannot be simply construed as either seeking pleasure or avoiding pain in the teleological sense, it is clear that many animals possess the neural hardware for experiencing pleasure and pain (Olds & Milner, 1954; Stellas, 1982). Hedonic processes and motivation are no doubt intricately related, but the relationship is highly complex and easy generalizations cannot be made with present knowledge. Accumulated evidence does suggest, however, that hedonic processes and their correlated neurological centers and neurohumoral systems (see German & Bowden, 1974) appear to be associated with reinforcement and learning processes (Hoebel & Teitelbaum, 1962; Margules & Olds, 1962; Olds & Milner, 1954), changes in drive level (Deutsch & Howarth, 1963) and appetence, autonomic responsivity (Halperin & Pfaff, 1982), the maintenance of biological homeostasis (Deutsch & Howarth, 1963), and the mediation of a host of specific motivational states—hunger, thirst, thermoregulation, sex, aggression, maternal behavior, and so on (Stellar, 1982). Clearly, pleasure and aversion are woven into the fabric of motivation, and despite the typical specificity of motivated behaviors, all involve the same hedonic processes—approach–withdrawal, reinforcement, and hedonic experience (Stellar, 1982).

In earlier sections, we saw that the limbic–hypothalamic complex was involved in many aspects of motivated behavior, and, not surprisingly, we find it center stage in the neurophysiology of pleasure and aversion. The early work of Olds and his colleagues on intracranial self-stimulation (ICSS) led to the postulation of neural centers for hedonic processes situated at various loci in the hypothalamus and limbic system. The parts of the brain susceptible to rewarding stimulation are far-ranging, but are pretty much centered upon the hypothalamus, which Konner (1982) calls the "central organ of motivation." Konner likens the reward system of the brain to a wheel, with the hypothalamus as the hub and various olfactory and limbic pathways as the spokes. These spokes radiate out into the olfactory bulbs and olfactory cortex, the septal area, the hippocampus, the anterior nucleus of the thalamus, the cingulate cortex, the hippocampus, and down into the limbic portion of the midbrain and even into lower brain-stem centers in the pons and medulla (Halperin & Pfaff, 1982; Olds, 1976). The highest rates of positive response to ICSS are found in the medial forebrain bundle of the lateral hypothalamus, with rates falling off in the medial hypothalamus and other midline structures such as the hippocampus and cingulate cortex.

The aversion centers of the brain have not received the massive attention accorded the pleasure pathways, and consequently their neurological substrates are not as well-mapped nor as well understood. Nevertheless, a composite picture of the aversion system emerges when we scan some of the major research findings. First, however, it is important to note that the aversion system mediates displeasure and discomfort across diverse response categories including physical pain (Mayer & Price, 1982), punishment, fear, avoidance, escape, frustration, and the displeasure associated with rage, anger, and irritable aggression (Moyer, 1976, 1981). Given these multiple criteria of displeasure, it is not surprising that the neuroanatomy of aversion is complex and that loci often vary in terms of particular response categories. Some of the more or less general areas associated with aversiveness or negative reinforcement include the medial, periventricular system of the hypothalamus (Olds,

1956; Stellar, 1982), the mesodiencephalic limbic area described by Nauta (1960, 1964), and electrode implantation in humans has implicated several other areas including the thalamic center median, cingulate gyrus, periaqueductal sites and mesencephalic tegmentum in unpleasant feelings ranging from anxiety, fear, rage, to intense aversion and aggression (Valzelli, 1981).

Using deeply implanted electrodes in the brains of severely disturbed psychiatric patients, Heath (1964, 1975, 1981) has greatly increased our understanding of the neuroanatomy and functional complementarity of both pleasure and displeasure. Of particular interest here are his findings on the subjective displeasure associated with experienced outbursts of fear, anger and rage (Heath, 1981). Profoundly aversive emotional reactions resulted in his patients when focal sites in the amygdala, hippocampus, and midline tegmental structures were stimulated. Fear was the predominant reaction, but violent rage responses, to the extreme of homicidal behavior, also were seen. It is noteworthy that these extreme reactions were correlated almost perfectly with brain stimulation; when current was on the reactions occurred, and when off they subsided. The patients were "regressed" and "progressed" at will, moving from extremely aversive high-amplitude electrical activity in the ventral hippocampus and medial amygdala one moment, to "abstract, unemotional" behavior the next with the termination of stimulation (Heath, 1981).

Stellar's Limbic Continuum.   Stellar (1954, 1982) has long argued that motivation is multifactorily determined with the hypothalamus and associated limbic mechanisms playing central roles. We find that the hypothalamic–limbic complex is involved in the full range of primitive response functions: eating, drinking, sleep, copulation, rage and attack, maternality, thermoregulation, grooming, and fear. Moreover, the hypothalamus and limbic structures control and/or mediate response output in all of the deep response modalities—motivational, emotional, behavioral, and in terms of pleasure/displeasure. We must conclude, then, that any theory addressing the underlying causes of behavior must necessarily feature the hypothalamic and limbic inputs into response output. Yet, with all the intricate interconnections across many different levels of function in the limbic system, a true understanding seems impossible at this time.

One way to introduce order in complex systems is to think hierarchically or in terms of continua, and Stellar (1982) accommodates us with the following "continuum of functions of the limbic system" (p. 386) proceeding from the most psychoneurologically primitive to most advanced:

1. physiological regulations
2. consumatory behavior

3. appetitive behavior
4. reward and reinforcement
5. pleasantness and unpleasantness

Little motivation is involved at the level of physiological regulation, but motivation plays a role at all of the higher levels. Consumatory behavior often is a servant of physiological regulation, but nevertheless is clearly motivated. Appetitive behavior reflects strong approach–avoidance tendencies that usually are unlearned or natural. Reward and reinforcement represent the next highest level of limbic functioning, and they are important in the acquisition of operant responses and are said to have incentive or hedonic value. At the highest (and most human) level, we have the subjective experiences of pleasure and displeasure, pleasure and pain. Stellar's continuum (or, more accurately, hierarchy) is an evolutionary one, and he reminds us that "behavior has developed over the long reaches of phylogeny and new properties emerged, gradually or abruptly, as new properties of the nervous system developed" (Stellar, 1982, p. 387). So we see that a meaningful phylogenetic hierarchy of functions may be constructed within the limbic–hypothalamic complex, without reference to the higher functions of the neocortex. Thus, we may argue that much of the activation and energy behind motivated behavior has been processed greatly at the diencephalic level (physiologically, behaviorally, affectively, operantly, and hedonically) before the neocortex enters the picture! Again, we see just how crucial the lower centers are in motivated behavior in both animals and human beings. Stellar (1982) sums it up very well:

> In humans, we have the reflexes and physiological regulations that automatically adapt the organism, we have approach and withdrawal, appetitive and consumatory motivated behavior, reward and reinforcement of learning, affective display, and hedonic experience. As in other vertebrates, the limbic system seems clearly involved in all of these hedonic processes, one would think all the more extensively for the more complex and highly evolved of them. (p. 405)

LEARNING AND BEHAVIOR

From our discussion of pleasure and aversion vis-à-vis motivation, we make an easy transition into the paleohedonics of learning. A thorough consideration of the concept of reinforcement is a crucial first step in effecting this transition. The concept of reinforcement has occupied center stage in most of the major theories of learning since Pavlov ushered in the age of learning theory with his ingenious conditioning experiments at the turn of the century (Miller, 1980). Pavlov went beyond the static reflexology of his day, and demonstrated how new reflex patterns (conditioned responses) could be acquired through a process later called *classical* or *respondent conditioning*. The classical conditioning paradigm involved the pairing of a neutral stimulus with a stimulus capable of eliciting a certain response naturally, and with sufficient pairings or "reinforcements," the neutral stimulus came to acquire response eliciting properties similar to the natural stimulus. The classic illustration of this phenomenon, of course, is the experimental dog that salivated reflexively (unconditioned response) upon presentation of meat paste (unconditioned stimulus), only to later salivate (conditioned response) to a bell tone (conditioned stimulus) once the association between the paste and tone had been conditioned. For our purposes, two points are noteworthy here: (a) the reinforcement in classical conditioning is primarily associative rather than hedonic, and (b) classical conditioning represents one of the most effective mechanisms whereby an animal may free itself from pure natural imperatives and develop more elaborate behavioral repertoires than those accorded by natural selection. Nevertheless, it may be assumed that these "new" responses are typically erected upon, and are elaborations of, the basic behavioral hardware (neurohumoral substrates) and software (species-typical dispositions, etc.) of the animal. Only in the laboratory-manipulated animal or the domesticated human are we likely to encounter arbitrary or trivial response acquisition; for the animal trying to survive in the wild, learning processes are efficient, economical, and adaptive, and elaboration above and beyond natural competencies is minimal.

The so-called Father of Behaviorism, John B. Watson, attempted to encompass the entirety of animal and human behavior within the confines of unconditioned and conditioned reflexes, and, as such, was a true elaborationist. He believed that humans are born with unlearned emotional responses (fear, love, rage) and rudimentary motor patterns that can be greatly expanded through conditioning. Moreover, novel behaviors could be learned *ad infinitum* through Pavlovian conditioning, and he became convinced that even the most complex human behavior could be theoretically reduced to conditioned reflexes. His approach proved to be overly reductionistic and restricted, but his stature as a historical figure in the behaviorist movement remains unquestioned.

E. L. Thorndike (1898) had earlier set the stage to move beyond Watson's sterile reductionism in his seminal research on the goal-directed escape behavior of cats. Thorndike shared Watson's hard-minded aversion to teleology and mentalism, but focus was less on the immediate causes of behavior than the past consequences of behavior. Through trial-and-error, Thorndike's cats eventually learned to escape from a box by operating a latch. Once the cat hit the release mechanism it was allowed to run out of the box and obtain food. It was noteworthy that the cats became increasingly efficient in effecting escape; that is, latencies became progressively shorter and escape movements smoother and more precise. Thus, escape movements became associated with certain consequences (freedom, food), leading Thorndike (1911) to formulate his famous Law of Effect:

> The Law of Effect is that: Of several responses made to the same situation, those which are accompanied or closely followed by satisfaction to the animal will, other things being equal, be more firmly connected with the situation, so that, when it recurs, they will be more likely to recur; those which are accompanied or closely followed by discomfort to the animal will, other things being equal, have their connections with the situation weakened, so that, when it recurs, they will be less likely to occur.

Thorndike's Law of Effect was the forerunner of the concept of reinforcement in operant conditioning, which is perhaps the most central concept in learning theory (see Miller, 1980). Thorndike's satisfiers are, of course, directly analogous to the broad class of positive reinforcers (stimuli that increase the probability of a specified response when presented contingent upon its occurrence), whereas his dissatisfiers are less directly analogous to negative reinforcers (stimuli that increase the probability of a specified response by their removal). Actually, as Nevin (1973) points out, Thorndike's "discomfort" was more akin to the modern definition of punishment (response-dependent discomfort) than to the concept of negative reinforcement. However, the details of these issues need not detain us here; of more importance is the fact that Thorndike laid the foundation for a hedonics of learning that ultimately brought learning processes within the provinces of modern behavioral biology and neuroscience.

The Hedonics of Learning

Earlier we addressed the hedonics of motivation, and it is becoming clear that a hedonics of learnings exists as well. Throughout the history of learning theory the relationship between reward and response acquisition has been a controversial one, inflamed by such questions as "is reinforcement drive-reducing or drive inducing," "can learning occur in the absence of reinforcement," "how and where in the brain does reinforcement cement associative bonds," and so on. Beginning with Olds' famous serendipitous discovery in 1953 that a rat that had previously received brain stimulation tended to return to the place of stimulation, and subsequent publication with Peter Milner of confirming evidence in 1954 (Olds & Milner, 1954), older questions faded into the background as researchers grabbed at the opportunity to place reinforcement on firm neurological footing. Olds himself quickly emerged as the champion of this new field of brain-stimulation reward, and it wasn't long before he and his colleagues began to map the pleasure and aversion areas of the brain. Areas capable of supporting reward or pleasure were found to be widespread in the brain:

> Stimulation could be applied at any location within a very broadly circum- scribed system, and this system was much the same in different mammals. . . . It was a continuous anatomical swath through the CNS, invading almost all the olfactory-paleocortical areas of the telencephalon and spreading thence across the floor of the forebrain and midbrain and then along a path that moved to near the roof of the medulla . . .

> The system was focused on the hypothalamus and its outposts. As the stimulating probes were planted closer and closer to the lateral hypothala- mus the rewarding effects of stimulation became more intense by all measures, and the thresholds were lowered. (Olds, 1976, pp. 4–5)

The neuroanatomy of pleasure and aversion in regard to motivation was discussed earlier, and we see here that the limbic–hypothalamic complex is not only fundamental to approach–avoidance tendencies, but is central to the learning process as well, for animals will learn and perform all kinds of responses in order to receive brain-stimulation reward. That pleasure could be obtained by direct stimulation of the brain was a counterintuitive notion (Miller, 1980), but Olds demonstrated that intra- cranial self-stimulation (ICSS) in high pleasure areas of the brain served as an exceptional reinforcer. Strong ICSS areas produced exceptionally high rates of response, and experimental subjects would often stimulate themselves into exhaustion. Moreover, when given the opportunity to choose between strong traditional reinforcers (food, water, or sex) and ICSS, experimental subjects typically chose the superordinate pleasure of brain stimulation. Clearly, Olds had hit upon a phenomenon of monumen- tal theoretical importance, but even today the functional significance of ICSS remains shrouded in mystery (Clavier & Routtenberg, 1980).

Many hypotheses have been forwarded (Routtenberg, 1980; Wauquier & Rolls, 1976) as to the whys and wherefores of ICSS, with perhaps the most prevalent being that brain-stimulation reward involves the direct stimulation of the brain's endogenous substrates of reinforcement or reward (Clavier & Routtenberg, 1980). This perspective assumes that natural reward areas exist in the brain that are normally indirectly stimulated by natural activities such as food or water intake, copulation, maternality, and so forth, but these can be stimulated directly through ICSS procedures. If this is true, then the pleasure experienced in ICSS may represent normal pleasures highly augmented by direct stimulation. This raises certain important questions: (a) are there specific and neuro-humorally distinct pleasure and aversion centers in the brain?, and (b) does ICSS affect specific neurons in those centers, or affect whole centers or mixtures of centers? Olds (1956) initially held that ICSS loci repre-sented pleasure centers in the brain, and that the end point of stimulation corresponded to the tip of the stimulating electrode (Clavier & Routten-berg, 1980). However, the finding (Olds, 1976; Olds & Olds, 1963) that most ICSS sites lay along well-known neuroanatomical pathways gradu-ally led to supplanting of the notion of "centers" for that of "pathways." However, many questions remained unresolved, because several differ-ent brain regions involving different pathways were related to ICSS (e.g., the medial forebrain bundle, substantia nigra, dorsal pons; Clavier & Routtenberg, 1980). Given the diversity of neural structures involved in ICSS, the main question was, "Do all these structures share a common functional significance in the reward physiology of the animal?"

All of the diverse and intersecting hedonic pathways probably do have a common functional significance at the behavioral level, that of guiding and rewarding performance of species-appropriate and survival-enhanc-ing action on the part of the animal. Nevertheless, we must remember that the true neurohumoral pathways of reward and aversion remain speculative, with the best picture at present being that of "multiple systems or components that serve different, but related functions" (Cla-vier & Routtenberg, 1980, p. 96).

Biochemistry of Reward. Reward behavior maintained by ICSS probes appears to share a common pharmacology based on catecho-lamine neurotransmission (Stein, 1978, 1980). The term *catecholamine* refers to a group of chemically related compounds, the most important of which are epinephrine, norepinephrine, and dopamine. Epinephrine is not commonly found in the brain, but a large body of research has confirmed norepinephrine and dopamine as the catecholamine neurotransmitters in the brain (Julien, 1981). Although the match is not perfect (Clavier & Routtenberg, 1980), there is a great degree of overlap between the anatomical and catecholamine pathways subserving ICSS (Clavier & Routtenberg, 1974; German & Bowden, 1974; Ungerstedt, 1971), and possibly reward in the more general sense as well. However, ICSS cannot be solely attributed to catecholamine (CA) transmission because: (a) some CA systems have been shown incapable of supporting ICSS; (b) the experimental elimination of a CA system known to subserve ICSS does not eliminate ICSS response; and (c) certain non-CA systems have been shown to be causally related to ICSS (Clavier & Routtenberg, 1980). The fairest conclusion to draw here is that CA and ICSS systems do overlap in the reward process, but in extremely complex ways.

These complications notwithstanding, it is clear that certain catecholamines, especially noradrenaline and dopamine, are involved in the mediation of brain-stimulation reward. Some of the most convincing evidence has come from research using psychotropic drugs that act on CA-containing neurons. Early in the game, Olds (1959) and later Stein (1964) found that ICSS could be manipulated predictably with psychotropic drugs. Generally, drugs that enhance CA neurotransmission enhance ICSS responsivity as well, whereas drugs that interfere with CA neurotransmission also interfere with ICSS. Examples of CA-enhancing drugs are d-amphetamine (Stein, 1964), cocaine (Crow, 1968), and phenethylamine in combination with a monoamine oxidase inhibitor (Stein, 1980); by contrast, the CA-inhibiting drugs include reserpine, chlorpromazine, haloperidol, and the CA synthesis inhibitor alpha-methl-para-tyrosine (Clavier & Routtenberg, 1980; Stein, 1980). It appears that these enhancing and inhibiting drugs produce general effects on the CA system, rather than affecting noradrenergic or dopaminergic neurons differentially. Recent research has tended to focus more on the precise roles of the NA and DA systems in the reward process, rather than upon which is more important. As Stein (1980) says: "Abolition of self-stimulation by disruption of either the NE (norepinephrine) or the DA system suggests that these systems act jointly rather than separately and that the activity of both systems is required for the successful performance of operant behavior" (p. 119).

Stein (1980) points out that reward appears to be associated with events that both increase drive (incentives) and reduce drive (satisfiers). He further suggests that the drive-induction versus the drive-reduction distinction may have a biochemical basis, with the catecholamines serving as the substrate for the former, and the opoid peptides (enkephalins) for the latter (see Table 8.3). Stein's induction–reduction hypothesis is an important one and he reviews a considerable body of research in its favor;

TABLE 8.3
Pharmacological Evidence for Two Types of Reward

Reward type	Abused drug	Behavioral effect	Neurochemical substrate
Incentive	Cocaine or amphetamine	Increases drive and arousal	Catecholamines
Satisfier	Morphine	Reduces drive and arousal	Opoid peptides?

Note: This table is adapted from Stein's (1980) Table II. Used with permission.

nevertheless, his model is a highly speculative one given present knowledge of the neurochemistry of reward. His model of the different roles of reward (see Table 8.4) is also speculative but extremely interesting, providing us with a cogent hypothesis on the differential roles of dopamine, noradrenalin, and the enkephalins in the reward process. In his analysis, neurohumorally mediated rewards act in several ways to influence operant behavior: they motivate, steer, and eventually terminate the response sequence through the provision of "satisfaction." As Table 8.4 shows, dopamine (activation), noradrenalin (steering), and the enkephalins (satisfaction) play different, but fundamental roles in the reward sequence. We see that the "reward" so fundamental to operant learning is not a unitary entity, but, rather, reflects a complex array of interrelated neuroanatomical and neurohumoral components located primarily in the limbic–hypothalamic pathways of the brain.

ICSS Areas and Memory Consolidation.   Learning always contains a memory component, for unless a response or response pattern is stored, at least temporarily, it is not learned. We have seen that many of the limbic-hypothalamic areas subserving reward are also often implicated in many other behavioral functions—motorial, motivational, emotional, sensory-perceptual, and so on. Routtenberg (1975; Clavier & Routtenberg, 1980; Routtenberg & Kim, 1978) has shown that another important functional system overlaps with the ICSS areas, that of memory consolidation. However, just as brain-stimulation reward is not a unitary phenomenon, there are probably different processes occurring with regard to memory formation in the different brain regions mutually supporting memory and ICSS. In other words, "just as there are many forms of reinforcement leading to the increased probability of behavioral occurrence, so too are there several different processes involved in the formation of memory" (Clavier & Routtenberg, 1980, p. 96).

The amygdala is a limbic structure that appears to support both ICSS

TABLE 8.4
Different Roles of Reward

Role	Behavioral effect	Putative Neurotransmitter
Incentive	Activate pursuit behavior	Dopamine
Reinforcement	Guide response selection via knowledge of response consequences	Noradrenalin
Gratification	Bring behavioral episode to satisfying termination	Enkephalin

Note: This table is adapted after Stein's (1980) Table III. Used with permission.

and memory formation (Goddard, 1964; Wurtz & Olds, 1963), and Bresnahan and Routtenberg (1972) have studied the effects of memory-disrupting electrical stimulation in this area in some detail. They found that the greatest disrupting effects occurred when the medial regions of the amygdala were stimulated. Bresnahan and Routtenberg suggested that the medial nucleus of the amygdala may play some role in the registration of short-term memory formation related to the experimental task, and that stimulation of the nucleus disorganizes the short-term process whereby information cannot be used efficiently for long-term storage. It should be noted that the disrupting stimulation was administered during learning and not retention, but the experimental animals actually learned the task as well as controls; where the deficit occurred was in the short-term memory to long-term memory consolidation.

Encouraged by these findings, Routtenberg and his colleagues have studied other ICSS regions regarding memory formation. Routtenberg and Malsbury (1969) and Huang and Routtenberg (1971) have shown that the region of the substantia nigra and pars compacta support high rates of ICSS, and, more recently, Routtenberg and Holzman (1973) found that stimulation of this area was memory-disruptive, with results quite similar to those found with the amygdala. This finding is particularly significant due to the fact that the substantia, pars compacta area is dopaminergic, has been related to human movement disorders, and participates in the control of consumatory behavior (Clavier & Routtenberg, 1980). Also, as with the amygdala, the effects of stimulation were postregistrational; that is, the animal was able to initially learn the response with no apparent interference in either acquisitional or motor processes, but disruption was evident in the retentional processes. Whatever the basic causal factors are in amygdaloid and SN memory disruption, it appears clear that they exert their effects after the learning trials *per se*.

In the aforementioned studies on the amygdala and SN, stimulation was applied during the learning trials, although memory disruption occurred later during the 24-hour retention phase. Similarly, Collier, Kurtzman, and Routtenberg (1977) applied stimulation to the entorhinal cortex (EC) while the animal was learning, but observed no subsequent effects on later retention performance. However, when this area was stimulated after learning had occurred, 24-hour retention performance was severely disrupted. Thus, it appears that the EC area is concerned explicitly with short-term memory or post-registrational processes leading to 24-hour retention performance. Clavier and Routtenberg (1980) interpret these results, in conjunction with those on the amygdala and SN, as supporting the notion of differential participation of brain structures involved in ICSS and memory formation. All three of these brain regions support ICSS, but each appears to have a slightly different effect on the retention process.

Future research on the ICSS-memory linkage will, no doubt, reveal exceptionally complex systems of facilitation and inhibition of retentional processes as new and more subtle brain loci are explored. At present, however, we may conclude, along with Clavier and Routtenberg, that ICSS systems definitely do participate in memory processes, and that this participation differs depending on the particular brain sites involved. For our purposes, this line of research is particularly significant, for it demonstrates a crucial neurophysiological link between the "pleasures" associated with reinforcement and the encoding of acquired information in the brain. Moreover, these learning-related processes are mediated, for the most part, by structures in the limbic-hypothalamic complex, which itself plays a central role so many other basic behavioral processes— motivation, emotion, and species-typical action patterns. Again, we see that "all roads lead to the limbic system" where the rudiments of behavior are concerned.

Hedonics of Species-Typical Behavior.   We recall Herrnstein's (1977a, 1977b) argument that much of an animal's behavior is self-reinforcing; that is, the mere performance of a phylogenetically conditioned, species-typical action may be inherently pleasurable in and of itself. Thus, an animal may be reinforced by more than the external, consumable objects that Skinner and the Skinnerians emphasize; the performance of certain actions may themselves produce highly pleasurable internal stimuli that keep those actions high in the animal's response hierarchy. The importance of this assumption cannot be overemphasized, for now we have a conceptual bridge between the generalism of individual learning theory, on the one hand, and the specifism of the ethologists on the other (Herrnstein, 1977a, 1977b). Armed with the idea that an animal phylogenetically prepared "to be itself" can derive pleasure from "acting as itself," we have a way of relating the great body of literature on reinforcement and learning to the day-to-day, species-characteristic behavior of organisms. To quote Herrnstein (1977a):

> When a response is to any degree self-reinforcing, to that degree it ceases to be arbitrary. Its form is then dictated by built-in contingencies of reinforcement, not easily shaped by the behavioral engineer. The study of innate response patterns, long the preserve of ethologists, is where behaviorists should look for understanding of behavior's intrinsic power to reinforce. (p. 601)

We have seen that motivation, emotion, and specific patterns of behavior are mediated, in large measure, by structures in the limbic-hypothalamic complex. We also have seen that pathways of endogenous pleasure are interspersed throughout the limbic-hypothalamic complex as well. It is tempting to speculate here that the neuroanatomy and neurophysiology of the brains of animals and humans are designed for the type of "self-reinforcement" postulated by Herrnstein. Clearly, many of the more advanced creatures appear to be designed as processers of pleasure, and it may well be that acting in accordance with natural prerogatives, performing instinctive actions, releasing innate drive energy, and so forth, may serve as internal stimuli that act upon the pleasure pathways of the brain. If this is true, one of the major causes of behavior would be experienced pleasure in being one's essential self in the general sense, and in performing innate behavior patterns in the specific sense. Thus, the feline predator, for example, derives pleasure not only from consuming the prey, but in all the anticipative and appetitive accompaniments of the hunt—the stalk, smelling and sighting the prey, chasing, pouncing and killing, and perhaps even in repelling competitors prior to eating.

We are beginning to see the concept of reinforcement in rather stark contrast to that of the classical and operant learning theorists; rather than merely representing an association between a natural response and a neutral stimulus, or an after-the-fact stimulus capable of maintaining high response probability, reinforcement, in the form of endogenous brain reward, is the innate means by which organisms are encouraged, on a probabilistic basis, to conform to the natural mandates of their respective species. It is, of course, presumed that this inherent system of rewarding phylogenetically correct responses evolved through natural selection and is conducive to species survival. Indeed, if animals had nothing other than classical or operant learning at their disposal, the survival of both individuals and species would be little more than a random process. However, furnished with species-appropriate behavioral programs and innate reward systems to assure performance of them, animals can apply hard-won evolutionary wisdom to the day-to-day challenge of survival.

A corollary to this argument is that animals and humans really learn much less than is commonly assumed, but, instead, spend the preponderance of their time performing either basic innate patterns of behavior, modified in varying degrees by experience, or basic patterns acquired early in ontogeny, modified in varying degrees by subsequent experience. In fact, it is quite possible that classical and operant learning principles apply more to the *performance* of responses than the *acquisition* of responses. (Brown & Herrnstein, 1975; Herrnstein, 1977a). Both animal and human behavior is relatively stable and predictable at the species or population level of analysis, and appears to be based far more on the elaboration of inherited programs and dispositions than it does on acquisition of novel responses *per se*. So, rather than being creatures created by learning, we are creatures who learn. We humans may vary in how we express our sexuality, our sociality, or our hostility, but we do not vary in whether we possess the software programs or the biogrammar subserving these adaptive patterns of behavior. Furthermore, we differ little socially or culturally in terms of what we find pleasurable and satisfying, finding pleasure, as do the animals, in performing phylogenetically adaptive means–ends actions (Mace, 1962; Pribam, 1980), and, in general, just begin good, competent members of our species. Although layers of cultural learning in the form of habits, fads, and fashions may obscure the underlying phylogenetic programs and their rewarding structures, they are there nevertheless, providing the essence of behavior.

Biological Constraints on Learning

In our discussion of the hedonics of learning, the neurophysiology of reward and the motivation-reward-behavior linkages mediated within the limbic–hypothalamic complex were emphasized. We saw that the processes of learning were constrained in many ways by species neurostructural "hardware" and innate "software" programming designed to maximize adaptation and survival. Learning is, thus, more than a simple, general mechanism for acquiring and storing information irrespective of phylogenetic or ecological considerations; it is nature's way of releasing organisms, in varying degrees, from the shackles of fixed, genetically controlled, elicitor-response pattern linkages, and allowing a modicum of response flexibility for more advanced species. Even in the most advanced species of all, *Homo sapiens,* response flexibility is relative, and the constraints of lower species superceded only to a degree. We humans share with the animals many of the pre-programmed "constraints" (Hinde & Stevenson-Hinde, 1973) and "biological boundaries" (Seligman & Hager, 1972) of learning, and, moreover, learning is usually adaptive and survival-targeted for both animals and humans. However, as we already know, humans have a greater capacity to decouple or disengage from natural imperatives than any other creature, and in this fact lies our uniqueness, our arbitrariness, and our domination of the world. Still, most of our behavior is "learned" via "class common" mammalian, and subcortical neurostructures (Oakley, 1983), and we continue to be phylogenetically constrained in terms of how we learn, what we want to learn, and what we ultimately learn.

The Innate Disposition to Learn.   Many experts believe there is an innate disposition to learn (Tinbergen, 1951), and, as Humphrey (1973) says, "Learning, it seems, may be its own reward" (p. 301). Imitation, for example, is a phylogenetically old form of learning (MacLean, 1976) that is effected with exceptional ease and possibly "enjoyed" by some of the higher "playful" and "curious" mammals (Humphrey, 1973). To quote

Aristotle: "From earliest childhood the instinct for imitation is natural to us, as is the universal pleasure in imitations. Man is superior to the other animals in being more imitative, and his first lessons are learned by imitation. Learning is very agreeable, not only to philosophers, but also to other men" (Poetics iv; also quoted in Humphrey, 1973, p. 302). Thus, it seems we are predisposed to imitate by having the innate motivation to do so, by possessing necessary behavioral equipment, and by deriving pleasure from the process. By virtue of being phylogenetically prepared to imitate, we are predisposed to readily and easily imitate early in life, and with minimal provocation.

Animals not only have a general predisposition to learn, but specific ones as well. Tinbergen (1951) describes how an adaptive response pattern (e.g., parenting in the herring gull) may be broken down into components with differing degrees of innate disposition. The herring gull possesses a number of innate reactions to the young, including brooding them, feeding them, and rescuing them if attacked. Moreover, the parents readily condition to their young, and after a five-day period will not accept strange offspring in their nests. They will actually neglect or kill any other young forced on them. Tinbergen (1951) says this capacity to "know" the chicks individually is remarkable, and is conditioned to minute cues beyond the sensibilities of the human observer. By contrast, as Tinbergen tells us, the herring gull's ability to distinguish its own eggs is amazingly poor, despite the fact that eggs of different gulls vary greatly in color and speckling. We find, therefore, that herring gulls are highly predisposed to learn their chicks, but poorly predisposed to learn their eggs.

Critical Periods in Learning.   Certain types of learning are constrained temporally, most notably in the case of imprinting and related processes (Hess, 1973; Salzen, 1970; see also chapter 5). Originally viewed as a sudden, irreversible attachment formed early in the life of birds (Lorenz, 1935) and as a unique form of learning (Hess, 1970) occurring during a sensitive period, the notion of imprinting has been expanded to include numerous processes: the learning of bird songs (Marler, 1972; Thorpe, 1961), mother–infant and infant–mother attachment in animals and humans (Bowlby, 1969; Freedman, 1974; Gray, 1958; Hess, 1973; Sluckin, 1965), food preferences and other primal preferences (Hess, 1973), development of the smile (Ambrose, 1963; Wolff, 1963), environmental imprinting (Thorpe, 1945), and various forms of pathology in animals and humans (Morris, 1969, 1971). No matter how much we may dicker about definition, irreversibility, and so on, imprinting and imprinting-like phenomena are phylogenetically old (Hess, 1973) preferences and predispositions that generally exert their effects early in life, and serve to channel and constrain subsequent behavior to a great degree. It is very likely that many of our fundamental preferences are learned in infancy prior to consciousness and language in accordance with the imprinting model. Such fundamental preferences may, of course, be elaborated *ad infinitum* through subsequent development and learning.

Species Differences in Learning.   Each species has its own particular set of constraints in the learning area. Assuming that learning is adaptive in the evolutionary sense, each mammalian species is programmed with the neural hardware and software to accomplish the basic tasks of food procurement, defense, reproduction, parenting, and so on. In accomplishing these tasks, however, each species draws upon its own motivational and motor systems in often highly stylized and specific ways. Such species–specific or species-typical releaser → action pattern coordinations are extremely important factors in the day-to-day behavior of less advanced species, and probably mix in with and are elaborated into complex human behavior as well.

An extensive review of species differences in learning readinesses and capabilities is not appropriate here, but we might summarize a few illustrations from Hinde (1973): (a) the herring gull does not respond to its eggs as we recall, but a related species, the guillemot, does respond; (b) species differ markedly in the amount of learning needed to recognize other members of their species; (c) some avian species need virtually no environmental stimulation to learn their songs, whereas others must imitate; (d) species vary widely in whether and, to what degree, "tools" are used; (e) different species of bees and fish differ widely in methods of localization and orientation; and (f) despite the reported achievements of chimpanzees, only humans have developed a verbal–symbolic language.

As Hinde (1973) aptly summarizes, these species differences are largely based on several basic factors: (a) inability of certain species to respond to certain categories of stimuli (e.g., the octopus compensates appropriately for objects it picks up, but cannot learn to distinguish objects differing only in weight); (b) general stimulus preferences (e.g., the monkey prefers objects it can touch, whereas the rat relies more on visual features); (c) response-specific preferences (e.g., the animal responds in a species-characteristic way to a given stimulus that another species would respond to differently). Different species will also select out certain specific elements of a stimulus complex, whereas another species will select other elements from the same complex; (d) reinforcement-specific preferences—as discussed earlier, species differ widely in what stimuli and responses they prefer or "enjoy"; and (e) response-reinforcer interactions (e.g., a rat will easily learn to escape from shock when allowed to run or jump, but can be trained only with difficulty to escape by pressing a lever).

Many more examples could be generated, but this brief overview should dispel any notion of a set of general laws of learning that apply to any and all organisms with equal facility. The constraints on learning are indeed enormous, particularly when one compares the whethers, whats, and hows of learning across different species.

Canalization and Development.   Although the term *canalization* initially referred to a nonassociative, sensitization type of learning in which a dominant innate pattern is strengthened and narrowed in action through mere repetition (Razran, 1971), it is more commonly associated with Waddington's (1957, 1961, 1962) theories of genetics and development. Waddington's (1962) notion of "canalization of development" was designed to deal with a puzzling fact of embryogenesis and maturation of species anatomical structures: Organisms, even primitive ones, are capable of far more phenotypic variation in anatomical traits that is actually exhibited. In other words, given potential variability inherent in the genotype, and additional variability potential through experience and genotype-experience interaction, why is it that anatomical traits within a given species are so constant, so "normal"? For species to remain in the "normal range of reaction" in trait development, it is necessary for great amounts of potential trait expression to be inhibited or constrained. As Vale (1980) says, there must be a mechanism to keep species members close enough to one another anatomically, physiologically, and behaviorally to produce viable offspring, and to accomplish this considerable suppression of variability is required.

Waddington (1957) notes that many alternative pathways exist for trait development, but only one can be followed; typically, the pathway selected will lead to normal phenotypic expression. Moreover, even when trait development is diverted from its pathway by major gene substitutions or environmental stresses (Vale, 1980), there is a strong tendency to return to the proper developmental "canal." Waddington (1957) depicts canalization in development as a ball (the phenotype) rolling through a set of valleys or canals. The deeper the canal the greater the canalization, and the more difficult it is for either genetic or environmental stresses to divert the rolling ball to another developmental pathway. Nevertheless, with sufficient stress traits may be de-tracked and slip into another, possibly abnormal canal. However, traits differ in strength of canalization, and, thus, some are exceptionally resistant to de-tracking whereas others are easily diverted. For example, Waddington (1962) summarizes the work of Fraser and his colleagues on canalization of three types of hair growth patterns in mice: primary facial whiskers, secondary facial whiskers, and body hair. Using resistance to variation induced by selective breeding procedures as the criterion of strength of canalization, Fraser found the primary whiskers to be highly canalized (variation resistant), the secondary whiskers moderately canalized, and the hair coat weakly canalized (variation susceptible).

Although the concept of canalization is typically associated with morphogenesis, it also represents a fruitful model for behavioral epigenesis and learning processes as well (Fishbein, 1976, 1984). Fishbein decries the lack of hard data on behavioral canalization, but persuasively argues that obvious behavioral constancies exist within species that are consistent with the canalization model. Further, canalization and learning are seen as related processes:

> Given that canalized behaviors are acquired as a function of experience, what is the relationship between canalization of behavior and learning? Learning was earlier defined as a set of functions or processes which progressively organize the individual's sensory experiences or motor activities, or both. These functions are set into motion when the individual intersects with the environment, enabling the individual to better coordinate his behavior with the environment. By this definition, all canalized behaviors are learned, but not all learned behaviors are canalized. That is, if the behavior is inevitably acquired by normal individuals raised in environments normal for the species, then it is canalized, e.g., learning to speak a language; but if it is not inevitably learned, e.g., playing the piano, then it is not canalized. (Fishbein, 1976, p. 115)

Based on Fishbein's argument, a learning continuum might be postulated beginning with maximally canalized and biologically constrained learning at one pole (fixed-action patterns, instincts, phylogenetically conditioned dispositions, behavioral dispositions, etc.) and proceeding up to highly variable, species-decoupled, self-conscious, and cultural forms of learning at the other pole. At the lower pole learning would be minimally susceptible to environmental influence and maximally susceptible to phylogenetic programming, while the opposite pattern would hold at the upper pole. What is evident here is that learning is not a unitary phenomenon for which one can postulate general laws transcending phylogenetic programming or species membership, nor can it be viewed as the "first cause" of any of the major response systems. Rather, learning refers to a wide range of complex and often interconnected processes that are concerned far less with novel response acquisition than with the modification and elaboration of pre-programmed, highly canalized, and species-adaptive traits and behavioral systems.

The Hierarchical Nature of Learning

Like all major behavioral systems, learning may be hierarchicalized phylogenetically. As mentioned in chapter 3, Razran (1971) postulates a phylogenetic hierarchy of learning involving 11 qualitatively different levels of function. Razran's model assumes that lower animals are capable of only the more phylogenetically primitive processes, more advanced animals are capable of both the primitive and certain of the advanced processes, and humans possess capability at all 11 levels. Also, as we recall from chapter 3, a complex calculus governs the systematic interrelationships of higher and lower systems in the learning hierarchy (e.g., higher levels arose from lower ones in the process of evolution, lower levels continue as subsystems within higher levels, higher and lower systems interact both antagonistically and synergistically, and so on). In Razran's comprehensive evolutionary model, the phylogenetic bases of learning and nonunitary nature of learning are etched very clearly. Learning is, thus, not a "thing" but a multifarious set of adaptive strategies for processing and storing adaptation-related information within the psychoneural information-processing capabilities of a given species.

Razran's 11 evolutionary levels include 2 nonassociative or preconditioned levels (habituation and sensitization), 3 of associative conditioning (aversive, classical, and reinforcing), 3 of perceiving (sensory preconditioning, configuring, and eductive types of learning), and 3 of thinking (symbosemic, sememic, and logicemic). The two nonassociative, three associative, three perceptual, and three cognitive forms of learning comprise four *superlevels* that Razran labels as *reactive, connective, integrative,* and *symboling* respectively. To quote:

> The quaternary compression highlights the chief qualitative transformation of the process [of learning] in its hundreds of millions of years of existence—namely, that connective conditioning, needing no encephalon and no cognition, is but one realm of learning, that the integrative learning of cognized and primarily cortical perceiving is another, and the capstone of learned symbolic thinking a third, with nonassociative or preconditioned mechanisms in the role of ultimate rudiments. (Razran, 1971, p. 311)

Although Razran's hierarchic levels of learning are qualitatively distinct, they all—save for habituation and sensitization, which are more reactions than learning—involve the formation of associations of one sort or another. Razran places the variations of classical and instrumental learning under the heading *associative* conditioning, whereas the variations of perceptual and symbolic learning are categorized as *associative superconditioning.* Whereas the category of associative conditioning includes familiar types, associative superconditioning includes lesser known and novel elements. The interested reader may wish to consult Razran directly for specific definitions of configural and eductive learning, the symbosemic, sememic, and logicemic forms of cognitive learning, and so on. Concern for space does not allow explication of these complex and subtle types of advanced learning here.

Plotkin and Odling-Smee (Odling-Smee, 1983; Plotkin & Odling-Smee, 1981) propose a multiple level model of evolution that features hierarchic information-gaining (learning) and information-using (performance) processes. A schematic outline of their model is shown in Fig. 8.1.

Evolutionary Level I consists of the primary genetic process subserving phylogenesis. At this level the unit of life that gains information is the population, and the place of storage is the gene pool. The sampling range on which Level I is based corresponds to the cumulative range of a population across environmental space and time. An individual organism may only gain access to the Level I store through inheritance, and then only a small fraction of the store's information is available. Modification of the Level I store occurs slowly over time principally as a function of natural selection. Level II consists of processes of plastic or open development, that is, by "variable epigenesis." Variable epigenesis allows the organism to fine tune itself to the local environment within the limits of its behavioral capabilities. The unit of life is the individual organism, but the precise location of the information store is debatable. Odling-Smee is somewhat vague about this, and merely suggests that Level II information is stored some way in the phenotype. Essentially, Level II seems to refer to a genetic-maturational unfolding that is not totally canalized, thereby allowing environmental inputs. Level III consists of individual learning where, again, the unit of life is the individual organism. Information at this level is stored in regions of the central

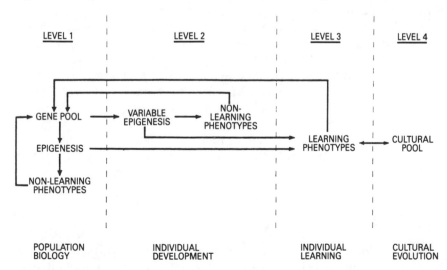

FIG. 8.1.   The four levels of evolution (from Plotkin & Odling-Smee, 1981).

nervous system controlling memory. The major difference between Levels II and III is that variable epigenesis is broader than learning because the former can affect almost any aspect of the developing phenotype, whereas the latter concerns itself entirely with modifying behavior (Odling-Smee, 1983). The final level, Level IV, refers to cultural evolution. At this level the unit of life is a culture, and the locus of information is the cultural pool of information stored in the memories of the culture's members.

In the aforementioned model, Level I information is relatively fixed and based on millenia of natural selection with great information loss along the way. Although the information stored at Levels II and III is less reliable than that of Level I, the organism makes up for the loss in terms of increased behavioral flexibility in adapting to the environment. At these higher levels, the organism can adjust itself to contemporary environmental demands, rather than having to rely on genetic information originally gained in the adaptive efforts of their ancestors. At the level of cultural evolution, the organism is even more freed from constraints on learning; here information may be transmitted both within and between generations (Plotkin & Odling-Smee, 1981), and there are no limits on the total amount of information stored. Unfortunately, there are two major disadvantages in Level IV information processing: (a) first, even though massive amounts of information may exist in the cultural store, individual members tend to differ greatly in their access to, and ability to assimilate the information potentially available. In humans, intelligence, socioeconomic level, and education represent important moderating variables in the quest for cultural information; and (b) an organism generally must be a "normal" member in good standing within a given culture if acquisition of cultural information is to be beneficial and adaptive. For deviant or atypical types, contact with an alien culture may have disastrous consequences. This point is discussed at greater length in chapter 12.

There are other evolutionary hierarchies of learning and related processes to consider, such as Slobodkin and Rapoport's (1974) notion of differential response depth, or Oakley's (1983) three types of mammalian information-processing (associative, representational, and abstract), but let us now move to the next chapter with the knowledge that learning is, indeed, both a phylogenetic and hierarchic phenomenon.

SUMMARY

The principles of motivation are central to any theory of the causes of behavior. Adaptive behavior must be motivated to occur, and each species has its own special, evolved motivational structures. It is assumed that human beings possess "innate" motivational hardware and software programs just as do other animals, but the human capacity to elaborate upon them is unique.

As is true of all behavioral systems, motivation can be characterized in terms of the regression–progression continuum. Thus, there are presumed to be primitive motives, advanced motives, and mixed motives between the two poles. Moreover, as with other behavioral systems, it is possible to phylogenetically progress motivationally toward the upper pole, or to regress down toward the lower pole. It is assumed that there are very few basic motives at the lower pole, but many derivative motives at the upper pole.

All motivated behavior falls into two fundamental categories, approach and withdrawal. Approach systems appear far more numerous and variegated than do the withdrawal systems. Being simpler and presumably requiring less neural mediation, the withdrawal modality appears to be more phylogenetically primitive than the approach modality (see chapter 5).

There appear to be remarkably few—but, nevertheless, extremely important—basic motive systems shared by animals and humans. Among these are: food procurement, aggression, reproduction, social-affiliation, and curiosity and exploration in the approach category, and pain-avoidance, threat avoidance, and fear in the withdrawal category.

The basic, phylogenetically conditioned motive systems receive varying degrees of elaboration in ontogeny across species. Phylogenetically primitive organisms may possess only a few of the basic motives in rudimentary form to begin with, and capacity for elaboration is minimal. More advanced organisms, by contrast, possess both a greater number of basic motive systems, and a greater capacity for system elaboration. Of course, *Homo sapiens* appear to be superiorly endowed both in terms of innate motivational structures and capacity for system elaboration.

The basic motive systems operate in terms of innate inhibition-release relationships. Motivational systems are, for all practical purposes, inactive most of the time until their energy is "released" by appropriate eliciting circumstances. Although each basic motive system comes with its own inhibition-release mechanisms, there is room for modification and elaboration of the system's inhibition-release dynamics through learning and experience. Again, however, little modification of innate contingencies occurs with primitive organisms, whereas considerable modification of inhibition-release patterns may be seen in more advanced animals. Human beings add a unique feature to the dynamics of inhibition and release; humans have the capacity to inhibit or facilitate motive discharge through cognitive activity.

Motives and motive systems seldom act independently of one another, and "mixes" and "blends" of motives, emotions, and behaviors, and so on are the norm. Types of mixes or interactions discussed were: coordinated motivational–behavioral systems, motivation and conflict, and hormonal and neural interaction.

There is great neuroanatomical and neurohumoral overlap between motivation and emotion. Motivation and emotion are generally mediated by lower brain centers in the limbic-hypothalamic axis, and may be viewed as part and parcel of the same result—the arousal, activation, and energizing of species-adaptive behavior. Motivation and emotion are thoroughly coupled in primitive mammals, but decoupling of the two occurs in higher animals, most notably humans.

Except for the most primitive creatures, the basic approach-avoidance tendencies are accompanied by the experiences of pleasure and aversion. Research has shown that neurohormonal hardware and software subserve hedonic processes, and, further, that these processes are associated with a number of important behavioral systems: reinforcement and learning, drive level, homeostasis, and a variety of specific motivational states. The pleasure and aversion pathways of the brain were discussed in some detail.

Given the importance of reinforcement in learning processes, the "hedonics of learning" is of major interest. Following the discovery by Olds in the mid-1950s that stimulation of certain brain areas in the rat was reinforcing, the field of brain-stimulation reward has flourished. Extensive research led to fairly precise mapping of reward and aversion areas of the brain. As with the neurochemistry of motivation and emotion, the hedonic pathways are located primarily in the limbic–hypothalamic complex. Biochemically, brain reward appears to share a common pharmacology based on catecholamine transmission. Although the match is not perfect, there is a great degree of overlap between the anatomical and catecholamine pathways subserving brain reward.

Pleasure plays a major role in motivating an animal to perform adaptive responses appropriate to its species. Acting as a member of one's species may be "self-reinforcing" (Herrnstein, 1977a, 1977b). This appears to be a crucial factor in assuring "appropriate" response output in both animals and humans.

Field and experimental research indicates that there are a number of biological constraints on learning, including the innate disposition to learn, critical period restrictions, species differences, and canalization of learning and development.

It is argued that *learning* refers to many different phylogenetically hierarchicalized processes. This assumption is discussed from the standpoints of Razran's 11 evolutionary levels of learning and Plotkin and Odling-Smee's multiple level model of evolution.

9

Hierarchical Analysis of Behavior and Misbehavior

Selfishness in general can be said to have evolved phyloge-netically from the lowest creatures to us. Selfishness has hardly been wiped out; in fact, the majority of anyone's daily acts are probably selfish. The point at which selfishness turns into wickedness, by human standards, is when it begins to hurt others. . . . In sum, selfishness, greed, *and* ambition *are expressions of 'normal' inclinations to selfishness; they are not, strictly speaking deviations from being human. They are . . . 'all too human.'*

—Maxwell (1984, pp. 222-223)

THE CAUSES OF BEHAVIOR

Rensch (1971) tells us that *"all scientific research is predominantly research into causes"* (p. 14), for causal factors are absent only in pure description, simple classification, and logical inference. He further avers that science operates in terms of universal laws, the most important of which is the law of causality. This law is predicated on the assumption of a universe governed by material cause–effect relationships independent of human perception and awareness. Such relationships are potentially discoverable through scientific research and causal inference, yet, as fallible humans, we can discern them only as partial processes (Rensch, 1972). Thus, in the area of animal and human behavior, scientists agree that behavior is caused, but great variation exists in discovering and defining the true causes operating.

From the foregoing chapters and the assumptions of the regression–progression model (see Appendix I), it is evident that behavioral causality is no simple, straightforward matter. Ignoring for the moment that actual, in vivo behavior is itself exceptionally complex and difficult to define, we find its causes even more complex and problematic. Given that behavior is not a thing or entity but a dynamically fluctuating complex of hierarchically interactive activities operating at a given time, the question of causes seems virtually unanswerable. Yet, within this maelstrom of activity a certain order exists, most of which is hidden within the neurohumoral hardware of the organism and not accessible to human perception.

How, then, may we lay claim to a science of behavior? There are two fundamental possibilities. The first and most popular approach is to collect the best empirical data possible and then to attribute causes to behavior that are congruent with prevailing theoretical, social, and moral paradigms (see Bailey, 1986a; Brodbeck, 1968). These attributions are analogous to the "ideologies" (collective belief systems held by the privileged, educated masses) described by Mannheim (1936), or Bergmann's (1950) "rationales" (viz. mixtures of factual judgment, value judgments, and value judgments masquerading as facts). We are speaking here of beliefs about causes rather than the true causes themselves. In this approach, the distinction between causal analysis and theoretical explanation often is quite blurred. Examples include Galen's humoral theory, ether theory, Mesmer's animal magnetism, Watson's radical behaviorism, McDougall's hormic psychology, Skinner's radical behaviorism (see Rychlak, 1968), human ethology, sociobiology, and, indeed, most of the social–psychological theories of human behavior. And yes, the phylogenetic regression–progression model belongs in the list as well. The issue is not whether a given model of human behavior contains ideological elements (Bergmann, 1951; Brodbeck, 1968), but, rather, how well the model agrees with known facts and how effective it is in stimulating the search for new facts. Using these criteria, some of the aforementioned models obviously fare much better than others. A second approach is to avoid broad theorizing and focus instead on empirical data derived from controlled experimental research. This approach is maximally effective in the physical sciences, but its effectiveness is severely limited in the causal analysis of behavior, especially complex human social behavior. The wheels of empirical science move very slowly, and the strict empirical approach cannot begin to keep pace with demands for answers in the areas of human aggression and crime, the quest for psychological health, the management of increasingly large populations, and so forth. Thus, it seems we must resort to theory and some degree of speculation in order to identify the most likely causes of our actions, hoping that empirical research will prove us more right than wrong in the long run.

The phylogenetic regression model attempts to deal with the dilemma by eclectically drawing from diverse information sources and piecing together what is hopefully a meaningful rationale for discussing the probable causes of human behavior. It is assumed that determination of the "true causes" of complex behavior is beyond the power of the present model or competing ones, so emphasis will instead be on developing well-reasoned theoretical arguments regarding behavioral causality.

The Multiple Determination of Behavior

As has been emphasized throughout, behavioral units of living organisms can never be attributed to a single cause. Reynolds (1981) articulates this principle very nicely vis-à-vis the behavior of higher primates and humans:

> In this conceptualization, innate motor components and innate contexts of activation, such as releasing signals, are constantly being integrated with conceptually stored information to produce a composite product . . . the properties of innate action, volitional control, and conceptual thinking are partial determinants of the behavioral product. (p. 73)

Rychlak (1968) discusses the complexities of causal analysis in some depth and reminds us that Aristotle postulated four different species of causes: material, formal, efficient, and final. Thus, the causes of a thing or a behavioral unit include the material substance involved, the formal blueprint by which the substance operates, the efficient actions necessary to implement the blueprint, and the ultimate purpose or intention for which the object or behavior was designed. All adaptive behavior appears to involve all four of these components, although the weighting of each varies greatly with the type of behavior, the species behaving, situational factors, and so forth. Among the causes subserving behavior, then, are what an organism is made of, its design characteristics, its functional capacity to implement its design characteristics, and its "purpose in being." The dromedary, for example, is a slightly built, one-humped member of the camel family, *Camelidae,* known for its fleetness of foot and endurance in the desert. What makes this interesting and peculiar creature what it is? In being what it is, what causes its remarkable consistency in morphology, constitution, and behavior? Conversely, what causes the dromedary not to lay eggs, build nests, eat worms, and warble lovely songs? Certainly, it makes no conscious effort to maintain its dromedariness or to avoid emulating the actions of other species; in actuality, it has little or no control over being itself. It is slave to its phylogenotypic programming more than anything else, programming that keeps its behavior within a narrow band of species propriety. It is slave to its physical morphology, its hormones, and its brain structures, and all the infinitude of intercoordinations among them.

The fact that dromedaries exhibit individual differences in morphology and behavior shows that the phylogenotype (see chapter 6) is not the whole story. Certainly, some of the individual differences may be attributed to trait characteristics inherited from parental genotypes. Many of the variations in size or function of physical structures, or variation in species-typical behavioral traits, would fall into this category. Moreover, much like the mule or draft horse, there are no wild dromedaries; the dromedary was selectively bred and domesticated to fulfill specific human needs. So added to its fundamental phylogenetic "camelness" are characters bred in and trained in by human design. The residue of individual variation remaining would be attributed to other environmental influences including epigenetic–maturational factors, species-constrained learning experiences, and adventitious learning experiences. In the dromedary, then, we see that behavior is determined primarily by the phylogenotype (its "camelness"), to a lesser degree by parental genotypes and selective breeding, and to yet a lesser degree by environment and learning. All of these causes combine and interact to define the dromedariness that distinguishes the dromedary from all other creatures.

The behavior of different species differs greatly in relative influence of the phylogenotype, parental inheritance, and experience. Although greatly influenced by species constraints (the phylogenotype) and intra-species variation based on patterns of parental inheritance, humans are undeniably more shaped and controlled by the environment than are other animals. Through species-constrained learning, imitation, cognitive learning, and adventitious learning, humans have substantial freedom to vary among themselves in innumerable ways. Moreover, human beings appear to possess the greatest freedom to transcend or decouple from (Alexander, 1979; Durham, 1979) natural, selection-tracked motivation; that is, a strongly felt wish or desire may be denied behavioral expression for moral or other reasons. Thus, what would be a cause of behavior for a lower animal (e.g., a strong urge for copulation in the presence of a willing partner) becomes a behaviorally passive, inner emotional feeling of frustration for the human being. As said before in different language, this ability to resist what would be determining causes in other animals is a defining element of our humanness. As we shall see, however, our ability to resist causes is a relative one.

From the regression–progression standpoint, final behavioral output is

determined by the phylogenotype (built-in structures and structure-function relationships), variation due to parental inheritance, and environmental factors, and, in humans, the ability to resist lower causes through
conscious will and moral sensibility. The actual operation of these categories of causes is overwhelmingly complex, however, and may be compre-
hended only in the abstract. When one takes into consideration the
inherent complexity of the innumerable inhibition-facilitation coordinations and interactions at each level of the hierarchically arranged human
organism, and the inhibition-facilitation interactions across levels, it
becomes immediately clear that the true causes of adaptive behavior are
presently not discernible, and that imposition of theory is required to
derive rational and meaningful causal imputations (Brodbeck, 1968). The
challenge, then, is to make the most reasonable causal statements possible within our limits of knowledge on how physical morphology, the
endocrine system, the brain, the environment, and interactions among
them lead to one hierarchical possibility over another.

Hierarchy and Behavioral Causality

What we have said so far implies that causes may be hierarchicalized just
like other aspects of behavior. Weiss (1969) eloquently argues against a
micro-precise causality or Newtonian reductionism where the true causes
presumably lie at the smallest units of analysis. Weiss (1969) decries the
view of a "Laplacian universe made up of a mosaic of discrete particles,
operating by the laws of micro-causality" (p. 28), and correctly concludes
that living organisms only can be understood macrodeterministically in
terms of their hierarchic systems dynamics. Indeed, most scientific laws
of behavior are macrodeterministic, that is, based on what Weiss calls
reliable correlations between macro-configural events over a given stretch
of time. For example, the human embryo goes through a highly predictable series of time-ordered metamorphoses at the macroscopic level of
analysis, yet there is no evidence of analogous lawful order at the level of
the cell or cell particles. This example illustrates what Weiss (1969) calls
the principle of the *"determinancy in the gross despite demonstrable
indeterminancy in the small"* (p. 31).

Weiss (1969) summarized his model of hierarchic determinancy as
follows:

> Applying the systems concept, an organism as a system reveals itself as
> encompassing and operating through the agency of subsystems, each of
> which, in turn, contains and operates through groups of systems of still lower
> order, and so on down through molecules into the atomic and sub-atomic
> range.

The fact that the top level operations of the organism thus are neither structurally nor functionally referable to direct liaison with the processes on the molecular level in a steady continuous gradation, but are relayed step-wise from higher levels of determinancy . . . through intermediate layers of greater freedom or variance to next lower levels of again more rigorously ascertainable determinancy, constitutes the *principle of hierarchical organization.* (p. 33)

Weiss is convincing in his argument that the behavior of living organisms is not reducible to chains of micro-precise cause–effect relationships. Nevertheless, lower processes do indeed influence higher ones, but indirectly through variable intermediary subsystems, which themselves enjoy a certain independence and degree of sovereignty over subordinate component units. For example, it is tempting to say that genes cause certain traits to occur, such as eye color, height, or even schizophrenia, but this is quite misleading. Genes are themselves systems composed of variable molecular component subsystems, and they affect phenotypic characters not by direct action, but through numerous variable, intermediary subsystems (Mayr, 1970; Scheller & Axel, 1984). Weiss (1969) concedes that an ordered progression does seem to exist from DNA through RNA to protein synthesis, but he asks how do we get from the gene to highly coordinated and highly organized action at the phenotypic level?

This question is beyond the scope of the present work, but it does raise an important point: Linear cause-effect relationships are, for all practical purposes, nonexistent in living organisms, and, therefore, animal and human behavior must be construed in something other than strict cause-effect terms. Despite its complexity and postulation of a number of speculative and poorly defined constructs ("wholes," "configurations," "levels," "information," and "information exchange," "control mechanisms," "regulators," etc.), the hierarchic-systems approach seems to be the best conceptual model we have to derive causal inferences about behavior.

The Regression–Progression Hierarchy

Consonant with the hierarchic-systems approach, the phylogenetic regression–progression model assumes that adaptive behavior is a function of numerous, interacting causes acting more or less simultaneously at many different levels of organismic functioning from sub-atomic particles through molecules, cells, progressively more complex cell systems (tissues, organs, organ systems, etc.), and even up to mental phenomena at the highest levels. Behavior, therefore, cannot be attributed to a cause producing an effect, but, rather, must be attributed to numerous contributing factors that, through their combined effects in the neurohumoral and neuromuscular systems of the body, lead to functional and species-appropriate modes of response. What, then, are some of these contributing factors, or better still, causal constraints? Causal constraints fall into three molar, generally overlapping categories: structural, priming conditions, and proximal elicitors.

Structural constraints, of course, as Aristotle noted, are those imposed by the design features of the organism. As our discussion of the dromedary illustrated, physical morphology is perhaps the greatest behavioral delimitor of all, determining, to a great degree, the major action parameters of the organism. Compare for a moment the common earthworm, the giraffe, and the human being. How much of the essence of each of these three kinds of living creatures can be accounted for (or "caused") just by sheer design features alone? Irrespective of motivation or environmental stimulation, earthworms, giraffes, and people differ greatly in virtually all areas of behavior and no amount of will or training can minimize these differences to any significant degree. We must, therefore, rule out motivation and learning as major defining causes of these species differences, and conclude that much of the behavior of animals is caused simply by what they are and what they are capable of doing in the first place. Furthermore, given the range of function and activity across all living organisms, a single member of a given species, whether primitive or advanced, really cannot do very much; that is, by virtue of its species membership and the design limitations thereof, it is severely constrained in its behavioral possibilities. Indeed, knowing the species membership of a given organism allows us, with considerable confidence, to determine its behavioral probabilities within its natural surroundings.

The behavior of all organisms is indisputably constrained by morphological design features, but how much is the behavior itself constrained by natural design? Here is where biological and environmental determinists come to a parting of the ways. If much of human behavior is instinctual or built-in from the beginning like physical morphology, then behavior would be primarily determined by these internal and innate structures and external causes would be of minimal significance. The so-called nature–nurture controversy has revolved around this issue of how much of our behavior is caused by innate, species universals and how much by external causes in the environment. We will not revive this sterile controversy here, but instead look for a richer and more sophisticated approach to the problem. For now, however, given the material reviewed in prior chapters, we conclude that: (a) there is a wealth of evidence supporting the notion that many behavioral propensities in humans are biologically based or built into the neurohumoral hardware and software of the nervous system; and (b) no sharp distinction can be drawn between behavior that is determined by internal causes and behavior that is externally determined.

Behavior also is constrained by the *priming conditions,* or cumulative factors affecting the immediate state of the phenotype (see chapters 6 and 7). Although an animal may have the behavioral potential to copulate at any time, it is likely to actually emit this behavior under a rather limited set of circumstances. Depending on internal readiness in terms of drive level, an animal may or may not initiate and/or perform the copulatory response when exposed to an appropriate sexual object. In this instance, the "readiness to release" normally inhibited sexual behavior becomes the crucial determinant, and external eliciting stimuli merely serve to set the process in motion. Which, then, is the "true cause" of the copulatory response—the complex, hierarchically arranged neurohumoral systems subserving the behavior, or the external eliciting stimuli. The PRP model accords causal status to both factors, but the internal readiness is by far the more important determinant. Both internal and external causes are generally necessary for adaptive behavior to occur, yet neither, taken alone, is a sufficient cause. But, just as the starting mechanism of a car defines far less carness than does the motor, transmission, and electrical system, the external elicitor explains less of the coordinated behavioral sequences it sets off than do the neurohumoral structures subserving those sequences.

Whereas an elicitor is defined literally as a stimulus that succeeds in actually setting off a response or response pattern, a priming stimulus or condition contributes to response readiness rather than setting off response discharge. A given readiness to respond at a given moment may be (and typically is) a function of many internal and external primers, all of which combine to make a given response pattern highly probable. It follows, then, that when priming is minimal external elicitors must be especially powerful for response discharge to occur, but, conversely, minimal elicitation is required when the organism is highly primed. So viewed, elicitors and primers are not absolutes, but are defined by their effects; hormonal secretions, for example, act as elicitors when they act on behavior more or less directly (e.g., as when injections of testosterone produce atypical male behavior in the female rat, but, more often, hormones serve a behaviorally passive priming function).

A variety of elicitors of phylogenetic regression were discussed in chapters 6 and 7, many of which have the capability to act as primers of behavior as well. Some of the major primers (or elicitors) for human behavior are tendencies toward certain responses inherited in phylogeny (the phylogenotype), tendencies toward certain species-unique responses (the transgenotype), tendencies inherited from parental genotypes, hormones, neurotransmitters, brain function and dysfunction, pain or fear, drugs, social releasers (when they affect the organism, but short of overt behavior), stressors of various sorts, and so on. Considering that primers are many, and further that they act in additive and combinatorial fashion, we are struck by the magnitude of internal causality and the fruitlessness of causal explanations based solely on external contingencies.

The foregoing notwithstanding, the role of *proximal elicitors* in behavioral causality cannot be denied. A proximal elicitor refers to a stimulus or stimulus configuration either in the internal or external environment that causes a response or response pattern to be discharged that otherwise would have remained dormant. The proximal elicitor causes response discharge much like a light switch causes the light to come on (viz., a small amount of patterned energy sets off a vastly greater amount of more complexly patterned energy within more complexly structured systems). Again, the reader is referred back to chapters 6 and 7 for more extensive discussion of elicitors.

In summary, behavior is a function of overlapping causes emanating from three levels of analysis—the level of inherent structural design, the level of motivational readiness, and the level of proximal elicitation. The phylogenetic regression–progression model assumes that adaptive behavior generally is caused by inputs from all three levels, and, further, that the conceptual significance of causes is greatest at the level of structure, next greatest at the level of readiness, and least of all at the level of proximal elicitation. One need only to attempt to elicit cat behavior from a dog or earthworm behavior from a giraffe to immediately confront the inherent limitations of stimulation in and of itself.

Some Special Complications

In Bailey (1986a) some of the biases in social science were discussed from the standpoint of the sociology of science. These included biases emanating from the assumptive base of science (e.g., empiricism, determinism, and research methodology), difficulties in humans being objective about themselves, difficulties in being objective about controversial social issues, the need for social science to justify itself, power issues, paradigm protectiveness, the hegemony of "environmentalism," and so on. The problem of objectivity is not limited to social scientists, however; the journalist Mary Hager (1982), in an invited paper in the *American Psychologist,* argues that the "Myth of Objectivity" plays a role in all human endeavors. As human beings, it is impossible for us to be totally dispassionate and objective about things that threaten our belief systems or act against our self-interest. Although objectivity is elusive for all of us, it is especially so for the social scientist who works in areas of greatest threat to the human ego.

To a great degree, the biases of social science revolve around different ways and means of identifying and explaining the causes of human behavior. Why humans act as they do is a touchy question for social scientists, political leaders, philosophers, theologians, and laypersons alike, for in the "true causes" of behavior lies our essence as human beings. Thus, we would expect people to be very defensive about what makes them tick, and this is indeed the case. Nowhere are the Freudian defense mechanisms of repression, denial, and rationalization more evident than in our feeble attempts to explain our own behavior and that of others. There is a powerful tendency for both scientists and laypersons to find certain causes of behavior far more palatable than others, and nowhere is this more evident than in causal inferences made about human misbehavior (e.g., crime, warfare, terrorism, sexual sadism, child molestation, and so on; see following chapters).

Generally, causal inferences must be thoroughly adjusted to things like the American democratic dream, environmentalism, prevailing theoretical paradigms, humanistic and theistic ideology, economic considerations, and one's own ego needs before people will listen to them, editors will publish them, or granting agencies will fund research on them (Bailey, 1986a; Mahoney, 1976). For example, many behavioral scientists of a century ago would be considered radical biological determinists, racists, and just bad people by contemporary standards (Gould, 1981), by virtue of their postulation of causes based on innate characters or atavism; yet, in their day, these same scientists were applauded for these views. Although we may rightfully hold these 19th-century scientists guilty of racism and elitism because of the ethnocentristic and self-serving social recommendations emanating from their theories, we cannot assess the validity of the theories themselves on that basis. A theory may be quite valid in its causal premises, and then be used for nefarious purposes unrelated to those essential premises. Indeed, how sure can we be that our current causal attributions will survive the ravages of time any better than those of Louis Agassiz, Samual Morton, Paul Broca, or Cesar Lombroso? Can we truly say that we understand the causal essences of love, crime, gender, or mental illness that much better than they? Certainly, we have accumulated far more scientific information, but our powerful need to adjust findings to nonscientific standards seems no less active than theirs.

One need not look far to find a wealth of examples of such adjustment. Rather than multiplying examples, however, we concentrate on what might be called "the hegemony of socialization." Many social scientists seem satisfied with explaining personality, mental illness, sex differences, criminality, intelligence, and most everything else with a single "cause"—differential socialization. Each of us is indeed socialized in the sense that our basic neurohumoral hardware and innate behavioral software programs are modified, extended, and/or suppressed by sociocultural influences, but this does not mean that the social environment acts as a unitary or direct cause. The phylogenetic regression model would include socializing influences in any postulated matrix of biosocial causes subserving complex human behavior, but such external influences are not always primary nor definitive. That we are socialized is tautological, but this tells us little about the epigenesis of complex, motivated behavior or the proximate causes of such behavior. As we have argued, the internal structural and priming conditions of the body are generally primary in explaining the whys of complex human behavior (especially adaptive behavior), whereas socializing influences are more likely to play modulatory and elaborative functions.

The use of socialization as a unitary causal construct is essentially a creation of modern social science, more specifically, American social science. As the term is used, it is a rationale to end all rationales, a simple and uniform way to facilitate communication among social scientists and give meaning to their perceptions. What it is not, however, is a rigorously defined construct capable of serving as the foundation for meaningful causal inferences. In many ways, the modern concept of socialization is analogous to the concept of instinct in the early 1920s—an all-inclusive, all-sufficient, eminently circular, and exquisitely convenient method of attributing causes in sympathy with the Zeitgeist. Both concepts operate at a low level of conceptualization, differing primarily in the relative weight given to innate versus learned causal attributions.

Some of the aforementioned points may be illustrated with a single brief example. In an analysis of the literature on sex differences in psychopathology, Eme (1979) reviews a wealth of evidence and reaches a remarkable conclusion: All sex differences in psychopathology are not due to differential socialization and biological factors deserve more attention in the area. It is remarkable that a conclusion so obvious required such careful and extensive documentation, but Eme was aware that the socialization hypothesis is an accepted truism among many social scientists. He acknowledged, for example, that the massive disparity between the sexes in aggression and antisocial behavior is most commonly explained by differential socialization, but argued that sex differences in activity level, biological disposition to aggression, possible greater ease of learning of aggression in the male, body type (greater mesomorphy in the male), and hormonal secretions cannot be ignored. More tellingly, although the case for biological mediation of the sex disparity was quite convincing, the socialization hypothesis received weak empirical support in any direct sense. That is, differential socialization could not be demonstrated in the form of specific environmental or social experiences that favored the learning of aggressiveness in males and unaggressiveness in females (e.g., learned fear of aggression in females, greater parental reinforcement of male aggression, female reinforcement of male aggression, and so forth).

The preceding chapters, with their fairly extensive discussion of the phylogenetic, genetic, neural, and humoral underpinnings of behavior, demonstrate rather clearly the impotence of gratuitously biological or social imputation of causes, and it is argued that a dynamic, hierarchical, and inclusive model, one appropriately sensitive to intercoordination of component structures within and between levels of the hierarchical system, is required. This approach lacks the stark simplicity of instinct or socialization as causal explanations, but opts instead to confront the complex matrix of mutually interacting causes—structural, state-of-the-organism, and triggering—that are implicated in all adaptive behavior. The "true causes" of human behavior and misbehavior will, no doubt, continue to elude us, but our best causal inferences will result when all we know about animals and human beings (their evolutionary heritage, neurohumoral states, learning histories, and eliciting conditions) are brought to bear on the problem.

A Comparison of Explanatory Models

Thus far we have implicitly contrasted the hierarchic-systems approach of the PRP model with rather simplistic and naive versions of the socialization hypothesis. Although invocation of the simplistic version is common in both the technical writing and everyday conversation of social scientists, there are, nevertheless, some quite rich and sophisticated socialization models. An excellent example is Bandura's (1978) thoughtful discussion of "reciprocal determinism" in relation to social learning theory. According to Bandura, causal processes in social learning theory are conceptualized in terms of reciprocal determinism, that is, the "continuous reciprocal interaction between behavioral, cognitive, and environmental influences" (p. 344). At the center of these mutually interacting causes lies the "self-system," a highly cognitive set of self-conceptions that exert regulatory influence over specific response tendencies. In his model, Bandura appropriately acknowledges the crucial importance of internal cognitive events (thoughts, expectations, beliefs, attitudes, etc.) as mediators of overt action. Yet, his approach is far more than a traditional, unidirectional S–O–R model with a special emphasis on the "O"; it goes beyond unidirectionality or even simple bidirectionality, and, instead, focuses on the interactive reciprocality that far more accurately characterizes complex human behavior.

The cognitive (neocortical) nature of Bandura's model is clear:

Social learning theory . . . analyzes behavior in terms of reciprocal determinism. The term *determinism* is used here to signify the production of effects by events, rather than in the doctrinal sense that actions are completely determined by a prior sequence of causes independent of the individual. Because of the complexity of interacting factors, events produce effects probabilistically rather than inevitably. In their transactions with the environment, people are not simply reactors to external stimulation. Most external influences affect behavior through intermediary cognitive processes. Cognitive factors partly determine which external events will be observed, how they will be perceived, whether they have any lasting effects, what valence and efficacy they have, and how the information they convey will be organized for future use. The extraordinary capacity of humans to use symbols enables them to engage in reflective thought, to create, and to plan foresightful courses of action in thought rather than having to perform possible options and suffer the consequences of thoughtless action. By altering the immediate environment, by creating cognitive self-inducements, and by arranging conditional incentives for themselves, people can exercise some influence over their own behavior. An act therefore includes among its determinants self-produced influences. (p. 345)

The phylogenetic regression–progression model shares Bandura's emphases on the reciprocal-interactive nature of causes, the probabilistic nature of behavior, the importance of cognitive and self-produced influences, the importance of self-regulatory processes, and so on. Although fundamentally congruent with Bandura's model, the PRP model differs in a number of ways:

1. The PRP model not only assumes that component causes interact reciprocally, but that they interact in hierarchical-systemic fashion.

2. The PRP model ranks causes hierarchically, proceeding from phylogenetically primitive causal inputs at the level of inherent neurohumoral structures up to refined thought more or less decoupled from the lower systems.

3. The PRP model assumes that primitive causes are more urgent, powerful, and reliable than advanced ones, whereas Bandura places more emphasis on advanced cognitive causality. Bandura seems to view the rational cognitive system as master of the lower centers, whereas, following Plutchik (1977), the PRP model sees the neocortex more as "slave" to lower needs.

4. Bandura seems to assume that the substructures of behavior are acquired through learning, primarily social learning, whereas the PRP model assumes that most of the basic substructures of behavior are present at birth and attain subsequent levels of complexity through elaborative maturational and learning processes.

5. As is true of most contemporary models of human behavior, Bandura's approach does not emphasize the "bad side" of human behavior, e.g., irrational processes, selfishness, gratuitous excesses in the areas of sex and violence, sudden discharge phenomena such as Monroe's (1978) dyscontrol syndrome or Mark and Ervin's (1970) epileptoid forms of violence (see chapter 10). Reynolds' (1979) critical analysis of the comparisons and contrasts between Bandura's essentially cognitive approach to aggression and that of the neurophysiologically oriented ethologists is instructive here. Whereas Bandura tends to emphasize intentions, social norms, ideational context, and suppositions about outcome, the ethologists (as exemplified by J. P. Flynn's research on the neurophysiology of aggression in cats) tend to focus more on motivation and phylogenetic programming of behavior in the brain (Reynolds, 1979). More like the ethological model, the PRP model was purposely designed to accommodate the phylogenetically primitive and "inhuman" aspects of human aggressive behavior.

So far, we have seen how the PRP model compares and contrasts with a good psychological model of causation. Let us now repeat the exercise with a good, solid biosocial model. In 1982, an entire issue of the *Journal of Social and Biological Structures* was devoted to discussion of the relations between the law, biology, and culture. Among the eminent invited participants was the German psychologist and evolutionary biologist, Hubert Markl. His paper was entitled, "Constraints on Human Behavior and the Biological Nature of Man." Rather than enumerating biological constraints on human nature, however, Markl focused instead on the lack of such constraints and the weaknesses and excesses of sociobiological explanations of human behavior. In so arguing, he delivered an excellent essay on the biosocial and biocultural determinants of behavior, with primary emphasis on sociocultural causality.

Markl's model and the PRP model share many fundamental assumptions, as the following quote shows:

> If sociobiological reasoning about the biological nature of man means anything at all, it refers to genetic constraints on the specific predispositions toward behavior. More specifically, it must refer to constraints on the behavioral development of the newborn: to epigenetic rules (Lumsden & Wilson, 1981) which owe their existence, if not directly to the individual's genes, then at least to the interaction of genes with external influences on prenatal ontogenesis. If an organism is without learning capacity, such an innate endowment would fully specify the possible behavioral potentials. But in humans we can (at least theoretically) differentiate between whole series of constraining and directing influences. Such constraints are, first of all, the blueprint for development contained in the genome of the zygote. The

directing influences are represented, second, by prenatal environmental influences on the developing embryo. Postnatally, at a third level, the child is subject to the directing influences of behavior modification in culture-dependent learning situations. At that stage, an intense richness of information is incorporated into the child's behavioral system through imitation learning, conditioning, cognitive self-structuring, and by formal teaching. Through these devices the individual can partake in the traditions of its culture. Thus, within the range of constraints imposed on the individual by its genes and its prenatal epigenesis, learning cultural traditions further narrows behavioral options. Each culture makes specific selections from the gamut of behavioral possibilities open to a human neonate. (p. 382)

Markl (1982) goes on to describe development as a continuous interactive process involving a complex mixture of genetic, fetal, cultural, and personal individualization. The outcome of this process "is a unique person with unique patterns of species-typical, culture-typical and personal capacities, constraints and inclinations" (p. 383). One can hardly argue with the thrust of these points, and clearly most of them are basically congruent with both the Bandurian and PRP models. There are certain differences in emphasis between the Markl and PRP models, however:

1. The main difference arises from differential weighting of primitive versus advanced causes. Markl chooses to emphasize the cognitive and cultural bases of behavior, and argues against strong biological determinism. He argues that the human being, by virtue of learning, experience, and imagination, is able to "escape" or decouple (see chapter 2) from its biological imperatives and enjoy "an amazing freedom of action." The PRP model basically agrees with this assumption, but with certain strong qualifications. First, humans have the potential for a degree of decoupling, but that potential is only marginally realized due to phylogenetic inertia, the ease with which regression occurs, and the numerous prerequisites necessary for a high level of phylogenetic progression (intelligence, strong cultural shaping, denial and control of lower motives, self-consciousness, etc.). Second, "escape" from our biological substructures is only relative under the best of circumstances, for in our moments of deepest and most profound reflection we remain tied to the structure-function intercoordinations of the body.

2. Markl (1982) implies hierarchical levels of causality (genetic blueprint, prenatal influences, and postnatal learning experience), but does not carry the reasoning very far. By contrast, the PRP model centers on the hierarchical analysis of behavioral causality.

3. As is true of most approaches to human behavior, Markl makes no provision for momentary changes in behavior; that is, the momentary

regressions and progressions so important for the PRP model are not addressed.

4. Again, along with many other experts on human behavior, Markl implies a disjunction between our animal and human natures; that is, we are fundamentally either a biological creature to be explained biologically, or a cultural creature to be explained culturally. He suggests, for example, citing Luckmann (1979), that Darwinian fitness may play little or no role in the everyday life of most individuals, and, further, that standards of cultural fitness may have supplanted biological ones. The PRP model emphasizes both biological and cultural causes of behavior, and more importantly, accords relative importance to each depending on the state of the organism (including the learning history) and eliciting conditions.

5. Both Bandura's and Markl's models fail to grapple with the question of why people are so inclined to misbehavior, noncultural, and acultural practices. Given that "deviance" often is defined arbitrarily or in terms of stereotypical labeling of individuals or subcultures, there still remains a large residue of culture-resistant behavior and nonconformity in modern society. The term *culture* is stretched to meaningless proportions when rape, child molestation, brutal murders, and vandalism are ascribed to cultural causes. In these instances, failure to behave culturally would appear to be the primary problem. We must ask, then, why there are so many cultural deviants in our midst, and if we are so above the animals, why, as MacLean (1978b) asks, do we continue to do the things animals do? The PRP model attempts to solve the riddle by assuming an animal nature in all people, but adds that individuals differ greatly in their mastery of the Beast. One's degree of mastery is a multiple function of genetic variation, learning (especially moral and cultural shaping), and situational circumstances. How else may we explain the timid choirboy who murders his parents in a violent rage or the catastrophic personality changes associated with drug use or brain damage? Service is done to no one when these and similar phenomena are cast into the wastebasket of unexplainable exceptions. From the standpoint of the PRP model, such exceptions are difficult, if not impossible, to successfully explain solely in terms of culturally or otherwise learned causes.

Levels of Explanation

The PRP model assumes that theoretical hierarchies of behavior may be generated indefinitely as long as they are meaningful and parsimonious. Following the hierarchic-systems approach advocated by Koestler, Powers, Weiss, Von Bertalanffy, and many others, living organisms are construed as hierarchies within hierarchies, microscopic systems embedded within larger systems seemingly *ad infinitum*. Thus, if one wishes to construct a hypothetical hierarchy for explanatory purposes, it is necessary to select from among a plethora of conceptual possibilities. The particular hierarchy derived is, of course, an abstract conceptualization nonisomorphic to the "true hierarchy" it approximates; it is merely a convenient way of organizing our thoughts in meaningful fashion. As theoretical constructions, they are judged not by their inherent truth value but by their functional and heuristic value.

In the preceding chapters, many hierarchical approaches have been mentioned, including Maslow's hierarchy of needs, MacLean's triune brain, Rado's dynamic cerebral system, Piaget's stages of cognitive dvelopment, Thorndike's levels of intelligence, Burt's hierarchy of abilities, Loevinger's levels of ego development, Kohlberg's stages of moral development, and so forth. Clearly, the hierarchical cat can be skinned many ways, and each thoughtful analysis provides us with a small glimpse of the greater reality. In this spirit, the following hierarchical levels of analysis were formulated: sociobiological, ego-psychological, cultural, philosophical, and spiritual. In this scheme, the sociobiological level accounts for the primitive, "animalistic" aspects of functioning, the spiritual level the highest and most phylogenetically advanced functioning, whereas the ego-psychological, cultural, and philosophical levels account for middle-range functioning. An overview of the scheme is shown on Table 9.1. As shown, the two lower levels constitute the broader paleopsychological level of functioning, and, analogously, the three higher levels constitute the broader neopsychological level.

The Sociobiological Level.   Given the breadth and scope of sociobiological theory, and its unwavering commitment to Darwinian fitness as the ultimate cause of behavior, the sociobiological level was chosen to occupy the ground floor of the theoretical hierarchy. For purposes of convenience, all of the approaches premised on evolutionary biology (ethology, biosocial anthropology, evolutionary psychiatry, etc.) are lumped under the heading of "sociobiology." Within the sociobiological arena, Dawkins' (1976a) theory of the selfish gene represents the most extreme argument for a genetic determinism. With his best hyperbole, Dawkins reduces the human being to a robot, a throwaway phenotype who is blindly compelled by selfish genes programmed to replicate themselves at any cost. When persons are so compelled, they are, by definition, behaving at a low level of phylogenetic regression (or fixation). But, as we already know, not all our behavior is directly coupled to our genetic imperatives, as Dawkins (1976a) recognizes in his final chapter: "for an understanding of modern man, we must begin by throwing out the gene as the sole basis of our ideas of evolution" (p. 205). The genes continue to exert control over our behavior, but a new and perhaps more

TABLE 9.1
Summary of Hierarchical Levels of Analysis

PALEOPSYCHOLOGICAL LEVELS

Sociobiological Level
Basic neurohumoral hardware of behavior
  Sex
  Aggression
  Fear
  Pleasure and pain
  Kinship, parenting, affiliation
Selfishness—asocial, antisocial
Fitness-targeted behavior (self and kin)
  Altruism—kin
  Xenophobia—strangers
Eruptions of once fitness-targeted behavioral segments
Stimulus control strong; releaser-fixed action pattern linkages strong
Little cognitive mediation of behavior
Little personal "freedom"

Ego-psychological Level
Egotism replaces primitive asocial selfishness
Self-interest is opportunistically disguised (reciprocal altruism)
Minimal cognitive mediation and modulation of behavior
Rudimentary self-consciousness
Rationalized hedonism
Some degree of freedom from biological imperatives

Cultural Level
Individual behavior guided by group norms and standards
Group needs supercede those of individual
Acceptance by group based on conformity to group norms

(Continued)

powerful force now dominates human action—that of culture. Here, Dawkins falls victim to an error that plagues discussions on biological versus cultural causation (Reynolds, 1981); he seems to imply a supplantation of genes by culture, and we are left with the feeling that culture has somehow won out over the Beast. By contrast, the PRP model assumes an ongoing, dynamic interaction of older and newer functions, governed by the principles of regression and progression.

Although culture is absent at the sociobiological level, all is not individual selfishness in the direct sense. A rudimentary social organization exists that revolves around primitive rules of kinship laid down in phylogeny (see chapters 2 and 5). In accordance with Hamilton's (1964) concept of inclusive fitness, an indirect form of selfishness comes into

TABLE 9.1 *(Continued)*

NEOPSYCHOLOGICAL LEVELS

Conformity to group reinforced by customs, mores, and legal strictures
Social structures aid the neocortex in controlling lower functions
Sociobiological and psychological needs are sublimated prosocially
Moderate self-consciousness; very limited self-reflection
Moderate freedom from lower drives, but now bound by social pressure
Rudiments of conscience—group defines "right" and "wrong"

Philosophical Level

Critical self-reflection
Critical analysis of cosmic questions—life, death, being, causality . . .
Love of learning, knowledge
"Search for truth"
Creative imagination
Rules of thinking—inductive and deductive logic
Independent thinking—freedom from both drives and culture
Refined sense of right and wrong—systematic ethics

Spiritual Level

Transcendent relationship with Supreme Being
Sacrifice of both personal and group needs to higher power
Concern with afterlife as well as present contingencies
Refined love for all humankind (agape)
Concern with purpose in life; eternal meanings
Truth and knowledge emanate as revelations from the Deity
The Deity aids the neocortex in controlling the drives of the "flesh"
Individual is freed from the world but bound by the Deity
Self-control is most reliable at this level

---

effect where individuals are motivated to maximize the Darwinian fitness of their close relatives as well as their own fitness. Thus, to behave altruistically toward close kin is to behave selfishly toward one's own genes carried by them; at this level of functioning social and group-oriented behavior are ultimately directed toward the asocial goal of perpetuating one's own genes and not toward survival of the group for its own sake. Only at the cultural level do we see social organization governed more by abstract and arbitrary prerogatives than by genes seeking to replicate themselves.

Therefore, at the hard sociobiological level of functioning, the individual is governed and guided by phylogenetically ancient, inherently selfish patterns of adaptation to the environment. When functioning at this level is more or less pure, as in extreme regression, the controlling and modulating powers of the higher levels are suspended, and ancient patterns are released in relatively large segments and part segments. In contrast to traditional sociobiological theory, the PRP model assumes that such patterns need not be fitness-targeted at the time of release, but may represent, instead, patterns that were once heavily fitness-targeted in phylogeny (see Barkow, 1983; Symonds, 1979) and are now retained, as vestiges with differing degrees of coherence, in the individual's reptilian and paleomammalian nervous systems. On occasions, however, when these once fitness-targeted patterns are, by virtue of appropriate internal and external conditions, placed again on the survival track, we would expect fairly coherent sequences of regressive behavior targeted by ultimate as well as proximate causes. Thus, a man who goes into an uncontrollable rage and attacks others in random fashion is not behaving adaptively at all, but, ironically, his behavior is being driven primarily by deep centers of the brain (see chapter 10) which mediated quite adaptive anger and attack behavior in his phylogenetic forbears. On the other hand, if a man draws upon his phylogenetically primitive rage and aggression centers to protect his family and belongings from plunderers, his actions are presumably survival-targeted, adaptive, and roughly homologous to similar patterns used by his phylogenetic ancestors in similar situations.

Therefore, phylogenetic regression to the sociobiological level may occur in two ways: release of once adaptive patterns in nonadaptive or maladaptive fashion, and release of once adaptive patterns that serve contemporary adaptive functions. In the former instance, inherently adaptive structure-motivation-behavior intercoordinations are nonadaptively or maladaptively decoupled, whereas in the latter instance old adaptive patterns subserve current adaptive behavior, albeit primitive adaptive behavior. This is a crucial distinction for several reasons:

1. First of all, it defuses the oft-cited criticism of sociobiology that behavior which is not clearly fitness-targeted must be explained in sociocultural rather than sociobiological terms. Much of Markl's (1982) critique of sociobiological determinism takes this form, but to demonstrate a weak link between current behavior and Darwinian fitness is not to discount the causal influence of once adaptive patterns and tendencies. The maladaptive release of bits and pieces of phylogenetically old patterns is common in phylogenetic regression, particularly in rage reactions (see chapter 10) and psychopathological reactions (see chapter 12). Generally, phylogenetically regressive patterns that are weakly targeted toward fitness are associated with chaotic and/or pathological releases,

whereas more strongly targeted ones reflect longer and more smoothly coordinated sequences of adaptive behavior.

2. Second, the distinction between inappropriate and maladaptive regressive release of vestigial functions versus the release of old adaptive patterns and their elaborations allows us to address the problem of momentary fluctuations in behavior. Everything a person does is not adaptive nor meaningful, and a microbehavioral analysis of a normal person's behavior over an hour's time would reveal much behavioral noise. Suppose we observe a hypothetical subject for an hour as he reposes in front of a televised football game, occasionally sipping beer and munching goodies. Our microbehavioral analysis would likely reveal little obvious adaptive behavior, a fairly large amount of once adaptive behavioral tendencies, and considerable meaningless action. Little adaptive behavior would be evident due to the absence of both internal priming and adequate eliciting conditions, and our subject would be freed to relax and cater to his immediate whims.

One whim would be eating strictly for pleasure, which represents a partial decoupling from the ultimately adaptive, tuned-to-the-environment, "pleasure in food-seeking and food-consumption" complex that characterized his evolutionary forbears. In this instance, pleasurable sensation and bits and pieces of the original, highly coordinated behavioral complex (hand-to-mouth behavior, salivating, chewing, swallowing, etc.) are pulled out and sacrificed to self-indulgence. Ironically, pleasurable experience originally designed to assure the performance of adaptive nutritional behavior has herewith degenerated into a maladaptive, life-threatening quest for proximal pleasure. Thus, we see that our subject's indulgent nibbling and drinking involves the employment of phylogenetically old patterns of motivation and action, but in minimally coordinated and adaptive fashion.

Similar reasoning would, no doubt, apply to our subject's emotional involvement in the game as manifested in screams of agony and delight, exhortations to "kill" the opposition, an overwhelming obsession with winning, and so on. Such colorful behavior is, of course, multiply determined, but the PRP model would focus on once-adaptive dominance ("need to win"), tribal togetherness ("our team"), and xenophobic (antipathy toward outsiders) tendencies as likely causal candidates. Thus, in explaining the whys of this irrational involvement in a mere athletic event, the PRP model would look for elaborations of old tendencies as the primary causes, with priming conditions (frustration, low self-esteem with compensatory need to "be on top," need to identify with a "tribal group," etc.) and proximal eliciting conditions (need to prevail over a cowatcher who is rooting for the other team, having money riding on the outcome, the actual sights and sounds of "combat" on the screen, etc.) making significant contributions as well. Little of this rich flow of behavior is necessarily adaptive in the sense of being survival-targeted, but it is eminently reasonable to assume that many of the underlying motive tendencies and overt actions involved represent segments of once adaptive patterns and/or elaborations and mixtures of those segments.

The aforementioned analysis merely skimmed over the multiplicity of true causes actually directing our subject's behavior over an hour's time, but our goal was merely to illustrate how once adaptive patterns continue to serve as causes of much contemporary human behavior. Indeed, it seems that old patterns may be drawn from in piecemeal fashion to meet any evanescent and nonadaptive need of the person. However, when threat to survival enters the picture, the bits and pieces of behavior strewn about may be immediately reconstituted into their original adaptive coordinations and enable the person to behave adaptively. This is, in fact, one of the major forms of phylogenetic regression as defined by the PRP model.

The Ego-Psychological Level.   At the ego-psychological level we move up from the more or less pure nonadaptive, maladaptive, or adaptive release of lower sociobiological functions. Now the relationship between lower sociobiological needs and overt behavior is mediated by mental activity of either a constraining or facilitating sort. Although this mental activity is basically functionalistic, acultural, amoral, and nonreflective, it, nevertheless, moves the person one small step away from strictly animal modes of functioning. Whereas cause–effect was more evident at the sociobiological level, some phylogenetically progressive self-restraint and resistance to lower urgencies is now possible. The individual continues to act selfishly in the sociobiological sense, but now, by virtue of limited decision making and processing of alternatives, self-interest can be disguised to a degree and attuned to long-range as well as immediate goals. Whereas the sociobiological level is roughly analogous to id level functioning in the Freudian scheme, the ego-psychological level is analogous to primitive ego functioning. At the ego-psychological level we encounter sociopathic rather than sociobiological functioning; instead of being motivated directly by primitive impulses, the individual denies himself just enough to convince others that motives higher than self-interest are operating (see Barkow, 1983, on the issue of self- and other-deception). In this way, the human being can maximize self-interest far more efficiently than the animal that must follow its natural inclinations and is not free to follow cognitively derived alternatives.

Wallach and Wallach (1983) are extremely critical of social scientists for sanctioning selfishness and hedonism in their human subjects, and they are especially incensed by mental health professionals who train their patients in the art of selfishness. Social scientists are correct in recognizing the inherent nature of human selfishness and pleasure-seeking, but their fatalism and capitulationism are unjustified. Human beings are compulsively selfish and sociopathic at the sociobiological and ego-psychological levels of functioning, but the PRP model tells us that a degree of freedom from these imperatives is possible with sufficient self-control and enculturalization. However, selfish strategies are easily reinforced and phylogenetic progression thwarted when therapists operate only at the opportunistic ego-psychological level of functioning.

The Cultural Level.   Self-interest begins to yield to the needs and requirements of the group as we reach the cultural level of functioning. Whereas group behavior at the sociobiological and psychological levels was erected upon inherently selfish kinship and tribal bonds, cultural behavior involves partial decoupling from the lower systems. As many writers have pointed out, however, culture never totally transcends biology; instead, culture typically refines, complements, and extends the biological underpinnings provided by natural selection. In fact, if culture violates biological prerogatives beyond certain limits, individual and social pathology may result. Nevertheless, culture is premised on sufficient freedom from lower compulsions to develop group-defined rules and norms of individual behavior and social organization. With culture, behavior becomes adjusted to arbitrary standards as well as natural ones, and conflict between old imperatives and new requirements is commonplace. Culture requires far greater self-control and cognitive mediation of behavior than do the sociobiological and ego psychological levels, for the prescribed rules of conduct must be learned, stored in memory and assimiliated into pre-existing cognitive structures, and then called forth and evaluated prior to action. Of course, this evaluative process is usually subconscious and eventually becomes habitual, but represents, nevertheless, a large step in phylogenetic progression. The cultural level is one of intellectual and behavioral conformity, yet is one that can be developed to a high level of refinement in terms of dress, etiquette, and custom (e.g., "haute culture").

The Philosophical Level.   From cultural conformity, we move to the philosophical level where true self-reflection and a questioning attitude about the universe are encountered for the first time. At this level, the full weight of human thought and imagination are brought to bear on questions of life and existence. The philosopher, by definition, loves to think and unravel the mysteries of nature, including the mysteries of his or her own consciousness. At this level the mind is truly turned back on itself, often revealing unpleasantries and conundrums beyond the grasp of the common man. Only the intelligent few indulge themselves with philosophic reflection, and then only for a fraction of their time. To seriously philosophize is to phylogenetically progress toward the acme of human experience, and for those few brief moments to imagine worlds infinitely beyond the comprehension of the most intelligent animal. From the din of impetuous and creative philosophic reflection come the great discoveries in science and art that have transformed the gap between man and animal to a great chasm. The practice of science or art should not be confused with the generation of creative ideas that open new avenues of research and expression; the former is a form of culture where one conforms to prevailing paradigms, whereas the latter is the product of less fettered human thought.

The Spiritual Level.   The levels discussed so far are similar to many of the levels and stages seen in other hierarchic approaches to personality and development. However, our most phylogenetically advanced level, the spiritual level, is rather novel and requires fuller explanation. The word spiritual is used here to describe a transcendent relationship with a power greater than oneself or, for that matter, a power greater than any human power. Religion, in its various forms from primitive animism and supernaturalism to modern theology, is a species–specific human trait par excellence, and appears to have no analogue at all in the animal world. Religion, in its higher forms,[1] brings us closest to a true transcendence of our animal nature, where concern shifts from the corporeal to the most abstract of concepts, God. In moments of highest piety in modern religions of both East and West, the selfish, egoistic needs of the individ-

---

[1]The phrase, "in its higher forms," is crucial here, for as correctly noted by an anonymous reviewer of this book, religion often involves "a blind unquestioning faith, and the uncritical acceptance of spiritual dogma . . . for the average person religion often represents little more than an intellectual and emotional crutch based on highly ritualized superstitious behavior." To this we might add the "actively regressive" elements of religious oppression, prejudice, terrorism, and warfare. In PRP theory, however, religion may be hierarchicalized like everything else, with primitive forms of object, animal, and quasi-human animism, magic and superstition, totemism, and idolatry occupying lower points on the regression–progression scale, and the more refined theologic, epistemic, moral, and cosmological expressions occupying the higher levels (see Table 9.1). Just as precious few people reach, for a few moments, the heights of phylogenetic progression in the cultural, philosophical, scientific, moral, and ethical aspects of life, so do precious few reach the human zenith of spiritual expression. At that hypothetical zenith of sacrifice, agape, and oneness with the Supreme Being, superstition, dogma, and ritualism would have long been left behind.

ual are submerged in the higher reality of the deity. Here, behavior is attuned to the deity and at the same time de-coupled from its normal fitness tracking. For the deity, the individual may be willing to sacrifice his life, the lives of his family members, material goods, and virtually anything else that might appease or propitiate the higher power. Religion appears to be the greatest of all motivators of human behavior, for there is nothing the true believer will not do or sacrifice in order to save his immortal soul.

Paradoxically, even though religion, in its highest forms, can motivate the most advanced behavior, it also can produce the most heinous and animalistic active regression where ideology provides the excuse for prejudice, oppression, and imperialism (see chapter 3). The phylogenetically progressive form of religion, thus, represents a rising above the lower needs and a genuine, unselfish commitment to a higher power that cannot be perceived, defined, or even imagined in its entirety. Although regressive slips occur in the most pious and loving people, the frequency and magnitude of phylogenetic regression would appear to be minimal in the likes of Buddha, Mahatma Ghandi, St. Augustine, or even in modern religionists like Mother Teresa, Billy Graham, or Pope John Paul II. Their deeply held religious beliefs seem to represent failsafe antidotes to our natural human tendencies toward avarice, prejudice, and violence. In his book, *The Evolution of Love,* Sydney Mellen (1981) sees the theme of love in Christianity as the primary reason for its extraordinary popularity over the centuries, and in his concluding comments wonders whether the teachings of Jesus hold hope for a world headed for ruin:

> Some of them [the young] seem to be drawn towards the life and teachings of Jesus, and doubtless what attracts them is not a church or a religion but simply the man Jesus as an embodiment of love, charity, and compassion. Perhaps they can salvage that human treasure from amid the ecclesiastical decay. (p. 290)

We sometimes forget that many of the great scientists and philosophers of the past were devout religionists who devoted much of their energy toward proving the existence of God. Distinctions between science and religion were minimized or ignored, and scientific discovery was seen as divine revelation. We are all familiar with the philosophical arguments of Thomas Aquinas regarding divine truth, Descartes "proof" of God's existence, or Locke's essay on the "Reasonableness of Christianity," but some may be surprised that two of the world's greatest scientists— Newton and Einstein—held a deep belief in a Supreme Being who created their object of study, an orderly, lawful universe. P. W. Bridgman (1958) noted that Einstein was a man who "could not bring himself to accept the idea that chance plays a fundamental role in the scheme of things, and who passionately exclaimed, 'Der Herr Gott wurfelt nicht' ('The Lord God does not throw dice')'' (p. 51). Newton not only believed that God created the universe, but that the movement of bodies in space acted, ultimately, in accordance with God's purpose. Rather than assuming that the unscientific theologizing of Newton and Einstein hindered their work, one could more cogently argue that their religious beliefs inspired them to devote their lives to the study of an orderly universe (Rychlak, 1968).

Apart from the philosophical questions surrounding the existence of God, there is little question that human beings have a powerful need to believe (Ostow & Scharfstein, 1954), and, as James (1896/1955) argued, an inherent right to believe as well. Further, the sociobiologist Wilson (1978) asserts:

> The predisposition to religious belief is the most complex and powerful force in the human mind and in all probability an ineradicable part of human nature. . . . It is one of the universals of social behavior, taking recognizable form in every society from hunter-gatherer bands to socialist republics. Its rudiments go back at least to the bone alters and funerary rites of Neanderthal man. At Shanidar, Iraq, sixty thousand years ago, Neanderthal people decorated a grave with seven species of flowers having a medicinal and economic value, perhaps to honor a shaman. Since that time, according to the anthropologist Anthony F. C. Wallace, mankind has produced on the order of 100 thousand religions. (p. 169)

Religion is indeed deeply rooted in human nature, and continues to thrive even in our sophisticated technological age. Of the over 4 billion people inhabiting the earth, 58 million are Roman Catholic, 316 million Protestant, 122 million Eastern Orthodox, 465 million Islamic, and 100 million Shinto and Taoist. Along with these major world religions, there are innumerable smaller religious bodies, sects, and splinter groups that have uncounted followers and supporters. Just within the United States there are over 150 major religious bodies (*World Book,* 1973). The United States is the second most religious country in the world—after India—and a 1977 Gallup Poll revealed that 94% of Americans believe in God or some higher being, and 31% reported having experienced a sudden religious awakening or conversion at some point in their lives. Despite the scientist's implicit belief that religion only appeals to the suggestible and uninformed, the numbers show that God, or some form of Supreme Being, is at the forefront of human consciousness for most of the people of the earth.

Assuming that religion, in its highest forms, is one of our most powerful motivators and phylogenetically advanced traits, is it not reasonable to further assume that religion stands in opposition to the expression of lower, animalistic needs and tendencies? Indeed, the history of religion is one of progressively forsaking pagan blood sacrifices, fertility rites, and tribal clannishness for self-control, elaborate and refined rituals and standards of etiquette, and professed love (agape) for the entire human family. As the course of religion progressed from the concrete, multiple gods of rivers, trees, lightning, animals, and later idols representing them, up to the abstract, philosophic entity of a God or Supreme Being, the lower needs slipped farther and farther into the background, and the Beast came under the control of the deity. In the terms of Paul the Disciple, the *flesh* was tamed by the *spirit,* and only such taming could keep the Beast at bay; the reasoning seemed to be, "Since the desires of the flesh are too powerful for the individual or secular social structures to reliably control in failsafe fashion, one must call upon the Supreme Being for strength and support." Thus, the inner psychological battle between one's own id, flesh, or the Beast, and the superego or neocortical inhibiting structures, was externalized into a more equitable battle between the Beast and God.

The PRP model places great emphasis on self-control, for by controlling our lower passions we are able to phylogenetically progress into a world of thought and mind and achieve some relief from the Darwinian fitness imperative. Moreover, the PRP model postulates that the spiritual nature of man is the most reliable "controller" of all, pitting not only the individual neocortex and cultural proscription against the Beast, but the infinite power of the deity as well. A corollary assumption is that reliable self-control, across societies, cultures, and the span of history, is impossible without the ultimate in cortical supplementation, obeisance to moral commandments of the deity. Indeed, even with such obeisance, supplemented by rules of law at the cultural level and concepts of virtue, justice, fairness, and humanity at the philosophical level, human self-control remains a fragile flower on a windblown meadow. Only within the system of eternal meanings and absolute morality of religious thought is any kind of lasting victory over the Beast conceivable, and only there for the truly pious few; compromise solutions at the levels of legal stricture, custom, or human morality, as history has amply shown, force self-control for a time, but slippage and regressions are all too common.

Campbell (1975) discussed these basic issues in his controversial Presidential Address before the American Psychological Association. The heart of his argument was that traditional religious moralizing is one of the great inhibitors of our natural selfishness and self-indulgence, and that such curbing of natural appetites is necessary for effective social functioning. Further, he chided social scientists for rejecting traditional religious teachings and substituting a hedonistic morality where selfishness and pleasure are elevated to the status of virtues:

The religions of all ancient urban civilizations (as independently developed in China, India, Mesopotamia, Egypt, Mexico, and Peru) taught that many aspects of human nature need to be curbed if optimal social coordination is to be achieved, for example, selfishness, pride, greed, dishonesty, covetousness, cowardice, lust, wrath. Psychology and psychiatry, on the other hand, not only describe man as selfishly motivated, but implicitly and explicitly teach that he ought to be so. They tend to see repression and inhibition of individual impulse as undesirable, and see all guilt as a dysfunctional neurotic blight created by cruel child rearing and a needlessly repressive society. They further recommend that we accept our biological and psychological impulses as good and seek pleasure rather than enchain ourselves with duty. (pp. 1103-1104)

Neither Campbell nor the present writer argue that repression of all pleasure or animal desire is healthy or desirable, and, indeed, the PRP model places considerable emphasis on healthy regressions and healthy access to one's inner nature (see chapter 12). However, when the focus shifts from psychological health and personal expression to self-control and its relations to cultural optimization and the most phylogenetically advanced forms of human thought, the issue of curbing of our inherently intrusive animal nature must be addressed. The question is, "In what setting does the most phylogenetically advanced forms of individual and social behavior occur—in a setting where the Beast is released from its cage and petted into submission, or one where the cage is reliably secured by 'repressive' religious moral proscriptions?" History and the chaos of our modern age seem to tell us that self-control is a tenuous thing even when supported by traditional religious morality, and without it law, custom, and lofty philosophic ideals are clearly insufficient to the task.

THE METHOD OF HIERARCHICAL ANALYSIS

The PRP model is clearly a hierarchical one, and its application implies a hierarchical analysis. It is assumed that living organisms are hierarchically organized, and further that the causes determining the behavior of organisms are hierarchically organized as well. However, the true causes determining the organism's dynamic flow of behavior cannot be fully grasped at our present level of understanding, and we must settle for causal explanations, rationales, and scenarios involving varying portions of fact, theory, and speculation. The only thing we can be certain of is that simple, cause–effect solutions are woefully inadequate to the task of explaining human behavior, most particularly human misbehavior. Although the PRP model is thought to apply to all forms of human behavior, it seems particularly applicable to that dark side of human nature left unaddressed by most of social science—the "inexplicable exceptions" of gratuitous violence, rapacity, and destructiveness that grow with the dawn of each new day.

An infinitude of possible causal rationales, hierarchical or otherwise, may be generated for a given sequence of human behavior. For the sake of simplicity, the PRP model chooses to concentrate on five hierarchical levels of analysis in attempting to explain the causes of behavior: the sociobiological, ego-psychological, cultural, philosophical, and spiritual levels. These levels are organized from most phylogenetically primitive (paleopsychology) to the most phylogenetically advanced (neopsychology), in accordance with the principles of the PRP model as outlined in earlier chapters and Appendix I. For the remainder of the book, *hierarchical analysis* refers to behavioral analysis using the five levels in accordance with the general principles of the PRP model.

Case Analysis: The "Inexplicable" Murders of Ted Bundy[2]

In an era of mass murderers, serial murderers, and torture killings, the case of Ted Bundy stands out as a macabre reminder of the depth of man's inhumanity. Our analysis of Bundy is a retrospective one, based on the intimate account of the "nice guy" turned bestial killer, *The Stranger Beside Me,* by Ann Rule (1980). Rule is a professional writer who befriended Bundy in 1971; at the time she was a "plumpish mother of four, almost forty, nearing divorce," and Ted was 24, "a brilliant, handsome senior in psychology at the University of Washington." They met as volunteer workers at Seattle's Crisis Clinic, and she felt herself immediately drawn to this "perfect man," this sensitive, empathic, caring, and gallant man who seemed to understand women so well. She was to remain faithful to Bundy to the end, although she became suspicious early in the game, and was admittedly manipulated and used by him, as were so many other women in his life. Even when the horrible facts of his inexplicable rampage of kidnappings, rapes, and mutilation-murders of beautiful young women were brought to light, Rule remained under his hypnotic power, seemingly incapable of confronting the causes of Bundy's Jekyll and Hyde transformation. Rule (1980) wrote:

> Ted has been described as the perfect son, the perfect student, the Boy Scout grown to adulthood, a genius, as handsome as a movie idol, a bright light in the Republican Party, a sensitive psychiatric social worker, a budding

---

[2]Much of the material in this section on Ted Bundy originally appeared in: Bailey, K. G. (1985). Ted Bundy: A paleopsychological analysis of a mass murderer. *New Trends in Experimental and Clinical Psychiatry, 1,* 41–62.

lawyer, a trusted friend, a young man for whom the future could hold only success.

He was all of these things, and none of them.

Ted Bundy fits no pattern at all; you could not look at his record and say: "See, it was inevitable that he would turn out like this."

In fact, it was incomprehensible. (p. 13)

Not being trained in behavioral science, Rule may be forgiven her admitted naivete and lack of objectivity, and her inability to generate causal statements as well. Unfortunately, her fatalistic resignation and puzzlement were no more than that of the plethora of mental health professionals who studied Bundy, many of whom were stricken with his charm and stood on his side prior to unequivocal determination of guilt. While Bundy was merely under suspicion, psychiatrists determined that he was "not psychotic, neurotic, the victim of organic brain disease, alcoholic, addicted to drugs, suffering from a character disorder or amnesia, and was not a sexual deviate" (p. 187). One woman psychologist, Dr. Patricia Lunneborg of the psychology department at the University of Washington, stated flatly that Bundy could not possibly be the killer, and that she intended to do everything possible to refute the "ridiculous" charges and innuendos made against him. Interestingly, once his guilt was undeniable, mental health experts immediately shifted to the conventional tack of attributing his behavior to psychiatric problems not noticed before. Although not mentally incompetent, he was now a sociopath with an "extensive history of self-defeating, unadaptable, antisocial behavior." Emphasis here was not so much on why the killings occurred in the first place, but on Bundy's current state of mind and competence to stand trial.

What, indeed, were the causes of Bundy's heinous acts? We can only surmise and speculate *ex post facto,* but Bundy's case represents an excellent one for hierarchical analysis using the PRP model. First, it is evident that "socialization" as an explanation is totally inadequate, for Bundy's personal history contains nothing remotely deviant enough to explain his actions (see Michaud & Aynesworth, 1983). Indeed, what social or environmental conditions have scientific research shown to be causes of gratuitous violence, except, perhaps, having been subjected to extreme violence oneself in childhood? Even there, being subjected to violence is a priming condition rather than a direct cause, for only a minority of abused children grow up to be gratuitously violent themselves. Certainly, hunger, poverty, abuse, frustration, exposure to violent models, living in a violent society, violence on television, the threat of atomic annihilation, and so forth, prime aggression in a probabilistic way, but the causal linkages are extremely obscure. Even if we assumed that Bundy had been subjected to all these misfortunes in great measure, we could in no way predict that he was destined to murder, sexually violate, and to mutilate scores of young women. From the standpoint of modern social science there is simply no way to explain the actions of a Ted Bundy, and perhaps this accounts for the curious silence of behavior experts on the subject of "incomprehensible" violence.

Ted Bundy's early life was not typical in every respect, but it certainly was not abnormal. Theodore Robert Cowell was born in a home for unwed mothers in Burlington, VT, on November 24, 1946. His mother was a "good girl" from a deeply religious family in Philadelphia, and his father, whom he never knew, was a graduate of Pennsylvania State University, an Air Force veteran, and a salesman. Although the Cowell family was disappointed by the illegitimate birth, the mother, Louise, was taken back into the middle-class home in Philadelphia. There a charade began where the grandparents became the "parents" and Louise assumed the role of "sister" to Ted. Ted adored his grandfather-father and apparently identified with him. However, to keep the secret intact, Louise moved to Tacoma, WA, when Ted was 4, and changed his name to Theodore Robert Nelson. Soon after, at a Methodist church function, Louise met Johnnie Culpepper Bundy, a small, mild-mannered cook, and they were married on May 19, 1951. Ted always considered himself a Cowell, however, and never really identified with the diminutive Johnnie. Yet, Johnnie accepted Ted as his son and made a strong effort to be a good father. Eventually, four half-siblings came along, two girls and two boys, but the bright and attractive Ted remained a clear number one in his mother's heart.

Ted's early childhood was not abnormal, but he did suffer doubts about his parentage, was moved about, had three different names before his fifth birthday, was pampered by his mother, was teased in school for his slenderness, and developed a rather introverted personality. He was pleasant, well-mannered, and generally liked by his peers, although he was picked up at least twice by juvenile authorities during his high school years on suspicion of auto theft and burglary. He graduated high school in 1965, and then attended the University of Puget Sound during 1965–66. The next year he transferred to the University of Washington where he began an intensive program in Chinese. While there he met Stephanie Brooks, who was to be a central figure in the deadly transformation of Ted Bundy. She was the beautiful and sophisticated daughter of a wealthy California family, and soon Ted was "in love." A year later she was to drop him because of his insecurity and aimlessness in life. Rule believes that this humiliating experience was a crucial turning point for Ted, a man who considered himself a possible descendant of royalty, a pampered child who was used to having his way. She speculates that Ted's later spate of killings represented a form of symbolic revenge against Stephanie; certainly it was noteworthy that all the victims were young, beautiful, and parted their long hair down the middle just like Stephanie. Yet, even if we grant a correlation here, "symbolic revenge" qualifies neither as a necessary nor a sufficient cause of the brutal murders; what must be explained are not Bundy's thoughts, wishes, or even his feelings but his behavior, for many a normal person has committed rape and murder in his own mind.

Certainly, Ted was highly motivated to even the score with Stephanie, but, paradoxically this led more to prosocial behavior than anything else! He became obsessed with "becoming someone" so that he could win Stephanie back, and then reject her as she had rejected him. He no longer cared about intensive Chinese, and moved, instead, into the political arena. In April of 1968, he was appointed Seattle chairman and assistant state chairman of the New Majority for Rockefeller. Conservative Republicans were charmed not only by Ted's charisma, but by his strongly traditional ideological stance on political and moral issues as well. It is clear here that Bundy's traditional, middle-class upbringing had produced a thin veneer of propriety and gallantry that made him the "perfect person" in the eyes of many. For the next few years, Ted's Horatio Alger-like metamorphosis continued, culminating in him being awarded a plum political job as assistant to Ross Davis, chairman of the Washington State Republican Party, in April 1973. He was now ready to repay Stephanie for her rejection. In late 1973, he contacted Stephanie, wooed her once again, and shortly afterward they were engaged to be married. Something was different about Ted, however; whereas his ardor was unquenchable before, he was now indifferent and hostile. Soon, the woman he had chased for 6 years was rudely cast out of his life.

The Murders.   So far we have a picture of an essentially normal young man, who is more remarkable for his positive than negative characteristics. He is handsome, intelligent, and well-liked, and has apparently overcome the burden of illegitimacy and the pain of rejection by his first love. Despite some early brushes with the law and his quest for revenge against Stephanie, there is nothing in his social background to explain or rationalize the murderous rage against women which, during the years from 1974 to 1980, led to the brutal deaths of at least 36 young women. The pathos began on November 25, 1973, with the disappearance of Kathy Devine, a teenager who was last seen hitchhiking on a street corner in Seattle's north end. On December 6th, her body was found, face down, in a forest area near Olympia, WA. Decomposition was far advanced, but the pathologist tentatively concluded she had been strangled and possibly her throat had been cut. Her jeans had been slit down the back with a sharp instrument suggesting she had been sodomized. As was typical of the cases to follow, the disappearance was sudden with no witnesses, the body was well-hidden and not discovered until long after the fact, and police investigators were left with little to go on.

The second victim was Joni Lenz, a young woman who lived in a basement room in an old house near the University of Washington. She was attacked as she slept on the night of January 4, 1974. When found she was unconscious and covered with blood, having been beaten in the head and face with a metal rod wrenched from the bed frame. When the bed covers were pulled away, the metal rod was found rammed into her vagina and into her internal organs. She had not literally been raped, but the sexual element in the attack was obvious. She appeared to be a chance victim upon whom the attacker vented a maniacal and inhuman rage incompatible with any definition of human conduct. Joni Lenz was to survive, but with residual brain damage and, no doubt, shattered views of what constitutes the human race.

Over the next 4 years the grisly pattern would repeat itself many times in Washington, Oregon, Utah, Colorado, and finally culminating in the infamous attack in the Chi Omega house on the University of Florida campus on January 14, 1978. Although the details varied from case to caes, the basic pattern was the same: Beautiful young women were sought out, then either abducted forcibly or tricked into entering Bundy's battered old Volkswagen, after which they were usually bludgeoned about the head with a crowbar or other blunt instrument, sexually brutalized, and often mutilated. The bodies often were transported a considerable distance (the front right seat of the Volkswagen was removed for easy transport of the victim) and then dumped in secluded wooded areas. For these victims, it was generally not known exactly when in the sequence they were killed, to what degree they were tortured and sexually abused before death, and the exact cause of death was not always clear. Were all the facts known, it is likely that the horrors suffered by these young women would stagger the imagination. A hint of what might have occurred emerged on March 1, 1975, when the skulls of several of the victims were found in a makeshift graveyard on Taylor Mountain, a thickly wooded mountain near North Bend, WA. It appeared that the killer had, month after month, come to the mountain to dispose of only the severed heads of his victims; why the victims were beheaded and what became of the bodies remains a mystery.

Bundy's final and most outrageous rampage came in Tallahassee, FL, on January 14, 1978. He had arrived on the Florida State University campus only a week earlier, and had obtained a room just blocks away from the Chi Omega sorority house. The Chi Omega house was the campus home for the brightest, the most beautiful, and most popular girls at the university, and security was good by college standards. On that fateful Saturday night, however, Bundy apparently gained entrance through a back door left open due to a malfunctioning lock. On his way in, he apparently picked up a large log from a woodpile outside, and it became the instrument through which he vented his rage. The first victim found was Karen Chandler, who came staggering out of her room with blood streaming down her face. Although grievously wounded, she would survive. Likewise, Kathy Kleiner would survive her severe head wounds as well. The injured girls shared the same room, which according to Rule (1980) "looked like an abattoir, with blood sprayed on the light walls. Bits of bark—oak bark—covered their pillows and bedclothing" (p. 234).

Lisa Levy and Margaret Bowman would not fare so well. Lisa appeared to have been strangled, had a large bruise on her right shoulder, and her right nipple had been bitten off. Moreover, there was a double bite on her left buttock, where her "killer had literally torn at her buttock with his teeth, leaving four distinct rows of marks where those teeth had sunk in" (Rule, 1980, p. 242). She had also been sexually assaulted with a blunt object that had been jammed into her body, tearing the rectal orifice and vaginal vault, and damaging other internal organs. This object turned out to be a Clairol hair mist bottle with a nozzle-top. Even Rule, who tried her best to rationalize Bundy's acts in her book, was shocked into disbelief: "The man who attacked Lisa Levy as she had lain asleep had struck her, strangled her, torn at her like a rabid animal, and then ravished her with the bottle. And then, apparently, he had covered her up and left her lying quietly on her side, the covers pulled up almost tenderly around her shoulders" (p. 242).

When found, Margaret Bowman lay on her face with a gaping wound on the right side of her head exposing the brain. A nylon stocking was tightly cinched around her neck, a neck that appeared half its normal size. Pieces of bark were strewn everywhere, glued to the girl's face by blood and all about the bed. Her panties lay on the floor at the end of the bed. It was evident that she had been dead for some time. In piecing the evidence together, it appeared that Bundy had, "in a grip of compulsive, maniacal fury," moved through the second floor of the Chi Omega house bludgeoning and killing his victims within a space of 15 minutes, with scores of witnesses nearby! It seemed that Bundy was completely out of control now, and he had forsaken the stealth and caution that had characterized his earlier murders.

Incredibly, "his blood lust unsatiated," he was to attack again within the space of an hour. This time, in an apartment only a fraction of a mile from the Chi Omega house, Cheryl Thomas was attacked as she slept. She suffered severe head wounds and all her clothes, except her panties, had been ripped off. Later examination revealed that her skull was fractured in five places, her jaw was broken, and her left shoulder dislocated. Also, her eighth cranial nerve was so damaged that she was not only deafened, but suffered problems in equilibrium as well. Yet, she was to survive.

In the wake of these horrors, we must ask the question Rule asks: "Rage, hate, animalistic mutilation. And why?" Indeed, why? Can anyone seriously believe that Bundy's actions were caused by some freakish event in his upbringing, or some combination of such events? Was it becàuse of his illegitimacy? His rejection by Stephanie? The frustration of never having known his father? For having been jeered by his classmates for his slenderness as a child? Because he subconsciously hated his mother? Because he resented authority? Because he was a "sexual psychopath"? Because he was an egotist who could not bear to be put down or humiliated? Because of his "fantasies," as Bundy himself thought?

The only thing clear here is that none of the aforementioned reasons even approach being either necessary or sufficient causes of Bundy's actions. It seems that we are forever frustrated in seeking human causes for inhuman actions. Ted Bundy, and those like him, represent a grievous threat to prevailing theories and models of aggression and violence, a fact apparently recognized by those hundreds of experts who write about every sort of nastiness except the worst kind. The fact that social scientists so carefully ignore the Ted Bundys of the world in their theorizing is itself an interesting phenomenon, perhaps explained in some measure by issues discussed by Bailey (1986a). It seems that social scientists wish to protect us from ourselves by discrediting theories of "innate aggression" and by explaining away extreme violence through rationalization, obfuscation, and simply turning their heads from the chaos that increasingly surrounds them. Vast increases in mass murders, serial killings, rapes, torture and mutilations, and other forms of extreme violence are among the most noteworthy social events of this century. The PRP model represents one, albeit imperfect, attempt to confront the problem.

Analysis From the PRP Model

The Sociobiological Level.   Proceeding from the notion that primitive causes are generally more powerful than advanced ones (see Appendix I), we first see how many causes of Ted Bundy's murderous behavior can be found at the sociobiological level of functioning. Our analysis revolves around two focal issues: First, Bundy's transformation from the "perfect man" to a crazed killer, and second, the motives operating at the time of the killings.

First, no man is perfect such that he has completely risen above and decoupled from the reptilian instincts and selfishness of the sociobiological level. The most normal of men, far more than women, appear to be gripped by irrational compulsions in the areas of sex and aggression (see chapter 12). This gender asymmetry becomes even more pronounced in the areas of sexual and aggressive psychopathology (see following chapters); one could reasonably assume, then, that for men regression to primitive, pathological levels of functioning increases the probability of dysfunctional release of phylogenetically old patterns of sexual and aggressive response. Also, in such regression, the sexual and aggressive components may fuse and blend in additive fashion, with catastrophic results. One cannot overlook the fact that women never demonstrate the extreme form of sexual sadism shown by Ted Bundy, where torture, body mutilation, and killing accentuate the sexual response and is accompanied by sexual orgasm. In fact, some psychoanalytic writers have speculated that women are far more likely to be sexually stimulated by sexual masochism rather than sadism (Deutsch, 1944; Fenichel, 1945; Freud, 1924/1948). Moreover, the stalk-attack-kill fixed action pattern (see chapter 11) seen in predatory animals, and in fragmented form in men in highly regressed states, is rarely if ever seen in women.

In Ted Bundy we see a perversion and caricaturization of phylogenetic maleness, with its inborn behavioral, motivational, emotional, and reward components mixed atypically and then released from their normal inhibition. Thus, Ted Bundy is not remarkable for the tendencies and predispositions carried deep within his brain, but he is indeed remarkable in that these tendencies were released in such grotesque fashion. It is not that Bundy "learned" to rip and tear at his victim like a predatory animal, but that all of the acquired social and moral inhibitions, positive social modeling, and ample reward for being a "perfect man" failed to prevent pathological release! The social sciences have found no evidence whatsoever that any environmental conditions exist, accidental or contrived, which could produce a raging killer like Ted Bundy, a killer who repeatedly risked his own life and forsook all identification with civilized society in order to satisfy his primitive cravings. What reward, other than the satisfactions accompanying the acts themselves, could have motivated such reprehensible behavior?

Some would question whether Bundy enjoyed his acts, or whether such enjoyment or satisfaction, if experienced, served as major causes of his behavior. Modern social science tells us little about such matters, but Krafft-Ebing's (1965) famous 19th-century work, *Psychopathia Sexualis,* provides many relevant insights. His in-depth case studies of rape, sexual sadism, necrophilia, body mutilation, and the like, revealed rather dramatically the pleasurable, compulsive nature of these acts. The case of Sergeant Bertrand, a sadist and necrophile, is a dramatic example. Bertrand was a "man of delicate physical constitution and peculiar character" who was "affected with destructive impulses, which he himself could not explain." At age 13, as he masturbated, he began to experience fantasies of killing women and defiling the corpses, and soon he began to mutilate the bodies of animals while masturbating. He declared that such actions produced "inexpressible pleasure." In 1847, being by accident in a graveyard, he was so overcome with passion that, despite the fact that people were nearby, he dug up a newly buried body and received satisfaction by hacking it with a shovel. A year later, he accidently came across the body of a 16-year-old girl, and, for the first time, performed coitus with the cadaver before cutting it up. He said later, "All that one could enjoy with a living woman is nothing in comparison with the pleasure I experienced" (Krafft-Ebing, 1965, p. 68). This example will suffice here, but Krafft-Ebing describes many more cases where a combination of violent and sexual motivation produced "indescribable pleasure" and "uncontrollable compulsions" far more powerful than normal sexual expression.

In theorizing about human misbehavior in general and Ted Bundy in particular, one cannot ignore the implications of Krafft-Ebing's findings. We must ask, "Where does the potential for deriving such 'indescribable pleasure' in performing such heinous acts come from?" Let us first approach the question in terms of the structural components, priming conditions, and proximal elicitors presumably operating at the sociobiological level in the case of Ted Bundy. In the prior chapters and in chapter 10 following, considerable evidence is assembled supporting the notion that the basic motivation-behavior-reward components of sex, aggression, and other species-related behavioral systems are innate and mediated by neural structures in the reptilian system and the limbic–hypothalamic complex. This "animal" part of human sexuality and aggression is rarely expressed in pure form, however, but is, in most people, shown in sublimated, disguised, elaborated, and culturally molded ways. At the deepest levels, then, people continue to possess atavistic residues of sexual and aggressive systems originally developed in the dim phylogenetic past. We cannot be sure just how many of these have been retained, nor how coherent the motivation-behavior-reward linkages continue to be. The PRP model argues that many of these primitive components continue to exist, however, in varying degrees of latency and activation in the reptilian and paleomammalian brain systems. Further, as argued in chapter 8, depending on priming and eliciting conditions, such primitive components may be released in whole or part, and in numerous combinations. Such releases may occur in adaptive sequences, targeted in terms of Darwinian fitness, or they may occur in piecemeal, nonadaptive or maladaptive abreactions. Many of Ted Bundy's epileptoid rampages would seem to be in this latter category.

Given the assumptions of the PRP model that primitive motives are more powerful than advanced ones, and that animals and humans derive pleasure in performing species-characteristic actions (see chapter 8; Appendix I), it follows that Bundy would derive pleasure from discharging primitive sexual and aggressive energy. The extremity of his compulsion is partially explained by the additive blending of the primitive sexual and aggressive components, thereby producing far greater pleasure than either taken alone (see Zillmann, 1984). All of this stands to reason; yet the more difficult question remains—"How can a civilized human being derive 'indescribable pleasure' from killing, torture, and mutilation?" Here it is necessary to postulate that which is anathema to the modern social scientist—human beings do bear the Mark of Cain in the form of residues of meat-eating and predatory behavior (see chapter 10: Bailey, 1985). The predatory biting and tearing, and possible cannibalism of the Ted Bundys of the world convict us all, and prove Raymond Dart right after all. Such socially reprehensible and self-destructive actions seem impervious to social explanations, but conform with ease to the idea of regressive release of primitive predatory motives, action patterns, and reward contingencies.

The Ego-Psychological Level.   The irresistible compulsions, the irrationality, and release of primitive predatory patterns involved in the stalking of Bundy's victims and the killings themselves seem to be best explained by massive regressions to the sociobiological level of functioning. At that level, self-awareness, free will, conscience, and humanity stood aside as autistic needs usurped all powers of the personality. Yet, little of Bundy's life was spent stalking and killing; in fact, most friends and acquaintances found him to be more charming and likeable than the average person. Certainly, he was a very adaptable person, both phylogenetically and ontogenetically. He was extremely effective at the psychological level of functioning, using his physical attractiveness and superficial charm to great personal advantage. It seemed that he specialized very early "in playing the role" of mannerly and courtly young man outwardly, while inwardly the opportunism and manipulativeness of the budding sociopath was at work. One suspects that the peculiar nature of his upbringing by a doting mother-"sister," and possibly some genetic predisposition to sociopathy from the biological father's side, helped set the stage for a person heavily fixated at the sociobiological and psychological levels of functioning. Thus, Ted Bundy learned to "act" with smoothness and propriety, but that deep identification with the human race characteristic of the phylogenetically advanced personality seemed to be absent.

Early in life Ted Bundy became an expert in maximizing his own pleasure and prerogatives at the expense of others. Yet, he was so smooth and devious and effused such "sincerity" that others, particularly women, were virtually at his mercy. He seemed to epitomize in his person the good emotions and behaviors of the psychological level—empathy, friendliness, gentleness, and concern for others. Unfortunately, his self-identity was changeable and erratic, and these good, essentially mammalian characteristics remained more instruments of manipulation than emergent realities. Thus, while wooing Stephanie, his lovemaking was "sweet and gentle," but his ardor dimmed and turned to hostility when she was no longer of use to him. Early in life an infrastructure of manipulativeness, lack of conscience, and lying was evident, and it broke clearly into the open with arrests for burglary and auto theft while in high school. Moreover, those who knew him well were aware that he could be arrogant and vengeful at times, and his obsession with avoiding humiliation belied a level of egocentrism only slightly above primitive sociobiological selfishness.

The Cultural Level. Motivationally and emotionally, actions at the sociobiological and psychological levels are little more than what one would expect from early *Homo sapiens* or perhaps even Neanderthal. These creatures, bereft of the refined self-awareness and informational content that characteristize modern man, were still able to behave in socially acceptable ways within prevailing social contexts, and at the same time maximize the fitness of their own phenotypes and those of close kin. Their social structures were functional and efficient, but were not culturally advanced in the sense of being revered and deified for their own sake. At some point in human history, certain cultural constructs sufficiently decoupled from fitness tracking and became ends in themselves, giving rise to arbitrary norms and rules of conduct. To abide by such rules was to forsake some of the "pure" selfishness of the sociobiological level and some of the disguised selfishness of the psychological level. Conformity became an end of itself, a shibboleth to be judged by.

During most of Ted Bundy's adult life, he operated very effectively at the cultural level. He was intellectually bright, and performed well in one of our culture's most sanctified institutions, the educational system. His brightness and quickness of mind made him a very valuable member of society, and this, no doubt, explains why his innocence was proclaimed by so many and his guilt denied until the bitter end. He was not only intelligent but intellectual, and others were often enthralled by his musings. He fared quite well in his forays into the American political system and, for a time, seemed destined to rise to great prominence. Again, his brightness, charm, ability to affect high culture, and professed belief in traditional values raised him to a prominent place in conservative political circles. It was at the cultural level that Ted Bundy became the "perfect man" as far as women were concered—he was polite, gallant, and attracted to humanitarian social causes. In his better moments, he was indeed a quite "cultured" man.

The Philosophical Level.   Few persons in the modern age spend much time at the philosophical level, and one doubts whether *Homo sapiens* or Neanderthal engaged in philosophical reflection at all. Functioning at this level requires, first, the derivation of abstract constructs like truth, justice, morality, being, mind, causality, freedom, deductive and inductive reasoning, and the like, and, second, persons of sufficient motivation, intelligence, and training to understand and contemplate them. Moreover, the true philosopher, as the Greek roots of the word denote, loves to think, learn, and reflect on the circumstances of his existence. To philosophize is not merely to accept the world, but to question it, to understand it; as Will Durant (1953) summarizes, "We shall define philosophy as a total perspective, as mind overspreading life and forging chaos into unity" (p. x).

There is little evidence that Ted Bundy spent much time at the philosophical level, despite possessing ample knowledge and ability. By reading between the lines, we see, perhaps, a glimmer of philosophical reflection in his prison poetry and letters to Ann Rule, which, nevertheless, appeared tainted by conscious attempts to manipulate the reader to his purposes. Even when the truth was out, Bundy remained in a survival mode fighting for his life and freedom, and never seemed to come to grips with the magnitude of his evil or the inhumanity of his acts. His actions were not to be pondered and measured against the lofty principles civilized people live by, but they were to be excused and rationalized to the advantage of Ted Bundy.

The Spiritual Level.   Bundy was raised in a religious home, but there is little evidence suggesting he ever experienced conversion or any kind of profound commitment to religion. Only while in jail, as a suspected murderer and defiler of women, did he turn to Bible reading and thoughts of God. These thoughts were always expressed to Ann Rule in writing, and not in personal conversation. Perhaps as the tragic story of his life neared its end, he may have pondered the afterlife, and thoughts of eternal damnation and possible forgiveness flashed across his mind. On the other hand, his frequent mention of God in his letters may have been one more subtle attempt at manipulation. The reader may decide for himself or herself as to whether Ted Bundy had reached a spiritual plane or not in the following poem from jail in Utah:

Sleep comes slowly
Read the words of the wholly (sic)
The scriptures bring peace

They talk of release
They bring us to God
In here that seems odd
But His gift is so clear
I find that He's near
Mercy and redemption
Without an exception
He puts me at ease
Jailer, do what you please
No harm can befall me
When the Savior does call me.
—Rule (1980, pp. 129–130)

One thing is for certain: Ted Bundy was seldom at the spiritual level during his life, and no semblance of spirituality was present as he stalked and murdered his victims. Nor for that matter was any semblance of culturality or philosophical reflection present either. At those times the sociobiological level rode supreme with some executive help from the opportunistic psychological system. Clearly, he had regressed away from the human aspects of his personality, leaving the animal side dominant.

Summary of Possible Causes

A number of possible causes of Bundy's "inexplicable" behavior has been discussed in terms of structural components, priming conditions, and proximal elicitors. Additionally, possible causes were discussed in terms of the five postulated levels of hierarchical analysis. Proceeding from the logic of the PRP model (see Appendix I), let us now summarize the matrix of postulated causes operating in Bundy's case (see Table 9.2).

The PRP model places primary emphasis on structural causes, that is, the neurohumoral and neurobehavioral phylogenetic givens of the animal or person. Material reviewed in the present book (see especially chapters 8 and 10) supports the notion that human beings are, by nature, selfish, sexual, aggressive, anxious, and pleasure-seeking creatures who behave in boorish ways when neocortical and cultural inhibitions are weak or dysfunctional. The PRP model postulates that we humans easily regress to these lower sociobiological functions when the delicate balance of excitatory and inhibitory functions of the body is disturbed in some way. Typically, such regressions are minor ones, but, depending on the matrix of factors operating, regressions may be catastrophic, as with Ted Bundy. Table 9.2 lists some of the possible structural causes contributing to Bundy's compulsive and irrational behavioral discharges. Assuming no extreme irregularities in neurohumoral functioning, Ted Bundy would share a "normal" phylogenetic maleness with other men at the structural level. It was not so much the possession of primitive drives (e.g., desire

TABLE 9.2
Summary of Possible Causes Contributing to Bundy's Behavior

Structural Level

Basic neurohumoral hardware with innate releaser-fixed action linkages
  Sex (overdeveloped sex drive?)
  Aggression (male predatory aggression; rage reactions)
  Fear
  Pleasure and pain
Mixing of primitive sexual and aggressive components
  Orgiastic pleasure in inflicting pain and harm
Schizophysiology (lower segments of triune brain gain temporary control)
Pathological release of segments of once-adaptive behaviors (regression)
Sociobiological selfishness
  Primitive self-interest and need satisfaction
  Xenophobia (hostility toward "outsiders")
  Pathological jealousy (sociobiological acquisitiveness of female?)

Priming Conditions

Problems in psychosocial development
  Illegitimate birth
  Charade of mother-"sister" and grandparents-"parents"
  Spoiled by mother-"sister"
  Ambivalence and resentment toward mother-"sister"
  Frustration because of being taken from beloved grandfather-"father"
  Resentment toward and rejection of foster father, Johnnie Bundy
  Absence of strong father figure in life
  Frequent moves in early years
  Confused self-identity and sex role development
  Teasing by peers at school
  Early problems with the law—burglary, car theft
Apparent failure to effect warm and loving "kinship" with human race
Possible genetic disposition to sociopathy on the natural father's side

(Continued)

for forceful possession of the female, selfishness, "predatory aggression," etc.) at the structural level that produced Bundy's monstrous behavior, but rather the fact that these drives were released from their normal inhibition.

Structural causes are interesting theoretically, but priming causes are perhaps of most practical interest. Structural causes lay the groundwork of behavioral potentialities, but priming causes often determine whether such potentialities actually find their way into overt behavior. Theoretically, given the sociobiological imperative to reproduce at all cost, men are all rapists in the deep recesses of their reptilian and mammalian brains, but, fortunately, few men actually rape and even fewer wantonly inflict physical injury on their victims. Thus, the existence of inherent

TABLE 9.2 *(Continued)*

Strong need to control others, especially women
Strong need to succeed, "be someone"
Obsession with avoiding humiliation
Rejection by Stephanie Brooks
Fantasies of revenge toward Stephanie
Use of alcohol and marijuana
Self-admitted "fantasies," implicitly of a gruesome nature
Positive internal stimulus feedback from the actual killings
    Positive feedback loops leading to progressively more violent murders

Proximal Elicitors for Actual Killing

Perceptual stimuli associated with stalk-attack-kill-mutilate sequence
    Nighttime—Bundy was a "night person"
    The excitement associated with the "hunt"
    Ongoing cognitions—planning, adjusting to contingencies, fantasies
    Feelings of frustration, hatred, sexual desire
Immediate effects of alcohol and/or marijuana
Similarities of victims to Stephanie Brooks
Positive feedback loops associated with actual killings
    Pleasurable experience
    Feedback from own behavior
    Feedback from victim's behavior

Note: The above table is based on material from Rule (1980). Note that the Structural Level of Table 9.2 is very similar to the Sociobiological Level in Table 9.1. This follows in that there is maximal structure-function overlap at phylogenetically primitive levels, and minimal analogous overlap at advanced levels. Also note that some causal contributors are included under more than one heading (e.g., alcohol is listed under both Primers and Elicitors). This follows in that primers and elicitors are not hard-and-fast categories, but are differentiated by their respective effects—a given stimulus condition is a primer when it merely increases response probability short of response discharge, while the same condition is an elicitor when it directly contributes—usually along with other elicitors operating concurrently—to response discharge.

potentialities to rape or to derive satisfaction from inflicting injury may not be as crucial as the priming conditions which additively wear away at the inhibitory apparatus. Once the inhibitory functions are sufficiently eroded, minimal eliciting stimuli are required for regressive outbreak of culturally dysfunctional behavior. Table 9.2 lists a large number of priming conditions that appeared to contribute to Ted Bundy's readiness to discharge vast reserves of sexual and aggressive energy with minimal external provocation. This long list, however, should not blind us to the fact that all of the primers in the world would not have caused his murderous behavior without the potentialities to rape, murder, and maim stored at the structural level of functioning.

    Proximal elicitors only came into effect when Bundy was actually in the field of behavior where certain sights, smells, tactile stimuli, and so forth, could impact his senses. Far more important were the internal motives that compelled him, perhaps from the poverty of external stimuli in his lonely room, to plan his next attack, assemble his deadly tools, remove the front right seat from the light brown Volkswagen, and then proceed out into the night in search of victims. Perhaps the sight of an attractive woman on television, the fantasy of a past attack, a pornographic picture, an item of female clothing, or some other proximal stimulus served to set off the sequence, but these events hardly qualify as differential causes of his behavior. These stimuli were trivial in and of themselves; they only achieved causal significance in being perceived by Ted Bundy, a man already highly primed for extreme violence.

In Ted Bundy's case, proximal stimuli appeared to achieve major causal importance once the stalk-rape-kill-mutilate sequence was set into effect by inner compulsion. Once the hunt began, external stimuli no doubt exerted guiding and arousing effects, and certainly stimulus conditions operated in terms of powerful, positive, closed feedback loops as he actually attacked his victims. His rampage through the Chi Omega house was that of a man completely out of control, that of a man completely controlled by inner compulsions, on the one hand, and overpowering feedback from his own behavior and that of the victim on the other. At the height of his frenzy, the only limit on his violence was a physical incapability to destroy or defile any further. At that point, he was at behavioral asymtote and all three levels of causes were at asymtote as well. Within the limits of his physical and behavioral phenotypes, acted upon to the highest degree by priming and eliciting conditions, he had phylogenetically regressed as low as a human being can possibly go. To refer to his behavior in those moments as in any way human is to unjustly discredit the human race.

In Ted Bundy, we see the failure of the higher cultural, philosophical, and spiritual levels to inhibit and block the discharge of phylogenetically primitive behavior. The higher levels may be held guilty only in the negative sense; they did not cause Bundy to kill, but failed to keep him from killing. For the heinous acts of a Ted Bundy, it is fruitless to search for primary causes in the form of upbringing, enculturalization, or socialization; these factors unquestionably contributed to his actions but not definitively so. Far more important was the breakthrough of noncultural and asocial behavior "learned" phylogenetically rather than ontogenetically.

Although the PRP model has provided a systematic and hopefully cogent analysis of the causes of Ted Bundy's actions, it has not answered the ultimate question of why he killed and maimed in the first place, and why multitudes of young men with backgrounds similar to his treat women with gentleness and respect. The answer to this question is beyond the scope of any existing theory or model, and we must continue to grope for answers in the netherworld of speculation. Whatever the answer proves to be, it is likely to reflect some accidental and improbable matrix of structural, priming, and eliciting causes that side with the powerful forces of regression against the counterforces of culture and humanity.

Postscript on Ted Bundy.   Of the many popular books about Ted Bundy, Michaud and Aynesworth's (1983), *The Only Living Witness,* is perhaps the most recent and objective account. Yet, after months of interviewing Bundy at the Florida State Prison, where he remains in what is perhaps the longest Death Row in the United States, Michaud and Aynesworth joined that large group of writers and psychiatric experts distinguished by their inability to understand or explain Bundy's actions. As Michaud and Aynesworth point out, all post-conviction theorizing has emphasized some sort of derangement or insanity, which, for the most part, was circularly derived from the heinousness and magnitude of the crimes. And despite their critical approach and hours of candid interviews with Bundy, Michaud and Aynesworth themselves could come up with little more than platitudes and metaphors: e.g., "arrested development," "immaturity," a "hunchback" within, an "entity" within, a "bright, dedicated killer," a "likeable, lovable homocidal mutant." Their frustrated and fruitless search for credible causes is summed up in their final chapter:

> It would be reassuring to say with finality what caused Ted to kill, to establish a link the way cigarette smoking has been connected to lung cancer. But his case resists categorization. There is no evidence of overt boyhood trauma, of physical abuse from women, of injuries beyond what any normal child is apt to sustain. (p. 322)

We must ask here whether the Bundy riddle can ever be solved without some theory of phylogenetic regression, without some theory of pathological release of phylogenetic maleness that takes into account evolved sex differences in the structures, primers, and elicitors which govern behavior. The hierarchical analysis performed previously represents one such approach, and it is hoped that our analysis will stimulate other writers and researchers to address the ever-increasing problem of pathological and "senseless" aggression and violence.

SUMMARY

We have now completed our explication of the principles and postulates of the phylogenetic regression–progression model. In so doing, we have discussed trends in the New Biology and brain science (chapter 2), defined phylogenetic regression and discussed the regression–progression continuum (chapters 3 and 4), described some of the correlates and elicitors of phylogenetic regression (chapters 5, 6, and 7), discussed motivation and learning from the perspective of the PRP model (chapter 8), and, lastly, we have theorized about the causes of behavior and performed a retrospective analysis of the causes of Ted Bundy's animalistic acts. In one sense, we have explicated the principles of the PRP model, and in a broader one we have hopefully set forth the rudimentary principles of a human paleopsychology or the science of phylogenetically primitive social behavior.

In the final three chapters, our focus is on the paleopsychological analysis of human aggression and psychopathology. Due to the prevailing philosophical and ideological positions of modern social science (see Bailey, 1986a), the dark side of human nature has been for the most part ignored, rationalized, or explained away. The PRP model draws material from diverse sources in an attempt to deal with the puzzling variability in behavior both within and between individuals. Ted Bundy dramatically illustrates how the most refined cultural behavior and the bloodlust of the primitive predator exist, in schizophysiological neurohumoral disharmony, in modern *Homo sapiens*. A fundamental premise of the PRP model is that any comprehensive theory of human behavior must necessarily confront the full range of causal influences—both "animal" and "human"—and not be limited to either pole of the primitive–advanced continuum. This is crucial in the areas of aggression and psychopathology, where phylogenetically old tendencies and predispositions play such fundamental causal roles.

10

The Mark of Cain:
Old Aggression in a New Age

QUOTES OF OUR TIME

Shortly before 4 p.m. last Wednesday, in 96 degree heat, James Huberty left his house after casually announcing to his wife, "I'm going to hunt humans."
—Leo, J., & Griggs, L., 1984, p. 90).

Two white men who admitted murdering a deaf black man because they found no game to kill on a drunken hunting expedition were sentenced to the maximum 25 years to life in prison yesterday.
—(Two Men, 1980, p. 6).

A 9-year-old boy who refused to share his bicycle was stabbed and beaten to death and three playmates have been arrested in what a prosecutor calls 'one of the most vicious' killings he's ever seen.
—("Children Kill," 1985, p. 1).

Subway gunman Bernhard Goetz said in an interview yesterday that before shooting four teenagers he felt like a mouse trapped by a cat, 'You know, a cat plays with a mouse before he kills it.'
—("Felt Like," 1985, p. 1).

The case of the Green River Killer is part of a grim parade of so-called serial murders . . . in more than 30 cases during the past decade, a lone murderer has killed at least half a dozen people, usually strangers.
—("River of Blood," 1984, p. 26).

Drifters Henry Lee Lucas, 47, and Ottis Elwood Toole, 36, were drawn together by more than mere loneliness or poverty . . . they roamed from

coast to coast on a seven-year spree of rape, mutilation, and murder that is unequalled in American police records. The two convicts have allegedly confessed to committing, separately and together, hundreds of murders.
—(Stanley, A., 1983, p. 47).

People are more likely to be hit, beat up, physically injured, or even killed in their own homes by another family member than anywhere else, and by anyone else, in our society. . . .
    Each year in the United States, at least six million men, women, and children are victims of severe physical attacks at the hands of their spouse or parents . . . Each year 2,000 children are killed by their caretakers.
—(Gelles, 1979, p. 1).

Detroit began cleaning up yesterday from a wave of violence that left one man dead, more than 80 injured and 34 jailed following a riot that erupted after the Tigers clinched their first World Series Title in 16 years.
—("More Than," 1984, p. 4).

Looting and vandalism erupted in downtown Philadelphia yesterday as crowds of young people left theaters showing martial arts films. At least 18 people were arrested . . . 5,000 people were in a three-block area during the hourlong disturbance.
—("Violence Erupts," 1985, p. 10).

Brussels, Belgium—At least 40 people were killed and more than 260 others were injured during a riot last night between fans of the British and Italian soccer teams about to play the Cup of Champions final.
—("Forty Die," 1985, p. 1).

Tunisia has long seemed a gracious outpost of moderation and stability in the developing world. . . . But when word came that the government was raising the price of bread by over 100%, the facade of stability cracked. Riots erupted last week . . . mobs composed mainly of teenagers and young men in their 20s rampaged through city streets, smashing shop windows and attacking post offices and banks.
—("Bourgiba Lets Them," 1984, p. 44).

BACKGROUND ISSUES

One often hears that human beings are the most violent creatures on earth, yet the very same creature that rapes, pillages, tortures, maims, wages war, and invents ever more deadly instruments of destruction is responsible for the breathtaking artistic and technological achievements of our age. On the one hand, human history has been dominated by the irascible, brutish ape that resides in each of us; that selfish, xenophobic, and aggressive component of human nature that seems to make territorial conflict and war inevitable. Yet, on the other hand, the human race is without peer in terms of love, compassion, yearning for peace, artistic sensibility, and thirst for knowledge. These seemingly irreconcilable facts force us to an obvious and inescapable conclusion: Each of us is neither the bloodthirsty killer ape of Raymond Dart or Robert Ardrey, nor simply the passive, peace-loving noble savage of Rousseau. We are, rather, both of these rolled into one mass of confused and contradictory feelings and dispositions.

In the problem of aggression, we see an excellent example of Paul MacLean's (1954a) concept of schizophysiology, where phylogenetically old and new parts of the brain coexist in perpetual disharmony and antagonism. The neocortically mediated social and religious values of most modern societies cry out for peaceful solutions to conflict and an end to senseless violence, but these cries often go unheard as the limbic and reptilian systems continue to rule over reason and good sense. Without involvement of the older and lower cognitive systems, there would be no true aggression, for aggression is neither an emotionless abstraction nor is it defined merely by its consequences as many psychologists imply. The true essence of aggression lies in its motive force, the substructures for which are, in large part, phylogenetically continuous with lower species and thoroughly wired-into the adaptive hardware of the organism. The higher cortical functions of intelligence, reflection, choice, language, imagination, and so forth, do not produce aggression, but rather serve to prime it, elicit it, inhibit it, elaborate it, and otherwise color its many manifestations.

Human aggression is, no doubt, species–specific as Holloway (1968b, 1974) correctly asserts, but not because it is something truly different or transcendent: Its distinctiveness more likely emanates from the capacity of the human intellect—through rationalization, obfuscation, and denial—to take the primal clay of aggression and shape it into some arbitrary creation of culture. So shaped, aggression may be viewed as anything from the pathological exception seen only in the deranged to the most exalted trait of the warrior. Underlying the neocortically transformed surface manifestations, however, are the older motivational–emotional realities of aggression without which the plagues of mankind—individual and collective violence—could not occur. Without the omnipresent readiness to engage in aggressive and hostile acts, the greatest problem of our age would be solved easily. As it is, we social scientists suffer one humiliation after another in our war against aggression and violence; it seems that the more we study the problem and defend human nature against the charge of "innate aggression," the more our romantic notions go up in the flames of crime, terrorism, and organized warfare. Perhaps it is time to acknowledge the phylogenetic Mark of Cain, and then proceed to erect new theories and seek new solutions from there.

The Reality of Cruelty and Destructiveness

That human aggression and violence are widespread is self-evident. In chapter 9, we analyzed a single case of extreme aggression in detail; let us now examine the frightful scope of the problem. A good starting place is Freeman's (1964) well-known essay, "Human Aggression in Anthropological Perspective." Drawing from Lewis Richardson's (1960) *Statistics of Deadly Quarrels,* Freeman tells us that approximately 59 million human beings were killed between 1820 and 1945 in wars, murderous attacks, and deadly quarrels. Freeman goes on to quote from T. A. Walker's, *A History of the Law of Nations:*

> When Basil II (1014) could blind fifteen thousand Bulgarians, leaving an eye to the leader of every hundred, it ceases to be a matter of surprise that Saracen marauders should thirty years later be impaled by Byzantine officials, that the Greeks of Adramyttium in the time of Malek Shah (1106–16) should drown Turkish children in boiling water, that the Emperor Nicephorous (961) should cast from catapults into a Cretan city the heads of Saracens slain in the attempt to raise the seige, or that a crusading Prince of Antioch (1097) should cook human bodies on spits to earn for his men the terrifying reputation of cannibalism. (in Freeman, 1964, p. 111)

Fromm (1973) refers to the "ample" and "horrifying" historical documentation that exists throughout civilized history for seemingly spontaneous and ruthless acts of killing and destructiveness. He says that, "Many of these occurrences give the impression of orgies of destruction, in which neither the conventional nor genuinely moral factors had any inhibitory effect" (p. 271). Indeed, as Fromm tells us, we humans have engaged in virtually every destructive act accessible to the human imagination, including various forms of torture, mutilation, disembodiment, crucifixion, human sacrifice, and so forth. Throughout history, mere killing has been one of the milder forms of destructiveness, when compared to the extremes of human cruelty seen in the death camps at Auschwitz and Ravensbrück or the catalog of atrocities outlined by Solzhenitsyn in the *Gulag Archipelago.* Many more instances of extreme human cruelty could be listed, but as Langer (1978) comments, to do so makes for dreary reading. Aside from the sheer magnitude of human cruelty, the fact that such wanton destructiveness exists at all is of major importance theoretically. Indeed, extreme cruelty and destructiveness in humans cannot be realistically deduced, *a priori,* from any of the socialization models, and only a few of the biopsychological models address the problem directly.

In the past, it was customary to hold romantic notions about the absence of true cruelty and destructiveness in animals, and to presumptively attribute these twin evils, instead, to the human species. The biologist Adolph Portmann (1943) expresses this view nicely:

when terrible things, cruelties hardly conceivable, occur among men, many speak thoughtlessly of brutality, of bestialism, or a return to animal levels . . . As if there were animals which inflict on their own kind what men do to men. Just at this point the biologist has to draw a clear line: these evil, horrible things are no animal survival that happened to be carried along in the imperceptible transition from animal to man; this evil belongs entirely on this side of the dividing line. (p. 63)

Recent studies in field primatology (Fossey, 1981, 1984; Goodall, 1979; Hausfater & Hrdy, 1984; Hrdy, 1977, 1979; Itani, 1984; Trudeau, Bergmann-Riss, & Hamburg, 1981) place Portmann's assumption of animal innocence in question, for considerable evidence of cruelty in the form of infanticide, cannibalism, and "warfare" has been found in monkeys and apes. It thus appears that the darker side of human nature is shared with our primate cousins, and is therefore phylogenetically continuous to some degree. In fact, among the higher primates (e.g., Old World Monkeys and apes) the higher the species phylogenetically, the more frequent and varied the intraspecific killing (Itani, 1984). So, rather than evolving out or being attenuated in the phylogenetic progression from ape to man, killing patterns in primates, like many other forms of social behavior, have become more complex and varied across situations. If we assume a more or less constant, innate killing potential in baboons, chimpanzees, and humans, then the baboon → chimpanzee → human phylogenetic "progression" from less to more killing could be parsimoniously explained by the elaborationist hypothesis (see chapters 8 and 9). That is, the primitive motive forces to kill and their associated behavior patterns may be homologous up through monkeys, apes, and humans, whereas the greater actual killing at higher levels is a product of greater intelligence and response elaboration within and across situations. Implied here is the notion that similarly evolved motivation–action structures (e.g., the killing potential) may be expressed quite differently as they are inhibited, filtered through, and elaborated through the level of brain function in the particular species phenotype.

In extreme cruelty and destructiveness we see a particularly wanton, brutal, and uncivilized type of aggression where the aggressor seemingly derives *pleasure* from inflicting pain or injury on others. Following Washburn and Hamburg (1972) and, less directly, Herrnstein (1977a, 1977b), a rationale for explaining pleasure in torture and killing was developed in chapter 5 (see also Bailey, 1985). At one level, atavistic elements, perhaps radiating mainly from reptilian/predatory roots phylogenetically, appear to provide much of the motive force for inhuman, irrational, and cold-blooded acts of violence that surround us each day. That pleasure is provided in destructiveness is crucial theoretically, yet social scientists have avoided this issue. Some writers in the humanities have, however, courageously addressed the problem, albeit in rather abstract, metaphorical terms. An excellent source here is Langer's (1978), *The Age of Atrocity: Death in Modern Literature*. In wrestling with the question of why one human being inflicts pain and suffering on another, Langer offers this eloquent apology: "I might venture the suggestion that as other resources for heroic transcendence fail, torture becomes the torturer's way of transcending his mortality by creating the illusion that the power to inflict pain on others somehow exonerates one from suffering the same fate" (p. 47). Perhaps there is a grain of truth in the strained assumption that torturing another person is a means of self-affirmation and transcending the fear of death, but these "advanced" causal attributions pale before the primitive causes that immanate from our inherent and pleasurable destructive urges, our racialism, our universal xenophobia.

The Problem of Senseless and Extreme Violence

Senseless, irrational, and extreme forms of violence pose severe problems for most existing theories of aggression and violence. If aggression is a set of learned, operant responses, or an arbitrary set of behaviors forced on the individual by a sick society, or a healthy adaptive social response (Ward, 1973), or a means of self-defense as Fromm (1973) argues, then there should be no sadistic murders, no torture, no terrorist bombings of innocent people, and no malicious vandalism. Bluntly stated, if the prevailing sociocultural theories of the genesis of aggression are true, then there would simply be no extreme cruelty or destructiveness! It requires artful mental gymnastics to blame society when a vicious rape or bludgeoning occurs, yet that has been the predominant approach of American social scientists for the past several decades. Given the unprecedented rise in both the frequency and brutality of crimes of violence during the tenure of the so-called environmentalistic theories of aggression, we must again confront the dilemma of whether to stick with accepted thinking or venture out into new, uncharted waters. Whatever approach we take, the lingering questions about the motivational whys of extreme cruelty and destructiveness must be confronted.

Phylogenetic regression theory assumes that extreme cruelty and destructiveness can only be fully understood when their primitive, regressive nature is taken into account. This does not imply that only atavistic causes are involved, but rather that they are the fundamental components in the complex matrix of proximal and ultimate causes producing the violent behavior. As we recall from earlier chapters, primitive response systems are: (a) often universal in the species, at least under extreme levels of stress or provocation; (b) closely tied to the body in the sense of neuromuscular, neurophysiological, and neurohumoral functioning; (c) generally elicited under high levels of primed motivation and emotion; (d) often accompanied by pleasurable experience; (e) composed of phylogenetically conditioned elicitor-response pattern linkages; and (f) often composed of extreme, all-or-none actions with short reaction times. We also recall that exaggerated gender asymmetry often is seen in regressed states, and nowhere is distinctive phylogenetic maleness seen more clearly than in the extremes of cruelty and violence. In fact, at the height of excitement of a particularly cruel attack of the stronger male on a weaker female or juvenile (e.g., see chapter 9 on Ted Bundy), we see phylogenetic regression perhaps in its purest form.

Examples of Extreme Regression.   A few illustrations of senseless violence are provided here to demonstrate how difficult it is to explain (or explain away) the more grievous instances of violence that assault us from the newspapers each day. Take, for example, the case of Lorne J. Acquin, a Canadian Indian, who was convicted of committing the worst mass murder in the history of the state of Connecticut by killing his foster brother's family ("Foster Brother," 1977). Dead were Cheryl Beaudoin, her children Frederick Allen, 11, Sharon Lee, 10, Debra Ann, 9, Paul Albert, 8, Roderick, 6, Holly Lyn, 5, Mary Lou, 4, and visiting Jennifer Santoro, 6. Family survivors were at a loss to explain the "why" of the killings. One survivor commented, "We loved him (Acquin) . . . he was a part of our family." Said another family member, "We can't believe he did it, because he was not a violent person and he loved those children." We can only imagine what compelling force drove Acquin to stab and beat his victims with such fury, victims whom, by every evidence, he dearly loved. Whatever the force, it was greater than love, greater than reason and logic, and greater than the will to live on Acquin's part. Here we have a heinous, brutal crime, that carries with it the total annihilation of innocent victims and the likely annihilation of the attacker himself. Yet, there was nothing to be gained and everything to lose for all concerned. Aside from the release of bestial compulsions over which the killer had little or no control, what other causes can we invoke to explain an atrocity of this magnitude?

Another example difficult to explain with conventional models is the case of the torture killing of a 17-year-old traffic offender by his teenage cellmates ("Cellmates," 1982). Christopher Peterman died of brain damage following an estimated 4½-hour period of torture and beating by five youths who were being held for non-violent crimes. Among other things, the youths allegedly burned toilet paper between the victim's toes. This attack would seem senseless and gratuitously malicious by anyone's standards, yet it is noteworthy that the attackers lacked a chronic history of violence against persons. One gets the impression that, once an attack begins, and the attacker has complete power over the victim and the inhibiting effects of counterattack are absent, the process is difficult to stop until it reaches its bloody conclusion. Again, especially in the absence of a prior history of violence, a release of pre-existing, pent-up aggression seeking expression appears more plausible than conventional learning or socialization explanations. Certainly acting as a group was an influential priming factor (see chapter 7), and perhaps none of the five boys would have tortured and killed alone, but this begs the question: We are still left with the question of what primal motives were released or augmented by the collective psychology of the situation.

The problem of extreme overreaction and inability to restrain the kill-and-destroy sequence once it begins sometimes produces tragic results in the law enforcement area. In chapter 7, we mentioned two highly sensational instances of extreme police overreaction to illustrate the effects of group regression, one in which nine Chicago policemen (see Bailey, 1978) were accused of murdering a 19-year-old youth by dragging him from his car and beating him to death. According to an eyewitness interviewed on national television, "They began hitting him while he screamed. . . . They pushed and tore at each other to get at the boy. . . . Once they got the taste of blood they were like wild animals tearing apart game. . . . Finally, they bashed his head in and killed him." In a more recent yet remarkably similar instance, five white Miami policemen were charged with the beating death of black insurance executive Charles McDuffie (see Porter & Dunn, 1984, for detailed account). Significantly, a policeman who witnessed the event used almost identical language to that of the witness in the previous example: The officers who surrounded McDuffie "looked like a bunch of animals fighting for meat."

It is important to note that dangerous high speed chases preceded both of the attacks described, and the officers were, consequently, in an extreme state of excitement prior to stopping the victims' vehicles. One suspects that the survival threat involved in the dangerous chases augmented the regressive behavior of the officers in at least two ways: first, by acting as a primer (or elicitor) of regression, and, second, by producing extreme hostility toward the violator for putting the officers and other people on the highway in danger in the first place. This suggests that an extreme state of excitement may contribute to, and possibly serve as an augmenter for, violent and destructive attacks. As a sometimes trainer of state police personnel in crisis management, this writer is well aware of the dangers posed by post-chase excitement. Experienced officers are careful to warn trainees of the hazards, and to urge them to think "self-control" before encountering the violator.

Among other theoretically significant instances of extreme violence are "rampage" and "berserk" killings, such as that of the drunken South Korean policeman who, after an altercation with his wife, went on an 8-hour grenade and shooting rampage in which 72 persons were killed and 35 others wounded ("Policeman," 1982). In the rampage reaction, we see a temporary but total loss of neocortical inhibition where the innate killing and destructive potential is released unchecked. Paradoxically, the dyscontrolled reaction is sometimes seen in the outwardly overcontrolled, quiet, conforming, "nice guy" who is described in glowing terms by family and friends (e.g., Ted Bundy, Lorne J. Acquin). Others may be described as seclusive, odd, and lacking in friends, but a history of criminal violence or trouble with the law is atypical. Many examples could be cited here, but few could top the infamous "Mass Murder at McDonald's" the summer of 1984. According to *Time* magazine (Leo & Griggs, 1984), a "frustrated misfit" named James Huberty, 41, strolled into a McDonald's restaurant near San Diego and calmly proceeded to fire hundreds of rounds into scores of helpless victims. When the shooting stopped, 21 persons were dead and 15 others wounded. Men, women, and children were victimized indiscriminately, and the gunfire was so rapid and continuous that policemen thought more than one gunman was inside. As with Ted Bundy, the attributed causes fail to mesh with the magnitude of the crime (e.g., divorce of parents, erratic job history, or failure to receive an appointment at a mental health clinic the day before the attack). Certainly, his social alienation and "sour personality" were priming factors, and no doubt the 96 degree temperature on that fateful Wednesday was part of the causal matrix, but we are left in puzzlement over the true causes of the incident.

Perhaps more puzzling than dyscontrolled rampages, however, is the phenomenon of thrill killings, epitomized in the ritual torture-killings of Sharon Tate and four of her friends by Charles Manson and his followers. According to Nash (1975), the leader of the killer band, Charles "Tex" Watson, used a pistol to shoot most of his victims, screaming, "I am the devil and I have come to do the devil's work" (p. 239). Once the victims were slain, their blood was used by the cultists to write demented slogans throughout the house. The killing spree was repeated only hours later when the same group invaded the home of Leno and Rosemary LaBianca, killed them, and again scrawled bloody messages on the walls. Whereas Manson and his followers came from the dregs of society, Italy was shocked in the mid-1970s by a series of "senseless" and "sadistic" crimes by the offspring of the new rich (" 'Thrill' Killings," 1976). These crimes appeared to be of the thrill variety and featured murder, torture, and gang rape. One case involved three male members of Rome's fast set who lured two girls to a seaside villa where they tortured and sexually abused them for 48 hours. One girl, age 17, was finally drowned in a bathtub, and the other, age 19, was left for dead after being beaten in the head with a tire iron. Italian sociologists and theologians labored to explain the wave of violence, but were placed at a grievous disadvantage by the senseless nature of the crimes and the privileged status of the attackers. It is doubtful that anyone was truly relieved by attributing the blame on "right wing politics," "new-facism," "the corrupted morals of Italy's consumer society," "rapid economic gains," or "the crumbling of middle class values" (" 'Thrill' Killings," 1976). Are we perhaps seeing here a type of malicious vandalism, a gratuitous, senseless destructiveness directed toward human bodies rather than inanimate objects? Phylogenetic regression theory does, in fact, place senseless killing and malicious vandalism in the same basic category—an atavistic recovery of propensities toward predatory destructiveness that goes far back into the phylogenetic history of our species (see Rosenzweig, 1981, for a similar formulation).

The Special Case of Vandalism.   Because vandalism is one of the most senseless forms of destructiveness, it should be discussed briefly at this point. *Vandalism* derives its name from the Vandals, a barbarous East German tribe of marauders who invaded Western Europe in the fourth and fifth centuries and eventually sacked Rome in 455. They are traditionally regarded as the great destroyers of Roman art, civilization, and literature, and their actions are considered synonymous with barbaric ignorance, tastelessness, and lack of sensibility. At some undefined point in time, vandalism came to mean willful, reckless, and usually malicious destruction of any and all types of property, and not just destructiveness toward *objects d'art.* Sociologists (Cohen, 1973) tell us that there are many different types of vandalism, each presumably having its own eliciting circumstances and underlying motivational structures. Cohen (1973), for example, lists five types: acquisitive, tactical, vindictive, play, and malicious. The first four types are thought to have special "meanings" for the vandal and fairly reasonable and credible motives can be identified: acquiring property, advancing a political cause, seeking revenge, and destructiveness in the context of "play" activities. However, with the fifth type, malicious vandalism, Cohen's attempts to sociologically rationalize the problem break down. Whereas the "fun" aspects of "play"vandalism are difficult to rationalize, the malicious type defies rationalization altogether. Cohen concedes that malicious vandalism "often carries the implication of not just hatred but of action *enjoyed for its own sake* and even action that is found amusing" (p. 48; italics added). Cohen goes on to say that a combination of hostility and fun are present in many cases of malicious vandalism. Then, as the reader virtually begs for an explanation of why this is so, Cohen retreats into the safe cover of lofty socializations like "boredom," "despair," "exasperation," "resentment," "failure," "frustration," and abstract metaphors like "breaking out" or "breaking clear." In addressing the crucial question of "why," Cohen makes his final retreat by squarely placing vandalism, especially the malicious type, into the netherworld of irresolvable complexity and abstraction: "So any answer to the question of 'Why do they do it?' can only be expressed at the most abstract level and cannot really do justice to the wide range of behavior that the term vandalism covers" (p. 51).

Cohen's sociological apologetics for malicious vandalism illustrates the predominant role of the social sciences in the gratuitous and senseless types of violence and destructiveness—that is, in *ex post facto* fashion, to explain away the causes of such behavior by blaming society or otherwise externalizing the problem. The most obvious questions remain unanswered, however: "Why does senseless destructiveness often give every evidence of being extremely pleasurable?"; "Why is a violent attack (against persons or objects) so difficult to stop once it is started?", and most important of all, "Why is extreme destructiveness seen almost entirely in males but not females?"

Philip Zimbardo's (1973) classic field experiments on "autoshaping" (vandalism on "abandoned" cars) place these questions in bold relief. His procedure was to take an old, dilapidated car, place it in strategic parts of the city, and then tabulate the frequency of spontaneous acts of vandalism directed toward it. For maximum effect, the car was provided with "releaser" cues to call attention to itself, such as no license plates, hood or trunk open, or a tire removed. For the car left in the Bronx, the results were startling—within 10 minutes the 1959 Oldsmobile received its first strippers, a father, mother, and 8-year-old son. Within 7 minutes this family had searched the car for valuables and had removed the battery and radiator. By the end of 26 hours, a steady parade of vandals had removed every detachable part of any value, and then, a few hours later, random destruction began in the form of window-breaking and other kinds of noninstrumental destructiveness. In less than 3 days, the car suffered 23 incidents of destructive contact and was, by then, reduced to a useless, battered hulk.

By contrast, a car similarly abandoned on the Stanford University campus remained over a week without incident. As Zimbardo reflected, it was obvious that releaser cues adequate in New York were inadequate at Stanford. Proceeding on the assumption that vandalism needs to be primed in some settings, Zimbardo and his male graduate students took a sledge hammer to the car themselves and waited for others to follow. Their wait was brief:

> First of all, there is considerable reluctance to take the first blow, to smash through the windshield and initiate the destruction of a form. But it feels so

good after the first whack, that the next one comes more easily, with more force, and feels even better. Although everyone knew the sequence was being filmed, the students got 'carried away' temporarily. Once one person had begun to wield the sledge hammer it was difficult to get him to stop and pass it on to the next eager pair of hands. Finally, they all attacked simultaneously. One student jumped on the roof and began stomping it in, two were pulling the door from its hinges, another hammered away at the hood and motor, while the last one broke all the glass he could find. They later reported that feeling the metal or glass give way under the force of their blows was stimulating and pleasurable. (Zimbardo, 1973, pp. 88–89)

Contrary to many writers, Zimbardo does not attempt to excuse vandalism, and he, perhaps echoing the concerns of the general populace, sees gratuitous destructiveness as a breaking down of the rules of social order that underlie civilization and communal life. Indeed, it is difficult to excuse brutal attacks on persons or property when the primary motivation for such acts is found in the pleasure derived from committing the acts themselves. Zimbardo (1973) was ever so close to the truth when he reflected, "It is pleasurable to behave at a purely sensual, physical, unthinking level—regardless of whether the act is making love or making war" (p. 90).

Definitional Issues

The kinds of human aggression discussed so far have been extreme, atypical, and often pathological. Many other kinds exist, however; so many in fact that the number of definitions is overwhelming, and many writers question whether aggression can be viewed as a unitary phenomenon (Moyer, 1976; Valzelli, 1981). Among the numerous attempts at definition are those by the learning-oriented psychologists (Bandura, 1973; Berkowitz, 1962; Buss, 1961; Cahoon, 1972; Dollard, Doob, Miller, Mowrer, & Sears, 1939), cultural anthropologists (Montagu, 1968, 1976), philosophers (Midgley, 1980; Shaffer, 1971), psychiatrists and psychoanalysts (Daniels, Gilula, & Ochberg, 1970; Fawcett, 1971; Frank, 1967; Fromm, 1973), historians, criminologists, and political scientists (Goldstein, 1975; Grundy & Weinstein, 1974; Hirschi & Gottfredson, 1980; Hofstadter & Wallace, 1971; Jeffrey, 1979; Rose, 1969), and a host of writers in the biological sciences. A good general definition that basically agrees with the thrust of the present chapter is given by Kahn and Kirk (1968): "*Aggressive drive is an inborn, biologically rooted, directionally oriented energizer of behavior that is elicited by frustration of other drives and needs necessary to the survival of the species and the individual organism. Aggressive drive functions to serve, support, and insure success of these other drives and needs by assertive means up to destructive force.*" (p. 569).

The phylogenetic regression–progression model is in agreement with Kahn and Kirk regarding the biological rootedness, drive and energy aspects, and the directionality of aggression, but there are differences regarding the mechanisms of elicitation. Kahn and Kirk imply that frustration of needs and drives necessary for survival is the *sine qua non* for eliciting aggression, but this ignores at least two types of aggressive behavior: first, where through injury to the brain or temporary brain dysfunction, primitive, noninstrumental aggression is released from its normal bondage, and second, those instances where pleasurable aggression is practiced for its own sake.

Perhaps this is a good juncture to speculate briefly on the genesis of the aggression system and its motivation-emotion-reward-behavior linkages in the brain. Far back in phylogeny when the rudiments of the aggression system were first formed, it was probably true that aggression was typically elicited by frustration of other drives; that is, aggression served as a kind of overseer of other drives, working to assure satisfaction of basic survival needs. These rudimentary aggression systems, no doubt, required some stimulation to set them into effect, and probably did not "spontaneously generate" aggressive drive in the absence of eliciting stimuli as some of the popular ethologists imply (Ardrey, 1966; Lorenz, 1967; Storr, 1968). However, these evolving motivation-emotion-reward-behavior linkages, with their wired-in interconnections in the brain and hormonal system, were by no means passive or pacific; rather, these aggressive systems provided hair-trigger readinesses to respond which, for all purposes, were something tantamount to spontaneous aggression. Probabilistically speaking, given the in-built readinesses on the one hand, and virtually constant threat and provocation on the other, animal aggression evolved to be immediately mobilized, frequent, and efficient. Further, in line with earlier discussion, we may presume that performance of aggressive behavior—in the manner of one's species—produced a sense of pleasure and enjoyment. So, rather than being a passive, inert system until met with threat or frustration, or a spontaneous generator of destruction, aggression is a powerful, phylogenotypically primed readiness, a normal and adaptive part of animal and human nature.

Primitive Aggression.   Our modified version of the Kahn and Kirk definition serves as the assumptive base for what we mean by *primitive aggression*. Primitive aggression refers basically to "natural" animal aggression as it evolved in the various nonhuman species, unmodified by language, thought, or culture. In animals, aggression operates in a direct, functional way, and is closely tied to and dependent upon special elicitorial and releasing conditions. At extremely regressed levels in humans, aggression may also operate in a similarly efficient, nonredundant, and survival-targeted fashion. Most human aggression, however, is based on the interaction between primitive reptilian and limbic carry-overs, and advanced linguistic and culture-mediated cognitions. This fact helps explain why man is more aggressive and violent than other animals, and why human aggression is so complex and multifaceted. Moyer (1976) points out that much of man's aggressive behavior is symbolic whereby others are hurt through sarcasm, gossip, or character assassination. One can even attribute "meaning" to some types of vandalism (Cohen, 1973; Ward, 1973), and ideology clearly plays a major role in warfare (especially religious warfare), political terrorism, political oppression, means of punishing criminals, racial and ethnic prejudice and persecution, street riots, insurrections, and violence in the name of morality, law, and order (Daniels et al., 1970; Grundy & Weinstein, 1974; Hofstadter & Wallace, 1971; Rose, 1969). Thus, human aggression includes a far greater range of responses than is seen in other animals, due to capability of the human neocortex to elaborate and extend upon the primitive aggression of the lower brain systems. We see here that the phylogenetically old aggressive tendencies of the reptilian and limbic systems are not lost; they merely wait for permission from the neocortex to rise into action once again.

Aggression Versus Violence.   So far we have used the terms *aggression* and *violence* interchangeably, but different qualities of meaning are implied in the two. Valzelli (1981) suggests that the term *aggression* be reserved for "normal" aggression, while *violence* be viewed as "abnormal" aggression. Normal aggression, of course, refers to primitive (as previously defined), species-typical, survival-targeted aggression within appropriate ecological contexts, whereas violence tends to be inappropriate, gratuitous, arbitrary, excessive, and destructive. This is an intuitively appealing distinction, save for one important exception—predatory aggression. Predatory aggression poses a severe dilemma for the biologist who loves animals, for it involves eminently normal species behavior that, nevertheless, culminates in the violent destruction of the prey animal. We are, therefore, forced to conclude that destructiveness is "normal" where predation is concerned, whereas destructiveness is, following Valzelli, abnormal in most other instances. As is emphasized later in the chapter, predatory aggression is exceptional in many ways, and may be a crucial factor in regressive forms of human cruelty and destructiveness. For now, however, we go with Valzelli's (1981) distinction between normal and abnormal aggression (violence), appropriately excepting predatory activity:

> *aggressiveness is that component of normal behavior which, under different stimulus-bound and goal-directed forms, is released for satisfying vital needs and for removing or overcoming any threat to the physical and/or*

psychological integrity subserving the self- and species-preservation of a living organism, and never, except for predatory activity, initiating the destruction of the opponent. (Valzelli, 1981, p. 64)

AGGRESSION, VIOLENCE, AND THE BRAIN

Valzelli (1981) tells us that proto-living organisms have, from the very beginning, fed and preyed upon one another and engaged in life-and-death competition, and it was through this primeval interplay of predatory aggression and defense against predation that the process of natural selection came into being (Sylvester-Bradley, 1976). This primal predatory theme is as old as life itself, and, consequently, as primitive neural matter evolved, inchoate versions of the attack-defense template were built into living organisms. Valzelli (1981) says that the earliest record of vertebrates is provided by *Heterostraci,* a tadpole-shaped creature of the class *Agnatha* that lived 460 million years ago. Its lack of grasping jaws and paired fins for fast swimming suggests it existed by passively ingesting bottom-mud rich in living and dead organic materials. The predatory activity of Agnatha was, thus, something short of active attack on prey, but was considerably more than the biochemical transformations and assimilation of non-living matter that characterized the "feeding" processes of Protozoans. With the appearance of the actively motile forms, the sedentary predation of Agnatha gave way to more active and aggressive creatures. About 60 million years after Agnatha, the *Acanthodian* fishes appeared, armed with formidable jaws, a large mouth, efficient teeth, paired terminal nostrils, and large eyes, all of which contributed to active hunting of prey. Perhaps it was at this point, some 400 million years ago, that a truly aggressive stalk-attack-kill-eat pattern came into existence. Such predatory aggression clearly predates all other forms of aggression by a wide margin, and many eons of evolutionary time would pass before neural circuits for protection of young, dominance, territoriality, and the like were wired into more phylogenetically advanced organisms.

We see that the morphological and neurological templates for predatory aggression were clearly drawn in fishes, and some, such as the *Chondrichthytes* (fishes with cartilaginous skeleton, such as the shark), have been among the world's most active and insatiable predators. Later, some of the world's most fearsome predators evolved during the age of reptiles, epitomized by the mighty *Tyrannosaurus,* the largest meat-eating animal that ever lived. The importance of these developments cannot be overestimated:

The line traced by evolution represents a continued need for meeting the demands of life. Competition and predatory behavior probably represent the major motivated states for several hundred million years. . . . This implies that primitive brains, and in particular those of the various animal forms from Gnathostomes to Reptiles included, must have been especially settled and adjusted for continuous hunting, aggression, and predatory behavior. (Valzelli, 1981, pp. 15–17)

It should be noted here that Paul MacLean (see chapter 2) and many others believe that many of the primal tendencies of reptiles continue to exist deep in the ancient parts of the human brain. This assumption is of crucial importance in applying phylogenetic regression theory to the problem of human aggression and violence, especially where extreme cruelty and destructiveness are involved.

The primitive reptilian brain, with its armamentarium of rigid instincts and automatisms, gradually merged into the mammalian limbic system that provided more adaptable and flexible means of self- and species-preservation. Many neuropsychological researchers agree that human aggression is, to a great extent, based on the interplay between the phylogenetically advanced neocortex and the phylogenetically primitive limbic system (MacLean, 1970, 1973a, 1976; Mark & Ervin, 1970; Monroe, 1978; Moyer, 1976; Restak, 1979; Scott, Cole, McKay, Leark, & Golden, 1982; Scott, Martin, & Liggett, 1982; Valzelli, 1981). For these writers, aggression is primarily a problem of brain function, as Mark and Ervin (1970) clearly state: "The organ of behavior is the brain, which means that in discussing violence we are actually talking about one of the ways brain function is expressed in behavior" (p. 4). Mark and Ervin draw upon W. B. Cannon's old notion of the fight or flight mechanism, and argue that any animal, regardless of species, can be expected to react to life-threatening stress with one of two general patterns of behavior, aggression or escape. This view implies that aggression at the limbic level is primarily defensive, or perhaps that it is elicited by frustration of survival needs as Kahn and Kirk (1968) propose. One cannot generalize too far on this point, for there are many limbically mediated forms of aggression that are not always defensive (viz., irritative, competitive, and intermale aggression; Moyer, 1976). Moreover, reptilian and limbic neurostructures and functions overlap considerably, and it is not always possible to clearly distinguish between, for example, primarily reptilian "offensive" functions (e.g., stalk-attack-kill-eat patterns) and primarily "defensive" limbic functions (e.g., escape, avoidance, dominance, territoriality, etc.). We recall here that MacLean (1970) includes in the limbic system some parts of the brain stem that have primary connections with the limbic cortex. Perhaps it is best to view the reptilian brain as housing the basic neurological hardware for aggression, whereas the limbic cortex serves to extend and elaborate aggressive behavior through the energizing and directing effects of emotions and feelings. The phylogenetic regression–progression model assumes that aggression (and violence moreso) is, at its foundations, reptilian, predatory, protoconscious, automatic, and instinctual.

Neuroanatomy of Predatory Aggression

The neuroanatomy of predatory aggression has been more thoroughly mapped by researchers than has any other type of aggression. Predatory aggression is controlled by many phylogenetically old neural systems in the brain, including the hypothalamus, thalamus, midbrain, hippocampus, and amygdaloid nuclei. As early as 1928 (cited in Johnson, 1972), Hess reported that highly emotional rage reactions, or "sham rage," could be induced by hypothalamic stimulation. Later researchers found that a number of predatory behaviors could be elicited by hypothalamic stimulation, but the particular site of stimulation appeared to determine the type and severity of response. When the lateral hypothalamus in cats is stimulated electrically, chemically, or presumably naturally by presentation of an appropriate prey animal, species–specific predatory patterns can be elicited with remarkable regularity (Moyer, 1976). Because stimulation of the lateral hypothalamus normally elicits predatory attack when the appropriate prey is present, Valzelli (1981) sees the response pattern as "feeding behavior displayed as predatory aggression." By contrast, stimulation of the anterior hypothalamus leads to a different type of aggression where the cat may ignore an available rat and, instead, viciously attack the experimenter or another person (Egger & Flynn, 1963). In fact, the now classic studies of the Yale group in the 1960s (Adams & Flynn, 1966; Egger & Flynn, 1963; Wasman & Flynn, 1962) dramatically revealed two distinct kinds of hypothalamic aggression: (a) stimulation of the lateral area that leads to the "normal" quiet, stalking, and biting attack, and (b) stimulation of the dorsomedial area that produced symptoms of feline rage involving high arousal, striking out with unsheathed claws rather than biting, and attacks on objects other than the prey animal. The evidence is thus quite strong that predatory aggression of the stalk-attack-kill type is mediated by the lateral hypothalamus in cats, and stimulation of this area produces similar killing behavior in a variety of other species (Moyer, 1976).

Although the lateral hypothalamus is intimately involved in predatory aggression, it is only one of many neurological structures involved in the predation syndrome. Other areas thought to be implicated in predatory behavior include the midline thalamus, posterior midline thalamus, lateral preoptic regions, midbrain ventral tegmental area, dorsolateral midbrain reticular formation, central pontine tegmentum, the amygdaloid nuclei, and portions of the cerebellum (Moyer, 1976). Of these various loci, the bilaterally represented amygdaloid nuclei play extremely important roles in both predatory and other forms of aggression. The amygdala and hypothalamus are intimately connected, and stimulation of the amygdala in cats can either facilitate or suppress attack depending on whether the hypothalamus is stimulated at the same time (Egger & Flynn, 1963). Further, if the areas of the amygdala that normally suppress attack are ablated, attack elicited by stimulation of the hypothalamus will be facilitated (Egger & Flynn, 1967). Although the amygdala does appear to have the capacity to facilitate predatory aggression, its role as an inhibitor may be more important.

There are many areas of the brain that serve to inhibit predatory and other kinds of aggressive behavior, and one often sees excitatory and inhibitory capacities housed in single structures such as the amygdala and the hypothalamus. For example, we have seen that stimulation of the lateral hypothalamus produces highly reliable predatory aggression in cats, but stimulation of the medial or ventromedial area stops both feeding behavior and predatory attack (Oomura, Ooyama, Yamamoto, & Naka, 1967), as does stimulation of the basolateral nuclei of the amygdala (Adamec, 1975a, 1975b, 1975c). With the amygdala, it seems that the centromedial nuclei serve to facilitate aggressiveness, whereas the basolateral nuclei serve the opposite function (Valzelli, 1981). Moreover, early studies showed that bilateral amygdalectomy all but eliminated the predatory tendencies in the cat (Summers & Kaelber, 1962) and the rat (Woods, 1956), and bilateral lesions of the amygdala "tames" a variety of innately hostile and vicious animals, which can be handled without gloves following surgery (Valzelli, 1981). Moreover, the same operation decreases competitive aggression in reptiles (Keating, Kormann, & Horel, 1970), and also serves to block internal competitive and dominance aggression in rats (Bunnell, 1966; Karli, 1974). In Klüver and Bucy's (1937) classic study, bilateral lesions in the temporal lobes (including the amygdala and hippocampus) produced a syndrome of hypoaggressiveness, hypersexuality, playfulness, and "stupidity." More recently, temporal lobe-amygdaloid lesions in squirrel monkeys caused a lowering of rank in the dominance hierarchy, and similar lesions have been found to impair many social behaviors, including aggressive threats and submissive gestures, in wild monkeys (Dicks, Myers, & Kling, 1969).

Our overview of predatory and related forms of aggression in animals, although very sketchy, revealed numerous and relatively well-defined neuroanatomical structures in the primitive reptilian and paleomammalian brains that function to excite or inhibit attack and kill behavior. Further, as Moyer (1976) points out, learning and experience are not essential to the basic predation response: "Effective, if not skilled, killing is reported for many predators that have never been exposed to prey. . . . Cats isolated from birth will attack rats (although less vigorously and less persistently than those nonisolated) when electrically stimulated in the lateral hypothalamus" (p. 142). Again, we stress that these structures themselves, by virtue of the fact that they exist and function so effectively and adaptively, define the reality of predatory aggression, at least in nonhuman species. At which time these complex neurostructures—and their complex interrelationships with the priming and eliciting conditions that affect them—are understood, then the basic essence of predatory aggression will be understood. That this degree of understanding has not been achieved should not discourage the search for the roots of primitive aggression, in both animals and humans, in the structure-primer-elicitor and motivation-emotion-reward-behavior interrelationships mediated in the lower centers of the brain.

Neuroanatomy of Human Aggression

Data on the neuroanatomy of human aggression are limited due to the necessary moral and ethical constraints on surgical intervention. Therefore, data on humans come more from clinical studies of brain disease and post-disease surgery than from controlled experimentation of the sort done with animals. Despite these limitations, a strong circumstantial case can be made for primitive, phylogenetically old brain structures intruding into many forms of human aggression. The phylogenetic regression–progression model assumes, as a working hypothesis, that the basic neurohumoral substructures of primitive aggression in animals, e.g., the amygdaloid nuclei, hypothalamus, and limbic system in general, serve similar and fundamentally homologous functions in humans, but the range and complexity of aggressive response in humans vastly exceeds that of even our closest phylogenotypic relative, the chimpanzee. Just as the small distinctly human transgenotype can, through the action of control genes (see chapter 6), produce a great chimpanzee–human differential phenotypically despite almost complete overlap phylogenotypically, so can chimpanzee and human aggression differ despite great overlap in the basic structure–function systems of the brain. Thus, although the primitive neuroanatomy of chimps and humans differs little, human aggression encompasses far more because of the inhibiting, facilitating, modulating, and elaborating functions of the human neocortex. Not surprisingly, loss of neocortical inhibition over the lower aggression centers through disease or injury is a major factor in pathological aggression or violence.

First, let us look at pathological aggression released by tumors of the brain. As Moyer (1976) summarizes, a considerable range of psycho-pathology results from brain tumors. For one thing, intracranial pressure may produce headache, nausea, vomiting, and psychotic symptoms including hallucinations, delusions, and various other kinds of cognitive impairment. When portions of the limbic system are involved, changes in personality and affect frequently occur, and the patient may experience inappropriate laughter, euphoria, or depression. Further, the patient may become hyper- or hypophragic (anorexic), and may exhibit hyper- or hyposexuality. Of special interest here is the well-documented evidence that limbic system tumors often involve increased irritability, temper outbursts, and even homocidal attacks of rage (Kletschka, 1966; Moyer, 1976). Noteworthy is the fact that these dyscontrolled outbursts are often totally out of keeping with the patient's premorbid personality, and seem to occur more or less involuntarily (viz., are not subject to conscious or willful neocortical control).

The temporal lobes of the neocortex and the limbic amygdaloid nuclei are intimately connected, with the more advanced temporal lobes serving as inhibitors of aggression. Thus, it is not surprising that temporal lobe tumors in human patients are associated with increased tension and aggressive behavior, ranging from intense sibling rivalry to unpredictable assaultiveness (Moyer, 1976). That the more extreme cases seem to involve at least partial release of atavistic behavior is evident in Sweet, Ervin, and Mark's (1969) and Mark and Ervin's (1970) descriptions of extremely violent patients with temporal lobe tumors. One of these, a short muscular man, attempted to kill his wife and daughter with a butcher knife. When brought to the hospital, he was in a full-blown rage reaction during which he snarled, bared his teeth, and tried to attack anyone who came close. The snarling and teeth-baring are, of course, particularly significant from the standpoint of regressive recovery of atavisms. Special X-ray films revealed that the tumor was underneath the right frontal lobe, and was thought to press directly on the anterior temporal lobe and the nearby limbic system. Upon removal of the tumor, the patient's symptoms disappeared and he peaceably returned to his job as a nightwatchman.

Malamud's (1967) study of 18 persons with limbic tumors revealed that all had some psychiatric disorder. Nine of them had tumors of the temporal lobe, of which two were assaultive, 2 were suicidal, 1 was both aggressive and suicidal, 1 had episodes of depression, 1 had episodic, uncontrollable fear, and 2 showed psychotic symptoms. These varied reactions reveal that temporal lobe and limbic system relations are complex, and, further, that temporal dysfunction is associated with many pathological outcomes, not just heightened aggression. Nevertheless, pathological aggression is one of the most likely results of temporal lobe tumors, and it is well-known that patients suffering from temporal lobe epilepsy often are prone to explosive and violent behavior (Blumer, Williams, & Mark, 1974; Gloor, 1960).

One of the most dramatic instances of temporal lobe pathology and extreme aggression was the celebrated case of Charles Whitman. Whitman was an introspective young man who was aware of his pathological motivations and sought help from a psychiatrist. In a letter written just hours before killing his wife and mother, Whitman complained of being a *victim* (Johnson, 1972; italics added) of many unusual and irrational thoughts. One is struck by the alien and intrusive nature of the uncontrollable urges Whitman experienced, and he did, indeed, appear to be victimized by the primitive neural discharges within his own brain. As we sadly recall, the morning following the killing of his wife and mother, Whitman climbed atop a tower at the University of Texas, armed with a high-powered rifle with a telescopic sight, and proceeded to kill 14 people and wound 24 others before being shot to death himself. Because of the extensive damage to his brain from gunshot wounds, the neuropathologist could not pinpoint the exact locus of Whitman's tumor, but it was probably in the medial part of one temporal lobe near the amygdaloid nucleus (Sweet, Ervin, & Mark, 1969).

Tumors in areas of the limbic system other than the temporal–amygdaloid complex may also result in irritable behavior, rage, and assaultiveness. Some of these areas include the white matter of the cingulate gyrus (Moyer, 1976), the cingulum and left frontal lobe (Malamud, 1967), the septal region (Zeman & King, 1958), the frontal lobe (Strauss & Keschmer, 1935), and, perhaps most significantly, the hypothalamus. Alpers (1937) reported on a patient with damage to the anterior hypothalamus who suffered extreme personality change and flew into rages over trivial matters. Reeves and Blum (1969) described a case of tumor destruction of the ventromedial hypothalamus that resulted in the hypothalamic syndrome seen in animals—overeating, obesity, and increased aggression. At times the patient would lose control without apparent provocation, and would hit, scratch, and attempt to bite the examiner. Killeffer and Stern (1970) reported on a similar case, and Sano (1962) analyzed data on 297 limbic tumors and concluded that irritability and rage attacks were frequent with damage to the anterior hypothalamus.

We have concentrated on effects of tumor damage in the limbic system on human aggression, but the problem may be approached from several other angles including clinical study of other diseases and physical trauma, brain stimulation, electroencephalography, and surgical intervention. Generally, these other approaches confirm the importance of limbic structures in subserving a wide range of phylogenetically primitive aggressive emotions and behaviors. Space does not permit a thorough review of all these approaches, and for more detail the reader should consult the excellent resource works available (Mark & Ervin, 1970; Monroe, 1978; Moyer, 1976; Valzelli, 1981). We round out our discussion of human aggression and the brain with a brief look at some of the more dramatic examples of clinical neuropathology.

Illustrative Clinical Syndromes.   Moyer (1976) discusses several clinical syndromes associated with extreme aggression, including rabies, encephalitis, epilepsy, and the Lesch–Nyhan syndrome. The word "rabies" is derived from a Latin word meaning rage, and the disease is caused by a filterable virus transmitted to the victim by the saliva of the infected animal. Severe brain damange often results, involving generalized neuropathy throughout the entire brain and localized lesions of the limbic system, especially in and around the temporal lobes. Moyer (1976) expresses some wonderment about the fact that the rabies virus so often attacks the specific centers of the nervous system relating to aggression, and, indeed, hyperaggressivity is the cardinal behavioral symptom of the disease.

Encephalitis lethargica is sometimes associated with severe conduct problems in children involving personality change, poor impulse control, and violent displays of temper. The behavior disorder is most common in children between the ages of 3 and 10, and Brill (1959) provides a graphic description of the symptom picture:

> A marked destructiveness and impulsiveness, with a tendency to carry primitive impulses into headlong action. Children who had previously been normally behaved would i.e., steal, destroy property, set fire, and commit various sexual offenses, without thought of punishment. The motivation was less comprehensible and less subject to immediate control than in the so-called psychopathies, but the capacity for real remorse was strikingly well retained. There was a marked instability of emotion which, coupled with disinhibition of action, led to aggression, usually against others, but occasionally against the patient himself, resulting in gruesome self-mutilation (p. 1167)

Moyer (1976) observes that the neural damage in encephalitis lethargica, although more localized and specific than in other encephalitic disorders, is still rather diffuse and, consequently, clear brain-behavior relationships have not been established. However, Brill (1959) reported that the hypothalamus, mesencephalon, and brain stem generally sustain neuron loss, and Himmelhock, Pincus, Tucker, and Detre (1970) suggest that the temporal lobes also are frequently involved. Moyer (1976) reminds us here that these neuroanatomical structures "have been shown to be important in the neural circuitry of aggression in animals" (p. 32).

The Lesch–Nyhan syndrome is another disorder of childhood that results in pathological aggressive behavior. Moyer (1976) tells us that affected children are retarded, spastic, and demonstrate the bizarre symptom of persistent, uncontrollable self-mutilation. Most pronounced is biting behavior where the cheek, lips, and fingers are so vigorously chewed that they are actually chewed away. Lesch–Nyhan patients appear to experience pain and are extremely distressed by and frightened by their own destructive behavior. Other people also are objects of their aggression, and they may pinch, hit, or bite anyone within range. The syndrome is a genetic disease of the male, transmitted as an X-linked recessive character. It results in a disorder of purine metabolism whereby enormous quantities of purine are produced. According to Moyer (1976), researchers have shown that large quantities of purines administered to rats will produce self-mutilation and aggression toward other rats, but, at present, little is known of the underlying causal mechanisms of the Lesch–Nyhan disease in humans. Once again, however, we see the capability of the brain to force and compel human beings to do the most gruesome things, even to bite and chew at one's own body.

Many acts of violence are of the epileptoid variety involving abnormal spontaneous activations of various neural systems of the brain. Such acts have been variously referred to as the limbic syndrome, dyscontrol syndrome, episodic violence, expressive aggression, and so forth (Monroe, 1978). Epilepsy and epileptoid syndromes may be caused by brain trauma, tumors, cerebral circulation defects, toxins, birth injury, or metabolic disturbances, but about two thirds are idiopathic, or of unknown causes. Even in normal persons, spontaneous abnormal discharges of overburdened neurological circuits may occur (Jonas, 1965), but in the genuine epileptic with known tissue damage or in the dyscontrolled individual with only soft sign neuropathy (Monroe, 1978), the discharges may be both frequent and severe. A variety of behavioral sequelae are associated with epilepsy, but the highest percentage of personality disorders appear to emanate from temporal lobe disorders. Although epileptics may show extreme fear, sexual dysfunction, or depression, there is abundant evidence for uncontrolled, impulsive, and assaultive behavior, especially in the temporal lobe or psychomotor types. Moyer (1976, p. 37) cites Gastaut (1954) who concluded that the "psychomotor epileptic behaves, in the interval between his fits, like an animal presenting a state of continuous rhinencephalic excitation, and during his fits, like an animal presenting a paroxysmal rhinencephalic discharge." Gastaut goes on to say that, in the interval between fits, the patient is likely to be impulsive, aggressive, and prone to violent outbursts. Other writers have commented on the suddenness, apparent absence of provocation, and extreme contrast with the patient's usual good-natured behavior, that characterizes outbursts in the psychomotor patient (Walker & Blumer, 1972).

THEORETICAL CONSIDERATIONS

As we recall from earlier chapters (see also Appendix I), any behavior, or, more specifically, any coordinated, circumscribed set of emotion-motivation-reward-behavioral response linkages, may be seen as occupying a point (or delimited area) on a phylogenetic primitive–advanced continuum. At the primitive pole, phylogenetically old characteristics are paramount, whereas at the phylogenetically advanced pole distinctly human ones predominate. We further recall that behavior is ongoing and dynamic, and innumerable momentary regressions and progressions are constantly occurring. We also recall that progression up the scale, or resistance to regression down the scale is largely a function of intelligence, broadly defined as the ability of the neocortex to do meaningful cognitive work. The presence of high intelligence does not guarantee advanced behavior, however, but it does make it more probable. The neocortex and its functional correlate intelligence play crucial roles in encouraging progression and discouraging regression by exerting direct inhibitory control over the naturally expressive lower centers and by exerting indirect inhibitory control over socially and culturally deviant behavior through the inculcation of moral and ethical prohibitions. When these inhibitory functions fail, even briefly, passive phylogenetic regression is likely to occur, and when the neocortex not only loosens control but willingly and actively does so, active phylogenetic regression is the likely result. In phylogenetic regression, feelings, motives, and/or behaviors once-adaptive (e.g., predatory aggression, xenophobia, territoriality, overvaluation of kin, nepotism) in phylogeny are recovered, which may be used either adaptively or maladaptively in the modern context. Let us now apply our model to some selected questions of interest in the area of aggression.

The Most Primitive Form of Aggression

We may first ask, "What is the most primitive form of aggression?" From theory, we may deduce that predatory aggression defines the primitive pole of aggression for humans just as it does for most other living creatures. This conclusion is based on well-supported facts that predatory aggression is: (a) the phylogenetically oldest form of aggression; (b) the behavioral parameter that has probably affected evolutionary development of living organisms more than any other (through selective action on both predators and prey); (c) the type of aggression most clearly represented in the primitive reptilian brain; and (d) it is the only form of aggression that characteristically involves the total destruction and annihilation of its object. Destruction is, thus, seen as a quintessential feature of predatory aggression, and is a natural consequence of the omnipresent kill-and-eat pattern in nature. Destructiveness, by contrast, may be seen as a generally pathological derivative or elaboration of the normal predatory pattern where pleasure is taken in stalking, killing, and mutilating. In destructiveness, predatory aggression jumps off its natural track as a provider of protein, and the pre-consumatory components of the pattern are enjoyed for their own sake. In humans, a range of destructiveness within the primitive predatory category may be seen, going from non-ritualized cannibalism, as was presumably practiced by early hominids (Ardrey, 1961, 1977; Dart, 1953/1973), on to ritualized cannibalism as presumably practiced by Neanderthal and some modern tribes, then a step "higher" to mutilation, torture, and killing not involving eating of the object, and, finally, predatory destructiveness partially sublimated into violent attacks on inanimate objects, as in vandalism, and, perhaps, into certain aspects of war at a higher level. Our conclusion, then, is that many aspects of gratuitous aggression radiate from a phylogenetically ancient predatory core deep within the reptilian brain, a brain that continues to exist in modern humans much as it did in its scaly originators millions of years ago.

Work by Andy and Stephan (1974) on the neuroanatomy of primate aggression suggests that structures strongly associated with predatory aggression, e.g., the diencephalon (thalamus and hypothalamus) and mesencephalon, exhibited the least progressive development in primate phylogeny, whereas structures weakly or marginally associated with predatory aggression, e.g., the hippocampus, septum, and amygdala, exhibited considerable enlargement going from primitive insectivores to man. Even these latter structures changed little, however, compared to the human neocortex that showed a rate of growth 156 times greater than that of the basal insectivore. Of special interest to our discussion is the fact that, upon electrical or chemical stimulation, the most integrated, aggressive attack was elicited from the least progressive structures, the diencephalon and mesencephalon; this means that the most phylogenetically primitive structures mediating aggression are the ones most likely to produce the purest atavistic responses when stimulated. By contrast, stimulation of the slightly more advanced structures—hippocampus, septum, and amygdala—tended to produce fragments or attenuated forms of aggression, whereas stimulation of the neocortex did not elicit aggression at all. However, aggression was facilitated by ablation of neocortical tissue, presumably because of loss of inhibitory capability.

Andy and Stephan conclude that injuries to, or developmental abnormalities associated with, the rudimentary structures subserving aggression may activate physiological states which cannot be controlled by the inhibiting action of the neocortex. If such problems exist in the lower structures, and the neocortex is damaged or malfunctions as well, "one would expect the acme of aggressive state to develop" (Andy & Stephan, 1974, p. 327). All of this provides ample support for our argument that segments and part-segments of primitive aggressive behavior may be elicited in regressive states where the neocortex fails in its inhibitory functions. To dramatize this point, let us look at the role the prototypic predatory behavior "biting" plays in extreme cases of phylogenetic regression in humans. Teeth-baring is a frequently used threat gesture in humans, especially under conditions of extreme provocation or anger, as in the case of Mark and Ervin's (1970) famous patient Julia, and actual biting of self or others is fairly common in mental patients and among those suffering damage to primitive brain centers (Brill, 1959; Greenbaum & Lurie, 1948; Reeves & Blum, 1969). Also, as discussed earlier, gruesome biting of self and others is a cardinal symptom of the Lesch–Nyhan syndrome, and we recall the biting attack of Ted Bundy in the Chi Omega house murders described in chapter 9. Ironically, it was Bundy's teeth marks and the damning testimony of the forensic odontologist, Dr. Richard Souviron, that contributed greatly to Bundy's eventual conviction and death sentence (Rule, 1980). Dr. Souviron has testified in at least two prior murder cases where the killer had applied numerous bites to his victims. Perhaps other explanations are possible here, but the notion of atavistic recovery of primitive predatory biting behavior seems to fit the facts quite well in these instances. Further, we may assume that such acts reside at or near the most regressed point on the phylogenetic regression–progression continuum. Indeed, what could be more regressive than to bite and tear at another human being with one's teeth?

Redundancy of Brain Structures Mediating Primitive Aggression

Another crucial question is, "Why are there so many different anatomic structures in the reptilian and paleomammalian brains that mediate predatory and other forms of aggression?" As we have seen, supernumerous structures have been implicated in aggression, including the thalamus, hypothalamus, amygdaloid nuclei, hippocampus, cingulate gyrus, stria terminalis, laterobasal septal nuclei, and several lesser areas (Moyer, 1976; Valzelli, 1981; Valzelli & Morgese, 1981). Why such redundancy? For one thing, such redundancy reveals just how phylogenetically ancient, how basic, how necessary, and how omnipresent aggression is as a means of adaptation and survival in animals and humans. It is doubtful that any other neurobehavioral system if so well-represented in the brain or so thoroughly integrated into the very being of the organism. Secondly, the large number of structures and large number of fairly specific functions associated with them reveal that aggression is not a unitary entity, but is rather a complex, multi-level, multifaceted system of generally adaptive "acting against" responses. This complexity and breadth of response allows the more advanced animal to meet diverse threats and challenges from the environment. Whereas the reptile may be phylogenetically limited to little more than simple predatory and defensive aggression, the advanced mammal possesses a large repertoire of threat-contingent acting-against responses including predatory aggression, dominance aggression, territorial aggression, maternal-protective aggression, irritative aggression, and sex-related aggression (Moyer, 1976; Zillmann, 1984). And thirdly, the advanced mammal not only possesses many different types of aggression, but is also capable of mixing types so the complexity of aggression is augmented almost beyond comprehension. In advanced mammals and humans, simple, pure, innate releaser → innate response pattern sequences are rarely seen, and, instead, we see different types of aggression and part-types intermixed in a dynamic flow of responsivity.

Mixing of Aggression Components

The issue of mixing aggression components is extremely important theoretically, because it helps explain why so many experts differ as to what aggression is, what causes it, and what is likely to control it. Researchers seldom speak of mixes, for it is difficult enough to isolate and identify single component systems to begin with, much less to show how they intermix and interact with each other. The prevailing approach has been for writers to emphasize single-cause approaches, such as the killer instinct (Ardrey, 1961; Dart, 1953/1973), learning processes (Bandura, 1973; Berkowitz, 1962), or a host of rather abstract economic, cultural, and ideological "causes" (Daniels et al., 1970; Grundy & Weinstein, 1974; Hofstadter & Wallace, 1971; Montagu, 1968). From the standpoint of phylogenetic regression theory, all of these disparate opinions are partially true, but none is totally true. The truth of human aggression is not to be found in any single cause, but rather in the symphonic interaction of many coterminous causes. Some causes are more fundamental than others, however, and our approach chooses to emphasize the phylogenetically old neurobiochemical substrates of aggression, with and upon which is added much through learning, socialization, and culture.

So far we have seen that neuroanatomical structures exist at the reptilian and limbic levels of brain functioning that both trigger and suppress aggressive behavior (see Valzelli, 1981, Table 2, p. 91 for an excellent summary). Inhibitory structures exist, then, at subneocortical levels as well as at the neocortical level. This fact allows for many complex interactions of excitory and inhibitory functions at subcortical levels alone, and once the vagaries of neocortical inhibition of lower centers are introduced, the matrix of interactional possibilities is further enlarged. Our conceptual causal matrix is further expanded when we consider the brain's ability to intermix the different types of aggression (predatory, dominance, irritative, etc.) in more advanced animals. Yet, mixing is not limited to excitation-inhibition interaction within and across levels or to interblending of aggression types; just as intriguing is the fact that different behavioral systems interact in important ways, as with the aggression–fear blend that characterizes agonistic behavior in animals (see chapter 5) or with the aggression-suppressing properties of fear in humans (Valzelli, 1981). It is especially interesting to note that the "negative" aggression system often interacts with the "positive" sexual and affectional systems (Zillmann, 1984) in courtship and copulatory behavior, domestic violence, rape and sexual perversion, love–hate ambivalences, and violent sexual passion. Valzelli (1981) points out, for example, that the neuroanatomical structures subserving aggression—the hypothalamus, amygdala, hippocampus, cingulate gyrus, and septal nuclei—also are implicated in pleasure, grooming, sexual, and parental care behaviors. All this is of enormous theoretical significance when we consider the mysteries of sadistic sexual murders, child battering, pleasure-in-destruction, and a host of other knotty problems. Purely and simply, there are specific mechanisms for sex, aggression, and parenting in the brain that overlap greatly neuroanatomically, and it should be no surprise, then, that behavioral mixtures emanating from them would occur. Even though learning and socialization are important, the primary causes of a sadistic rape or child battering would seem to lie mainly in our schizophysiological, ambivalent, mixed-up brains with their closely juxtaposed centers for both "negative" and "positive" behaviors.

Behavioral and Emotional Hierarchies

A major implication of the PRP model is that most behavioral systems can be set into hierarchies, and this is particularly true of aggression and violence. No single hierarchy is likely to totally characterize a behavioral system such as aggression, sexuality, or fear; many subsystem hierarchies may be generated depending on whether affective, motivational, neurological, or overtly behavioral factors are emphasized. As recalled, in chapter 4 we outlined the all-inclusive grand hierarchy, or primitive-advanced continuum, which includes all behavioral systems and their component subsystems in ongoing, dynamic interaction. From this rather general and abstract vantage point, aggression would be, at those times when the person is perceptibly aggressive as compared to something else, merely a figure in the broader ground of total responsivity. One may be more specific, however, and extract component hierarchies form the larger, more inclusive one. In chapter 5, for example, the following hierarchy was generated: predatory aggression → dominance aggression →· assertiveness → intellectual aggression → mastery. This hierarchy applies fairly well to humans from the standpoint of decreasing neocortical involvement and proportionately increased subneocortical involvement with descent down the scale.

The specific hierarchy above focuses primarily on overt *behavior* in the areas of predatory destructiveness, dominance, etc., but humans are unique in their capacity to *feel* aggressive yet not behave aggressively outwardly. Human beings are aggressive enough to begin with, but we would be much more so if we acted on every aggressive urge or motive. Observation tells us that human beings are far more often frustrated and angry than aggressive, and we may all be thankful for that fact. Nevertheless, the internal dynamics of feeling, emotion, and motivation that fall short of salient external action are crucial to understanding human and individual psychology. A simple, specific hierarchy of aggressive emotion or motivation, then, might look like this: rage → anger → annoyance. This motivation–emotion centered hierarchy is extremely important for understanding the day-to-day social behavior of humans, where people suffer almost constant annoyance in controlled silence, but may occasionally regress into anger or rage under sufficient provocation. It is crucial as to whether such a regression-to-rage or anger engages the behavioral system or not; it if does, an attack on persons or objects may occur, but, if not, the response may be limited to "silent rage" or at worst an explosive temper tantrum. This distinctively human capacity for decoupling the motivation-behavior relationship is a two-edged sword; on the one hand, silent rage is far better than dyscontrolled rage from the standpoint of social order, but, on the other, it is at the root of many forms of medical and mental pathology.

The foregoing analysis presumes that anger and annoyance are outgrowths and elaborations of the broadly represented primitive rage centers of the brain, modified and modulated by the higher centers, especially the neocortex. As we ascend the hierarchy from primitive rage, learning, self-control, and cultural influence play increasingly important roles, to where, at the level of annoyance, the rage factor is minimal and cognitive factors primarily define the source of negative feeling. For example, one may be annoyed by poor postal service, inferior wine, loud TV commercials and an infinitude of other, often arbitrary circumstances. However, as we descend from annoyance to anger and rage, arbitrary elements progressively drop out and real or perceived threats to survival become paramount. At least, this is typically true for the normal person; indeed, one cardinal characteristic of the psychotic is the expression of rage or anger in inappropriate contexts, where the strong feeling has become disattached from its survival tracking. Such de-tracked rage is dramatically illustrated by one of this writer's patients who went into a 2-day rage attack because a cafeteria waitress refused to honor a simple request to put the tuna fish on the plate instead of in a cardboard cup!

By virtue of its broad representation in the brain, as with predatory aggression, it is clear that the rage response is inherently adaptive and crucial to survival in the wild. Rage appears to be an immediate, relatively total, highly aroused, and almost automatic mode of responding to threat in almost any shape or form. Although future research will surely discover many more eliciting stimuli for rage, the present list is impressive: pain, physical wounding, physical blows, frustration, food removal, sleep deprivation, morphine deprivation in addicted rats, and excessive heat (Moyer, 1976; Valzelli, 1981). It seems that numerous threats elicit attack behavior in animals, and rage is the emotional component of the attack (Valzelli, 1981). Also, rage occurs when the rage-inhibiting structures of the brain are lesioned, as in the sham rage in cats following decorticalization (Woodworth & Sherrington, 1904), or damage to any of the many limbic structures (ventromedial hypothalamus, basolateral amygdala, septal nuclei, dorsal hippocampus, etc.) which act to suppress aggression. All this suggests that rage is a primitive and adaptive form of self-protection in animals and humans, and, further, that both its neurological triggers and suppressors are primarily limbic and not neocortical (see Boddy, 1978, p. 175 for discussion). This may explain why rage is so difficult to stop when initiated, and why it is so resistant to will-power and conscious control.

Normal Versus Pathological Aggression

We close this chapter with a brief discussion of some of the differences between normal and abnormal aggression in both animals and humans. Based on principles developed in earlier chapters, our distinctions revolve around the following 2 × 3 conceptual matrix: (animal:human) × (presently adaptive behavior: once adaptive behavior: never adaptive behavior). Thus, we presume that both animals and humans exhibit "presently adaptive," "once adaptive," and "never adaptive" action tendencies, and the type and form of these tendencies determines, in large measure, whether expressed aggression is normal or abnormal.

Presently Adaptive and Never Adaptive Aggression in Animals. In relatively primitive animals, aggressive behavior is almost always adaptive; that is, both appropriate to its species and appropriate to the immediate context calling for aggressive response. Said another way, the innate motivation-emotion-reward-behavior response patterns remain within their species-typical survival tracking and are emitted only in survival-related contexts. For example, species-typical aggressive response to predatory attack, territorial encroachment, or wounding would be *presently adaptive* according to our definition. However, when such presently adaptive motives or action tendencies slip out of their normal survival tracks and are used in species-inappropriate and idiosyncratic fashion, we have *never adaptive* aggression. We say "never" because the de-tracked or short-circuited behavior probably never played an adaptive role at any time in phylogeny. When a given species, for example, evolves sharp hooves, deadly canine incisors, or specific killing skills, as with the large feline predators, we cannot be sure that these weapons will never be used nonadaptively or accidentally against mates or offspring. That such weapons are seldom used, as Lorenz (1967) tells us, is not the issue. Even in the most pathologically violent human being, aggression is adaptive most of the time—it is the pathological exception, not the norm, that makes a Ted Bundy, Henry Lee Lucas, or John Wayne Gacy.

As a general rule, we may say that any animal, including species *Homo,* which possesses the neurohumoral hardware and correlative software behavioral programs for normal, presently adaptive behavior, can and probably will exhibit some pathological, never adaptive eruptions from those programs. Very often, deviant or stressful priming and eliciting conditions are implicated in the de-tracking from presently adaptive to never adaptive behavior. Many examples could be given here, but we concentrate on one dramatic illustration. "Cannibalism" is a disorder often seen in confined domestic fowls that is manifested in feather picking, toe picking, or comb, wing, tail, or vent picking. The condition occurs in all breeds of domestic fowl, and may have some adaptive element because a genetic disposition appears to exist in certain species (Ferguson, 1968). However, as Ferguson points out, the disorder appears to emanate primarily from disruption of normal dominance pecking under circumstances of social stress:

Social stress is a main causal factor of cannibalism. Social organization based on unidirectional pecking is well recognized as a normal behavioral activity. Under normal circumstances this mutual imposition and acceptance of the peck order is conducive to social stability and therefore to the well-being of the flock. . . . When social tensions occur, these may lead to excessive pecking reactions and this in turn to cannibalism. (p. 193)

Once Adaptive Tendencies Pathologically Expressed.   Just as presently adaptive tendencies may be pathologically expressed never adaptively, so may once adaptive tendencies. "Once adaptive" refers to predispositions, action patterns, and so on, which once played significant roles in the phylogeny of the organism (see chapter 9). Such once adaptive patterns may be seen in presently living species in one of three ways: (a) adaptively (e.g., a person experiences anger when a bag of groceries is stolen from his/her car); (b) nonadaptively (e.g., a person feels mildly annoyed after dropping a bag of groceries); and (c) maladaptively (e.g., a person physically attacks the bag boy who dropped the groceries). In the first case, anger tendencies, developed early in phylogeny and mediated by phylogenetically old areas of the brain are regressively recovered, but remain in their normal self-protective, survival-tracking; in the second case they are similarly elicited, but for no obvious adaptive purpose; and in the third case they are recovered, but subsequently derailed from their survival-tracking and pathologically expressed. Some degree of phylogenetic regression is always implied in once adaptive patterns (see chapter 11 also on this issue), for they were developed in phylogeny prior to the ontogeny of the individual organism and must be called up from subneocortical brain structures into action.

In the next chapter, we see that predatory aggression, territorial aggression, and dominance aggression were once omnipresent adaptive strategies in our evolutionary ancestors, and the hardware and software programs for these strategies continue to exist in us today. That they are often covered by layers of social and cultural learning, or that they are generally neocortically inhibited does not diminish their importance as major causal agents of adaptive, nonadaptive, and maladaptive aggressive behavior in modern humans. In fact, how much of human aggression is learned as novel responses, and how much is comprised of once adaptive mechanisms and tendencies modified and elaborated through learning? We might also ask, "How much aggression would be learned without predispositions and readinesses which were acquired early in phylogeny and presently housed in primitive parts of the brain?" Again, we argue that access to the environmentally new is less important than access to the phylogenetically old is explaining the causes of human aggression.

The Special Case of Infanticide.   Until publication of Hrdy's (1979) seminal article in *Ethology and Sociobiology,* it was widely assumed that infanticide in animals and humans was the pathological result of overpopulation and other ecological pressures. To the contrary, Hrdy postulated that infanticide is often an adaptive response that, on the average and over the lifespan, serves to increase the chances of survival and reproductive success of the individual responsible. Thus, ultimate causes are involved that may incur adaptive advantage to the killer in several possible ways (Hausfater & Hrdy, 1984): (a) exploitation of the young as a food source; (b) sexual selection that increases individual reproductive opportunities by eliminating dependent offspring of a prospective mate; (c) removal of a potential competitor for resources; and (d) parental behavior that maximizes lifetime reproductive success at the expense of present offspring. Variations of these strategies have been observed in numerous species, including insects and insect larvae, fish, frogs, eagle chicks, mice, rats, hyenas, monkeys, apes, and humans (Hausfater & Hrdy, 1984; Itani, 1984).

Rapidly accumulating evidence shows that infanticide is neither rare nor aberrant in nature, and can be caused by parents, other kin, non-kin, or by adults or other immatures (Michener, 1985). The methods of aggression may be direct (overt killing) or indirect (neglect), and the victim may or may not be cannibalized. Although cannibalism has been observed in a variety of primate species, including the great apes, it is not clear whether the killing or the eating is the primary motivation of the behavior. Itani (1984) suggests that killing may be primary and eating secondary in primate cannibalism, but he warns that insufficient data exist for firm conclusions at this point. Regardless of the relative weighting of killing-to-eating, it is clear that the certain components of the predatory stalk-kill-eat system is brought to fore when infanticide involves cannibalism. Following our earlier policy of placing destructive violence into the general category of predatory aggression, we argue that all forms of infanticide involve a predatory component at the neuropsychological level; that is, disinhibition of the reptilian predatory system, or portions thereof, would seem necessary to provide the motivation and killing responses for the infanticide and/or cannibalism sequence. There is some evidence that patterns of cannibalism are correlated with species dietary habits in primates (Itani, 1984), and we suspect that further research will confirm the now tentative connection between infanticide/cannibalism and discharge (or part-discharge) of the predatory system of the brain.

Although infanticide and other forms of intraspecific killing are clearly exacerbated (primed) by ecological stresses, as in the Gombe chimps (Goodall, 1979) and the imperiled mountain gorilla (Fossey, 1981), it seems they are adaptive and functional more often than not. Whether or not infanticide and/or cannibalism emanates from the predatory system is arguable, but less controversial is the presently adaptive nature of these behaviors for both animals (Hausfater & Hrdy, 1984) and humans (Chagnon, Flinn, & Melancon, 1979; Dickemann, 1979). Whereas animals and pre-technological human populations may practice presently adaptive forms of infanticide as a matter of course to maximize individual or inclusive fitness, what about persons at the highest levels of civilization? Here is where the notion of once adaptive tendencies enters the picture. Although infanticide operates on a lesser scale in the more modern populations, and cannibalism is a rare anomaly in virtually all human populations, the reptilian and hypothalamic–limbic complexes of all adult humans share the same killing potential that was once used to manipulate offspring for individual adaptive purposes. Thus, through the process of phylogenetic regression, the most educated and effete modern human, under severe elicitorial conditions, may recover once-adaptive infanticidal emotions and motivations that may or may not lead to overt action. Unfortunately, the statistics on child-battering, neglect, abuse, and child-killing (Bolton, 1983; Guttentag & Secord, 1983; Helfer & Kempe, 1974; Leavitt, 1974) indicate that such once adaptive emotions and motivations are emerging more and more into the behavioral system. Simply speaking, dispositions (or portions of them) that were once adaptive, but that remain under strict suppression in normal humans, are released under stress or provocation and enter, albeit very briefly, into action found supremely reprehensible and criminal by our society.

Infanticide is especially problematic because its evolutionary roots are adaptive, but its social limbs and branches are socially repugnant to the highest degree in our society. We see that socially repugnant forms of aggression cannot be equated with abnormality in every case. We were earlier forced to except predatory aggression from abnormality, and now infanticide (whether or not it is a form of predatory aggression) must follow suit. Clearly, it is important to distinguish between what is socially defined as pathological, and what is pathological from the standpoint of natural, adaptive species behavior. Following this distinction, human infanticide may be construed in several ways.

1. As a normal and even desirable action in certain societies, both pre-technological and modern. For example, female infanticide has been widely practiced in both ancient and modern societies, and extremely high rates in India and China, over the past few centuries, have been documented (Guttentag & Secord, 1983). Interestingly, some of the highest rates recorded occurred among the highest castes in Northern India during late 18th and early 19th centuries, where daughters were disposed of because it was feared they would not be successful in marrying up in the caste system. In these instances, the natural tendency to infanticide is supported by social custom and tradition. From our perspective, these would be instances of active phylogenetic regression (see chapter 3).

2. As a socially repugnant action without redeeming qualities, even if adaptive from a strict biological viewpoint. Certainly, a human parent

guilty of infanticide in America would receive precious little sympathy from the court or society even if monumental gains in individual or inclusive fitness were, in fact, realized at the expense of the infant. In this instance, the infanticidal motivation and behavior are alien and repugnant to the offender as well as society at large, and the why is a total mystery for all concerned. Here the once adaptive tendencies emerge through passive phylogenetic regression, and somehow slip through the counterforces of internal inhibition and culture. This model conforms to the frequent observation that child abusers or killers often appear essentially normal save for the offending act itself.

3. As a never adaptive consequence of possessing the neurohumoral hardware for killing behavior that may erupt, either totally or in bits and pieces, in psychosis, brain damage, or other conditions of pathological, nonadaptive dysrelease. In these instances, the question of whether infanticidal behavior is supported or not supported socially is moot. Here the problem is primarily a structural one—the once adaptive neurohumoral structures for killing misfire due to damage or dysfunction in the structures themselves, or due to analogous damage or dysfunction in the higher inhibiting structures. On the surface level, such "sick" behavior is explained circularly by the presence of sickness, thereby providing an explanatory escape hatch not available when the offender is normal as in 2.

Using infanticide for illustration, we see that human killing behavior can be dissected into at least three categories: one being both biologically adaptive and socially acceptable; one being biologically adaptive but socially unacceptable; and one being neither biologically adaptive nor socially acceptable. When speaking of pathological aggression, then, we must make appropriate distinctions between pathological behavior that is socially defined versus that which emanates from neurohumoral structures which serve contemporary adaptive functions or that once served adaptive functions in phylogeny.

SUMMARY

Human beings are, at one and the same time, the most violent and compassionate creatures on earth. This paradox is at least partially explained by the schizophysiological nature of the human nervous system that is characterized by ambivalence and antagonism both within and between phylogenetically older and newer levels of functioning. At the limbic or paleomammalian level, for example, both excitatory and inhibitory functions are housed within certain structures, e.g., the hypothalamus and amygdaloid nuclei, but just as important are the excitatory and inhibitory relationships existing between the limbic system and the neo-cortex. These complex neuropsychological interrelationships are the foundation stones of human behavior and once we understand them the loving and hating propensities of mankind are stripped of some of their mystery.

The writings of Derek Freeman, Eric Fromm, Alexander Solzhenitsyn, and many others amply document the extent of human destructiveness, and their catalogue of violent acts staggers the mind. Indeed, as Fromm (1973) points out, human beings have performed, at one time or another, every horrible and destructive act accessible to the human imagination. In fact, mere killing is mundane and anticlimactic compared to the extremes of man's inhumanity—torture, mutilation, disembodiment, crucifixion, human sacrifice, infanticide, and so on. The fact that these acts occur at all, and worse still that they have occurred with such great frequency throughout history, leaves us little choice but to assume a blemish on human nature, to accept the Mark of Cain as a given.

Phylogenetic regression theory presumes that the metaphorical Mark of Cain has credence due to the likelihood that our hominid ancestors were, from the beginning, aggressive, clannish, and xenophobic, and further from the fact that propensities for extreme violence have been recently discovered in our closest primate relatives, the chimpanzees and gorillas. All of this suggests that much of human aggression is phylogenetically continuous with our prehuman ancestors, the substrates for which were built into our nervous systems through eons of evolution. Therefore, there is no such thing as human aggression, only aggression performed by human phenotypes. Such aggression is greatly influenced by socialization and culture, but the primal causes of aggression lie deep within the recesses of the ancient reptilian and limbic brains. From these deep recesses emanate the primal motive forces which provide the impetus and energy for aggressive behavior.

Extreme violence is particularly important from our theoretical perspective, but there are many other forms of aggression. Given the variegated tapestry of aggression, Moyer (1976) concluded that aggression is not a unitary phenomenon. Among the many forms are predatory aggression, competitive aggression, territorial aggression, maternal aggression, and sex-related aggression (Moyer, 1976; Valzelli, 1981; Zillmann, 1984). Of the various forms, predatory aggression stands out as the phylogenetically oldest type and is the only one involving total destruction of the object of attack. Most importantly, phylogenetic regression theory proposes that predatory aggression may lie behind the pleasure-in-destruction seen in the mystifying extremes of human violence (e.g., torture, brutal murders, thrill killings, gang attacks, and perhaps even in the more perverse acts of vandalism).

The neuroanatomy of predatory aggression has been mapped in considerable detail by researchers. Predatory aggression is controlled by a number of phylogenetically old neural systems in the brain, including the hypothalamus, thalamus, midbrain, hippocampus, and amygdaloid nuclei. Many of these old reptilian and paleomammalian structures are shared by animals and man, and atavistic recovery of biting and attack behavior is fairly common in certain clinical syndromes in humans—tumors in the temporal and amygdaloid regions, rabies, certain types of encephalitis, the Lesch–Nyhan syndrome, and certain epileptoid syndromes. Of particular theoretical interest is the fact that these patients are typically incapable of controlling their spontaneous aggressive outbursts through exercise of will or mental concentration; indeed, such alien and atavistic outbursts are often more frightening to the patient than anyone else.

Several theoretical issues were discussed. First, it was concluded that predatory aggression is the most primitive form of aggression in both animals and humans. This conclusion was based primarily on the fact that predatory aggression was, by a wide margin, the first form of aggression to evolve in phylogeny. Also, its wide representation in the lower brain structures, its important role as a major parameter of evolution, and its inherent destructiveness were cited in the argument.

A second theoretical issue centered on the fundamental importance of aggression in the everyday affairs of humans. The fundamental importance of aggression as a mediator of behavior is revealed in the extreme redundancy of structures controlling aggression in the brain. If aggression is not central to human social behavior, why so much neural redundancy and so many aggression-related structures in the brain? Assuming the number of structures = importance of function line of argument, it appears likely that aggression, in its many forms, is the most important of the primitive motivation-emotion-reward-action pattern systems. This conclusion would seem to hold until which time the neurohumoral structures subserving fear, sexuality, parenting, play, and so on, prove to be more numerous and redundant than those subserving aggressive behavior.

Other theoretical issues discussed included the mixing of aggression components, behavioral versus emotional hierarchies, and distinctions between normal and pathological aggression. Regarding the latter distinction, of especial importance were the distinctions drawn between *presently adaptive* aggression, *once adaptive* aggression, and *never adaptive* aggression. In distinguishing between normal and abnormal aggression in humans, it is necessary to consider presently adaptive, once adaptive, and never adaptive factors against prevailing social and cultural definitions of normality and abnormality. This 2 (culturally normal vs. abnormal) × 3 (presently, once, never) conceptual model was applied to the problem of infanticide in animals and humans.

11
Paleopsychological Bases of Aggression in Humans

Aggressive behavior is so widespread in the animal kingdom that it is virtually universal in some form or another in almost every animal which has the necessary motor apparatus to fight or inflict injury. It is absent or rare in only those invertebrates such as some worms and oysters which have no means of inflicting damage, whereas it is common in most arthropods and vertebrates which have appendages, claws, teeth, or other structures capable of damaging movements. Lobsters, crayfish, spiders, most insects, and most vertebrates are all capable of severe aggressive behavior, which can be seen in both natural and experimental conditions.

—Southwick (1970b, p. 2)

GENERAL OVERVIEW

So far we have discussed the extremes of aggression and the evolved neuroanatomical structures that subserve aggressive and violent behavior. Now we look at adaptive aggression as it evolved *au naturel* in animals, and then go a step further and show how this primitive or old aggression continues to intrude into the affairs of mankind. Given the neuroanatomy and neurochemistry (Brain & Benton, 1981; Valzelli, 1984; Valzelli & Morgese, 1981) of aggression and the dynamics of MacLean's triune brain, we are forced to conclude that old aggression has not disappeared or evolved out of the human nervous system, but continues on in the hidden recesses of the reptilian and limbic systems.

We have seen that aggression is not a unitary entity, but is rather composed of several different subtypes (Moyer, 1976; Valzelli, 1981). Nevertheless, old aggression can be categorized into three primary areas: predation, territoriality, and dominance. Phylogenetic regression theory assumes that these three parameters of primitive aggression, taken singly or in various combinations, accounts for most aggressive behavior in both animals and humans. In humans, however, the picture is complicated by the elaborating effects of social learning and culture, but it is not uncommon for persons to regress to predatory destructiveness, territorial insularity, or raw dominance–submission relations when adequately stressed or provoked.

A major goal of the phylogenetic regression–progression model is to establish deductive principles by which the sudden within-person transitions from peaceable, culturally constrained behavior to autistic emotionality and hyperaggressiveness may be explained. At present, no theory addresses this issue in any detail, and precious few theories even consider the matter at all. Most writers, even biologically oriented ones, seem hesitant to confront the Beast, and the typical pattern is to thoroughly discuss the evolutionary and neurobehavioral bases of aggression in animals, and then, in the final few pages, to conclude that all this really has little or nothing to do with the sociocultural complexities of human aggressive behavior. In recent years, the psychobiological apologists (Benton, 1983; Passingham, 1982; Scott, 1981; Tedeschi, Melburg, & Rosenfeld, 1981; Washburn & Dolhinow, 1983) have supplanted the sociological apologists of yesteryear (Lewis & Towers, 1972; Montagu, 1968, 1976, 1978), but the result is the same—the Beast no longer exists and has been supplanted by neocortically mediated, socially conditioned, thinking man who has the ability to decide whether or not to be aggressive. For example, Scott (1981) tells us:

One major conclusion can be drawn. Human agonistic behavior has changed as a result of both genetic and cultural evolution. Even if we could reconstruct the agonistic behavior of our remote ancestors accurately, this would still not give us a picture of modern human nature. If any destructive tendency has survived out of the remote past, it is fearful and over-defensive behavior that is no longer appropriate in modern civilized life. (p. 154)

Similarly, regarding territoriality, Passingham (1982) says, "There is little profit to be gained from discussing territoriality in man as if we had or had not inherited some *propensity* from our primate ancestors. . . . It would be more accurate to say that we are capable of dividing up land and protecting it, and that like other animals we only do so where it would pay" (p. 391). A page later, Passingham says, "We will learn nothing of value about these [territoriality, protection of property, etc.] by studying animals. The only factor in common is that both animals and people make *decisions* as to when it will and when it will not be worth challenging another individual to secure something that is prized" (p. 320; italics added). And then following a brief discussion of warfare, Passingham (1982) reaches his penultimate conclusion: "The reason why man is the only primate that conducts wars is that only man is *able* to do so. There is no cause to suspect the monstrous presence of a 'beast within.' Our trouble is that we are too clever for our own good" (p. 330). Whereas Passingham exhibited unsurpassed scholarship and rigorous conceptual analysis throughout all but the final pages of his outstanding book, it seemed that he groped for rationalistic, instrumentalistic, and humanistic escape hatches when discussing the nature of human aggression. Similar last-page disclaimers are found in most other books addressing the psychobiology of aggression, but we must ask whether this is because there really is no legitimate reason to suspect the Beast-within, or whether it is required that such discussions end on a positive note or otherwise not offend the collective human sense of self. It is noteworthy that the apologetic writers seldom, if ever, address the mounting crisis of extreme human aggression (e.g., torture, mutilation, senseless and pleasure killing, rape, child abuse and molestation, and other crimes of passion). It does not seem possible for purely sociocultural, or even predominantly sociocultural, theories and assumptions to cogently explain such extreme and senseless forms of destructiveness. If sociocultural apologetics are to hold, they must confront the Beast in a Ted Bundy or Henry Lee Lucas, and explain it away in convincing fashion. So far, this has not been done.

The phylogenetic regression–progression model assumes that the Beast exists, in each of us, in the form of propensities, readinesses, and pre-programmed patterns that were developed in phylogeny and are presently housed in the neurohumoral hardware and software of the reptilian and paleomammalian brains. Moreover, we escape from the Beast or gain access to it through the processes of phylogenetic progression and regression (see Appendix I; chapters 3 and 4). Rather than acquiring the Beast through the learning of novel and arbitrary responses, its rudiments are "learned" phylogenetically, but the final behavioral product reflects the complex elaboration of basic response patterns by social and cultural forces (chapters 8 and 9). Much of this complex elaboration involves learning to inhibit our naturally spontaneous basic animality, and bringing it under the control of rules of law, custom, morality, and culture in general. In this view, we never totally transcend our basic animality; rather, it continues to influence us in subconscious, sublimated, and disguised ways. However, under stress, provocation, or other appropriately eliciting conditions (chapters 6 and 7), segments or part-segments of the Beast may return in relatively pure forms as the mantle of culture is shed in the regressive process.

In discussing whether the Beast-of-aggression still exists in human beings, it is necessary to consider the tripartite classification system of presently adaptive, once adaptive, and never adaptive behavior outlined in the prior chapter. As we saw with infanticide, infant killing serves contemporary adaptive functions in certain modern populations; that is, it remains on its original survival tracking and yields benefits in individual or inclusive fitness for the killer. Perhaps more common is the situation where normally suppressed once adaptive killing potential is released under certain circumstances of stress and provocation. The release of this potential, once strongly survival-tracked in phylogeny, may or may not serve any adaptive role in the modern context. More than likely, such release will be dysfunctional and maladaptive; e.g., the killing action slips off its "normal" survival track and becomes part of a complex dysfunctional mixture of structural, priming, and eliciting conditions whereby "senseless" infanticidal behavior is released. In those instances where violence is released as a pathological by-product of the mere fact that powerful centers of aggression exist in the brain, then we have "never adaptive" responsivity. Just as never adaptive misfiring of powerful aggression systems no doubt occurred as these systems were evolving in early species, so may such misfirings occur in modern humans. Infanticidal behavior or other extreme aggression of this type was, theoretically speaking, never survival-tracked in early phylogeny nor is it survival-tracked in its modern expression. Once we look at human aggression in these three ways, the either–or approach of the nature–nurture antagonists, or the often superficial and homocentric arguments of the apologists for human aggression lose much of their thrust. From our perspective, phylogenetically conditioned killing and destructive potential indeed exists and is always with us, housed deep within the primitive levels of the brain. However, it may be suppressed, modified, and elaborated numerous ways, and its outward manifestations may fall either into the presently adaptive, once adaptive, or never adaptive categories.

Presently adaptive and once adaptive functions often are difficult to distinguish, but there are several distinguishing criteria: (a) presently adaptive functions exhibit essentially uninterrupted continuity from lower species to the human level. For example, it is likely that males have been more aggressive than females, progressing upwardly from chimpanzees, through *australopithecus*, *erectus*, Neanderthal, etc., and on up to modern *Homo*. Thus, what was adaptive in earlier times continues to be presently adaptive today, although the survival-tracking is, no doubt, less firm in humans than in lower species. By contrast, killing nonrelatives or strangers who posed survival threat or threat to resources was probably once adaptive, but there is far less clear phylogenetic continuity for this adaptive strategy in modern humans than for nigh-universal sex differences in aggression. Therefore, killing strangers remains on once adaptive status and is normally suppressed, while the sex differential in aggression is phenotypically expressed with nearly as much power in most modern populations as in earlier times; (b) presently adaptive strategies are generally seen with far greater frequency within individuals and across populations than are the once adaptive strategies. It is, of course, tautological that functions less suppressed (the sex differential) are going to be more frequently seen than those more suppressed (killing the stranger); and (c) phylogenetic regression is required to recover the dormant once adaptive strategies, whereas presently adaptive strategies operate nearer to the person's modal level of functioning. For example, acting within one's phylogenetically conditioned sex role is modal for most people, whereas a regression to predatory destructiveness, xenophobia, and so on would be required to elicit the normally suppressed kill-the-stranger response.

PRIMITIVE AGGRESSION TYPE 1: PREDATION

The Dynamics of Animal Predation

Following the continuity assumption just discussed, we would suspect that the phylogenetically older a carryover is, the more likely it will be expressed in once adaptive rather than presently adaptive form. That is, the carryover will typically exist in latent form and will require phylogenetic regression for recovery. As the phylogenetically oldest form of aggression, by a wide margin, it follows that predatory aggression in humans typically exists in behaviorally latent, once adaptive forms. Thus, the fact that predatory aggression is rarely seen in original form, or that it does not play a central role in most post hunting-and-gathering societies, is not *prima facie* evidence for its disappearance somewhere in phylogeny. The phylogenetic regression–progression model assumes that predatory tendencies continue to exist in humans, largely in the reptilian brain, which emerge in extreme aggression against persons and objects (chapter 10). Although predatory aggression may be less obvious than in earlier times, it nevertheless serves as a foundation stone of human nature.

In exploring this foundation stone, let us now look at the dynamics of animal predation. First, we may ask ourselves whether predatory activity qualifies as an act of aggression. In pursuing this question, we quickly find ourselves faced with a troublesome paradox; despite the fact that predation involves the destruction of one animal for another, and despite the chasing, biting, tearing, and ferocity, the act is often viewed as a benign quirk of nature. Lorenz (1967), for example, extolls the survival value of predatory violence, and states that "The inner motives of the hunter are basically different from those of the fighter" (p. 25). Although this is literally true, it does not absolve the predator form the "guilt" of true aggression; it merely shows that the fighter and predator are both aggressive, but in different ways. In a similar vein, Carrighar (1971) sees predation as a kind of cosmic poetry, a symphony of life and death played without guile or malice. From another perspective, Wilson (1971) sees interspecific aggression as being less emotionally intense than that between members of the same species. Hence, not only is the predator accorded more positive intentions than the more bellicose, emotional intraspecific competitor, it often is viewed as nature's benefactor, improving stock by weeding out the weak and inferior, and serving to help keep populations within limit. And so our paradox is complete: predator–prey violence is the most prevalent cause of injury and death in animals (Southwick, 1970b), but as a necessary instrument of individual and species survival, it is not a true form of aggression.

In recent times, researchers (Brain, 1981; Moyer, 1976; Ursin, 1981; Valzelli, 1981) have appropriately placed predation within the family of aggressive behaviors in animals. As Moyer (1976) tells us, "*predatory aggression* is the attack behavior that an animal directs toward the injury or destruction of the prey. It is aggressive in that it leads to the injury or destruction of the prey" (p. 135). Yet, Moyer further says that predatory aggression has little in common with other classes of aggression, and that the predatory tendencies of a given animal do not allow one to predict aggressiveness toward targets other than prey, such as conspecifics or humans. From a number of perspectives we see that predatory aggression, although a genuine form of aggression, is somehow different, a special case. In the prior chapter, we concluded that predatory aggression is the phylogenetically oldest form of aggression; it has played a central role—perhaps the most central role—in the phylogenetic development of most living creatures; it is mediated by numerous and well-defined neurostructures in the reptilian and paleomammalian brains; its neurostructures have changed less in phylogeny than those for other forms of aggression; and, it is the only form of aggression that characteristically involves the destruction of its object. These distinctions do not disqualify predation as a form of aggression; much to the contrary, it is the oldest, the most omnipresent, and possibly the most theoretically important form of aggression in nature.

That predatory aggression is a major parameter of nature is shown by the number and variety of its instruments and the corresponding defenses against them. Street (1971), in his book *Animal Weapons,* shows the extent to which life and survival in many species depend on effective weaponry and defensive capability. A partial listing of techniques serves to make the point: horns, teeth, spines, suckers, projectiles, lures, traps, stings, poisons, and electrical shock on the offensive side, and burrowing, shells, camouflage, and warning coloration on the defensive side. As Lorenz (1967) informs us, the use of lethal weaponry is usually inhibited in conspecific fighting, whereas horns, teeth, and so forth are put to effective use against predators or prey. Eibl-Eibesfeldt (1970) describes how certain antelopes will gore a lion with horns that play a purely nonlethal role in highly ritualized intraspecific combat, and the giraffe uses its short horns to fight rivals while its more deadly hooves are reserved for the eating enemy. Although powerful weapons are not normally used directly against conspecifics, they enter the picture indirectly in maximizing threat gestures (teeth baring, etc.) and giving special form to certain well-controlled aggressive encounters (horn-locking, non-lethal biting, butting rather than pinching with claws in the fiddler crab, etc.). This, by the way, is one more reason to wonder why predation has been viewed as less aggressive than aggression within species, since the facts indicate that the evolved instruments of aggression are used against interspecifics and not used against conspecifics!

Despite its unique character, the predator–prey relationship stands high among nature's laws and might be considered the quintessence of the animal world. The very existence of many animals depends on the day-to-day outcome of the dynamics of predation, and to eat another or to avoid being eaten accounts for a great amount of behavior in the wild. Predation's frequency, however important, is not the whole story, for it is in the attack and flight, danger and deception, and competition and concealment that we see the defining characteristics of each species expressed in their most salient forms.

Up From the Killer Ape?

If predation is so central to animal existence and behavior, then is it not reasonable to assume that predatory dynamics are equally important for man, who evolved with no less blood on his hands? This seemingly obvious question forms the basis for one of the greatest controversies of this century in social science, and is one of the more malevolent variations of the nature–nurture issue. Whenever questions of man's baser

nature are brought to fore, advocates for the defense—humanistic psychologists, anthropologists, and sociologists—rush to quell the rumor,
whereas certain of the more pessimistic evolutionary prosecutors dog-
gedly present what, for them, is proof for the case. In no other area, save
possibly for the issue of race and intelligence, are the antagonists so
locked in opposition as in the case of human aggression, especially
predatory aggression. Most agree that man evolved as a hunter, and many
agree that man is a rapacious, omnivorous creature whose capability for
violence exceeds all others. The humanist argues, however, that man's
misdeeds resulted from the adoption of the agrarian way and subsequent
development of an unnatural form of social organization called *civilization*. Prior to these perversions man was an amiable herbivore who might
have accidently dined on a mouse or two and little more. Even if he did
kill, it was a pleasureless, perfunctory act motivated by nothing more
than a physiological need for protein. Certainly he was not a bloodthirsty
killer who not only killed, but had to kill.

Evolutionary reconstructions of man's predatory nature are complicated by two major obstacles: First, the fossil evidence regarding man's
predecessors is very fragmented and incomplete. Because all of man's
direct forbears are extinct, it is not possible to resolve any issue of man's
nature short of controversy, and what are cited as facts are, in reality,
personal deductions based on scraps of evidence. Thus, the rightness or
wrongness of evolutionary reconstructions reflects the theorist's reputation, his or her skill in argument, and reader receptivity to a great degree.
Secondly, the evidence is fragmented and incomplete regarding man's
closest living relatives, the monkeys and apes. Indeed, little was known of
primates in the wild until the work of Zuckerman, Carpenter, Hall,
DeVore, Washburn, Schaller, Goodall, Teleki, Fossey, Hrdy, and others.
Although the evidence is incomplete both phylogenetically and comparatively, it is clear that as new data accumulate the differences between
humans and closely related species are being reduced rather than increased. Thus, as we gain in knowledge the "romantic fallacy" of human
uniqueness and the "illusion of man's central position in nature" (Ardrey,
1970) have begun to yield to the realization that the ape–human gap is not
so large after all (see Gallup & Suarez, 1983, Table 1.1 for an up-to-date
summary of animal–human similarities in mentation and behavior).

Given that many ape–human similarities were observed only in the past
few decades, many misconceptions about primates and the uniqueness of
human nature were bound to arise. Among these misconceptions were
that primates are really not that aggressive generally, and predation has
little if any significance in primate social life. Both of these notions are
easily refuted. There is little argument that monkeys are quite aggressive,
especially the baboons and macaques, but there are those who argue that

man's closest relatives, the great apes, are so unaggressive as to negate any possibility of innate aggression in humans (see Lewis & Towers, 1972, for an extreme view). The gorilla and chimpanzee spend much more time on the ground than other apes (Dolinhow, 1972), and are much more humanlike in their genetics, morphology, and social behavior. Also, the overlap between man and chimpanzee in genetic make-up, brain structure and behavior is truly remarkable (Goodall, 1982; chapter 6). Therefore, if these creatures are basically unaggressive, so the argument goes, then man is likely to be similarly unaggressive in an evolutionary sense.

The mountain gorilla certainly appears to be unaggressive much of the time, but he can be rough if pushed too far. The threat that he might be aggressive seems to reinforce dominance and leadership in the silver-backed male, and perhaps the evolutionary process substituted implicit cues in the form of brute size and capacity to intimidate for overt aggression. Still, as Dian Fossey (1981, 1984) showed, a darker side of gorilla behavior—including infanticide and other forms of extreme intra-specific aggression—can come out under stress or disruption of normal patterns. Moreover, there is recent evidence that some gorilla infanticide may be a "normal" and adaptive reproductive tactic by which the killing male enhances his chances for gaining breeding females (Fossey, 1984). With the chimpanzee, there is less ambiguity regarding potential for aggression and predatory violence. Goodall's (1971, 1972) early observation on the Gombe Stream suggested that chimpanzees belonging to the same community seldom direct lethal aggression toward one another, but controlled aggression is used by dominant males to assure their position, and these males, when frustrated, may attack other members of the group. Although familiar chimpanzees were not frequently violent toward one another, they did exhibit a wide range of frenetic and clamorous aggressive behaviors that included (Goodall, 1972) "temper tantrums," "glaring," "slapping and stamping," "the bipedal swagger," "the attacking charge," "stamping on the back," "lifting, slamming, and dragging," "biting," "hair-pulling," and so on. In this tense atmosphere, females, lower ranking males, and the young must emit a wide range of appeasement gestures to avoid attacks from the dominant males.

Whereas lethal aggression is infrequent among familiar chimpanzees, murderous attacks may occur between members of different communities. For undetermined reasons (Goodall, 1979), the original community of chimps studied by Goodall began to divide in 1970. By 1972, two distinct communities had separated, one established in the southern part of the home range and the other in the north. For a time things were peaceful, with between-community antagonism limited to loud displays by males patrolling the common boundary. Then in early 1974, a gang of five chimps from one community caught a single male from the other and subjected him to a vicious 20-minute attack (Goodall, 1979). The victim suffered innumerable wounds from hitting, kicking, and biting, and later disappeared into the jungle never to be seen again. Shortly thereafter, several other gang attacks by young males occurred, including the severe beating of an old male, who presumably later died, and the killing of an old female. The pattern of attacks led Goodall to suspect that a rare phenomenon was being recorded—"the gradual extermination of one group of animals by another, stronger, group" (Goodall, 1979, p. 608). Goodall was shaken by these startling new findings, and expressed her surprise that "chimpanzees might, deliberately and systematically, kill one another" (p. 620). She concludes the 1979 article, by stating that "our new awareness of chimpanzee violence compels us to acknowledge that these ape cousins of ours are even *more* similar to humans than we thought before" (p. 620).

Marler (1976) believes violence in animals has been underestimated, and he argues that, once the "quiet" violence of dominance relations, territoriality, infant neglect and abandonment, and withholding of food resources are considered, "a great deal of animal mortality must have an element of social causation" (p. 240). All this suggests that aggression is a major moderator of animal social behavior, with certain of the consequences being pathological and stress-induced and others being adaptive and survival-tracked. In fact, Bernstein and Gordon (1974) speculate that "excessive" primate aggression (beyond what is needed for predation or self-defense) may be the very force "which *bonds* primates to one another" (p. 307; italics added) and helps maintain their social structure. Bernstein and Gordon enumerate many aspects of adaptive aggression in primates, including defense against predators, competition for resources, territorial repulsion of threatening intruders, dominance relations, competing for sexual access, the establishment and maintenance of social order, and sex-role socialization. Bernstein and Gordon are aware of the nonadaptive and pathological effects of extreme and uncontrolled primate aggression, but they conclude that "the complete absence of aggression would be equally disastrous" (p. 311).

Clearly, primates exhibit generous amounts of both adaptive and maladaptive aggression in the wild, but what about the specific case of predatory aggression? It is true that hunting and meat-eating are infrequent phenomena in primates, but relative frequency is a poor measure of social or functional importance. Having a baby is an infrequent occurrence in humans, yet there is no more important social phenomenon than the blessed event, which, interestingly, wanes in excitement with frequency. More important is the functional significance of a behavioral event that, although infrequent, may go to the very roots of an animal's existence. Such is the case for primate predation. It is well-known that baboons kill and eat newborn gazelles, half-grown hares, nestling birds, and other small animals (Washburn & DeVore, 1961a), but their diet is overwhelmingly vegetarian with meat accounting for less than 1% of food intake. Nevertheless, Washburn and DeVore state: "The readiness to eat meat is present, however, and it is easy to see how the acquisition of a simple weapon by *Australopithecus* could expand the baboon kind of diet to include the killing of many more small creatures" (p. 94). In another paper, Washburn and DeVore (1961b) enumerate the many contrasts between the social behavior of baboons and early man, and conclude that many of the differences can be attributed to the more well-developed patterns of hunting in hominids. It is ironic that early man's distinctiveness was so strongly based on being a better predator than his distant cousin the baboon.

Hunting in Chimpanzees.   Speculation about the hominid transition from herbivore to hunter can be carried further when the object of study is the chimpanzee rather than the baboon. Early studies by Washburn, DeVore, and others led to the presumption of baboons merely stumbling upon occasional prey, and there was little talk of active hunting behavior. Goodall's (1971) observation on chimpanzees also showed them to be occasional meat eaters who sometimes appeared to capture their prey almost by accident. At other times, however, their hunting seemed more purposeful and deliberate, and involved "remarkable cooperation" among the participants. One form of cooperation involved the apparent blocking of the cornered victim's escape routes by several chimpanzees stationing themselves appropriately at the bases of nearby trees. Goodall (1971) only observed two actual instances of chimpanzees killing prey, however: One in which a red Colobus monkey was seized and torn to pieces, and another spectacular instance where a juvenile baboon was stalked and killed amid the screaming hunting cries of the chimps and the roaring of agitated male baboons. Once the baboon was slain by having its head slammed onto some rocks, other chimps in the valley, attracted by screams and cries that "typifies a hunt and kill," quickly appeared to join in the revelry. The resulting feast gave every impression of being a singularly enjoyable event: "Chimpanzees nearly always eat meat slowly, usually chewing leaves with each mouthful as though to savor the taste for as long as possible" (Goodall, 1971, p. 206).

One could argue that Goodall's observations fail to make the case that chimpanzees are by nature hunters and lovers of meat, for predation was not the central focus of her study and even the best researcher must have his or her data confirmed by others. Whatever doubt remained was dispelled by the work of Geza Teleki (1973) in his book, *The Predatory Behavior of Wild Chimpanzees.* Building on Goodall's work and his own field studies at Gombe in 1968 and 1969, Teleki showed that chimpanzees preyed upon six different species in the area, with young baboons being most preferred. Further, predatory behavior proved to be a group activity involving males exclusively in the pursuit phase, mostly males in the capture phase, and eventually all members of the group in the consumption phase. Although the whole sequence is a cooperative venture, the relative unaggressive sharing in the consumption phase was one of its most remarkable aspects. Here the usual rules of rank and priority failed to hold, and an alpha male might be seen begging food from a subordinate who would flee under other circumstances. An additional feature of crucial importance was the chimpanzee's passion for baboon brains, a dietetic preference documented in detail by both Goodall and Teleki. One cannot overestimate the significance of this specific finding and the general conclusion that the chimpanzee, although the hunter only 10 or so times a year, is a hunter nevertheless and a member of the exclusive fraternity of carnivores. Marler (1973), in a review of Teleki's book, sums up the situation quite well:

> There can be no doubt that predatory behavior is deeply rooted in the social life of the chimpanzee. The meat eating of nonhuman primates can no longer be dismissed as casual omnivory. The opened baboon skulls from which brains are eagerly removed are remarkably like those found by Raymond Dart with australopithecine remains. (p. 572)

Chimpanzee predation is accepted as a given in Goodall's recent writings, and, similar to our formulation, she even hints that certain cases of chimpanzee infanticide may involve the predatory system. One of the most disquieting discoveries at Gombe occurred when an adult female, Passion, killed and ate the new infant of Gilka, whose first baby had mysteriously disappeared when about a month old (Goodall, 1979). Gilka had been sitting with her infant when Passion appeared and charged her. Gilka fled and Passion seized and killed the baby, whereupon she and her own two offspring, Pom (adolescent female) and Prof (infant male) consumed the flesh. The following year, Gilka again gave birth, but the baby met the same fate, this time at the hands of Pom, who had learned well from her mother. Several other infants were killed and still others vanished. Passion and Pom were the prime suspects, and, in one instance, Goodall actively intervened to save an infant from their murderous intentions. Goodall declined to speculate at length on the causes of this apparently aberrant behavior, but she did note that Passion and her offspring "behaved as if the baby were normal prey" (Goodall, 1979, pp. 612–613). She also noted that calmness, begging, and sharing occurred during the eating of the infant, as would occur in the consumption of normal prey. It seems that "normal," presently adaptive predatory tendencies somehow slipped out of their natural tracking and were directed toward inappropriate prey objects. Indeed, the entire sequence would have been quite normal had the victims been infant baboons rather than infant chimpanzees.

The Dartian Hypothesis.   We now come to the most crucial question of all—were our primordial ancestors innately aggressive, carnivorous predators, and if so, have these propensities been transmitted genetically up the hominid line to the most aggressive creature of them all, modern man? For a number of writers the answer is a firm yes on both counts, although the range of opinion goes all the way to those who deny any form of innate aggression in either man or his forbears. The affirmative case began with Dart, the discoverer of *Australopithecus africanus,* who is the most fervent spokesman for the theory of man as predator. Once the idea struck home, after many years of sifting through fossil remains at various sites in southern Africa, Dart proceeded with what his university compeers saw as a savage and relentless attack on the image of man. A sampling from his paper (Dart, 1953/1973), "The Predatory Transition from Ape to Man," will show why his colleagues were inclined to dismiss his work:

> The australopithecine deposits of Taungs, Sterkfontein and Makapansgat tell us in this way a consistent, coherent story not of fruit-eating, forest-loving apes, but of the sanguinary pursuits and carnivorous habits of proto-man. (p. 30)

> The loathsome cruelty of mankind to man forms one of his inescapable, characteristic and differentiative features; and it is explicable only in terms of his carnivorous, and cannibalistic origin. (p. 32)

> On this thesis man's predecessors differed from living apes in being confirmed killers: carnivorous creatures, that seized living quarries by violence, battered them to death, tore apart their broken bodies, dismembered them limb from limb, slaking their ravenous thirst with this hot blood of victims and greedily devouring livid writhing flesh. (p. 34)

Amid these gems of overstatement, Dart argued that "the chief cultural tools of the Australopithecinae were clubs formed by the long limbs of antelopes" (p. 30), and, further, that "accuracy in hitting and hurling, which the apes lack but which men universally possess, is an inherited instinct" (p. 35). So, if we are to believe Dart, australopithecus was a weapon-toting, stone-throwing hunter, a carnivorous consumer of flesh whose heritage demanded the use of deadly aggression for survival.
We may rightfully accuse Dart of hair-raising hyperbole, and we may be

repelled by his gory literary reconstructions, but his central thesis (viz., man's predatory nature) is not easily dismissed. Man as predator is not a new idea, for as early as 1917 Carveth Read suggested that pre-hominids might have had the characteristics of a predatory wolf-like primate, much like the baboon, and earlier James (1911) referred to "the rooted bellicosity of human nature," and he saw man as "the most formidable of all beasts of prey, and indeed, the only one that preys systematically on its own species." Long before Dart, cannibalism was widely recognized as a sordid blemish on the human condition, but few could force themselves to view the practice as part and parcel of man's baser nature. Freeman (1964) acknowledged cannibalism to be "one expression of man's carnivorous nature" which "was probably once a universal practice" (p. 113), and Hogg (1958) documented the extent of the practice over the centuries. The existence of cannibalism is consistent with the Dartian thesis of the killer instinct, but its prevalence throughout history does not, of course, prove the thesis.

Man the Hunter

Although writers differ sharply on the issue of man as predator, most agree that man was a hunter throughout most of hominid evolutionary development. As we recall from chapter 4, approximately 99% of human evolution occurred within the hunting and gathering mode (Campbell, 1979), and as Laughlin (1968) summarized, "Hunting is the master pattern of the human species" (p. 304). By referring back to Table 4.10, we see that hunting and gathering dominated all major phases of human prehistory, including diet, mating, reproductive behavior and parenting, social behavior and kinship ties, perceptual and mental functioning, social order and politics, in-group and out-group relations, and so on. As argued in chapter 4, many of our basic tendencies (e.g., motivation-emotion-reward-behavior linkages) are by-products of the phylogenetic shaping that occurred in the hunting and gathering phase, and it is to them that we most often regress when under stress. Such regressions allow access to the warmth, cooperativeness, playfulness, and sharing of the quintessential hunter–gatherer, but there is a darker side also: Hunting is a predatory activity, and there can be no hunting without killing. The dispositions and behavioral tendencies that serve the hunter include, as a central component, a killing potential, an evolved capability and willingness to destroy other species for one's own benefit. This often pleasure-inducing, killing potential still resides deep in our reptilian and mammalian brains, and continues to serve certain presently adaptive functions (e.g., present-day hunting and killing of animals for food). More problematic is the occasional regressive return of the killing potential in the once adaptive or never adaptive modalities. Here the once adaptive killing potential may slip out of its normal suppression under stress (e.g., an urban business-man who has never hunted may kill another person), or aspects of the killing potential that were never adaptive may be released through psychosis, drugs, psychosis, or local dysfunction in the predatory aggression centers of the brain.

Concluding Comment

In conclusion, it seems undeniable that man possesses the neuropsychological substrates for predatory aggression and that he has been a hunter throughout most of his existence, but what about the killer ape, the mythological Grendel whose lust for blood is an all-consuming, cosmic obsession? Phylogenetic regression theory views the killer ape notion as an exaggerated, oversimplified, caricature of the truth, but, yet, true to a degree. At no time in human history was man, as a matter of practice, a rampaging, bloodthirsty monster genetically programmed for random killing. Neither is man endowed with a spontaneous, cyclic drive to injure and kill that must be periodically satisfied. But man possesses the ready capacity to kill, and probably always has. The predatory theme runs deep in human protohistory making cruelty, destructiveness, and pleasure-in-violence highly probable but not necessarily inevitable. At least, violence is not inevitable for individuals, but the outlook is not so optimistic where populations are concerned, especially stressed or socially disordered populations (Shepard, 1973).

PRIMITIVE AGGRESSION TYPE 2:
TERRITORIALITY

Spatial Aggression

The use of space is one of the most fundamental aspects of animal behavior. To exist an animal must occupy space, and the animal's movement in space defines its behavior. This movement is typically obstructed by, or conversely facilitated by animate and inanimate objects in the environment, and individual behavior must be viewed in the context of complex, mutually inclusive spatial relationships. Animal spacing is influenced by a host of nonrandom internanimal and object-animal parameters such as affiliation, attachment, and aggression on the individual level, and geographic locus, group movement, and species dispersion at the population level. Spacing parameters underlie and give character to the social structure of many species, and social behavior in the ontogenetic sense, and survival in the phylogenetic sense depend largely on effective use of space.

Organisms are functionally and spatially distributed into intricate, encompassing ecosystems at the most general level of analysis, multi-species communities at the next biotic level, and single-species niches at the most fundamental level (Andrewartha & Birch, 1954). Individual and species roles are stable and well-defined in the interrelationships that comprise the overall ecosystem, and much of this consistency emanates from interspecies predatory competition. Most animal spacing involves food-seeking movements or predator avoidance either through direct maneuver when in actual proximity, or by virtue of numerous anticipatory behaviors. Obviously, distance and spacing are important elements in predator–prey dynamics, with the predator being motivated to close distance between it and the prey, and the prey motivated to do the opposite. Hediger (1964) says that the be-all and end-all of a wild animal's existence is flight from enemies, and the particular "escape reactions," "defense reactions," and "critical reactions" involved are species–specific and subject to definite laws, both qualitatively and quantitatively. Each of these reactions is based on a measurable inter-animal distance factor: The escape reaction is elicited by approach to within the flight distance, the defense reaction by approach to within the defense distance, and the critical reaction (exhibited when escape is prevented in some way) by approach to within the critical distance.

The predator–prey interplay represents one of the many ways adaptive aggression acts to regulate and organize animals into spatial and social systems. Possibly more than any other factor, predatory aggression determines where most animals are and what they are doing at a given time. Adaptive aggression also plays an important role in mediating a host of intraspecific behavioral processes, including spatial regulation among conspecifics. According to Glen McBride (1971):

> Aggression is the most common behavior used to control spacing areas. It may be overt, or formalized into mild threats and avoidance. The stimuli releasing aggression are never simply those from conspecifics, but always include a distance component, that is, the neighbor must be in the spacing area. The distance component of aggressive stimuli is so general that one has little difficulty in arguing that intraspecific aggressiveness evolved to keep conspecifics spaced for any of the many functions served by spacing. (pp. 53–54)

Aggression is involved, at varying degrees of subtlety and directness, in most of an animal's actions relative to its conspecifics. If a member of a gregarious species, it will maintain a conservative social distance (Hediger, 1964), meaning the maximum distance the animal will move away from the group. Among other things, this constricted social distance serves as a protection against predator aggression, for the animal is able to quickly retreat into the safety of the group when threatened. Social distance is sometimes controlled by dominant members of the group who demand social proximity from subordinates, as is often seen in the despot-harem grouping in baboons. As McBride (1971) points out, the living space of gregarious animals falls somewhere between the outer limits of social distance and the personal fields of nearby neighbors. Even if the closely spaced conspecifics do not defend well-defined geographic territories, aggressive encounters may occur when personal fields or "body territories" are overly encroached upon.

Territorial Defense

Animals may be seen as operating in their respective *ranges* (the total area the animal traverses), *territories* (areas defended), *core areas* (areas typically occupied), and *homes* (areas where animals sleep). Of these various spatial areas, the territory is most important theoretically and is the place where adaptive aggression is most intensely expressed. Nowhere is controlled aggression more clearly seen than in the establishment and maintenance of individual and, in some instances, group territories. Amid the many functions and definitions of territory discussed in the literature, the notion of defense stands uppermost, and is its most defining characteristic.

As an evolved social mechanism, territoriality must be functional in some way, and Carpenter (1958) lists no less than 32 distinct adaptive properties of territorial behavior, including (a) protection against predators; (b) reinforcement of dominance and selective breeding of the strong; (c) reduction of sex-related fighting and killing; (d) helps in warning and repelling trespassers; (e) facilitates protection of nest and young; and (f) helps prevent overpopulation and aids in species dispersion over available space. The spacing element is certainly a cardinal function of territory from the standpoints of groups and populations, whereas the protection functions relate more specifically to individuals and small aggregations of animals. Hediger (1961) suggests another rather novel function, that of insuring close confinement of conspecifics in groups so they can model after each other and benefit from mutual experience. More recently, Pontius (1976) hypothesized that territory fosters adaptation and survival by preventing unstructured overstimulation of certain subcortical structures (especially the limbic system and septal region) that play important roles in emotion, motivation, and species propagation. Of all the many adaptive functions of territory, however, reduction of injury due to intraspecific fighting stands out as one of the most important; here, as in the dominance hierarchy, we see nature's way of using controlled aggression to reduce uncontrolled or dyscontrolled aggression. Although a given animal may be frequently called upon to repel territorial intruders by threat or actual fighting, overall aggression is reduced in the long run due to fairly stable spatio-territorial relations that develop among species members.

A *territory,* most simply defined, is an area occupied by a particular animal. Most definitions in the literature, however, are more complex, and certain of the functions of territory often enter the definition. Carpenter (1958) sees territoriality as a "behavioral system which is expressed in a spatial-temporal frame of reference" (p. 228), whereas Hediger (1964) defines territory "as an area which is first rendered distinctive by its owner in a particular way and, secondly, is defended by it" (p. 9). Mayr (1935) defined territory as an area occupied by a male of a species that is defended against intrusions by male conspecifics, within which the defender makes himself conspicuous. One of the best and simplest definitions, according to Hediger (1964), is that of Noble (1939) who defined territory as any defended area. In his excellent review of the literature on territory in birds, Armstrong (1965) discussed a number of definitions that emphasize the reproductive and bonding aspects of territorial behavior, but he concluded that defense against competitors of the same species is the most essential feature of territory.

Whether one is speaking of territory, territoriality, territorialism (Armstrong, 1965), field of repulsion (Kummer, 1971), repulsion by advertisement (Wilson, 1971), or whatever, aggression in the form of threat and/or fighting is involved. Consequently, Brown (1964), suggests that territoriality is most accurately regarded as site-dependent aggressiveness. Similarly, Eibl-Eibesfeldt (1970) says that ownership of territory is often a prerequisite for aggressive behavior, whereas Carpenter (1958) states that "attack, encroachment, and defense constitute important aspects of territoriality, and so do challenge, vocalization, song, and other display or signalling activities" (p. 229). Also of considerable importance is the fact that an animal is capable of more effective counteraggression when in its territory, and success in fighting increases with closeness to the territory's center (Armstrong, 1965). So it seems that territory ultimately leads to lower levels of aggression, but it allows its defender to rise to supernormal heights of aggression when faced with a trespasser.

Establishment of a territory involves demarcation as well as defense. Territorial demarcation falls under four basic headings (Hediger, 1961): optical, acoustical, olfactory, and combinations of the three. The optical modality is predominant in lower vertebrates, such as fish and reptiles, whereas birds tend to employ both the optical and acoustical modalities. Mammals up to prosimians tend to favor olfactory types of marking, but the primates, including humans, demonstrate great variability in methods of demarcation. A number of higher primates employ raucous vocalizing to repel intruders, whereas man uses every conceivable technique to designate boundaries. Visual markers such as signs, fences, geographic boundaries, and so forth are preferred by humans, but vocal and even olfactory methods are sometimes used (Hediger, 1961; Hereford, Cleland, & Fellner, 1973). With humans vocal responses ("Would you please not use my yard for a pathway?") serve as a second line of defense when the weaker, implicit visual markers (shrubs, tree lines, yard markers, etc.) fail to do their job.

The Question of Human Territoriality

Considerable controversy has arisen in recent years over attempts to extrapolate from animal territoriality to human spatial behavior. Whether or not humans are territorial in the simplistic sense is debatable, but there is no question that man shows a wide range of behaviors appropriately characterized as territorial (Mehrabian, 1976). Whereas Ardrey's (1966) speculations about the underlying mechanisms of human territoriality remain unproven, his examples and illustration stand firm, for history itself is a chronicle of the establishment and disestablishment of individual, group, and national boundaries through the use of invasion and defense. Hence, the argument is not about facts, but the interpretation of facts. Ardrey postulates a phylogenetic, instinctive basis for human territoriality, which has been severely criticized by social and biological scientists alike (Crook, 1968; Holloway, 1968c; Klopfer, 1968; Montagu, 1968). Still, one of the experts (Etkin, 1967) states that "There is a striking resemblance between territoriality as it appears in animal societies and the reactions of human groups to their 'native soil' " (p. 140). In a later chapter of Etkin's book, Freedman (1967) discusses territoriality in primitive hunting peoples, and further comments on the territorial aspects of teenage gangs in American cities. Davis (1968) likewise reflects on the primate nature of human gangs (e.g., rank and territorial characteristics) that he suspects is based on innate, evolved aggressive tendencies. Eibl-Eibesfeldt (1972) also believes "Many features of human territorial behavior point to out ancient primate heritage" (p. 75), and he asserts that humans defend both individual and group territories (see also Eibl-Eibesfeldt, 1979). Tinbergen (1968) is much more cautious about generalizing from animals to humans and considers individual and pair territories to be of limited importance to man. However, he believes man behaves very much like a group-territorial species.

Washburn and Hamburg (1972) argue that territorial defense in the classic sense is not typical of monkeys and apes, and Jolly (1972) correctly points out that "territorial defense has arisen over and over, by convergent evolution in unrelated lines of primates as an adaptation to particular niches, whereas even closely related species may differ in their territorial behavior" (p. 171). But what of our closest relatives the chimpanzees? Goodall's (1979) observations on the Gombe chimpanzees found not only startling evidence of infanticide, cannibalism, warfare, and genocide, but chimpanzee territoriality as well. More recently, in discussing social order and possessiveness in chimpanzees, Goodall (1982) stated, "Chimpanzees are territorial: adult males regularly patrol boundaries, chasing off or even killing strangers" (p. 357). In reviewing what he called the "Gombe Holocaust," Desmond (1979) concludes, "Chimpanzees *can* be aggressively territorial, much more so than was previously realized" (p. 223). Desmond also commented on murderous attacks on interlopers from neighboring groups, where "chimpanzee compassion" was conspicuously absent. All of this seems to refute earlier assertions that chimpanzees are nonterritorial and lacking in intragroup and intergroup spatial consciousness. Certainly, chimpanzees are not territorial in the urgent, reflexive form seen in birds. The large neocortex of the chimpanzee produces a far more elaborate and flexible territoriality, one not thoroughly bound by blind instinct or stimulus control.

As a nonterrestrial, or mobile terrestrial species, as the case may be, primates are unlikely to show the site-dependent aggressiveness Brown (1964) describes, but this actually enables them to use aggression in a wider range of contexts. In primates we see a greater rather than lesser use of the spatial aggression McBride (1971) sees as the hub of primate social organization. Along with repulsion of predators and reinforcement of stability and control within social groups—both of which involve distance parameters and spatial aggression—intergroup repulsion and antagonism to the stranger (Marler, 1976) are equally indigenous to the primate way of life. It is here, and not in site-dependent territorial defense, that we have cause to believe once adaptive, spatially mediated aggression has entered the human heart through the primate family tree. That primate social grouping and dispersion are largely based on spatial aggression and intergroup hostility is amply supported in numerous primate field studies (Carpenter, 1964; Dolinhow, 1972; Jay, 1967; Jolly, 1972; Kummer, 1971). Following a review of the existing literature, Washburn and Hamburg (1972) commented, "It is our belief that intergroup aggression in primates had been greatly underestimated" (p. 287). They further state, "Intergroup aggression either leads to one group's having the resources of an area at its exclusive disposal, or at least creates a situation in which one is much more likely to obtain food in one area" (p. 286).

Thus it appears that spatial regulation in primate species is largely governed by intergroup hostility, which is itself attuned to available food resources in a particular area. These fundamental baseline parameters of primate social life are interesting to weigh in relation to Bigelow's (1972) analysis of the role of intergroup conflict in human evolution. He argues that intergroup competition may have been more vital to hominid evolution than mere hunting, for "keeping other humans off the hunting grounds" would seem a necessary precondition for ready access to game and avoidance of starvation. He takes issue with the speculation that early hominid groups were so widely dispersed that lethal competition was improbable, and reminds us that, "The relatively sudden disappearance of Neanderthal man coincides with the appearance of *Homo sapiens* in western Europe, and we cannot ignore the very obvious implications of this coincidence" (p. 9). One could easily interpret these aspects of Professor Bigelow's theory as a variation of the Dartian hypothesis expressed in spatial and group terms. Whether or not Dart or Bigelow are right in their assumptions, it is more than probable that early man was no less prone to hostility, in-group versus out-group repulsion, and spatial aggression than were his primate predecessors.

Body Territory.   Even if we assume mankind is naturally inclined toward spatial aggression and the establishment and defense of group territories (Tinbergen, 1968; Valzelli, 1981), it does not necessarily follow that individual territorialism is likewise a part of human nature. Nevertheless, it is likely that some degree of once adaptive individual territoriality, even of the hard, site-dependent sort, continues to play a role in the spatial affairs of humans. That it is seldom expressed in pure form is not a negating factor; its overt expression is more likely seen in muted, socially moderated, and socially elaborated forms where deep, intrinsic motivational forces yield, to a degree, to external demands. One indirect, outward manifestation of inner territoriality is seen in the protection of one's own body. It is reasonable to assume that one's body, and the body buffer zone (Kinzel, 1970) immediately surrounding it represents a kind of portable territory which is readily defended at the slightest intrusion. Lyman and Scott (1967) coined the term "body territory" to describe this basically site-independent, geography-free concept that is highly analogous to the sociofugal spacing mechanisms seen in animals. Body territory includes the space encompassed by the external human body and the anatomical space of the body, the latter of which is "the most private and inviolable of the territories belonging to an individual" (p. 241). For Lyman and Scott, body territory is only one of several facets of human territoriality, and they provide a provocative analysis of control of space in public areas, the home, and certain group interactions. Along with these public territories, home territories, interaction territories, and body territories, there are three types of reaction to encroachment: turf defense, insulation, and linguistic collusion. All of this suggests that human beings are motivated to develop territories, motivated to define criteria for encroachment, and motivated to defend these areas when encroached upon.

The Northwestern University anthropologist Edward T. Hall has also been very effective in exploiting the notion of human territoriality. His work (1959, 1961, 1963, 1969, 1971) helped bridge the chasm between hard ethological empiricism on the animal side and tender anthropological speculation on the human side. With a rigorous anthropological point of view and a deep empathy for ethological theory, Hall brought human territoriality into the mainstream of modern social science in a more credible way than the so-called popularizers of ethological concepts. In his seminal *The Hidden Dimension* (1969), Hall built upon the foundations laid by Christian and Calhoun in crowding and stress, and Hediger in the spatial world of animals. Venturing farther across the barbed wire of disciplinary boundaries than most, Hall acknowledged the fundamental importance of the biological "infraculture" embedded in human territoriality, and argued that by observing animals we can "learn an amazing amount that it translatable to human terms" (Hall, 1969, p. 7). And those hoping to apply ethological notions to human space behavior, might take as their credo the following quote from chapter one of *The Hidden Dimension:* "Thus any attempt to observe, record, and analyze proxemic systems, which are parts of modern cultures, must take into account the behavioral systems on which they are based as expressed by earlier life forms" (p. 4).

Concluding Argument

From this brief review of animal and human territoriality, it appears probable that certain aspects of animal territoriality continue to intrude into the affairs of man, but this does not imply the presence of a coherent, thoroughly wired-in "territorial instinct" that constantly presses for expression irrespective of circumstances. Phylogenetic regression theory does assume that various once adaptive territorial tendencies in humans are phylogenetically continuous with lower animals, but they are variable in form and presumably mediated through a number of subneocortical structures. Human territoriality is thus not a single, evolved entity, but rather a set of self-, kin-, and property-protecting propensities that involve a shifting amalgam of several primitive motive sources depending on particular eliciting circumstances. Along with pure, site-dependent aggression of the sort seen in animals, there are other likely once adaptive contributors including spatial aggression, sociobiological selfishness (de-

fense of one's own genes, body, material possessions, etc.), inclusive
fitness (defense of kin), xenophobia and ingroup–outgroup antipathy, and
no doubt a host of other factors. When social learning, cultural influences,
and the capacity of the neocortex to refine and elaborate old prerogatives
are brought into the picture, we begin to see why experts disagree on the
"causes" of human territoriality.

A Conceptual Hierarchy.   A good primitive-to-advanced or regression–
progression hierarchy for territoriality might go as follows: site-dependent
aggression → spatial aggression → proxemics and personal space → self or
egocentric territoriality → conceptual territoriality. Strict site-dependent
aggression would appear to be oldest and purest form, followed by a more
general spatial aggression that mediates many aspects of social behavior
but is not restricted to a single geographic locus. These two primitive
forms have a long phylogenetic history, and encompass most of the
distance-related aggressive behavior of animals. With humans, these two
forms are seldom obvious, but they still serve as the covert motive
sources for the more advanced, neocorticalized expressions of territoriality. For example, at the third level, proxemics and personal space, once
adaptive territorial aggression is modified considerably by cultural learning; nevertheless, the underlying biogrammar or infraculture of space is
basically the same across cultures even though great surface variability
may be present. Indeed, in most cultures individuals are highly motivated
to defend one's home area, one's own body, one's immediate kin, and
one's life-sustaining material goods, but how these things are defended
differs from culture to culture.

   With proxemics and personal space we move well into distinctively
human expressions of territoriality (see Edney, 1974). There is a massive
literature on proxemics and personal space (Altman, 1975; Baldassare,
1978; Edinger & Patterson, 1983; Evans & Howard, 1973; Hayduk, 1978;
Mehrabian, 1976; Patterson, 1968; Scheflen, 1976; Sommer, 1969), and
this is where most of the empirical research on human space behavior is
concentrated. The proxemics–personal space level is one where social
learning, cultural learning, values, prejudices, preferences, and the like
help mediate, with the help of the lower emotional–motivational centers,
our sociospatial interactions. At the next level, self or egocentric territoriality, we move from a spatial concept of territory to a psychological one:
"to facilitate the study of co-mingling—at least in American society—it is
useful to extend the notion of territoriality into claims that function like
territories but are not spatial and it is useful to focus on situational and
egocentric territoriality" (Goffman, 1972, p. 29). Certainly it makes sense
to assume that defense of self, along with defense of body, is a major
motivating force in humans. The last level, conceptual territoriality, is the

most novel and it allows us to expand the notion of territoriality to include the personalization of and defense of ideas and concepts. John B. Calhoun discussed conceptual territories in his 1968 address at the Meeting of the American Association for the Advancement of Science:

> The experience of things becomes transformed into concepts about them until evolution produces a conceptual space in which values are related to relationships between abstract ideas rather than to ways of behaving in relation to physical situations. The responsible choice among ideas forming one's conceptual space replaces the search for resources in physical space. Commitment to abstract values which guide action replaces aggressive defense of physical objects incorporated into one's ego. Compassion—the understanding support of others with differing values—replaces submission to aggressive action. Evolutionary progression tends to increase the time and energy devoted to *conceptual space*. (Calhoun, 1971, p. 329; italics added)

PRIMITIVE AGGRESSION TYPE 3: DOMINANCE

Animal Aggression and Social Order

Defense of territory and competition for rank are the two most important forms of intraspecific aggression, and both represent the use of force to produce harmony and stability where chaos would otherwise reign. Once established, territory serves to protect the defender in many ways, whereas social rank serves to provide order in close-knit social groups. The reinforcement of order and stability in social relationships is of major adaptive significance, because a social group is by its very nature a systematic ordering of separate individuals into a relatively stable whole. Such ordering is basically vertical and resulting social ranks are influenced by many factors including gender, strength, size, age, seniority, fearlessness, health, concentration of hormones, and individual training (Dimond, 1970). Dolinhow (1972) further suggests that individual rank is based on "personality," experience, and kinship ties as well as sheer physical ability.

Most animals are inherently competitive and a great amount of fighting, especially among males, occurs in the wild. This fighting is typically neither senseless nor maladaptive, however, but is rather involved in competition for dominance and social rank, for food and water, for choice of females, for mating privileges, and for self-protection (Valzelli, 1981; Van Kreveld, 1970). Given the many reasons to fight and the animal's ready motivation to engage in competitive aggression, one wonders how social order is maintained or how so few animals are seriously injured or killed in such encounters. The mystery is solved when we look at the controls nature has placed on competitive aggression, the most important of which is the ranking hierarchy. Van Kreveld (1970) lists some of the adaptive functions of social ranking: First, the socially ranked group is highly integrated and can act as a unit when faced with external threat; second, aggression and aggressive displays are reduced in the ranked groups; and third, weaker, less capable, and aberrant members of the group have less access to resources in ranked groups and are thus more likely to be selected out of the gene pool. We see why Valzelli (1981) and others (Bernstein & Gordon, 1974) conclude that competitive aggression and the dominance hierarchy are vital for the establishment and regulation of social behavior in animals, including primates.

Before delving more deeply into dominance and status, some terms should be clarified. Moving from primitive-to-advanced, let us consider dominance, dominance hierarchy, social rank, and status. The most restricted and concrete term is *dominance,* which we define as winning in a threat–submission encounter, or a series of such encounters. The *dominance hierarchy* refers to the establishment and maintenance of a peck order or linear rank order that is based primarily on success in dominance encounters involving overt threat. *Social rank* is a more complex and enduring social phenomenon that builds upon dominance and the dominance hierarchy, but is not identical to them. Certainly in higher animals and primates, stable social rank is influenced by many moderating factors, as Dimond (1970) and Dolhinow (1972) pointed out. Thus, whereas dominance is temporary and the dominance hierarchy stable only in the absence of challenge and confrontation, social rank remains relatively enduring as long as the animal's personality and presence are respected by the group.

The *status hierarchy* is the most advanced form of social ordering. Here the individual's experience, personality, reputation, and kinship ties confer a specialness, an attitude of respect not typically seen in dominance or even high social rank alone. This explains the enigma of why a sickly old baboon or chimpanzee may exert firm and authoritative leadership in the group without ever resorting to physical violence. Some animals appear to enjoy status and respect in the group largely by virtue of the knowledge they possess; this is, indeed, a far cry from enforcing dominance or achieving social rank through threat, intimidation, or even personal charisma. Frans de Waal (1982) discussed the relationship between personality and social status in chimpanzees, and his description of the old female Big Mamma is instructive here. Big Mamma was the oldest chimp in the group studied, and her threatening gaze, large physical size, and "all-comprehending manner" earned her great respect in the community. As de Waal described, her "central position is comparable to that of a grandmother in a Spanish or Chinese family. When tensions in the group reach their peak, the combatants always turn to her—even the adult males" (p. 56). Even though Big Mamma scored high on intimidation, there seemed to be something more at work—perhaps a chimpanzee respect for age and wisdom that conferred great social status.

We have seen that dominance and submission relationships are major structural components of social rank and, to a lesser degree, social status. Particular dominance–submission patterns are typically species–specific and are among the more characteristic and definitive elements of the animal's behavioral repertoire. Social dominance is usually decided by fighting, bluffing, or passive submission in an initial encounter between a pair of individuals, or early in a series of encounters (Collias, 1944). How this is accomplished, however, varies considerably from species to species, but in most cases there is an exchange of signals rather than blows. Eibl-Eibesfeldt (1961, 1970, 1972) describes the various releasing signals mediating dominance and submission in animals. Generally the threatening opponent will try to look larger and more intimidating by raising itself high and spreading its mane, skinfolds, fins, or feathers as the case may be, or it may threaten by a display of weapons (teeth, claws, horns, etc.). The loser in the encounter, by contrast, attempts to appease the victor by exhibiting submissive postures that often are the mirror image of the threat posture. Darwin (1872/1896) called this phenomenon the principle of antithesis. Dogs, for example, assume a very erect posture with the spine straight and the ears and tail high when threatening; in contrast, when submitting, the spine becomes concave and the animal prostrates itself. According to Marler (1956), the principle of antithesis explains submissive posturing better than does the more dramatic notion that the animal is trying to expose a vulnerable part of its body to the victor (Lorenz, 1967).

As well as signaling submission to terminate combat, an animal may also emit certain appeasement gestures that mitigate hostility and help reduce the likelihood of a fight in the first place. A common form of appeasement is the greeting gesture, which is seen in a variety of species and has become high ritualized in primates, especially the chimpanzee. One form of chimpanzee greeting is the hold-out-hand gesture which occasionally leads to mutual clasping reminiscent of the human handshake (Goodall, 1972). It is usually initiated by the low ranking animal, who reaches palm up toward the higher ranking animal in a kind of begging gesture. The dominant animal then extends its hand and clasps the waiting hand of the subordinate, thereby communicating calmness and reassurance. Eibl-Eibesfeldt (1970), speaking like a good psychoanalyst, suggests that this form of greeting probably derives from an "infantile search for contact." The socially complex chimpanzee uses many other appeasement and reassurance gestures including sexual presenting (both heterosexual and ipsisexual), bowing and crouching, submissive kissing, submissive mounting, various screams and squeaks, and many forms of touching and patting (Goodall, 1972). These appeasement gestures often are elicited by ritualized aggressive behavior that typically characterizes social encounters between unfamiliar or unfriendly chimps. For example, it is not uncommon for a male chimpanzee to make an initial approach with hair and penis erect (de Waal, 1982), thereby eliciting stylized appeasement and submissive behavior from lower ranking chimps nearby. Wickler (1967), incidentally, provides a detailed analysis of phallic symbolism and its relation to dominance and threat in both animals and humans. He reveals that many simians use genital display as a threat signal, and further postulates a close connection between ownership of territory, social dominance, and male genitalia.

Because communication of threat via threatening signals and display is not always sufficient to maintain social rank or move up the ladder, a certain amount of fighting must occur. Nevertheless, much of the fighting is of the sham or ritualized type described by Lorenz (1967) and other ethologists. Eibl-Eibesfeldt (1961) provides numerous examples of tournaments, rituals, and ceremonials that allow competition for rank to occur without serious injury to either of the combatants. Male cichlids, for example, perform a ritual fight that begins with threat and proceeds to non-injurious bodily contact: First, the fish fan their tails to propel currents of water toward each other; next, they grasp each other with their thick-lipped mouths and begin to push and pull; and finally, one fish gives up and swims away unharmed. Eibl-Eibesfeldt (1961) also provides graphic examples of rattlesnake wrestling, ceremonial fighting in the Galapagos lava lizard, and species–specific combat in isolation-reared Norway rats. These examples illustrate how animals typically avoid serious injury in the quest for dominance, and further how social ranking and ritualization help reduce lethal aggressiveness.

Dominance and submission are characteristic of nearly all vertebrates in a dyadic situation, but not all animals develop social ranking hierarchies. Avian species are among the most territorial and rank-conscious of nature's creatures, and, in fact, Schjelderup-Ebbe's (1935) description of the "peck order" in domestic chickens is possibly the first detailed account of social dominance in animals. The peck order emerges from numerous contests between pairs of chickens that eventually results in a linear hierarchy wherein the topmost chicken (the alpha) may peck all others below, the next bird down (the beta) may peck all but the topmost bird and so on down to the bottom-most bird (the omega) that is pecked by all and pecks none in return. As Guhl (1956) informs us, once the peck order is determined, total pecking decreases in frequency as members of the hierarchy come to know their superiors. In a socially unstable flock without an established peck order, Guhl found more fighting and wounding, and less eating and weight gain. As discussed earlier, without a pecking order domestic fowl will often exhibit cannibalistic behavior and other kinds of pathological aggression (Ferguson, 1968). Ironically, a series of highly aggressive encounters between individuals eventually leads to greater stability, order, and less overall aggression within the group. As is true of all forms of social order, a price must be paid—here by those of lower rank who are occasionally abused by those of higher rank and often denied equal access to the finer things of life. Some lower ranking chickens become so oppressed by their superiors that they are unable to mate and suffer from what Guhl (1956) calls "psychological castration."

Primate Leadership.   Social order in animal groups is accomplished in many ways, including the linear ranking hierarchy; however, in most instances we still see controlled aggression as the primary regulatory agent. For example, the emergence and maintenance of leadership in animals involves controlled aggression on the part of both the leader (avoidance of excessive force, bullying, etc.) and the follower (acceptance of authority, submissiveness, avoidance of provocation, collectively or individually, etc.). The submissive animal actually controls aggression to a greater degree than does the dominant one, for the surest way to avoid danger is via escape or avoidance, the prime *modus vivendi* of the weak and powerless. Fortunately, the leaders themselves often are not prone to fierce attacks on their followers; rather, they govern through overt threat, potential threat (Dolinhow, 1972), controlled aggression (Hall, 1964), and a variety of implicit cues that assert dominance effectively but nonviolently.

Kummer (1971) see social ranking and primate leadership as examples of social role behavior. When baboons, for example, are confronted with a predator, the large adult males immediately group together and assume the role of protectors until the danger has passed. Kummer says such concerted defensive actions by baboon groups against jackals, dogs, and leopards have been observed repeatedly. Whereas the protective role is temporary and tied to predatory attack, the role of leader is usually a more stable and permanent arrangement. The silver-backed male mountain gorilla epitomizes the role of benign despot, and is generally able to maintain strict discipline with little overt aggression (Schaller, 1963). Much of the group's daily routine is structured by this typically gentle behemoth, and his tight control is managed with remarkable subtlety. Although gorilla aggression normally ranges from a brief stare to physical contact in the form of nonlethal biting and wrestling, the leader seldom resorts to more than stylistic posturing, facial communication, and limited vocalizing to get his way. Although this idyllic picture of gorilla social stability and restrained aggressiveness may be the norm, gorilla pacifity can degenerate into extreme violence under stressful ecological conditions. As we recall from earlier discussion, stressed mountain gorillas exhibited leadership struggles, infanticide, and murderous attacks on weaker members of the group similar to the internecine strife of the Gombe chimps (Fossey, 1981, 1984). Thus, we see that social hierarchy, leadership, and other social role modalities in primates are not failsafe mechanisms, but, when functioning smoothly and free from pathological stress, they do help reduce the overall amount of group aggression.

One cannot overemphasize the importance of social ordering in primate social behavior (Bernstein, 1970). Zuckerman (1932) stated many years ago that "Every ape or monkey enjoys a position within a social group that is determined by the interrelation of its own dominant characteristics and those of its fellows. The degree of its dominance determines how far its bodily appetites will be satisfied" (pp. 233–234). Hall (1965) points out that high-ranking male primates have first priority for food and sexual favors, and they repay their subordinates by reducing in-group fighting, by protecting mothers and infants from others in the group, by protecting the group from predators, and by taking initiative in matters of leadership. The alpha animal accomplishes these many feats with the aid of the group's rapt attention and sensitivity to his whims, whether they be for the moment agonistic or altruistic. Chance and Jolly (1970) argue that the direction of attention toward the protective adult male is an evolved behavioral structure in primates, and, further, that a similar "attention structure" (see Chance, 1976) probably operates in humans as well. In this regard, Abramovitch (1976) studied the attention structure in preschool children by recording the direction of social glances vis-à-vis social rank. Social rank was defined by wins and losses in property fights. Consistent with the primate model, high-ranking children received disproportionately greater visual attention from other children than did those of low rank. Although it remains controversial as to whether direction of glances in children reflects dominance, a different social structure associated with dominance, or an entirely different social structure (Abramovitch, 1980), Abramovitch's findings are intriguing from the standpoint of possible phylogenetic continuity of the primate attention structure.

Social Cooperation.   Whether in the form of a single "control animal" (Bernstein, 1966), or the oligarchic "control hierarchy" (Hall & DeVore, 1965) noted in male baboons, rank, status, and leadership are central to primate social order. Yet, societies are built less on the leader than the led, for rare is the king who can ignore the collective wrath of his subjects.

Every leader is vitally dependent on the cooperation of his or her charges, and their willingness to submit to authority forms the real basis of social order. Crook (1971) states that social cooperation has only recently emerged as an important area of primate research. Primate social cooperation is expressed in a myriad of ways: (a) male agreements among central hierarchy members and other all-male groupings; (b) follower agreement to have a variety of feeding, sexual, and spatial behaviors monitored and controlled by the leader; (c) follower agreement to focus attention on minute cues emanating from the leader, so his whims may be properly accommodated; and (d) follower agreement to suppress aggression, especially aggression directed toward the leader.

This last form of cooperation is of crucial importance to the present discussion. It shows that primate social organization is premised, in large measure, on inhibition of aggressive tendencies, and the leader serves as a prime-inhibitor of aggression. We see that cooperation involves severe restrictions on individual freedom and inequities at every level of analysis, for to be ordered and organized is to be submissive and stratified to some degree. As Crook (1971) tells us: "All these cases of cooperation occur nevertheless, in a highly competitive situation giving rise to the various types of hierarchy, classes, and castes" (p. 249), and he questions whether animals may not, in fact, practice cooperation as a subterfuge for gaining rank. He further asks whether animals may not perhaps mitigate the lethal effects of direct competition by indirect competition mediated through cooperation. Said another way, sociobiological selfishness and competitive self-interest may continue to operate at the deeper levels of primate society, even if cooperation reigns at the level of overt behavior. Crook believes that consideration of these issues will go a long way in revealing how primate studies are relevant to human behavior. Crook (1971) concludes his discussion with some very interesting speculations about human evolution:

> We may infer that far from being a remote analogy to human life, the social sorting process in baboon and macaque groups, the emergence of kinship, role, and the social mobility of the male players may be a very close homolog of the early social systems of proto-hominids. Upon such a basis the acculturation and communication processes were added as human society emerged into its primitive forms. Competition-contingent cooperation may thus lie at the root of our behavioral heritage—but it lies there in no simple instinctual sense. (p. 256)

Anthropologists have made much of the cooperative nature of hunting and, as we have seen, many experts believe hunting played a central role in hominid evolution, particularly in terms of tool use, brain development, and language. Bigelow's (1972) theory of hominid evolution places the issue of cooperation in a new light, for as we recall he saw intergroup competition and aggression as more basic to proto-hominid intragroup togetherness than cooperative hunting. Brain and language development are probably the most definitive precipitates of human evolution, and Bigelow thinks that the capacity to inhibit in-group aggression enabled cooperation and communication to emerge in a way that widened the gap between humans and other primates.

Thus, self- and group control are not only at the foundation of social order, they apparently acted as catalysts and possible causal agents for the development of cortical complexity and speech. The emergence of cooperation and communication was, therefore, not a purely felicitous undertaking of the noble savage, but rather the natural outcome of internal social control on the one hand, and effective defense against antagonistic, competitive outsiders on the other. In this regard, Bigelow (1972) says, "The evolution of linguistic capacities, therefore would have served to reinforce territorial and other segregating forces during prehistoric times. And greater linguistic capacities, therefore would have simultaneously increased the social cohesion *within* each separate group. Conceptual and emotional differences between us and them would have been accentuated" (p. 43).

Even with his well-developed internal controls, man required external restraints on his selfishness and aggressiveness, for cooperativeness was not an end in itself. As Tiger and Fox (1971) tell us: "Man added no new genetic qualities and lost no old ones in the areas of aggression and violence. He is still the angry and conciliatory primate; he still strives to dominate and outdo his rivals; he still resorts to bloody combat to gain his ends—in all this he is no different" (p. 211). Here we return, full circle, to the notions of dominance and leadership (viz., nature's use of controlled aggression to dampen uncontrolled aggression). As with other primates, early humans maintained social order through social ranking (and status) and submission to the power and authority of leaders:

> The basic features of all human social and political organizations can be discerned in the social organization of non-human primates. In humans, as in monkeys, the maintenance of peace *within* a given group is achieved through a dominance hierarchy. The differences involve degrees of complexity, not any fundamentally distinct attributes peculiar to humans alone. (Bigelow, 1972, p. 30)

Dominance and Social Rank in Humans.   Robert Ardrey (1970) carried the idea of human dominance to its extreme in *The Social Contract*, and he later suggested (Ardrey, 1971) that dominance may have more affect on human social structure than the "territorial imperative." Freedman (1967) likewise emphasizes the importance of dominance in humans, and speaks of the "rivalrousness of the four-year-old," and the pleasure of achieve-ment and status in adults. The same line of thought is seen in Breger's (1974), *From Instinct to Identity,* and following an excellent chapter on our primate heritage, he concludes: "In a sense *dominance is the monkey and ape forerunner of government"* (p. 61). This proposed animal domi-nance-human politics link has spawned a new and exciting discipline called *biopolitics* (Watts, 1981; Wiegle, 1979), which is heavily rooted in ethological theory and field primatology. To quote R. D. Masters (1976), one of the major writers in the area:

> From an ethological perspective, politics can be defined as behavior which simultaneously partakes of the attributes of dominance and submission (which the human primate shares with many other mammals) and those of legal or customary regulation of social life (characteristic of human groups endowed with language). (p. 197)

Masters goes on to say, "political life is the arena of 'agonistic' (aggres-sion and dominance-oriented behavior) directed to the establishment, maintenance or change of social rules" (p. 207). From Ardrey to the modern biopolitician, we see a clear implication: Human civilization and the infrastructure of social order underlying it are derivative from and elaborations of a dominance–submission template that originated early in phylogeny and reached full flower in our primate progenitors.

In a book entirely devoted to human dominance, Maclay and Knipe (1972) relate dominance in animals to a wide range of human social behavior including the transference relationship between patient and therapist, bullying, humiliation, obedience, susceptibility to propaganda, submissiveness, assertiveness, hereditary class ranking systems, and what they call industrial ranking systems. From these examples, we see there is no dearth of opinion as to the importance of dominance in child behavior, adult behavior, and the formation and maintenance of group structures going all the way from dyadic units, through group hierarchies, to governments and societies. Although all of the suggested linkages may not hold, there appears good reason to assume that much human social behavior is indeed derivative of the phylogenetically older dominance, submission, and leader–follower systems.

Implications for Human Study

Most of the empirical research on human dominance and social ranking has been done with young children. In the first half of the present century, child researchers focused on numerous aspects of aggressive behavior, but the ethological concepts of dominance and territory were neglected (Smith & Connolly, 1972). The English psychologist W. C. McGrew

(1972) was one of the first to study dominance behavior in children systematically, and he published the now well-known *An Ethological Study of Children's Behavior*. An edited book (Blurton-Jones, 1972) of similar title was published in the same year, but it dealt only peripherally with dominance and ranking behavior. Building upon the work of Thompson (1967), Esser (1968), Parten (1933), and others, McGrew (1972) studied dominance hierarchies in carefully observed but statistically small groups of young children. He found that a reliable dominance hierarchy for boys could be derived from the analysis of quasi-agonistic encounters involving winning or losing at something. In these encounters, the winning boy gained or retained possession of an object or space, whereas the losing boy lost or failed to gain possession (girls did not participate in enough property fights for a female hierarchy to develop). Aggressive interactions occurred mainly between the more dominant males, and dominance ranking was found to be correlated with number of wins. Moreover, dominance ranking was significantly and positively correlated with adult ratings of the subjects on variables like aggressiveness, activity, and sociability. Armed with these exploratory but consistent findings, McGrew (1972) concluded, "The usefulness of a dominance hierarchy comes from its power to help explain a group's social behavior or from its power to provide organization to otherwise puzzling phenomena" (p. 122).

In the 1970s, a number of articles on dominance in children appeared in American journals of child development, and the momentum has continued into the 1980s. The words "ascendance," "dominance," "submission," "status," and so on have been part of the traditional parlance of psychology for many years, but the ethologically inspired use of these terms is quite new (Rajecki, 1983). William Hartup's (1970) extensive review of the empirical literature in child psychology on group formation, group functioning, peer influence, popularity, leadership, and peer status, led him to comment: "individual differences inevitably produce differentiation of status positions; children's peer groups always possess a hierarchical structure," and further, "status differentiation is a universal attribute to group functioning" (p. 370). Clearly, psychologists were moving closer to the ethological formulations, and it wasn't long before rather clear-cut similarities in the dominance and submissive behavior of monkeys, apes, and children were noted (e.g., see Table 4.1 in Rajecki, 1983). Also, as with other primates, children aggressively compete for resources; in fact, Smith and Green (1975) estimated that about 70% of all aggression between peers in their study was over property. Strayer and Strayer (1976) identified a dominance hierarchy in preschoolers based on attacks and threats, and then found the outcomes of property fights could be predicted by the attack-threat ranking. The majority of wins, of course, went to the child previously classified as dominant in the property fights. It would appear that dominance is "presently adaptive" for children just as it is for non-human primates. Indeed, Rajecki (1983) cited a large number of writers who all reported that the most desirable areas in children's environments were occupied or controlled by those high in their respective dominance hierarchies.

Rajecki (1983) summarizes some of the dominance-related phenomena that are important features of a child's social life: (a) the gain or loss of scarce resources; (b) societal consequences in the form of differential opportunity and access; (c) the role of social signaling in social conflict; and (d) the relation of rank to social monitoring (attention structure) in the group. Clearly, dominance and submission play important presently adaptive roles in the everyday lives of children, just as does, for example, spontaneous play behavior. By virtue of lesser psychoneural development and lesser enculturalization in children, theory would predict more consistent survival tracking of basic primate patterns in the young as compared with the more culturally constrained adult. The more developed symbolic cognition of the adult also produces greater distance and decoupling from phylogenotypic patterns, which may explain the paucity of ethological studies with human adults (Austin & Bates, 1974; Zivin, 1983). Even though adults may decouple from phylogenetic dominance imperatives in their more cultured moments, however, these imperatives remain on once adaptive status ready to be recovered by phylogenetic regression—especially under conditions of ecological deterioration or stress (see Rajecki, 1983).

The turmoil and emotionality of adolescence would seem to be an ideal time for the re-emergence of once adaptive dominance relations as major mediators of social behavior. Much has been written on dominance and social ranking relations in gangs of adolescent males (Davis, 1968; Suttles, 1968; Thrasher, 1963; Whyte, 1943; Yablonsky, 1970), but systematic empirical research in the area is limited (Savin-Williams & Freedman, 1977). In the most comprehensive work on young adolescents, Savin-Williams (1976, 1977, 1980) developed a primate-based dominance matrix based on measures of personality, social characteristics, and verbal agonism in commands and ridicule. Among the traits possibly linked to hierarchical position were athletic ability, physical fitness, chronological age, peer-related popularity, intelligence, physical pubertal status, and creativity. Significant correlations with rank were found for the first four trait characteristics, but Savin-Williams (1980) placed only athletic ability in a major explanatory role. Because athletic ability is a composite of several fitness parameters (physical strength, size, agility, good general health, physical attractiveness, etc.), one is not surprised at its influential role in mediating dominance in adolescents.

Given the apparent central role of dominance in adolescent social relations, we may ask, "What happens when the young person is deprived of status in the peer group?" DeVore (1971) draws what Eisenberg (1971) calls "astonishing parallels" between subadult baboon males and human adolescent males in terms of identity conflict and status deprivation. There is, DeVore (1971) says:

> a kind of delayed social maturity in the young male baboon which is, I submit, the classic opportunity for frustration and, indeed, we find in such groups that the most aggressive animals are these young subadult males constantly quarrelling with the females and constantly being put down by the adult males. In some respects, they are totally disruptive—the juvenile delinquents of the primate world. (p. 305)

It is tempting to digress on the many conceptual possibilities suggested by status deprivation, but space is limited. Clearly, the primate dominance complex in humans is important in both normal and abnormal behavior in young children, adolescents, and adults, and researchers have only begun to scratch the surface in the area. We have emphasized dominance processes in children here, but many more vistas remain to be explored. One major point of convergence between ethology and the social sciences is in the field of social psychology (Rajecki, 1977). In-group versus out-group sociofugality, the dynamics of dominance and status, and the far-reaching implications of controlled aggression in leadership and authority, all go to the core of human social behavior. For example, the in-group versus out-group factor would seem relevant to the analysis of prejudice, race relations, group attitudes, bystander apathy, and the structuring of social classes. Dominance and status dynamics seem relevant to areas such as birth order, dyadic relations (marriage, friendship, leader–follower relations, etc.), person perception, social comparison processes, trait similarity (same status) versus trait complementarity (different status), and a host of other possibilities. Furthermore, the primate leader–follower paradigm no doubt bears some relation to the analysis of conformity, obedience, and compliance, fear behavior, persuasion, small group processes, and perhaps even job satisfaction. Many of these issues are being presently explored (Krames, Pliner, & Alloway, 1978; Omark, Strayer, & Freedman, 1980; Rajecki, 1977), while others await the creative application of the New Biology.

SUMMARY

Without the capacity to aggress, an animal would be at a severe disadvantage in self-protection, protection of family and offspring, competing for sexual access, or procuring food in the case of the predator. There are many kinds of phylogenetically old or primitive aggression, but most can be fitted into three molar categories: predation, territoriality, and dominance. Phylogenetic regression–progression theory postulates that most human aggression is derived from these three motivation-emotion-reward-behavior templates. Such human derivatives and elaborations may be expressed in any one of the three modalities described in the preceding chapter: presently adaptive, once adaptive, or never adaptive.

Predation unquestionably plays a central role in the animal world, but can we say man is a predator? Raymond Dart, Robert Ardrey and others have argued or implied that modern humans evolved from an earlier "killer ape," whereas most social scientists assert the opposing view that man evolved from inherently amiable, herbivorous primate ancestors. Recent observations of chimpanzee hunting, meat-eating, gang attacks, intergroup antipathy, "warfare," and infanticide provide circumstantial support for the Dartian thesis of man-as-predator, but the killer-ape notion is another matter. We argue that man is a predator and hunter by nature who, under certain circumstances, appears to derive enjoyment from killing, but he is not a killer ape programmed for random murder and destruction. The predatory theme runs deep in human nature, making cruelty, destructiveness, and pleasure-in-violence highly probable, but not necessarily inevitable.

Aggression is a major moderator of spacing and territoriality in many animals. Such aggression may be used to control spacing areas or to protect the animal or its relatives in the case of territorial defense. There are numerous adaptive advantages of territorial behavior (Carpenter, 1958), among which is the overall reduction in aggression once stable territorial relationships develop. We see here nature's way of using controlled aggression to maintain order and keep lethal aggression to a minimum.

Ardrey (1966) argues that humans possess a territorial instinct that lies at the base of human greed, xenophobia, prejudice, and warfare. Phylogenetic regression theory assumes a more complex scenario. Certain territorial tendencies in humans probably are phylogenetically continuous with lower animals, but they are variable in form and presumably mediated, in differing degrees, through all levels of brain functioning (reptilian, mammalian, and neocortical). Thus, human territoriality is not a single evolved entity, but a set of self-, kin-, and property-protecting propensities emanating from several primitive motive sources.

Dominance and social ranking represent additional ways that aggression is used to keep fighting and unnecessary killing within limits. Whereas territory primarily serves to protect the defender, dominance and social ranking helps provide order in close-knit groups. Proceeding from primitive to advanced, there are various levels of dominance and ranking: (a) dominance—this refers to a single threat-submission encounter, or several such encounters, where a winner and a loser emerges; (b) dominance hierarchy—this refers to the establishment and maintenancce of a linear rank order through the use of overt aggression or threat; (c) social rank—this is much like the dominance hierarchy, but is more subtle and stable. Further, it is moderated by the animals' "personalities" and experience as well as sheer fighting ability; and (d) the status hierarchy—this is the most advanced form of social ordering in animals and reflects the individual's personality, reputation, experience, and kinship ties. It connotes a specialness and attitude of respect which goes far beyond physical intimidation. Of the four levels, the status hierarchy would seem most analogous to typically human ways of ranking individuals.

Several authors have emphasized the importance of status dynamics in human behavior. Ardrey (1971) exploited the notions of dominance and status in humans in *The Social Contract,* and Breger (1974) asserted that *"dominance is the monkey and ape forerunner of government"* (p. 61). Other writers have applied primate models of dominance (and status) to a wide range of concerns: children's social behavior (Rajecki, 1983; Zivin, 1983), adolescent social behavior (Savin-Williams, 1976, 1977, 1980); adult social behavior and self-esteem (Barkow, 1975; Maslow, 1937), the objective benefits of rank for the individual (Savin-Williams & Freedman, 1977), and politics and government (Watts, 1981). It was concluded that many other applications of the dominance model are possible in social psychology and other disciplines specializing in human social behavior.

12

The Paleopsychology
of Pathological Processes

No zoologist, as far as I know, has ever observed that animals rape in their natural habitat, the wild. Sex in the animal world, including those species that are our closest relations, the primates, is more properly called "mating," and it is a cyclical activity set off by biologic signals the female puts out. Mating is initiated and "controlled," it would seem, by the female estrous cycle. When the female of the species periodically goes into heat, giving off obvious physical signs, she is ready and eager for copulation and the male becomes interested. At other times there is simply no interest, and no mating.

—Brownmiller (1975, pp. 12–13)

DEFINITIONS AND THEORY

In chapter 9, five hierarchical levels of analysis were formulated: socio-biological, ego–psychological, cultural, philosophical, and spiritual. The sociobiological level is more broad than traditional sociobiology, and includes the evolved neurohumoral hardware of the person and the evolved software programs that guide primitive behavior (pleasure, pain, kinship, selfishness, sex, aggression, fear, etc., see Table 9.1). The ego–psychological level builds on the sociobiological level, allowing distinctly human forms of egotism to replace raw selfishness and animalistic modes of functioning. These first two levels comprise the paleopsychology of the person (viz., the primitive, phylogenetically continuous, and minimally modified and minimally elaborated deep structure of behavior). Paleopsychology thus refers to the phylogenetically old psychology of the individual, those structures, tendencies, and predispositions carried over from both our nonhuman and early hominid ancestors. At the sociobiological level, chimpanzee–human or phylogenotypic differences are minimal or absent, whereas the ape→human bridge was crossed in moving to the ego–psychological level. It is reasonable to assume that the opportunism, rationalized selfishness, hedonism, and rudimentary self-consciousness of the ego–psychological level defined the psychology of the first hominids (e.g., *Australopithecus afarensis* or *africanus*). Generally speaking, then, regression to the sociobiological level would produce something roughly analogous to chimpanzee functioning, whereas regression to the ego-psychological level would recover something roughly analogous to early hominid modes of functioning.

It is commonly assumed that we human beings have transcended our basic animality, enabling us to function primarily at the neopsychological levels of culture, philosophical reflection, and spirituality. Careful observation, however, reveals a great gap between what modern humans can do and what they actually do most of the time. Even the most intellectually elite individuals, living in the most technologically advanced societies, seldom operate above the level of cultural conformity and social habit, and rare is the person who ponders the philosophical or spiritual-cosmological implications of his or her acts as they occur. We humans like to think our every act is the product of rational thought and objective choice, and we recoil from the notion that we are slaves to pleasure or survival-targeted tendencies that operate below conscious awareness. Yet, Crook (1980) infers that "most adult human beings actually comprehend few of their sources of action and impulse and are often far from knowing consciously what they are about; what we profess to know is usually a rationalization of what has impelled or directed us from within" (p. 283; also see Barash, 1979, and Burrow, 1937/1974, for similar views). All we have considered to this point indicates that will-power, self-reflection, and the rational intellect are minor causes of behavior, for they generally guide rather than produce response output. As discussed in earlier chapters, the structural hardware of the organism, its evolved software programs, and the primers and releasers that affect them, comprise the main components of the causal matrix determining most day-to-day behavior.

In this final chapter, we focus on pathological processes, and we see that the rudiments of much human pathology are found at the paleopsychological levels of functioning. Of central importance, of course, is how these rudiments interact, synergistically and antagonistically, with the higher functions of self-consciousness and culture. Our focus is on human pathology in advanced technological cultures, where the conflict between paleopsychological and neopsychological prerogatives stands out most clearly. Such pathology may be divided into two molar categories: (a) regressions, broadly speaking, to paleopsychological levels, and (b) failures to successfully renunciate, modulate, elaborate, or transcend our old natures in ways that produce social and cultural reinforcement. Modern humans must meet their own needs and the demands of culture at the same time, and conflict is the inevitable result. There is little place in the modern university, scientific laboratory, operating room, or summit meeting for the unmodified human primate; proper performance in these arenas requires thoroughgoing suppression of our natural apeness, and the slightest regression into simian irascibility, sexuality or xenophobia may have catastrophic results. Only under culturally prescribed circumstances (e.g., vacations, hunting and fishing trips, play and athletics, the privacy of one's own home) may our apeness emerge in carefully modulated form, and censure or scandal be avoided.

Whereas our primitive ancestors were merely required to behave in accordance with natural mandates, modern man is burdened with a multiplicity of neoadaptive as well as paleoadaptive demands. The history of humankind is essentially one of progressing from simple adaptation to the natural environment (physical and social) to adaptation to the (often) unnatural demands of culture. In contrast to the natural environment, which operates independently of human intellect and consciousness, human culture increasingly came to reflect the arbitrariness and whim of creative imagination. Now added to the clean and straightforward criterion of reproductive viability were added potentially endless cultural criteria for tribal acceptance and success. Although these new criteria for social survival were bound only by the limits of human imagination, they tended to fall into three molar categories: conformity, order, and productivity. The *sine qua non* of primitive culture is conformity, and without conformity there is no culture. Once the criteria of conformity (racial characters, kinship affiliations, customs, mores, ritual, tradition, etc.) are sufficiently met to assure acceptance, then a certain social order will naturally follow. In early man, conformity and social order were probably one and the same, but as the early hominids merged into *Homo,* social order increasingly became an end in itself requiring self-conscious rules, regulations, and primitive law. Finally, as culture came to dominate the lives of human beings, one could not merely be, but one must produce, one must be something. This last cultural shibboleth, productivity, has hypertrophied in modern culture to the point of pathology, carrying the message that human worth is measured in dollars, material wealth, and production of goods (Fromm, 1976). This phylogenetically recent emphasis on productivity has elevated abstract intelligence over biological intelligence, with the result that social rewards are disproportionately accorded to the highly intelligent minority (Herrnstein, 1973). In the modern meritocracy, virtually all of us are relative failures, each falling short of his or her own aspirations and cultural expectations.

The phylogenetic regression model assumes that much of human physical and psychological pathology emanates from failure to reconcile our old and new natures. Our solution, however, is not simply regression to natural eutopias, or removal of cultural roadblocks to instinctual expression as Freud espoused. We should be true to our biological natures and tolerant of self-expression, as Crook (1980) says, but the demands of culture must be met if we are to enjoy its benefits. We must concede that modern technological culture is here to stay, and recognize that the phylogenetic clock cannot be turned back. Cultural pressures to conform, maintain social order, and produce cannot be escaped, but within those constraints a happy, satisfying, and relatively pathology-free life is possible. Such good health is not easily attained, however, for rare is the person who emerges from the crossfire between nature and culture unscathed in some way. The healthiest of us engages in occasional skirmishes of neurotic conflict, self-doubt, depression, and alienation, whereas the career criminal, the psychotic, the child molester, the rapist, the murderously violent, and other cultural failures wage major wars they often lose. At the center of our conflicted inner worlds is the primeval schizophysiology, the eternal war between the Beast and our humanity that has stalked the evolution of modern Technological Man.

The PRP Model of Pathology

Several principles of pathology may be derived from the phylogenetic regression model. These principles are summarized in Table 12.1. As shown, these principles fall under four categories: structure–function anomalies, anomalous phylogenetic continuity, regression–progression anomalies, and ecological imbalances.

Structure-Function Anomalies. The human paleophenotype is composed of physical, behavioral, and mental characteristics that were acquired through natural selection at varying points in phylogeny. Most of these characters or structure–function systems no doubt evolved for rather specific reasons to meet rather specific ecological demands. This does not mean, however, that entirely new characters evolved each time the environment changed and placed new adaptive demands on the human organism—this would be extremely imparsimonious and inefficient. Given the rich reptilian, mammalian, and paleoprimatological heri-

TABLE 12.1
Paleopsychological Model for Pathological Processes

Summary of Principles

Structure–Function Anomalies

Damage and/or dysfunction in normal structure–function systems of body
  1. Genetic abnormalities
  2. Hormonal abnormalities
  3. Neurotransmitter abnormalities
  4. Neurological abnormalities
Pathological dysrelease of never-adaptive tendencies and patterns
Pathological dysrelease of once-adaptive tendencies and patterns

Phylogenetic Continuity and Abnormality

Culture-dissonant releases and elaborations of phylogenetically old tendencies
  1. Of presently adaptive tendencies
  2. Of once-adaptive tendencies

Regression–Progression Anomalies

Pathological fixations on regression-progression continuum
Pathological depth of regression
Pathological frequency of regression
Erratic and labile regressions and progressions
Inflexibility of movement on regression-progression continuum

Ecological Imbalances and Incongruities

Failure to achieve ecological fit
Suboptimum and supraoptimum environmental conditions
Abnormal environmental conditions
Failure to sufficiently satisfy evolved need systems (physical, emotional, and mental)
Failure to meet social and cultural demands

tage of the early hominids, selective processes, in all likelihood, typically built upon and elaborated upon older systems in facing new challenges. This helps explain why the body's basic structure–function systems (genetic processes, hormonal and neurotransmitter systems, and neuropsychological organization) are shared with the other higher primates; indeed, aside from the large neocortex and language capacity, we find few human novelties phylogenetically (see Gallup & Suarez, 1983). Thus, it follows that damage or dysfunction at the primary structure–function level will likely release aspects of our essential apeness, or even more primitive processes, which are normally so subtly interwoven into complex human behavior as to escape notice.

Such releases may be of the once-adaptive or never-adaptive types. As recalled from chapter 10, once-adaptive refers to tendencies or dispositions that once played important adaptive roles somewhere in phylogeny, but that are generally latent in the human paleophenotype. Through phylogenetic regression, once-adaptive tendencies may be recovered with often pathological results. For example, seduction of barely pubertal girls was once probably highly adaptive in hominid phylogeny, but is illegal in most modern societies. Never-adaptive refers to neutral or maladaptive behavior that emanates from once-adaptive neurostructures or behavioral tendencies. For example, part of the normal sexual-reproductive system in an early hominid male might, because of brain damage or other dysfunction, never-adaptively misfire in the form of satyriasis or incestuous activity. Similar never-adaptive sexual misfiring may occur in modern males whose reproductive systems are little different from their hominid ancestors. The main point here is that a once-adaptive biostructural system may misfire never-adaptively, both in ancestral species or in later species that possess the system as well.

Once-adaptive and never-adaptive releases often occur in the context of brain damage or dysfunction. If damage or dysfunction is mild and primarily disinhibitory, then release of once-adaptive patterns is likely; with severe damage, however, motivation-emotion-reward-behavior patterns are not only released, but released in disjointed and maladaptive fashion. Whereas well-integrated dominance aggression might be released under the influence of alcohol (disinhibited once-adaptive pattern), situation-inappropriate rage and violence may occur with direct damage to the aggression centers of the brain (never-adaptive dysrelease, see chapter 10). In addition to aggressive dysrelease, many other pathological reactions appear caused by, or exacerbated by, brain dysfunction or atypical brain function: delinquency and sociopathy (Gabrielli & Mednick, 1980; Gorenstein, 1982), schizophrenia (Levy, Kurtz, & Kling, 1984; Seidman, 1983; Stevens, 1982), sexual anomalies (Langevin, 1983), obsessive–compulsive neurosis (Turner, Beidel, & Nathan, 1985), depression and mania (Jampala & Abrams, 1983; Silberman, Weingartner, Stillman, Chen, & Post, 1983; Sackeim, 1983), and disturbed cortico-limbic psychic functioning (Joseph, 1982). Also, of particular interest is the disinhibitory model of psychopathology developed by Gorenstein and Newman (1980) that focuses on the relation between septal dysfunction and a number of psychopathological syndromes (e. g., psychopathy, hysteria, hyperactivity, impulsive personality, and alcoholism).[1]

---

[1]The psychotic trigger reaction described by Pontius (1984) is one of the best examples of pathological dysrelease patterns. Pontius suggests that the reaction emanates from a seizure-like imbalance between frontal lobe and limbic systems. Pontius proposed this new

Phylogenetic Continuity and Psychopathology. Numerous animal models of psychopathology have been formulated (Bolton, 1983; Fox, 1968; Green, 1983; Harlow & Mears, 1979; Keehn, 1979a, 1979b; Kornetsky & Markowitz, 1975; Matthyesse & Haber, 1975; Reese, 1979; Reite & Caine, 1983; Zubin & Hunt, 1967) and Wenegrat's (1984) sociobiological analysis of abnormal behavior is especially noteworthy. Moreover, given the great phylogenotypic overlap between humans and chimpanzees, and the fundamental formative influence of the hunting and gathering phase of human evolution, we must ask to what degree our basic animality, apeness, and pastorality affects our normality and abnormality. In modern technological societies abnormality often is arbitrarily defined by deviation from cultural norms, but such deviation may or may not be maladaptive from the paleopsychological standpoint. All successful societies require some minimal congruence between paleoadaptive and neoadaptive or cultural requirements (e. g., sexual and reproductive activity must be allowed in some form), but societies vary greatly in degree of congruence. Where congruence is high, adaptive demands in terms of intelligence, learning, and productivity are low, for one must merely be his or her essential hunting and gathering self to meet cultural standards. Most modern societies, however, are highly incongruent in their paleoadaptive versus neoadaptive demands, with natural apeness and natural humanness being held in very low esteem. A progressive society composed of regressive and disconforming individuals is a contradiction in terms, and here we confront the great dilemma of modern man: Man cannot be totally himself and a creature of advanced culture at the same time.

Psychological health and happiness, then, become matters of reconciling natural humanness with the arbitrariness and burgeoning demands of an advanced, aggressive, and competitive culture. Those lacking in sufficient youth, motivation, intelligence, education, family background and privilege, and so forth, tend to fall by the wayside and either develop psychopathology or have it attributed to them. These "failures" lack or

---

diagnostic concept following detailed case analyses of eight patients who either committed or attempted murder in epileptic-like states. The psychotic trigger reaction apparently:

represents a seizure-like phenomenon of brief duration, with autonomic nervous system (hypothalamic?) symptoms, at times with a transient, slightly altered state of consciousness, and with only a slight and at the most brief memory impairment surrounding the homocidal episode which typically is well remembered. There can also be some depersonalization and hallucinations of colored rims around objects, which may appear to be larger than they are and visual, auditory, or somatic "formed hallucinations". After the homocidal attack several of these patients felt drained of all energy. All but one felt intense remorse, and all felt they were responsible for their violent acts during which they experienced a severe loss of control, which they were at a complete loss to explain, inasmuch as these acts were out of character compared with their usual behavior. In all eight patients the homocidal acts were the first which had occurred in their lives (Pontius, 1984, p. 327).

have not learned the necessary skills to renunciate, modulate, or elaborate their natural humanness in ways considered valuable by society.
Such persons often are eminently successful in the paleoadaptive area,
often producing larger families and more elaborate extended kinship
networks than those successful at the neopsychological level of intellectual productivity. The successful individual in advanced societies exerts
constant control over his or her paleopsychological resources, and is able
to select presently adaptive, situation-appropriate responses and use
them in culturally approved ways. For example, assertiveness and even
aggression are appropriate in certain contexts, and the person who knows
when and how to regress to the innate wellsprings of aggressiveness will
be socially successful, whereas unconstrained expressions are likely to be
socially repulsive or even criminal. Great discernment and flexibility is
required in these matters, for culture can be whimsical in telling us what is
right and wrong at a given time. The case of the "Subway Vigilante,"
Bernhard Goetz is a case in point (Leo, 1985). In the days immediately
following his shooting of four threatening black teenagers, Goetz was
hailed by the press as a hero and crime fighter, but, as emotions cooled,
popular opinion reversed and he became a bloodthirsty assassin. Modern
society does, indeed, demand intelligence and thoughtfulness in choosing
between socially rewarding possibilities and socially punitive ones.

We see that both individual and social pathology revolve around the
continuity problem. The healthy and socially rewarded individual must
carefully select from a broad repertoire of presently adaptive and once-
adaptive behavioral possibilities at any given time, and once chosen, the
behavioral response must be properly dressed for the occasion; that is,
powerful sexual attraction must be transformed into ostensibly harmless
sexual banter, a flash of anger must be suppressed and transformed into
stylized assertiveness, fear must give the appearance of being overcome,
and so forth. Seldom may the older tendencies be expressed in unadulter-
ated terms; indeed, what we call social skill is basically the capacity to
transform unpresentable emotions and actions into presentable ones.
Thus, one goal in avoiding or treating individual or social pathology is to
refine the coupling or interface between natural man and unnatural
culture, so that social reward is maximized for the individual and order
and productivity maximized in the individual's various reference groups
(family, community, and society at large).

Regression–Progression Anomalies. Several principles of pathology
naturally follow from the basic PRP model. First, the model implies that
fixations on the regression–progression continuum are possible. If behavior reflects ongoing, momentary regressions down and progressions up
the continuum as proposed, then it follows that some persons have wider

response continua than others (e.g., from deeply primitive to highly advanced, as with Ted Bundy). Other persons may have truncated continua congenitally or otherwise (e. g., the mentally retarded, brain-damaged, severely psychotic), while still others may be paleopsychologically fixated and never progress to neopsychological levels of functioning (e. g., the feral children of fact and fancy; Lane, 1976; Maclean, 1979). In modern society, severe phylogenetic fixations are rarely encountered, for almost all persons have the capacity and experiential background to sample culture in some degree.

Much more common are deep regressions that may occur in essentially normal persons who possess sufficient ego-strength to progress back at will, and sufficient cultural sensitivity to avoid being labeled deviant for their activities (e. g., persons who engage in private perverse sexual activities, or who use hard-core pornography with no apparent ill effects). However, given the Pandora's box or release implications of the PRP model, it is hypothesized that few persons are able to deeply regress to primitive levels of sexuality or violence without residual effects, sometimes more or less permanent ones (see Malamuth & Donnerstein, 1984, on the effects of violent pornography). The common notion that once one kills it is much easier to kill again (Kagan, 1984) is consistent with a regression→release explanation, as is the paradox of sexual hyperactivity (rather than sexual avoidance) that sometimes occurs in persons raped or sexually molested (Yates, 1982). Equally paradoxical is the frequent finding that abused children are at extreme risk for being abusing parents themselves. Having been helpless victims of violence, one might expect abused children to learn passive, avoidant, and phobic responses, making them less likely than average to abuse. To argue that the abused abuser has simply modeled violent responses is to beg the question: The behaviors may be modeled, but what of the motivation to harm and hurt? It seems that recourse to a release explanation of some kind is needed to deal with the motivational issue here.

Overly frequent, dyscontrolled, and labile regressions are generally associated with severe psychopathology (viz., psychosis, brain damage, and primitive psychopathy). In these instances, movement on the phylogenetic continuum is under little or no conscious control, and is symptomatic of underlying pathological processes typically at the structural level of analysis (genetics, hormones, neurotransmitters, neurophysiology, etc.). Such passive regressions are both effects and causes, and they act to severely disrupt the normal human nature–culture coupling that defines normality for Technological Man. The peculier disinhibitory characteristics of the schizophrenic, for example, produces frequent, deep, and labile regressions that represent a pathological kaleidoscope of presently adaptive, once adaptive, and never adaptive responses. In the schizophrenic, we see nigh-total failure of neoadaptive processes and a resurgence of pathologically mixed and situation-inappropriate paleological processes (Arieti, 1970). The caricatures of dominance and territoriality (Esser, Chamberlain, Chapple, & Kline, 1965; Horowitz, Duff, & Stratton, 1964; Sommer, 1959), obsessive concern with oral-predatory themes, fantasies of mutilation and destruction, hypertrophied xenophobia of the paranoiac, confused sex-role behavior and sexuality, and the tonic immobility of the catatonic (Gallup & Maser, 1977), seem to reflect processes that were once-adaptive sometime in phylogeny, but are inadequately recovered and integrated in the schizophrenic. In them, we see pathological depth, frequency, and lability of regression in bold relief.

At the other extreme is inflexibility of movement on the regression–progression continuum. The rigidity and tension of the neurotic, the character armor (Reich, 1945) and ingrained habit patterns of the personality disorder, and certain other symptoms of schizophrenia (e. g., concreteness, stereotypy, rigidity, perseveration) would fall in this category. The normal individual can laugh, play, love, express sexuality, express anger and hostility, and otherwise regress in controlled and situation-appropriate fashion. Some persons develop controlled or adaptive regression to a fine art (actors and other showpersons, prize fighters, professional wrestlers, police and military personnel, charismatic public speakers, etc.), whereas most of us are consigned to a dreary sameness of habit and behavior. As argued in chapter 8, most of us spend more time performing old habits than in learning new ones, and only a few enviable people develop artistry in benign regression. Such artistry is notably absent in virtually all forms of psychopathology, save for the sociopath who employs regressive charisma for personally adaptive, but socially offensive purposes. For most disturbed and nonnormal individuals, motivation-emotion-reward-behavior patterns are compulsively repetitious, self-defeating, and illogical on the face of it. Only when we approach the problem paleopsychologically do we see older patterns of logic and adaptation operating.

Ecological Imbalances.   There are limits to the cultural imposition of neoadaptive demands on the human body and mind. As primates and hunter–gatherers by nature, we must achieve at least minimal organism–environment ecological fit in order to survive, and achieve a fit within a limited, optimal range for good psychological health and freedom from stress (Zentall & Zentall, 1983). We humans are chained to our biology, but the links are flexible; we stretch the chain slightly and experience invigorating tension, moderately and experience stress and tension, but if we pull too hard the chain may break, producing severe physical disease, psychosis, or death. So, degree of ecological fit defines yet another perspective on physical and mental pathology thoroughly consistent with the phylogenetic regression–progression model.

Altman (1976) outlined the major features of an ecological model for interpersonal behavior and personality: (a) behavior cannot be understood apart from its intrinsic relationship with the physical environment; (b) there is mutual and dual impact between person and environment; (c) person–environment relations are dynamic and constantly changing; and (d) person–environment relations occur at several levels of psychological functioning, but act as a coherent system. The biologist Edwin Willems (1974) similarly described the central thrust of "behavioral ecology": "Complex interrelationships and interdependencies within organism-behavior-environment systems and the behavioral, adaptive dependencies between organism and habitat are among the central interests of the ecological perspective on behavior" (p. 152). In a later paper, Willems (1977) listed several other points of interest: (a) human behavior must be conceptualized and studied at levels of complexity atypical of social science; (b) this complexity lies in systems of relationships that link person, physical environment, and social environment; (c) such systems may change abruptly or over long periods of time; (d) tampering with any part of the system will probably affect the whole system; (e) simple intrusions may produce unintended and possibly pathological effects; and (f) long-term harm may follow from short-term good. Willems' points seem to imply that optimum ecological fit is painfully achieved, tenuously held, and easily lost or altered with small changes in the environment. Obviously, this has important implications for any theory of pathological processes.

The ecobehaviorist often speaks of organism-environment relations, but less is said of what constitutes the organism. One purpose of this volume is to define human nature, that is, the structures, tendencies, and predispositions, present at birth in inchoate form, which interact with experience to produce "normal," representative members of species *Homo sapiens*. Moreover, we have argued that human nature encompasses far more in the way of phylogenetic inertia, phylogenetically conditioned hardware and software programs, and phylogenotypic overlap with closely related primate species than many have hitherto presupposed. Ecological fit, therefore, requires as many concessions of the environment to the human primate as vice versa. Not only must all humans have access to sufficient water, food, shelter, breathable air, and other physical resources for organismic survival, certain psychological needs must be met as well for mental well-being: love, kinship, and belongingness; competence, self-esteem, and perceived control over the environment; sexual expression, sex-role actualization, and reproductive actualization; privacy, protection, and territorial integrity; and meaning-in-existence in the broader sense (Crook, 1980). Moreover, maintaining some link with the wild would seem advisable, given the eons of time our primeval ancestors adapted themselves to the savannas, woods, and jungles. Even if the domesticated, urban, workaday ecological fit is abominable for most of us, partial re-establishment of the older fit is possible via our leisure and sporting activities. Indeed, many of our leisure activities are unabashed reversions to pre-technological modes of comaraderie, competition, and sheer physical (as opposed to mental) exertion.

Implications for Psychological Health and Ill Health. A regression–progression perspective on psychological health may be deduced from the aforementioned principles. More specifically, two perspectives may be deduced: (a) one for the natural organism-environment relations that characterized pre-cultural and pre-technological societies, and (b) one for the unnatural conditions of domestication in modern man. Under the natural conditions that prevailed for virtually all of hominid evolutionary development, human beings strove to adapt to an environment minimally influenced by creative intellect. That is, ecological conditions arose through the random processes of nature for human beings just as for all other animals. Said another way, our ancestors followed "a course of fitness maximization through engaging in 'appropriate' behaviors that accord with the norm generated by evolution" (Barash, 1981, p. 88). Early humans, like other animals, sought food, protected themselves, reproduced and parented their young, and otherwise fought the sociobiological battle of survival. Adaptation was a straightforward matter of achieving sufficient ecological fit whereby the probability of consigning one's own genes to future generation could be maximized. At this inchoate stage, little self-consciousness (Jaynes, 1976), self-monitoring, or effort to adjust oneself to arbitrary adaptive requirements of culture were evident. However, as evolution progressed and the human brain enlarged, increasingly complex social and cultural environments were imposed that taxed the adaptive capabilities of cultural man, forcing him to perform at near capacity in many areas (Crook, 1980). In essence, culture instituted new and theoretically endless requirements for acceptance and success that were added to the natural adaptive requirements that go with being a mammal and primate (Tinbergen, 1973).

A natural environment-to-cultural environment continuum may be inferred, proceeding from the earliest humans to the most modern of modern humans: minimal self-consciousness, minimal self-monitoring, motivational spontaneity, and biological survival targeting would define the primitive pole, whereas maximal self-consciousness, self-monitoring, controlled and non-spontaneous motivation, weak survival tracking, and strong adaptation to ideological requirements would define the advanced pole. Primitive man was merely required to adapt at the lower pole: He was required to do little more than live out biologically ordained roles and conform to very limited socially imposed rules and regulations. Early man and woman were thus psychologically healthy in the mere living of their natural mammalian, primatological, and hunting and gathering roles within a culturally relaxed and nonreflective context. It is difficult to imagine identity confusion, neurotic conflict, emotional constriction, social alienation or existential crises in these early people. Aside from the physically sick or infirm, each person was needed and each had a place in the local scheme of things. No doubt there were some deviant and maladaptive individuals in the earliest and most culturally relaxed stages of hominidization, but the criteria for failure were difficult to meet by modern standards. In primitive man, psychopathology was probably more or less confined to structure-function anomalies of the never-adaptive sort (e. g., conditions caused by faulty genetic, biochemical, or neurological functioning). If primitive man was fortunate enough to be physically healthy, he had a very good chance of being mentally and emotionally healthy as well.

Unfortunately, because of pressures to adapt to culture as well as the natural environment, good physical health does not guarantee good psychological health in the modern human. Given the organism-culture interplay in modern humans, psychological health and ill health tend to fall into four conceptual categories: (a) biological success–cultural success; (b) biological success–cultural failure; (c) biological failure–cultural success; and (d) biological failure–cultural failure. Optimum mental health would, of course, be found in those modern humans who are not only physically and structurally sound and capable of effectively pursuing biologically relevant goals (McGuire & Essock-Vitale, 1981, 1982; McGuire, Essock-Vitale, & Polsky, 1981), but culturally successful as well. Cultural success is defined here in the broad sense as the establishment of consistent patterns of social reward, and in the precise sense as the incorporation of, assimilation of, and masterful application of the explicit and implicit rules of culture. Obviously, the biological failure–cultural failure represents the most pathological combination, as seen in the process schizophrenic, severe brain disorders and dementias, and severe mental retardation.

Choice between the middle two combinations is less straightforward. In highly technological cultures such as our own, one can be highly successful socially despite physical and even mental infirmities. That is, a highly intelligent person can meet the three standards of culture—conformity, order, and productivity—very well, sometimes because of physical disabilities not in spite of them. Indeed, in chapter 4, we used Stephen

Hawking, the brilliant young physicist who is paralyzed from the neck down, as a quintessential example of Technological Man. And, as we recall (Boslough, 1984), Hawking did not begin to use the full power of his intellect until emotional-motivational interference from his healthy body had been excluded, allowing "pure mind" to operate. By contrast, a cultural "failure" living in a healthy body is subject to much derision and rejection in our culture. Among these would be those of low intelligence, the uneducated, a large portion of the criminal element, and the alienated, dispossessed, and oppressed. Social failure is defined here relative to the dominant culture in a given society, and such failure may occur because of or irrespective of the personal qualities of the individual. Being born into the untouchable class in India or into the so-called underclass in American forebodes failure for the most inherently talented and resourceful. Nevertheless, many such persons may be very successful in subcultural groups which value physical skills over mental ones, as in warfare, gang behavior, primitive agricultural groups, and some forms of athletics. In our society, certain athletes may enjoy great success in society at large by virtue of their hypertrophied physical skills, but such outcomes are statistically improbable.

What, then, are the specific characteristics of optimum psychological health in modern culture? First and foremost, the individual must reconcile his or her biological heritage with the explicit and implicit demands of our technological culture. To do so, he or she must be sufficiently integrated at the structural level and sufficiently intelligent to assimilate and integrate cultural information, on the one hand, and suppress lower motivational interference on the other. Regression–progression activities would be appropriately modulated in the healthy person, with optimal access at both ends of the general continuum and an absence of movement anomalies (e. g., pathological fixations, extreme or labile regressions, or inflexibility of movement). That is, access to the lower sexuality, aggression, love, play, and fear systems would be evident, but in culturally congruent and neocortically modulated ways. Indeed, reduced or aberrant accessibility to these natural systems may be one major cause of psychopathology in neurosis, depression, family disturbances, crime, and a host of other problems. The optimally healthy person has access to the higher centers as well as the lower ones, and his or her cultural success is likely erected on phylogenetic progressions that contribute to society via production of material or mental goods. Higher mental activity also can be satisfying and fulfilling in itself once the neocortex has been thoroughly programmed with cultural information and cognitive schemas. There is some evidence, however, that far more pleasure is experienced in using previously acquired information than in its initial acquisition (Bailey, Burns, & Bazan, 1982), and some forms of concentrated higher activity

(e. g., studying) may be perceived as unpleasurable (Bazan, 1980; Burns, 1979, 1984).

The optimally healthy person also will achieve a good ecological fit wherein the basic physical and psychological needs of the organism mesh appropriately with environmental contingencies. We should note here that the ecological fit for the physical phenotype is basically the same for the modern individual as for early man; that is, a minimal fit in terms of diet, exercise, rest, clean air, social climate, and freedom from noxious stimulation is required for survival, and a fit in the optimal range is required for good physical health. Indeed, the fields of holistic medicine and health psychology are, in large measure, devoted to re-establishing phylogenetically natural modes of living in such areas as diet, exercise, rest, social behavior, and environmental quality. Thus, in the field of holistic medicine the general model for prevention and treatment is relatively straightforward: re-establish natural modes of functioning. In mental health fields, this simple model does not hold because individuals must adapt to culture as well as the natural environment. Prevention and treatment of psychiatric and psychological problems, therefore, requires focus on the environment-culture interplay, or, more specifically, the individual's success or failure in reconciling his or her biological demands with both the natural environment and technological culture (viz., biological success–cultural success). The quality of such reconciliation is relative, and it is doubtful that many persons are eminently successful in terms of both physical and psychological health. Certainly, in our technological culture many people opt for cultural success over biological success for rather obvious financial reasons.

Methods of Analysis

In subsequent sections, we analyze several pathological processes from the perspective of the phylogenetic regression–progression model. These illustrative analyses are intended to enrichen rather than supplant or compete with existing models of psychopathology. Although the PRP model has implications for psychopathology in general, only a small sample of model-relevant disorders is discussed here. Each analysis follows a four-step procedure.

First, the possible causal roles of structure–function anomalies are briefly discussed. It makes little sense to invoke higher level learning or cognitive constructs if the disorder is primarily genetic, chromosomal, or neurohumoral. However, because so few human psychiatric problems are exclusively structural (e. g., Huntington's chorea or the Lesch–Nyhan syndrome), none of our analyses are limited to this level.

Second, the syndrome or condition is analyzed from the standpoint of phylogenetic continuity. As with structure-function analysis, this approach would seem consonant with the principle of parsimony, which urges us to employ lower order concepts as long as possible before invoking more complex higher order ones. This approach is also consistent with the principles of hierarchical organization that postulate that higher processes arise from lower ones, lower levels continue as subsystems within higher levels, higher levels are more functionally efficient but lower levels more universal, and higher levels typically but do not invariably control lower levels (Razran, 1971). Primary emphasis is on phylogenetic continuity in the form of elaborations of older systems, presently adaptive patterns, and regressive recovery of once-adaptive patterns.

Third, the problem is analyzed in terms of the logic of the regression–progression continuum, and anomalities thereof. Analysis centers on the type, frequency, and quantity of movement on the R–P continuum.

Fourth, the problem is analyzed vis-à-vis degree of ecological fit and the environment–culture interplay. Where possible, the problem is classified into one of the four combinatorial possibilities of biological success–failure versus cultural success–failure.

ILLUSTRATIVE ANALYSES:
DISORDERS OF THE SEX-AGGRESSION LINKAGE

The Paraphilias

DSM-III (1980) states that the essential feature of the subclass of psychosexual disorders called *paraphilias* is that unusual or bizarre imagery or acts are necessary for sexual excitement. DSM-III furthers says such imagery or acts tend to be "insistently and involuntarily repetitive" and generally involve preference for nonhuman objects for arousal, sadistic or masochistic activity, or sexual activity with nonconsenting partners. Generally, paraphilic imagery or activity is a prerequisite for sexual excitement and orgasm. Specific paraphilias listed in DSM-III include fetishism, transvestism, zoophilia, pedophilia, exhibitionism, voyeurism, sadism, and masochism. Some paraphiliacs express little shame or anxiety over their activities, whereas others admit guilt and depression and recognize the deviant nature of their disorder. Noteworthy is the compulsive motivation involved and the patient's limited freedom to control deviant thoughts and actions.

In *Three Essays on the Theory of Sexuality,* Freud (1905/1953c) developed the first unified theory of sex perversion, its origin in infant sexuality, and its impact on early development (Rada, 1978). In Freud's view, adult genitality in the form of heterosexual intercourse defined normal sexuality, and perversion represented a continuation of infantile sexual desires and practices into adult life. All infants are autoerotic, narcissistic, and "polymorphous perverse" by nature (Fenichel, 1945), and adult perversion, thus, reflected pathological psychosexual fixations and/or regressions to infantile patterns. Exhibitionism, voyeurism, bisexuality, and fusion of partial impulses (masochism and sadism) are all part of the normal infant sexual repertoire, but these tendencies become subdued, sublimated, and neutralized as the ego and superego arose in the process of socialization. In the normal adult, these infantile tendencies are generally repressed but may be partially expressed in fantasy or sexual foreplay, whereas in the neurotic the repression is more severe and serves as the basis of neurotic symptom formation: "The neurosis is, so to say, the negative of the perversion" (Freud, 1905/1953c, p. 165). In the Freudian model, the normal person strikes a proper balance between sexual desire and repressive social forces and, therefore, enjoys partial access to infantile sexuality; by contrast, the neurotic gives in to social repression and denies himself sexual expression, whereas the pervert does not, or cannot, yield to social restriction and expresses infantile needs more or less directly. On the face of it, the distinction between normal recovery of infantile patterns and perversion is rather unclear, but the exclusiveness of sexual object, compulsive motivation, and fixation of symptoms spotlight the pathologic nature of the perversions (Rada, 1978).

The phylogenetic regression–progression model accepts the basics of the Freudian analysis, but goes a step further—the regression to earlier patterns in perversion is phylogenetic as well as ontogenetic. We must ask, "Where do the original infantile patterns come from?". The most reasonable answer would be, "From the basic mammalian and primate hardware and software programming built into the brain through eons of evolution." If this is basically true, then what we call infantile sexuality would be a complex amalgamation of prehuman, human, and experiential components. The issues of fixation and regression, thus, take on new meanings: We now must ask which adult manifestations are primarily phylogenotypic, transgenotypic, or experientially acquired. Zillmann (1984), for example, discusses the sex–aggression linkage in detail and comments frequently on the biting and scratching that often accompanies pre-copulatory and copulatory activity in both animals and humans. We have discussed the theoretical significance of biting in reference to the phylogenetic bases of orality and extreme aggression in earlier chapters, and sexual biting appears also to have a phylogenetic component. On the one hand, it may arise from pathological recovery of once-adaptive or never adaptive predatory patterns (e. g., Ted Bundy, chapter 10), or, more typically, from mammalian or primatological mouthing patterns in showing affection or expressing aggressivity in the mating process. Whereas sexual biting is widespread and often violent in many species, it is generally less severe in more phylogenetically advanced animals, and is generally muted in both chimpanzees and humans (see Zillmann, 1984). Although muted, sexual biting, and perhaps other kinds of sexual aggression, indicate that human sexuality, whether normal or perverse, is not totally human after all.

Structural Considerations.   As Hughlings Jackson (Taylor, 1931) argued, and many others have implied (Bakan, 1971; Barash, 1981; Bolton, 1983; Demaret, 1979), there are few truly "abnormal" conditions; rather, psychopathology is more often natural or essentially normal action tendencies abnormally expressed. From this perspective, the paraphilias would be viewed as perversions of essentially normal sexuality (Wilson, 1983) at the level of structure. Indeed, at the most concrete level, they are behavioral anomalies of essentially normal male orgasmic or ejaculatory functioning (Langevin, 1983). Thus, one could theoretically be an extreme paraphiliac in the absence of neuropathology or other structural anomalies, through, for example, the mere accidental learned (imprinted) connection between normal sexual desire and some inanimate object (Wenegrat, 1984). Certain questions remain, however, as to why accidents of such severity are so statistically rare, so addictive (Hatterer, 1980), and so disproportionately male. Yalom (1980), for example, reports that he was unable to find a single case of female fetishism in the psychiatric literature, and the other paraphilias are also rarely seen in women (Al-Issa, 1982). As in any complex behavior, an array of (often gender-linked) priming and proximate causes is involved that act to release tendencies, which then interact with social and cultural demands. Specific pathological syndromes are, thus, composed of particular combinations of components at various levels, each with its own causal element. Fetishism, for example, appears caused by the phylogenotypic and neurophysiological priming components of male sexuality at one level, by acquired primers at another level (e. g., acquired bond between sexual motivation and inanimate object), and by proximal eliciting stimuli (e. g., sight of the arousing object).

Whereas most paraphilias are normal tendencies expressed abnormally, endocrinological imbalances, brain damage, psychosis and other pathological conditions may increase the likelihood of sexual deviation by diminishing internal controls (Langevin, 1983). For example, brain damage in areas not directly involved in sexuality may release presently adaptive or once-adaptive patterns in socially proscribed forms, while direct damage to septal (Gorenstein & Newman, 1980) and other sexual areas may release never-adaptive and situation-independent patterns.

Also, psychosis, mental retardation, and senility may increase the like-hood of inappropriate behavior such exhibitionism (Coleman, Butcher, & Carson, 1980), and excessive use of alcohol and drugs are major primers of both violent and nonviolent sexual offenses (Langevin, 1983). Epstein (1961) noted a possible connection between temporal lobe epilepsy and fetishism and transvestism in men, and Hoenig and Kenna (1979) noted a similar connection with transsexualism. Wilson (1983) reviewed research by a Czechoslovakian team that revealed a relationship between a wide range of male sexual deviations and minor temporal lobe damage. Such damage appeared to affect later sexual preferences if it occurred before age 3.

Phylogenetic Continuity.   Certain aspects of the paraphilias provide fairly clear examples of phylogenetic continuity of motivation-emotion-reward-behavior patterns from animals to humans. Indeed, few, if any, of the paraphilias are distinctly human, and their roots descend deep into the animal world. As Stoller (1975) states, "aberrant sexual practices are found throughout animal species and are ubiquitous in human behavior" (p. ix). We may also be phylogenetically prepared for the paraphilias, much as we are for phobic and other behaviors (Rosenhan & Seligman, 1984). First, let us look at our closest relative, the chimpanzee, and then at more distant relatives. Recall that phylogenetic continuity may be expressed in at least two ways: (a) in structures, motives, or actions that serve presently adaptive functions for both our nearest relatives and ourselves (e. g., sexual seeking, preference for young, healthy sexual partners, pleasure-in-sex); and (b) in structures, motives, or actions which were once-adaptive in our progenitors, but are now typically suppressed in deference to culture (e. g., spontaneous sexual expression, nudity, public copulation or masturbation, group participation in copula-tion).

What are some of the chimpanzee (phylogenotypic) sexual characters that are presently or once-adaptive in humans? A brief list of chimpanzee sexual characteristics is provided in Table 12.2. Some of the chimpanzee characteristics listed are clearly phylogenetically continuous with human sexuality, whereas others are not. The most obvious noncontinuous or transgenotypic characters revolve around sexuality in the human fe-male—loss of estrus, uninterrupted sexual receptivity, greater emphasis on orgasm, lesser promiscuity and greater object preference. The phylo-genotype:transgenotype ratio is larger for the human male, who lacks analogous phylogenetic advances in sexual physiology and behavior. Gender aside, a great amount of overlap exists between chimpanzee and human sexuality. Large chimpanzee:human differences appear to exist because of the constraining effects of culture. The real question is not

TABLE 12.2
Some Aspects of Chimpanzee Sexuality

Some evidence of infantile sexuality—autoeroticism, masturbation

Female has menstrual cycle of 35 days and exhibits genital swelling for about 14 days of cycle

Genital swelling is powerful visual sexual cue for males

Males exhibit genital exploration and sniffing, courtship patterns, and desire for copulation during swelling, but generally lose interest with decrease in swelling. However, genital inspection may occur with a nonreceptive female

Females often permit a variety of sexual liberties (genital inspection, fondling, etc.) for old and young males alike

Both males and females are sexually promiscuous and permanent pair bonds are absent; however, both sexes often show copulatory preferences. Some couples even seem to court, "dance," and "date" for brief periods (de Waal, 1982)

Females often permit copulation with several males in succession; generally, each will wait his turn with little "jealousy"

Copulation is often public, but some couples seek privacy; copulating couples are frequently "sexually harassed" by juveniles who are "fascinated" with adult sexuality

Some temporary consort relationships develop and such couples may sleep together and travel together; sometimes a male will force the female into the consort relationship

Male usually initiates sexual encounter, but females sometimes initiate even to the point of helping the male achieve erection

Male initiates encounter by exposing his erect penis to female

Copulation brief (15 seconds or so), with vigorous thrusting movements; the female will often emit a high-pitched scream at the climax of copulation. Females are sometimes left "unsatisfied" and press the exhausted partner for more sexual activity. Some adolescent females exhibit almost manic rushes of sexual activity at times

Males are usually socially dominant, but females may be dominant during estrus. Sex may have calming effect on male, and female uses sex to exert some control over male aggression. Males sometimes assume female presenting posture to defuse male aggression.

Incest is typically avoided, especially mother–son incest. Young females seem most attracted to unfamiliar males, and especially avoid old, familiar males (who might be their father)

Homosexuality appears to be very rare in chimpanzees

Note: References for Table 12.2 included de Waal, 1982; Goodall 1971, 1972; Mitchell, 1979.

how similar our overt behavior is to the chimpanzee, but how similar how private and deepest wishes are. For example, as the omnipresence of pornography shows, more humans males wish to inspect the female's genitals than actually do; by contrast, there is little inclination, imaginal or otherwise, of the human female to inspect the genitals of the male (Symonds, 1979). This particular gender difference seems clearly phylogenetically continuous, but learning and experiential factors are crucial to its expression in humans. Here phylogeny determines the "what" of the tendency and learning the "how" of its expression.

Regression–Progression Anomalies.   The phylogenetic regression model assumes that humans will regress to the chimpanzee template for sexuality if left to their own devices, if severely stressed, or if primitive sexuality is pathologically released in some way (alcohol, brain damage, psychosis, etc.). With sexual "liberation," we do not progress to higher levels of Platonian romance, but instead regress to promiscuity, pleasure-in-sex, group sex, temporary liaisons, and obsession with genitalia and orgasm. Indeed, by virtue of active regression modern humans can, with the help of manuals and paraphenalia, achieve levels of imaginative sexual expression a chimpanzee might envy! Our concern here, however, is not with the sexual libertine who may be subculturally "normal," but with the "abnormal" paraphiliac as described in DSM-III.

All of the paraphilias appear to have phylogenetically continuous elements that may be regressively recovered, but the dynamics of some are more complex than others. Voyeurism and exhibitionism are perhaps the most straightforward examples, requiring simple regression to chimpanzee genital inspectionism and penile exhibitionism. Genital exploration is a salient sexual behavior in male chimpanzees, and Goodall (1972) reported that one male chimp inspected 18 times in a 10-minute period! Penile exhibition also is very common in chimpanzees, both to initiate sexual activity (de Waal, 1982) and as a dominance gesture. Interestingly, penile exhibitionism, perhaps as a show of masculinity, is the most common sex crime in America (Rosenhan & Seligman, 1984). Of course, human exhibitionism and voyeurism are only partially explained by regression, but access to the phylogenotype would seem to be a necessary precondition. At the primitive level, these are disorders of phylogenetic maleness, and no society has produced females more inclined to them than males. At the chimpanzee level and possibly below, these activities once served important adaptive roles in the reproductive process, and may even serve some adaptive function in human males today. In all probability, however, regressive recovery of once-adaptive functions is a more important cause of exhibitionism and voyeurism than current adaptive function. In fact, both are copulation substitutes or displacements, and serve to reduce rather than increase individual or inclusive fitness.

The other paraphilias are more complex, generally because of displacement of sexual object as well as intrusion of once-adaptive patterns. The least object displacement occurs in pedophilia, where age of the object is the criterion of deviance. Pedophiles are primarily oriented toward children of the opposite sex in the 8-to-10 year range, but about one-third are homosexually oriented and prefer slightly older children (DSM-III, 1980). Phylogenetic continuity is more apparent for the heterosexual than homo-sexual pedophile, who prefers looking and fondling not unlike that seen between adult male chimpanzees and prepubertal females. Goodall (1971) says that true homosexuality is extremely rare in chimpanzees, but there is considerable ipsisexual play and romping of a quasisexual sort. Al-though regression may explain some of the motivational-behavioral components of homosexual pedophilia, other constructs (e. g., genetics, biochemistry, learning) are required to explain the deviant object choice.

One other model-congruent paraphilia might be mentioned—zoophilia. Object displacement in this condition is more severe than in homosexual-ity because it involves cross-species sexual activity. As in other paraphi-lias, "normal" sexual seeking and desire for orgasm remain intact, but the copulatory act becomes disattached from its normal object and the ultimate aspect of sexuality (viz., reproduction) is voided. Most paraphi-lias represent diversions of normal sexuality into abnormal outlets, but why one becomes a voyeur and another a zoophiliac is a difficult ques-tion. This dilemma is similar to that in psychosomatic medicine (e. g., "Why does X amount of stress affect one organ system in patient A and another in patient B?"). Presumably, some combination of somatic com-pliance, priming conditions, and eliciting stimuli is involved in both cases, but we can only speculate on the exact causal array. As Schumer (1983) tells us, there are many unanswered questions surrounding the whys of the paraphilias, and certainly a close analysis of the specific learning and family of the paraphiliac is required (Stoller, 1975). Much can be said, however, without resort to high level constructs of learning and socializa-tion. In the zoophile, for example, normal, "chimpanzee" sexuality may be diverted from the normal sexual object because of mal-imprinting to extraspecies objects, as often occurs with animals (Meyer-Holzapfel, 1968; Morris, 1969; Wilson, 1983), or simply because no consenting human object is available. Whatever the causes, substitute sexual objects, even fetishes (Epstein, 1969, 1975), are frequently used by animals, and we should not be surprised that the same occurs with humans. Zucker-man (1932) described a female chimpanzee that used a cat as sexual partner, and Yerkes and Yerkes (1929) told how Congo, an immature female gorilla, showed prolonged sexual interest in a dog toward which it performed pseudomale behavior. Whatever the true causes of zoophilia in humans, cross-species sexual activity has considerable precedent in nature.

Our goal is not to reformulate the paraphilias in line with the phyloge-netic regression model, but to demonstrate the model's potential for explaining certain components of the disorders. Clearly, object choice, sexual identity, courtship, foreplay, and copulatory practices, and many other aspects of human sexuality are ontogenetically flexible and greatly influenced by socialization and cultural pressure. Yet, the phylogenotype is the foundation structure for diverse expressions at the level of behavior, and regressions and progressions, of varying degrees of subtlety, are part of the overall picture.

Ecological Imbalances.   Many modern clinicians view the "victimless" paraphilias (e. g., fetishism, transvesticism) as harmless sexual variations requiring no treatment (see Haslam, 1979), and one textbook writer in abnormal psychology (Schumer, 1983) refers, rather sanguinely, to the paraphilias as "sexual pluralities." These views emanate from a strong commitment to cultural relativism where normality and abnormality are solely defined by prevailing cultural norms and beliefs. The ecological approach represents a quite different approach to psychopathology. It asks not only whether a given behavior pattern is culturally acceptable or unacceptable in the abstract, but whether it increases or decreases the biological fitness of the behavioral agent and/or alters the social environment, favorably or unfavorably, for self or kin in some way. From the ecological perspective, there are no true individuals who may pursue their atypical inclinations "as long as they don't harm anyone else"; rather, all behavior occurs within larger physical and social contexts, and there is no clear line between self-initiated action on the one hand, and effect on social structures on the other. Ecologically, then, it would be extremely unlikely than any compulsive paraphilia would be totally "harmless" such that it had no significant effect on the agent's overall ecological fit or on the reproductive patterns of self or kin. For one thing, the sexual deviate's fertility and fecundity may be affected by celibacy, lesser tendency to marry, marital disruption, or reduced coital frequency (Mc-Falls, 1979). According to Wilson (1983), such reduced reproductive success may even have eugenic effects, presumably by weeding out unhealthy phenotypes.

In chapter 7, we discussed how differences between people act as elicitors for aggression, prejudice, and conflict. Nowhere is this more true than with sexual preferences and idiosyncracies, perhaps because of the central role of sexuality in the reproductive process and ecological fitness. Even liberal-minded social scientists, who speak benevolently of sexual pluralism in the abstract, may hold quite different views about sexual deviation in their sons or daughters. Irrespective of cultural values, there is a phylogenetic bias for heterosexual intercourse in all humans, and a similar bias against deviations that interfere with intercourse *per se* or with the species-typical male–female social interactions and courtship rituals that lead to intercouse. From an evolutionary standpoint, we must ask where sexual pluralism or "do your own thing" would have taken

Australopithecus or *Homo erectus?* Obviously, such fitness de-tracking would have been disastrous in the early stages of evolutionary development, and it may have long-term negative consequences for modern *Homo sapiens*. How much can the hypothetical masturbation–intercourse ratios, animal–human versus human–human intercourse ratios, physical object–human intercourse ratios, and so on, of early man be altered short of ecological imbalance in modern man? This is an empirical question, but from the perspectives of phylogenetic inertia and ecological fit, a relatively small margin of error would be predicted.

As we recall, the maximally healthy person in our modern technological society is successful both biologically and culturally (viz., there is good ecological fit at both primitive and advanced levels of functioning). Most paraphiliacs are relative failures at both these levels; biologically, because of interference with normal reproductive patterns, and culturally, because of reduced social reinforcement associated with "different" or "deviant" status. Even with the so-called "harmless" paraphilias of fetishism or transvestism there is great risk of ostracism and social rejection if caught in the act, and, consequently, secrecy imposes severe limits on freedom of expression. Much less social tolerance is reserved for the exhibitionist, voyeur, sadist, and masochist, who often risk life and limb, as well as their social reputations, to pursue their compulsive preferences. Stoller (1975) makes much of human intelligence, imagination, and the ability to choose alternate pathways to sexual satisfaction, and he denigrates the notion of phylogenetic continuity in the paraphilias. Yet, how much free will is involved in beating, body mutilation, self-exposure, or obsessive attraction to female shoes? Indeed, the paraphilias, at the moment they are performed, represent one of the least free modes of human expression—so unfree, in fact, that one questions the essential humanness of their causal structure. At worst, these primitive compulsions lead to both biological and social failure, and at best, under the most fortuitous circumstances of secrecy and tolerance, they allow a tenuous modicum of cultural, but not biological, success. One may be a cultural success by fooling others, but Mother Nature is not so easily fooled.

The Special Case of Rape[2]

Rape is one of the clearest examples of intrusion of mixtures and part-combinations of once-adaptive patterns into modern social life. Contrary to the overgeneralized and highly politicized counter-myth that "rape is

---

[2]Following completion of the manuscript, an anonymous reviewer commented that, "Two recent papers in the journal *Ethology and Sociobiology* (Shields & Shields, 1983; Thornhill & Thornhill, 1983) provide strong support for the author's analysis of rape as a byproduct of an adaptive strategy". Although both papers are consistent with the approach taken here,

an act of violence," rape is more likely a disorder of phylogenetically normal sexual seeking in the male of the species (see Symonds, 1979; Wenegrat, 1984; Wilson, 1983). That force or aggression is used to effect sexual access does not, *ipso facto,* make rape purely, or even predominantly, aggression for aggression's sake. Also, the fact that rape is uniformly perceived as violent by female victims (Atkeson, Calhoun, Resick, & Ellis, 1982; Burgess & Holmstrom, 1974) does not allow unequivocal deductions about the rapist's motives. As recalled from chapter 10, aggressive drive is unique in that its primary function is to guarantee the satisfaction of other survival needs of the organism (Kahn & Kirk, 1968), and it is therefore no surprise that aggression is used for sexual access to unwilling partners. As Zillman (1984) avers, connections between sex and aggression are omnipresent, but these connections are more often functional than accidental. The use of aggression for sexual access is seen throughout nature, and human prehistory and history provide abundant examples of male competition for access and forcible rape of the female (Zillmann, 1984). Moreover, the view that women want to be violated is hardly recent, but as old as history itself:

> Perhaps she will struggle first . . . yet she will wish to be beaten in the struggle. . . . You may use force; women like you to use it; they often wish to give unwillingly what they like to give. She whom a sudden assault has taken by storm is pleased, and counts the audacity as a compliment. (Ovid, *Artis amatoriae,* i, 665-675; Cited in Zillman, 1984)

Because use of force for sexual access is seen throughout the animal kingdom and throughout human history, we must inquire about its adaptive functions. More specifically, we must ask, "in the course of human evolution, did variation in male sexual aggressiveness covary with success in reproduction, and if so, in which direction?" On the face of it, the

---

the Thornhill and Thornhill analysis is especially noteworthy. They hypothesized that, "human rape is an evolved facultative alternative that is primarily employed when men are unable to compete for resources and status necessary to attract and reproduce successfully with desirable mates . . . males that cannot effectively compete may employ rape as the *only* behavioral alternative, or depending on circumstances of relative status and family composition, they may incorporate rape into a repertoire of other behavioral patterns." (1983, p. 137, italics added). In this view, the evolutionary benefits/costs of rape versus other alternatives is the crux of the matter, and it follows that men lacking in socially acceptable reproductive alternatives are at the greatest risk to rape. It also follows that male violence, aggression, or control are means and not ends in the rape scenario. Harming the female or even exerting control for the sake of control confers no reproductive benefits to the rapist; such behavior is evolutionarily adaptive only when it increases the likelihood of inseminating the "desirable" female. That some rapists are gratitiously violent, or that few rapes produce offspring, does not negate the adaptive nature of rape in a probabilistic sense. For the social loser, some chance of reproductive success with the desired female may be better than no chance.

sexually aggressive male would have the advantage in consigning his genes to future generations, whereas his more demure brother would be at a singular disadvantage. The sociobiologist David Barash (1979) says that rape is common among many animals, and it may be an especially effective adaptive strategy for bachelors who have been excluded from normal reproduction. Although aware of the surface complexities of human behavior, Barash tentatively suggests that "human rapists, in their own criminally misguided way, are doing the best they can to maximize their fitness" (p. 55). Sociobiologists have typically depicted the human male as a sexually aggressive depositor of sperm who is not particularly prone to altruism toward either females or offspring, unless it serves some reproductive advantage in terms of inclusive fitness. As Wilson (1978) says, "It pays males to be aggressive, hasty, fickle, and undiscriminating" (p. 125) in the sexual arena, and further, "If a man were given total freedom to act, he could theoretically inseminate thousands of women in his lifetime" (p. 124). All this suggests that the human male, at the deeper levels of motivation, is impelled by once-adaptive urges to spread his millions of sperm as widely as possible throughout femaledom, without great regard for the consequences.

Many questions are begged by the previous analysis: (a) why do only a small proportion of modern males resort to rape for sexual access?; (b) why do the demographics of rape vary culturally and from one period of history to another?; and (c) when is rape psychopathological and when not? The phylogenetic regression–progression model may help shed some light on these and related questions.

Structural Considerations.   To what extent is rape attributable to genetics, biochemistry, and the neuropsychology of behavior, and, more generally, to disorders of phylogenetic maleness? Further, what particular mixtures and combinations of primitive motive-emotion-reward-action pattern structures are involved in the rape syndrome? The evidence is sketchy regarding the biostructural causality of rape, but it is likely that future research will strengthen rather than weaken the biological link. Genetic, biochemical, and neurological priming influences on aggression in animals is well-documented (Brain & Benton, 1981; Mandel, Kempf, Mack, Haug, & Puglisi-Allegra, 1981; Moyer, 1976; Sandler, 1979; Scott & Fuller, 1965; Valzelli, 1981), but the case is less clear for the human species. Despite the paucity of experimental data on human variation in aggression, it is highly probable that inherited neural and endocrinological differences resonate with differences in human aggression (Moyer, 1976). The biology of sexuality is also well-documented in nonprimates (Beach 1974, 1976a, 1976b; Bermant & Davidson, 1974; Ford & Beach, 1951; Fox, 1968; Ghiselin, 1974) and nonhuman primates (de Waal, 1982; Jolly,

1972; Mitchell, 1979; Symonds, 1979), but, again, direct genetic or bio-chemical causes are difficult to isolate for humans. Although genetic variation may contribute to cultural differences in sexual expression (Ginsberg, 1965), others argue that the inherited aspects of human sex are nearly formless, and only by enculturalization does sex assume meaning. Such plasticity exists only at the level of overt behavior, however, for all humans are of the same cloth in terms of the structural interconnections that subserve sexual behavior and define its essential character (e. g., those species–specific interconnections between the central nervous system, autonomic nervous system, endocrine secretions, and peripheral sex organs).

Of most interest here are the structural connections between sex and aggression that may play a part in human rape. Sex and aggression have been intimately connected throughout phylogeny; more specifically, there are many specific connections between these two motive systems for a given species (Zillman, 1984). In many animal species, the sex–aggression connection is expressed in intermale competition for access to females and, less frequently, in forcible conquest of the female. Males lacking in either drive system, or in the ability to properly modulate the connections between them, would be at a serious disadvantage in the reproductive process. Sex and aggression are linked in all human cultures, but the differential weighting of each and the dynamic interaction of these two drive systems are quite culturally variable. For example, some cultures de-emphasize both sex and aggression, others emphasize one over the other, and still others emphasize both (Zillman, 1984). Anthropologists and ethnographers generally extoll the benefits of sexually permissive societies and warn of the dangers of sexual repression, and Prescott (1977) postulated a causal relationship between repressed sexuality and heightened social aggression. Zillmann's (1984) careful review of the area, however, led to different conclusions: (a) ethnographers tend to project their own view of what constitutes the ideal relationship between sex and aggression onto other peoples; (b) prior to exposure to the ethnographer's values, sexually "repressive" and sexually "liberal" cultures may be equally satisfied with their modes of expression; (c) sexual repression may be a consequence of aggressiveness rather than its cause; and (d) the culturally ideal balance of sex and aggression remains to be discovered.

Ideology to the contrary, sexual permissiveness and promiscuity are not the cures for extreme aggression and rape. As Zillmann (1984) points out, textbooks on human sexuality portray Polynesian cultures, such as the sexually active inhabitants of Mangaia, as prototypes of sexual paradise. Yet, even in Mangaia, where sexual activity among young people is actively encouraged, there are conflicts over adultery and forcible rape, even gang rape (Marshall, 1971), is in evidence. Thus, even in sexual paradise, rules and regulations are required to keep conflict to a minimum, and to protect females from unwanted male intrusions. The universality of male rape and its universal absence in the female is, no doubt, partially attributable to gender differences in neuropsychological programming at the structural level. It appears that human males, as the sexual seekers, are designed for both stronger sexual (Eysenck, 1982) and aggressive responsivity (Holliday, 1978) than human females, and a specific male predisposition to employ aggression for sexual access may be inbuilt as well. Rather than men being taught to rape, they must be taught not to rape, and no society has been totally successful in discouraging this age-old, once-adaptive male strategy.

Although rapists are not a unique group in terms of physical and structural characteristics (Rada, 1978), the mesomorphic body type (Cortés & Gatti, 1972; Lindzey, 1967) and elevated blood testosterone (see Langevin, 1983; Rada, 1978 for thorough reviews) may moderate the aggressive component in some cases, and various forms of brain damage and dysfunction may prime certain individuals for sexual and/or aggressive pathology (Entwhistle & Sim, 1961; Erickson, 1945; Mark & Ervin, 1970; Monroe, 1978; Williams, 1969), including rape (Langevin, 1983; Rada, 1978). A rough causal link between high levels of testosterone and both sexual and aggressive pathology is fairly well-established, but only in the more extreme cases. In one study, for example, Rada, Laws, and Kellner (1976) found that the plasma testosterone level of rapists and child molesters were within normal limits, but significantly higher levels were found a subgroup of the most violent rapists. Interestingly, the highest testosterone level occurred in the only offender who murdered his victim during the rape. As with the paraphilias discussed earlier, damage to the temporal lobes and the temporo-limbic functional system appears related to hypersexuality and other sexual–aggressive pathology (Blumer, 1970; Blumer & Walker, 1975; Mark & Ervin, 1970; Monroe, 1978; Terzian & Ore, 1955). Unfortunately, little of this work was done exclusively on rapists (Langevin, 1983), but reasonable extrapolation to the more dyscontrolled rapists seems warranted. Rapists range from those seemingly normal psychiatrically to those classified as intractable sociopaths, psychotics, and brain damaged. The diagnostic challenge is to separate out the once-adaptive and presently adaptive patterns, which may be released by "normal" proximal elicitors or disinhibitory forms of brain dysfunction, and from never-adaptive patterns emanating from direct damage to the sex–aggressive centers.

Phylogenetic Continuity.   We have seen that ample phylogenetic precedent exists for male rape of females but not vice versa. Rape is an effective male adaptive strategy in the animal world, which allows the male to deposit sperm with minimal energy expenditure and personal cost (Barash, 1979; Symonds, 1979). If a degree of phylogenetic continuity in the rape strategy exists between nonhuman and human beings, then that continuity would be a partial cause of human rape. That human rape is embedded within a complex cultural matrix would not negate the fundamental causal significance of the older tendency working at unconscious or minimally conscious levels of the personality. This assumption implies that all men, by virtue of their phylogenetic maleness, are inclined toward rape at some level in the quest to actualize their sexual prerogatives (e. g., through desire, fantasy, or, more rarely, in actual behavior). Given the prevalance of rape in history, the apparent increased frequency of rape in the recent era of sexual freedom and availability of violent pornography (Court, 1984), and the experimental research showing that sexual excitedness may be increased by rape and/or pain content (Farkas, 1979; Malamuth, 1981; Malamuth & Check, 1980; Malamuth, Heim, & Feshbach, 1980), and, further, that acceptance of force in sexual conquest is quite high in normal males (Abel, Barlow, Blanchard, & Guild, 1977; Koss, 1983; Tieger, 1981), there seems good reason to assume animal–human continuity in the rape strategy.

In discussing phylogenetic continuity of the rape motive structure, our concentration is on relevant aspects of chimpanzee sexual behavior. Phylogenotypic analysis of the human rape strategy by comparison to the chimpanzee model is impeded greatly by the large transgenotypic differences in female reproductive physiology. Obviously, chimpanzee–human differences in female sexuality (e.g., lack of estrus, concealment of ovulation, well-developed capacity for orgasm, and "continuous receptivity" in the human female; see chapter 4) are correlated with chimpanzee:human differences in male sexual behavior, thereby obscuring phylogenetic continuity. In other words, if chimp and human males were exactly the same sexually, human males would behave differently because of the human female's shaping influence. Nevertheless, chimpanzee and human males are fundamentally similar in sexuality at primitive levels of functioning (e. g., both are sexual seekers, both employ aggression for sexual access—most typically against one another—, both are possessive of females, both are promiscuous by nature, and, for both, sexual access is influenced by dominance and status). Sexual access is anything but democratic for both chimpanzee and human males, with mature and high-ranking males in both species enjoying copulatory advantage over immature and low-ranking males.

In chimpanzees (Goodall, 1973, 1975) and other primate species, one finds a considerable number of low-ranking, peripheral, usually adolescent males who are not attractive to females or who are discouraged from copulation by intimidating superiors. They are forced to "sneak a little on the side" (de Waal, 1982) or "steal a quick-copulation" when opportunity arises (Goodall, 1982). Such "stealing" would certainly constitute rape by human standards (see Alexander, 1979; Wenegrat, 1984). In fact, Symonds (1979) speculates that if we could somehow assess the feelings of nonhuman primate females, many copulations that appear normal to the human observer might be perceived as rapes by the compromised female! How many human rapes are those of peripheralist males whose restricted access to females leads to "stealing" copulatory privileges otherwise inaccessible? That aggression and force are used to effect the act should not confuse us as to its essentially sexual and reproductively adaptive nature. In the immature or low-ranking chimp or human male, sexual need may be at its highest, but access to desired copulatory partners is reciprocally low. Of relevance are the findings that human rapists are often lacking in heterosexual skills (Segal & Marshall, 1985), are unable to effectively carry out the culturally determined seduction or courtship sequence, and often are from the lower social classes. The likelihood of rape, then, could be viewed as a function of the ratio of strength of sexual (proximate motivation) and reproductive (ultimate motivation) need to availability of desired partners. "Desired partners" is a crucial concept here, for the male sexual need is seldom highest for the most available partner, e. g., wife or girlfriend; much to the contrary, normal human males (and some females) appear to achieve maximal sexual excitement in affairs and other "dangerous" liaisons with more or less unfamiliar partners. For the human male, sex can be maximally exciting without love, commitment, or familiarity, and most males, in fantasy or reality, engage in a lifelong quest for the ideal sexual partner, who is never really found. In this quest, the male is the victim of his own sociobiological imperatives, but this in no way condones male victimization of the female for sexual purposes.

Rape reflects a breakdown of inhibitions over sexual and aggressive impulses in the human male, impulses that have come up through the primate family tree and reside in the inner psyches of all men. These impulses to copulate with or impregnate unfamiliar females would appear inherited, but rape as a coherent pattern is, of course, not inherited. Various forms of trickery, force, and coercion are used by chimpanzee males to effect copulation with desired females, but actual rape is rare (de Waal, 1982). What seems to be phylogenetically continuous from chimpanzee male to human male is not rape *per se,* but the readiness to use any available method, including force, to copulate with desired females.

Regression–Progression Anomalies.   Many rapists are married men who may appear quite normal to the observer, even to the wife (Rada, 1978). Even sociopathic rapists with long criminal histories, or pathological rapists who employ excessive force or who derive sadistic pleasure from the attack do not typically come across as lustful animals driven to defile at any cost. A regression from the normal, socially constrained modes of self-presentation is required to release the presently, once-, or never-adaptive motive and action segments that constitute the primary components of the causal matrix. Each rape is different from all others and the specific motives and *modus operandi* of the rapist show individual variations, but all rapes share a common denominator—all involve a regression from surface modes of functioning to primitive, autistic modes of interconnected sexual and aggressive functioning. Rape requires active and extreme involvement of the mutually enhancing limbic sexual and aggression systems, and it is unlikely that a true rape can occur if either one of these two systems is operating at diminished capacity. As outlined in chapter 5, regression typically involves reduced self-consciousness, reduced inhibition and increased spontaneity, increased pleasure-seeking and pain avoidance, diminished control over aggression, and increased access to sexual motivation. In chapter 8, we also discussed the inhibition-release characteristics of psychoneural functioning, and the hierarchical and within-level complexity of even the most rudimentary motive systems (e. g., sexual behavior in the male rat). In regression, motive systems such as sex and aggression, which normally operate fairly independently in socialized humans, may temporarily regain their phylogenetic integrity in once-adaptive form. In most modern males, however, the desire for sexual conquest is well-modulated and in a state of reliable suppression, and release of sufficient motivation for rape would be quite unlikely.

In the peripheral male or social failure, rape motivation may be closer to the surface, and may be expressed in presently adaptive rather than once-adaptive form. Although use of force for sexual access is commonly seen in privileged males, it is probable that other successful, albeit less direct, strategies could have been used with similar results; in this case, once-adaptive techniques were used but not required. By contrast, force may be the only means by which the social loser has access to the "ideal" female (e. g., young, healthy, and of high social status; see Symonds, 1979; Wenegrat, 1984 from the sociobiological standpoint); in this case, regression to old methods of stealing sex is presently adaptive, for it may, in fact, confer some reproductive advantage on the rapist. This analysis may help explain some of the empirical data on rape regarding social class, the use of unnecessary violence, and the extremity of hatred toward women seen in many rapes. Although rapists come from all socioeconomic status (SES) levels, many are young males from the lowest levels of intellectual functioning, education, and social standing (Dietz, 1978; Gibbons, 1973; Lesse, 1979; Segal & Marshall, 1985).

Interestingly, rape victims also tend to come from low SES levels (Hayman, Lanza, Fuentes, & Algor, 1972; Miller, Moeller, Kaufman, Divasto, Pathak, & Christy, 1978), are often black (Amir, 1971; Hayman, 1970) and adolescent (Peters, 1976), and are likely to have a history of psychiatric care (Burgess & Holmstrom, 1974). Moreover, similar to the rapist, the victim may score low on measures of social competence and present a picture of vulnerability (Myers, Templer, & Brown, 1984). These findings indicate that sheer desirability is only one of many interacting primers and/or elicitors in rape; others include low threat value and availability of the victim.

At lower SES levels, aggression often is used to gain access to resources not otherwise available (Moffitt et al., 1981; Wolfgang, 1966), and the female is one such resource. Excessive violence is less simply explained, but how often is just the right level of aggression seen in assault, murder, abduction, armed robbery, or prison escapes? Once inhibitions are sufficiently lowered (see chapter 10), primitive motivation spills forth in rivers not droplets, and we should not be surprised that excessive force often is part of the limbic fear–sex–aggression discharge in the sexual attack.

The phylogenetic regression–progression model postulates that nigh-complete atavistic patterns can be recovered in certain extreme regressions (e. g., the predatory biting attacks of Ted Bundy, chapter 10), but, more typically, bits and pieces of old patterns are subtly integrated into the ongoing stream of behavior. Moreover, such bits and pieces may emanate from the motivational, emotional, reward, and/or action pattern areas of the brain, both within and across functional behavioral systems (fear, sexuality, aggression, etc.). To complicate matters further, these lower emanations are in constant synergistic and antagonistic interaction with the higher cognitive centers, which provide a human persona for what are sometimes quite inhuman actions. Thus, to be precise, all human rapes are complex neuropsychological events involving complexes of higher and lower components that may, in theory, be disentangled causally. Although each individual case of rape has its own complex causal matrix, the PRP model assumes that lower, once-adaptive or presently adaptive aspects of phylogenetic maleness are always a part of the picture, and often are the overriding consideration.

From this perspective, the various forms of rape (e. g., the anger, power, and sadistic rapes; Groth, 1981; Groth & Birnbaum, 1979) are potentially analyzable into their component structures. Few theorists have subjected rape to subtle causal analysis; more often, smidgeons of empirical data have been used to debate the molar question of whether rape is an act of sex or aggression. Obviously, rape is an act of fear, sex, aggression, and a host of other motives and emotions, and certainly is not simply "an act of aggression" for its own sake as Brownmiller (1975) and Groth (1981) stipulate. It does little good to mouth the complexities of rape and then confidently put all the eggs in the aggression basket; in fact, Symonds (1979) argues that ignoring the sociobiological sexual imperatives in rape may actually promote rape in the long run. As Symonds (1979) states, "Every interview with a rapist I have seen or read suggest to me that rapists have mixed motives, and that part of that mixture is sex" (p. 282). Rapists seem to enjoy discussing the power aspects of rape, and they tend to understate the sexual element which represents the female's power over them. Moreover, given the popularity of the "rape-as-aggression" counter-myth, the rapist's ramblings about anger and power may get a more sympathetic ear from professionals than revelations about uncontrollable lust (Wenegrat, 1984).

Until the time each man can have all the sex he wants with whom he wants, rape will continue to exist. Rape is primarily a result of male frustration in being designed for promiscuous sex on the one hand while being totally dependent on the female to carry out this natural imperative on the other. Male sexuality cannot be understood by a rational calculus derived from frequency of intercourse, quality of orgasm, number of available partners, or even passion of the partner; the male of the species is designed to spread his sperm far and wide, and this goal is neurohumorally and neuropsychologically supported by high sex drive, hypersensitivity to minute sexual stimuli, and an inherent desire for a multiplicity of sex partners. No amount of masturbation, conjugal bliss, or illicit liaisions can totally satisfy what is, in essence, a powerful, unconscious, phylogenetically prepared longing to produce the most offspring with the most desirable females available. All men are frustrated in this schizophysiological quest, but the privileged male has far better chance of avoiding pathological regressions.

It is important to note that this universal male frustration is not purely sexual in the orgiastic sense; each male wants to "possess" the female both sexually and as a subject in his fantasied "kingdom." Each male wants to be an alpha male, for with alpha status comes all the things men long for—unlimited sexual access to the female, domination over the female, domination over other males and juveniles, and control of physical resources. From this perspective, many rapes reflect a falsely self-attributed alpha status that is enforced or "proven" at any cost. Although absurd by modern cultural standards, many men, in their deepest wishes, see themselves as alpha males who own their wives and children, and who are, in fact, kings of their castle. Failure to recognize this male need is, no doubt, a major factor in divorce and the uneasy relations between the sexes. Rightly or wrongly, the alpha chimpanzee and silverback gorilla enjoy such ownership privileges, such privileges have been enjoyed by most men throughout history, and, until the past few years, women were content to let men play the game of sexual superiority. Unfortunately, humans do not relinquish their older prerogatives easily, and rape, wife and child abandonment, and even nonsexual criminality may be regressive ways of regaining lost alpha status for many males.

Ecological Considerations.   Although male use of force for sexual access has deep roots in phylogeny, vicious, sadistic, and gratuitously violent rapes are primarily anomalies of modern man. Even in modern times, however, gratuitously violent rapes are infrequent compared to so-called anger and power rapes (Groth, 1981); in fact, in the Groth, Burgess, and Holmstrom (1977) sample, over 60% of rapes fell in the power category, which features "possession" of the female rather than desire to hurt, whereas 30% involved brutality of the anger-retaliation type and 5% of the even more brutal sadistic type. Thus, the majority of rapes seem consistent with the phylogenetic continuity and regression argument, where ecologically distressed males give in to their universal imperative to possess the desired female. Such males may be extensively primed for such release through genetic and/or socially conditioned proneness to delinquency and criminality (Langevin, 1983), excess secretion of serum testosterone (Rada, 1978), alcohol and drug abuse (Langevin, 1983), social alienation and deprivation, and perhaps even the ready availability of violent pornography (Malamuth & Donnerstein, 1984). Moreover, a host of other developmental primers of rape have been discussed in the literature: rejecting, controlling, seductive, and punitive mothers; passive, distant, uninvolved, and sometimes cruel fathers; rape as a defense against sexual inadequacy, dependency needs, or homosexual wishes; conflicted latency and adolescent stages of social development; high frequency of sexual perversion during adolescence; displacement of hostility onto victim; and so on (see Rada, 1978, for discussion). A similar host of sociological causes of rape have been postulated, many of which build upon Durkheim's notion that crime is a normal and inevitable feature of organized society (Dietz, 1978): breakdown of normative values in those individuals unable to act in accordance with them (Robert Merton's, 1968, anomie theory); differential opportunity (Cloward, 1959); differential association (e. g., "keeping bad company"; Sutherland & Cressy, 1966); the delinquent subculture; (Cohen, 1955); and deviant "role careers"; (Gibbons, 1973). No doubt all of these developmental and social factors, and, many more heretofore undiscovered, are ecological stressors and priming conditions for rape. What inevitably remains unexplained, however, is why one male in sordid circumstances rapes whereas another in worst circumstances does not (Schumer, 1983).

The phylogenetic regression model assumes that proneness to rape is a universal male character, use of force for sexual access is very common across cultures, most men "rape" at the fantasy level, a small proportion of men actually rape, and an even smaller proportion are likely to use pathological violence in commission of the rape. The differing frequencies and types of actual rapes, therefore, appear to be a function of male sexual seeking, on the one hand, and the priming and eliciting conditions that determine whether and how such seeking is expressed. This perspective implies that rape frequencies and types should differ culturally and subculturally, should differ from one historical period to another within cultures and subcultures, and should resonate with ecological imbalances such as crowding, poverty, slum life, sexual permissiveness and access to pornography, social acceptance of aggression and violence as means to ends, warfare and other forms of social malaise or upheaval, racism and prejudice, sexism and sexual oppression, and a sense of meaningless or hopelessness in life. Any stress or strain that weakens the thin veneer of culture and morality will increase the probability of social deviations of all types, including rape. Societies as well as individuals suffer ecological crises where the physical and psychological phenotypes of the constituent members do not mesh or fit with the prevailing environment. Contemporary American society, with its glorification of competition and violence, exploitation of sexuality, and its readiness to excuse violent and criminal acts as accidents of rearing or circumstance, is an ideal breeding ground for Tennysonian, tooth-and-claw methods to satisfy personal needs. In this setting, we should not be surprised that rape has increased more rapidly in the last decade than any other type of violent crime (Coleman, Butcher, & Carson, 1980).

SUMMARY

Paleopsychology is defined as the phylogenetically old psychology of the individual, those structures, tendencies, and predispositions carried over from both our nonhuman and early hominid ancestors. The phylogenetic regression–progression model assumes that both normal and abnormal behavior in humans is, in large measure, erected on these paleopsychological foundations. Of central importance is how the paleopsychological foundation structures interact, synergistically and antagonistically, with the higher, neopsychological functions.

Chapter focus was on the paleopsychological–neopsychological interplay in advanced technological cultures where conflict between the phylogenetically old and new stand out most clearly. This nature–culture conflict produces psychopathology through two major processes: regressions to phylogenetically older, culture-dissonant patterns, and failures to successfully renunciate, modulate, elaborate, or transcend our old natures.

The history of mankind is one of progressing from simple adaptation to the natural environment to adaptation to (often) unnatural culture. As culture became the measure of human worth, there were increasing pressures for conformity, order, and productivity. Consequently, abstract intelligence came to supplant biological intelligence as the major moderator of success.

The phylogenetic regression–progression model of psychopathology emphasizes four categories of analysis: structure-function anomalies, anomalous phylogenetic continuity, regression-progression anomalies, and ecological imbalances (see Table 12.1). Each of these categories was discussed in some detail.

Given the natural organism-culture interplay in modern humans, psychological health and ill health tends to fall into four conceptual categories: (a) biological success–cultural success; (b) biological success–cultural failure; (c) biological failure–cultural success; and (d) biological failure–cultural failure. Optimum psychological health, of course, goes with category a above, whereas the most pathological combination falls in category d. The psychological health implications of categories b and c are less obvious. In modern societies, however, the biological failure–cultural success combination would appear more generally beneficial than the biological success–cultural failure combination.

For illustration, the PRP model of psychopathology was applied to two pathological conditions—the paraphilias and rape. The paraphilias are compulsive sexual disorders that involve methods of achieving orgasm in ways other than heterosexual intercourse. These include fetishism, transvestism, zoophilia, pedophilia, exhibitionism, voyeurism, sadism, and masochism. Of these, fetishism, exhibitionism, voyeurism, pedophilia, and zoophilia were discussed in some detail.

Rape represents one of the clearest examples of intrusions of once-adaptive patterns into modern social life. Rape is described as primarily a disorder of phylogenetically normal sexual seeking in the male. Recorded history indicates that male use of force for sexual access is universal, but gratuitously violent rapes are atypical and pathological. However, it is often difficult to determine when rape is or is not "adaptive" for the rapist in terms of individual or inclusive fitness.

As with the paraphilias, the probability of rape is influenced by priming and eliciting factors operating within the categories of structure, phylogenetic continuity, regression-progression anomalies, and ecological imbalances. Within this complex matrix of phylogenetic, ontogenetic, and social-developmental causes are, perhaps, some answers to the questions of why rape is a universal male character, why some men rape and others do not, and why a minority of men use gratuitous violence in committing rape. Our analysis, using the four conceptual categories, represents an initial and rudimentary attempt to squeeze out a few possible answers. Much more empirical and theoretical work will be needed, however, before definitive answers will be forthcoming.

Appendix
The Regression-Progression Model: Assumptions, Subassumptions, and Corollaries

The overarching assumption of the phylogenetic regression-progression model is that *all behavior may be viewed as falling somewhere on a hypothetical continuum (or hierarchy) proceeding from the most phylogenetically primitive to the most phylogenetically advanced patterns of response.* *Behavior* is very broadly defined, referring to any and all forms of response output and not just motor output. Behavior, thus, may refer to motivational urges with no obvious external manifestations, emotional feelings, specific motor patterns, or even thoughts and other mental phenomena. Behavior may only be separated into it conative and cognitive components arbitrarily, however, for actual *in vivo* behavior invariably involves mixtures and integrations of numerous constituent components. So, taken literally, the phylogenetic regression-progression continuum is, in reality, composed of motivation-emotion-motor pattern-reward linkages, each of which differs in some degree from the other in terms of phylogenetic primitiveness or advancedness. Many propositions may be derived from these basic assumptions, and the following summary attempts to place some of the more salient derivations into meaningful order.

I. Assumption I: Behavior is not a discrete entity, or a set of discrete entities, but an ongoing stream of dynamic and fluctuating motivation-emotion-behavior-reward linkages that merely appear as discrete events to the human observer.

A. *Subassumption IA:* to occur, meaningful or adaptive behavior must be motivated.

1. *Corollary IA1:* motivation, in both animals and humans, is primarily defined by, and derivative of, the evolved neurohumoral hardware and software programs which, on a probabilistic basis, serve to facilitate appropriate and adaptive response output of a given species to environmental demands.

2. *Corollary IA2:* acquired motives may be seen in higher species, most especially in human beings, but these are typically secondary to and/or derivative of the primitive motivational structures postulated in IA1.

B. *Subassumption IB:* higher animals are equipped with emotions and feelings which help energize and direct adaptive and species appropriate behavior.

1. *Corollary IB1:* the emotional components in behavior are primarily defined by, and derivative of, the evolved neurohumoral hardware and software programs which, on a probabilistic basis, serve to facilitate appropriate and adaptive response output of a given species to environmental demands.

C. *Subassumption IC:* animals and humans are equipped with inbuilt, species-typical action patterns and behavioral tendencies that are core components of adaptive, species-appropriate response output.

1. *Corollary IC1:* the motoric components in behavior are primarily defined by, and derivative of, the evolved neurohumoral hardware and software programs which, on a probabilistic basis, serve to facilitate appropriate and adaptive response output of a given species to environmental demands.

2. *Corollary IC2:* the more phylogenetically advanced the animal, the less fixed are the inbuilt motor patterns (see footnote 2, chapter 4, for discussion of phylogenetic advancedness).

3. *Corollary IC3:* the more phylogenetically advanced the animal, the more inbuilt behavioral patterns are modifiable by learning and experience.

D. *Subassumption ID:* the approach-avoidance behavior of higher animals (including humans) is guided by the experiences of pleasure and displeasure, broadly defined.

1. *Corollary ID1:* the reward (pleasure) and aversive (displeasure) components of adaptive behavior are primarily defined by, and derivative of, the neurohumoral hardware and software programs which, on a probabilistic basis, serve to facilitate appropriate and adaptive response output of a given species to environmental demands.

a. *Subcorollary ID1a:* neurohumoral reward pathways have evolved primarily to facilitate reliable and frequent *performance* of species-typical adaptive responses. Presumably, aversion plays some analogous function in discouraging species-atypical behavior, as well as mediating avoidance responses.

    b. *Subcorollary IDIb:* neurohumoral reward and aversion pathways also serve, to a lesser extent, as facilitators of response acquisition (learning), and possibly memory consolidation as well.

2. *Corollary ID2:* both animals and human beings spend far more time in the *performance* of responses than in *learning* them.

    a. *Subcorollary ID2a:* the performance-learning differential is a direct function of the phylogenetic advancedness of a given animal; that is, the more advanced an animal the more new responses it learns relative to the performance of old ones (e. g., phylogenetically conditioned responses or responses or preferences learned early in ontogeny, as with imprinted responses).

II. Assumption II: each hypothetical motivation-emotion-behavior-reward integration comprising the ongoing stream of behavior postulated in Assumption I falls at a point on the PRP continuum, although only for an infinitesimal, immeasurable fraction of a second. Actually, to be fully consistent with Assumption I, it is permissible to assume that a given motivation-emotion-behavior-reward coordination "fluctuates within a given band" on the PRP continuum, rather than occupying a specific point for a brief time.

III. Assumption III: the span of a given organism's PRP continuum and its freedom to traverse that continuum basically are determined by its inherent species characteristics.

    A. *Subassumption IIIA:* primitive organisms operate only within the lower segments of the PRP continuum, and capability to progress up the scale is severely constrained. Such primitive organisms quickly reach the upper asymtote of phylogenetic advancement, beyond which no progress is possible.

    B. *Subassumption IIIB:* advanced organisms operate within a wider PRP continuum than do primitive organisms.

1. *Corollary IIIB1:* the more phylogenetically advanced the species, the wider its PRP continuum.

2. *Corollary IIIB2:* even though more advanced organisms possess the potential to operate at the more advanced levels of their wider continua, they more often operate within the more inherently pleasurable and secure lower levels of functioning.

3. *Corollary IIIB3:* due to possessing both the greatest inherent compe-

tence, and the greatest ability to learn new competencies, human beings possess the widest PRP continuum of all animals.

a. *Subcorollary IIIB3a:* despite possessing unmatched potential for advanced behavior, humans, like the advanced nonhumans, prefer to spend most of their time enjoying the pleasures and securities of the primitive levels of functioning. Phylogenetic advancement, even for a very talented human being, is hard-won ground tenuously held.

C. *Subassumption IIIC:* advanced animals not only possess a wider PRP continuum, but they are more "free" (from blind instinct, etc.) to traverse it. Whereas a primitive animal may be fixated at lower levels of functioning, the advanced animal has some freedom to progress up or regress down the scale.

1. *Corollary IIIC1:* human beings not only possess the widest PRP continuum, but they—by virtue of greater inherent competence, greater capacity to augment competence through learning, self-consciousness, culture, etc.—are the most free of all animals to progress up the continuum or actively regress (see Chapter 3) down it. Humans, are thus the most flexible and variable of all creatures. Again, however, this freedom is only relative, and is strongly constrained phylogenetically, though less so than is the case with other animals.

D. *Subassumption IIID:* biological intelligence refers to the innate endowment of an animal vis-à-vis the width of its PRP continuum and capacity for traversing that continuum. Said another way, biological intelligence is a function of animal's inherent hierarchical range of competencies, and ability (freedom) to select from those competencies relative to environmental demands.

E. *Subassumption IIIE:* abstract intelligence refers to the capacity to transcend biological intelligence, and to assimilate and use information that is not coded in the genes, and that is not necessarily adaptive nor survival-targeted. Said another way, *abstract intelligence provides a means for extending the PRP continuum beyond the innate givens indefinitely through the exercise of mind.* It is through such exercise of mind that humans have phylogenetically progressed to where a mighty gap exists between ourselves and our closest nonhuman relatives.

1. *Corollary IIIE1:* due to the unmatched complexity and flexibility of function of the human brain, human beings possess a greater capacity for abstract intelligence than any other animal.

2. *Corollary IIIE2:* in humans, abstract intelligence provides the potential for phylogenetic progression, but does not guarantee it. In fact, the PRP model assumes that most human beings typically operate far below their inherent potential for abstract intelligence.

3. *Corollary IIIE3:* generally, abstract intelligence helps to inhibit

phylogenetic regression through its capability for producing and using moral and ethical information.

4. *Corollary IIIE4:* abstract intelligence may ally itself with the processes of regression, producing what is termed *active phylogenetic regression.*

IV. Assumption IV: learning is a complex, multifaceted, and nonunitary process of response acquisition that is, in large measure, based on evolved neurohumoral hardware and software programs that serve to facilitate appropriate and adaptive response output within a given species.

A. *Subassumtion IVA:* the primary function of learning is the refinement and elaboration of pre-programmed response patterns, tendencies, and dispositions.

B. *Subassumption IVB:* learning is more often *inhibitory* than *facilitory;* that is, given the great number of responses potentially available to even the simplest organism at a given moment, massive response suppression is necessary for ordered and appropriate behavior to occur.

1. *Corollary IVB1:* the more complex and advanced the organism, the greater the response possibilities; thus, the more advanced the organism, the greater the need for response suppression.

2. *Corollary IVB2:* given Corollary IVB1, it follows that man, as the most phylogenetically advanced creature, is the greatest specialist in response inhibition.

3. *Corollary IVB3:* it is presumed that the exaggerated inhibitory character of human behavior is a major factor in the human psychology and mental functioning. Indeed, it seems that man is, by nature, a very inhibited being.

4. *Corollary IVB4:* following from Corollary IVB3, learning *not to release* pre-existing patterns and tendencies (e. g., sex, aggression, etc.) is a major factor in human development and personality.

C. *Subassumption IVC:* learning processes within a given species are primarily a function of that particular species *constraints* on learning.

1. *Corollary IVC1:* following Seligman and Hager (1972), a given species may be prepared, nonprepared, or contraprepared to perform certain responses.

a. *Subcorollary IVC1a:* prepared responses are the easiest to learn, nonprepared responses the next easiest, and contraprepared responses the most difficult to learn.

b. *Subcorollary IVC1b:* responses which are prepared are the most pleasurable to learn, nonprepared responses the next most pleasurable, and contraprepared responses the least pleasurable (and most aversive) to learn.

D. *Subassumption IVD:* the so-called types of learning may be phylogenetically hierarchicalized as may most other basic systems of behavior. Gregory Razran's (1971) 11 evolutionary levels of learning illustrate this subassumption very well.

E. *Subassumption IVE:* morphogenetic and psychogenetic trait epigenesis occur, in great measure, in accordance with the principle of canalization. Development is thus a directed process leading to the growth and refinement of adaptive behavior systems.

1. *Corollary IVE1:* given Subassumption IVE, we may assume that human development and socialization are not random nor arbitrary; that is, human beings develop, in great measure, in ways they must develop, rather than merely in ways that the culture or environment dictate.

V. *Assumption V:* progression up the PRP scale or regression down it are complex and dynamic phenomena, but are, nevertheless, subject to certain regularities.

A. *Subassumption VA:* progression up the PRP scale is generally far more difficult than regression down it.

1. *Corollary VA1:* progression is generally unnatural and requires external learning and pressures, whereas regression is a return to natural, species-wide modes of response.

2. *Corollary VA2:* progression initially has little to build on in the nervous system, and supporting internal structures must be learned.

3. *Corollary VA3:* regression requires little in the way of learned new structures, but, rather, represents a *release* of motivational energy and motor responses encoded in phylogeny and stored in the nervous system.

4. *Corollary VA4:* the release of phylogenetically prepared tendencies and dispositions (regression) is generally more pleasurable than phylogenetic progression, which is based on *inhibition* of phylogenetically old tendencies.

B. *Subassumption VB:* phylogenetic progression is facilitated by a number of internal and external conditions:

1. *Corollary VB1:* in humans, phylogenetic progression is facilitated by good physical health and a well-integrated nervous system.

2. *Corollary VB2:* in humans, phylogenetic progression is potentially facilitated by high-quality nervous systems (e. g., high biological and abstract intelligence) capable of acquiring, storing, and flexibly using information, especially cultural information.

3. *Corollary VB3:* in humans, the level of phylogenetic progression reached is primarily an interactive function of the quality of the nervous

systems operating and the quality and quantity of culturally-relevant information available.

a. *Subcorollary VB3a:* in humans, phylogenetic progression is facilitated by the quality and availability of formal educational systems, and the degree to which individuals profit from those systems.

b. *Subcorollary VB3b:* in humans, phylogenetic progression is generally facilitated by the levels of social, cultural, and religious values reached by a given normative group, and the success of that normative group in transmitting those values to its members.

C. *Subassumption VC:* phylogenetic regression is facilitated by a number of internal and external conditions.

1. *Corollary VC1:* phylogenetic regression is facilitated by poor health, fatigue, nervous system dysfunction, or any other internal condition where the inhibition of primitive response systems fails.

a. *Subcorollary VC1a:* individuals may be genetically predisposed to phylogenetic regression either in terms of genetic pathology or in terms of genetic variation in normal trait structure (activity level, aggression, extroversion, etc.).

b. *Subcorollary VC1b:* phylogenetic regression may be facilitated or primed by ingestion of certain chemical agents that reduce inhibitory control over the primitive neural centers (amphetamines, ethyl alcohol, hallucinogenic drugs, etc.).

2. *Corollary VC2:* theoretically, one of the most potent elicitors of phylogenetic regression is *stress,* or more specifically, *threat to the survival of the individual.*

3. *Corollary VC3:* whereas human beings have little innate programming for the facilitation of phylogenetic progression, humans are generously endowed with innate programming for phylogenetic regression.

a. *Subcorollary VC3a:* human beings are endowed with both the tendencies to respond to certain releasing stimuli and the correlated motor patterns for appropriately responding to such stimuli. When a phylogenetically old response pattern is released by an equally phylogenetically old releasing stimulus pattern, this is an instance of phylogenetic regression.

4. *Corollary VC4:* phylogenetic regression may be released or facilitated by *mental activity,* e.g., internal-representational thoughts, wishes, dreams, daydreams, and so forth, in a direct elicitorial sense, or indirectly by "priming" thoughts, wishes, dreams, etc., which serve to erode inhibition over primitive tendencies.

5. *Corollary VC5:* phylogenetic regression may be facilitated by *subcortical supplementation* where the observed release of primitive emotion and behavior in others leads to similar release in the subject. Riots, mob behavior, gang attacks, etc., illustrate this process.

a. *Subcorollary VC5a:* subcortical supplementation is far more powerful in its effects than is cortical supplementation. That is, it is far easier to produce phylogenetic regression than progression through social stimulation.

D. *Subassumption VD:* the motivation-emotion-behavior-reward content recovered in phylogenetic regression is either presently-, once-, or never-adaptive.

1. *Corollary VD1:* presently-adaptive refers to phylogenetically-old tendencies and predispositions which continue to play contemporary adaptive roles. Phylogenetic continuity is essentially unbroken. Examples include use of aggression to protect self or kin, sexual attraction to opposite sex, and maternal parenting behavior.

2. *Corollary VD2:* once-adaptive refers to normally latent ancestral tendencies and predispositions which may be partially recovered through phylogenetic regression. Under normal circumstances, phylogenetic continuity is broken at the level of overt behavior, but remains in varying degrees of intactness at motivational, emotional, and hedonic levels; once regression occurs, continuity (across some or all levels) may be re-established temporarily. Examples include sexual promiscuity, especially in males, male preference for barely pubertal females, kill-the-stranger response, prejudice toward persons who are different, and clear re-differentiation of phylogenetically-conditioned sex roles under severe stress or social breakdown.

3. *Corollary VD3:* never-adaptive behavior refers to tendencies and predispositions recovered in regression which were not adaptive in ancestral species nor do they serve current adaptive functions. Generally, never-adaptive responses are released from neuropsychological structures that once served adaptive functions in phylogeny, but that misfire in some way, usually as a consequence of brain damage or dysfunction. Examples include rage responses and other forms of gratuitous or excessive violence that were maladaptive in the past and continue to be maladaptive in the present, nonadaptive but not maladaptive forms of behavioral noise that emanates from structures that are themselves inherently adaptive (e. g., excessive chatter, awkward or excessive movements, emotional or thought flooding of nonpathological type), and obsessions of various types (sex, acquisitiveness, narcissism, etc.) that emanate from basically normal psychological systems. In never-adaptive responses, phylogenetic continuity is indirect: the neurohumoral *structures* are phylogenetically continuous, but the maladaptive or nonadaptive behaviors emanating from them are not continuous.

References

Abel, G. G., Barlow, D. H., Blanchard, E. B., & Guild, D. (1977). The components of rapists' sexual arousal. *Archives of General Psychiatry, 34,* 895–903.

Abramovitch, R. (1976). The relation of attention and proximity to rank in preschool children. In M. R. A. Chance & R. P. Larsen (Eds.), *The social structure of attention* (pp. 153–176). New York: Wiley.

Abramovitch, R. (1980). Attention structures in hierarchically organized groups. In D. R. Omark, F. F. Strayer, & D. G. Freedman (Eds.), *Dominance relations.* New York: Garland.

Adamec, R. (1975a). The behavioral basis of prolonged suppression of predatory attack in cats. *Aggressive Behavior, 1,* 297–314.

Adamec, R. (1975b). The neural basis of prolonged suppression of predatory attack. 1. Naturally occurring physiological differences in the limbic systems of killer and non-killer cats. *Aggressive Behavior, 1,*315–330.

Adamec, R. (1975c). Behavioral and epileptic determinants of predatory attack behavior in the cat. *Canadian Journal of Neurological Science, 2,* 457–466.

Adams, D. B., & Flynn, J. P. (1966). Transfer of an escape response from tail shock to brain-stimulated attack behavior. *Journal of the Experimental Analysis of Behavior, 9,* 401–408.

Ainsworth, M. (1969). Object relations, dependency, and attachment: A theoretical review of the infant-mother relationship. *Child Development, 40,* 969–1025.

Aldis, O. (1975). *Play fighting.* New York: Academic Press.

Alcock, J. (1975). *Animal behavior: An evolutionary approach.* Sunderland, MA: Sinauer.

Alexander, F. (1960). Introduction. In Sigmund Freud, *Group psychology and the analysis of the ego.* New York: Bantam Books.

Alexander, R. D. (1974). The evolution of social behavior. *Annual Review of Ecology and Systematics, 5,* 325–383.

Alexander, R. D. (1975). The search for a general theory of behavior. *Behavioral Science, 10,* 77–100.

Alexander, R. D. (1977). Evolution, human behavior, and determinism. *Proceedings of the Biennial Meeting of the Philadelphia Science Association, 1976, 2,* 3–21.

Alexander, R. D. (1979). Evolution and culture. In N. A. Chagnon & W. Irons (Eds.), *Evolutionary biology and human social behavior: An anthropological perspective* (pp. 59–78). North Scituate, MA: Duxbury.

Alexander, R. D., & Noonan, K. N. (1979). Concealment of ovulation, parental care, and human social evolution. In N. A. Chagnon & W. Irons (Eds.), *Evolutionary biology and human social behavior: An anthropological perspective* (436–453). North Scituate, MA: Duxbury.

Alexander, R. D., Hoogland, J. L., Howard, R. D., Noonan, K. M., & Sherman, P. W. (1979). Sexual dimorphisms and breeding systems in pinnipeds, ungulates, primates, and humans. In N. A. Chagnon & W. Irons (Eds.), *Evolutionary biology and human social behavior: An anthropological perspective* (pp. 402–435). North Scituate, MA: Duxbury.

Al-Issa, I. (Ed.). (1982). *Gender and psychopathology.* New York: Academic Press.

Allport, F. H. (1924). *Social psychology.* Cambridge: Houghton Mifflin.

American Psychiatric Association. (1980). *Diagnostic and statistical manual of mental disorders,* Third Edition. Washington, DC: APA.

Alpers, B. J. (1937). Relation of the hypothalamus to disorders of personality. *Archives of Neurology and Psychiatry, 38,* 291–303.

Altman, I. (1975). *The environment and social behavior: Privacy, personal space, territory, and crowding.* Monterey, CA: Brooks/Cole.

Altman, I. (1976). Some perspectives on the study of man-environment systems. In H. Proshansky, W. Ittelson, & L. Rivlin (Eds.), *Environmental psychology: People and their physical settings.* (2nd ed., pp. 27–37). New York: Holt, Rinehart & Winston.

Altmann, S. A. (1967). The structure of primate social communication. In S. A. Altmann (Ed.), *Social communication among primates* (pp. 325–362). Chicago: University of Chicago Press.

Ambrose, J. A. (1963) The concept of a critical period for the development of social responsiveness. In B. M. Foss (Ed.), *The determinants of infant behavior II* (pp. 201–225). London: Methuen.

Ambrose, J. A. (Ed.). (1969). *Stimulation in early infancy.* New York: Academic Press.

Amir, M. (1967). Alcohol and forcible rape. *British Journal of Addiction, 62,* 219–232.

Amir, M. (1971). *Patterns of forcible rape.* Chicago: University of Chicago Press.

Andrewartha, H. G., & Birch, L. C. (1954). *The distribution and abundance of animals.* Chicago: University of Chicago Press.

Andy, O. J., & Stephan, H. (1974). Comparative primate neuroanatomy of structures relative to aggressive behavior. In R. L. Holloway (Ed.), *Primate aggression, territoriality, and xenophobia* (pp. 305–330). New York: Academic Press.

Ardrey, R. (1961). *African genesis.* New York: Dell.

Ardrey, R. (1966). *The territorial imperative.* New York: Dell.

Ardrey, R. (1970). *The social contract.* New York: Atheneum.

Ardrey, R. (1971). Discussion of session I. In A. H. Esser (Ed.), *Behavior and environment: The use of space in animals and men* (pp. 48–49). New York: Plenum.

Ardrey, R. (1977). *The hunting hypothesis.* New York: Bantam.

Aries, P. (1962). *Centuries of childhood: A social history of family life.* (R. Baldick, Trans.) New York: Vintage.

Arieti, S. (1970). The structural and psychodynamic role of cognition in the human psyche. In S. Arieti (Ed.), *The world biennial of psychiatry and psychotherapy* (Vol. I, pp. 3–33). New York: Basic Books.

Arieti, S. (1976). *Creativity: The magic synthesis.* New York: Basic Books.

Aristotle. (1952) In Vol. 8 of R. M. Hutchins (Ed)., *Great books of the western world.* Chicago: Encyclopedia Britannica.

Arlow, J. A., & Brenner, C. (1964). *Psychoanalytic concepts and the structural theory.* New York: International Universities Press.

Armstrong, E. A. (1965). *Bird display and behavior: An introduction to the study of bird psychology.* New York: Dover.

Atkeson, B. M., Calhoun, K. S., Resick, P. A., & Ellis, E. M. (1982). Victims of rape: Repeated assessment of depressive symptoms. *Journal of Consulting and Clinical Psychology, 50,* 96–102.

Austin, W. T., & Bates, F. L. (1974). Ethological indicators of dominance and territory in a human captive population. *Human Forces, 52,* 447–555.

Bailey, K. G. (1978). The concept of phylogenetic regression. *Journal of the American Academy of Psychoanalysis, 6,* 5–35.

Bailey, K. G. (1985). Phylogenetic regression and the problem of extreme aggression. *Journal of Social and Biological Structures, 8,* 207–224.

Bailey, K. G. (1986a). *Models and myths in social science.* Unpublished manuscript, Virginia Commonwealth University.

Bailey, K. G. (1986b). *A kinship model for psychotherapy.* Unpublished manuscript, Virginia Commonwealth University.

Bailey, K. G., Burns, D. S., & Bazan, L. C. (1982). A method for measuring "primitive" and "advanced" elements in pleasures and aversions. *Journal of Personality Assessment, 46,* 639–646.

Bailey, K. G., Caffrey, J. V., Jr., & Hartnett, J. J. (1976). Body size and implied threat: Effects on personal space and person perception. *Perceptual and Motor Skills, 43,* 223–230.

Bailey, K. G., Hartnett, J. J. & Gibson, F. W. Jr. (1972). Implied threat and the territorial factor in personal space. *Psychological Reports, 30,* 263–270.

Bailey, K. G., & Millbrook, J. M. (1984). "Primitiveness" and "advancedness" of pleasures and aversions in relation to WAIS indices. *Journal of Clinical Psychology, 40,* 295–299.

Bailey, K. G., Tipton, R. M., & Taylor, P. F. (1977). The threatening stare: Differential response latencies in mild and profoundly retarded adults. *American Journal of Mental Deficiency, 31,* 599–602.

Bakan, D. (1971). *Slaughter of the innocents: A study of the battered child syndrome.* Boston: Beacon Press.

Baker, J. R. (1974). *Race.* New York: Oxford University Press.

Baldassare, M. (1978). Human spatial behavior. *Annual Review of Sociology, 4,* 29–56.

Bandura, A. (1973). *Aggression: A social learning analysis.* Englewood Cliffs, NJ: Prentice-Hall.

Bandura, A. (1978). The self-system in reciprocal determinism. *American Psychologist, 33,* 344–358.

Barash, D. P. (1977). *Sociobiology and behavior.* New York: Elsevier.

Barash, D. P. (1979). *The whisperings within: Evolution and the origin of human nature.* New York: Harper & Row.

Barash, D. P. (1981). The sociobiologic paradigm. In C. Eisdorfer, D. Cohen, A. Kleinman, & P. Maxim (Eds.), *Models for clinical psychopathology* (pp. 63–94). New York: Spectrum.

Bardin, C. W., & Catterall, J. F. (1981). Testosterone: A major determinant of extragenital sexual dimorphism. *Science, 211,* 1285–1294.

Barkow, J. H. (1975). Prestige and culture: A biosocial interpretation. *Current Anthropology, 16,* 553–572.

Barkow, J. H. (1980). Biological evolution of culturally patterned behavior. In J. S. Lockard (Ed.), *The evolution of human social behavior* (pp. 277–296). New York: Elsevier.

Barkow, J. H. (1983). Begged questions in human evolution. In G. C. L. Davey (Ed.),

Animal models of human behavior: Conceptual, evolutionary, and neurobiological perspectives (pp. 205–222). New York: Wiley.

Barlow, N. (Ed.). (1985). *The autobiography of Charles Darwin, 1809–1882.* London: Collins.

Barnett, S. A. (1967). *Instinct and intelligence: Behavior of animals and man.* Englewood Cliffs, NJ: Prentice-Hall.

Bates, D. G., & Lees, S. H. (1979). The myth of population regulation. In N. A. Chagnon & W. Irons (Eds.), *Evolutionary biology and human social behavior: An anthropological perspective* (pp. 273–389). North Scituate, MA: Duxbury.

Bateson, P. P. G. & Hinde, R. A. (Eds.). (1976). *Growing points in ethology.* London: Cambridge University Press.

Bazan, L. C. (1980). *An initial construct validation for a scale measuring behaviors on an advanced-primitive continuum.* Unpublished master's thesis, Virginia Commonwealth University.

Beach, F. A. (1942). Male and female mating behavior in prepuberally castrated female rats treated with androgens. *Endocrinology, 31*,673–678.

Beach, F. A. (1967). Cerebral and hormonal control of reflexive mechanisms involved in copulatory behavior. *Physiological Reviews, 47,* 289–316.

Beach, F. A. (1974). Human sexuality and evolution. In W. Montagna & W. A. Sadler (Eds.), *Reproductive behavior* (pp. 333–365). New York: Plenum.

Beach, F. A. (1976a). Cross-species comparisons and the human heritage. *Archives of Sexual Behavior, 5,* 469–485.

Beach, F. A. (1976b). Sexual attractivity, proceptivity, and receptivity in female mammals. *Hormones and Behavior, 7,* 105–138.

Beal, J. B. (1974). Electrostatic fields, electromagnetic fields, and ions-Mind/body/environment interrelationships. In J. G. Llaudado, A. Sances, & J. H. Batocletti (Eds.), *Biologic and clinical effects of low-frequency magnetic and electrical fields.* Springfield, IL: Charles C. Thomas.

Beer, C. G. (1963). Ethology—The zoologist's approach to behavior. Pt. I. *Tuatara, 11,* 170–177.

Beer, C. G. (1964). Ethology—The zoologist's approach to behavior. Pt. II. *Tuatara, 12,* 16–39.

Benton, D. (1983). Do animal studies tell us anything about the relationship between testosterone and human aggression? In G. C. L. Davey (Ed.), *Animal models and human behavior: Conceptual, evolutionary, and neurobiological perspectives* (pp. 281–298). New York: Wiley.

Berent, S. (1981). Lateralization of brain function. In S. B. Filsov & T. J. Boll (Eds.), *Handbook of clinical neurology* (pp. 74–101). New York: Wiley.

Bergmann, G. (1951). Ideology. *Ethics, LXI,* 205–218.

Berkowitz, L. (1962). *Aggression: A social psychological analysis.* New York: McGraw-Hill.

Berkowitz, L. (1969). Simple views of aggression. *American Scientist, 3,* 372–383.

Bermant, G., & Davidson, J. M. (1974). *Biological bases of sexual behavior.* New York: Harper & Row.

Bernard, L. L .(1924). *Instinct: A study in social psychology.* New York: Henry Holt.

Bernstein, I. S. (1966). Analysis of a key role in a capuchin (*Cebus albifrons*) group. *Tulane Studies in Zoology, 13,* 49–54.

Bernstein, I. S. (1970). Primate status hierarchies. In L. A. Rosenblum (Ed.), *Primate behavior* (pp. 71–109). New York: Academic Press.

Bernstein, I. S., & Gordon, T. P. (1974). The function of aggression in primate societies. *American Scientist, 62,* 304–311.

Berofsky, B. (1973). Free will and determinism. In P. P. Wiener (Ed.), *Dictionary of the history of ideas* (pp. 236–242). New York: Charles Scribner's Sons.

Bigelow, R. (1972). The evolution of cooperation, aggression, and self-control. In J. K. Cole & D. D. Jensen (Eds.), *Nebraska symposium on motivation* (pp. 1–58). Lincoln: University of Nebraska Press.

Bindra, D. (1976). *A theory of intelligent behavior.* New York: Wiley.

Bitterman, M. E. (1965). The evolution of intelligence. *Scientific American, 22,* 92–100

Blinkov, S., & Glezer, I. I. (1958). *The human brain in figures and tables: A quantitative handbook.* New York: Basic Books.

Blumer, D. (1970). Changes of sexual behavior related to temporal lobe disorders in man. *Journal of Sex Research, 6,* 173–180.

Blumer, D., & Walker, A. E. (1975). The neural basis of sexual behavior. In D. F. Benson & D. Blumer (Eds.), *Psychiatric aspects of neurologic disease* (pp.   ). New York: Grune & Stratton.

Blumer, D. P., Williams, H. W., & Mark, V. H. (1974). The study and treatment, on a neurological ward, of abnormally aggressive patients with focal brain disease, *Confinia Neurologica, 36,* 125–176.

Blumer, H. (1951). Collective behavior. In A. McC. Lee (Ed.), *New outline of the principles of sociology* (pp.   ). New York: Barnes & Noble.

Blurton-Jones, N. (Ed.). (1972). *Ethological studies of child behaviour.* London: Cambridge University Press.

Boddy, J. (1978). *Brain systems and psychological concepts.* New York: Wiley.

Bogen, J. E. (1977). Some educational implications of hemispheric specialization. In M. C. Wittrock (Ed.), *The human brain* (pp. 33–152). Englewood Cliffs, NJ: Prentice-Hall.

Boice, R. (1981). Captivity and feralization. *Psychological Bulletin, 89,* 407–421.

Bokun, B. (1977). *Man: The fallen ape.* Garden City, NY: Doubleday.

Bolles, R. C., & Faneslow, M. S. (1982). Endorphins and behavior. *Annual Review of Psychology, 33,* 87–101.

Bolton, F. G., Jr. (1983). *When bonding fails: Clinical assessment of high-risk families.* Beverly Hills, CA: Sage.

Boslough, J. (1984, February). Inside the mind of a genius. *Reader's Digest,* pp. 118–124.

Bourgiba (1984). Let them eat bread. *Time,* January, p. 44.

Bowlby, J. (1952). *Maternal care and mental health.* (2nd ed.). Geneva: World Health Organization.

Bowlby, J. (1958). The nature of the child's tie to his mother. *International Journal of Psycho-Analysis, 39,* 350–373.

Bowlby, J. (1960). Symposium on 'psychoanalysis and ethology' II. Ethology and the development of object relations. *International Journal of Psycho-Analysis, 41,* 313–317.

Bowlby, J. (1969). *Attachment and loss. Vol. I. Attachment.* New York: Basic Books.

Bowlby, J. (1973). *Attachment and loss. Vol. II. Separation.* New York: Basic Books.

Brace, C. L. (1967). *The stages of human evolution: Human and cultural origins.* Englewood Cliffs, NJ: Prentice-Hall.

Bradshaw, J. L., & Nettleton, N. C. (1983). *Human cerebral asymmetry.* Englewood Cliffs, NJ: Prentice-Hall.

Brain, P. F. (1981). Differentiating types of attack and defense in rodents. In P. F. Brain & D. Benton (Eds.), *Multidisiplinary approaches to aggression research.* (pp. 53–78). Amsterdam: Elsevier/North Holland.

Brain, P. F., & Benton, D. (Eds.). (1981). *Multidisiplinary approaches to aggression research.* Amsterdam: Elsevier/North Holland.

Branigan, C. R., & Humphries, D. A. (1972). Human non-verbal behavior, a means of communication. In N. Blurton-Jones (Ed.), *Ethological studies in child behavior* (pp. 37–64). Cambridge: Cambridge University Press.

Breger, L. (1968). Motivation, energy, and cognitive structure in psychoanalytic theory. In J. Marmor (Ed.), *Modern psychoanalysis* (pp. 44–65). New York: Basic Books.

Breger, L. (1974). *From instinct to identity*. Englewood Cliffs, NJ: Prentice-Hall.

Bresnahan, E., & Routtenberg, A. (1972). Memory disruption by unilateral low-level subseizure stimulation of the medial amygdaloid nucleus. *Physiological Behavior, 9,* 513–525.

Bridgman, P. W. (1958). Determinism in modern physics. In S. Hook (Ed.), *Determinism and freedom in the age of modern science* (pp. 43–63). New York: New York University Press.

Briere, J., Downes, A., & Spensley, J. (1983). Summer in the city: Weather conditions and 'psychiatric emergency-room visits. *Journal of Abnormal Psychology, 92,* 77–80.

Brill, H. (1959). Postencephalitic psychiatric conditions. In S. Arieti (Ed.), *American Handbook of Psychiatry* (Vol. II, pp. 1163–1174). New York: Basic Books.

Broca, P. (1878). Anatomie comparée des circonvolutions cérébrales. Le grand lobe limbique et la scissure limbique dans la série des mammifères. *Review of Anthropology, 7,* 385–498.

Brockett, C. A. (1982). *Effects of incubation in low creative individuals*. Unpublished Master's thesis, Virginia Commonwealth University.

Brodbeck, M. (1963). Meaning and action. *Philosophy of Science, 30,,* 309–324.

Brodbeck, M. (Ed.). (1968). *Readings in the philosophy of the social sciences*. New York: Macmillan.

Brown, J. L. (1964). The evolution of diversity in avian territorial systems. *Wilson Bulletin, 76,* 160–169.

Brown, J. (1977). *Mind, brain, and consciousness*. New York: Academic Press.

Brown, R. (1965). *Social psychology*. New York: Free Press.

Brown, R., & Herrnstein, R. J. (1975). *Psychology*. Boston: Little, Brown.

Brownmiller, S. (1975). *Against our will: Men, women, and rape*. New York: Bantam Press.

Bruner, J. S. (1972). Nature and uses of immaturity. *American Psychologist, 27,* 687–708.

Bruner, J. S., Jolly, A., & Sylva, K. (Eds.). (1976). *Play: Its role in development and evolution*. New York: Basic Books.

Buchenholtz, B. (1956). The motivating action of pleasure. *Journal of Nervous and Mental Disease, 123,* 569–577.

Buchenholtz, B. (1958). Models for pleasure. *Psychoanalytic Quarterly, 27,* 307–326.

Buchenholtz, B., & Naumberg, G. W. (1957). The pleasure process. *Journal of Nervous and Mental Disease, 125,* 396–402.

Bunnell, B. N. (1966). Amygdaloid lesions and social dominance in the hooded rat. *Psychonomic Science, 6,* 93–94.

Bunney, W. E., Pert, A., Rosenblatt, J., Pert, C. B., & Gallaper, D. (1979). Mode of action of lithium: A Some biological considerations. *Archives of General Psychiatry, 36,* 898–901.

Burgess, A. W., & Holmstrom, L. L. (1974). Rape trauma syndrome. *American Journal of Psychiatry, 131,* 981–986.

Burns, D. S. (1979). *The construction and initial validation of a scale measuring behaviors on an advanced-primitive continuum*. Unpublished master's thesis, Virginia Commonwealth University.

Burns, D. S. (1984). *The construction and initial validation of an objective scale measuring behaviors on a primitive-advanced continuum*. Unpublished doctoral dissertation, Virginia Commonwealth University.

Burrow, J. W. (1968). Editor's introduction. In Charles Darwin (1859), *The origin of the species*. Baltimore, MD: Penquin.

Burrow, T. (1974). *Perspectives in social inquiry*. New York: Arno Press. (originally published 1937)

Buss, A. H. (1961). *The psychology of aggression*. New York: Wiley.

Cahoon, D. D. (1972). A behavioristic analysis of aggression. *Psychological Record, 22*, 463–476.

Cairns, R. B. (1979). *Social development: The origins and plasticity of interchanges*. San Francisco: Freeman.

Calhoun, J. B. (1962). Population density and social pathology. *Science, 206*, 139–146.

Calhoun, J. B. (1971). Space and the strategy of life. In A. H. Esser (Ed.), *Behavior and environment: The use of space by animals and men* (pp. 329–387). New York: Plenum.

Callen, K. (1980). Women degraded in media wasteland: Cantor. *ADAMHA News, VI*, 5–7.

Campbell, B. G. (Ed.). (1972). *Sexual selection and the descent of man*. Chicago: Aldine.

Campbell, B. G. (Ed.). (1979). *Humankind emerging* (2nd ed.). Boston: Little, Brown.

Campbell, D. E., & Beets, J. L. (1978). Lunacy and the moon. *Psychological Bulletin, 85*, 1123–1129.

Campbell, D. T. (1975). On the conflicts between biological and social evolution and between psychology and moral tradition. *American Psychologist, 30*, 1103–1126.

Cantwell, M. (1983). The offender. In M. W. Zawitz (Ed.), *Report to the nation on crime and justice: The data* (pp. 29–40). Washington, DC: U. S. Department of Justice.

Caplan, A. L. (Ed.). (1978). *The sociobiology debate*. New York: Harper & Row.

Carpenter, C. R. (1958). Territoriality: A review of concepts and problems. In A. Roe & G. G. Simpson (Eds.), *Behavior and evolution* (pp. 224–250). New Haven, CT: Yale University Press.

Carpenter, C. R. (1964). *Naturalistic behavior of nonhuman primates*. University Park: Pennsylvania State University Press.

Carrighar, S. (1971). *Wild heritage*. New York: Ballantine Books.

Carthy, J. D., & Ebling, F. J. (Eds.). (1964). *The natural history of aggression*. New York: Academic Press.

Cattell, R. B. (1971). *Abilities: Their structure, growth, and action*. Boston: Houghton Mifflin.

Cell mates charged in teen's death. (1982, June). *Richmond Times-Dispatch*, p. 2.

Cerbus, G. (1970). Seasonal variation in some mental health statistics: Suicides, homocides, psychiatric admissions, and institutional placement of the retarded. *Journal of Clinical Psychology, 26*, 60–63.

Cerbus, G., & Travis, R. J. (1973). Seasonal variation of personality of college students as measured by the MMPI. *Psychological Reports, 33*, 665–666.

Chagnon, N. A. (1979). Is reproductive success equal in egalitarian societies? In N. A. Chagnon & W. Irons (Eds.), *Evolutionary biology and human social behavior: An anthropological perspective* (pp. 374–401). North Scituate, MA: Duxbury.

Chagnon, N. A., Flinn, M. V., & Melancon, T. F. (1979). Sex-ratio variation among the Yąnomamö Indians. In N. A. Chagnon & W. Irons (Eds.), *Evolutionary biology and human social behavior: An anthropological perspective* (pp. 290–320). North Scituate, MA: Duxbury.

Chagnon, N. A., & Irons, W. (Eds.). (1979). *Evolutionary biology and human social behavior: An anthropological perspective*. North Scituate, MA: Duxbury.

Chance, M. R. A. (1967). Attention structure as the basis of primate rank orders. *Man, 2*, 503–518.

Chance, M. R. A. (1976). Attention structure as the basis of primate rank orders. In M. R. A. Chance & R. R. Larsen (Eds.), *The social structure of attention* (pp. 11–28). New York: Wiley.

Chance, M. R. A., & Jolly, C. J. (1970). *Social groups of monkeys, apes, and men*. London: Thames & Hudson.

Charlesworth, W. R. (1979). Ethology: Understanding the other half of intelligence. In M. von Cranach, K. Foppa, W. Lepenies, & D. Ploog (Eds.), *Human ethology: Claims and limits of a new discipline* (pp. 491–529). London: Cambridge University Press.

Cherry, C. M., Case, S. M., & Wilson, A. C. (1978). Frog perspective on the morphological difference between humans and chimpanzees. *Science, 200*, 209–211.

Children kill boy, 9, who refused to share. (1985, August). *Richmond Times-Dispatch*, p. 1.

Chitty, D. (1957). Self-regulation of numbers through changes in viability. *Cold Springs Harbor Symposia on Quantitative Biology, 22*, 277–280.

Chitty, D. (1960). Population processes in the vole and their relevance to general theory. *Canadian Journal of Zoology, 38*, 99–113.

Christian, J. J. (1950). The adreno-pituitary system and population cycles in mammals. *Journal of Mammology, 31*, 247–259.

Clavier, R. M., & Routtenberg, A. (1974). Ascending monoamine-containing fiber pathways related to intracranial self-stimulation: Histochemical fluorescence study. *Brain Research, 72*, 25–40.

Clavier, R. M., & Routtenberg, A. (1980). In search of reinforcement pathways: A neuroanatomical oddyssey. In A. Routtenberg (Ed.), *Biology of reinforcement: Facets of brain stimulation reward* (pp. 81–108). New York: Academic Press.

Cloward, R. A. (1959). Illegitimate means, anomie, and deviant behavior. *American Sociological Review, 24*, 164–176.

Cobb, S. (1965). Brain size. *Archives of Neurology, 12*, 555–561.

Cofer, C. N., & Appley, M. H. (1964). *Motivation: Theory and research*. New York: Wiley.

Cohen, A. K. (1955). *Delinquent boys: The culture and the gang*. New York: Free Press.

Cohen, S. (1973). Property destruction: motives and meanings. In C. Ward (Ed.), *Vandalism*, New York: Van Nostrand Reinhold.

Coleman, J. C., Butcher, J. N., & Carson, R. C. (1980). *Abnormal psychology and modern life* (6th ed.). New York: Scott, Foresman.

Collias, N. E. (1944). Aggressive behavior among vertebrate animals. *Physiological Zoology, 17*, 83–123.

Collias, N. E. (1956). The analysis of socialization in sheep and goats. *Ecology, 37*, 228–239.

Collier, T. J., Kurtzman, S., & Routtenberg, A. (1977). Intracranial self-stimulation derived from entorhinal cortex. *Brain Research, 137*, 188–196.

Collins, J. J. (1981). *Alcohol use and criminal behavior: An executive summary*, Washington, DC: U. S. Department of Justice.

Comfort, A. (1971). The likelihood of human pheromones. *Nature, 239*, 432–449.

Commins, S., & Linscott, R. N. (1947). *Man and man: The social philosophers*. New York: Random House.

Constable, G. (Ed.). (1973). *The neanderthals*. New York: Time-Life Books.

Coon, C. S. (1939). *The races of Europe*. New York: Macmillan.

Coon, C. S. (1971). *The hunting peoples*. Boston: Little, Brown.

Cortés, J. B., & Gatti, F. M. (1972). *Delinquency and crime: A biopsychosocial approach*. New York: Seminar Press.

Count, E. W. (1973). *Being and becoming human: Essays on the biogram*. New York: Van Nostrand Reinhold.

Court, J. H. (1984). Sex and violence: A ripple effect. In N. M. Malamuth & E. Donnerstein (Eds.), *Pornography and sexual aggression* (pp. 143–172). Orlando, FL: Academic Press.

Cranach, M. von. (Ed.). (1976). *Methods of inference from animal to human behavior*. Chicago: Aldine.

Cravens, H. (1978). *The triumph of evolution: American scientists and the heredity-environment controversy, 1900–1941*. Philadelphia: University of Pennsylvania Press.

Crook, J. H. (1968). The nature and function of territorial aggression. In M. F. A. Montagu (Ed.), *Man and aggression* (pp. 141–178). London: Oxford University Press.

Crook, J. H. (1971). Sources of cooperation in animals and man. In J. F. Eisenberg & W. S. Dillon (Eds.), *Man and beast: Comparative social behavior* (pp. 235–260). Washington, DC: Smithsonian Institution Press.

Crook, J. H. (1980). *The evolution of human consciousness*. London: Oxford University.

Crow, T. J. (1968). Enhancement by cocaine of intracranial stimulation in the rat. *Life Sciences, 9*, 375–381.

Damon, W. (1977). *The social world of the child*. San Francisco: Jossey-Bass.

Daniels, D. N., Gilula, M. F., & Ochberg, F. M. (Eds.). (1970). *Violence and the struggle for existence*. Boston: Little, Brown.

Dart, R. (1973). The predatory transition from ape to man. In Maple, T., & Matheson, D. W. (Eds.), *Aggression, hostility, and violence*. New York: Holt, Rinehart & Winston. (Originally published 1953)

Darwin, C. (1865). *The movements and habits of climbing plants*. London: John Murray.

Darwin, C. (1875). *Insectivorous plants*. London: John Murray.

Darwin, C. (1896). *The expression of the emotions in man and animals*. New York: Appleton. (originally published 1872)

Darwin, C. (1968). *The origin of the species*. Baltimore, MD: Penguin. (originally published 1859)

Darwin, C. (1981). *The descent of man, and selection in relation to sex*. Princeton, NJ: Princeton University Press. (originally published 1871)

Davey, G. C. L. (Ed.). (1983). *Animal models of human behavior: Conceptual, evolutionary, and neurobiological perspectives*. New York: Wiley.

Davis, D. E. (1964). The physiological analysis of aggressive behavior. In W. Etkin (Ed.), *Social behavior and organization among vertebrates* (pp. 53–74). Chicago: University of Chicago Press.

Davis, D. E. (1968). An inquiry into the phylogeny of gangs. In E. L. Bliss (Ed.), *Roots of behavior: Genetics, instinct, and socialization in animal behavior* (pp. 316–320). New York: Hafner.

Dawes, R. M. (1980). Social dilemmas. *Annual Review of Psychology, 31*, 169–193.

Dawkins, R. (1976a). *The selfish gene*. New York: Oxford University Press.

Dawkins, R. (1976b). Hierarchical organisation: a candidate principle for ethology. In P. P. G. Bateson & R. A. Hinde (Eds.), *Growing points in ethology* (pp. 7–54). London: Cambridge University Press.

de Beer, G. R. (1958). *Embryos and ancestors* (3rd ed.). Oxford: Clarendon Press.

de Chardin, T. (1959). *The phenomenon of man*. New York: Harper/Colophon.

de Lacoste-Utamsing, C., & Holloway, R. (1982). Sexual dimorphism in the human corpus callosum. *Science, 216*, 1431–1432.

Demaret, A. (1979). *Éthologie et psychiatrie: Valeur de survie et phylogenese des maladies mentales*. Brussels: Pierre Mardaga.

Demarest, J. (1983). The ideas of change, progress, and continuity in the comparative psychology of learning. In D. W. Rajecki (Ed.), *Comparing behavior: Studying man studying animals* (pp. 143–180). Hillsdale, NJ: Lawrence Erlbaum.

de Riencourt, A. (1974). *Sex and power in history*. New York: Dial/James Wade.

Desmond, A. J. (1979). *The ape's reflexion*. New York: Dial Press.

Deutsch, H. (1944). *The psychology of women: A psychoanalytic interpretation* (Vol. 1). New York: Grune & Stratton.

Deutsch, J. S., & Howarth, C. I. (1963). Some tests of a theory of intracranial self-stimulation. *Psychological Review, 70*, 444–460.

DeVore, I. (1971). The evolution of human society. In J. F. Eisenberg & W. S. Dillon (Eds.), *Man and beast: Comparative social behavior* (pp. 297–312). Washington, DC: Smithsonian Institution Press.

de Waal, F. (1982). *Chimpanzee politics: Power and sex among apes*. New York: Harper & Row.

Diamond, I. T., & Hall, W. C. (1969). Evolution of the neocortex. *Science, 164*, 251–262.

Dickemann, M. (1979). Female infanticide, reproductive strategies, and social stratification: A preliminary model. In N. A. Chagnon & W. Irons (Eds.), *Evolutionary biology and human social behavior: An anthropological perspective* (pp. 321–368). North Scituate, MA: Duxbury.

Dicks, D., Myers, R. K., & Kling, A. (1969). Uncus and amygdala lesions: effects on social behavior in the free ranging rhesus monkey. *Science, 165,* 69–71.

Diener, E., Fraser, S. C. Beaman, A. L., & Kelem, R. T. (1976). Effects of deindividuation variables on stealing among Halloween trick-or-treaters. *Journal of Personality and Social Psychology, 33,* 178–183.

Dietz, P. E. (1978). Social factors in rapist behavior. In R. T. Rada (Ed.), *Clinical aspects of the rapist* (pp. 59–117). New York: Grune & Stratton.

Dimond, S. J. (1970). *The social behavior of animals.* New York: Harper Colophon Books.

Dimond, S. J. (1979). Performance by splitbrain humans on lateralized vigilance tasks. *Cortex, 15,* 43–50.

Dion, K. L. (1970). *Determinants of unprovoked aggression.* Unpublished doctoral dissertation, University of Minnesota.

Dipboye, R. L. (1977). Alternative approaches to deindividuation. *Psychological Bulletin, 84,* 1057–1075.

Divale, W. T., Harris, M., & Williams, D. T. (1978). On the misuse of statistics: A reply to Hirschfield et al. *American Anthropologist, 80,* 379–386.

Dobzhansky, T. (1937). *Genetics and the origin of species* (1st ed.). New York: Columbia University Press.

Dobzhansky, T. (1973). Nothing in biology makes sense except in the light of evolution. *American Biology Teacher, 35,* 125–129.

Dolinhow, P. (Ed.). (1972). *Primate patterns.* New York: Holt, Rinehart, & Winston.

Dollard, J., Doob, L. W., Miller, N. E., Mowrer, O. H., & Sears, R. R. (1939). *Frustration and aggression.* New Haven, CT: Yale University Press.

Duff, C. (1930). *This human nature.* New York: Cosmopolitan Book.

Duke, J. T. (1976). *Conflict and power in social life.* Provo, UT: Brigham University Press.

Dumond, D. E. (1975). The limitations of human population: A natural history. *Science, 187,* 713–721.

Dunlap, K. (1919). Are there any instincts? *Journal of Abnormal Psychology, 14,* 35–50.

Dunstone, J. J., Cannon, J. T., Chickson, J. T., & Burns, W. K. (1972). Persistence and vigor of shock-induced aggression in gerbils (*Meriones unguiculatus*). *Psychonomic Science, 28,* 272–274.

Durant, J. R. (1981). The beast in man: An historical perspective on the biology of human aggression. In P. Brain & D. Benton (Eds.), *The biology of aggression* (pp. 17–47). The Netherlands: Sijthoff, Leiden.

Durant, W. (1953). *The pleasures of philosophy.* New York: Simon & Schuster.

Durden-Smith, J., & deSimone, D. (1983). *Sex and the brain.* New York: Warner Books.

Durham, W. H. (1979). Toward a coevolutionary theory of human biology and culture. In N. A. Chagnon & W. Irons (Eds.), *Evolutionary biology and human social behavior: An anthropological perspective* (pp. 39–58). North Scituate, MA: Duxbury.

Eccles, J. C. (1970). *Facing reality: Philosophical adventures by a brain scientist.* New York: Springer-Verlag.

Eckholm, E. (1985). Pygmy chimp readily learns language skill. *New York Times,* June, pp. A–I, B1.

Edinger, J. A., & Patterson, M. L. (1983). Nonverbal involvement and social control. *Psychological Bulletin, 93,* 30–56.

Edney, J. J. (1974). Human territoriality. *Psychological Bulletin, 81,* 959–973.

Eggan, J. (1926). Is instinct an entity? *Journal of Abnormal and Social Psychology, 21,* 38–51.

Egger, M. D., & Flynn, J. P. (1963). Effect of electrical stimulation of the amygdala on hypothalamically elicited attack behavior in cats. *Journal of Neurophysiology, 26,* 705–720.

Egger, M. D., & Flynn, J. P. (1967). Further studies on the effects of amygdaloid stimulation and ablation on hypothalamically elicited attack behavior in cats. In W. R. Adey & T. Tokizane (Eds.), *Progress in brain research* (Vol. 27, pp. 165–182). Amsterdam: Elsevier.

Ehrhardt, A. A., & Meyer-Bahlburg, H. F. L. (1981). Effects of prenatal sex hormones on gender-related behavior. *Science, 211,* 1312–1318.

Ekman, P., & Friesen, W. V. (1975). *Unmasking the face: A guide to recognizing emotions from facial expressions.* Englewood, NJ: Prentice-Hall.

Eibl-Eibesfeldt, I. (1961). The fighting behavior of animals. *Scientific American, 205,* 112–122.

Eibl-Eibesfeldt, I. (1972). *Love and hate.* New York: Holt, Rinehart & Winston.

Eibl-Eibesfeldt, I. (1970). *Ethology: The biology of behavior* (1st ed.). New York: Holt, Rinehart, & Winston.

Eibl-Eibesfeldt, I. (1975). *Ethology: The biology of behavior* (2nd ed.). New York: Holt, Rinehart & Winston.

Eibl-Eibesfeldt, I. (1979). *The biology of peace and war: Men, animals, and aggression.* New York: Viking Penguin.

Eibl-Eibesfeldt, I., & Hass, H. (1967). Neue Wege der Humanethologie. *Homo, 18,* 13–23.

Eisenberg, J. F. (1971). Introduction (Part 3). In J. F. Eisenberg & W. S. Dillon (Eds.), *Man and beast: Comparative social behavior* (pp. 263–272). Washington, DC: Smithsonian Institution Press.

Ellsworth, P. C., Carlsmith, J. M., & Henson, A. (1972). The stare as a stimulus to flight in human subjects: A series of field experiments. *Journal of Personality and Social Psychology, 21,* 302–311.

Elmadjian, F., Hope, J. M., & Lamson, E. T. (1957). Excretion of epinephrine and norepinephrine in various emotional states. *Journal of Clinical Endocrinology, 17,* 608–620.

Eme, R. F. (1979). Sex differences in childhood psychopathology. *Psychological Bulletin, 86,* 574–595.

Engel, G. L. (1977). The need for a new medical model: A challenge to biomedicine. *Science, 196,* 129–136.

Entwhistle, C., & Sim, M. (1961). Tuberous sclerosis and fetishism. *British Medical Journal 2,* 1688–1689.

Epstein, A. W. (1961). Relationship of fetishism and transvestism to brain and particularly temporal lobe dysfunction. *Journal of Nervous and Mental Disease, 133,* 247–253.

Epstein, A. W. (1969). Fetishism: A comprehensive review. In J. Masserman (Ed.), *Dynamics of deviant sexuality.* New York: Grune & Stratton.

Epstein, A. W. (1975). The fetish object: Phylogenetic considerations. *Archives of Sexual Behavior, 4,* 303–308.

Erickson, T. (1945). Erotomania (nymphomania) as an expression of cortical epileptiform discharge. *Archives of Neurological Psychiatry, 53,* 226–231.

Erikson, E. H. (1950). *Childhood and society.* New York: Norton.

Esser, A. H. (1968). Dominance hierarchy and clinical course of psychiatrically hospitalized boys. *Child Development, 39,* 147–157.

Esser, A. H. (Ed.). (1971). *Behavior and environment.* New York: Plenum.

Esser, A. H. Chamberlain, A. S., Chapple, E. D., & Kline, N. S. (1965). Territoriality of patients on a research ward. In J. Wortis (Ed.), *Recent advances in biological psychiatry* (Vol. III, pp. 37–44). New York: Plenum.

Essock-Vitale, S. M., & Fairbanks, L. A. Sociobiological theories of kin selection and reciprocal altruism and their relevance to psychiatry. *Journal of Nervous and Mental Disease,* 1979, *167,* 23–28.

Essock-Vitale, S. M., & McGuire, M. T. Sociobiology and its potential usefulness in psychiatry. *McLean Hospital Journal,* 1979, *IV,* 2, 69–81.

Essock-Vitale, S. M., & McGuire, M. T. Predictions derived from the theories of kin selection and reciprocation assessed by anthropological data. *Ethology and Sociobiology,* 1980, *1,* 233–243.

Etkin, W. (1967). *Social behavior from fish to man.* Chicago: University of Chicago Press.

Evans, R. I. (1975). *Konrad Lorenz: The man and his ideas.* New York: Harcourt, Brace, & Jovanovich.

Evans, G. W., & Howard, R. B. (1973). Personal space. *Psychological Bulletin, 80,* 334–344.

Eysenck, H. J. (1982). Gender, genes, and psychopathology. In I. Al-Issa (Ed.), *Gender and psychopathology* (pp. 266–279). New York: Academic Press.

Fahrbach, S. A., & Pfaff, D. W. (1982). Hormonal and neural mechanisms underlying maternal behavior in the rat. In D. W. Pfaff (Ed.), *The physiological mechanisms of motivation* (pp. 253–285). New York: Springer-Verlag.

Fairbanks, L. A. (1977). Animal and human behavior: Guidelines for generalization across species. In M. T. McGuire & L. A. Fairbanks (Eds.), *Ethological psychiatry: Psychopathology in the context of evolutionary biology* (pp. 87–110). New York: Grune & Stratton.

Farkas, G. M. (1979). *Trait and state determinants of male arousal to descriptions of coercive sexuality.* Unpublished doctoral dissertation, University of Hawaii.

Fawcett, J. (Ed.). (1971). *Dynamics of violence.* Chicago: American Medical Association.

Felt like a mouse trapped by cat on subway, Goetz says. (1985, March). *Richmond Times-Dispatch,* p. 1.

Fenichel, O. (1945). *The psychoanalytic theory of neurosis.* New York: Norton.

Ferguson, W. (1968). Abnormal behavior in domestic birds. In M. W. Fox (Ed.), *Abnormal behavior in animals* (pp. 188–207). Philadelphia: Saunders.

Festinger, L., Pepitone, A., & Newcomb, T. (1952). Some consequences of de-individuation in a group. *Journal of Abnormal and Social Psychology, 47,* 382–389.

Fichtelius, K., & Sjölander, S. (1972). *Smarter than man? Intelligence in whales, dolphins, and humans.* New York: Pantheon.

Fincher, J. (1976). *Human intelligence.* New York: Putnam.

Fishbein, H. D. (1976). *Evolution, development, and children's learning.* Pacific Palisades, CA: Goodyear.

Fishbein, H. D. (1984). *The psychology of infancy and childhood: Evolutionary and cross-cultural perspectives.* Hillsdale, NJ: Lawrence Erlbaum Associates.

Fisher, H. E. (1982). *The sex contract: The evolution of human behavior.* New York: William Morrow.

Ford, C. S., & Beach, F. A. (1951). *Patterns of sexual behavior.* New York: Harper & Row.

Forty die in soccer match riot in Brussels. (1985, May). *Richmond Times-Dispatch,* p. 1.

Fossey, D. (1981). The imperiled mountain gorilla. *National Geographic, 159,* 501–523.

Fossey, D. (1984). Infanticide in mountain gorillas (*Gorilla gorilla Beringei*) with comparative notes on chimpanzees. In G. Hausfater & S. Blaffer-Hrdy (Eds.), *Infanticide: Comparative and evolutionary perspectives* (pp. 217–236). New York: Aldine.

Foster brother charged in deaths in Connecticut. (1977, July). *Richmond Times-Dispatch,* p. 12.

Fox, M. W. (1968). *Abnormal behavior in animals.* Philadelphia: Saunders.

Fox, R. (1967). *Kinship and marriage: An anthropological perspective.* Harmondsworth and Baltimore: Penguin.

Fox, R. (1971). The cultural animal. In J. F. Eisenberg & W. S. Dillon (Eds.), *Man and beast: Comparative social behavior* (pp. 273–296). Washington, DC: Smithsonian Institution Press.

Fox, R. (1972). Alliance and constraint: Sexual selection and the evolution of human kinship systems. In B. Campbell (Ed.), *Sexual selection and the descent of man* (pp. 282–331). Chicago: Aldine.

Fox, R. (1975). Primate kin and human kinship. In R. Fox (Ed.), *Biosocial anthropology* (pp. 9–36). New York: Wiley.

Fox, R. (1979). Kinship categories as natural categories. In N. A. Chagnon & W. Irons (Eds.), *Evolutionary biology and human social behavior: An anthropological perspective* (pp. 132–144). North Scituate, MA: Duxbury.

Fox, R. (1980). *The red lamp of incest.* New York: E. P. Dutton.

Frank, J. D. (1967). *Sanity and survival.* New York: Random House.

Freedman, D. G. (1961). The infant's fear of strangers and the flight response. *Journal of Child Psychology and Psychiatry, 4,* 242–248.

Freedman, D. G. (1964). Smiling in blind infants and the issue of innate vs. acquired. *Journal of Psychology and Psychiatry, 5,* 171–184.

Freedman, D. G. (1965). Hereditary control of early social behavior. In B. M. Foss (Ed.), *Determinants of infant beahvior III* (pp. 149–159). London: Methuen.

Freedman, D. G. (1967). A biological view of man's social behavior. In W. Etkin (Ed.), *Social behavior form fish to man* (pp. 152–188). Chicago: University of Chicago Press.

Freedman, D. G. (1971). An evolutionary approach to research on the life cycle. *Human Development, 14,* 87–89.

Freedman, D. G. (1974). *Human infancy: An evolutionary perspective.* New York: Wiley.

Freedman, D. G. (1979). *Human sociobiology: A holistic approach.* New York: Free Press.

Freedman, J. L. (1973). The effects of population density on humans. In J. Fawcett (Ed.), *Psychological perspectives on crowding* (pp. 209–240). New York: Basic Books.

Freedman, J. L. (1976). *Crowding and behavior.* San Francisco: Freeman.

Freeman, D. (1964). Human aggression in anthropological perspective. In J. D. Carthy & E. T. Ebling (Eds.), *The natural history of aggression* (pp. 109–119). New York: Academic Press.

Freud, S. (1938) Totem and taboo. In A. A. Brill (Ed.), *The basic writings of Sigmund Freud* (pp. 807–930). New York: Modern Library. (originally published 1913)

Freud, S. (1948). The economic problem of masochism. *Collected Papers, 5,* 255–268. London: Hogarth Press. (originally published 1924)

Freud, S. (1952). *An autobiographical study.* New York: Norton. (originally published 1935)

Freud, S. (1953a). *On aphasia.* New York: International Universities Press. (originally published 1891)

Freud, S. (1953b). Interpretation of dreams. *Standard Edition, Vol. 4 & 5,* London: Hogarth Press. (originally published 1900)

Freud, S. (1953c). Three essays on the theory of sexuality. *Standard Edition, Vol. 7.* London: Hogarth Press. (originally published 1905)

Freud, S. (1955). Group psychology and the analysis of the ego. *Standard Edition. Vol. 8.* London: Hogarth. (originally published 1921)

Freud, S. (1957). Project for a scientific psychology. *Standard Edition, Vol. I.* London: Hogarth Press, (originally published 1895)

Freud, S. (1960). The psychopathology of everyday life. *Standard Edition, Vol. 6.* London: Hogart Press (originally published 1901)

Freud, S. (1961). Civilization and its discontents. *Standard Edition, Vol. 21,* London: Hogarth Press. (originally published 1930)

Freud, S. (1963a). Reflections upon war and death. In P. Rieff (Ed.), *Sigmund Freud: Character and culture* (pp. 107–133). New York: Collier. (originally published 1915)

Freud, S. (1963b). Why war? In P. Rieff (Ed.), *Sigmund Freud: Character and culture* (pp. 134–147). New York: Collier. (originally published 1932)

Freud, S. (1964). Analysis: Terminable and interminable. *Standard Edition, Vol. 23.* London: Hogarth. (originally published 1937)

Freud, S. (1969). *A general introduction to psychoanalysis*. New York: Simon & Schuster. (originally published 1920)

Freud, S. (1964). Analysis: Terminable and interminable. *Standard Edition, Vol. 23*. London: Hogarth. (originally published 1937)

Friedman, H., Becker, R. O., & Bachman, C. H. (1963). Geomagnetic parameters and psychiatric hospital admission. *Nature, 200*, 626–628.

Friedman, H., Becker, R. O., & Bachman, C. H. (1965). Psychiatric ward behavior and geophysical parameters. *Nature, 205*, 1050–1052.

Fromm, E. (1941). *Escape from freedom*. New York: Rinehart.

Fromm, E. (1973). *The anatomy of human destructiveness*. New York: Holt, Rinehart, & Winston.

Fromm, E. (1976). *To have or to be?*. New York: Harper & Row.

Fuster, J. M. (1980). *The prefrontal cortex: Anatomy, physiology, and neurophysiology of the frontal lobe*. New York: Raven.

Gabrielli, W. F., & Mednick. S. A. (1980). Sinistrality and delinquency. *Journal of Abnormal Psychology, 89*, 654–661.

Gallup, G. G., Jr. (1974). Animal hypnosis: Factual status of a fictional concept. *Psychological Bulletin, 81*, 836–853.

Gallup, G. G., Jr., & Maser, J. D. (1977). Tonic immobility: Evolutionary underpinnings of human catalepsy and catatonia. In J. D. Maser & M. E. P. Seligman (Eds.), *Psychopathology: Experimental models* (pp. 334–357). San Francisco: Freeman.

Gallup, G. G., & Suarez, S. D. (1983). Overcoming our resistance to animal research: Man in comparative perspective. In D. W. Rajecki (Ed.), *Comparing behavior: Studying man studying animals* (pp. 5–26). Hillsdale, NJ: Lawrence Erlbaum Associates.

Gandossy, R. P., Williams, J. R., Cohen, J., & Harwood, J. H. (1980). *Drugs and crime: A survey and analysis of the literature*. Washington, DC: U. S. Department of Justice.

Gardner, E. (1963). *Fundamentals of neurology*. Philadelphia: Saunders.

Gardner, H. (1983). *Frames of mind: The theory of multiple intelligences*. New York: Basic Books.

Gastaut, H. (1954). Interpretation of the symptoms of "psychomotor" epilepsy in relation to physiologic data on rhinnencephalic function. *Epilepsia, 3*, 84–88.

Gazzaniga, M. S. (1977). Review of the split brain. In M. C. Wittrock (Ed.), *The human brain* (pp. 89–96). Englewood Cliffs, NJ: Prentice-Hall.

Gazzaniga, M. S., Bogen, J. E., & Sperry, R. W. (1962). Some functional effects of sectioning cerebral commissures in man. *PNAS, 48*, 1765.

Gazzaniga, M. S., Bogen, J. E., & Sperry, R. W. (1963). Laterality effects in somesthesis following cerebral commissurotomy in man. *Neuropsychologica, 1*, 209–215.

Gazzaniga, M. S., Bogen, J. E., & Sperry, R. W. (1965). Observations in visual perception after disconnection of the cerebral hemispheres in man. *Brain, 88*, 221.

Gazzaniga, M. S., & Sperry, J. E. (1967). Language after section of the cerebral commissure. *Brain, 90*, 131.

Gelles, R. J. (1979). *Family violence*. Beverly Hills, CA: Sage Publications.

Gergen, K. J., Gergen, M. M., & Barton, W. H. (1973, October). Deviance in the dark. *Psychology Today*, pp. 129–130.

German, D. C., & Bowden, D. M. (1974). Catecholaminergic systems as the neural substrate for intracranial self-stimulation. *Brain Research, 73*, 381–419.

Geschwind, N. (1965). Disconnexion syndromes in animals and man. *Brain, 88*, 237–294; 585–644.

Geschwind, N., & Galaburda, A. M. (Eds.), *Cerebral dominance: The biological foundations*. Cambridge, MA: Harvard University Press, 1984.

Ghiselin, M. T. (1973). Darwin and evolutionary psychology. *Science, 179*, 964–968.

Ghiselin, M. T. (1974). *The economy of nature and the evolution of sex*. Berkeley, CA: University of California.

Gibbons, D. C. (1973). *Society, crime, and criminal careers* (2nd ed.). Englewood Cliffs, NJ: Prentice-Hall.

Gibson, K. R. (1977). Brain structure and intelligence in macaques and human infants from a Piagetian perspective. In S. Chevalier-Skolnikoff & F. E. Poirer (Eds.), *Primate biosocial development: Biological, social, and ecological determinants* (pp. 113–158). New York: Garland.

Ginsberg, B. E. (1965). Coaction of genetical and nongenetical factors influencing sexual behavior. In F. A. Beach (Ed.), *Sex and behavior* (pp. 53–75). New York: Wiley.

Glick, S. D. (Ed.). *Cerebral lateralization in nonhuman species*. Orlando, FL: Academic Press, 1985.

Gloor, P. (1960). Amygdala. In J. Field (Ed.), *Handbook of physiology, Section I: Neurophysiology* (Vol. 2, pp. 1395–1420). Washington, DC: American Physiological Society.

Goddard, G. V. (1964). Amygdaloid stimulation and learning in the rat. *Journal of Comparative and Physiological Psychology, 58*, 23–30.

Goffman, I. (1972). *Relations in public*. New York: Harper & Row.

Goldstein, J. H (1975). *Aggression and crimes of violence*. New York: Oxford University Press.

Goodall, J. van Lawick. (1971). *In the shadow of man*. Boston: Houghton Mifflin.

Goodall, J. van Lawick. (1972). A preliminary report on expressive movements and communication in the Gombe stream chimpanzees. In P. Dolhinow (Ed.), *Primate patterns* (pp. 25–84). New York: Holt, Rinehart & Winston.

Goodall, J. van Lawick. (1973). Cultural elements in a chimpanzee community. *Proceedings of the 4th International Congress of Primatology I*, 144–184. Basel: Karger.

Goodall, J. van Lawick. (1975). The chimpanzee. In V. Goodall (Ed.), *The quest for man* (pp. 131–169). New York: Praeger.

Goodall, J. (1979). Life and death at Gombe. *National Geographic, 155*, 592–621.

Goodall, J. (1982). Order without law. *Journal of Social and Biological Structures, 3*, 353–360.

Goode, W. J. (1963). *World revolution and family patterns*. New York: Free Press.

Goodman, M. (1975). Protein sequence and immunological specificity. In W. P. Luckett & F. S. Szalay (Eds.), *Phylogeny of the primates* (pp. 219–248). New York: Plenum Press.

Gordon, R. A. (1980). Research on IQ, race, and delinquincy: Taboo or not taboo? In E. Sagarin (Ed.), *Taboos in criminology* (pp. 37–66). Beverly Hills: Sage.

Gorenstein, E. E. (1982). Frontal lobe functions in psychopaths. *Journal of Abnormal Psychology, 91*, 368–379.

Gorenstein, E. E., & Newman, J. P. (1980). Disinhibitory psychopathology: A new perspective and a model for research. *Psychological Review, 87*, 301–315.

Goudge, T. A. (1967). George John Romanes. In P. Edwards (Ed.), *The encyclopedia of philosophy* (pp. 205–206). New York: Macmillan.

Gould, S. J. (1977). *Ontogeny and phylogeny*. Cambridge, MA: Harvard University Press.

Gould, S. J. (1981). *The mismeasure of man*. New York: Norton.

Graves, C. W. (1966). Deterioration of work standards. *Harvard Business Review, 44*, 117–128.

Gray, P. H. (1958). Theory and evidence of imprinting in human infants. *Journal of Psychology, 46*, 155–166.

Green, S. (1983). Animal models in schizophrenia research. In G. C. L. Davey (Ed.), *Animal models of human behavior: Conceptual, evolutionary, and neurobiological perspectives* (pp. 315–338). London: Wiley.

Greenbaum, J. V., & Luria, L. A. (1948). Encephalitis as a causative factor in behavior disorders in children. *Journal of the American Medical Association, 136*, 923–930.

Greenwald, A. (1980). The totalitarian ego: Fabrication and revision of personal history. *American Psychologist, 35*, 603–618.

Griffin, D. R. (1976). *The question of animal awareness: Evolutionary continuity of mental experience*. New York: Rockefeller University Press.

Groth, N. A. (1981). Rape: The sexual expression of aggression. In P. F. Brain & D. Benton (Eds.), *Multidisciplinary approaches to aggression research* (pp. 465–476). Amsterdam: Elsevier/North Holland.

Groth, N. A., & Birnbaum, H. (1979). *Men who rape: The psychology of the offender*. New York: Plenum Press.

Groth, N. A., & Burgess, A. W., & Holmstrom, L. (1977). Rape: Power, anger, and sexuality. *American Journal of Psychiatry, 134*, 1239–1243.

Grundy, K. W., & Weinstein, M. A. (1974). *The ideologies of violence*. Columbus, OH: Charles E. Merrill.

Guhl, A. M. (1956). The social order of chickens. *Scientific American, 194*, 424–446.

Guilford, J. P. (1967). *The nature of human intelligence*. New York: McGraw-Hill.

Guttentag, M., & Secord, P. F. (1983). *Too many women? The sex ratio question*. Beverly Hills, CA: Sage.

Haeckel, E. H. (1866). *Generelle morphologie des organismen*. Berlin: Reimer.

Haeckel, E. H. (1874). *Anthropogenie oder Entwickelungsgeschichte des Menschen*. Berlin: Englemann.

Haeckel, E. H. (1900). *The riddle of the universe*. New York: Harper.

Hager, M. G. (1982). The myth of objectivity. *American Psychologist, 37*, 576–579.

Hall, E. T. (1959). *The silent language*. New York: Doubleday.

Hall, E. T. (1961). The language of space. *Journal of the American Institute of Architects, 35*, 71–74.

Hall, E. T. (1963). A system for the notation of proxemic behavior. *American Anthropologist, 65*, 1003–1026.

Hall, E. T. (1969). *The hidden dimension*. New York: Doubleday.

Hall, E. T. (1971). Environmental communication. In A. H. Esser (Ed.), *Behavior and environment: The use of space by animals and men* (pp. 147–256). New York: Plenum.

Hall, K. R. L. (1964). Aggression in monkey and ape societies. In J. D. Carthy & F. J. Ebling (Eds.), *The natural history of aggression* (pp. 51–64). London: Academic Press.

Hall, K. R. L. (1965). Social organization of old world monkeys and apes. *Symposium of Zoological Society of London, 14*, 265–289.

Hall, K. R. L., & DeVore, I. (1965). Baboon social behavior. In I. DeVore (Ed.), *Primate behavior: Field studies of monkeys and apes* (pp. 53–110). New York: Holt, Rinehart & Winston.

Hall, K. R. L., & Goswell, M. J. (1964). Aspects of social learning in captive patas monkeys. *Primates, 5*, 59–70.

Halperin, R., & Pfaff, D. W. (1982). Brain-stimulated reward and control of autonomic function: Are they related? In D. W. Pfaff (Ed.), *The physiological mechanisms of motivation* (pp. 337–376). New York: Springer-Verlag.

Halstead, W. C. (1951). Biological intelligence. *Journal of Personality, 20*, 118–130.

Hamilton, E. (1942). *Mythology*. New York: New American Library.

Hamilton, W. D. (1964). The genetic evolution of social behavior: Parts I and II. *Journal of Theoretical Biology, 7*, 1–52.

Handy, R. (1967). Ernst H. Haeckel. In P. Edwards (Ed.), *The encyclopedia of philosophy* (pp. 399–402). New York: Macmillan.

Harlow, H. F. (1969). Age-mate or peer affectional system. In D. S. Lehrman, R. A. Hinde, & E. Shaw (Eds.), *Advances in the study of behavior* (Vol. 2). New York: Academic Press.

Harlow, H. F. (1971). *Learning to love*. San Francisco: Albion.

Harlow, H. F., & Mears, C. (1979). *The human model: Primate perspectives*. New York: Wiley.

Harris, M. (1977). *Cannibals and kings: The origins of cultures.* New York: Random House.

Hart, B. L. (1967). Testosterone regulation of sexual reflexes in spinal male rats. *Science, 155*, 1283–1284.

Hartup, W. W. (1970). Peer interaction and social organization. In P. H. Mussen (Ed.), *Carmichael's manual of child psychology.* New York: Wiley.

Haslam, M. T. (1979). *Psychosexual disorders: A review.* Springfield, IL: Thomas.

Hass, H. (1970). *The human animal.* New York: Putnam.

Hatterer, L. J. (1980). *The pleasure addicts.* New York: Barnes & Noble.

Hausfater, G., & Hrdy, S. B. (1984). *Infanticide: Comparative and evolutionary perspectives.* New York: Aldine.

Hawthorne, N. (1981). Rappaccini's daughter. In W. Pronzini, B. N. Malzberg, & M. H. Grenberg (Eds.), *Arbor House treasury of horror and the supernatural* (pp. 32–61). New York: Arbor House.

Hayduk, L. A. (1978). Personal space: An evaluative and orienting review. *Psychological bulletin, 85*, 117–134.

Hayes, K. J. (1962). Genes, drives, and intellect. *Psychological Reports, 10*, 299–342.

Hayman, C. R. (1970). Sexual assaults on women and girls. *Annals of Internal Medicine, 72*, 277–278.

Hayman, C. R., Lanza, R., Fuentes, R., & Algor, K. (1972). Rape in the District of Colombia. *American Journal of Obstetrics and Gynecology, 113*, 91–97.

Heath, R. G. (1964). Developments toward new physiologic treatments in psychiatry. *Journal of Neuropsychiatry, 5*, 318–331.

Heath, R. G. (1975). Brain function and behavior: Emotion and sensory phenomena in psychotic patients and experimental animals. *Journal of Nervous and Mental Disease, 160*, 159–175.

Heath, R. G. (1981). The neural basis for violent behavior: Physiology and anatomy. In L. Valzelli & G. Morgese (Eds.), *Aggression and violence: A psychobiological and clinical approach* (pp. 176–194). Centro Culturale e Congressi Saint Vincent.

Hediger, H. (1961). The evolution of territorial behavior. In S. L. Washburn (Ed.), *Social life of early man.* New York: Viking Fund Publications in Anthropology.

Hediger, H. (1964). *Wild animals in captivity.* New York: Dover.

Helfer, R. E., & Kempe, C. H. (Eds.). (1974). *The battered child* (2nd ed.). Chicago: University of Chicago Press.

Heilbrun, A. B. (1982). Cognitive models of criminal violence based upon intelligence and psychopathy levels. *Journal of Consulting and Clinical Psychology, 50*, 546–557.

Hereford, S., Cleland, C. C., & Fellner, M. (1973). Territoriality and scent-marking: A study of profoundly retarded enuretics and encopretics. *American Journal of Mental Deficiency, 77*, 426–430.

Herrick, C. J. (1933). The functions of the olfactory parts of the cerebral cortex. *Proceedings of the National Academy of Science, 19*, 7–14.

Herrick, C. J. (1956). *The evolution of human nature.* Austin: University of Texas Press.

Herrnstein, R. J. (1973). *IQ in the meritocracy.* Boston: Atlantic Monthly Press.

Herrnstein, R. J. (1977a). The evolution of behaviorism. *American Psychologist, 32*, 593–603.

Herrnstein, R. J. (1977b). Doing what comes naturally: A reply to Professor Skinner. *American Psychologist, 32*, 1013–1016.

Hess, E. H. (1959). Imprinting. *Science, 130*, 133–141.

Hess, E. H. (1970). The ethological approach to socialization. In R. A. Hoppe, G. A. Milton, & E. C. Simmel (Eds.), *Early experiences and the processes of socialization* (pp. 19–36). New York: Academic Press.

Hess, E. H. (1973). *Imprinting: Early experience and the developmental psychobiology of attachment.* New York: Van Nostrand Reinhold.

Hewes, G. W. (1977). Language origin theories. In D. M. Rumbaugh (Ed.), *Language learning by a chimpanzee* (pp. 3–53). New York: Academic Press.

Hiiemae, K. M. (1978). Mammalian mastication: A review of the activity of the jaw muscles and movements they produce in chewing. In P. M. Butler & K. A. Josey (Eds.), *Development, function, and evolution of teeth*. New York: Academic Press.

Hiiemae, K. M., & Kay, R. F. (1973). Evolutionary trends in the dynamics of primate mastication. In M. R. Zingeser (Ed.), *Craniofacial biology of primates*. *In Symposia of Fourth International Congress of Primatology* (Vol. 3). Basel: Karger.

Hill, S. Y. (1980). Introduction: The biological consequences. In *Research Monograph No. 1: Alcoholism and alcohol abuse among women: Research issues*. Rockville, MD: National Institute of Mental Health.

Himmelhoch, J., Pincus, J., Tucker, G., & Detre, T. (1970). Sub-acute encephalitis: Behavioral and neurological aspects. *British Journal of Psychiatry, 116*, 531–538.

Hinde, R. A. (1959). Some recent trends in ethology. In S. Koch (Ed.), *Psychology: A study of a science* (Vol. 2, pp. 561–611). New York: McGraw-Hill.

Hinde, R. A. (1970). *Animal behaviour: A synthesis of ethology and comparative psychology*. New York: McGraw-Hill.

Hinde, R. A. (1973). Constraints on learning: An introduction to the problems. In R. A. Hinde & J. Stevenson-Hinde (Eds.), *Constraints on learning* (pp. 1–19). New York: Academic Press.

Hinde, R. A. (1974). *Biological bases of human social behavior*. New York: McGraw-Hill.

Hinde, R. A., & Stevenson-Hinde, J. (Eds.). (1973). *Constraints on learning*. New York: Academic Press.

Hines, M. (1982). Prenatal gonadal hormones and sex differences in human behavior. *Psychological Bulletin 92*, 56–80.

Hirschi, T., & Gottfredson, M. (Eds.). (1980). *Understanding crime: Current theory and research*. Beverly Hills, CA: Sage.

Hobhouse, L. T. (1901). *Mind in evolution*. London: Macmillan.

Hockett, C. F. (1960). The origin of speech. *Scientific American, 203*, 88 ff.

Hoebel, B. G., & Teitelbaum, P. (1962). Hypothalamic control of feeding and self-stimulation. *Science, 135*, 375–377.

Hoenig, J., & Kenna, J. C. (1979). EEG abnormalities and transsexualism. *British Journal of Psychiatry, 134*, 293–300.

Hofstadter, R., & Wallace, M. (Eds.). (1971). *American violence: A documentary history*. New York: Random House.

Hogg, G. (1958). *Cannibalism and human sacrifice*. London: Robert Hale.

Holcomb, W. R., & Adams, N. (1982). Racial influences on intelligence and personality measures of people who commit murder. *Journal of Clinical Psychology, 38*, 793–796.

Holland, T. R., Beckett, G. E., & Levi, M. (1981). Intelligence personality, and criminal violence: A multivariate analysis. *Journal of Consulting and Clinical Psychology, 49*, 106–111.

Holliday, L. (1978). *The violent sex: Male psychobiology and the evolution of consciousness*. Guerneville, CA: Bluestocking Books.

Holloway, R. L. (1968a). The evolution of the primate brain: Some aspects of quantitative relations. *Brain Research, 7*, 121–172.

Holloway, R. L. (1968b). Human aggression: The need for a species-specific framework. In M. Fried, M. Harris, & R. Murphy (Eds.), *War: The anthropology of armed conflict and aggression* (pp. 29–48). New York: Natural History Press.

Holloway, R. L. (1968c). Territory and aggression in man: A look at Robert Ardrey's *Territorial Imperative*. In M. F. A. Montagu (Ed.), *Man and aggression* (pp. 96–102). London: Oxford University Press.

Holloway R. L. (Ed.). (1974). *Primate aggression, territoriality, and xenophobia: A comparative perspective*. New York: Academic Press.

Holzman, P. S. (1970). *Psychoanalysis and psychopathology*. New York: McGraw-Hill.

Horowitz, M. J., Duff, D. F., & Stratton, L. O. (1964). Body buffer zone. *Archives of General Psychiatry, 11*, 651–656.

Hrdy, S. B. (1977). *The Langers of Abu: Female and male strategies of reproduction.* Cambridge, MA: Harvard University Press.

Hrdy, S. B. (1979). Infanticide among animals: A review, classification, and examination of the implications for the reproductive strategies of females. *Ethology and Sociobiology, 1,* 13–40.

Huang, Y. H., & Routtenberg, A. (1971). Lateral hypothalamic self-stimulation pathways in *Rattus norvegicus. Physiological Behavior, 7,* 419–432.

Huizinga, J. (1976). Play and contest as civilizing functions. In J. S. Bruner, A. Jolly, & K. Sylva (Eds.), *Play: Its role in development and evolution* (pp. 675-687). New York: Basic Books.

Humphrey, N. K. (1973). Predispositions to learn. In R. A. Hinde & J. Stevenson-Hinde (Eds.), *Constraints on learning* (pp. 301–304). New York: Academic Press.

Humphrey, N. K. (1976). The social function of intellect. In P. P. G. Bateson & R. A. Hinde (Eds.), *Growing points in ethology* (pp. 303–318). London: Cambridge University Press.

Hutt, S. J. (1970). The role of behaviour studies in psychiatry: An ethological viewpoint. In S. J. Hutt & C. Hutt (Eds.), *Behaviour studies in psychiatry* (pp. 1–23). Oxford: Pergamon Press.

Huxley, T. H. (1896). *Man's place in nature.* New York: Appleton.

Irons, W. (1979). Natural selection, adaptation, and human social behavior. In N. A. Chagnon & W. Irons (Eds.), *Evolutionary biology and human social behavior: An anthropological perspective* (pp. 4–38). North Scituate, MA: Duxbury.

Itani, J. (1984). Intraspecific killing among non-human primates. *Journal of Social and Biological Structures, 5,* 361–368.

Izard, C. E. (1971). *The face of emotions.* New York: Appleton-Century-Crofts.

Izard, C. E. (1977). *Human emotions.* New York: Plenum.

James R., & Griffin, A. (1968). Seasonal admission rates in Texas mental hospitals. *Journal of Clinical Psychology, 24,* 190.

James, W. (1911). *Memories and studies.* London: Longmans, Green & Co.

James, W. (1955). The will to believe. In D. J. Bronstein, Y. H. Krikorian, & P. P. Weiner (Eds.), *Basic problems of philosophy* (pp. 431–438). Englewood Cliffs, NJ: Prentice-Hall. (Originally published 1896)

Jampala, V. C., & Abrams, R. (1983). Mania secondary to left and right hemisphere damage. *American Journal of Psychiatry, 140,* 1197–1199.

Jay, P. C. (Ed.). (1968). *Primates: Studies in adaptation and variability.* New York: Holt, Rinehart & Winston.

Jaynes, J. (1969). The historical origins of 'ethology' and 'comparative psychology'. *Animal Behavior, 17,* 601–606.

Jaynes, J. (1976). *The origin of consciousness and the breakdown of the bicameral mind.* New York: Houghton Mifflin.

Jeffrey, C. R. (1979). *Biology and crime.* Beverly Hills, CA: Sage.

Jensen, A. R. (1972). *Genetics and education.* New York: Harper & Row.

Jerison, H. J. (1973). *Evolution of the brain and intelligence.* New York: Academic Press.

Jerison, H. J. (1976). Paleoneurology and the evolution of the mind. *Scientific American, 234,* 90–101.

Jerison, H. J. (1977). Evolution of the brain. In M. C. Wittrock, (Ed.), *The human brain.* Englewood Cliffs, NJ: Prentice-Hall.

Johanson, D. C., & Edey, M. (1981). *Lucy: The beginnings of mankind.* New York: Simon & Schuster.

Johanson, D. C., & White, T. D. (1979). A systematic study of early African hominids. *Science, 203,* 321–330.

Johnson, R. N. (1972). *Aggression in man and animals.* Philadelphia: Saunders.

Johnson, S. C. (1981). Bonobos: Generalized hominid prototypes or specialized insular dwarfs. *Current Anthropology, 22,* 363–375.

Johnson, S. D., Gibson, L., & Linden, R. (1978). Alcohol and rape in Winnipeg, 1966–1975. *Journal of Studies on Alcohol, 39,* 1887–1894.

Jolly, A. (1972). *The evolution of primate behavior.* New York: Macmillan.

Jolly, C. (1970). The seed-eaters: A new model of homonid differentiation based on a baboon analogy. *Man, 5,* 5–26.

Jonas, A. D. (1965). *Ictal and subictal neurosis: Diagnosis and treatment.* Springfield, IL: Thomas.

Joseph, R. (1982). The neuropsychology of development: Hemispheric laterality, limbic language, and the origin of thought. *Journal of Clinical Psychology, 38,* 4–33.

Julien, R. M. (1981). *A primer of drug action.* San Francisco: Freeman.

Jung, C. G. (1946). *Psychological types or the psychology of individuation.* New York: Harcourt, Brace. (Originally published 1922)

Kagan, D. (1984). Serial murderers. *Omni, 6,* 200.

Kahn, M. W., & Kirk, W. E. (1968). The concepts of aggression: A review and reformulation. *Psychological Record, 18,* 559–573.

Kalat, J. W. (1975). Original sin and/or original virtue. *Contemporary Psychology, 20,* 705–706.

Karli, P. (1956). The Norway rat's killing response to the white mouse. *Behavior, 10,* 81–103.

Karli, P. (1974). Aggressive behavior and its brain stem mechanisms (as exemplified by an experimental analysis of the rat's mouse-killing behavior). In J. de Wit & W. W. Hartup (Eds.), *Determinants and origins of aggressive behavior* (pp. 277–290). The Hague: Mouton.

Kaufman, C. (1960). Symposium on 'psychoanalysis and ethology' III. Some theoretical implications from animal behaviour studies for the psycho-analytic concepts of instinct, energy, and drive. *International Journal of Psycho-Analysis, 41,* 318–325.

Keating, E. G., Kormann, L. A., & Horel, J. A. (1970). The behaviorial effects of stimulating and ablating the reptilian amygdala *(Caiman sklerops). Physiology and Behavior, 5,* 55–59.

Keehn, J. D. (Ed.). (1979a). *Origins of madness: Psychopathology in animal life.* Oxford: Pergamon.

Keehn, J. D. (Ed.). (1979b). *Psychopathology in animals: Research and clinical implications.* New York: Academic Press.

Kelso, A. J. (1970). *Physical anthropology.* Philadelphia: Lippincott.

Kerferd, G. B. (1967). Aristotle. In P. Edwards (Ed.), *The encyclopedia of philosophy.* New York: Macmillan.

Key, W. B. (1974). *Subliminal seduction.* New York: New American Library.

Key, W. B. (1981). *The clam plate orgy.* New York: The New American Library.

Killeffer, F. A., & Stern, E. (1970). Chronic effects of hypothalamic injury. *Archives of Neurology, 22,* 419–429.

Kimura, D. (1979). Neuromotor mechanisms in the evolution of human communication. In H. D. Steklis & M. J. Raleigh (Eds.), *Neurobiology of social communication in primates* (pp. 197–219). New York: Academic Press.

Kinder, E. F (1927). A study of nest-building activity of the albino rat. *Journal of Experimental Zoology, 47f,* 117–161.

King, M. C., & Wilson, A. C. (1975). Evolution at two levels in humans and chimpanzees. *Science, 118,* 107–116.

Kinsbourne, M. (1981). The development of cerebral dominance. In S. B. Filsov & T. J. Boll (Eds.), *Handbook of clinical neuropsychology* (pp. 399–417). New York: Wiley.

Kinzel, A. F. (1970). The body buffer zone in violent prisoners. *American Journal of Psychiatry, 127,* 59–64.

Kirkman, F. B. (1937). *Bird behavior.* London: Nelson.

Kletschka, H. D. (1966). Violent behavior associated with brain tumor. *Minnesota Medicine, 49,* 1853–1855.

Klopfer, P. H. (1968). From Ardrey to altruism: A discourse on the biological basis of human behavior. *Behavioral Science, 13,* 399–401.

Klüver, H., & Bucy, P. C. (1937). Psychic blindness and other symptoms following bilateral temporal lobectomy in Rhesus monkeys. *American Journal of Physiology, 119,* 353–353.

Koestler, A. (1967). *The ghost in the machine.* New York: Macmillan.

Koestler, A., & Smythies, J. R. (1969). *Beyond reductionism: New perspectives in the life sciences.* New York: Macmillan.

Kohlberg, L. (1964). Development of moral character and moral ideology. In M. L. Hoffman & L. W. Hoffman (Eds.), *Review of child development research* (Vol. 1, pp. 383–432). New York: Russell Sage Foundation.

Köhler, W. (1925). *The mentality of apes.* London: Routledge & Kegan.

Kohne, D. E. (1975). DNA evolution data and its relevance to mammalian phylogeny. In W. P. Luckett & F. S. Szalay (Eds.), *Phylogeny of the primates* (pp. 249–261). New York: Plenum Press.

Kolb, L. (1971). Violence and aggression: An overview. In J. Fawcett (Ed.), *Dynamics of violence* (pp. 7–18). Chicago: American Medical Association.

Kolb, B., & Whisaw, I. Q. (1980). *Fundamentals of human neuropsychology.* San Francisco: Freeman.

Konner, M. (1982). *The tangled wing: Biological constraints on the human spirit.* New York: Holt, Rinehart & Winston.

Kornetsky, C., & Markowitz, R. (1975). Animal models and schizophrenia. In D. J. Ingle & H. M. Shein (Eds.), *Model systems in biological psychiatry.* Cambridge, MA: MIT Press.

Kosewski, M. (1979). The prison as an aggressive social organization. In S. Feshbach & A. Fraçczk (Eds.), *Aggression and behavior change: Biological and social processes* (pp. 208–228). New York: Praeger.

Koss, M. P. (1983). The scope of rape: Implications for the clinical treatment of victims. *The Clinical Psychologist, 36,* 88–91.

Krafft-Ebing, R. von. (1965). *Psychopathia sexualis* (Translated from 12th German edition). New York: Stein & Day.

Krames, L., Pliner, P., & Alloway, T. (Eds.). (1978). *Aggression, dominance, and individual spacing.* New York: Plenum.

Kris, E. (1952). *Psychoanalytic explorations in art.* New York: International Universities Press.

Kristal, M. B. (1980). Placentophagia: A biobehavioral enigma (or *De gustibus non disputandum est*). *Neuroscience and Biobehaviorial Reviews, 4,* 141–150.

Kummer, H. (1971). *Primate societies: Group techniques of ecological adaptation.* Chicago: University of Chicago Press.

Kuo, Z. Y. (1921). Giving up instincts in psychology. *Journal of Philosophy, 18,* 645–666.

Lane, H. (1976). *The wild boy of Aveyron.* Cambridge, MA: Harvard University Press.

Langer, L. L. (1978). *The age of atrocity: Death in modern literature.* Boston: Beacon.

Langevin, R. (1983). *Sexual strands.* Hillsdale, NJ: Lawrence Erlbaum Associates.

Latimer, B. M., White T. D., Kimbell, W. H., Johanson, D. C., & Lovejoy, C. O. (1981). The pygmy chimpanzee is not a living missing link in human evolution. *Journal of Human Evolution, 10,* 475–488.

Laughlin, W. S. (1968). Hunting: A biobehavioral system and its evolutiory importance. In R. B. Lee & I. DeVore (Eds.), *Man the hunter* (pp. 304–320). Chicago: Aldine.

Laughlin, C. D., & d'Aquili, E. G. (1974). *Biogenetic structuralism.* New York: Columbia University Press.

Leaky, R. E., & Lewin, R. (1977). *Origins.* New York: Dutton.

Leavitt, J. E. (Ed.). (1974). *The battered child: Selected readings.* Morristown, NJ: General Learning Press.

Le Bon, G. (1960). *The crowd.* New York: Viking. (Originally published 1895)

Lee, R. B., & DeVore, I. (Eds.). (1968). *Man the hunter*. Chicago: Aldine.

Legg, C. R. (1983). Interspecific comparisons and the hypothetico-deductive approach. In G. C. L. Davey (Ed.), *Animal models of human behavior: Conceptual, evolutionary, and neurobiological perspectives* (pp. 225–246). New York: Wiley.

Lenneberg, E. H. (1967). *Biological foundations of language*. New York: Wiley.

Leo, J. Low profile for a legend. (1985, January). *Time*, pp. 54–55.

Leo, J., & Griggs, L. (1984, July). Sudden death. *Time*, pp. 90–91.

Leon, M., Croskerry, P. G., & Smith, G. K. (1978). Thermal control of mother-young contact in rats. *Physiology and Behavior, 21*, 793–811.

Lesse, S. (1979). The status of violence against women: Past, present and future factors. *American Journal of Psychotherapy, 33*, 190–200.

Lévi-Strauss, C. (1968). *The elementary structures of kinship*. Boston: Beacon Press.

Levy, A., Kurtz, N. & Kling, A. S. (1984). Association between cerebral ventricuclar enlargement and suicide attempts in chronic schizophrenia. *American Journal of Psychiatry, 141*, 438–439.

Lewin, K. (1951). *Field theory in social science*. New York: Harper.

Lewis, J., & Towers, B. (1972). *Naked ape or homo sapiens?* New York: New American Library.

Ley, R. G., & Bryden, M. P. (1981). The right hemisphere and emotion. In G. Underwood & R. Stevens (Eds.), *Aspects of consciousness* (Vol. 2, pp. 215–240). New York: Academic Press.

Lindzey, G. (1967). Behavior and morphological variation. In J. N. Spuhler (Ed.), *Genetic diversity and human behavior* (pp. 227-240). Chicago: Aldine.

Lockard, R. B. (1971). Reflections on the fall of comparative psychology: Is there a message for us all? *American Psychologist, 26*, 168–179.

Locke, J. (1952). An essay concerning human understanding. In R. M. Hutchins (Ed.), *Great books of the western world* (Vol. 35, pp. 85–395). Chicago: Encyclopedia Britannica. (Originally published 1690)

Loevinger, J. (1976). *Ego development*. San Francisco: Jossey-Bass.

Lombroso, C. (1887). *L'homme criminel*. Paris: Alcan.

Lombroso, C. (1897). *The female offender*. New York: Appleton.

Lorenz, K. (1931). Beiträge zur Ethologie der sozialer Corviden. *Journal of Ornithology, 79*, 67–127.

Lorenz, K. (1935). Der Kumpan in der Umvelt des Vogels. *Journal of Ornithology, 83*, 137–214; 289–413.

Lorenz, K. (1943). Die angeborenen Formen möglicher Erfahrung. *Zeitschrift fur Tierpsychologie, 5*. 235–409.

Lorenz, K. (1950). The comparative method of studying innate behavior patterns. In Society for Experimental Biology, Symposium No. 4: *Physiological mechanisms in animal behavior* (pp.   ). New York: Academic Press.

Lorenz, K. (1952). *King Solomon's ring*. New York: Thomas Crowell.

Lorenz, K. (1964). *Man meets dog*. Baltimore, MD: Penquin.

Lorenz, K. (1967). *On aggression*. New York: Bantam Books.

Lorenz, K. (1972). The enmity between generations and its probable ethological causes. In M. W. Piers (Ed.) *Play and development* (pp. 64–118). New York: Norton.

Lorenz, K. (1973). The comparative study of behavior. In K. Lorenz & P. Leyhausen (Eds.), *Motivation of human and animal behavior: An ethological view* (pp. 1–31). New York: Van Nostrand.

Lorenz, K. (1982). *The foundations of ethology: The principle ideas and discoveries in animal behavior*. New York: Simon & Schuster.

Lorenz, K., & Leyhausen, P. (1973). *Motivation of human and animal behavior*. New York: Van Nostrand.

Lorenz, K., & Tinbergen, N. (1957). Taxis and instinctive action in the egg-retrieving behavior of the greylag goose. In C. H. Schiller (Ed.), *Instinctive behavior: The development of a modern concept* (pp. 176–206). New York: International Universities Press.

Low, B. S. (1979). Sexual selection and human ornamentation. In N. A. Chagnon & W. Irons (Eds.), *Evolutionary biology and human social behavior: An anthropological perspective* (pp. 462–486). North Scituate, MA: Duxbury.

Lowry, R. J. (Ed.). (1973). *Dominance, self-esteem, ad self-actualization: Germinal papers of A. H. Maslow.* Monterey, CA: Brooks/Cole.

Luce, G. (1971). *Biological rhythms in human and animal physiology.* New York: Dover.

Luckmann, T. (1979). Personal identity as an evolutionary and historical problem. In M. von Cranach, K. Foppa, W. Lependies, & D. Ploog (Eds.), *Human ethology: Claims and limits of a new discipline* (pp. 56–74). Cambridge, London: Cambridge University Press.

Lumsden, C. J., & Wilson, E. O. (1981). *Genes, mind, and culture.* Cambridge, MA: Harvard University Press.

Lumsden, C. J., & Wilson, E. O. (1983). *Promethean fire: Reflections on the origin of mind.* Cambridge, MA: Harvard University Press.

Lyman, S. M., & Scott, M. B. (1967). Territoriality: A neglected dimension. *Social Problems, 15,* 236–249.

MacAndrew, C., & Edgerton, R. (1964). The everyday life of institutionalized idiots. *Human Organization, 23,* 312–318.

Mace, C. A. (1962). Psychology and aesthetics. *British Journal of Aesthetics, 2,* 3–16.

MacFarlane, A. (1977). *The psychology of childbirth.* Cambridge, MA: Harvard University Press.

Mackay, C. (1980). *Memoirs of extraordinary popular delusions and the madness of crowds.* New York: Harmon. (Originally published 1841).

Maclay, G., & Knipe, H. (1972). *The dominant man.* New York: Delta.

Maclean, C. (1979). *The wolf children: Fact or fantasy?* New York: Penquin.

MacLean, P. D. (1949). Psychosomatic disease and the "visceral brain". Recent developments bearing on the Papez theory of emotion. *Psychosomatic Medicine, 11,* 338–353.

MacLean, P. D. (1952). Some psychiatric implications of physiological studies on the frontotemporal portion of the limbic system (Visceral brain). *Electroencephalography and Clinical Neurophysiology, 4,* 407–418.

MacLean, P. D. (1954a). The limbic system and its hippocampal formation. Studies in animals and their possible application to man. *Journal of Neurosurgery, 11,* 29–44.

MacLean, P. D. (1954b). Studies on the limbic system ("visceral brain") and their bearing on psychosomatic problems. In R. A. & E. Wittkower (Eds.), *Recent developments in psychosomatic medicine* (pp. 101–125). London: Sir Isaac Pittman & Sons.

MacLean, P. D. (1955). The limbic system ("visceral brain") in relation to central gray and reticulum of the brain stem. *Psychosomatic Medicine, 17,* 355–366.

MacLean, P. D. (1957a). Chemical and electrical stimulation of the hippocampus in unrestrained animals. I. Methods and EEG findings. *Archives of Neurological Psychiatry, 78,* 113–127.

MacLean, P. D. (1957b). Chemical and electrical stimulation of hippocampus in unrestrained animals. II. Behavioral findings. *Archives of Neurological Psychiatry, 78,* 128–142.

MacLean, P. D. (1958a). The limbic system with respect to self-preservation and preservation of the species. *Journal of Nervous and Mental Disease, 127,* 1–11.

MacLean, P. D. (1958b). Contrasting functions of the limbic and neocortical systems of the brain and their relevance to psychophysiological aspects of medicine. *American Journal of Medicine, 25,* 611–626.

MacLean, P. D. (1962). New findings relevant to the evolution of psychosexual functions of the brain. *Journal of Nervous and Mental Disease, 135,* 289–301.

MacLean, P. D. (1964). Mirror display in the squirrel monkey, *Saimiri sciureus. Science, 146,* 950–952.

MacLean, P. D. (1967). The brain in relation to empathy and medical education. *Journal of Nervous and Mental Disease, 144,* 374–382.

MacLean, P. D. (1968a). Ammon's Horn: A continuing dilemma. Forward in S. Ramón y Cajal, *The structure of Ammon's Horn.* Springfield, IL: Charles C. Thomas.

MacLean, P. D. (1968b). Alternative pathways to violence. In L. Ng (Ed.), *Alternative to violence.* New York: Time-Life Books.

MacLean, P. D. (1970). The triune brain, emotion, and scientific bias. In F. O. Schmitt (Ed.), *The neurosciences: Second study program* (pp. 336–349). New York: Rockefeller University Press.

MacLean, P. D. (1972a). Cerebral evolution and emotional processes: New findings on the striatal complex. *Annals of the New York Academy of Science, 193,* 137–149.

MacLean, P. D. (1972b). Implications of microelectrode findings on exteroceptive inputs to the limbic cortex. In C. H. Hockman (Ed.), *Limbic system mechanisms and autonomic function* (pp. 115–136). Springfield, IL: C. C. Thomas.

MacLean, P. D. (1973a). A triune concept of the brain and behavior. In T. Boag & D. Campbell (Eds.), *Hincks memorial lectures* (pp. 6–66). Toronto: University of Toronto Press.

MacLean, P. D. (1973b). The brain's generation gap: Some human implications. *Zygon Journal of Religious Science, 8,* 113–127.

MacLean, P. D. (1975a). Role of pallidal projections in species-typical display behavior of squirrel monkey. *Transactions of the American Neurological Association, 100,* 29–32.

MacLean, P. D. (1975b). Sensory and perceptive factors in emotional functions of the triune brain. in L. Levi (Ed.), *Emotions—their parameters and measurement* (pp. 71–92). New York: Raven Press.

MacLean, P. D. (1976). The imitative-creative interplay of our three mentalities. In H. Harris (Ed.), *Astride the two cultures. Arthur Koestler at 70* (pp. 187–213). New York: Random House.

MacLean, P. D. (1977a). An evolutionary approach to brain research on prosematic (nonverbal) behavior. In J. S. Rosenblatt & B. R. Komisaris (Eds.), *Reproductive behavior and evolution* (pp. 137–164). New York: Plenum.

MacLean, P. D. (1977b). On the evolution of three mentalities. In S. Arieti & G. Chrzanowski (Eds.), *New dimensions in psychiatry: A world view* (pp. 305–328). New York: Wiley.

MacLean, P. D. (1978a). Effects of lesions of the globus pallidus on species-typical display behavior of squirrel monkeys. *Brain Research, 149,* 175–196.

MacLean, P. D. (1978b). A mind of three minds: Educating the triune brain. In the *Seventy-seventh Yearbook of the National Society for the Study of Education* (pp. 308–342). Chicago: University of Chicago Press.

MacLean, P. D. (1978c). Why brain research on lizards? In N. Greenberg & P. D. MacLean (Eds.), *Behavior and neurology of lizards* (pp. 1–10). Washington, DC: National Institute of Mental Health.

MacLean, P. D. (1981). Role of transhypothalamic pathways in social communication. In P. Morgane & J. Panksepp (Eds.), *Handbook of the hypothalamus* (Vol. 3, pp. 259–287). New York: Marcel Dekker.

MacLean, P. D. (1982a). A triangular brief on the evolution of brain and law. *Journal of Social and Biological Structures, 5,* 369–379.

MacLean, P. D. (1982b). On the origin and progressive evolution of the triune brain. In E. Armstrong & D. Falk (Eds.), *Primate brain evolution: Methods and concepts* (pp. 291–316). New York: Plenum.

MacLean, P. D. (1986). Culminating developments in the evolution of the limbic system: The thalamocingulate division. In B. K. Doane and K. E. Livingstone (Eds.), *The limbic system: Functional organization and clinical disorders.* New York: Raven Press.

MacLean, P. D., & Delgado, J. M. R. (1953). Electrical and chemical stimulation of frontotemporal portion of the limbic system in the waking animal. *Electroencephalography and Clinical Neurophysiology, 5,* 91–100.

MacLuskey, N. J., & Naftolin, F. (1981). Sex differentiation of the central nervous system. *Science, 211,* 1294–1303.

Mahoney, M. J. (1976). *Scientist as subject: The psychological imperative.* Cambridge, MA: Ballinger.

Malamud, N. (1967). Psychiatric disorders with intracranial tumors of the limbic system. *Archives of Neurology, 17,* 113–123.

Malamuth, N. M. (1981). Rape fantasies as a function of exposure to violent-sexual stimuli. *Archives of Sexual Behavior, 10,* 33–47.

Malamuth, N. M., & Check, J. V. P. (1980). Sexual arousal to rape and consenting depictions: The importance of the woman's arousal. *Journal of Abnormal Psychology, 89,* 763–766.

Malamuth, N. M., & Donnerstein, E. (1984). *Pornography and sexual aggression.* Orlando, FL: Academic Press.

Malamuth, N. M., Heim, M., & Feshbach, S. (1980). Sexual responsiveness of college students to rape depictions: Inhibitory and disinhibitory effects. *Journal of Personality and Social Psychology, 38,* 399–408.

Malmo, R. B. (1975). *Our emotions, needs, and our archaic brain.* New York: Holt, Rinehart & Winston.

Mandel, P., Kempf, E., Mack, G., Haug, M., & Puglisi-Allegra, S. (1981). Neurochemistry of experimental aggression. In L. Valzelli & L. Morgese (Eds.), *Aggression and violence: A psychobiological and clinical approach* (pp. 61–71). Centro Culturale e Congressi Saint Vincent.

Mannheim, K. (1936). *Ideology and utopias.* New York: Harcourt, Brace & World.

Margules, D. L., & Olds, J. (1962). Identical feeding and rewarding systems in the lateral hypothalamus in rats. *Science, 157,* 274–275.

Mark, V. H., & Ervin, F. R. (1970). *Violence and the brain.* New York: Harper & Row.

Markl, H. (1982). Constraints on human behavior and the biological nature of man. *Journal of Social and Biological Structures, 3,* 381–387.

Marler, P. (1956). Behavior of the chaffinch. *Behaviour Supplement, 5,* 1–184.

Marler, P. (1968). Aggregation and dispersal: Two functions in primate communication. In P. C. Jay (Ed.), *Primates: Studies in adaptation and variability* (pp. 420–438). New York: Holt, Rinehart & Winston.

Marler, P. (1972). A comparative approach to vocal learning: Song development in white-crowned sparrows. In M. E. P. Seligman & J. L. Hager (Eds.), *Biological boundaries of learning* (pp. 336–376). New York: Appleton-Century-Crofts.

Marler, P. (1973). Review of G. Teleki's *The predatory behavior of wild primates. Science, 182,* 572.

Marler, P. (1976). On animal aggression: The roles of strangeness and familarity. *American Psychologist, 31,* 239–246.

Marris, P. (1974). *Loss and change.* New York: Pantheon.

Marshall, W. (1971). Sexual behavior on Mangaia. In D. S. Marshall & R. C. Suggs (Eds.), *Human sexual behavior: Variations in the ethnographic spectrum* (pp.   ). New York: Basic Books.

Marx, K., & Engels, F. (1976). Manifesto of the communist party. *Collected Works* (Vol. 6, pp. 476–517). New York: International Publishers. (Originally published 1848).

Maslow, A. H. (1937). Dominance-feeling behavior, and status. *Psychological Review, 44,* 404–429.

Maslow, A. H. (1942). Dominance-feeling and sexuality in women. *Journal of Social Psychology, 16,* 259–294.

Maslow, A. H. (1943). A theory of human motivation, *Psychological Review, 50,* 370–396.

Maslow, A. H. (1954). *Motivation and personality.* New York: Harper & Row.

Masters, R. D. (1976). The impact of ethology on political science. In A. Somit (Ed.), *Biology and politics* (pp. 197–223). The Hague: Mouton.

Matarazzo, J. D. (1972). *Wechler's measurement and appraisal of adult intelligence.* Baltimore, MD: Williams & Wilkins.

Matthyesse, S., & Haber, S. (1975). Animal models of schizophrenia. In D. J. Ingle & H. M. Shein (Eds.), *Model systems in biological psychiatry.* Cambridge, MA: MIT Press.

Maxwell, M. (1984). *Human evolution: A philosophical inquiry.* New York: Columbia University Press.

Mayer, D. J., & Price, D. D. (1982). A physiological and psychological analysis of pain: A potential model of motivation. In D. W. Pfaff (Ed.), *The physiological mechanisms of motivation* (pp. 433-471). New York: Springer-Verlag.

Mayr, E. (1935). Bernhard Altum and the territory theory. *Proceedings of Linnean Society, N.Y.* (Nos. 45, 46).

Mayr, E. (1970). *Populations, species, and evolution.* Cambridge, MA: Belknap Press of Harvard University Press.

Mayr, E. (1972). The nature of the Darwinian revolution. *Science, 176,* 981-989.

Mayr, E. (1977). Darwin and natural selection. *American Scientist, 65,* 321-327.

Mazur, A. (1983). Hormones, aggression, and dominance in humans. In B. B. Svare (Ed.), *Hormones and aggressive behavior* (pp. 563-576). New York: Plenum.

McBride, G. (1971). Theories of animal spacing: The role of flight, fight and social distance. In A. H. Esser (Ed.), *Behavior and environment: The use of space by animals and men* (pp. 53-68). New York: Plenum.

McBride, G., King, M., & James, J. W. (1965). Social proximity effects of galvanic skin responses in adult humans. *Journal of Psychology, 61,* 153-157.

McClelland, D. C., Davis, W. N., Kalin, R., & Wanner, E. (1972). *The drinking man.* New York: Free Press.

McDougall, W. (1920). *The group mind.* New York: G. P. Putnam.

McDougall, W. (1926). *An introduction to social psychology.* Boston: John W. Luce.

McFalls, J. A. Jr. (1979). *Psychopathology and subfecundity.* New York: Academic Press.

McFie, J. (1975). *Assessment of organic impairment.* London: Academic Press.

McGee, M. C. (1979). Human spatial abilities: Psychometric studies and environmental, genetic, hormonal, and neurological influences. *Psychological Bulletin, 86,* 889-918.

McGrew, W. C. (1972). *An ethological study of children's behavior.* New York: Academic Press.

McGuire, M. T. (1979). Sociobiology: Its potential contributions to psychiatry. *Perspectives in Biology and Medicine, 23,* 50-69.

McGuire, M. T., & Fairbanks, L. A. (Eds.) (1977). *Ethological psychiatry: Psychopathology in the context of evolutionary biology.* New York: Grune & Stratton.

McGuire, M. T., & Essock-Vitale, S. M. (1981). Psychiatric disorders in the context of evolutionary biology: A functional classification of behavior. *Journal of Nervous and Mental Disease, 169,* 672-686.

McGuire, M. T., & Essock-Vitale, S. M. (1982). Psychiatric disorders in the context of evolutionary biology: The impairment of adaptive behaviors during the exacerbation and remission of psychiatric illnesses. *Journal of Nervous and Mental Disease, 170,* 9-20.

McGuire, M. T., Essock-Vitale, S. M., & Polsky, R. H. (1981). Psychiatric disorders in the context of evolutionary biology: An ethological model of behavioral changes associated with psychiatric disorders. *Journal of Nervous and Mental Disease, 169,* 686-704.

McLeod, B. (1984). In the wake of disaster. *Psychology Today, 18,* 54-57.

Mead, M. (1968). Introductory remarks. In M. Mead, T. Dobzhansky, E. Tobach, & R. E. Light (Eds.), *Science and the concept of race* (pp. 3-9). New York: Columbia University Press.

Mead, M. (1971). Innate behavior and building new cultures. In J. F. Eisenberg & W. S. Dillon (Eds.), *Man and beast: Comparative social behavior* (pp. 371-381). Washington, DC: Smithsonian Institution Press.

Meerlo, J. A. M. (1962). The dual meaning of human regression. *Psychoanalytic Review, 49,* 77-86.

Meerlo, J. A. M. (1967). Communication and mental contagion. In L. Thayer (Ed.), *Communication: Concepts and perspectives* (pp. 1-23). Washington, DC: Spartan Books.

Mehrabian, A. (1976). *Public places and private spaces: Psychology of work, play, and living environments.* New York: Basic Books.

Mellen, S. L. W. (1981). *The evolution of love.* San Francisco: Freeman.

Melvin, K. B., Cloar, F. T., & Massingill, L. S. (1967). Imprinting of bobwhite quail to a hawk. *Psychological Record, 17,* 235-238.

Menaker, E. (1956). A note on some biologic parallels between certain innate animal behavior and moral masochism. *Psychoanalytic Review, 43,* 1.

Merton, R. K. (1968). *Social theory and social structure.* New York: Free Press.

Meyer-Holzapfel, M. (1968). Abnormal behavior in zoo animals. In M. W. Fox (Ed.), *Abnormal behavior in animals* (pp. 476-503). Philadelphia: Saunders.

Michaud, S. G., & Aynesworth, H. (1983). *The only living witness.* New York: Linden Press/Simon & Schuster.

Michener, G. R. (1985). Violence against the young. *Science, 227,* 743-744.

Midgley, M. (1980). *Man and beast: The roots of human nature.* New York: New American Library.

Milgrim, S. (1970). The experience of living in cities. *Science, 167,* 1461-1468.

Miller, J., Moeller, D., Kaufman, A., Divasto, A., Pathak, P., & Christy, J. (1978). Recidivism among sex assault victims. *American Journal of Psychiatry, 135,* 1103-1104.

Miller, N. E. (1980). Introduction: Brain-stimulation reward and theories of reinforcement. In A. Routtenberg (Ed.), *Biology of reinforcement: Facets of brain-stimulation reward* (pp. 1-10). New York: Academic Press.

Milner, B. (1967). Discussion of the subject: Experimental analysis of cerebral dominance in man. In C. H. Millikan & F. L. Darley (Eds.), *Brain mechanisms underlying speech and language* (pp. 122-132). New York: Grune & Stratton.

Mitchell, G. (1979). *Behavioral sex differences in nonhuman primates.* New York: Van Nostrand Reinhold.

Mitchell, G. (1981). *Human sex differences: A primatologist's perspective.* New York: Van Nostrand Reinhold.

Mizuno, T., & Yugari, Y. (1975). Prophylactic effect of L-5-hydroxytryptophan on self-mutiliation in the Lesch-Nyhan syndrome. *Neuropädiatrie, 6,* 13-23.

Moffitt, T. E., Gabrielli, W. F., Mednick, S. & Schulsinger, F. (1981). Socioeconomic status, IQ, and delinquency. *Journal of Abnormal Psychology, 90,* 152-156.

Money, J., & Ehrhardt., A. A. (1972). *Man & woman, boy & girl.* Baltimore: Johns Hopkins University Press.

Money, J., Hampson, J. G., & Hampson, J. L. (1957). Imprinting and the establishment of gender role. *Archives of Neurological Psychiatry, 77,* 333-336.

Monroe, R. R. (1978). *Brain dysfunction in aggressive criminals.* Lexington, MA: Lexington Books.

Montagu, M. F. A. (Ed.). (1968). *Man and aggression.* London: Oxford University Press.

Montagu, M. F. A. (1976). *The nature of human aggression.* Oxford: Oxford University Press.

Montagu, M. F. A. (1978). *Learning non-aggression*. Oxford: Oxford University Press.

Moos, S. W. (1964). The effects of "fohn" weather on accidents rates in the city of Zurich (Switzerland). *Aerospace Medicine, 35*, 643-645.

More than 80 hurt, 1 killed in Detroit. (1984, October). *Richmond Times-Dispatch*, p. 4.

Morishige, W. K., Pepe, G. J., & Rothchild, I. (1973). Serum luteining hormone, prolactin, and progesterone levels during pregnancy in the rat. *Endocrinology, 92*, 1527-1530.

Morris, D. (1967). *The naked ape*. New York: McGraw-Hill.

Morris, D. (1969). *The human zoo*. New York: Dell.

Morris, D. (1971). *Intimate behavior*. New York: Random House.

Moyer, K. E. (1976). *The psychobiology of aggression*. New York: Harper & Row.

Moyer, K. E. (1981). A physiological model of aggression with implications for control. In L. Valzelli & L. Morgese (Eds.), *Aggression and violence: A psychobiological and clinical approach* (pp. 72-79). Centro Culturale e Congressi Saint Vincent.

Myers, M. B., Templer, D. I., & Brown, R. (1984). Coping ability of women who become victims of rape. *Journal of Consulting and Clinical Psychology, 52*, 73-78.

Naftolin, F. (1981). Understanding the bases of sex differences. *Science, 211*, 1263-1265.

Nash, J. (1970). *Developmental psychology: A psychobiological approach*. Englewood Cliffs, NJ: Prentice-Hall.

Nash, J. R. (1975). *Bloodletters and badmen*. (Book 3). New York: Warner Books.

Nauta, W. J. H. (1960). Some neural pathways related to the limbic system. In E. R. Rainey & D. S. O'Doherty (Eds.), *Electrical studies on the unanesthetsized brain* (pp. 1-16). New York: Hoeber.

Nauta, W. J. H. (1964). Some efferent connections of the prefrontal cortex in the monkey. In J. M. Warren & K. Akert (Eds.), *The frontal granular cortex and behavior* (pp. 397-409). New York: McGraw-Hill.

Needham, R. (1971). Remarks on the analysis of kinship and marriage. In R. Needham (Ed.), *Rethinking kinship and marriage* (pp. 1-34). London: Tavistock.

Neisser, U. (1966). *Cognitive psychology*. Englewood Cliffs, NJ: Prentice-Hall.

Nevin, J. A. (Ed.). (1973). *The study of behavior: Learning, motivation, emotion, and instinct*. Glenview, IL: Scott, Foresman.

Night of Terror. (1977, July). *Time*, pp. 12-22.

Noble, G. K. (1939). The role of dominance in the social life of birds. *Auk, 56*, 263-273.

Numan, M. (1974). Medial preoptic area and maternal behavior in the female rat. *Journal of Comparative and Physiological Psychology, 87*, 746-759.

Numan, M., Rosenblatt, J. S., & Komisaruk, B. R. (1977). Medial preoptic area and onset of maternal behavior in the rat. *Journal of Comparative and Physiological Psychology, 91*, 146-164.

Oakley, D. A. (1983). Learning capacity outside the neocortex in animals and man: implications for therapy after brain injury. In G. C. L. Davey (Ed.), *Animal models of human behavior: Conceptual, evolutionary, and neurobiological perspectives* (pp. 247-266). New York: Wiley.

Odling-Smee, F. J. (1983). Multiple levels in evolution: an approach to the nature-nurture issue via "applied epistomology". In G. C. L. Davey (Ed.), *Animal models of human behavior: Conceptual, evolutionary, and neurobiological perspectives* (pp. 135-158). New York: Wiley.

Olds, J. (1956). Pleasure centers in the brain. *Scientific American, 193*, 105-116.

Olds, J. (1959). Studies of neuropharmacological effects by electrical and chemical manipulation of the brain in animals with chronically implanted electrodes. In P. B. Bradley, P. Deniker, & C. Redsuco (Eds.), *Neuropsychopharmacology* (pp. 20-32). Amsterdam: Elsevier.

Olds, J. (1976). Reward and drive neurons: 1975. In A. Wauquier & E. T. Rolls (Eds.), *Brain-stimulation reward* (pp. 1-27). New York: Elsevier.

Olds, J., & Milner, P. (1954). Positive reinforcement produced by electrical stimulation of septal area and other regions of the rat brain. *Journal of Comparative and Physiological Psychology, 47,* 419-427.

Olds, M. E., & Olds, J. (1963). Approach-avoidance analysis of rat diencephalon. *Journal of Comparative Neurology, 120,* 259-295.

Omark, D., Strayer, F. F., & Freedman, D. (Eds.). (1980). *Dominance relations.* New York: Garland Press.

Oomura, Y., Ooyama, H., Yamamoto, T., & Naka, F. (1967). Reciprocal relationships of the lateral and ventromedial hypothalamus in the regulation of food intake. *Physiology and Behavior, 2,* 97-115.

Oppenheimer, J. (1973). Recapitulation. In P. Wiener (Ed.), *Dictionary of the history of ideas* (pp. 56-59). New York: Charles Scribner's.

Ornstein, R. E. (1977). *The psychology of consciousness.* New York: Harcourt Brace Jovanovich.

Orton, S. T. (1928). Specific reading disability-strephosymbolia. *Journal of the American Medical Association, 90,* 1095-1099.

Osborne, R. T., Noble, C. E., & Weyl, N. (1978). *Human variation: The biopsychology of age, race, and sex.* New York: Academic Press.

Ostow, M., & B. Scharfstein (1954). *The need to believe: The psychology of religion.* New York: International Universities Press.

Paasonen, M. K., MacLean, P. D., & Giarman, N. J. (1957). 5-Hydroxytryptamine (serotonin, enteramine) content of structures of the limbic system. *Journal of Neurochemistry, 1,* 326-333.

Paluck, R. J., & Esser, A. H. (1971). Territorial behavior as an indicator of changes in clinical behavioral condition of severely retarded boys. *American Journal of Mental Deficiency, 76,* 284-290.

Papez, J. W. (1937). A proposed mechanism of emotion. *Archives of Neurological Psychiatry, 38,* 725-743.

Park, R. E., & Burgess, E. W. (1921). *Introduction to the science of sociology.* Chicago: University of Chicago Press.

Parsons, T. (1966). *Societies: Evolutionary and comparative perspectives.* Englewood Cliffs, NJ: Prentice-Hall.

Parsons, T., & Bales, R. F. (1954). *Family, socialization, and interaction process.* Glencoe, IL: Free Press.

Parten, M. (1933). Social play among preschool children. *Journal of Abnormal and Social Psychology, 28,* 136-147.

Passingham, R. E. (1982). *The human primate.* San Francisco: Freeman.

Patterson, M. L. (1968). Spatial factors in social interactions. *Human Relations, 21,* 351-361.

Pelletier, K. R. (1977). *Mind as healer, mind as slayer.* New York: Delta.

Pernanen, K. (1976). Alcohol and crimes of violence. In B. Kissen & H. Begleiter (Eds.), *The biology of alcoholism, Vol. 4: Social aspects of alcoholism* (pp. 351-444). New York: Plenum Press.

Pert, C. B., & Snyder, S. H. (1973). Opiate receptor: Demonstration in nervous tissue. *Science, 179,* 1011-1014.

Peterfreund, E. (1971). *Information, systems, and psychoanalysis: An evolutionary biological approach to psychoanalytic theory.* New York: International Universities Press.

Peters, J. J. (1976). Children who are victims of sexual assault and the psychology of offenders. *American Journal of Psychotherapy, 30,* 398–421.

Peters, R. (1980). *Mammalian communication: A behavioral analysis of meaning.* Monterey, CA: Brooks/Cole.

Pfaff, D. W. (1982). Neurobiological mechanisms of sexual motivation. In D. W. Pfaff (Ed.), *The physiological mechanisms of motivation* (pp. 287–318). New York: Springer-Verlag.

Pfeiffer, J. E. (1969). *The emergence of man.* New York: Harper & Row.

Pfeiffer, J. E. (1980). Current research casts new light on human origins. *Smithsonian, 11,* 90–106.

Piaget, J. (1948). *The moral judgment of the child.* Glencoe, Illinois: Free Press (originally published in 1932).

Piaget, J. (1962). *Play, dreams, and imitation in childhood.* New York: Norton.

Piaget, J. (1964). *The origins of intelligence.* New York: International Universities Press.

Pilbeam, D. (1984). The descent of hominoids and hominids. *Scientific American, 250,* 84–96.

Pincus, F. L. (1969). *Risky and conservative group shifts: Conformity leadership or responsibility diffusion?* Unpublished doctoral dissertation, University of California, Los Angeles.

Plotkin, H. C. (1983). The function of learning and cross-species comparisons. In G. C. L. Davey (Ed.), *Animal models of human behavior: conceptual, evolutionary, and neurobiological perspectives* (pp. 117–134). London: Wiley.

Plotkin, H. C., & Odling-Smee, F. J. (1981). A multiple level model of evolution and its implications for sociobiology. *The Behavioral and Brain Sciences, 4,* 225–268.

Plotnik, R., Mir, D., & Delgado, J. M. R. (1971). Aggression, noxiousness, and brain stimulation in unrestrained rhesus monkeys. In B. E. Eleftheriou & J. P. Scott (Eds.), *The physiology of aggression and defeat* (pp. 143–222). New York: Plenum Press.

Plutchik, R. (1977). Cognitions in the service of emotions: An evolutionary perspective. In D. K. Candland, J. P. Fell, E. Keen, A. I. Leshner, R. M. Tarpy, & R. Plutchik (Eds.), *Emotion* (pp. 189–211). Monterey, CA: Brooks/Cole.

Plutchik, R. (1979). Universal problems of adaptation: Hierarchy, territoriality, identity, and temporality. In J. B. Calhoun (Ed.), *Perspectives on adaptation, environment, and population* (pp. 223–226). New York: Praeger.

Plutchik, R. (1980). *Emotion: A psychoevolutionary synthesis.* New York: Harper & Row.

Policeman on rampage kills at least 72, then self. (1982, April). *Richmond Times-Dispatch,* p. 12.

Pontius, A. A. (1976). Neuro-psychiatric hypothesis about territorial behavior. *Perceptual and Motor Skills, 24,* 1232–1234.

Pontius, A. A. (1984). Specific stimulus-evoked violent action in psychotic trigger reaction: A seizure-like imbalance between frontal lobe and limbic systems? *Perceptual and Motor Skills, 1984, 59,* 299–333.

Porter, B., & Dunn, M. (1984). *The Miami riot of 1980: Crossing the bounds.* Lexington, MA: Lexington Books.

Portmann, A. (1943). *Grenzen des Lebens.* Basel: Friederich Reinhardt.

Powers, W. T. (1973). *Behavior: The control of perception.* Chicago: Aldine.

Prescott, J. W. (1977). Phylogenetic and ontogenetic aspects of human affectional development. In R. Gemme & C. C. Wheeler (Eds.), *Progress in sexology: Selected papers from the proceedings of the 1976 International Congress of Sexology.* New York: Plenum.

Prestrude, A. M. (1975, April). *Parasympathetic concomitants of tonic immobility.* Paper presented at the Southwestern Psychological Association, Houston.

Pribam, K. H. (1980). Cognition and performance: The relation to neural mechanisms of consequence, confidence, and competence. In A. Routtenberg (Ed.), *The biology of reinforcement: Facets of brain-stimulation reward* (pp. 11–38). New York: Academic Press.

Prideaux, T. (1973). *Cro-Magnon Man.* New York: Time-Life Books.

Quadagno, D. M., Briscoe, R., & Quadagno, J. S. (1977). Effect of perinatal gonadal hormones on selected nonsexual behavior patterns: A critical assessment of the nonhuman and human literature. *Psychological Bulletin, 84,* 62–80.

Rada, R. T. (1975). Alcoholism and forcible rape. *American Journal of Psychiatry, 132,* 444–446.

Rada, R. T. (Ed.). (1978). *Clinical aspects of the rapist.* New York: Grune & Stratton.

Rada, R. T., Laws, D. R., & Kellner, R. (1976). Plasma testosterone levels in the rapist. *Psychosomatic Medicine, 38,* 257–268.

Rado, S. (1969). *Adaptational psychodynamics: Motivation and control.* New York: Science House.

Rajecki, D. W. (1977). Ethological elements in social psychology. In C. Hendrick (Ed.), *Perspectives on social psychology.* Hillsdale, NJ: Lawrence Erlbaum Associates.

Rajecki, D. W. (1983). Successful comparative psychology: Four case histories. In D. W. Rajecki (Ed.), *Comparing behavior: Studying man studying animals* (pp. 67–107). Hillsdale, NJ: Lawrence Erlbaum Associates.

Rapaport, D. (1953). On the psychoanalytic theory of affects. *International Journal of Psycho-Analysis, 34,* 177–198.

Rapaport, D., & Gill, M. M. (1959). The points of view and assumptions of metapsychology. *International Journal of Psycho-Analysis, XL,* 153–162.

Rasmussen, K. (1931). The Netsilik Eskimos: Social life and spiritual culture. *Report of the fifth Thule expedition, 1921–1924.* Copenhagen: Gyldendalske Boghandel.

Ratner, S. C. (1967). Comparative aspects of hypnosis. In J. Gordon (Ed.), *Handbook of clinical and experimental hypnosis.* New York: Macmillan.

Razran, G. (1971). *Mind in evolution.* Boston: Houghton & Mifflin.

Read, C. (1917). On the differentiation of the human from the anthropoid mind. *British Journal of Psychology, 8,* 395–422.

Reese, W. G. (1979). A dog model for human psychopathology. *American Journal of Psychiatry, 136,* 1168–1172.

Reeves, A. G., & Blum, F. (1969). Hyperphragia, rage, and dementia accompanying a ventromedial neoplasm. *Archives of Neurology, 20,* 616–624.

Reich, W. (1945). *Character analysis.* New York: Orgone Institute Press.

Reite, M., & Caine, N. G. (Eds.). (1983). *Child abuse: The nonhuman primate data.* New York: Alan R. Liss.

Rensch, B. (1957). The intelligence of elephants. *Scientific American, 196,* 44–49.

Rensch, B. (1971). *Biophilosophy.* New York: Columbia University Press.

Rensch, B. (1972). *Homo sapiens: From man to demigod.* New York: Columbia University Press.

Restak, R. M. (1979). *The brain: The last frontier.* New York: Warner Books.

Reynolds, P. C. (1981). *On the evolution of human behavior: The argument from animals to man.* Berkeley, CA: University of California Press.

Reynolds, V. (1967). *The apes.* New York: Harper Colophon.

Reynolds, V. (1979). Comments on papers by Flynn et al. and Bandura. In M. von Cranach, K. Foppa, W. Lepenies, & D. Ploog (Eds.), *Human ethology: Claims and limits of a new discipline* (pp. 357–364). London: Cambridge University Press.

Rheingold, H. (1967). A comparative psychology of development. In H. W. Stevenson, E. H. Hess, & H. L. Rheingold (Eds.), *Early behavior: Comparative and developmental approaches* (pp. 279–293). New York: Wiley.

Richardson, L. F. (1960). *Statistics of deadly quarrels.* London: Stevens & Sons.

River of blood. (1984, April). *Time,* p. 26.

Robinson, H. B., Woods, S. C. & Williams, A. E. (1979). The desire to bear children. In J. S. Lockard (Ed.), *The evolution of human social behavior* (pp. 87–106). New York: Elsevier.

Roizen, J., & Schneberk, D. (1978). Alcohol and crime. In M. Aarens, T. Cameron, J. Roizen, R. Roizen, R. Room, D. Schneberk, & D. Wingard (Eds.), *Alcohol, casualities, and crime.* Berkeley: Social Research Group.

Roper, M. K. (1969). A survey of the evidence for intrahuman killing in the Pleistocene. *Current Anthropology, 10,* 427–459.

Romanes, G. J. (1882). *Animal intelligence.* London: Kegan, Paul, & Co.

Romanes, G. J. (1883). *The mental evolution in animals.* London: Kegan, Paul, Trench, & Co.

Romanes, G. J. (1888). *Mental evolution in man.* New York: Appleton.

Rose, M. R. (1983). Hominid evolution and social science. *Journal of Social and Biological Structures, 6,* 29–36.

Rose, J. E. & Woolsey, C. N. (1948). The orbitofrontal cortex and its connections with the mediodorsal nucleus in rabbit, sheep, and cat. *Research Publication of the Association of Nervous and Mental Disease, 27,* 210–232.

Rose, T. (Ed.). (1969). *Violence in America: A historical and contemporary reader.* New York: Random House.

Rosenhan, D. L., & Seligman, M. E. P. (1984). *Abnormal psychology.* New York: Norton.

Rosenzweig, M. R., & Leiman, A. L. (1982). *Physiological psychology.* Lexington, MA.: D. C. Heath.

Rosenzweig, S. (1981). Toward a comprehensive definition and classification of aggression. In P. F. Brain & D. Benton (Eds.), *Multidisciplinary approaches to aggression research* (pp. 17–22). Amsterdam: Elsevier/North Holland.

Rotton, J., & Kelly, I. W. (1985). Much ado about the full moon: A meta-analysis of the lunar-lunacy research. *Psychological Bulletin, 97,* 286–306.

Routtenberg, A. (1975). Significance of intracranial self-stimulation for memory consolidation. In P. B. Bradley (Ed.), *Methods in brain research* (pp. 453–474). New York: Wiley.

Routtenberg, A. (Ed.). (1980). *Biology of reinforcement: Facets of brain-stimulation reward.* New York: Academic Press.

Routtenberg, A., & Kim, H. J. (1978). The substantia nigra and neostriatum: Substrates for memory consolidation. In L. L. Butcher (Ed.), *Cholinergic-monoaminergic interactions in the brain* (pp. 305–331). New York: Academic Press.

Routtenberg, A., & Holzman, N. (1973). Memory disruption by electrical stimulation of substantia nigra, pars compacta. *Science, 181,* 83–85.

Routtenberg, A., & Malsbury, C. (1969). Brainstem pathway of reward. *Journal of Comparative and Physiological Psychology, 68,* 22–30.

Rubin, R. T., Reinisch, J. M., & Haskett, R. F. (1981). Postnatal gonadal steroid effects on human behavior. *Science, 211,* 1318–1324.

Rule, A. (1980). *The stranger beside me.* New York: Norton.

Rumbaugh, D. M. (1970). Learning skills of anthropoids. In L. A. Rosenbloom (Ed.), *Primate behavior* (pp. 1–70). New York: Academic Press.

Rumbaugh, D. M. (Ed.). (1977). *Language learning by a chimpanzee.* New York: Academic Press.

Rychlak, J. F. (1968). *A philosophy of science for personality theory.* New York: Houghton Mifflin.

Sackeim, H. A. (1983). Possible reversed affective lateralization in a case of bipolar disorder. *American Journal of Psychiatry, 140,* 1191–1193.

Sagan, C. (1977). *The dragons of Eden: Speculations on the evolution of human intelligence.* New York: Ballentine Books.

Sai, F. T. (1984). The population factor in Africa's development dilemma. *Science, 226,* 801–806.

Salzen, E. A. (1970). Imprinting and environmental learning. In L. R. Aronson, E. Tobach, D. S. Lehrman, & J. S. Rosenblatt (Eds.), *Development and evolution of behavior* (pp. 158–178). San Francisco: Freeman.

Sandler, M. (Ed.). (1979). *Psychopharmacology of aggression.* New York: Raven Press.

Sano, K. (1962). Sedative neurosurgery: With special reference to posteromedial hypothalamotomy. *Neurologia medico-chirurgica, 4,* 112–142.

Sarich, V. M. (1968). The origin of hominids. In S. L. Washburn & P. C. Jay (Eds.), *Perspectives on human evolution* (Vol. 1). New York: Holt, Rinehart & Winston.

Sarich, V. M. (1984). Pygmy chimpanzee systematics: A molecular approach. In R. L. Susman (Ed.)., *The pygmy chimpanzee: Evolutionary biology and behavior* (pp. 43–48). New York: Plenum Press.

Sarich, V. M., & Cronin, J. E. (1976). Molecular systematics of the primates. In M.

Goodman & R. E. Tashian (Eds.), *Molecular anthropology* (pp. 141–170). New York: Plenum Press.

Sarich, V. M., & Wilson, A. C. (1967). An immunological time scale for hominid evolution. *Science, 158,* 1200–1203.

Satinoff, E. (1982). Are there similarities between thermoregulation and sexual behavior? In D. W. Pfaff (Ed.), *The physiological mechanisms of motivation* (pp. 217–251). New York: Springer-Verlag.

Savage-Rumbaugh, E. S. (1984). *Pan paniscus* and *Pan troglodytes:* Contrasts in preverbal communicative competences. In R. L. Susman (Ed.), *The pygmy chimpanzee: Evolutionary biology and behavior* (pp. 395–414). New York: Plenum Press.

Savage-Rumbaugh, E. S., Rumbaugh, D. M., & Boysen, S. (1978). Symbolic communication between two chimpanzees *(Pan troglodyte)*. *Science, 201,* 641–644.

Savin-Williams, R. C. (1976). An ethological study of dominance formation and maintenance in a group of human adolescents. *Child Development, 47,* 972–979.

Savin-Williams, R. C. (1977). Dominance in a human adolescent group. *Animal Behaviour, 25,* 400–406.

Savin-Williams, R. C. (1980). Dominance and submission among adolescent boys. In D. R. Omark, F. F. Strayer, & D. G. Freedman (Eds.), *Dominance relations.* New York: Garland Press.

Savin-Williams, R. C., & Freedman, D. G. (1977). Bio-social approach to human development. In S. Chevalier-Skolnikoff & F. E. Poirier (Eds.), *Primate bio-social development: Biological, social, and ecological determinants* (pp. 563–602). New York: Garland Press.

Schaller, G. B. (1963). *The mountain gorilla: Ecology and behavior.* Chicago: Aldine.

Scheflen, A. E. (1976). *Human territories: How we behave in space-time.* Englewood Cliffs, NJ: Prentice-Hall.

Schneider, D. M. (1968). *American kinship.* Englewood Cliffs, NJ: Prentice-Hall.

Scheller, R. H., & Axel, R. (1984). How genes control an innate behavior. *Scientific American, 250,* 54–62.

Schildkraut, J. J. (1965). The catecholamine hypothesis of affective disorders: A review of supporting evidence. *American Journal of Psychiatry, 122,* 509–522.

Schjelderup-Ebbe, T. (1935). Social behavior of birds. In C. Murchison (Ed.), *Handbook of social psychology* (pp. 947–972). Worcester, MA: Clark University Press.

Schneirla, T. C. (1959). An evolutionary and developmental theory of biphasic processes underlying approach and withdrawal. In M. R. Jones (Ed.), *Nebraska Symposium in Motivation* (pp. 1–42). Lincoln, NE: University of Nebraska Press.

Schumer, F. (1983). *Abnormal psychology.* Lexington, MA: Heath.

Schur, M. (1953). The ego in anxiety. In R. M. Lowenstein (Ed.), *Drives, affects, and behavior* (pp. 67–103). New York: International Universities Press.

Schur, M. (1955). Comments on the metapsychology of somatization. *Psychoanalytic Study of the Child, 10,* 120.

Schur, M. (1958). The ego and the id in anxiety. *Psychoanalytic Study of the Child, 13,* 190.

Schur, M. (1960). Phylogenesis and ontogenesis of affect- and structure-formation and the phenomenon of repetition compulsion. *International Journal of Psychoanalysis, XLI,* 275-287.

Schwartzman, H. (1978). *Transformations.* New York: Plenum Press.

Scott, J. P. (1958). *Aggression.* Chicago: University of Chicago Press.

Scott, J. P. (1962). Hostility and aggression in animals. In E. L. Bliss (Ed.), *Roots of behavior: Genetics, instinct, and socialization in animal behavior* (pp. 167-178). New York: Harper & Row.

Scott, J. P. (1981). The evolution of function in agonistic behavior. In P. F. Brain & D.

Benton (Eds.), *Multidisciplinary approaches to aggression research* (pp. 129-158). Amsterdam: Elsevier/North Holland.

Scott, J. P., & Fuller, J. L. (1965). *Genetics and the social behavior of the dog.* Chicago: University of Chicago Press.

Scott, M. L., Cole, J. K., McKay, S. E., Leark, R., & Golden, C. J. (1982, August). *Neuropsychological performance of sexual assaulters and pedophiles.* Paper presented at the annual convention of the American Psychological association, Washington, DC.

Scott, M. L., Martin, R. L., & Liggett, K. R. (1982, August). *Neuropsychological performance of persons with histories of assaultive behavior.* Paper presented at the annual convention of the American Psychological Association, Washington, DC.

Segal, Z. V., & Marshall, W. L. (1985). Heterosexual skills in a population of rapists and child molesters. *Journal of Consulting and Clinical Psychology, 53,* 55-63.

Seidman, L. J. (1983). Schizophrenia and brain dysfunction: An integration of recent neurodiagnostic findings. *Psychological Bulletin, 94,* 195-238.

Seligman, M. E. P., & Hager, J. L. (Eds.). (1972). *The biological boundaries of learning.* New York: Appleton-Century-Crofts.

Sells, S. B., & Wills, D. P. (1971). *Accidents, police incidents, and weather: A further study of the city of Fort Worth, Texas.* (Tech. Rep. 15). Fort Worth TX: Texas Christian University, Institute of Behavioral Research.

Selye, H. (1978). *The stress of life.* New York: McGraw-Hill.

Shaffer, J. A. (Ed.). (1971). *Violence.* New York: David McKay.

Shepard, P. (1973). *The tender carnivore and the sacred game.* New York: Charles Scribner's Sons.

Sherrington, C. S., (1947). *The integrative action of the nervous system* (2nd Ed.). New Haven: Yale University Press.

Shields, W. M., & Shields, L. M. (1983). Forcible rape: An evolutionary perspective. *Ethology and Sociobiology, 4,* 115-136.

Sighele, S. (1901). *La foule criminelle.* Paris: Alcan.

Silberman, E. K., Weingartner, H., Stillman, R., Chen, H., & Post, R. M. (1983) Altered lateralization of cognitive processes in depressed women. *American Journal of Psychiatry, 140,* 1340-1344.

Simons, E. L. (1977). *Ramapithecus. Scientific American, 236,* 28-35.

Simonds, J. F., & Kashani, J. (1979). Drug abuse and criminal behavior in delinquent boys committed to a training school. *American Journal of Psychiatry, 136,* 1444-1448.

Singer, P. (1982). *The expanding circle: Ethics and sociobiology.* New York: New American Library.

Singer, J. E., Brush, C., & Lubin, S. C. (1965). Some aspects of deindividuation: Identification and conformity. *Journal of Experimental Social Psychology, 1,* 356-378.

Skinner, B. F. (1966a). Contingencies of reinforcement in the design of culture. *Behavioral Science, 11,* 159-166.

Skinner, B. F. (1966b). The phylogeny and ontogeny of behavior. *Science, 153,* 1205-1213.

Skinner, B. F. (1975). The shaping of phylogenic behavior. *Acta Neurobiologiae Experimentalis, 35,* 409-415.

Skinner, B. F. (1977). Herrnstein and the evolution of behavior. *American Psychologist, 32,* 1006-1012.

Slobodkin, L. B., & Rapoport, A. (1974). An optimal strategy of evolution. *Quarterly Review of Biology, 49,* 181-200.

Slotnick, B. M. (1975). Neural and hormonal basis of maternal behavior in the rat. In B. E. Eleftheriou & R. L. Sprott (Eds.), *Hormonal correlates of behavior.* New York: Plenum Press.

Sluckin, W. (1965). *Imprinting and early learning.* Chicago: Aldine.

Smith, F. V. (1965). Instinct and learning in lamb and ewe. *Animal Behaviour, 13,* 84-86.

Smith, P. K., & Connolly, K. (1972). Patterns of play and social interaction in preschool children. In N. G. Blurton Jones (Ed.), *Ethological studies of child behaviour* (pp. 65-96). London: Cambridge University Press.

Smith, P. K., & Green, M. (1975). Aggressive behavior in English nurseries and play groups: Sex differences and responses of adults. *Child Development, 46,* 211-214.

Smith, W. J. (1969a). Displays of *Sayornis phoebe. Behavior, 33,* 283-322.

Smith, W. J. (1969b). Messages of vertebrate communication. *Science, 165,* 145-150.

Snyder, S. H. (1980). *Biological aspects of mental disorder.* New York: Oxford University Press.

Snyder, S. H., & Bennett, J. P. (1976). Neurotransmitter receptors in the brain: biochemical identification. *Annual Review of Physiology, 38,* 153-175.

Solecki, R. S. (1973). Introduction. In G. Constable (Ed.), *The neanderthals* (p. 7). New York: Time-Life Books.

Sommer, R. (1959). Studies in personal space. *Sociometry, 22,* 247-260.

Sommer, R. (1969). *Personal space: The behavioral basis of design.* Englewood Cliffs, NJ: Prentice-Hall.

Southwick, C. H. (Ed.). (1970a). *Animal aggression: Selected readings.* New York: Van Nostrand Reinhold.

Southwick, C. H. (1970b). Conflict and violence in animal societies. In C. H. Southwick (Ed.), *Animal aggression: Selected readings* (pp. 1-13). New York: Van Nostrand Reinhold.

Spencer, H. (1850). *Social statics.* New York: Appleton.

Spencer, H. (1879). *The data of ethics.* New York: Rand McNally.

Spencer, H. *The principles of psychology* (3rd ed.). New York: Appleton, 1895.

Springer, S. P., & Deutsch, G. (1981). *Left brain, right brain.* San Francisco: Freeman.

Stanley, A. (1983, Nov.). Catching a new breed of killer. *Time,* p. 47.

Stebbins, G. L. (1982). *Darwin to DNA, molecules to humanity.* San Francisco: Freeman.

Stein, L. (1964). Self-stimulation of the brain and the central stimulant action of amphetamine. *Federation Proceedings, 23,* 836-841.

Stein, L. (1978). Reward transmitters: Catechcholamines and opioid peptides. In M. A. Lipton, A. DiMascio, & K. F. Killam (Eds.), *Psychopharmacology: A generation of progress* (pp. 569-581). New York: Raven.

Stein, L. (1980). The chemistry of reward. In A. Routtenberg (Ed.), *Biology of reinforcement: Facets of brain-stimulation reward* (pp. 109-132). New York: Academic Press.

Stellar, E. (1954). The physiology of motivation. *Psychological Review. 61,* 5-22.

Stellar, E. (1982) Brain mechanisms in hedonic processes. In D. W. Pfaff (Ed.), *The physiological mechanisms of motivation* (pp. 377-407). New York: Springer-Verlag.

Stenhouse, D. (1973). *The evolution of intelligence.* New York: Harper & Row.

Stephan, H., & Andy, O. J. (1969). Quantitative comparative neuroanatomy of primates: An attempt at phylogenetic interpretation. *Annals of the New York Academy of Science, 167,* 370-387.

Stephan, H., & Andy, O. J. (1970). Data on size of the brain and of various brain parts in insectivores and primates. In C. R. Noback & W. Montagna (Eds.), *The primate brain* (pp. 289-297). New York: Appleton-Century-Crofts.

Stevens, J. R. (1982). Neuropathology of schizophrenia. *Archives of General Psychiatry, 39,* 1131-1139.

Stoller, R. J. (1975). *Perversion: The erotic form of hatred.* New York: Random House.

Storr, A. (1968). *Human aggression.* London: Penguin.

Strauss, I., & Keschner, M. (1935). Mental symptoms in cases of tumor of the frontal lobe. *Archives of Neurology and Psychiatry, 33,* 986-1005.

Strayer, F. F., & Strayer, J. (1976). An ethological analysis of social agonism and dominance relations among preschool children. *Child Development, 47,* 980-989.

Street, P. (1971). *Animal weapons*. New York: Taplinger Press.

Stroebel, C. F. (1967). A biologic rhythm approach to psychiatric treatment. In *Proceedings of the Seventh Medical Symposium*. York Town Heights, NY: IBM Press.

Stroebel, C. F. (1969). Biologic rhythm corelates of disturbed behavior in the rhesus monkey. In F. H. Rholes (Ed.), *Circadian rhythm in nonhuman primates*. New York: Karger.

Sue, D. W. (1981). *Counseling the culturally different: Theory and practice*. New York: Wiley.

Summers, T. B., & Kaelber, W. W. (1962). Amygdalectomy: Effects in cats and a survey of its present status. *American Journal of Physiology, 202*, 1117-1119.

Sutherland, E. H., & Cressey, D. R. (1966). *Principles of criminology* (7th Ed.). Philadelphia: Lippincott.

Suttles, G. D. (1968). *The social order of the slum*. Chicago: University of Chicago Press.

Sweet, W. H., Ervin, F., & Mark, V. H. (1969). The relationship of violent behaviour to focal cerebral disease. In S. Garattini & E. B. Sigg (Eds.), *Aggressive behaviour* (pp. 336-352). New York: Wiley.

Swindler, D. R. (1980). A synopsis of primate phylogeny. In J. S. Lockard (Ed.), *The evolution of human social behavior* (pp. 31-48). New York: Elsevier.

Sylvester-Bradley, P. C. (1976). Evolutionary oscillation in prebiology: Igneous activity and the origins of life. *Origins of Life, 7*, 9-18.

Symonds, D. (1979). *The evolution of human sexuality*. New York: Oxford University Press.

Takemoto, Y. (1968). The application of imprinting to psychodynamics. *Science and Psychoanalysis, 12*, 166-183.

Tavolga, W. N. (1970). Levels of interaction in animal communication. In L. Aronson, E. Tobach, D. S. Lehrman, & J. S. Rosenblatt (Eds.), *Development and evolution of behavior* (pp. 281-302). San Francisco: Freeman.

Taylor, J. (Ed.). (1931). *Selected writings of John Hughlings Jackson, Vol. 1*. London: Hodder & Stoughton.

Taylor, I., Walton, P., & Young, J. (1973). *The new criminology: For a social theory of deviance*. London: Routledge & Kegan Paul.

Tedeschi, J. T., Melburg, V., & Rosenfeld, P. (1981). Is the concept of aggression useful? In P. F. Brain & D. Benton (Eds.), *Multidisciplinary approaches to aggression* (pp. 23-38). Amsterdam: Elsevier/North Holland.

Teleki, G. (1973). *The predatory behavior of wild chimpanzees*. Lewisburg, PA: Bucknell University Press.

Terzian, H., & Ore, G. D. (1955). Syndrome of Klüver and Bucy reproduced in man by bilateral removal of temporal lobes. *Neurology, 5*, 373–380.

Thomas, H. (1937). *The story of the human race*. Garden City, NY: Garden City Publishing.

Thompson, D. H. (1967). *An ethological study of dominance hierarchies in preschool children*. Unpublished manuscript, University of Wisconsin.

Thorndike, E. L. (1898). Animal intelligence: An experimental study of the associative processes in animals. *Psychological Monographs, 2*, 109.

Thorndike, E. L. (1911). *Animal intelligence: Experimental studies*. New York: Macmillan.

Thornhill, R., & Thornhill, N. W. (1983). Human rape: An evolutionary analysis. *Ethology and Sociobiology, 4*, 137–173.

Thorpe, W. H. (1945). The evolutionary significance of habitat selection. *Journal of Animal Ecology, 14*, 67–70.

Thorpe, W. H. (1961). *Bird song: The biology of vocal communication and expression in birds*. Cambridge: Cambridge University Press.

Thorpe, W. H. (1974). *Animal nature and human nature*. London: Methuen.

Thrasher, F. M. (1963). *The gang*. Chicago: University of Chicago Press.

'Thrill' killings shaking Italy. (1976, April). *Richmond Times-Dispatch*, p. 6.

Tidd, C. W. (1960). Symposium on 'psychoanalysis and ethology' I. Introduction. *International Journal of Psycho-Analysis, 41,* 308–311.

Tieger, T. (1981). Self-related likelihood of raping and the social perception of rape. *Journal of Research in Personality, 15,* 147–158.

Tiger, L. (1969). *Men in groups.* New York: Random House.

Tiger, L. (1970a). Dominance in human societies. *Annual Review of Biology and Systematics.* 1,

Tiger, L. (1970b). The possible origins of sexual discrimination. *Impact of Science on Society, 20,* 29–44.

Tiger, L. (1975). Somatic factors and social behavior. In R. Fox (Ed.), *Biosocial anthropology* (pp. 115–132). New York: Wiley.

Tiger, L. (1979). *Optimism: The biology of hope.* New York: Simon & Schuster.

Tiger, L., & Fox, R. (1966). The zoological perspective in social science. *Man, 1,* 75–81.

Tiger, L., & Fox, R. (1971). *The imperial animal.* New York: Holt, Rinehart & Winston.

Tiger, L., & Shepher, J. (1975). *Women in the Kibbutz.* New York: Harcourt Brace Jovanovich.

Tinbergen, N. (1936a). Zur Soziologie der Silbermöwe. *(L. a. argentatus Pontopp). Beitrage Fortpflanzungsbiologie Vogel. 12,* 89–96.

Tinbergen, N. (1936b). Eenvoudige proeven over de zintuigfuncties van larve en imago van de geelgerande watertor. *De Levende Natuur, 41,* 225–236.

Tinbergen, N. (1951). *The study of instinct.* New York: Oxford University Press.

Tinbergen, N. (1953a). *Social behavior in animals.* New York: Wiley.

Tinbergen, N. (1953b). *The Herring Gull's world.* London: Methuen.

Tinbergen, N. (1968). On war and peace in animals and man. *Science, 160,* 1411–1418.

Tinbergen, N. (1973). Functional ethology and the human sciences. *Proceedings of Royal Society of London, 182,* 385–410.

Tinbergen, N. (1976). Ethology in a changing world. In P. P. G. Bateson & R. A. Hinde (Eds.), *Growing points in ethology* (pp. 507–527). London: Cambridge University Press.

Tinbergen, W. A., & Tinbergen, N. (1972). Early childhood autism: An ethological approach. *Zeitschrift für Tierpsychologie* (Supplement), *10,* 1–53.

Tobias, P. V. (1971). *The brain in hominid evolution.* New York: Colombia University Press.

Toch, H. H. (1969). *Violent men.* Chicago: Aldine.

Toch, H. H. (1983). The management of hostile aggression: Seneca as applied social psychologist. *American Psychologist, 38,* 1022–1026.

Tomkins, S. S. (1963). *Affect, imagery, consciousness. Vol. II. The negative effects.* New York: Springer.

Trivers, R. L. (1971). The evolution of reciprocal altruism. *Quarterly Review of Biology, 46,* 35–57.

Trivers, R. L. (1972). Parental investment and sexual selection. In B. H. Campbell (Ed.), *Sexual selection and the descent of man* (pp. 136–179). Chicago: Aldine.

Trivers, R. L. (1974). Parent-offspring conflict. *American Zoologist, 14,* 246–264.

Tromp, S. W., & Bouma, J. J. (1973). *Study of the possible relationship between atmospheric environment, suicide, and suicide attempts in the western part of the Netherlands* (Period 1954–1969). (Monograph Series, No. 12). Leiden, The Netherlands: Biometerological Research Center.

Trudeau, M. B., Bergmann-Riss, & Hamburg, D. A. (1981). Towards an evolutionary perspective on aggressive behavior: The chimpanzee evidence. In D. A. Hamburg & M. B. Trudeau (Eds.), *Biobehavioral assets of aggression* (pp. 27–40). New York: Alan R. Liss, Inc.

Turner, S. M., Beidel, D. C. & Nathan, R. S. (1985). Biological factors in obsessive-compulsive disorders. *Psychological Bulletin, 97,* 430–450.

Turnbull, C. (1972). *The mountain people.* New York: Simon & Schuster.

Two men draw life terms for shooting man as prey. (1980, February). *Richmond Times-Dispatch*, p. 6.

Uexküll, J. von. (1909). *Umwelt und innenleben der Tiere*. Berlin.

Uexküll, J. von. (1957). A stroll through the worlds of animals and men. In C. H. Schiller (Ed.), *Instinctive behavior: The development of a modern concept* (pp. 5–80). New York: International Universities Press.

Ulrich, R. E. (1966). Pain as a cause of aggression. *American Zoologist, 6*, 643–662.

Ulrich, R. E., & Azrin, N. H. (1962). Reflexive fighting in response to aversive stimulation. *Journal of the Experimental Analysis of Behavior, 5*, 511–520.

Ulrich, R. E., Wolff, P. C., & Azrin, N. H. (1964). Shock as an elicitor of intra- and interspecies fighting behavior. *Animal Behavior, 12*, 14–15.

Ungerstedt, U. (1971). Sterotaxic mapping of the monoamine pathways of the rat brain. *Acta Physiologica Scandinavia* (Suppl.), *367*, 1–48.

Ursin, H. (1981). Neuroanatomical basis of aggression. In P. F. Brain & D. Benton (Eds.), *Multidisciplinary approaches to aggression research* (pp. 269–294). Amsterdam: Elsevier/North Holland.

Uzoka, A. F. (1979). The myth of the nuclear family: Historical background and clinical implications. *American Psychologist, 34*, 1095–1106.

Vale, J. R. (1980). *Genes, environment, and behavior: An interactionist approach*. New York: Harper & Row.

Valzelli, L. (1980). *An approach to neuroanatomical and neurochemical psychophysiology*. Torino, Italy: C. G. Edizioni Medico Scientifiche s. r. l.

Valzelli, L. (1981). *Psychobiology of aggression and violence*. New York: Raven Press.

Valzelli, L. (1984). Reflections on experimental and human pathology of aggression. *Progress in Neuro-Psychopharmacology and Biological Psychiatry, 8*, 311–325.

Valzelli, L., & Morgese, L. (Eds.). (1981). *Aggression and violence: A psychobiological and clinical approach*. (Proceedings of the First Saint Vincent Special Conference, October 14/15, 1980). Centro Culturale e Congressi, Saint Vincent.

van den Berghe, P. L. (1979). *Human family systems: An evolutionary view*. New York: Elsevier.

van den Berghe, P. L. (1980). The human family: A sociobiological look. In J. S. Lockard (Ed.), *The evolution of human social behavior* (pp. 67–86). New York: Elsevier.

van Hooff, J. A. R. A. M. (1967). The facial displays of the catarrhine monkeys and apes. In D. Morris (Ed.), *Primate ethology* (pp. 7–68). London: Wiedenfield & Nicholson.

Van Kreveld, D. (1970). A selective review of dominance-subordination relations in animals. *Genetic Psychology Monographs, 81*, 143–173.

Verbrugge, L. M., & Taylor, R. B. (1976). *Consequences of population density: Testing new hypotheses*. Baltimore: Johns Hopkins Center for Metropolitan Planning and Research.

Viaud, G. (1960). *Intelligence: Its evolution and forms*. New York: Harper.

Violence erupts in Philadelphia. (1985, April). *Richmond Times-Dispatch*, p. 10.

Vine, I. (1970). Communication by facial-visual signals. In J. H. Crook (Ed.), *Social behaviour in birds and mammals: Essays on the social ethology of animals and man* (pp. 279–354). New York: Academic Press.

von Bertalanffy, L. (1968). *General system theory*. New York: George Braziller.

Voss, H. L., & Hepburn, J. R. (1968). Patterns in criminal homicide in Chicago. *Journal of Criminal Law, Criminology, and Police Science, 59*, 499–508.

Waddington, C. H. (1957). *The strategy of genes*. London: Allen & Unwin.

Waddington, C. H. (1961). *The nature of life*. New York: Atheneum.

Waddington, C. H. (1962). *New patterns in genetics and development*. New York: Columbia University Press.

Waddington, C. H. (1967). *The ethical animal*. Chicago: University of Chicago Press.

Walker, A. E., & Blumer, D. (1972, March). *Long term effects of temporal lobe lesions on sexual behavior and aggressivity.* Paper presented at the Houston Neurological Symposium on Neural Bases of Violence and Aggression, Houston, TX.

Wallace, R. A. (1979). *The genesis factor.* New York: William Morrow.

Wallach, M. A., & Wallach, L. (1983). *Psychology's sanction for selfishness: The error of egoism in theory and therapy.* San Francisco: Freeman.

Ward, C. (Ed.). (1973). *Vandalism.* New York: Van Nostrand Reinhold.

Warden, C. J. (1951). Animal intelligence. *Scientific American, 184,* 64–68.

Warren, J. M. (1977). Handedness and cerebral dominance in monkeys. In S. Hrarnad, R. W. Doty, L. Goldstein, J. Jaynes, & G. Krauthamer (Eds.), *Lateralization in the nervous system.* New York: Academic Press.

Washburn, S. L. (1978a). Human behavior and the behavior of other animals. *American Psychologist, 33,* 405–418.

Washburn, S. L. (1978b). The evolution of man. *Scientific American, 239,* 194–208.

Washburn, S. L., & DeVore, I. (1961a). Social behavior of baboons and early man. In S. L. Washburn (Ed.), *Social life of early man* (pp. 91–105). New York: Wenner-Gren Foundation.

Washburn, S. L., & DeVore, I. (1961b). The social life of baboons. *Scientific American, 204,* 62–71.

Washburn, S. L., & Dolhinow, P. C. (1983). Comparison of human behaviors. In D. W. Rajecki (Ed.), *Comparing behavior: Studying man studying animals* (pp. 27–42). Hillsdale, NJ: Lawrence Erlbaum Associates.

Washburn, S. L., & Hamburg, D. A. (1972). Aggressive behavior in old world monkeys and apes. In P. C. Dolhinow (Ed.), *Primate patterns* (pp. 276–296). New York: Holt, Reinhart & Winston.

Washburn, S. L., & Lancaster, C. S. (1968). The evolution of hunting. In R. B. Lee & I. DeVore (Eds.), *Man the hunter* (pp. 293–303). Chicago: Aldine.

Washburn, S. L., & Moore, R. (1980). *Ape into human: A study of human evolution.* Boston: Little Brown.

Wasman, M., & Flynn, J. P. (1962). Directed attack elicited from hypothalamus. *Archives of Neurology, 6,* 220–227.

Watson, R. I. (1973). Investigation into deindividuation using a cross-cultural survey technique. *Journal of Personality and Social Psychology, 25,* 342–345.

Watts, M. W. (1981). Editor's notes and introduction. In M. W. Watts (Ed.), *Biopolitics: Ethological and physiological approaches* (pp. 1–14). San Francisco: Jossey-Bass.

Wauquier, A., & Rolls, E. T. (Eds.). (1976). *Brain-stimulation reward.* New York: Elsevier.

Weber, M. (1947). *The theory of social and economic organization.* New York: Oxford University Press.

Wechsler, D. (1958). *The measurement and appraisal of adult intelligence* (4th Ed.). Baltimore: Williams & Wilkins.

Wechsler, D. (1971). The concept of collective intelligence. *American Psychologist, 26,* 904–908.

Wechsler, H. (1980). Introduction: Summary of the literature. In *Alcoholism and alcohol abuse among women: Research issues.* Rockville, MD: NIMH Research Monograph No. 1.

Weigert, E. (1956). Human ego functions in the light of animal behavior *Psychiatry, 19,* 4.

Weiss, P. A. (1969). The living system: Determinism stratified. In A. Koestler & J. R. Smythies (Eds.). *Beyond reductionism: New perspectives in the life sciences* (pp. 3–55). New York: Macmillan.

Weitzman, E. D., & Luce, G. (1970). Biological rhythms: Indices of pain, adrenal hormones, sleep, and sleep reversal. In NIMH, *Behavioral sciences and mental health* (pp. 319–332). Washington, DC: U.S. Government Printing Office.

Wells, H. G., Huxley, J. S., & Wells, G. P. (1934). *The science of life.* New York: Literary Guild.

Wenegrat, B. (1984). *Sociobiology & mental disorder*. Menlo Park, CA: Addison-Wesley.

Werner, H. (1948). *Comparative psychology of mental development*. New York: International Universities Press.

White, N. (Ed.). (1974). *Ethology and psychiatry*. Toronto: University of Toronto Press.

White, E., & Brown, D. M. (1973). *The first men*. New York; Time-Life Books.

Why you do what you do—Sociobiology: A new theory of behavior. (1977, August). *Time*, pp. 54, 63.

Whyte, W. F. (1943). *The streetcorner society*. Chicago: University of Chicago Press.

Wickler, W. (1967). Socio-sexual signals and their intra-specific imitation among primates. In D. Morris (Ed.), *Primate ethology* (pp. 69–147). Chicago: Aldine.

Wickler, W. (1972). *The sexual code: The social behavior of animals and men*. Garden City, NY: Doubleday.

Wiegle, T. C. (1979). *Biopolitics: Search for a more human political science*. Boulder: Westview Press.

Willems, E. P. (1974). Behavioral technology and behavioral ecology. *Journal of Applied Behavior Analysis, 7,* 151–165.

Willems, E. P. (1977). Steps toward an ecobehavioral technology. In A. Rogers-Warren & S. F. Warren (Eds.), *Ecological perspectives in behavior analysis* (pp. 39–62). Baltimore, MD: University Park Press.

Williams, D. (1969). Temporal lobe syndrome. In P. J. Vinken & G. W. Bruyn (Eds.), *Handbook of clinical neurology* (Vol. II, pp. 700–724). New York: Wiley.

Wilson, A. C. (1978). Frog perspective on the morphological difference between humans and chimpanzees. *Science, 200,* 209–211.

Wilson, A. S. (1974). Psychologic effects of magnetic and electrical fields. In J. G. Llaurado, A. Sances, Jr., & J. H. Battocletti (Eds.), *Biologic and clinical effects of low-frequency magnetic and electrical fields*. Springfield, IL: Charles C. Thomas.

Wilson, E. O. (1971). Competitive and aggressive behavior. In J. F. Eisenberg & W. Dillon (Eds.), *Man and beast: Comparative social behavior* (pp. 181–218). Washington, DC: Smithsonian Institution Press.

Wilson, E. O. (1975). *Sociobiology: The new synthesis*. Cambridge, MA: Harvard University Press.

Wilson, E. O. (1978). *On human nature*. Cambridge, MA: Harvard University Press.

Wilson, G. (1983). *Love and instinct*. New York: William Morrow.

Wilson, J. D., George, F. W., & Griffin, J. E. (1981). The hormonal control of sexual development. *Science, 211,* 1278–1285.

Wilson, P. J. (1980). *Man, the promising primate*. New Haven: Yale University Press.

Wittgenstein, L. (1963). *Philosophical investigations*. Oxford: Basil Blackwell.

Wolff, P. H. (1963). Observations on the early development of smiling. In B. M. Foss (Ed.), *Determinants of infant behavior* (pp. 113–134). London: Methuen.

Wolff, P. H. (1969). The natural history of crying and other vocalizations in early infancy. In B. M. Foss (Ed.), *Determinants of infant behavior* (pp. 81–109). London: Methuen.

Wolfgang, M. E. (1958). *Patterns in criminal homicide*. Philadelphia: University of Pennsylvania Press.

Wolin, S. J. B. (1980). Introduction: Psychosocial consequences. In *Alcoholism and alcohol abuse among women: Research issues*. Rockville, MD: NIMH Research Monograph No. 1.

Woods, J. W. (1956). "Taming" of the wild Norway rat by rhinecephalic lesions. *Nature, 178,* 869.

Woodworth, R. S., & Sherrington, C. S. (1904). A pseuoaffective reflex and its spinal path. *Journal of Physiology, 31,* 234–243.

Woolsey, C. N. (1958). Organization of somatic and sensory areas of the cerebral cortex. In H. F. Harlow & C. N. Woolsey (Eds.), *Biological and biochemical bases of behavior*. Madison: University of Wisconsin Press.

World Book. (1973). Chicago: Field Enterprises Educational Corp.

Wurtz, R. H. & Olds, J. (1963). Amygdaloid stimulation and operant reinforcement in the rat. *Journal of Comparative and Physiological Psychology, 56*, 941–949.

Wymer, J. (1982). *The paleolithic age*. New York: St. Martin's Press.

Wynne-Edwards, V. C. (1962). *Animal dispersion in relation to social behavior*. New York: Hafner.

Wynne-Edwards, V. C. (1965). Self-regulating systems in populations of animals. *Science, 147*, 1543–1548.

Yablonsky, L. (1970). *The violent gang*. Baltimore: Penquin.

Yakovlev, P. I. (1970). The structural and functional "trinity" of the body, brain, and behavior. *Topical Problems in Psychiatry and Neurology, 10*, 197–208.

Yalom, I. D. (1980). *Existential psychotherapy*. New York: Basic Books.

Yarczower, M., & Hazlett, L. (1977). Evolutionary scales and anagenesis. *Psychological Bulletin, 84*, 1088–1097.

Yates, A. (1982). Children eroticized by incest. *American Journal of Psychiatry, 139*, 482–485.

Yerkes, R. M., & Yerkes, A. W. (1929). *The great apes: A study of anthropoid life*. New Haven: Yale University Press.

Young, P. T. (1973). *Emotion in man and animal*. Hunting, NY: Robert E. Krieger.

Young, R. M. (1967). Animal soul. In P. Edwards (Ed.), *The encyclopedia of philosophy* (pp. 122–127). New York: Macmillan.

Yunis, J. J., & Prakash, O. (1982). The origin of man: A chromosomal legacy. *Science, 215*, 1525–1530.

Zeman, W., & King, F. A. (1958). Tumors of the septum pellucidum and adjacent structures with abnormal affective behavior: An anterior midline structure syndrome. *Journal of Nervous and Mental Disease, 127*, 490–502.

Zentall, S. S., & Zentall, T. R. (1983). Optimal stimulation: A model of disordered activity and performance in normal and deviant children. *Psychological Bulletin, 94*, 446–471.

Zillmann, D. (1984). *Connections between sex and aggression*. Hillsdale, NJ: Lawrence Erlbaum Associates.

Zimbardo, P. G. (1969). The human choice: Individuation, reason, and order vs. deindividuation, impulse, and chaos. In W. J. Arnold & D. Levine (Eds.), *Nebraska Symposium on Motivation* (Vol. 17, pp. 237–307). Lincoln: University of Nebraska Press.

Zimbardo, P. G. (1973). A field experiment in autoshaping. In C. Ward (Ed.), *Vandalism* (pp. 85–90). New York: Van Nostrand Reinhold.

Zivin, G. (1983). Hybrid models: Modifications in models of social behavior that are borrowed across species and up evolutionary grades. In D. W. Rajecki (Ed.), *Comparing behavior: Studying man studying animals* (pp. 181–202). Hillsdale, NJ: Lawrence Erlbaum Associates.

Zubin, J., & Hunt, H. F. (Eds.). (1967). *Comparative psychopathology: Animal and human*. New York: Grune & Stratton.

Zucker, R. A. (1968). Sex-role identity patterns and drinking behavior of adolescents. *Quarterly Journal of Studies on Alcohol, 29*, 868–884.

Zuckerman, S. (1932). *The social life of monkeys and apes*. London: Kegan Paul.

Author Index

Subject Index